# THE ILLUSTRATED GUIDE TO … S
# TOP COUNTER-TERRORI… …ORCES



Samuel M. Katz

603-609 Castle Peak Road
Kong Nam Industrial Building
10/F, B1, Tsuen Wan
New Territories, Hong Kong
Fax : (852)2411 0587



We welcome authors who can help expand our range of books. If you would like to submit material, please feel free to contact us.

We are always on the look-out for new, unpublished photos for this series.
If you have photos or slides or information you feel may be useful to future volumes, please send them to us for possible future publication.
Full photo credits will be given upon publication.

**ISBN 962-361-602-3**
Printed in Hong Kong

## Acknowledgments

A book of this nature would be impossible to produce, let alone write and refine, without the help of a small army of people through whose kindness, friendship, dedication and pride in their units has enabled me to separate fact from fiction, myth from reality, the information presented in the following pages would never have made it to the printed form.

In the United States I would like to thank Lieutenant Linda O'Brien, Metro-Dade Police Department Miami, Florida; Jerry Keller, Sheriff, Las Vegas Metropolitan Police and Lieutenant Gary Schofield, Las Vegas Metropolitan Police S.W.A.T Detail/Organized Crime Bureau; Lieutenant Larry D. McCoy, Metropolitan Police Department, Emergency Response Team; P.O. Joe Savage, Portland Oregon Police Bureau, S.E.R.T.; Special Agent I. Ray McElhaney, Federal Bureau of Investigation; William M. Dempsey, U.S. Marshals Service; Lieutenant Linda Hunt and P.O. Pete Sicilia, Seattle Police Department Tactical Operations Division, Seattle, Washington E.R.T; Kansas City Police Chief Steven Bishop and Captain William Massock, commander of the T.R.T.; and Lieutenant John P. Kennedy, Department of Police, City of Chicago, Hostage/Barricaded/Terrorist Incident Coordinator.

A very special thanks needs to be given to Sergeant Al Preciado of the Los Angeles Police Department's SWAT Platoon, as fine a guide through the world and mind of a SWAT officer as could be found anywhere; and, a very special thanks to Lieutenant Bob Sobocienski (my "Rabbi"), of the New York City Police Department's Emergency Service Unit, along with Inspector John Harkins, Captains Curt Wargo, Tom Martin, and Ralph Pascullo; Lieutenants Mike Libretto, Richard Greene and George Shanley; and, Detective Denis Burke and P.O. Kris Brandt.

In Europe, I would like to thank the commander of the Polish GROM, Colonel Slawomir Petelicki for his kind and generous efforts on my behalf; Dr. L. Borer, ***Polizeikommando des Kanton Aargau***, Switzerland; Markus Atzenweiler, ***Kantonspolizei Zürich***, Switzerland; Bernhard Aeppli; Colonel B., St. Augustin; Eugen Egli, Switzerland; Henning Thiesen, National Commissioner of the Danish Police, Denmark; Erwin Derntl, Steyr Mannlicher Aktiengesellschaft, Austria; Oberst Johannes Pachter, ***Gendarmerie Einsatzkommando Cobra***, Austria; Brigadier-General C. Clausen, Austrian Embassy, Washington DC; C.W.O. Hervé Madec, French Embassy, Brigadier-General Guy Pouliquen, French Embassy, Washington DC; Lieutenant Eddie Huybens, Colonel Vanden Broeck, Gendarmerie Commandement -P. R. C., Belgium; Brigadier General André G. De Smet, Defense, Military, Naval and Air Attaché, Belgian Embassy, Washington DC; Colonel Jean-Pierre I. Bastin - Belgian Embassy; Colonel Jiri Giesl, assistant Defense Attaché, Embassy of the Czech Republic, Washington DC; Lieutenant-Colonel Kai P. Vainio, Assistant Defense, Military, Naval and Air Attaché, Embassy of Finland; David Reynolds, Photo Press Defence Pictures, Great Britain; J.M. Coldrick, Metropolitan Police Service, Great Britain; Captain Simon Haselock, Royal Marines Public Relations, Great Britain; Paola Imperiale, Consul at the Italian Consulate in New York; General Maurizio Coccia, Military Attaché, Italian Embassy, Washington DC; Police Division Superintendent Jon Birger Berntsen, Oslo ***Politikammer Beredskapstroppen Deltatroppen***, Norway; Tom Nilssen, Headquarters Defence Command Norway; Captain José Celestino Da Silva, Portuguese Navy, The Naval Attaché, Embassy of Portugal, Washington, D.C.; Mr. Robert Pasman, Public Relations Dept., Royal Netherlands Marine Corps; Major J.A. Dijkstra, RNLMC; José Cigüenza Gabriel, Teniente Coronel Jefe Relaciones Públicas DRISDE, Ministerio De Defensa, Madrid, Spain; Rear-Admiral Francisco Nuñez, Defense Attaché, Embassy of Spain, Washington DC; Brigadier-General Michael von Rosen, Office of the Armed Forces Attachés, Embassy of Sweden, Washington D.C.; WO Hans H. Weber, For the Defense, Military, Naval and Air Attaché, Embassy of Switzerland, Washington, DC; W. Schad, SIG Swiss Industrial Company, Small Arms Division, Switzerland; and Steve Zaloga.

In Canada I would like to thank J.C. Picard, Inspector, Royal Canadian Mounted Police, Ottawa, Ontario; Major Ric Jones, Director General Public Affairs, National Defence Headquarters, Canada; Lieutenant Andrew Pope, Office of the Director of Public Affairs; and Ron Volstad.

In Australia I would like to thank Johny Flowers, for his efforts on my behalf, as well as Gary Duncan and A.E. Elliot; in South America I would like to thank Admiral Alvaro Campos, Defense Attaché, Embassy of Colombia, Brigadier-General Celso Suarez Martinez, Bogata, and Coronel Rafael Morales Gomez, Director of the fine Colombian publication ***Fuerzas Armadas***; Commander Alfredo Astiz, Jefe Del Servicio De Fuerzas Especiales, Argentina; Commandante "P," Brigade "Halcon", Argentina; Brigadier-General Tomas Angeles Dauahare, Defense, Military and Air Attaché, Embassy of Mexico; and, Major-General Paulo Fabiano Do Prado Soares, military attaché at the Brazilian Embassy in Washington D.C.

In Asia, I would like to offer very special thanks to H.R.H Brigadier Abdullah Bin Al-Hussein, Royal Jordanian Special Forces; Major Shadi Majali, Royal Jordanian Special Forces; Moray Taylor-Smith, Taiwan; Peter Randall, Hong Kong; Superintendent Eric Bar-Chen, Israel National Police HQ, Superintendent Yehoshua Bauer, Border Guard Spokesman's Office, Israel; and Commander David Tzur, Israel National Police; Ken Conboy; Brigadier TS Shergill, Military Attaché, Embassy of India; Mr. Goro Aoki, Police Attaché, Embassy of Japan; in Hong Kong, Peter Randall, Eric Lockyear Police Public Relations Branch; and, David Maxwell for his kind help.

In Africa I would like to thank Commissioner Shedrach Kiruki CBS, Police Headquarters, Kenya; Al J. Venter, South Africa; and, Captain Barkhuizen, Public Relations Dept. South Africa Police Media Liaison, ***Suid-Afrikaanse Polisie, Openbare Betrekkinge, Nediaskakeling***. I would also like to offer special thanks to Robert Pitta for his kind efforts on my behalf.

All opinions and conclusions are my own - Samuel M. Katz - NEW YORK - SEPTEMBER 1995.

# CONTENTS

## MIDDLE EAST & AFRICA



## ASIA & OCEANIA

# INTRODUCTION

Snipers from the New York City Police Department's Emergency Service Unit peer through the scopes of their Remington M24 7.62mm sniper's rifle. (Samuel M. Katz)

*It* has happened to every air traveler. Sitting in row 31, aisle C, and trying to pass the time of a dreadful trans-Atlantic flight, one daydreams. Thoughts of smacking the two crying kids a few rows ahead enters one mind, and more amorous thoughts are evoked by the blonde applying lipstick on the other side of the aisle. Then, of course, there is that one guy who just doesn't look right. He is sweating and is clutching his briefcase too tightly on his lap. Is he just a creep or is he about to announce a holy war and hijack the flight to the sunny shores of Beirut or the sweet skyline of downtown Teheran? Has he planted a powerful bomb inside his shaving kit that, at a pre-determined altitude, will turn the aircraft of aluminum and steel into a flesh-caked jigsaw puzzle of slivers and fragments? Cursing the moment you decided to book your flight, you pray that your fears are media-hyped paranoia. You begin thinking that the high-tech gadgets that airports now employ can sniff out a bomb, detect a gun hidden in an attaché case. But then you remember the "rent-a-cop" security guards manning the X-ray device--chewing gum and talking among themselves as you went through the procedure. Maybe they missed the bag with the bomb, maybe they were paid to. You remember Pan Am 103 and smoking craters around Lockerbie. You want desperately to get off but it is too late. Will this plane be hijacked? Will it be blown out of the sky? Why didn't you just stay at home? WHO WILL RESCUE US SHOULD WE BE HIJACKED? God how I hate to fly!

Years ago, soldiers fought wars and police officers arrested thieves and murderers--their roles were fairly basic and conventional. Then, on July 24, 1968, Palestinian terrorists hijacked an El Al Boeing 707 from Rome to Algiers. At that moment airline passengers became hostages and pawns in the international designs of desperate men whose motives might differ from region to region, country to country, but whose end result usually leaves innocent people dead and lives forever shattered. Military and police forces were left with little recourse, other than to pick up the pieces and vow to do more the next time. Several nations, such as Israel and Great Britain, created counter-terrorist entities the very first time their citizens were taken hostage; most other nations opted to wait until after the 1972 Munich Olympics.

***"They'll kill us off one by one. Don't cry, do something! Attack Them!,"*** spoken by a mourner at the funeral of one of the eleven Israeli athletes butchered by Black September terrorists in the infamous Munich Massacre. Two Olympians were killed in the initial terrorist assault and the nine surviving Israeli hostages, beaten and resigned to a violent death, had been bound and blindfolded inside a military chopper parked on a dark and damp tarmac in a secluded corner of a military airfield. When Bavarian police impotently attempted to rescue the hostages, the Palestinian terrorists, realizing that a victory parade in Damascus would be denied them, turned their automatic weapons on the hostages and cut them down in a gory orgy of ballistic might. For good measure, the terrorists gave their dead charges a fiery send-off, hurling incendiary grenades inside the bullet-marked helicopter. At the time, Munich was a zenith of criminal barbarity in the name of politics and international revolution. To most, the brazen and gleeful orgy of human destruction in the name of national liberation seemed too brutal and senseless to accept as fact.

As a result of the Munich Olympic massacre, virtually every nation on this planet has organized, trained and funded sophisticated and highly trained counter-terrorist forces - some of these units belong to military formations, others are elements of police and gendarmeries. This book is an attempt to list each of the world's ***principal*** counter-terrorist units - from those who are tasked to rescuing hostages seized by gun-toting revolutionaries with their own murderous agendas, to units tasked with hunting down terrorists far from friendly shores, and terminating them with extreme prejudice. From Entebbe to Mogadishu, from London to the Derry, from Port-au-Prince to Panama, the world has become unsafe for terrorists and their masters.

Many security officials argue that the world has changed a lot since the 1972 Munich Olympic Massacre, and the creation of the world's counter-terrorist forces, the units featured in the following pages of this book, are a testament to the revolutionary transformation of military and police units from conventional one-dimensional professionals into operators. But the world of terrorism has also changed since 1972. Today, in fact, Munich seems painfully innocent. Terrorists don't take hostages anymore and are disinterested with the publicity involved in having humiliated nations bow to their demands. In this New World Order, the terrorists' objective is to kill as many innocent victims as possible. No negotiations, no press conferences, no proclamations in Third World forums. The more innocent dead, the greater the victory, with the world transformed into one large indiscriminate battlefield - from the World Trade Center in downtown Manhattan to the plush avenues of Buenos Aires, from the jungles of Panama to the plush rolling hills of Scotland. We had all better take cover. Indiscriminate bloodshed has become the norm. We are all in the cross-hairs.

Although the Israeli athletes murdered in Munich were innocent victims, they were also representatives of a nation embroiled in a war of survival. But the six men who were killed in the February 26, 1993, bombing of the World Trade Center in downtown New York City, or the 1000 people seriously injured in the blast, did not represent any nation; they weren't flag bearers in some global competition. They were workers, fathers and mothers. The one hundred people killed in Buenos Aires in July 1994 when the seven-story office building which housed the Argentine Israel Mutual Association was destroyed by a Renault Traffic van crammed with nearly a ton of Grade-A high-explosives were not soldiers in a national campaign, but workers and students, clerics and children. Housewives strolling their children about in the cool winter's air just happened to be in front of 633 Pasteur Street in Buenos Aires when they were incinerated. These victims possessed no politics, no allegiances. The very fact that they were innocent and in the wrong place and the wrong time made them ***ideal*** targets. "It's madness," claimed one Argentine police officer who couldn't believe the level of destruction and loss of human life, "they won't be satisfied until we are all dead, and we don't know how to fight them!"

One day later, twenty-one more were dead. This time Jewish businessmen in Panama were killed when their commuter plane was destroyed by a bomb as it flew over the jungle town of Colon. Days after that, an Audi sedan parked outside the Israeli embassy in London blew up in a massive fire ball. Fifteen were injured, and nerves forever shattered.

Back in the good old days, when the who's who of revolutionary evil were based in Beirut and a pudgy Venezuelan playboy known to the world as "Carlos" was the king of his trade, there was a certain code of law and order in the world of terrorism. Unless you were a diplomat from one of the several dozen countries that was on the terrorist black list, unless you were an airline passenger traveling to or from Israel, your chances of being at the wrong end of a terrorist's gun were remote. In fact, unless you were of some major importance where killing you or taking you hostage would serve some larger propaganda purpose, terrorism was something that happened far away, "in the desert somewhere," and was brought home by the local news. In those turbulent though predictable days, men received their orders from Moscow Central and the KGB as international terrorism was but one extended battlefield of the Cold War. Today, as the KGB battles organized crime on the streets of Moscow, terrorists receive their orders from secretive offices in Iran where a total holy war, not global revolution, is preached. In his heyday, guerrilla chieftain Yasir Arafat coordinated differing and bickering factions into a dangerous army and succeeded in perpetrating such infamous acts as the Munich Olympic Massacre; today, a humbled Arafat coordinates garbage collection and postal service in the Gaza Strip and Jericho. The world has changed so dramatically in the last few years, yet who ever thought that both law enforcement officials and the average citizen would miss those days of mid-air hijackings? Today, if terrorists have targeted a particular individual, they won't simply walk into his--or her--office and place a bullet between his eyes, and they won't even bother sending a letter bomb through the post: they'll simply blow up the building where the target works, and potentially the entire neighborhood, as well. Terrorists are now looking into nuclear and biological weapons.

When French secret service agents arrested a middle-age man with a cellulite problem and the distinction of being one of the world's most wanted men in the Sudan this summer, it marked the end to what was a golden twenty-five years in the world of international terrorism. "The Munich Olympic Massacre and that whole period of violence was both the terrorists' shining moment and the beginning of the end for their publicity grabbing stunts," claimed Y.,* a senior Israeli counter-terrorists officer. "Sure hostages were taken following Munich, but virtually every nation on earth invested in the creation of super-secret mission-impossible commandos who could be summoned

Operators from Belgium's ESI take-down a suspected terrorist. (Courtesy: ESI)

A dead Black September terrorist killed by Israeli special forces in the Jordan Valley. (IDF Spokesman)

The "Country Club Massacre"--Tel Aviv, March 11, 1978. (IGPO)

at a moment's notice to rescue hostages and kill terrorists virtually anywhere in the world." The Israelis, trailblazers in the field, first rescued hostages on board a hijacked aircraft near Tel Aviv in 1972; unwilling to play the terrorist's game, the commandos dressed as mechanics in white coveralls and stormed the aircraft, killing the hijackers and rescuing 100 hostages. Four years later, Israeli commandos captured the world's attention with "Operation Thunderball," the July 4, 1976, rescue raid at Entebbe. The Germans, eager to erase the stigma of the Munich fiasco, formed an elite counter-terrorist unit, GSG-9, and subsequently rescued a hundred hostages held on board an aircraft in Somalia in 1977. British commandos from the Special Air Service assaulted the Iranian embassy in London to rescue hostages, and Dutch, French, Belgian and Spanish units have also performed "mission impossible" type exploits to save hostages and kill terrorists. The formation of these counter-terrorist units served notice to the terrorists. There would be no more Munichs, no more massacres.

Today, these black clad special forces dynamos have become too much of a match for the terrorist armies that once instilled fear and dread in the minds of so many. Prior to the 1994 World Cup games, for example, American law-enforcement took extraordinary steps to prepare for the potential onslaught. SWAT units received military training from the Army and Navy Special Forces, and from allied foreign services, intelligence files were searched and possible terrorist groups monitored. From New Jersey to Los Angeles, counter-terrorist teams put on very public displays with policemen rappelling from helicopters and firing their weapons into rooms where simulated hostages were being held. It made for great TV, but its true message was clear. The attacks never came. Like all the Olympic games that have since followed Munich, like all major televised events that seem ripe for attack, the terrorists never struck. Even at the height of the Gulf War, when paranoia about Saddam Hussein's secret armies virtually killed trans-Atlantic air travel and resulted in shotgun wielding police guarding New York rail stations, the attacks never materialized. The commandos--or operators, as they are known in the trade--are too good, too proficient, in the fine art of rescue; terrorists don't really hijack airliners and trains anymore, they don't try to seize ocean liners, and want nothing to do with being locked in an enclosed space waiting for a rescue assault to begin. If Entebbe proved anything it was that even the most remote stretch of Africa couldn't protect the terrorist from the long and innovative arm of a nation determined to seek justice and revenge.

Terrorists know that hostage-taking operations are no-win scenarios that will either result in their capture or very bloody death. So, still intent on inflicting death and mayhem throughout the world, they have resorted to a more remote (though more lethal) venue: the suicide and car bomber. The indiscriminate bomber, the master destructive technician, has replaced the cold-hearted killer. This new phase in the terrorist evolutionary chart began one sun-soaked Mediterranean afternoon in April 1983 when a young man, high on amphetamines and promises of paradise, crashed his pickup truck (crammed with a ton of explosives) through the gates of the American embassy in Beirut. The building was destroyed and fifty people were killed, including a good portion of the CIA station in the city. Following the bombing, a leftist newspaper was told by a caller that the U.S. embassy attack was "part of the Iranian revolution's campaign against imperialist targets throughout the world." America, and the west, failed to read the handwriting on the wall.

Six months later, the U.S. Marine barracks in Beirut evaporated in a mushroom cloud of destruction and the lives of 247 Marines were lost. That same day, fifty-four French paratroopers were also killed when another suicide bomber drove his vehicle through the French barracks in the city. The age of the car-bomber had begun. Through proxy--in this case Hizbollah, the Lebanese-Shiite Party of God--Iran had fired its first salvo against the Western world (primarily the United States and Israel) in which massive loss of life was objective number one, strategic targets receiving specific attention being objective number two, and the execution of total war being objective number three. The precedent had been set. From the flaming remnants of Pan Am 103 falling out of the winter's night sky over the Scottish hamlet of Lockerbie in December 1988, to the attempted destruction of the Israeli embassy in Bangkok in 1993. The new face of terror is Iran.

What makes fighting terrorism so difficult today is the fact that the conventional terrorist profile of a professional revolutionary is no longer valid. Gone are the days when men like Carlos, flamboyant guns for hire with the penchant for the high life, roamed the capitals of Europe playing at casinos, bedding young and impressionable girls, and living in KGB supplied safe-houses on an endless supply of drugs and Swiss francs. Gone are the terrorists educated in the camps of Lebanon and in the espionage dens of Eastern Europe, and when women, used their sexual charm and lethal designs, perpetrated some of the deadliest outrages in European and Middle Eastern history. Terrorist today are no longer guided by ideology, or patriotism, but rather by an unflinching and violent devotion to their faith. In the case of Iran, it is terrorism in the name of Islam, and its army are the faithful spread out to the four corners of the earth.

The new face of terror is a man like Mohammed Salameh, one of the coconspirators in the 1992 World Trade Center bombing in New York City. Salameh wasn't a glamorous playboy and he wasn't trained in Moscow. He was an immigrant to the United States meeking out a newcomer's existence. He wasn't rich, or an evil genius--he was arrested, in fact, for being stupid enough to request a refund on a deposit paid on the van used to transport the bomb. Salameh was, however, dangerous and a murderer. A zealot and Islamic fundamentalist who blindly followed the preaching of his spiritual leaders, Salameh was part of a network of part-time terrorists, immigrant plants, who used their adoptive homes and the rights and luxuries these adoptive nations provided, to mount a Jihad, or holy war. Salameh and his group did not receive Semtex explosives from diplomatic couriers and KGB companies, but rather from off the shelf products purchased in chemical supply houses with credit cards and money orders. They opted for simplicity over the technically brilliant--the most bang for the buck. "These guys made the big mistake of shitting where they ate," said one seasoned New York City Police lieutenant involved in the World Trade Center case. "These guys were amateurs who didn't even flee the country the day of the blast. They didn't bomb the building with their passports in hand and first-class tickets booked. They went home, they went to their mosques and jobs. Only the ring leader, the man who coordinated the offensive, got the hell out of there to Iran, Iraq or wherever." The forces of justice proved that its reach was long. That man was Ramzi Ahmed Yousef, and he was brought back to the United States from Pakistan on February 8, 1995, in order to stand trial for his crimes of murder and destruction.

Salameh and his gang of bombers believed that their cause was righteous and the powers of their faith would protect them. They foolishly failed to appreciate the effectiveness of modern law enforcement. Salameh and company were convicted and sentenced to 240 years in prison. Salameh and his partners were followers of blind Egyptian-cleric Omar Abdel Rahman, the man alleged to be the mastermind to both the Anwar es-Sadat assassination and the World Trade Center bombing, also believed to be the ring leader of a more aggressive wave of attacks scheduled to take place in New York, including the destruction of the United Nations and the Federal building in Manhattan, the destruction of tunnels and bridges, and the assassinations of U.S. senator Alfonse D'Amato and Egyptian President Hosni Mubarak. The conspirators in the ring, captured by New York City Police and Federal agents as they mixed their explosives, are scheduled to stand on trial in December. A similar Palestinian terrorist ring consisting of immigrants in St. Louis, Missouri, though belonging to the Abu Nidal faction, was arrested a month after the World Trade Center bombing for conspiring to car-bomb the Israeli embassy in Washington D.C.

An EOD officer from Austria's Gendarmerieeinsatzkommando Cobra detonates a suspected terrorist bomb. (GEK Cobra)

Also troubling is the use of the indigenous immigrant population for clandestine--almost overt at times--support and operations is the fact that it gives virtually every nation on earth--in North and Latin America, Europe and Asia--the potential for being turned into a Beirut or a Bosnia. When speaking of the London embassy bombing, Israeli Prime Minister Yitzhak Rabin said, "There is no doubt in my mind that we face a wave of extreme Islamic radical terrorist movements in the Arab-Muslim countries. They have an infrastructure in Europe, the United States and in Latin America". In fact, the Brazilian town of Foz do Iguaço, a town known for the spectacular Iguaço Falls, one of South America's greatest natural wonders, was the target of a massive intelligence effort by at least a half dozen intelligence services investigating the Buenos Aires and Panama bombings. Sitting on the border between Brazil, Argentina and Paraguay, Foz do Iguaço possesses Brazil's third-largest Arab community, with an Arab population of 12,000--the majority being Shiite immigrants from Lebanon. A lawless town where an Israeli-made Uzi submachine gun can be purchased for $2,500--no questions asked--is believed to be Hizbollah's operational base for mounting attacks in South America. Terrorists and smugglers battling spies and commandos in the jungle is almost the material of a James Bond movie, but truth is stranger and more frightening than fiction.

The combination of terrorism, religion inspired zealousness and roving immigrant mercenaries is a daunting phenomenon. Even the Israelis, as battle-hardened as they come in the fight against terrorism, are visibly frightened by the indiscriminate nature of the new wave of religion-inspired mayhem. The terrorists seem undaunted and brazen by what they can achieve, who they can target, and how many they can actually kill in a single attack. On April 6, Israeli Remembrance Day, the northern Israeli town of Afula was described as a slaughterhouse when nineteen-year-old Raid Zaqarna, a terrorist from the armed wing of Hamas, detonated 385 lb. of explosives, propane gas tanks and three-inch steel nails planted in his car and blew himself up along with a school bus that had pulled up beside his car at a traffic light. Nine were killed in the attack, and fifty-two injured. "Two boys were on fire like torches," claimed a witness who rushed to give

An operator from the Italian GIS takes down an airliner crammed with hostages during maneuvers in Germany. (Samuel M. Katz)

medical care to the wounded, "body parts and blood were scattered for nearly a hundred meters." A day later, on Israel's independence day, a suicide bomber with several sticks of dynamite strapped to his body, blew himself up on board a bus in the town of Hadera. Six were killed in the blast, and twenty wounded. Like similar car-bombers, Israeli security official believed that the terrorists were inundated with amphetamines and doses of "rewards awaiting them as martyrs in paradise" before pulling the pin, an M.O. that Argentine security officials privately believe describes the bomber who blew himself up and the AIMA on July 18, 1994.

Hamas, which means zeal in Arabic, has claimed to fight the peace process with the fires of hell and a drowning sea of blood. Supported by fundamentalists in Jordan, Iran, Egypt and the Sudan, as well as by revenues collected primarily in the United States and Europe, Hamas vows to make good on their threat with an army of soldiers eager to martyr themselves. In fact, Israeli and Panamanian investigators believe that the destruction of the commuter aircraft was one of the first Hamas operations overseas, carried out by a passenger, a suicide-bomber, who had carried the bomb on board with him. Hamas has become so brazen and so confident of its abilities, that it also targets Israeli secret service agents, and has killed several in a sophisticated and highly professional counter-espionage campaign.

It took security officials nearly a decade to safeguard the first group of targets that terrorists used to attack with impunity--airliners, airport and embassies. In the wake of the Marine Barracks bombing in Beirut in October 1983, buildings deemed as high-risk were upgraded to include concrete barriers to prevent some crazy suicidal terrorist from taking a building down, but the World Trade Center was bombed by a vehicle parked in an underground garage. "The World Trade Center was designed to survive all of the fury of the almighty," claims one FBI agent active in the investigation, "and look at what damage was inflicted on the building by one van crammed with explosives. Once terrorists begin bombing office buildings and other civilian and commercial interests, it is economically and physically impossible to provide ample, even adequate, protection." "What are you going to do, stop all parking and vehicular traffic in downtown areas because one building houses one office that one group overseas has a problem with?," the agent asks sarcastically. "These guys aren't deterred by roadblocks or barriers, if they can't strike out at the office then they'll drive out to the suburbs and blow up the director's house and his family."

Many believed that once the Cold War ended and Moscow was removed from the equation, state-sponsored terrorism would end. But Moscow's control over the world's underground armies was a blessing in a disguise. The Kremlin and its satellites provided weapons, money and support but the strings attached to the revolutionary were made of steel and a rigid code of behavior was adhered to at all times. Today, terrorism has but one true patron saint--a pariah nation bent on punishing the west for its sins against Islam and Palestinians; a nation with the natural resources and martyrdom mentality to not only see body counts on city streets reach astronomical levels, but one with apocalyptic beliefs bent on acquiring nuclear technology.

Teheran's involvement in much of the world's terrorism is so troubling because its behavior is so fanatic, its policies so violent and anti-Western. The more the world moves toward a global community and rapprochement the more radical the Iranian government becomes in its cries for a full-fledged Jihad. Ironically, events like the ground-breaking agreement between Israeli Prime Minister Rabin and PLO Chairman Yasir Arafat on the White House lawn, the peace agreement

A Portuguese commando trains in the art of assaulting a terrorist safe-house near Lisbon.

between Israel and Jordan and hints of a deal between Syria and Israel only increase the likelihood that the ante of destruction will be dramatically raised in the months to come. One by one, blood enemies are making peace. The British and the IRA, embroiled in centuries of religious strife, have reached a tentative cease-fire and even Iraqi dictator Saddam Hussein has stated his desire to reach peace with Israel, a country which he bombarded with SCUDs only a few years back. Iran finds itself in a small neighborhood of radical rejectionist states getting ever smaller. Its only means of power is violence, and the more isolated it becomes, the more aggressive the Iranian desire to achieve a nuclear potential of some kind.

For years, the United States toyed with thoughts of mutual assured destruction and first-strike capabilities in formulating its nuclear policy against the Soviet Union. But what use is an arsenal of intercontinental ballistic missiles against a group of individuals with plutonium, a briefcase, and the technology--and homicidal desire--to remove a city. What is to stop Iran, by proxy, from delivering a nuclear device into the United States and removing a city should Washington not atone for its past sins or acquiesce to some new outrageous demands? If Iran, through Hizbollah and Hamas or its other proxies, is willing to killing one or two hundred courtesy of a suicide bomber, what is to stop it from taking out a portion of Manhattan or Washington D.C.? This toned down doomsday scenario, even in light of recent bombings, was once viewed as alarmist paranoia but today is considered the gravest of threats to world security. The proliferation of nuclear materials from the former Soviet Union to such countries as Libya, North Korea and Iran, and their subsequent turning over of such material to terrorist groups, was one of the main reasons behind the Federal Bureau of Investigation opening a large office in Moscow.

There will soon be a day, many counter-terrorist officials fear, when the Ford Ecoline van crammed with a ton of high-explosive will look like a measly firecracker, and the destruction of the AIMA complex in Buenos Aires will resemble an act of vandalism rather than a major terrorist attack. A nuclear cloud hangs over the world and counter-terrorist agencies around the world are scrambling to find a response, an answer, anything to meet this threat. "If they ever do get their hands on the material and technology and the means to detonate a nuclear device," claims an American official, speaking on terms of anonymity who has a gloomy view of what the future holds, "terrorists probably won't make the first nuclear strike in a large European or American city, but rather in remote towns in Africa or South America where they have already built a support and operating infrastructure." The July 18 Buenos Aires bombing is a perfect example. The terrorists three primary objectives in destroying the AIMA were to lash out against the Arab-Israeli reconciliation (no matter where), to kill as many Jews as possible, and to instill a sense of fear and dread among a strong and vibrant Jewish population. Although in the wake of the bombing 200,000 Argentine braved the winter's rain and chill to protest the killings, the seeds of fear, one of terrorism's most cherished objectives, had already taken root. Journalists made an insidious effort to distinguish between the "Jews" killed in the blast and innocent Argentine citizens, and a neighborhood group protested the proposed site of the new Israeli embassy in Buenos Aires (the old one went up in a truck-bomb's fireball of destruction two years earlier) arguing that they didn't want car bombs to go off in ***their*** neighborhood. Residents from the prosperous Belgrano R District now want to have several synagogues dismantled and moved "far away." The shock waves have even spread to neighboring Brazil, home to 150,000 Jews. A nation that prides itself on racial and religious tolerance, heavily armed police units blocked the streets leading up to a Sao Paulo synagogue a few weeks back, stopping and moving cars of residents and searching worshippers in metal detectors; even searching bags containing prayer books and shawls. Even in New York City, home to the world's largest and most vibrant Jewish community, the repercussions of the recent wave of terrorism could not be ignored. "Fear is no longer something that people endure overseas," claimed a New York City detective assigned to protective duty around a Jewish landmard in Manhattan, "it is now something we live and breathe on a daily basis."

New York as possible ground zero for terrorist bombings is a daunting and tell-tale scenario. There wasn't a soul on the planet who could have imagined that the American heartland, Oklahoma City, Oklahoma, would be the sight of one of the most horrific acts of terrorism ever perpetrated in the last twenty years, but on April 19, 1995, at 9:06 A.M. local time, a truck crammed with a home-made bomb weighing nearly 5,000 lb. exploded outside the Alfred P. Murrah Federal Building. The nine-story structure, which included a day-care center, was decimated by the blast which had a destructive range of eight city blocks. The exact death toll in Oklahoma City will, perhaps, never be known. It is expected to surpass 200.

At first, all eyes pointed on the Middle East following the destruction of the federal center in Oklahoma City. Truck bombs, after all, has become the specialty of Hizbollah, Hamas and the Islamic Jihad. Soon, however, it became evident that this was the work of a domestic group or cell of individuals, one determined to wage war against the United States Government in retaliation for Waco, and a whole litany of right-wing issues. Terrorism, it appeared, had taken a sick turn for the worse--when perpetrated from within, its destructive waves create a haunting sense of vulnerability and fear that forever changes the face of the nations it strikes.

In the wake of the "bomber" replacing the "hostage-taker," police and security officials have little choice but to be vigilant and hope that their investigative skills and preventative measures make the terrorists incapable of functioning freely. Few terrorists, however, are deterred by any police or security measures. All that these governments can do is prepare and rally the forces required to battle the threat. But responding to terrorist attacks today is only good in picking up the pieces, searching through the rubble for survivors, and corpses. Nations will have to become more aggressive in their intelligence-gathering operations, in the covert missions, and the realization that this is a nasty, ugly war which must be fought without the restrictions and code of behavior imposed by democratic values. "Otherwise," claims one German counter-terrorist officer from the country's famed GSG-9 unit, "there will be no hostages to rescue, there'll be no rubble, no bodies to bury. Only a nuclear cloud and a point of chaotic no-return."

Some security officials have argued that many counter-terrorist units are now obsolete since the complexion of terrorism has changed

SWAT officers in Taipei, Taiwan, engage in martial arts practice--cold-killing still comes in handy even in this age of laser-sights and heavy ordnance.

so drastically since Munich, Entebbe and Mogadishu. Yet there will always be a need for men wearing Nomex coveralls and black balaclavas to storm an aircraft, raid a safe-house or lurk in the night against the forces of destructive evil. Perhaps the need for such forces was most eloquently summed up by a senior Argentine officer from the country's "***Brigade Halcon***" counter-terrorist following the blast in Buenos Aires. "Our objective should not be to make the streets of our cities safe from possible terrorist attack," he said, "but rather to make the world unsafe for the terrorists."

This is the story of the men who have volunteered to take on this daunting task.

## Argentina

The *"Brigada Especial Operativa Halcon"* patch.

It began as a cool and cloudy winter's July morning in the Argentine capital--it would end with one hundred people killed in Buenos Aires, and nearly twice as many seriously wounded. Outside a seven-story office building housing the Argentine Israel Mutual Association, a Renault Traffic van crammed with nearly a ton of Grade-A high-explosives detonated into a blast of blinding light and ear-shattering noise. When the dust settled and the ambulances and rescue workers reached the scene, it looked like a war zone--like London after the blitz. Terror, in the Middle Eastern variety, had come to Argentina. It had come a year and a half earlier to Buenos Aires when a car-bomb demolished the Israeli embassy, but only thirty were killed. This time the toll was horrific. The dead were not soldiers in a national campaign, but workers and students, clerics and children. Housewives strolling their children about in the cool winter's air just happened to be in front of 633 Pasteur Street in Buenos Aires when they were incinerated. These victims possessed no politics, no allegiances. The very fact that they were innocent and in the wrong place at the wrong time made them ***ideal*** targets. "It's madness," claimed one Argentine police officer who still cannot believe the level of destruction and loss of human life, "they won't be satisfied until we are all dead.... we don't know how to fight them!"

One entity that knows how to fight terrorism in Argentina is the Buenos Aires Police Department's ***"Brigada Especial Operativa Halcon"*** (Falcon Special Operations Brigade). Formed in 1986, the unit was originally created to provide the new and fledgling Argentine democracy with a small, though highly professional police elite capable of dealing with criminal terrorism--not the political opposition and the subsequent "dirty war" that had ravaged much of Argentine society previously under the command of the generals. ***"Brigada Especial Operativa Halcon"*** was to be an ***apolitical*** force tasked with one sole objective--assist the police in heavy tactical situations, be they terrorist, criminal or narcotics related, and to execute "special operations" and intervention in all those cases where the ordinary police cannot cope with the situation. They would be expertly trained in hostage-rescue and assault, and be airborne, heliborne and SCUBA qualified. Officers selected for the unit were to be the smartest and most innovative police officers owning (at least some) military experience.

Today, ***"Brigada Especial Operativa Halcon"*** consists of seventy-five operators. Directly commanded by the commander of the Buenos Aires Police Department, a "Comisario General," who determines where and when the unit needs to be deployed. The unit commander is a Comisario, and only the most experienced and innovative police special operations officers are allowed to ascend through the ranks to command ***"Brigada Especial Operativa Halcon."*** The brigade commander is responsible not only for leading the unit through its day-to-day tasks of intervening in tactical police situations and the deterring and prevention of terrorism, but is also tasked with forging and maintain links to allied units throughout the world. One of the brigade commander's most important tasks is selecting new recruits for the unit and supervising the training course.

Training, for volunteers already owning special forces experience, is six months long, and divided into three two-month sessions or stages. The first stage, basic, is among the most grueling and arduous--candidates are put through an exhaustive regimen where they are trained and tested in physical attributes, combat diving, combat shooting, explosives, parachuting, heliborne insertion, fast-roping and rappelling, survival instruction, and special weapons and tactical equipment. Throughout this phase and the second "intermediate" stage, candidates also study theoretical subjects including: urban operational tactics, first aid, communications, operational analysis, intelligence gathering and reconnaissance, EOD, and crisis intervention and negotiations techniques. The last phase includes advanced intelligence gathering and combat techniques, including other skills such as electronics, sniping and high-speed driving techniques. The attrition rate in the course is high (the exact number is

During joint-training with the U.S. Army's 1st SFOD-D at Fort Bragg, North Carolina, operators from ***"Brigada Especial Operativa Halcon"*** fast-rope from a MH-60 chopper. (Courtesy: Brigada Especial Operativa Halcon)

With Delta Force operators looking on, ***"Brigada Especial Operativa Halcon"*** operators fast-rope to the top floor of a five-story wooden "shooting house" in the compound at Fort Bragg, North Carolina. (Courtesy: Brigada Especial Operativa Halcon)

Once inside, the teams get to work. Here, as operators purify the top-floor, ***"Brigada Especial Operativa Halcon"*** shooters assault a first-floor room with Glock automatics. (Courtesy: Brigada Especial Operativa Halcon)

classified), but those who pass are awarded a special forces certificate and allowed a spot on a ***"Brigada Especial Operativa Halcon"*** team.

***"Brigada Especial Operativa Halcon"*** consists of five combat teams with fifteen operators in each. Within each team, there are two snipers, a paramedic, a hostage-negotiator, an EOD expert, a communications specialist, an intelligence specialist and eight assaulters. In large scale scenarios, the unit can be deployed as a massive intervention squad, but the usual deployment is team strength, to assist detectives and other police units assaulting a known drug location where the criminals are known to be heavily armed, and in freeing hostages held by barricaded subjects. In cases when the unit is deployed against terrorists, both domestic subversive groups and foreign "visitors" who just happened to bring explosives and weapons with them, the ***"Brigada Especial Operativa Halcon"*** operates in conjunction with the nation's intelligence service, the SIDE, and often works side-by-side with military intelligence and military special operations units. As the unit is also tasked with VIP protection, of both visiting and local dignitaries as well as government officials, it is called out on assignment all year round.

***"Brigada Especial Operativa Halcon"*** utilizes a combination of foreign weapons and equipment, and indigenously produced uniforms and protective gear. Unlike most counter-terrorist and hostage-rescue units, ***"Brigada Especial Operativa Halcon"*** does not consider the family of Heckler and Koch MP5 9mm submachine guns as a staple of their existence, and deploys only a handful. For close-quarter combat, the unit favors a 9mm handgun--the Austrian-produced Glock Model 17 is the favorite. When heavier firepower is used, the favored weapon is Italian-produced Franchi SPAS 12 12-gauge shotgun. The unit's primary automatic weapon and sniping weapon is the Heckler and Koch G3 GS/1 7.62mm sniping rifle.

Falcon Brigade's international contacts are vast and inclusive. Beyond the boundaries of South America, where the unit enjoys close ties to virtually all special police intervention units in Chile, Brazil, Uruguay, Paraguay and Venezuela, Falcon has maintained particularly close ties to American law-enforcement and military units. Brigade members have ventured to Los Angeles to train with the LAPD SWAT Platoon, to Florida to train with the Metro-Dade County SRT and the Broward County's Sheriff's Office SWAT unit. Falcon Brigade also enjoys a close-knit relationship with the FBI's HRT and the DEA

The two-man purifying team cleans out a room of any bad guys--note operators carrying Glock Model 18 9mm automatics and carrying additional 12-gauge shells for the team members carrying the shotgun. (Courtesy: Brigada Especial Operativa Halcon)

counter-terrorist intervention unit and has trained with both at their instructional facility at Quantico, Virginia. Falcon Brigade has also trained with United States Marine Corps at Camp Lejeune, South Carolina, and with the U.S. Army's 1st SFOD-D and 7th Special Force Group (Airborne) at Fort Bragg, North Carolina, as well as with 7th Group in Fort Sherman, Panama. As Falcon Brigade is also tasked with maritime counter-terrorism, the unit has frequently trained with the U.S. Navy's NAVSPECWARCOM Dev Group at Little Creek NAB, Virginia. Falcon Brigade also enjoys a close-training relationship with Germany's GSG-9 and Spain's GEO.

Back in Argentina, there is a strange aura of trepidation which has cast its shadow over Buenos Aires. Mothers are frightened to take their children outside, and threats from Lebanon about future bombings has caused many of the city's citizens to modify their behavior. Suspicion now rules where confidence once walked the city streets, and all must endure an inevitable sense of vulnerability and doom that all the policemen in the world cannot restore. "Our objective should not be to make the streets of our cities safe from possible terrorist attack," replies a senior Argentine officer from the country's "***Brigade Especial Operativa Halcon***" counter-terrorist unit, "but rather to make the world unsafe for the terrorists." Only time will tell what the future holds for Argentina in this, the latest battleground of the Arab-Israeli conflict, but it is certain that ***"Brigade Especial Operativa Halcon"*** will be at the ready, in the forefront of any struggle.

Excellent rear-view of ***"Brigada Especial Operativa Halcon"*** operators (and the equipment they bring into the field) acting in concert to create a lethal firepower combination. (Courtesy: Brigada Especial Operativa Halcon)

***"Brigada Especial Operativa Halcon"*** operators display their firing skills and the proper prone firing position. (Courtesy: Brigada Especial Operativa Halcon)

Carrying a Heckler and Koch G3 GS/1 7.62mm sniping rifle and wearing night vision goggles, a ***"Brigada Especial Operativa Halcon"*** prepares to enter a darkened room for dark-conditions target shooting inside the base "shooting house" near Buenos Aires. (Courtesy: Brigada Especial Operativa Halcon)

Inside the "shooting house," already peppered with 9mm holes and buckshot blasts, ***"Brigada Especial Operativa Halcon"*** enjoy some live-fire shooting. (Courtesy: Brigada Especial Operativa Halcon)

A ***"Brigada Especial Operativa Halcon"*** sharpshooter receives some assistance from the team leader during tactical maneuvers in Buenos Aires. (Courtesy: Brigada Especial Operativa Halcon)

Interesting series of photographs of a four man assault team (the two gunmen, the operator carrying the 12-gauge shotgun and the operator with the Heckler and Koch G3 GS/1) check their gear before storming a house, and then the assault begins--the lead member carrying the body bunker enters through the front door followed (almost hugged) by his cover man, as the two operators with the heavier firepower follow closely behind. (Courtesy: Brigada Especial Operativa Halcon)

## Brazil

*Foz do Iguaço, a town known for the spectacular Iguaço Falls, sits near one of South America's greatest natural wonders. Nestled on the border between Brazil, Argentina and Paraguay along the Parana River, Foz do Iguaço (and Ciudad del Este, just across the Parana River in Paraguay) are large town known as an out of the way resort for vacationers throughout Latin America and a town possessing Brazil's third-largest Arab community, with an Arab population of 12,000--the majority being Shiite immigrants from Lebanon. It is as lawless a town that can be found anywhere in South America--an Israeli-made Uzi submachine gun can be purchased for $2,500--no questions asked! Smuggler move liquor, electronic goods, cocaine, refugees--even babies--among the three countries, and brothel owners pay sex slave trader for teenage girls kidnapped from the countryside. Arms dealers peddle weapons and high explosives freely; and, according to Foz do Iguaço Police Chief Remy Gubert, Jr., "Millions of dollars worth of sophisticated weapons arrive each year from Miami in sealed drums inside cargo ships, and are distributed to smugglers throughout the region." Most important, however, Foz do Iguaço is believed to be Hizbollah's operational base for mounting attacks in South America. Terrorists and smugglers battling spies and commandos in the jungle is almost the material of a James Bond movie, but truth is stranger and more frightening than fiction. It is a town that is the target of a massive intelligence effort by at least half a dozen intelligence services in search of the bombing of the Jewish cultural center in Buenos Aires on July 18, 1994, and the bombing of a Panamanian commuter plane one day later.*

*It is 120° in the shade in a jungle paradise and the sun has yet to disappear to the west. At a nearby military base, three dozen operators, all wearing heavy and sticky black Nomex coveralls, converge on a wooden shooting house to prepare for the raid--intelligence reports several of the suspects wanted for the bombing of the Buenos Aires Jewish center are hiding. They are in Foz do Iguaço, in a poor neighborhood, inside a safe-house believed to be guarded by close-surveillance cameras, men with MP5s, and booby-traps. The operators check their own MP5s, and rehearse the assault over and over again. No one wants to die this blistering summer's day. The unit commander wanted the men inserted by a helicopter, a fast-rope assault would be the fastest, but the sounds of a chopper's beating blades would be a tip-off and alert the bad guys to run. Instead, they will pull up to the targeted house in commercial vans--five in all.*

*The operators wait until sunset before racing through the dusty streets of the shanty town in their vans at speeds in excess of 70mph. They reach their target unnoticed, and deploy through the main door and up the stairs in seconds. A shotgun blast blows the lock off of one door and a flash-bang grenade is tossed into the apartment's foyer. A blinding flash and a cloud of cordite is followed by the operators checking each and every room for signs of life--the potential for a deadly confrontation. There are seven rooms in all and it takes less than 40 seconds for the entire apartment, building and surrounding block to be secure. Police units are later called in for investigative support, but the bad guys had been warned. There was no one in the apartment, though large sums of cash and forged documentation were seized.*

*The operators return to their vans, unsling their MP5s and head back to base for the debriefing. They are disappointed but not discouraged. After all, they are members of the Brazilian Army's 1st Special Forces Battalion Counter-Terrorism Detachment, and each soldier knows that they will be very busy in the months to come. According to Brazilian Federal Police, since 1992 over 1,000 fundamentalist Shiites have arrived illegally in Ciudad del Este and Foz do Iguaço prompting police and army units, including the 1st Special Forces Battalion Counter-Terrorism Detachment to search Arab-owned ranches, gun shops and residences throughout the area,*

1st Special Forces Battalion Counter-Terrorism Detachment unit emblems, and the tools of their trade. (Courtesy: Brazilian Army 1st Special Forces Battalion Counter-Terrorism Detachment)

An operator, in full riot gear with gas mask, poses for the camera while clutching his MP5 SD3 9mm submachine gun. Note indigenous battle harness and holster for .45 automatic. (Courtesy: Brazilian Army 1st Special Forces Battalion Counter-Terrorism Detachment)

1st Special Forces Battalion Counter-Terrorism Detachment operators on the range. (Courtesy: Brazilian Army 1st Special Forces Battalion Counter-Terrorism Detachment)

***as well as cattle ranches bought by Arabs from Lebanon in recent years along Brazil's unpatrolled border with Uruguay.***

In 1953, following the hijacking of a civilian aircraft to the deepest stretch of the Amazon jungle, the Ministry of Aviation formed a special intervention squad to deal with hijackings or criminal acts of a political nature involving civilian aviation and the unit was under the command of the Força Aérea (Air Force). The unit was trained in surrounding and securing an airfield, storming an aircraft and executing tactical missions against the hijackers; the unit also possessed negotiators. In terms of a modern counter-insurgency force, a special forces entity was formed under the overall command and control of an air-ground division, in order to provide a guerrilla like force should it be needed in defense of the country from both irregular forces (such as rebels) as well as against terrorists and narco-terrorists. It was not until 1983, however, that a purely anti-terrorist and hostage-rescue force was established and incorporated into the Brazilian military's order of battle. That unit is the ***Destacamento Contra-Terror do 1º Batalhão de Forças Especiais - BFEsp - do Exército Brasileiro***: The Brazilian Army's 1st Special Forces Battalion Counter-Terrorism Detachment.

An all volunteer force, the 1st Special Forces Battalion Counter-Terrorism Detachment is similar to the U.S. Army's 1st SFOD-D in make-up, recruitment, mandate and training. Only those paratroop and special forces soldiers showing exemplary performance are even allowed to volunteer for service in the unit, and they must endure a grueling fourteen-day selection process where soldiering skills are examined and put through rigorous examination; according to unconfirmed reports, the attrition rate during this grueling process is as high as 90%. The counter-terrorist course lasts a full thirteen weeks, and is carried out at a top-secret facility near Rio de Janeiro. The course includes expert marksmanship, combat diving, combat shooting, explosives, parachuting, heliborne insertion, EOD, fast-roping and rappelling, survival instruction, and special weapons and tactical equipment. Because of Brazil's varied geographic landscape, extra emphasis is placed on intelligence-gathering and long-range reconnaissance--especially the stalking of a target in impassable jungle terrain. 1st Special Forces Battalion Counter-Terrorism Detachment operators are expert jungle warriors and taught to survive in the wild for weeks at a time. As expert in the art of jungle survival as the most experienced Amazon hunter, 1st Special Forces Battalion Counter-Terrorism Detachment operators have trained in the Amazon with the most notorious local tribes and are as expert in killing with a machete and dagger, as they are with a MP5 on full auto. Interestingly enough, because of Brazil's chaotic and often congested roadways, 1st Special Forces Battalion Counter-Terrorism Detachment trainees are taught high-speed and evasive driving techniques; according to "unconfirmed" reports, German instructors from Mercedes Benz have traveled to Brazil to teach operators the skill of "combat driving."

The 1st Special Forces Battalion Counter-Terrorism Detachment operators function in large teams, believed to consist of twenty-four operators. Their principal weapon is the Heckler and Koch MP5 family of 9mm submachine gun--the MP5 SD3 suppressed variant being the favored weapon. Shotguns deployed by the unit include the indigenous 12-gauge ENARM Pentagun shotgun, and the Remington M870 Mark 1 U.S. Marine Corps shotgun. The favored sniping weapon is the Heckler and Koch PSG-1 7.62mm marksman rifle, and the unit handgun is the American Colt .45 Model 1911A1 automatic.

1st Special Forces Battalion Counter-Terrorism Detachment foreign contacts are believed to be limited, and obviously center on cross-training with Portugal's GOE. The 1st Special Forces Battalion Counter-Terrorism Detachment is also believed to have trained with the U.S. Army's 1st SFOD-D and 7th Special Force Group (Airborne) at Fort Bragg, North Carolina, and the U.S. Navy's NAVSPECWARCOM Dev Group at Little Creek NAB, Virginia.

It should be noted that other branches of the Brazilian military deploy small elite units also capable of executing counter-terrorist missions, including the ***Grupos Especiais de Resgate de Marinha do Brasil*** (Brazilian Marine SOG), the ***Esquadrões de Resgate e Salvamento da Força Aérea Brasileira*** (Air Force Special Forces), and the ***Grupos de Ações Táticas Especiais*** of the various military police battalions stationed throughout the country. The 1st Special Forces Battalion Counter-Terrorism Detachment also trains and functions with various federal, state and municipal police agencies inside Brazil.

Stoic portrait of a 1st Special Forces Battalion Counter-Terrorism Detachment fire-team, posing at the entrance to their base near Rio de Janeiro. (Courtesy: Brazilian Army 1st Special Forces Battalion Counter-Terrorism Detachment)

1st Special Forces Battalion Counter-Terrorism Detachment operators practice and perfect their rope deployment along a drill tower. Expert ropesmen, unit members are renown for ability to climb enormous heights in split-second speeds. (Courtesy: Brazilian Army 1st Special Forces Battalion Counter-Terrorism Detachment)

Unit operators practice their low-light firing skills at their home base indoor firing range. Note Brazilian flag patches worn on the right upper sleeves. (Courtesy: Brazilian Army 1st Special Forces Battalion Counter-Terrorism Detachment)

Exciting photograph of a 1st Special Forces Battalion Counter-Terrorism Detachment team creating a human ladder in order to deploy over a wall obstacle. (Courtesy: Brazilian Army 1st Special Forces Battalion Counter-Terrorism Detachment)

# Canada

Canada first thought of establishing a national para-military/police counter-terrorist force in 1972, following the Munich Olympic Massacre. The Black September attack in Munich and the subsequent botched rescue attempted at Fürstenfeldbruk Airport had special significance for the Canadians since they would be hosting the 1976 Summer Olympics in Montreal. As a result, in 1975, the Canadian government authorized the Royal Canadian Mounted Police (RCMP) to create a hostage-rescue unit; the official mandate was a "trained means of intervention to domestic armed and barricaded situations." The unit, called the Emergency Response Teams of the RCMP, first borrowed its initial tactics and strategies from already existing North American police departments (such as the Los Angeles Police Department's SWAT unit, and the New York City Police Department's Emergency Service Unit). Military tactics, taken from instruction given by the Canadian military--especially the 1st Special Service Force. Initially, the RCMP ERTs consisted of seven-man teams--***all volunteers***--that included two snipers armed with high-powered weapons, such as M16A1 5.56mm assault rifles fitted with high-powered scopes and other military-issue sniper weapons such as the Canadian C3A1 7.62mm sniping rifle. As far as hostage-rescue forces go, the ERT was a small-scale stop-gap meant to prevent a repeat of the Munich Massacre. The 1976 Summer Games were peaceful and without incident, even though Palestinian terrorist groups did threaten to attack the Israeli team, and several threats were made against the South African squad. In addition to the ERTs who perform this function on a national level, a team functioned in each province--especially in the National Capital Region (NCR) of Ottawa where the RCMP employed a full-time ERT on permanent stand-by status. This team's responsibility was to provide an immediate and decisive response to

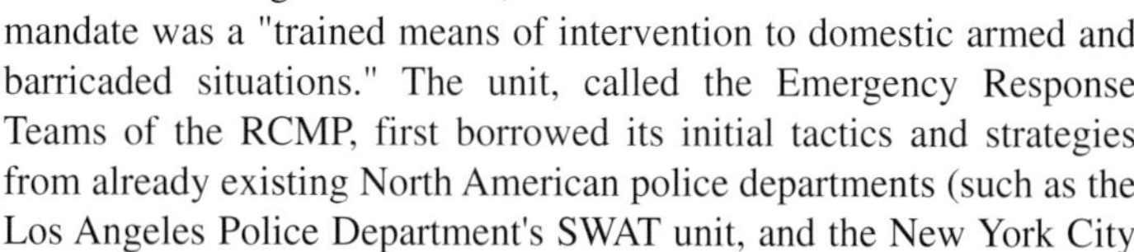

A senior RCMP officer discusses counter-terrorist tactics with two SERT operators during demonstrations in western Canada. The RCMP's SERT enjoyed a tremendous reputation as a force not to be crossed, and as a result enjoyed a tremendous deterrent psychological edge against "bad guys" planning operations in Canada. Note that operators are armed with MP5s and Browning Hi-Power 9mm automatics. (Courtesy: Ottawa Citizen)

SERT operators prepare to fast-rope down a RCMP chopper--the vast stretches of Canada made the unit's air mobility an important weapon in their order of battle. (Courtesy: Ottawa Citizen)

The Insertion!" Kicking up a blinding whirlpool of dirt and debris, a RCMP chopper deploys a force of SERT operators. (Courtesy: Ottawa Citizen)

Wearing their full black kit, including Kevlar body armor, assault vest, and obligatory balaclava, a three man SERT shock troop prepare to enter a "killing house." Note Heckler and Koch MP5s carried, and Brownings carried on hip/upper thigh holster. (Courtesy: Ottawa Citizen)

any terrorist attack against an embassy, consulate or government buildings in the capital.

Following the surge of international terrorism in the mid-1980s, especially hijackings, aircraft bombings and seajackings, the RCMP decided that it needed a larger, and more responsive type of force to meet and neutralize any terrorist situation on Canadian soil, or even perhaps to end terrorist situations involving Canadian nationals abroad. In May 1986, the RCMP formed its Special Emergency Response Team (SERT). Initially, the SERT was a fifty-man size force which consisted of the most capable volunteers already in ERT service. Eventually, however, the size of the force grew to be seventy-two-strong.

The SERT was a true hostage-rescue force similar in mandate and structure to Germany's GSG-9 and the FBI's HRT; it, in fact, received supplemental training from these units, as well as from Britain's Special Air Service, the U.S. Army's 1st Special Forces Operational Detachment-Delta, and, it has been suggested, several other European and "Asian" counter-terrorist forces. The SERT borrowed the tactics of many of these forces, including much of the equipment these forces carry into a situation--from the Heckler and Koch MP5 9mm submachine gun used by virtually every HRU around the world, to the British G60 Stun Grenade.

Service attachment to the SERT was strictly on a voluntary basis or regular duty officers with several years of experience in the RCMP. The SERT selection process was considered to be the most arduous in all of Canada, rivaling even the extremely difficult and highly selective process used by the Canadian military when selecting candidates for its elite 1st SSF. Training for all those who passed the selection process included four months of combat and tactical instruction, with snipers receiving an additional two months of training. A SERT tour of duty consisted of a three year rotation, although the options existed for an extended length of duty dependent solely on the officer maintaining his combat and profession proficiency.

The SERT was never operationally deployed in its seven years of activation. In April 1993, the SERT was ordered to disband, as responsibility for counter-terrorist work and hostage rescue operation was transferred to a newly created and top-secret unit of the Canadian Department of National Defense; Canadian reports have indicated that this unit is called “Joint Task Force Two.”

The SERT enjoyed very close relations with the FBI's HRT, Britain's Scotland Yard and various European counter-intelligence and counter-terrorist organizations and agencies; they have also enjoyed close-ties with the Israelis. It is believed that these national alliances, especially now with the U.S. Army and Britain's SAS, continue with the newly formed Canadian military counter-terrorist unit.

Close-quarter target practice for a four-man SERT squad. Note varied firing positions including combat prone pose for operators firing the MP5, and single-hand firing position for the operators clutching their 9mm Brownings. (Courtesy: Ottawa Citizen)

"Bang.....your dead!" A terrorists worst nightmare--an aim-light with their forehead for a target. On a floor littered with 9mm shell casings, SERT members hone their already razor-sharp marksmanship skills. (Courtesy: Ottawa Citizen)

# Colombia

*The orange Latin sun had yet to make its complete and brilliant appearance over the town center, but an eerie glow had set in over the wooden buildings as the squad moved in. They were fifteen in all, crouched down in an uncomfortable stance laden down by Kevlar body armor, gear and weaponry, connected to one another by powerful Motorola communication devices and peering around the corners through holes in their knitted caps doubling as balaclavas. Their camouflage was "urban BDU," a pattern of gray, black and white that seemed not quite to blend in with the brightly painted walls of the surrounding buildings. It didn't matter. The men hadn't planned to be there all that long anyway.*

*Slinking through the square, they positioned themselves around a small two-story dwelling, painted blue with red window sills. While a sharpshooter climbed a nearby bar to perch himself, and his PSG-1 rifle, on a balcony covered with different color light bulbs, the squad readied itself for the assault. Already, all fingers were slowly caressing the blue steel trigger housing of their German-produced Heckler and Koch MP5SD3 9mm submachine guns, and left eyes squeezing through infra-red scopes. At the commandante's signal, the assault begins. A small C-4 charge blows the front door wide open and three rows of three men race in their weapons blazing. The sharpshooter has unleashed five rounds of 7.62mm fire, as well, and the cover force on the ground outside provided a 270° field of fire. The ballistic display lasted all of seventy-three seconds.*

AFEU operators, clad in black Nomex coveralls, assault an outdoor TAC house at their home base near Bogota. (Courtesy: Colombian Armed Forces)

Covering one another with MP5s, two AFEU entry-teams prepare to enter the unknowns behind the front door of a shooting/TAC house; the AFEU has been forced to exercise entries in hundreds of instances. (Courtesy: Colombian Armed Forces)

Carrying an assortment of weapons, from suppressed MP5s to Remington 700 sniper rifles, AFEU operators in their urban camouflage fatigues, parade for inspection during a late-night morale-boosting ceremony prior to an early A.M. deployment in Bogota. (Courtesy: Colombian Armed Forces)

*At the end of display, the commandante signaled the end to the exercise with a rousing thumbs up. It had been an awesome show. As a few dozen officers, wearing neatly pressed olive uniforms with golden ranks and rainbows of medals examined the mock-up killing house, they noticed that the cardboard cut-outs meant to substitute for hostages had been rendered intact without a scratch while the cut-outs acting as terrorists had been peppered with dozens of well-placed holes, 7.62mm and 9mm in size; most rounds weren't wasted on what would have been body shots--they were all aimed at the head with a between-the-eye focus.*

*Once again, the men of the AFEU had proven why they are Colombia's best.*

Few countries have endured the scourge--and price--of internal

As an instructor looks on, AFEU operators perfect the art of a ladder assisted entry into a TAC house near Bogota at Facatativa.. Note gas masks worn, as well as protective headphones. (Courtesy: Colombian Armed Forces)

A Colombian Air Force UH-60 races toward a jungle LZ which will also be used by AFEU officers as a forward CP during a raid against a Cali cartel drug lab. (Courtesy: Colombian Armed Forces)

UNASE operators from "Rural Cundinamarca" meticulously move about a semi-deserted villa in the Colombian hills in search of wanted drug lords; note suspect, center, cuffed and secured next to an operator peering down the sights of his M-16A1 5.56mm assault rifle. (Courtesy: Colombian Armed Forces)

terrorism than has the Central American nation of Colombia. Caught in the crossfire of the turmoil of Latin American politics and coupled with the violence and uncontrolled fortune of the cocaine cartels and their drug economy, Colombia has been ***the*** epicenter of the world's battle against narco-terrorism. Cartels in Medellin, Cali and other sections of the country have set off car bombs in the crowded boulevards of Bogota (killing dozens), assassinated police officers, judges, newspaper editors and even political candidates, and have kidnapped and extorted just about anyone in the country worth seizing in the middle of the night. The narco-terrorists have literally turned the country into a giant fortress with the interior a lawless and often brutally violent feudal state.

Beyond the scope of Colombian narco-terrorists and cocaine-cartels involved in violence, the nation's principal terrorist group is the ***Movimiento 19 de Abril***, or 19th of April Movement also known as "M-19." Headquartered in Cali, the group's political objectives include to lead a vanguard struggle against the Colombian "bourgeoisie" and American "imperialism," along the lines of the communist struggles in southeast Asia. To achieve its goals, M-19 resorts to extorting funds from narcotics producers and distributors and on occasion will even cooperate and safeguard narcotics facilities and shipments. With an estimated membership of 1,000 hard-core supporters, and operational fronts in Putumayo Province (in the south), Tolima Province (in the west) and in the capital city of Bogota, the group's reach is nationwide. M-19 was formed on April 19, 1970, and expanded quite quickly after 1977 when its members received training and support from the Argentine Montoneros and the Uruguayan Tupamaros, as well as from the Cubans and Libyans; it is believed that M-19 officers received training from the PLO in Lebanon prior to 1982.

M-19's most infamous operation was the November 1985 attack on Bogota's Palace of Justice by nearly thirty heavily armed terrorists, including several young and highly attractive women sporting Uzi submachine guns and fragmentation grenades. The terrorists took an astounding 500 hostages, including many members of the Supreme Court and the Council of State. Colombian military units, including mechanized units firing 106mm recoilless rifles, counterattacked killing nearly twenty of the terrorists and freeing 400 hostages in a mad dash under a hail of flying ordnance, choking dust and an engulfing stench of death and cordite. When the siege ended, fifty hostages lay dead, including eleven members of the supreme court. Eleven soldiers had also died in the battle, and all the terrorists were killed. It was the worst terrorist incident in Colombian history and a turning point.

Colombian military and police units have been among the world's busiest in combating drug gangs and terrorists, guerrillas and revolutionaries. They are also among the world's most experienced. Colombia's principal counter-terrorist unit is the ***Agrupacion De Fuerzas Especiales Urbanas*** ("Urban Counter-Terrorist Special Forces Group, or AFEU). Unlike other units of its kind, the AFEU is neither army, police or navy, but rather a highly successful conglomerate of every facet of the Colombian defense and security community. The AFEU was formed on April 8, 1985, when Colombian military units, including mechanized forces, were unable to respond to the M-19 guerrilla attack on the Palace of Justice in Bogota. A small unit by Colombian standards, its total strength does not exceed 100-men, the unit is divided into six fifteen-man squads (two officers and thirteen operators), and includes weapons, operations, intelligence and quartermaster officers and NCOs. Although the AFEU accepts volunteers from every branch of the Colombian armed forces (as well as Metropolitan Police and National Guard) the unit is under the direct control of the ***Commandante de las Fuerzas Armadas*** (Commander of the Armed Forces), and the unit is headquartered at the ***Escuela de Caballeria*** (Cavalry School) near Bogota.

All volunteers to the AFEU undergo a strict and most grueling selection process. Only those soldiers, airmen, sailors and policemen displaying the highest intelligence, most disciplined physical attributes and best weapons skills are even allowed to try out for the unit, and all potential candidates are screened for leftist political affiliations and any potential ties to any of the nation's cocaine cartels. Those who survive the seven-day process begin an exhaustive six-month training course that has the candidates trained to split-second perfection in any and all aspects of counter-terrorism and hostage rescue. Training is conducted north of Bogota, at Facatativa, and includes rescue assault training to free hostages being held inside buildings, on board buses, planes, trains and even ships; special emphasis is placed on unit marksmen and the use of snipers for commencing rescue operations. Fast-roping and rappelling skills are emphasized, as are EOD skills and high-speed driving. Another AFEU specialty and tasked mandate is VIP protection, and in this function, according to one officer in the U.S. Army's 7th Special Forces Group (Airborne), "The unit is as expert as they come." AFEU operators are also renowned for their martial arts skills, especially cold-killing and hurling daggers. The unit's principal weaponry include the MP5 family of 9mm submachine guns; M16A2 5.56mm and Galil 7.62mm assault rifles; M60 7.62mm light machine guns; Glock, Beretta and Browning 9mm pistols; and, Remington M870 Mark 1 U.S. Marine Corps 12-gauge shotguns. As they face a determined and often heavily armed litany of opponents, AFEU operators also carry M79 40mm grenade launchers into action, as well as M72 66mm LAW rockets. AFEU snipers prefer Remington's 700 7.62mm sniper weapon system.

Much of the AFEU's operations since the unit was created in 1985 have been countering narco-terrorists, and indeed the unit captured notorious drug traffickers Carlos Lehder Rivas in February 1987 and Pablo Escobar in 1994. In February 1990, the AFEU was deployed to Cartagena during the first anti-drug summit attended by South American leaders and U.S. President Bush. During the summit, the AFEU secured and controlled Cartagena airport, established sniper

Faces camouflaged and guns on full-auto, UNASE operators deploy for action to secure a drug lord's villa and his armed defenders. Note second photograph and subdued individual. (Courtesy: Colombian Armed Forces)

UNASE operators from "Rural Cundinamarca" stand on guard atop a villa rooftop after securing it from a heavily armed drug gang. Note characteristic UNASE black coveralls, and black baseball cap. (Courtesy: Colombian Armed Forces)

UNASE operators, in their urban warfare camouflage, engage mock terrorists during a training exercise. (Courtesy: Colombian Ministry of Defense)

positions at the ***"Casa de Huespedes"*** ("Guest House") where the leaders were meeting. Prior to the summit, the AFEU raided several hundred "alleged" narco-terrorist safe-houses and villas.

Another special Colombian counter-terrorist unit, a force tasked with combating politically related kidnapping and extortion incidents, was formed in the summer of 1991. After an astounding number of kidnappings were recorded in a single summer in the capital of Bogota, Colombia, President Gaviria announced the creation of the ***Unidad Antisecuestro y Extorcion*** (Anti-Extortion and Kidnapping Unit, or UNASE) for operations exclusively in Bogota. According to material released in the still vibrant Colombian press, the UNASE consists of thirty-five operators--a colonel commands the unit, four officers command strike teams, fifteen NCOs maintain discipline and operational readiness, as well as double as squad team deputies, and fifteen operators, or special agents, fill the ranks. The unit was created to respond, within minutes, to any report of a terrorist-inspired kidnapping inside the Bogota city limits as well as in the nearby jungle suburbs. Their vehicles include armored squad cars and the use of Metropolitan Police helicopters. The unit can best be described as "half-detective, half-hostage-rescue." UNASE operators hunt down the kidnappers using any and all police skills and tricks "up their sleeves," and are drawn from a pool of the best detectives in the Metropolitan Police. But once they track down where the kidnappers and their hostages are, UNASE operators are specifically and expertly trained in the art of hostage-rescue having received extensive training from UEI personnel in Madrid.

UNASE equipment is standard Colombian special operations fare, with all personnel carrying Beretta 9mm automatics as personal side-arms, M16A2 and Israeli-produced Galil 5.56mm assault rifles, G3 7.62mm assault rifles, and MP5 9mm submachine guns.

On August 29, 1991, the UNASE turned operational putting on a dramatic "dog and pony" show for much of the Colombian defense and internal security establishment. So impressed were senior officers with the display that General Fabio Campo Silva, commander of the Metropolitan Police, suddenly announced the creation of two similar units in the northern cities of Bucaramangara and Barranquilla; more units have since been formed throughout the entire country. Because urban and rural work is so different in Colombia, from raiding safe-houses in high-rise apartment building to assaulting a jungle drug location, two types of UNASEs exist--one responsible for a city and one responsible for a stretch or rural (jungle and mountain) terrain.

Urban UNASE units are divided as follows:

- Investigative Section
- Intelligence Section
- Operational (Tactical) Section
- Technical Section
- Administrative Section

Rural UNASE units are divided as follows:

- Command and Operations Group
- Investigations Group
- Intelligence Group
- Evaluation and Analysis Group
- Communications and Electronics Group
- Crime Scene Group
- Transportation Group

The UNASE's first operational deployment came on October 7, 1991, when it responded to a drug cartel's kidnapping of a high-profile businessman in Bogota. The gang was tracked down and terminated in a brief fire-fight and the businessman released unharmed. Since then, they have been summoned several hundred times to tactical situations inside the country's larger cities of Bogota, Cali and Medellin, as well as in rural jungle locales where counter-terrorist skills and jungle warfare experience are the difference between the successful execution of a mission and the unit being forced to bury several of its own.

## Mexico

In June 1983, the then chief of Mexico's Capital Police, Colonel Ramon Mota Sanchez, proposed the creation of a special police unit to combat organized crime and criminal violence--narco-terrorism, and the violence that it brought, had become epidemic. Once established, however, the unit evolved into an organization charged with high-risk missions requiring the special training, equipment and skills associated with urban counter-guerrilla actions and anti-terrorism. It was according to one Mexican security expert, "half SWAT, half-special ops, all daredevil!" The unit, designated with the mysterious and supposed to be deterring "Force F" title, eventually became known as is known quite affectionately as the "Zorros." Commanded by a police colonel who is directly subordinate to the Secretary General For Protection and Highway Administration of the Federal District, the "Zorros," a 350-man squad, is based just due north of Mexico City close to the Secretary's headquarters. According to ***American*** intelligence reports, it consists of 350 counter-terrorist commandos equipped with M16A2 5.56mm assault rifles, CAR-15s, Smith and Wesson 12-gauge shotguns, 30-06 rifles, HK33 5.56mm submachine guns, and, of course, the counter-terrorist staple, the Heckler and Koch MP5 9mm submachine gun, as well as Beretta 9mm pistols; the unit also deploys tactical grenades, stun devices, and tear gas."Zorros" operators deploy for operation in full battle kit, camouflaged fatigues or black coveralls, complete with Kevlar body armor, load bearing equipment and the obligatory black balaclava. The troopers are usually deployed by the Mexican police's fleet of UH-1 and Jet Ranger choppers, or armored deployment vehicles, such as modified 4x4 trucks.

"Force F/Zorros" is a purely volunteer force--all applicants must be physically fit, considered expert in all tactical aspects of their work, and willing to specialize (sniper, EOD, communications). The unit is organized along conventional military lines, divided into what is known as "urban commando squads," "emergency ordnance disposal squads," and "sniper and marksmanship squads." They are in many ways similar to an American municipal SWAT unit, as they are tasked with counter-terrorism, hostage-rescue, EOD tasks, and the isolation and apprehension of violent criminals (something required more and more frequently in Mexico these days). Typically, they carry out five "jobs" a day--deactivating explosive devices left behind by rival drug gangs, rescuing hostages and kidnapped individuals, seizing terrorists and violent criminals, and raiding drug houses or those suspected of belonging to activists, guerrillas and sympathizers to the ***Ejercito Zapatista de Liberacion Nacional*** (the "Zapata Army of National Liberation" or EZLN), the underground liberation army that, in 1994, achieved extraordinarily effective achievements in the border state of Chiapas when it occupied one city, three towns and two villages with a ad-hoc army, many of whose soldiers were armed with nothing more than swords, spears and guts.

In terms of true counter-terrorist ability, the "Zorros" first gained prominence during the 1986 World Cup Soccer tournament when it protected the entire international festival and tournament from any potential and perceived threat; the unit also displayed its intervention skills for journalists in a display meant, in the words of a former "Zorros" officer, "To send the bad guys a message." The message was received--no terrorist attacks were attempted.

The "Zorros," obviously, enjoy its closest cooperation with American counter-terrorist, special operations units. The unit trains regularly with the FBI HRT at the Quantico, Virginia, facility, as well as visits to the "compound" at Fort Bragg for courses with the Army's 1st SFOD-D. The "Zorros" also send officers on fact-finding missions to various municipal SWAT units throughout the United States, especially to forces in California (Los Angeles and San Diego), Texas and Florida where the local units have officers who are native Spanish speakers. The "Zorros" have also entered in joint-training programs with other Latin American counter-terrorist and hostage-rescue units, including Argentina's ***Brigade Especial Operativa Halcon***, Chile's GOPE, and Venezuela's Special Intervention Squad. It has also been rumored that Spanish advisors, from the GEO and UEI, have been posted to the "Zorros" training facilities on regular intervals.

## U.S.A. - U.S. Federal Bureau of Investigation Hostage-Rescue Team (HRT)

***March 1994, East Rutheford, New Jersey. Little more than a year after a small, though determined, group of terrorists struck at a symbol of the United States of America in the bombing of the World Trade Center, all American law-enforcement eyes turned to Giants Stadium just across the Hudson River from New York City. That June, the world, literally, would be making its way to the United States of America to celebrate the international game of football--soccer. The 1994 World Cup was to be played in a nation that although did not play the game as a national sport, was the international media epicenter. When the tournament would commence on a warm day in Chicago, the eyes of the worlds--literally--would be focused on what happened on a select group of grass playing fields from California to the Atlantic shore. Such worldwide press was ripe for exploitation, for a statement. It is the type of global village scenario that makes law-enforcement officials reach for the antacids and makes the mouths of terrorists water.***

The coat of arms of the Federal Bureau of Investigation. (Courtesy: FBI Public Information Office)

The FBI badge. (Courtesy: FBI Public Information Office)

***The Federal Bureau of Investigation (FBI) was not willing to let any incident or any group spoil the games, and the display in East Rutheford was proof for the pudding. Outside Giants Stadium, as members of the world press gathered with recorders on and shutters ready, several dozen men, in black Nomex fatigues with body armor and black Fritz helmets ran through a course of obstacles with MP5s in hand; they fast-roped down the sides of the stadium facade, raced through a series of drainage pipes slinking about as if encountering a determined terrorist foe, and posed for the cameras with their weapons and gear in hand. Their MP5s were equipped with suppressers and with specially-designed flash-lights and laser aim-point devices, and several vans, all unmarked, supported the unit with a wide-array of space-age technology and state-of-the-art equipment. The FBI was proclaiming that should any individual or group attempt to interfere with the World Cup, they would encounter a determined and highly capable force of combatants.***

The concept of a federal American counter-terrorist and hostage-rescue unit is a fairly recent idea when compared to the European and Israeli models. Although the Munich Olympic Massacre was a scenario studied and examined by American law enforcement agencies, it was done primarily on the municipal level involving city SWAT units and State Police response teams; the kind of terrorism that groups like the militant Black Panthers and the Symbionese Liberation Army professed and executed was handled more by local police units rather than heavily armed federal agents. Yet following the 1975 OPEC incident in Vienna, following Entebbe and Mogadishu, American law enforcement realized that some sort of response on a federal level would eventually be needed; a hijacking situation did involve more than the "regular" SWAT team, and the use of "a" military unit to deal with a hostage incident in the United States requires a direct order from the president.

The true impetus behind the creation of the FBI's counter-terrorist unit, however, was the 1984 Olympics in Los Angeles, and the fact that many felt that it was a grave mistake to have left the security for the 1980 Winter Games, held in Lake Placid, New York, in the hands of local and state agencies. Even though global tensions were high during the 1980 Games, especially in light of the Soviet invasion of Afghanistan and the crisis in Iran, more tangible threats to American internal security would follow: including the mysterious Libyan hit teams, the bombing of the American embassy and Marine barracks in Beirut; these attacks all brought the possibility of terrorism to America's shores from a distant nightmare to a comprehensible reality.

An HRT special agent prepares to fire his Heckler and Koch HK 33E 5.56mm assault rifle during winter-time exercises in Virginia. The HRT prefers the Heckler and Koch family of weaponry to those of any other manufacture. (Courtesy: FBI Public Information Office)

Cover and concealment police officer's most trusted bit of training at the academy. Here, during counter-terrorist ambush training, HRT operators cover one another as the lead agent (right) prepare to move ahead with MP5 in hand. (Courtesy: FBI Public Information Office)

The potential for a large-scale terrorist attack during the 1984 Los Angeles Olympics prompted the creation of the Federal Bureau of Investigation's counter-terrorist and hostage-rescue force--a force that would become known as the HRT, or "Hostage Rescue Team." It was to be based at the FBI facility at Quantico, Virginia, just over the Potomac River from the nation's capital. Even though security for the 1984 Games would eventuality be charged to the LAPD's SWAT Platoon, the FBI HRT soon developed for itself a second-to-none reputation for tactical skill and professional standards. Created in late 1983 under authorization of William Webster, initial training for the HRT was completed in August 1983, and the unit became fully operational one month later. From the onset, it was decided that negotiations would be the team's first and primary strategy, and indeed, the unit's abilities was augmented by the fact that the bureau maintained a highly-trained hostage negotiator in each of its fifty-nine field offices.

By its very mandate, the HRT was to be more than just a tactical assault unit specializing in rescue work. The mission of the HRT extends past rescue operations, and involves the complete gamut of federal criminal justice jurisdictions. This includes rescue, apprehension, crime scene searches and testifying in court. In this capacity, the HRT is a national asset available to every field office across the country, required to function in both urban and rural settings. It's motto is simple and an apt description of its function: "To Save Lives."

When the FBI command decided to create the HRT, it did not want to implement an on-call force of agents who, through training and time, would lose their investigative skills and instincts. As a result, the unit became a carefully selected fifty-man squad of ***experienced*** FBI Special Agents, and team Agents spend about fifty-percent of their time training and fifty-percent doing criminal investigations.

Wearing their characteristic black coveralls and specially produced tactical assault vests, HRT officers make the most of a piece of cover found on the Quantico obstacle course as they let loose with three-round bursts of 9mm fire from their MP5s. (Courtesy: FBI Public Information Office)

Amid the backdrop of used tires helping absorb the blast of stun devices, fragmentation grenades and an endless barrage of 9mm and 5.56mm fire, HRT operators deploy for a "house clearing" exercise at the unit base in Quantico, Virginia. (Courtesy: FBI Public Information Office)

In November 1987, the two longest simultaneous sieges of U.S. prisons occurred, resulting in the largest crisis management mobilization in FBI history, and included the deployment of the HRT. These sieges provided a unique opportunity to test the entire range of hostage negotiation concepts, as taught by the FBI, in two parallel situations--two sieges in response to an agreement between the U.S. Department of Justice and Cuba that approximately 2,500 of the 125,000 Cubans who arrived in the United States during the Mariel boatlift would be returned to their homeland. Many of the potential deportees were incarcerated in the Oakdale, Louisiana Correctional Facility (OCF) and the U.S. Penitentiary in Atlanta, Georgia, (USPA). To these prisoners, deportation meant return to the cruel and inhumane conditions they had experienced during their imprisonment in Cuba. Although the 987 Cuban inmates in Oakdale were told that the agreement would have little impact on them, inmate informants began to warn guards that a riot might occur. Measures were taken to respond to a violent incident, but OCF's design did not allow for a "lock down" of prisoners. On Saturday, November 21, 200 inmates carrying homemade weapons (primarily shanks) rushed the front entrance of the facility, only to be repelled by guards using tear gas. This confrontation continued with inmates taking fifty-four prison employees hostage, of which twenty-six escaped or were released within the first three hours, and one was later released because of injury. The remainder were held hostage for the next nine days. Two days later, 1,370 Cuban detainees in Atlanta rioted, setting fires to buildings and taking seventy-five hostages.

While the HRT stood ready to enter the prison and end the hostage-taking ordeal through tactical means, the FBI and the Federal Bureau of Prisons (BOP) handled the crisis with meticulous patience and uncanny good will; the standoff ended days later after a grueling period of give and take and high-level negotiations. FBI officers on the scene knew that had the HRT entered the fray, the situation would have ended sooner, but also feared that several hostages, inmates and agents would have been killed, as well. The two incidents represented watershed marks for the HRT--they would try, through the most controlled patience permitted, to refrain from using deadly force in an incident. Their motto is to save lives, not to take them and, as a law-enforcement agency, albeit on a federal level, there is no such thing as acceptable casualties. Two recent incidents involving the HRT illustrate the difficulties and sometimes impossibility of restraint.

The first incident involved a 1992 hostage-siege and stand-off outside a ranch in Ruby Ridge, Idaho, when a white-separatist named Randy Weaver refused to surrender on weapon charges to U.S. Marshals. A U.S. Marshal and Weaver's son were killed in a shoot-out, and eventually several hundred FBI agents including the entire fifty-man HRT were called to the scene. In a controversial move far removed from federal guidelines, HRT commander Richard Rogers issued orders to his snipers that they should fire on any armed adult in the vicinity of the besieged cabin. One HRT sniper, Lon Horiuchi, fired on Weaver as he stood outside the cabin, but the shot only slightly wounded the separatist and, instead, killed his wife, Vicki, who was standing behind the targeted individual, and who the sniper could not see. On January 6, 1995, the Director of the Federal Bureau of Investigation Louis Freeh disciplined twelve agents for improper judgment and neglect of duty during the 1992 shoot-out.

The second use of deadly force by the HRT and the FBI came in May 1993, in Waco, Texas, outside the compound of David Koresh and the Branch Davidians. The ordeal, which began over a month earlier when four Bureau of Alcohol, Tobacco and Firearms agents were killed in a botched raid on the Davidian compound, ended after the FBI stormed the complex when negotiations failed to end the siege. The siege and subsequent killings at Waco is now a classic case of negotiations, hostage-rescue and siege warfare worthy of an entire book (it has been studied by over a hundred police agencies inside the United States), the HRT was deployed primarily in a sniper role--it was hoped that the HRT's marksman would be able to systematically eliminate targets they saw throughout the compound with weapons and therefore allow agents moving in on the fortified house and structures to retrieve the innocent children being held there. Of course, tear gas was deployed by the FBI, as was a combat engineer's vehicle (CEV). Hours later, HRT snipers and observers saw a white flag being produced, signaling that their patience and efforts had worked and that the entire ordeal would end without additional loss of live--especially without the loss of the children still inside. One of the followers, however, soon started a fire that quickly engulfed the entire compound in a fiery act of mass suicide and murder; "Children are like hostages," Koresh had uttered, "since they can't make decisions for themselves."

Waco was a tragic incident in the history of American law enforcement and a senseless loss of life that might have been averted. HRT snipers, men capable of hitting a quarter-inch target at 200 meters, had Koresh in their sights on several occasions, but because of the agency's rules of engagement forbidding them to fire on anyone unless they are not directly threatened themselves, they were legally restrained from "taking him down." Just how close the HRT adhered to its policy and motto of "To Save Lives" was perhaps best illustrated by the fact that agents feared the Koresh would feed the children (the hostages the agents were most concerned with) poison in a copy of the Jonestown Massacre in Guyana. HRT officers on the scene were all carrying anticyanide kits with them, and were prepared to rush the compound under fire and administer them to the dying children should the situation have presented itself.

Even though the Idaho and Waco sieges and debacles have been the source of great controversy for the HRT in terms of the amount of lethal force employed, the HRT has it as a clear pillar of its operational doctrine that it prefers negotiating over tactical assault. As a matter of training and policy, the FBI preaches restraint and the need to negotiate perhaps more than any other similar unit around the world, and certainly more than American municipal police SWAT units. In a situation such as an airline hijacking, for example, the FBI HRT would not go in unless the terrorists are slaughtering the hostages in a mad and uncontrolled orgy of violence; in a scenario such as the GIGN's rescue of AF 8969, FBI officials have told local law enforcement officials that they simply would not go in. Nevertheless, HRT agents train in taking down a hijacked airliner, bus or train on a year-round basis.

The HRT does, nevertheless, prepare for its tactical deployments being as explosive, effective and lethal as possible. The unit's training facility and home base at Quantico, Virginia, is considered among the world's most advanced--certainly on par with the GSG-9 facility at St. Augustin, the GEK Cobra base near Vienna, and the GIGN's base at Satory. The HRT possesses classrooms with intelligence material on virtually all the world's major and minor terrorist groups, information on the latest technology and tools employed in the fight against terrorism and in the art of hostage rescue, and maintains outdoor and indoor firing ranges and "killing houses" where tactical scenarios can be replicated under optimum conditions.

As a state-of-the-art counter-terrorist team with facilities considered among the world's best, the FBI HRT has forged ties with an army of international counter-terrorist and hostage-rescue teams, as well as close working ties to the hundreds of American municipal and state SWAT and tactical response units, as well as to military units. The HRT has trained with the U.S. Army's 1st SFOD-Delta and the U.S. Navy's SEAL Team SIX, and has instructed and trained with (or by) the Bureau of Alcohol, Tobacco and Firearms, the U.S. Secret Service, the U.S. Drug Enforcement Agency, the U.S. Customs Service, the

Amid cut-out targets, FBI HRT operators practice tending to a wounded terrorist taken in custody during a unit assault and wounded by unit firepower. Even though the HRT will deploy lethal force when necessary, it is still dedicated to saving lives, even those of terrorists and hostage-takers, so that they may be brought to justice at a later date. (Courtesy: FBI Public Information Office)

During take-down exercises, an HRT officer surprises a "terrorist" at the unit outdoor killing house--distracting the hostage-taker so that the hostage can be secured. (Courtesy: FBI Public Information Office)

U.S. Department of Energy, the Los Angeles Police Department SWAT Platoon, elements of the NYPD's Emergency Service Unit; officers from the Washington D.C. Police Department's Emergency Response Team (ERT), the Metro-Dade County SRT and SWAT and tactical response teams from over 100 jurisdictions throughout the United States, Mexico, Canada and other locations throughout the world--from the Sultanate of Oman to Hong Kong.

FBI HRT operators are proponents of the Heckler and Koch family of MP5 9mm submachine guns, and deploy them exclusively on virtually all jobs with the MP5A5E and MP5 SD3 being the most popular. The unit's primary assault rifle is the M16A2 and CAR-15 5.56mm assault rifle, though the HK33E is gaining popularity among HRT agents. Although the unit does not deploy shotguns on most jobs, HRT mobile command centers and arsenal trucks do carry Remington Mk. 870s, and the unit's primary sniper weapon is the Remington M40A1 7.62mm sniper weapon; the unit has experimented with Steyr police rifle, as well as the Heckler and Koch PSG-1. Browning Hi-Power 9mm pistols were once the favored side-arm of choice in the unit, but that has since been replaced by the Glock family of 9mm pistols.

Interesting view of the personal equipment carried by HRT officers in the field, including Protec helmets, Kevlar body armor and assault vests. Removable American flag patches are worn at all times. (Courtesy: FBI Public Information Office)

## U.S.A. - U.S. Marshals Service Special Operations Group (SOG)

The U.S. Marshals Service is the nation's oldest and most versatile federal law enforcement agency. Dating back to the year 1789 when George Washington appointed the first thirteen U.S. Marshals; the Marshals were created by the first Congress in the Judiciary Act of 1789, the very same legislation that established a federal judicial system. The Marshals Service has served the nation for over 200 years through a variety of vital law enforcement activities, and virtually all Federal law enforcement initiatives ***today***[1] involve the U.S. Marshals Service, including: the custody, care and transportation of Federal suspects and prisoners; the tracking and apprehension of Federal criminals who jump bail, violate parole or escape from prison; protection of courts, judges, attorneys and witnesses; enforcement of court orders; and, management of seized assets. Headquartered in Arlington, Virginia, the U.S. Marshals Service directs the activities of ninety-five district offices and personnel stationed in over 350 locations throughout the United States, including all fifty states and a stretch of territory from Guam to Puerto Rico, as well as the U.S. Virgin Islands and various other offices spread across the globe. Each district, it should be added, is headed by a Presidentially appointed U.S. Marshal. Approximately 3,500 Deputy Marshals and career employees perform the following nationwide day-to-day mission of the service.

The Marshals Service Patch.

Deputy U.S. Marshals carry out hundreds of special missions yearly that are related to the Service's broad federal law enforcement and judicial security responsibilities and the service maintains a highly specialized counter-terrorist apprehension and deterrence task force. The Special Operations Group (SOG) is that force. It is a specially trained and highly disciplined tactical unit, and a self-supporting response team that is fully-equipped with "alert equipment" and capable of responding to emergencies anywhere in the United States or its territories within six hours after receiving the order to assemble; to achieve this task, the Special Operations Group can call upon the support of local and state agencies, as well as of U.S. military units to aid and assist with transport. Most of the Deputy Marshals who have volunteered to be SOG operators serve as full-time Deputies in Marshals Service offices throughout the nation, and remain on-call twenty-four-hours-a-day for SOG missions. SOG missions include apprehending fugitives, dignitary protection, court security, transporting high-profile and dangerous prisoners, witness security and asset seizures.

The Special Operations Group dates back to April 1971. At that time, the Marshals Service was tasked by a Federal Court order to remove violent demonstrators from the island of Culebra, Puerto Rico; the mission was successfully completed, but it illustrated the need for a specially trained group of Deputy Marshals who could readily--and tactically--respond to such situations no matter when or where their services were needed. As a result, SOG was born at the request of the Attorney General. The first SOG training was conducted in 1971 in Los Fresno, Texas. There, at what had been at one time the Border Patrol Training Academy, selected Deputy Marshals trained--for the most part---in riot control and the tactics of urban confrontation, techniques, that by today's standards of violent crimes, seems prehistoric. Some of the assignments undertaken by SOG in those early and formative years included: (1) The violent May Day riot in Washington, D.C. in 1972; (2) Restoration of law and order at the American Indian Reservation at Wounded Knee, South Dakota in 1973; (3) The relocation of, and security for Vietnamese refugees on the Island of Guam in 1975; (4) Searching for survivors in Guyana after the Jonestown massacre in 1981; (5) Restoring law and order in the Virgin Islands after Hurricane Hugo struck in 1989; (6) Support of the military operation "Just Cause" in Panama, and the subsequent transport of Manuel Noriega to the United States to face drug trafficking charges in December 1989 (as well as providing security to the court where his trial was held); and, (7) Assisting the Los Angeles Police Department and the California National Guard in restoring order in Los Angeles after the riots that resulted from the Rodney King verdict. The group provided tactical teams to Los Angeles, Houston and Washington, DC. to support "Operation Gunsmoke," a ten-week multi-agency fugitive manhunt of the country's most violent and hard-to-find fugitives, and also participated in "Operation Trident," a nationwide sweep of the country's "most wanted fugitives" that netted 5,700 arrests in nine weeks in the summer of 1993; several of those seized were notorious drug traffickers, narco-terrorists, seized in locals as diverse as Miami, New Orleans, Honduras and Medellin, Colombia. Recently, Marshals and heavily armed tactical teams have been on-call to provide extra security to abortion clinics that have been targeted by extremely violent and fanatic Right-to-Life groups using terrorist-like tactics.

In 1983, the SOG Training Center and base for operations was established at Camp Beauregard, Louisiana. It became the base not only for SOG Basic and Advanced Training, but also a place where other federal, state, and local law enforcement agencies could receive tactical law enforcement training from Special Operations instructors. Since 1986, SOG instructors have also conducted training for foreign police officers under the State Department's Anti-Terrorist Program. As a result, hundreds of police officers from countries around the world (including Bolivia, Poland, the Philippines, and Turkey) have received training in anti-terrorism tactics, security procedures, and other specialized tactical skills. The SOG maintains a small, full-time operational cadre stationed at the Marshals Service Tactical Operations Center at Camp Beauregard, Louisiana, the "Harvard of American law enforcement tactical training," where all SOG deputies undergo extensive, specialized training in tactics and weaponry.

Service in the Special Operations Group is purely voluntary, and every Deputy who applies for SOG training is carefully screened and evaluated. Of those who undertake the SOG Basic Course, less than fifty-percent usually complete it, and they must meet rigorous standards of physical and mental ability when applying and prove their worth and true makeup throughout the lengthy instruction. The training requires physical and mental toughness, and the ability to perform under intense stress, "But," according to an SOG instructor featured in a rare televised interview, "it is nothing when compared to the streets." The training regimen, all three months of it, resembles a combination of the Los Angeles Police Department SWAT Platoon instruction and the Federal Bureau of Investigation's HRT School. Heavy emphasis is given to tactical assault and dynamic entries, and both units have cross-trained with the SOG. SOG operators and teams train incessantly in the execution of tactical assaults and entries into fortified strongholds (such as a barricaded fugitive or a booby-trapped drug stash location) and train in rappelling and fast-roping techniques and heliborne insertion and extraction. SOG operators are among the world's most proficient pistol handlers and marksman. While the SOG deploys the Heckler and Koch MP5 family of 9mm submachine gun, many operators prefer the Colt Firearms 9mm Colt submachine gun; a weapon which embodies the same straight line construction and design as the well-known Colt M16A2 5.56mm assault rifle. Initially, the United States Drug Enforcement Agency (DEA) adopted the weapon after extensive testing, and soon after several U.S. military and law enforcement agencies also adopted the sleek and reliable weapon--including the Marshals Service; it is also believed that the SOG carries KAC 9mm Suppressed Colt submachine guns, as well. Another SOG favorite is the Ingram Mac-10 submachine gun. The SOG's primary assault rifle is the CAR-15 5.56mm, and marksman carry M16A2s with scopes and the Remington M-24 system. The principal handgun is the Glock Model 19 and the Beretta M9 (though .357 Magnum's are a personal favorite of many SOG operators), and the shotgun of choice is the Ithaca 12-gauge DS Police Special shotgun.

Although most SOG operations are carried out with great secrecy and usually under the cover of darkness, their "jobs" are numerous and transcend the entire American continent and throughout the world. It should be noted that the Marshals Service has been designated by the U.S. Department of Justice as the primary U.S. agency to apprehend fugitives wanted by foreign nations and believed to be in the United States; in turn, the Marshals Service also tracks and apprehends, with the assistance of local authorities, U.S. fugitives who are thought to be in hiding in foreign countries. The Marshals Service maintains a liaison representative at Interpol Headquarters in Lyons, France, as well at the El Paso Intelligence Center in Texas.

The Marshals Service maintains a protective counter-terrorist program in its "Missile Escort Program" (MEP). Deputy Marshals provide security and law enforcement assistance to the Department of Defense and the U.S. Air Force during the movement of Minuteman and cruise missiles between military facilities. Deputies in selected districts are specially trained to assist with this program. They assisted in 611 missions in 1992 alone. This program is supervised by the Service's Office of Special Services.

It should also be noted that many of the Marshals everyday operations, especially Judicial Security and Federal Witness Protection involves heavy tactical work. Federal courts and judges under threat are protected by an elaborate and often heavily armed M16-toting U.S. Marshals presence; Marshal snipers, often on-loan SOG agents, will often add security to court houses ringed with agents and police officers. In 1993 alone there were 496 serious threats lodged against members of the judicial community, some requiring around-the-clock protective details. Protecting Federal prisoners, often the targets of very real threats from organized crime families, terrorist groups and drug cartels is also an involved and highly specialized form of counter-terrorist warfare and one that the U.S. Marshals perform remarkably well.

February 8, 1995: Outside the Manhattan Corrections Center in downtown New York City, in sub-freezing temperatures, U.S. Marshals man a vigil as Ramzi Ahmed Yousef, mastermind of the World Trade Center bombing, is brought back from Pakistan to stand trial in the United States.

[1] The Congress and the Presidency have called upon the Marshals to perform unusual and extraordinary missions, such as registering enemy aliens during times of war, sealing the American border against armed expeditions aimed at foreign countries, and handling the exchange of spies with the Soviet Union and the Communist-bloc during the Cold War.

# U.S.A. - The United States Army Military

The forces under the USSOCOM umbrella--the 1st SFOD-Delta (Airborne) falls under the command of JSOC (upper right hand corner).

***Lower Manhattan, New York City: Spring 1994: NYPD Emergency Service Unit squads had been notified not to respond to calls from concerned citizens about men dangling off of thirty-story skyscrapers in the middle of the night--the U.S. Army was conducting maneuvers while the city slept. Intrigued, city cops headed down to the Wall Street area to find men wearing black Nomex coveralls armed with MP5s rappelling off the ledge, monitored by men, in civilian dress, carrying two-way radios and peering through field glasses. "Eagle-Seven, this is base, Over!" The commander, called sir, by the people around him had ordered the operators to climb up to the thirtieth floor of the skyscraper again, and to rappel down to the twentieth floor and deploy poised for action. There was reason for the madness and just cause for the unit to depart their secured surroundings at Fort Bragg, North Carolina--no matter how sophisticated and realistic a training base can be, the "real thing" can never be replicated. The soot and grime along the ledges, the pigeon shit, the grease and chemicals left behind by workmen. Should terrorists seize a portion of a skyscraper in a major urban center, the rappelling tower in the North Carolina countryside just won't be sufficient prefatory material. It is what brought these operators to the Big Apple and they were determined to keep their exercise a quiet endeavor.***

***This was no ordinary exercise in Manhattan and this was no ordinary unit. As the New York City Police Department officers looked on in amazement and awe, the operators went through the motions of their instruction and exercises with greater energy and gusto as the early morning hours stretched into the amber emergence of dawn. Daylight meant that their time was up and they'd be heading back to North Carolina on a military flight. When morning hit the Wall Street, only a handful of people had known that they were ever there in the first place. After all, they are known in USSOCOM circles simply as "The Boys in Black."***

Whether they like it or not, the U.S. Army 1st Special Forces Operational Detachment-Delta is undoubtedly the most famous counter-terrorist unit in the world--even though they have yet to pull of a significant hostage-rescue operation along the lines of Entebbe, Mogadishu or Princess Gate; one British operator, demanding anonymity dared called the unit "Always a bridesmaid, though never a bride." They are nevertheless the men--and women?--of "Delta" and

A Delta operator demonstrates and displays his uniform, load bearing equipment and ubiquitous MP5 A2 9mm submachine gun. While Delta uniforms and equipment change and evolve on a daily basis, their basic uniform for overseas deployment consists of green fatigues or overalls, and personally selected specially produced load-bearing equipment and pouches. (Courtesy: Terry Griswald)

the mere mention of the name is enough to invoke images of the large-scale and the extravagant, massive firepower and the entire brunt of the American military behind it. The U.S. Army's 1st SFOD-Delta (Airborne) owns a unique international reputation that is part-hype, part self-promotion and part myth. They are, undoubtedly the most discussed unit in the world and the one that has trained the most smaller-nation counter-terrorist units the world over. They are, however, an enigma--not even officially recognized as existing as a unit even though it recruits through official army publications.

Like most counter-terrorist units around the world, "Delta" was born out of tragedy, yet it's very creation was mired by one of the most painful chapters in the modern American military history. In late 1977, years after most European nations began to cultivate indigenous counter-terrorist units of their own, President Jimmy Carter authorized the creation of an American counter-terrorist unit. It was five years after the Munich massacre, a year after Entebbe, and the German operation at Mogadishu had just gone down. America was woefully lagging behind much of the world, but trends in terrorism indicated that future attacks promised to become bolder and would involve far many more hostages. When sanctioning the creation of this indigenous American force, President Carter had asked his military and Justice Department officials to look through the files and find a man around whom this new force could be built--until the Pentagon intervened, there was talk of having this unit under the control of the Federal

Bureau of Investigation. Eventually, the name of a charismatic and highly capable officer reached the men President Carter had tasked with coordinating the creation of this force. His name was Colonel Charles Beckwith and America's response to terrorism, and the force that he would command would come to be known as Delta Force.

Colonel Charles Beckwith was born in Atlanta, Georgia in 1929 and turned down a chance to play football with the Green Bay Packers in order to take an R.O.T.C. commission in the U.S. Army. An early volunteer for the U.S. Army's Special Forces, even before they became the now legendary "Green Berets," Beckwith was a man with specific special operations talents that his superiors noticed and admired. In 1963 he was among the first U.S. Army officers to be liaisoned over to the British 22 Special Air Service Regiment--an experience that would forever change his life as well as the course of United States special operations thinking, planning and execution. While with the SAS in the Malayan jungles, Beckwith studied and learned (it was reported that the SAS had taught him eighty-six ways to kill another human being), admired and desired the opportunity to copy. That opportunity would come in 1965 when he was deployed to the Republic of Vietnam in command of the mysterious "Delta Project," a forebear of today's 1st SFOD-Delta (Airborne). Noted for his command of Army Special Forces personnel in country, especially at the siege of the Plei Me Special Forces camp in 1965 and during a rescue operation at Bong San in 1966, where then Major Beckwith took a 12.7mm round in the gut. Although wounded and almost declared dead by army surgeons, Beckwith bounced back and continued his service in the military including a return to Vietnam as commander of a battalion of Screaming Eagles in the 101st Airborne Division. His aggressive sense of duty and objective, his single-mindedness and overall interest with the professional execution of his mission (as opposed to the easy road up the ladder of command) earned him the affection of his troops, the respect of his contemporaries and the admiration of his superiors. It also earned him the name "Chargin' Charlie," a nickname that would follow him his entire life.

Following Vietnam, Beckwith returned to Fort Bragg but the world had become a far more hostile area for United States interests throughout the world. Terrorists that used to strike only at Israel, the British, or the Germans, were now finding a large and tempting target in the United States--not inside the confines of the fifty states but rather in Europe, in the Middle East and in Asia. The first harbinger that a crisis was developing for American interests was the March 1, 1973 takeover of the Saudi Arabian embassy in Khartoum, the Sudan, by Black September terrorists in which the American ambassador, Clee Noel, was singled out as a hostage and brutally murdered. American officials were left to the devices and skills of local police, military and intervention units. The Sudanese were grossly incapable of mounting any rescue and, as a result, hostages died.

In 1975, the seizure of the supply ship S.S. ***Mayaguez*** and the lengthy and muddled U.S. response once again displayed the American inability to mount a rescue operation. Time, for the creation of a national hostage-rescue force, was desperately running out. By 1977, and a year into the Carter administration in Washington D.C., an Israeli ***military*** unit, ***Sayeret Mat'kal***, had pulled off two incredible operations, including the Entebbe raid 3,000 miles from her national borders, the Dutch BBE had pulled off a rescue on board the besieged train at Du Pont, the French GIGN had successfully rescued a group of schoolchildren in Djibouti and, in Mogadishu, GSG-9 had exorcised

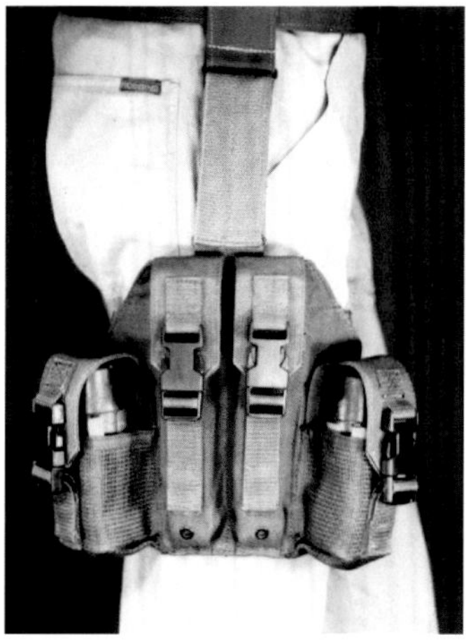

An Eagle Industries hip pouch--useful for carrying extra clips of MP5 ammo and flash-bang and smoke canisters--in widespread use with 1st SFOD-Delta operators. (Courtesy: Terry Griswald)

Interesting view of a Delta-inspired and Delta-used assault vest, featured Kevlar body armor protection and enough carrying power to carry clips for the operator's individual MP5, M4 or 12-gauge shotgun. (Courtesy: Terry Griswald)

In "Wally's World," Delta operators fast-rope down a 160th Special Operations Aviation Regiment (Airborne) MH-60 Pave Hawk atop a modified "TAC House" at SOTF. The structure is not believed to be the facility's notorious "House of Horrors." (Courtesy: Brigade Halcon)

1st SFOD-Delta (Airborne) operators fast-rope down a hovering MH-60 Pave Hawk from the U.S. Army's 160th Special Operations Aviation Regiment (Airborne) during insertion and extraction training at Fort Bragg. Few counter-terrorist units the world over are as lavishly equipped as Delta, and even fewer can rely on the muscle of a military might like the U.S. military for support, transport and facilities around the world. (Courtesy: Brigade Halcon)

the ghosts of Munich and rescued a plane load of hostages held aboard a Lufthansa airliner. Should a TWA flight be seized by foreign terrorists, or should any citizens, be they tourists or dignitaries, be assaulted or seized overseas, America had no coordinated response.

From the moment the first word was released concerning the failed Bavarian sniper effort at Fürstenfeldbrük, there were those in the U.S. special operations community who began contemplating the birth of an American counter-terrorist response. Much of the thought process came out of Fort Bragg, North Carolina, home to the U.S. Army's Special Forces command, and from Coronado NAB near San Diego where the U.S. Navy SEALs were headquartered. Vietnam had been the ideal testing ground for special operation deployments and strategies, but filtering forces through a jungle was a far different ballgame than a precision-strike rescue operation. After the GSG-9 rescue at Mogadishu, President Carter was quoted as asking the Pentagon, and General Bernard Rogers in particular, if the Americans possessed a similar capability. Most generals serving on the Joint Chiefs of Staffs and in the various operational offices and command knew the answer to be a resounding "negative." No officer, however, had it within him to tell the President of the national inability, and eventually the impetus to create an indigenous response unit was issued. The man to receive the call was Colonel Charles Beckwith.

The initial U.S. military counter-terrorist program was known under the code-name of "Blue Light." What was significant about Blue Light was its cohesive manner in which specific talent was sought and meshed to achieve a specific objective. The U.S. military following the Vietnam War was a force being rebuilt in both its equipment and doctrine with an emphasis on professionalism--with the draft abolished in 1973, the U.S. military was, for the first, an all volunteer service. The army improved but it was a slow and laborious process. "Blue Light," an effort to form a cohesive U.S. Army Rangers, Special Forces and U.S. Navy SEAL counter-terrorist effort, was rivaled by a plan by the 5th Special Forces Group (Airborne), the group responsible for the Middle East and North Africa, to handle all of the counter-terrorist and hostage-rescue scenarios. Finally, there was a plan by Colonel Beckwith at Fort Bragg to create a separate--black--unit along the lines of the British 22 SAS. From his post at TRADOC (Training and Doctrine Command), Beckwith formulated his vision and his unit--one to be called the 1st Special Forces Operational Detachment-Delta.[1] Both the 5th Special Forces Group (Airborne) and the forces under the "Blue Light" program were already inside their respective units, but Beckwith wanted a new breed of fighter in the 1st SFOD-Delta. He was not seeking men who had signed up in order to be eligible for the G.I. Bill, but rather veterans who had survived the Vietnam debacle in the service and who yearned to do something different in a world whose balance of power was shifting from conventional and nuclear to the masked man holding innocents--and nations--hostage.

When Beckwith received the authorization for the 1st Special Forces Operational Detachment-Delta (Airborne), headquartered in Fort Bragg, he faced problems and considerable obstacles. Firstly, the chain of command linking the unit to any ongoing scenario was laboriously muddled and bureaucratically prone to tragic delays--Beckwith had lobbied for the 1st SOF-Delta (Airborne) to be placed under the control of the Army's Chief of Staff, not Forces Command. Beckwith realized that the fewer people controlling his unit's operations and deployments the more efficiently and effectively they could react to a crisis overseas. In recalling how the SAS did things, basically getting whatever they wanted, Colonel Beckwith wanted to remove Murphy's Law from counter-terrorist special operations and to have this unit in command and control of all its intelligence-gathering, signals and supply levels. Beckwith was hoping to remove the "have been" and the "what if's" of Son Tay from the mantle of American special operations, though, ominously, the bungling of Son Tay would hang over Delta's head.

The Son Tay operation should have been the U.S. Army's "Entebbe." The November 21, 1970 raid was a bold attempt to rescue American POWs held captive north of Hanoi by the North Vietnamese, but the operation failed for the simple reason that the intelligence had been off--very off! After months of research, analysis, intelligence-gathering and coordination with Army and Air Force special operations, the task force succeeded in flying the 400 miles behind enemy lines to reach the prison camp but the prisoners had since been moved. Men like Beckwith and the subordinates he had hand picked to get the 1st SFOD-Delta (Airborne) off the ground realized the mistakes of Son Tay, separate intelligence units dictating the movements of separate military entities, could prove a fatal combination in any significant hostage-rescue strike; in this case the special forces units at Son Tay were lucky as casualties were nil. Time was of the essence in such operations, as was decisiveness and officers

Delta snipers peer through the sights of their Heckler and Koch PSG-1 7.62mm sniping rifles and fire single shots through the heads of their cut out targets on the second floor, while operators on the ground prepare to storm the mock-up TAC House. (Courtesy: Brigade Halcon)

The Austrian-produced Steyr Pinzsgaur six-wheeled transport vehicle--***the*** 1st SFOD-Delta vehicle of choice for overseas deployments. (Courtesy: Steyr Ltd.)

During a CTC (Combat Team Competition) in Germany, Delta operators, characteristic in their olive flight coveralls, pose with new-found friends in the Belgian Gendarmerie's ESI. (Courtesy: Gendarmerie Public Relations)

who had the courage and conviction to suit up and move out without Pentagon case studies--a unit had to be ready to deploy the moment they were needed and the intelligence afforded the commanding echelon to formulate a plan. If this new American counter-terrorist unit was going to work, Delta would have to call virtually all the shots. Beckwith wouldn't get his wish. Delta fell under the command and control of the JFK Special Warfare School and Center, the XVIII Airborne Corps, and the Department of the Army. According to Beckwith, in his memoirs, "Laid out on blackboard, it looked like the schematic for a Chinese fire drill."[2]

At first, Colonel Beckwith was told to recruit the men for his unit from the ranks of 5th Special Forces Group (Airborne), responsible for the Middle East, Near East and North Africa, and from 7th Special Forces Group (Airborne), responsible for Latin America. It was a stop-gap. Eventually, Delta would recruit from the entire U.S. Army--just as the 22 SAS does; the SAS accepts volunteers from the Parachute Regiment, the Royal Horse Artillery, the Royal Highland Fusiliers and the Royal Engineers (even, in rare cases, the Royal Air Force). Beckwith, in fact, did not want to recruit "ready-made" operators, but rather he wanted to mold new ones out of existing soldier stock. The selection process that Beckwith initially chose was almost a carbon copy of the 22 SAS Regiment's patented means for weeding out those without potential from those whose beret will eventually bear the "Who Dares Wins" motto. By April 1978, Beckwith had conducted four selection courses and out of the nearly 200 applicants who had volunteered fifty-three were selected.

Delta training was a nineteen week course of intense physical instruction, tactical training and practical instruction. Delta operators were taught how to ski and dive, drive race cars and locomotive engines, and were expected to know how to pick locks, and disappear when sought. They were trained to be part covert intelligence agent and part shooter. Shooting, in fact, became a Delta obsession. At the unit "House of Horrors," the lavish Killing House built specially for the unit, Delta operators spent nearly ten hours a day perfecting their skills at assaulting a secured target and rescuing hostages from heavily armed terrorists. Delta operators learned the A-Zs of commercial airliners and were trained to not only know how to assault a civilian airliner, but how to fuel one up and load the aircraft with hydraulic fuel; training was carried out at major metropolitan airports, such as O'Hare in Chicago and John F. Kennedy in New York City. Delta operators became expert in assaulting a commuter train and clearing it

CINCJSOC at the time of the ***Achille Lauro*** seajacking and CINCUSSOCOM at the time of the Persian Gulf War, General Carl Stiner--one of the most influential U.S. military thinkers and commanders in the sphere of special operations counter-terrorist operations. Note Israeli jump wings worn over the right breast pocket. (USSOCOM Public Affairs Office)

of terrorists (without harming hostages, of course), and assaulting seized buses. Delta operators flew to major cities to practice rappelling down the sides of skyscrapers and towers, flew to the Rocky Mountains for winter warfare exercises, and learned the art of underwater insertion in Florida and in California with the U.S. Navy SEALs. Whenever Colonel Beckwith had a question or needed some additional inspiration, he would simply venture to Hereford to visit his contacts in 22 SAS and his new friend, Colonel Ulrich Wegener, at GSG-9 St. Augustin, Germany. Within months, Colonel Beckwith arranged exchange programs with the 22 SAS, GSG-9, France's GIGN and Israel's ***Sayeret Mat'kal***. Delta had joined the international community.

Unlike other military counter-terrorist forces around the world, Delta would not be concerned with domestic incidents of hostage-taking and terrorism--that was the domain of the Federal Bureau of Investigation and local law enforcement SWAT units.

The day that Delta completed its certification exercises, on November 4, 1979, a news flash came over the wires from Teheran. The American Embassy had been overrun by a mob led by the Revolutionary Guard and the embassy staff, along with the Marine Corps Security Guard Contingent, had been taken hostage. In all, fifty-two Americans had been kidnapped and it was unclear if the Iranians were torturing them, treating them well, or preparing them for summary executions. Colonel Beckwith and staff had long predicted that the targeting of Americans would result in such a scenario. Within hours, Delta was placed on full alert and contingency plans prepared. Colonel Beckwith had always predicted that Delta's baptism of fire would be taking down an American airliner isolated on some desert tarmac. He never envisioned that it would involve assaulting an American embassy and having to evade a half-million man army in order to pull the operation off.

There have been books and films examining Operation Rice Bowl (Eagle Claw), the planned American rescue operations of the hostages held in Iran, and the finger of blame over the death and destruction at "Desert One" has reached to the highest pinnacle of power in Washington. While the tragedy of the Desert One landing strip on April 24, 1980, supersedes any and all other aspects of the valiant and quite innovative approach to pulling off what even the most daring military commanders would consider an impossible mission, Colonel Beckwith and his staff had assembled a cohesive, doable, and ingenious rescue blue-print that not only indicated the level of professionalism that the Delta operators could display in covert actions, but a level of skill in pulling off a tactical race against the clock that no other military unit--SINCE--has even attempted to replicate.

Beckwith, the overall ground commander of the operation, had a series of obstacles to overcome if Operation Rice Bowl, the rescue's code-name, was ever to be pulled off. He had to (a) gather and analyze enough intelligence to formulate a plan; (b) get the ground forces into Iran; (c) have transport ready ***in country*** to evacuate the rescued hostages and the military personnel; and, (d) have logistics in place, ***in country***, that would facilitate the transport of the operators to Teheran, and then their rescued citizens back to the transport liaison area. It was a daunting task if ever there was one but Beckwith was relentless and innovative. He drew up his contingencies, had them approved by the top brass while at the same time training his men for the mission at hand.

The units selected for this epic endeavor trained for six months in order to coordinate their skills and techniques in assaulting the embassy grounds, eliminating the Revolutionary Guard gunmen, and securing a mad escape through the mad traffic of a checkpoint-filled Teheran several hundred miles away to the Iranian desert. The plan was a complex puzzle-work of interlocking objectives and stages: From a landing strip in the Iranian desert, the Delta task force would be ferried by chopper to Teheran where they would hook up with operators who had covertly smuggled their way in country. Much as ***Sayeret Mat'kal*** had done in April 1973 in "Operation Spring of Youth" (see Israel Chapter) in the eventuality of a major screw-up once inside the enemy's capital the Delta operators in country would rent cars, prepare escape routes and plant diversions and aversions to any Iranian plans of pursuit. Most ominously, the rescue raid could not be executed solely by Delta--it would involve the United States Navy and their RH-53D Sea Stallion choppers and their fleet of warships and aircraft carriers, it would also involve the U.S. Air Force and their fleet of C-130 Hercules tankers and C-141 transports, and it would involve the 75th Ranger Regiment (Airborne), as security for the desert

A Delta operator demonstrates the proper firing position for aiming his Heckler and Koch Offensive Handgun Weapon System (OHWS), including a .45 caliber ACP pistol, sound suppresser and laser aiming module. (Courtesy: Heckler and Koch)

During survival training in the West Virginia blue hills, Delta operators prepare to feast on a wild pig found rummaging in the forest--Delta operators are expected to be able to survive in any condition--whether it be in the wilderness in sub-zero temperatures or in the cosmopolitan surroundings of a European capital city. (USASOCPA)

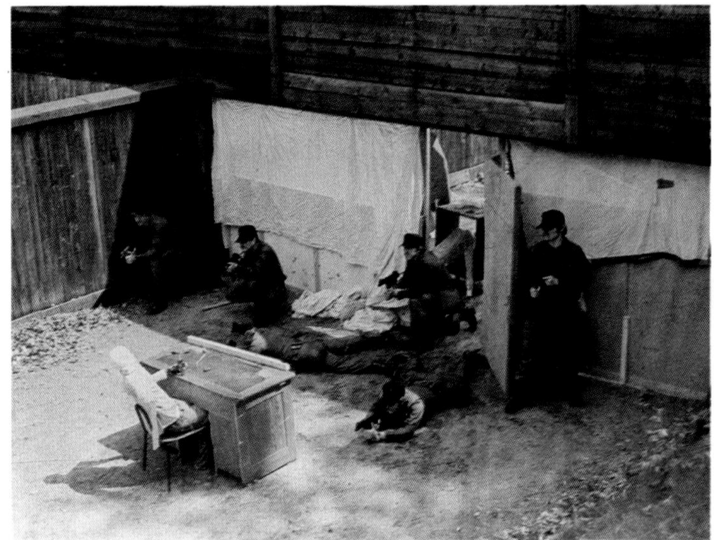

Delta operators, armed with the once favored Walther MP-K 9mm submachine, empty their magazines with fire directed at mannequins simulating terrorists, while keeping the mannequins simulating a hostage clear of 9mm holes. (Courtesy: Terry Griswald)

During insertion exercises in Fort Bragg, North Carolina, 1st SFOD-Delta operators deploy from the rear of a 160th Special Operation Aviation Regiment (Airborne) Chinook MH-47. (USASOCPA)

airfield. Colonel Beckwith felt that he could field, at the most, 120 operators, and additional forces, such as teams from 5th Special Forces Group (Airborne) to assault the Iranian Foreign Ministry.

At first, Beckwith hoped that his operators would be involved in a selective shoot with the hostage-takers, and as a result had trained his men to the point of excellence in the art of .45 caliber quick-shoot take downs with their accurized Colt automatic pistols; accurizing the famed .45s simply meant that loose-fitting parts from mass-produced models were replaced by custom-produced components that would withstand extreme conditions and use. After observing his operators go through the daily ritual at the "House of Horrors," and seeing them fire their 500 rounds daily, Beckwith realized that pistols would not be enough. A M3A1 Colt .45 submachine gun, also accurized variants, would be carried, as well, in case a shoot-out with the Revolutionary Guard had to be handled.

From Delta's end of the preparation cycle, all went well. The unit perfected its door breaching skills and entering a structure in minimum time, clearing it of all hostiles, and then proceeding to empty the hostages from the facility and bringing them to safety for the trek back to the refueling site and the hop back to the carrier U.S.S. ***Nimitz***. There were problems with the aviation aspect of the mission, however, and U.S. military inter-service bickering was threatening the very chances of the operation to be pulled off successfully. Colonel Beckwith had demanded that the U.S. Navy supply him with aces, "fly-by-the-seat-of-their-pants" aviators who could land on a dime, fly through 23mm antiaircraft streams, and not by deterred by the overall danger of the mission. The RH-53D pilots were combined force of mine-clearing flyers who were anything but "fly-by-night." Their training revealed flaws in their abilities to mount special operations sorties, and all but one of the original groups of Marine Corps and U.S. Navy aviators had to be replaced. Additional flyers were also needed as the task force commanders soon realized that they would need more than the six Sea Stallions originally ordered for the raid; additional aircraft meant more pilots, and flyers for this sortie were hard to come by. Six C-130s were also needed for transport and refueling, and two AC-130 gunships would be called into play: when the Delta operators were on the ground in Teheran, one AC-130 would circle the embassy providing overhead artillery support to meet any scenario, while the second gunship would circle over Teheran's Mehrabad International Airport, to make sure that the two "still-flying" F-4 Phantoms in Khomeini's Air Force would not be scrambled.

Seven dry runs of Operation Rice Bowl were conducted in the Arizona desert. Colonel Beckwith had divided his Delta task force into Red, Blue and White troops. In the actual raid, Red and Blue teams were to seize and secure the grounds of the U.S. Embassy and rescue the hostages and White Troop was to act as tactical back-up and secure the perimeter around the embassy against any Iranian Revolutionary Guard counter-attack. The dress rehearsals in Arizona replicated all aspects of the mission: how Delta would be flown to the Desert One landing strip, how they would then be flown to the staging area (and how the helicopters would be hidden), how they would be driven into Teheran, scale and storm the embassy, and then rescue the hostages, deal with any Iranian intervention. During the rehearsals and, indeed, for the operation itself, the operators wore black field jackets and jeans, with Kevlar body armor and black woolen caps. It was an odd uniform, but one that might come in handy should something go wrong in downtown Teheran.

By early April 1980, when U.S. Air Force meteorologists had seen a window of opportunity, D-Day was marked as April 24. The Delta operators were psyched for action--they were well aware of the odds against them pulling off the raid but they knew that they had spent the last three years not only proving their worth as a unit but, in essence, preparing for this incredible test. All went well--the trip to Egypt from where the Delta operators would set out from on their C-130 journey to the Iranian desert and the initial launch of the choppers from the flight deck of the ***Nimitz.*** The events of April 24, 1980 are now engraved in the history books as one of most tragic in modern American military history. Mechanical difficulties in several of the Sea Stallions led to Beckwith having to abort the mission at Desert One as much of his 120-man task force was sitting inside the belly of their RH-53Ds ready for the low-level hop to Teheran. Without enough choppers he couldn't ferry enough men to the rescue and, as a result, was forced to abort the raid. As the aircraft were poised to taxi and take-off back to base and back to the U.S.S. ***Nimitz***, a RH-53D crashed into a C-130. The resulting explosion killed eight servicemen and wounded dozens more. The mission had ended even before it had begun and the United States had been embarrassed beyond the scope of having their diplomats and embassy personnel STILL held hostage.

Four days after the debacle at Desert One, President Carter visited the Delta operators at Fort Bragg in a secretive and highly emotional ceremony honoring the dead and wounded.

President Carter ordered that another rescue mission be planned and executed, this one code-named Snow Bird, but the Iranians had secretly moved the hostages to various locations throughout Iran predicting another American face-saving military move. America's window of opportunity to end its hostage ordeal militarily had been lost forever.

If the failed raid in Iran did anything, it got the Pentagon to review its own handling of multi-service special operations. Navy ships, Marine pilots, army operators and air force ground personnel spelled disaster and the men wearing the stars on their shoulders should have foreseen the impending signs of doom. If anything was crystal clear following the debacle at Desert One, it was the fact that different services bickering and lobbying for a role in a major covert special operations was nothing more than a means of self-serving grandstanding as opposed to getting the job done professionally. In the SAS, if the British embassy in Teheran had been seized, the Royal Marines would not have lobbied to have their aviators fly in the SAS in order to boast of nothing more than representation. It was clear to all involved in Operation Rice Bowl, especially to Colonel Beckwith, that the most important lesson to be learned from the debacle at "Desert One" was the need to coordinate a cohesive special operations command. Following Iran, significant changes were made in the United States Special Operations community, eventually leading to the formation of the United States Special Operations Command (USSOCOM) based at MacDill Air Force base, in Tampa, Florida, that controls all three "conventional" branches of the American special operations community: USASOC, the United States Army Special Operations Command headquartered at Fort Bragg, North Carolina; USAFSOC, the United States Air Force Special Operations Command at Hurlburt, Field, Florida; and; USNAVSOC, the United States Navy Special Operation Command. JSOC, pronounced ***Jaysock***, the Joint Special Operations Command, based at Pope Air Force Base inside of Fort Bragg, became responsible for America's truly covert special operations units--the 1st SFOD-Delta (Airborne) and the U.S. Navy's SEAL Team SIX. Delta's air travel, at least in terms of helicopter insertion and extractions, would be the order of the day of a newly formed unit, the "Night Stalkers," the ominous title of the U.S. Army's 160th Special Operations Aviation Regiment (Airborne) based at Fort Campbell, Kentucky, the helicopter force tasked specifically with ferrying U.S. Army special operations units behind enemy lines on covert strikes with their compliment of MH-47, MH-60 and AH-6J/MH-6J reconnaissance/attack choppers.

From 1981 until 1989 Delta expanded both in size and its capabilities. It increased its exchange program with the SAS and GSG-9, strengthened ties and training visits were forged with the Israelis, as well as with virtually all the world's counter-terrorist units--from the Australian SAS to the Italian GIS. The U.S. Government was still apprehensive about its top-secret Delta entity and how to use it--in tactical terms, and there was still so much in-fighting inside the halls of power, between the various military and intelligence agencies that controlled Delta deployments around the globe, that little got done. In 1982, for example, following the December 17 kidnapping of General James Dozier in Italy, reported bickering between the CIA and NSC virtually shut down American efforts--and abilities--to locate the kidnapped general and facilitate an American-led (Delta) rescue attempt.

Delta's best opportunity to participate in a large-scale counter-terrorist victory was, again, thwarted but this time by the politics of international terrorism the manner in which sovereign nations, and their cowering leaders, allow a small band of men armed with AK-47s and murderous intentions to hold countries hostage. On December 4, 1984, for example, Delta was called to assault a Kuwaiti Airlines jumbo jet hijacked en route to Pakistan, but logistic difficulties at Fort Bragg stalled the deployment. On June 14, 1985, Shiite Muslim terrorists hijacked TWA Flight 847 from the Mecca of international terrorist strikes, Athens International Airport, and commandeered it to Mohammed Boumadiene International Airport in Algiers. Delta, as planned, deployed at a moments notice out of Pope Air Force Base at Fort Bragg, but when the hijacked aircraft arrived in Algiers, Algerian authorities refused to let Delta attempt a rescue on her soil. The terrorists went on to brutally murder a U.S. Navy diver, Robert Stetham, and take the Jewish hostages on to Beirut where they became pawns in a two-week diplomatic crisis which saw Israel release 300 Shiite prisoners and President Reagan declaring that "America does not deal with terrorists."

Delta's closest actual contact with international terrorists came on October 11, 1985, at Sigonella Naval Air Station in Sicily in what is, certainly, one of the most ***bizarre*** endings to one of the most successful

A pre-fabricated tactical assault Puzzle Palace. During rappelling exercises outside a skyscraper mock-up at SOTF, Delta operators prepare to assault a fourth-floor room by making their entry through outdoor windows. (Courtesy: Terry Griswald)

Delta operators, armed with Walther MP-Ks 9mm submachine guns, position themselves outside the "House of Horrors" TAC house before an assault. (Courtesy: Terry Griswald)

A Delta operator, wearing his desert pattern camouflage fatigues, lowers himself down from a U.S. Air Force Special Operations MH-53 Pave Low chopper during a "dog and pony" show for visiting generals from NATO. (Courtesy: Terry Griswald)

chapters in America's history of battling terrorists. On October 6, 1985, four terrorists from the Abu Abbass Faction of the Palestine Liberation Front seized the Italian cruise-liner S.S. ***Achille Lauro*** during a pleasure cruise of the Mediterranean off of Egypt and Israel; there were 750 passengers on board the boat, as well as 315 crew members. Most of the passengers on board were Americans, mainly Jewish-Americans from the New York Tri-State area, who were on holiday, and 666 of them left the cruise on October 7 for a ground tour of the pyramids. The terrorist plan, a retaliatory strike for the October 1, 1985, Israeli air raid on PLO headquarters in Tunis, was for them to land at the Israeli port of Ashdod, take over the facility and hold everyone hostage in order to secure the release of some 1,000 Palestinians being held in Israeli prisons. The terrorists took over the ship when, in their guise of being Norwegian students, a ship steward delivering room service discovered the four cleaning their weapons and readying their grenades. In all, the four gunmen took 97 passengers and the entire crew captive. The ship left its Egyptian mooring for a mad dash around the Mediterranean. The terrorists threatened to kill everyone on board unless demands were not met.

Upon release of the news concerning the hijacking of, the Italian GIS was put on full alert, as were Israeli special operations units; Israeli military intelligence monitored the ship's movements, as did IDF/Navy vessels and patrol craft. Although the attack was supposed to have targeted Israel and the ship was of Italian-registry, it was clear that this was an American problem--the Americans had been singled out, especially those with Jewish-sounding names. The Sixth Fleet was notified, as was the 1st SFOD-Delta at Fort Bragg, North Carolina, and the U.S. Navy's SEAL Team SIX (see below) for possible deployment

Some improvised room clearing techniques--from the outsidepracticed by Delta operators in the North Carolina summer. Note the weapon of choice is the old favorite M1911 Colt .45 caliber pistol. (Courtesy: Terry Griswald)

to the Mediterranean in order to mount a rescue operation. At first, the Italian Ministry of Defense had notified the U.S. military that the GIS would engineer a rescue assault--***Carabinieri*** divers would reach the passenger ship, climb on board and then storm the compartments in search of the terrorists. The Italians, however, balked at actually engaging the Palestinians, fearing possible future reprisals against Italian targets; it would, ominously, be a harbinger of worse to come.

Brigadier-General Carl Stiner, the special operations genius in charge of the JSOC, had briefed both an advance element of SEAL Team SIX and the 1st SFOD-Delta (Airborne) and headed with the task force to Sigonella NAS in Sicily to set up a on-shore command post for any possible action; according to reports, a breakdown in a JSOC jet caused for the unit's deployment to the Middle East to be delayed for eighteen hours and resulted in the joint JSOC task-force to deploy without helicopters.[3] If the ***Achille Lauro*** was to be stormed in port, it would be Delta's job; if it were to be assaulted in mid-water, SEAL Team SIX would get the call.

Over the course of the next two days, the Palestinian terrorists tormented the crew and, off the coast of Syria, took sixty-nine-year-old Leon Klinghoffer, an American-Jew in a wheelchair, and shot him in the head at point blank range; laughing, they then tossed his body and wheelchair into the Mediterranean. The murder of Klinghoffer was a point of no return for the terrorists. It was time to give themselves up before a tactical end to the raid-gone-wrong was executed by the Americans, Italians or Israelis; they quickly arranged for PLF chairman Abu Abbass, in Egypt to end the ordeal, to facilitate a "diplomatic end" to the crisis. Abbass arranged a deal with the Egyptians for safe passage, and in exchange for promising to leave Egypt as quickly and quietly as possible, was promised an aircraft and armed escort out of the country. For the Egyptians, and the government of President Hosni Mubarak, it was the simplest way to end the embarrassing incident; after all, no one knew that Klinghoffer had been murdered in cold blood.

As the Egyptian government ferried the four gunmen to an air base near Cairo, the American ambassador Nicholas Veliotes boarded the ship to see if the American citizens on board had, indeed, been treated well. When he learned of Klinghoffer's murder, he radioed his aide on shore with the now famous message: " Leon Klinghoffer was murdered by the terrorists off of Tartus when they were trying to get the attention of the Syrians. In my name, I want you to call the foreign minister, tell him what we've learned, tell him the circumstances, tell him that in view of this and the fact the we--and presumably--they didn't have those facts, we insist that they prosecute those sons of bitches."

The four hijackers, Abu Abbass and several heavily armed Egyptian counter-terrorist operators from Force 777 (who were to make sure that the terrorists left Egypt, as well as to protect them from any "third" power intervention) were at Al Maza Air Force Base northeast of Cairo preparing to board an Egyptair Boeing 737 for the quick flight out of the country to Tunis. Egyptian President Hosni Mubarak, eager to rid his country of the incident, told the Americans that the terrorists had already left Egyptian soil when ***he*** learned of Klinghoffer's murder. It was a lie and the Americans knew it; Israeli SIGINT monitors had been eavesdropping on Mubarak's communications. The U.S. Embassy was alerted by Ambassador Veliotes' message, as was one Lieutenant-Colonel Oliver North at the National Security Agency (NSA) who had been monitoring the ongoing events with the Israelis through secure SIGINT means; JSOC was also notified that the terrorists were getting away with murder and the top brass wanted some decisive action out of Washington. They got it. President Reagan authorized a mid-air interception of the Egyptian aircraft and for it to be diverted to Sigonella, where an advance team of Delta operators and SEAL Team SIX personnel, along with Brigadier-General Stiner, were waiting. With Israeli SIGINT assistance, the Egyptian aircraft was intercepted over the Mediterranean by F-14s from the U.S.S. ***Saratoga*** and, as planned, forced down to Sigonella where it was met by a ring of SEAL Team SIX and Delta operators, in Kevlar body armor, aiming their weapons at the aircraft and its human bounty. As General Stiner approached the aircraft, eager to remove the terrorists and Abu Abbass from the aircraft to an awaiting C-141 Starlifter, a ***Carabinieri*** contingent arrived on the tarmac; with weapons drawn, they surrounded the JSOC task force ordering the Americans to stand down and turn the Palestinians over to Italian jurisdiction. As General Stiner and the ***Carabinieri*** commander spent the better part of an hour yelling at one another (with Stiner's four-letter word tirade), a tense stand-off ensued with the Italians aiming their weapons at the Americans, and half the Americans aiming back at the Italians, and the other half securing the terrorists and Egyptians on board the aircraft.

Stiner, after checking with Washington on his SATCOM, was forced to turn the terrorists over to the Italians, realizing full well that Abu Abbass would probably be let loose in some back-channel deal engineered by a frightened Italian government. He was right. Although General Stiner personally followed the aircraft ferrying Abu Abbass to Rome in a piston aircraft, he would connect to an aircraft flying him to Belgrade and safety. The JSOC task force returned to the United States without bringing the murderers of Leon Klinghoffer to face American justice.

Delta would be active in the Middle East, in covert operation (with the Israelis, it has been suggested) in search of American hostages in Lebanon; in covert counter-narcotics operations in Latin America and to El Salvador to help search for the kidnapped daughter of President José Napoleón Duarte; and, in Panama, in 1989, when during "Operation Urgent Fury" a force of Delta operators and MH-6 pilots from the 160th Special Operations Aviation Regiment (Airborne) rescued American businessman Kurt Muse. When Iraq invaded Kuwait on August 2, 1990, and the United States was deployed to the Gulf en mass for Operation Desert Shield, USSOCOM commander General Stiner ordered the creation of three counter-terrorist strike forces to be on alert status in case the terrorist armies on Saddam Hussein's payroll decided to expand the conflict overseas: one focused on southwest Asia; one on Europe and the other on the United States proper. Delta operators were also detailed to serve as General Norman H. Schwarzkopf's bodyguards in Riyadh. As terrorist strikes did not take place, the JSOC units, under Brigadier-General Wayne Downing (a former Ranger), looked for work and Delta ended up joining the 22 SAS Regiment and the British Royal Marines SBS on SCUD-hunting sorties in Western Iraq.

Atop a "killing house" on the SOTF compound, operators from the 1st SFOD-Delta (Airborne) fast-rope from a Delta aviation platoon Bell-212 chopper. (Courtesy: Terry Griswald)

During Operation Desert Shield, instructors from the U.S. Army's 5th Special Forces Group (Airborne) and the 1st SFOD-Delta observe as Saudi special forces demonstrate what their American teachers have taught them in the art of tubular assaults. (USASOCPA)

Delta's most recent large-scale deployment, on October 3, 1993, was in Somalia when a combined force of approximately sixty Rangers and Delta operators was flown to the Olympic Hotel in downtown Mogadishu by MH-60 Pave Hawk choppers of the 160th Special Operations Aviation Regiment (Airborne) in a desperate last bid attempt to seize warlord Aidid; several previous night-time assaults had failed in bringing in the elusive target. Midday operations was not what the Night Stalkers were all about, but orders were orders. Once the Rangers and Delta operators fast roped down the choppers, they swiftly entered the hotel and seized twenty top Aidid lieutenants, but Somali gunners on the roof fired RPG anti-tank rockets at the hovering MH-60 Pave Hawks, and three were shot down. A four-hour fire-fight erupted around the hotel and wounded and surrounded Rangers attempted to set up a defensive perimeter while trying, in vain, to save the lives of the shot down 160th aviators spread out amid the wreckage; graduates of survival school, 160th aviators are also expert shots with their trademark German-made Heckler and Koch MP5 9mm submachine guns. Chief Warrant Officer Michael Durant, severely wounded and captured by Somali gunmen, was an aviator with the "Night Stalkers." Two of his comrades in the unit, CWO Clifton Wolcott and CWO Donovon Briley were killed in the debacle; their bodies were tied up and dragged through the streets of Mogadishu is a ghoulish display. Three Delta operators were killed in the close-quarter melee: Staff-Sergeant Daniel D. Busch, Master Sergeant Timothy L. Martin, and Sergeant 1st Class Earl R. Filmore, Jr. The U.S. Army, to this day, refuses to acknowledge that the three fatalities were Delta operators, instead claiming that they were assigned to Headquarters and Headquarters Company of the U.S. Army's Special Operations Command (USASOC) at Fort Bragg, North Carolina.

Delta's last known deployment was to Haiti in "Operation Uphold Democracy." The operators went in before the massive U.S. presence to safeguard American diplomats and key installations, as well as to serve as bodyguards to United Nations officials, visiting American politicians, and U.S. military commanders; they were characteristic in their BDUs (no insignia, of course), tactical load bearing vests and CAR-15 5.56mm assault rifles. The Delta operators were relieved by Polish counter-terrorist/hostage-rescue operators from GROM.

The exact size and order of battle of the 1st SFOD-Delta (Airborne) remains classified top-secret, though it is known that the unit is larger than an average Special Forces Group, and far more extensively connected to the rest of the forces under the JSOC and USSOCOM umbrella. It has been rumored that there are close to 2,500 personnel working "behind the wall" at the SOTF (pronounced ***Sodif***) compound on McKellars Road. The 1st SFOD-Delta (Airborne) consists of three operational squadrons, one support squadron, one signal squadron, and an aviation platoon, secretly headquartered at a base in the Virginia hills, and consisting of approximately twelve specially modified AH-6/MH-6s, and divided into red, white and blue platoons; other Delta aviation needs are handled by the U.S. intelligence community, the United States Air Force Special Operations Command, and the U.S. Army's 160th Special Operations Aviation Regiment (Airborne). According to publish accounts, there is also a "Funny Platoon" made up of special undercover operatives, and it is the only JSOC operational unit to include women. The women are most useful on overseas assignments where the sight of a man and a woman is likely to spark less curiosity and suspicion than two long-haired individuals in cowboys boots clutching a holster and wearing a beeper!

Delta's home at SOTF is also referred to--lovingly--as "Wally's World," since it is a special operations amusement park of untold expense, and it is considered the flagship special operations training facility in the world--far more elaborate and extensive than Hereford, in the United Kingdom, and far more technologically advanced than St. Augustin, in Germany. Little is known about what exists behind the fortified electronic barbed-wore fence at SOTF, but the standard facilities are known to be among the finest in the world--the "House of Horrors," the Delta Force killing house, the indoor range, the rappelling tower,[4] mock-ups of buses and trains that might need to be assaulted, and some of the most sophisticated sniper ranges to be found anywhere in the world. The "House of Horrors" is also home to the

Kuwait, Saudi and JSOC (see black beret) officers confer at a training site in Saudi Arabia as Delta operators put on a class for their Arab allies in counter-terrorist techniques. (USASOCPA)

As Saudi counter-terrorist troopers go through the motions of attempting to scale-down the side of a TAC House near the front-lines, instructors from Delta look on and offer their criticisms and suggestions. (USASOCPA)

Kuwaiti fifth-columnists, interestingly enough being trained in the art of ***terrorist-techniques*** by Delta and JSOC instructors, undergo a refresher course in assault weapons days before the commencement of the ground war. (USASOCPA)

Delta operators attempt to safely teach Kuwaiti resistance fighters the art of building entry and rope work. (USASOCPA)

unit's "aircraft room": a portion of a wide-bodied airliner suspended by steel cables from the ceiling. The section of an actual commercial airliner is fitted with authentic aircraft seats and mannequins, dressed as holiday travelers, playing the role of hostage. Delta operators are taught to ski in the Colorado Rockies, and taught to drive like daredevils at the Charlotte Motor Speedway.

According to various sources, all of Delta's equipment for overseas deployments, from 9mm tracer rounds for their MP5s to Steyr-Pinzsgaur vehicles, are crated and places in palettes ready to load onto a C-130 or C-141 at a moment's notice. Their J-2 platoon is staffed by intelligence officers and NCOs, mostly special forces veterans, who are fluent in just about every language in the world and experts in the tactics and idiosyncrasies of many of the world's most notorious terrorist groups.

In terms of firepower, few military counter-terrorist units can rival what Delta can bring to bear into a scenario--from the old standard Heckler and Koch MP5 to the 2.75-inch rockets carried by a 160th Special Operations Aviation Regiment (Airborne) MH-6 "Little Bird" light attack chopper. As a military unit, Delta was a force lavished with a large-and seemingly endless--black budget, though it attended to acquisitions with a frugal touch. For years, the favored weapon among the Delta operators were the Heckler and Koch family of MP5s 9mm submachine guns--especially the MP5 A3 and the MP5 SD3. Throughout most of their deployments, the operators found the MP5 to be an accurate, reliable and easy-to-use weapon that would serve them well in virtually any scenario; firing over 3,000 rounds per week, most Delta operators have come to consider their MP5s as extensions of their bodies. Slowly, however, the 1st SFOD-Delta (Airborne) is phasing out their MP5s in favor of a weapon with a true assault rifle load--the M4 5.56mm carbine. Tested in Haiti and on numerous anti-narcotics assignments in South America, the M4 carbine is a sturdy and accurate weapon considered to be the best weapon available in the 5.56mm caliber--even better than the similar Swiss-produced SIG SG 550/551 SP 5.56mm assault rifle. Insiders believe that in a matter of months, Delta will switch entirely to the M4. For years, the Delta handguns of choice were the old standard .45 caliber Colt M1911 automatic, and the M9 Beretta 9mm pistol, although many operators carried whatever they wanted, especially the exceptional SIG Sauer P228 9mm pistol, and the .357 Magnum. In 1994, however, it was announced that Heckler and Koch of Sterling, Virginia, was awarded the contract for the Offensive Weapon Handgun System (OHWS) for USSOCOM. The OHWS consists of a .45 ACP caliber semiautomatic pistol, a detachable flash and noise suppresser and a laser aiming module (LAM). The 1st SFOD-Delta (Airborne) shotgun of choice is the Mossberg "Cruiser 500" 12-gauge shotgun--often fitted with the Mag-Lite extension. Considered by many to be among the best snipers in the world, Delta operators favor the Heckler and Koch PSG-1, the Remington M40A1, and the Barett 12.7mm M50; the M14, the old standard 7.62mm rifle that Colonel Beckwith commenced with in 1977, is still carried by many Delta operators.

As will be seen later in this chapter in terms of SEAL Team SIX, the 1st SFOD-Delta possesses among the most sophisticated and lavish means of deployment found anywhere in the world. Under the umbrella command of USSOCOM, JSOC can call into play virtually every unit in the U.S. military should it be needed in assisting a Delta deployment. Transport could be via a C-5A Galaxy from MAC, one of the Sixth Fleet's carriers or destroyers, from C-130s from the United States Air Force Special Operations Command (USAFSOC), or from the helicopters of the U.S. Army's 160th Special Operations Aviation Regiment (Airborne). Unlike other counter-terrorist units around the world that are sometimes hindered by their limited means of transport, Delta can get to anywhere it needs to, anywhere in the world, with a phone call. In addition, tactical support aviation elements, like the wings in USAFSOC and the 160th Special Operations Aviation Regiment (Airborne) permit Delta units stationed in harms way to call in air support under the most dangerous and volatile of operational circumstances.

Little ***accurate*** information is available on the ***current*** 1st SFOD-Delta (Airborne) selection process, and what the actual training program is like. Nevertheless, recent Delta recruitment material published in U.S. Army publications does shed some light on this program. According to recent recruitment material and even an article in "Special Warfare Magazine," the 1st Special Forces Operational Detachment-Delta, or Headquarters Company USASOC, as the Army refers to them when they don't choose to mention the words "Delta Force," is currently recruiting worldwide for soldiers to plan and conduct special operations even though the U.S. military still does not confirm the unit's existence. Recruiting is also underway for Department of Defense, JCS, DA, USASOC and USSOCOM staff positions. Among the requirements for service with 1st Special Forces

Operational Detachment-Delta are:

- Volunteer
- Army active-duty, Reserve or National Guard
- Male
- U.S. Citizen
- Pass a HALO/SCUBA physical and eye examination
- No limiting physical profile
- Airborne qualified or volunteer for airborne training
- Pass a background security investigation and have (at least) a secret clearance
- Minimum age of 22
- No history of disciplinary infractions
- Must pass the five-event physical fitness qualification test (inverted crawl; run, dodge, and jump; push-ups; sit-up; and two-mile run) and 100-meter swim, all while wearing fatigues and boots.

**NCO Requirements Are:**

- Rank of sergeant (E-5) to sergeant first class (E-7)
- Four years minimum service
- Two years of remaining service in enlistment contract

**Officer Requirements Are:**

- Captain or Major
- Advanced-course graduate
- College-graduate (BA or BS)
- Minimum of 12 months successful command (company, battery, troop, Special Forces A-detachment, or aviation platoon).

Seeking a spot in Delta is called, in the USSOCOM jargon, as a "try out," and try outs are usually held twice a year, in the West Virginia mountains at Camp Dawson, home to the 19th Special Forces Group (Airborne). The selection process is a brutal test in survival and coping, and Delta instructors are seeking those who can mentally survive the most arduous of conditions--the physical and the psychological.

In another official U.S. Army publication, Military Intelligence, an article appeared with the following heading: ***"Delta Seeks Intelligence NCOs,"*** and the recruitment drive featured the following information and requirements: "Intelligence NCOs at Delta perform a variety of tactical and operational functions directly related to the accomplishments of Delta's rapid response, special operations missions. These positions are characterized by a high level of individual responsibility, access to national level intelligence systems and worldwide missions. Successful applicants in MOSs 96B and 96D must have good analytical skills, a strong practical background in either tactical or strategic intelligence, and the ability to write and brief well. Specialization and language skills are helpful but not required. MOS 97B applicants should have a strong tactical background, with the strategic level counter-intelligence background. Intelligence NCOs who complete a tour of duty at Delta find that they are well prepared for intelligence positions at either the tactical or strategic level, involving either analytical or leadership roles. They are also highly competitive with their peers.

Beyond the myth and speculation, the 1st SFOD-Delta (Airborne) recruitment, selection and training process remains close to what Colonel Beckwith had institutionalized back in November 1977--a system based quite closely to the SAS selection process. Beckwith had tremendous affection for the Special Air Service and tried to replicate it in any way shape and form that he could in his new entity.

The 1st SFOD-Delta (Airborne) maintains close ties to the international "who's who" of counter-terrorist and hostage-rescue units. The unit's closest ties are believed to exist with the 22 SAS Regiment, as well as with GSG-9 in Germany, the Australian SASR TAG, and Canada's newly formed military counter-terrorist force (the *exact* designation of which is still classified top-secret). The 1st SFOD-Delta (Airborne) also maintains close ties with Israel's ***Sayeret Mat'kal***, South Korea's 707th Special Mission Battalion, the Spanish GEO, Italy's GIS, Jordan's SOU, Egypt's Force 777, Argentina's Brigade Halcon, and, both before and after "Operation Uphold Democracy" in Haiti, the Polish GROM. Delta also maintains close ties to national law enforcement tactical units, including the FBI's HRT, DEA and Customs Service teams, and, it is believed municipal SWAT units in several large cities.

Although Haiti was the last confirmed deployment of the 1st SFOD-Delta (Airborne), unit operators are routinely deployed to trouble spots around the world as tactical security teams for American diplomats. One such case was the protection of U.S. senators in Sarajevo during a diplomatic fact-finding mission to the besieged Bosnian capital. The senators, wearing their standard civilian garb, were surrounded and protected by M4-toting guards--presumably from Delta. Officially, however, at the time of this book's writing, the U.S.

An impromptu counter-terrorist class inside a Saudi schoolhouse taken over by JSOC as a special operations training center near the Kuwaiti frontier. 5th Group, Delta and JSOC instructors demonstrate the art of room entry to a squad of Saudi special forces personnel. (USASOCPA)

In Fort Bragg, Delta operators fast-rope down the sides of a specially modified Bell-212 of the unit's aviation platoon. (Courtesy: Terry Griswald)

The SEAL Team SIX patch--for the unit that doesn't exist.

The Navy SEALs Trident badge--issued to all those who have made it through BUD/S and who have made it on a team, even SEAL Team SIX.

Army has yet to acknowledge that the U.S. Army's 1st SFOD-Delta (Airborne) even exists.

Also not existing publicly in the JSOC order of battle is the U.S. Navy's own counter-terrorism unit, SEAL Team SIX; the team is also known as "Dev Group" in certain naval circles. Unlike Delta, a unit that recruits from the entire U.S. Army, SEAL Team SIX recruits solely from those men who have already completed BUD/S and are certified special operations material.

The U.S. Navy SEALs (Sea Air and Land) are by far the most famous of the world's underwater warriors, and certainly the world's largest and most lavishly trained and equipped. On January 1, 1962, President Kennedy commissioned the first two SEAL teams. Their primary strength was unit cohesion, a highly accurate intelligence network, stealth-like assaults and deadly firepower--the enemy was never to know what hit them. Their baptism of fire was the precarious seas, rivers and rice paddles of Vietnam. Their ability to pop up out of the darkened abyss of a North Vietnamese shoreline, eliminate a sentry and then proceed to reconnoiter a target deep behind enemy lines was the mandate of their existence; even though they never numbered more than a few hundred men, the SEALs proved to be an enormous addition to America's massive Vietnam order of battle.

The first SEAL members were former U.S. Navy UDT (Underwater Demolition Teams) veterans needed to form the cohesive command cadre for this unit, as well as UDT trainees in the middle of the training eager for the adventure of this new seaborne, underwater and airborne commando component. SEAL training ensured that each commando was a proficient killer with his bare hands, as well as with any type of conventional--or unconventional--weapon conceivable. Those skills, as well as all their underwater infiltration and extraction techniques, would be crucial.

In Vietnam, the men of SEAL Teams ONE and TWO participated in a varied role as underwater saboteurs, intelligence operatives, raiders, and long-range scouts. They employed a wide variety of techniques and equipment ranging from small craft (which were heavily armed and armored) to bamboo river sampans; they deployed from beneath the depths of the South China Sea, to the murky muddy rivers of the Mekong Delta. They participated in thousands of operations, often eliminating their Viet Cong or North Vietnamese Army foes with a commando dagger or garrote, or an instantaneous, though highly dedicated, eruption of fire-power. They permeated fear among the ranks of the North Vietnamese and VC, causing every sentry to pay extra attention to noises and movements in the bush. Their potential tied down thousands of North Vietnam's best soldiers who were forced to perform guard duty on shore-line installations in eager anticipation of a SEAL raid.

Vietnam was the SEALs' "Aberdeen Testing Grounds," proving what was possible, and what needed to be done to make the impossible part of their operational play book. Special craft, such as the "Boston Whalers," were developed to retrieve stranded SEAL teams in mid-water, and coordinate tactics with U.S. Navy SEAL helicopters, Bell-205 Seawolves, were also established and penned into the SEALs operational manual. Most importantly, for the stubborn minds and appropriation committee chairmen in Washington, the SEALs distinguished tours of duty in Southeast Asia proved the skeptics wrong. The U.S. Navy was, indeed, capable of seaborne and underwater special operations. The world's mightiest military fleet had the most capable commando element, as well. Following the war, the SEALs expanded to five teams; their amphibious brand of hit-and-run warfare was markedly perfected.

Although the SEALs also spearheaded the assaults on Grenada and Panama, their most publicized deployment was during "Operation Desert Shield/Storm." During the early days of Iraqi occupation of Kuwait, SEAL commandos landed on the heavily defended shoreline and conducted reconnaissance mission in the heart of enemy territory. SEAL frogmen landed on the beaches of Kuwait City, often under the noses of Iraqi troops, and conducted "personalized" reconnaissance forays through the streets of the Kuwaiti capital. They monitored Iraqi troop movements, shoreline defenses and, most importantly, made contact with and provided intelligence and morale support to the fledgling Kuwaiti resistance. The SEALs contact in Kuwait was the most reliable source of HUMINT (Human Intelligence) filtering to Schwarzkopf's special operations commander in the gulf, who would soon develop into one of the most important members of the American's command staff. From his Riyadh HQ, Colonel Johnson dispatched his army of secret warriors to various locations throughout the from for intelligence-gathering forays. The information the SEALs would provide would prove crucial in the planning and execution of "Operation Desert Storm."

In the weeks prior to the liberation of Kuwait, SEAL units, commanded by Captain Ray Smith (at the time of this book's writing, the CINCNAVSPECWARCOM), mounted dozens of missions against the Kuwaiti shore, perfecting the "art of deception." From their heavily defended base on the Saudi coast at Ras al-Mis'hab, SEAL teams were tasked with providing the Iraqis with the impression that the 17,000 U.S. Marines, floating off shore in an armada of ships, were poised for an amphibious assault. The deception was to cause Iraqi commanders to position tens of thousands of men along the Persian Gulf waters, opening a huge gap far from the main allied thrust and depleting the Iraqi defenses around southern Kuwait and Iraq. For months, the SEALs left small markers along the shore to "hint" that the area was being primed for a major assault; Iraqi sentries constantly reported the sounds of motors in the water and muffled blasts. The fact that their missions, deep in the heart of enemy territory, were carried out with little or no support was standard operating procedure. As one SEAL commander would later say, "Being left alone with our butts constantly left out to dry is part of our trade!"

The day before the ground war began on February 24, 1991, a six-man SEAL team infiltrated the Kuwaiti shore armed with an ample supply of C-4 explosives. The objective of their mission, code-named "Operation Deception," was simple; cause a diversion loud enough to distract the Iraqis and cause them to react while giving the first allied units enough time to slice across the minefields along the Kuwaiti and Iraqi frontiers. Iraqi generals were to be convinced that an amphibious landing was underway, and rush thousands of troops to the beach in response. The operation worked. Two Iraqi divisions, among the best troops stationed in occupied Kuwait, were removed from the front lines opposite the Saudi frontier, and far away from poised allied troops. The SEALs' operation was a brilliant success.

Becoming a member of a SEAL team is not easy, and is not for the average soldier or sailor. In fact, SEAL selection and training is considered among the most difficult in the world. All volunteers are first subjected to a seven week pre-training weeding out period and then the notorious Basic Underwater Demolitions/SEAL ("BUD/S") training which can last up to twenty-four months. It is considered one of the most difficult training regimens anywhere in the world and is designed to push both bodies and minds to their breaking point; accordingly, BUD/S has a 60% attrition rate. The first phase of BUD/S is the physical conditioning and drown-proofing of the SEAL candidates. It is also in this phase that candidates learn the essentials of teamwork--the true secret behind the success or failure of the SEAL teams operationally. BUD/S has been the target of countless studies by foreign military units, military psychiatrists and other management specialists in an effort to find out how the tortuous physical demands and psychological pressures helps to distinguish those with potential from those who just couldn't be relied upon in a special ops mission deep behind enemy lines. "If you could dissect the perfect SEAL and divide him into three equal parts," claims a BUD/S instructor, "then he would consist of one-third adequate physical strength, one-third pure and infrangible will, and one-third teamwork." A candidate's physical strength is important--but only marginally. Although to many the image of a SEAL is that of a muscle-bound commando who can bench-press 500 lb. with little difficulty, his will and his desire to transcend pain and hardship, is an all-important trait that cannot be honed in a gym or weight room. Strength is important, but it will not motivate. Equally important is the BUD/S trainee's knowledge that he is ***nothing*** without his mates, and he is only a cog in a much larger machine. If he works properly and if he is maintained, the team will function better--meaning that their chances of executing their mission--and surviving--behind enemy lines is increased. If he forgets the notion of teamwork and lets down the other cogs of the machinery, then he and the team will fail. There is a saying in the SEALs that there is no "I" in the word SEAL or Team!

Rear-Admiral Raymond C. Smith, CINCNAVSPECWARCOM, at the time of this book's writing (PH3 Layne/U.S. Navy)

Operator practice a slow and deliberate stealth approach to a target courtesy of a SEALs Mk VII SDV. (U.S. Navy)

Phase One of BUD/S culminates in the infamous six day "Hell Week" during which the candidates are divided into 5-7 man boat crews and then have their minds and bodies pushed beyond any human endurance; much of the strenuous physical examination is done with no sleep. The initial aspect of torture and physical hardship is designed to weed out those who are simply in the wrong place--sailors and boatsmen who are not team material. Hell Week is a concentrated attrition process where only the strong, only the strong-willed and only those willing to perform as part of a team, can survive. It is during Hell Week that the BUD/S catch-phrase, "The Only Easy Day Was Yesterday," rings a muscle-aching and ironic truth.

There is one more aspect of the first Phase meant to weed out those completely unsuited for life as a SEAL--underwater acclimation or "Drown-proofing" in the SEALs vernacular. Drown-proofing is carried out in the third week of Phase One and consists of the following: In a huge swimming pool, with his wrists and ankles bound, a candidate must keep afloat for twenty minutes; bob up and down to the bottom of the deep pool for five minutes; perform flawless underwater back flips for five minutes; dive down and retrieve a face mask with one's teeth; and, finally swim quickly (with hands and ankles still bound) for 100 yards.

The second phase of BUD/S involves an underwater and SCUBA course. The training for this phase is as intense as the first portion, but far less intensive. Candidates are no longer pushed to fail, but rather to succeed. The students commence their diving course and subsequent regimen in the NAB's huge 50-foot, 100,000 gallon dive tower. Once the basic diving skills are mastered and an instructor feels comfortable with a student's progression, he advances toward the Draeger gear and the world of re-breathers. The final aspect of the diving instruction in the plush expanses of the Pacific Ocean off the San Diego coast. The first hints of operational diving are also introduced during this phase, as BUD/S candidates are ordered to infiltrate the sprawling San Diego harbor and execute mock attacks against bridges, civilian freighters and even tourist ferries. The entire phase lasts nearly eight weeks, though according to one British SBS officer who had visited BUD/S at the sprawling Coronado NAB, "Much of the emphasis here is one diving, re-breathing material, and other aspects of underwater warfare, and not enough on combat swimming." "Nevertheless," the SBS officer admits grudgingly, "the facility at Coronado is state-of-the-art."

The third and final phase of BUD/S is the land warfare section which involves underwater/amphibious infiltration and land warfare skills. The curriculum of this third phase includes: basic weaponry; basic marksmanship; combat shooting; explosive charges, EOD, and sabotage techniques; night-fighting and ambush; patrolling; long-range reconnaissance; intelligence-gathering; communications and radio procedures; heliborne insertion and extraction; small unit tactics and skills; and, built-up combat (though it should be mentioned that the actual A-Z curriculum is classified and not released for publication). It is in this phase that the candidates make their transition from volunteer into operator. The last few weeks of Phase Three is the most classified aspect of the training and carried out on the rocky spaces of St. Catalina Island, and is classified top-secret. It is here that the theoretical aspects of the entire BUD/S training is translated into

Operators are lowered down on from a specially modified special operations Bell-205 Seawolf as they prepare their weapons for a possible live-fire entry. (U.S. Navy)

An operator takes aim with his Heckler and Koch PSG-1 7.62mm sniper rifle--the most reliable and favored marksman's tool in the SEAL Team SIX arsenal. (Courtesy: Heckler and Koch)

operational terms. True special ops tradecraft is taught and mastered, including (it is believed) joint operations with other American SF units, and the more covert and operational aspects of America's intelligence community, such as the Central Intelligence Agency (CIA), the National Security Agency (NSA) and the Defense Intelligence Agency (DIA). It is also in this final phase that the SEAL candidate is introduced to NAVSPECWARCOM's multi-faceted fleet of fast insertion boats (such as the Fountain 42-foot High Speed Boat) and covert delivery vehicles ranging from locking out of U.S. Navy's fleet of submarines, and the MK. VIII SDV (special delivery vehicle).

Upon successful completion of BUD/S, the former candidate turned operator is sent to Fort Benning, Georgia, to U.S. Army Jump School, and then a six week probationary period with his team; it is during this phase that the new SEAL undergoes what is known as STT, or SEAL Tactical Training, an advanced and condensed version of Phase Three where the actual intricacies of a team's operational procedure are studies and mastered. After jump school, after STT and after a year of non-stop pressure and instruction, the operator is awarded the "Trident," the SEALs emblem in an emotional, though highly contained, ceremony inside the commander's quarters. The Trident, also known in the SEALs' vernacular as the "Budweiser" for its resemblance to the Anheuser-Busch beer logo is the ultimate symbol of a SEALs' worth and is, perhaps, the most coveted insignia in the entire U.S. Navy.

Currently, SEAL strength is approximately 2,000 men, and all units are under the control of the Naval Special Warfare Command (NAVSPECWARCOM),[5] which is divided into two distinctive groups known as Naval Special Warfare Groups (NSWG). A NSWG consists of several SEAL Teams; boat squadrons operating marine transport vehicles; swimmer delivery vehicles, the small two-man midget submarines; and a light attack squadrons. Naval Special Warfare Group 1 with its SEAL Team ONE, SEAL Team THREE and SEAL Team FIVE are based at Coronado, California, and responsible geographically for the Pacific and Asian nations; each SEAL team comprises approximately 30 officers and 200 enlisted men. Each of NSWG-1's Teams is geared toward a specific task and location. SEAL Team Three, for example, is equipped with the Chenowth Desert Patrol Vehicle (DPV), the heavily armed dune buggy that proved so successful during the Gulf War. NSWG-1 also consists of a detachment of SEALs based at Kodiak, Alaska; SDV Team ONE; and, a detachment of SEALs based at Pearl Harbor, Hawaii. NSWG-1 also consists of Special Boat Squadron 1, and Special Boat Units 11, 12 and 13.

During Operation Desert Shield, operators from SEAL Team EIGHT teach a class of Marines the art of boarding a hostile vessel, searching it for contraband and terrorists, and securing any bad guys that might be found. Naturally, it helps to bring on board a few MP5s and a 12-gauge shotgun for good measure. (U.S. Navy)

The largest command is NSWG-2, and it consists of Naval Special Warfare Units Two, Four, Six and Eight. Based at Little Creek NAB, Norfolk, Virginia, NSWG-2 controls the operations and activities of SEAL Team TWO (whose area of responsibility include Europe, Africa and three Middle Eastern countries), Seal Team FOUR (Southern Theater of Operations, including all of South America), and SEAL Team EIGHT (whose are of responsibility include Europe, Africa and three Middle Eastern countries); NSWG-2 also commands SDV Team TWO, and Special Boat Squadron 2, with its Special Boat Units 20, 22, 24, and 26.

When, following the failed rescue attempt by the U.S. Army's Delta Force of the American hostages held in Iran in April 1980, the need for improved anti-terrorist capabilities was desperately required by Washington, the U.S. Navy duly sanctioned the creation of a sixth SEAL team: SEAL Team SIX, a 175-man unit placed on permanent alert to respond to terrorist attacks against American targets worldwide. The man tasked with creating the navy's version of Delta was a charismatic and courageous officer named Lieutenant-Commander Richard Marcincko. A larger-than-life figure in the U.S. Naval Special Warfare community, Marcinko had lobbied his superiors to create a specialized unit to combat terrorism, especially maritime hostage-rescue, and in August 1980 Lieutenant-Commander Marcinko received authorization to command and create this force and vowed to have it operational within months. Calling this new unit SEAL Team SIX (there were already six platoons in Teams ONE and TWO that

.An operator demonstrates the proper firing position for the Heckler and Koch MP5 Navy model--a weapon made famous by SEAL Team SIX. (Courtesy: Heckler and Koch)

Operators from SEAL Team EIGHT, weapons poised (even if unloaded) perfect the timing and synchronization needed when entering a fortified cabin of a hostile ship. Although SEAL Team SIX is the U.S. Navy's unofficial official counter-terrorist entity, SEAL Team EIGHT is invaluable back-up. (U.S. Navy)

received counter-terrorist instruction), he searched the U.S. Navy SEAL Teams on both the West and East coasts in search for talent--innovative volunteers where sought, as well as those with natural skills for intelligence and undercover work, those who spoke numerous languages, and those who might look like naturals wearing earrings and jeans when on covert assignments overseas. SEAL Team SIX would be based at the SEALs Little Creek, NAB, and be operational within six months of the first selection trials--equal in intensity and grueling pace to Colonel Beckwith's first Delta selection in 1977. Training was harsh and professions oriented. As the operators under Marcinko's watchful eyes were ***already*** operators, having passed BUD/S, jump school and the rigors of underwater naval special warfare instruction, they could be pushed beyond what was considered the envelope--even for SEALs Now they needed to be deadly accurate with MP5s and .357 Magnums, they needed to know the A-Zs of storming a seized off-shore oil platform, reaching a hijacked passenger liner or naval vessel, and taking it back, compartment by sealed compartment. It was arduous training carried out at a brutal pace. Eighteen-hour days were commonplace and Marcinko stressed the attributed of weight-training to his men, as upper body strength was a most crucial element of reaching any waterborne target. For their first three years as a unit, SEAL Team SIX fired a reported 2,500 rounds of ammunition each week, threw hundreds of grenades and stun devices, and trained with the 1st SFOD-Delta, the U.S. Air Force Special Operations Wings, and the 160th Special Operations Aviation Regiment (Airborne). Marcinko also trained his men with the British SBS "M Squadron," the Dutch BBE and 7 NL SBS, the French GIGN, the Italian GIS and the Italian Navy's ***Incursori,*** Israel's Flotilla 13, Australia's 1st SASR TAG, and the Republic of Korea's 707th Special Missions Battalion.

Throughout the 1980's, SEAL Team SIX would be on-call on dozens of occasions: they were nearly ordered to storm the hijacked Italian cruise liner ***S.S. Achille Lauro*** in 1985, and had prepared a rescue raid into Beirut to rescue the American hostages. Marcinko's term as SEAL Team SIX commander ended in 1984 when he was issued with a suspension following disciplinary infractions by his men, though then given a plum command--a top-secret U.S. Navy counter-terrorist effort to test the security at U.S. Navy installations throughout the world. The unit was known as Red Cell, and eventually became infamous throughout the U.S. Navy as a brutal rogue force, and would result in Marcinko being convicted for the misappropriation of defense funds while commander of Team SIX (not to mention countless charges of brutal behavior) Marcincko would detail this story in his best-selling autobiography, Rogue Warriors.

A special SEALs boarding team was sanctioned in 1988, and was known as SEAL Team EIGHT; trained along similar lines with SEAL Team SIX, SEAL Team EIGHT became an on-call force tasked with boarding hostile and suspicious vessels. They were highly active during Operation Desert Shield/Storm in boarding vessels believed to be breaking the United Nations embargo against Iraq. SEAL Team SIX also operated inside Iraq once General Schwarzkopf opted to listen to CINCUSSOCOM, General Stiner, and despatch JSOC units to Iraq.

The SEALs, including the operators from SEAL Team SIX, deploy around the world courtesy of the warships of the various U.S. Navy warships and carrier groups, as well as courtesy of a whole network of U.S. Air Force aircraft and airlift commands. The Special Boat Units (SBUs) are an unsung, though integral, element of the SEALs capabilities. SBU personnel are not SEALs, they are sailors, but they are trained in unique aspects of naval special warfare and afford the SEALs the ability to reach their targets--be they shoreline or riverine. Some vessels currently used by the SEALs include the heavily armed long-range Patrol Coastal class craft built by the Bollinger Shipyards; the boats, there should be thirteen in service by the summer of 1995, can carry eight SEALs along with its crew of twenty-four, and is a fast moving support platform for NAVSPECWARCOM missions, complete with a MK 38 25mm gun; a Stinger SAM station, and posts for four support weapons. Other Special Boat Unit craft include the PB MK III patrol boats; RIBs; and IBS (Inflatable Boat Small) and CRRC (Combat Rubber Raiding Craft) Zodiacs. Recently, USSOCOM, has ordered the SOC (Special Operations Craft) MK V, a fast patrol boat that can ferry a force of up to twenty SEALs toward an objective at speeds of up to forty knots.

U.S. Navy SEAL deployments worldwide are supported by NAVAL SPECIAL WARFARE UNITS (NSWUs) that support forward deployed operational detachments. NSWU-1 is in Guam (formerly in Subic Bay, the Philippine Islands; NSWU-2 is in Scotland, though will shortly move to a new headquarters in Europe; NSWU-4, Rossey Roads, Puerto Rico; NSWU-8 is in Panama; and NSWU-10, Rota, Spain.[6] The SEALs maintain close ties to foreign naval special warfare units in NATO, and allied nations in the Mediterranean, Latin America and the Pacific. The SEALs' closest ties are with the British SBS; in fact, there is a SEAL contingent permanently based in Scotland, and the two units exchange officers (an SBS officer is posted to the SEALs, and a SEAL is posted to the SBS). In fact, this joint exchange of men and knowledge exists between the SEALs and the famed German ***Kamphschwimmers***; the French Jaubert Commandos; the Italian ***Incursori***; and, the Australian SAS Regiment's Tactical Assault Group (TAG). Close links also exist between the SEALs and Israel's Flotilla 13, as well as between the U.S. Navy SEALs and the Argentine and Brazilian ***Buzos Tacticos***, and the naval special warfare units of South Korea, the Philippines, and Thailand, and Norway, Denmark, Greece, Jordan, the Netherlands, Belgium, Spain, Turkey, Tunisia, Morocco, Malaysia, Indonesia, Singapore, and Brunei. The SEALs also train (and mount missions) with the U.S. Army's Special Forces Groups (Airborne) and 75th Ranger Regiment (Airborne), the Air Force Special Operations Community, and the U.S. Marine Corps Recon battalions (the SEALs consider themselves the best warriors in the USSOCOM community, since reaching their target is part of their operational and physical challenge). The SEALs have also trained with several municipal SWAT units, including those in New York City, Los Angeles, Miami and Atlanta, as well as with the FBI's HRT counter-terrorist team. The training with the SWAT units is particularly important to the SEALs, since the cops have become expert in close quarter combat and in the art of urban warfare (not to mention gaining entry to fortified rooms and buildings).

The SEALs operations are at the cutting edge of the U.S. national security requirements and not solely limited to the ocean depths and the enemy's shoreline. Recently, five SEALs (believed to be from SEAL Team SIX) were awarded the Silver Star for their role in the October 3, 1993, fire-fight in Mogadishu between forces loyal to Somalia warlord Mohammed Farah Aidid and a task force of Delta Force operators and U.S. Army Rangers. The SEALs received no press about their activities and operations in Somalia, but they were there--in the thick of the hail of bullets--in Mogadishu that fateful morning as part of Task Force Ranger. The medals were presented in a ceremony in Washington D.C., and then chief of naval operations Admiral Frank B. Kelso II presented the awards and stated, "As a result of the courage, commitment and utter professionalism of these men, many other brave comrades serve today, who might otherwise have been lost." General Wayne A. Downing, the USSOCOM commander, proudly said, "You men did your duty, for your country, for your units, and your comrades."

Prior to an actual ship-boarding mission, a SEAL Team EIGHT operator gathers his thoughts as his team-members gather their gear and hardware. (U.S. Navy)

SEAL Team SIX operators use virtually the entire line of Heckler and Koch hardware, from the specially produced MP5 Navy and the MP5K-PDW. The favorite weapon of SEAL Team SIX operators, however, is the .357 Magnum revolver, an ideal close-quarter weapon for operations inside fortified cabins.

[1] As per his memoirs, Beckwith recalled the reason behind his name: Special Forces Groups have an "A" (Alpha) Detachment commanded by a captain, a "B" (Bravo) Detachment commanded by a major, and a "C" (Charlie) Detachment commanded by a lieutenant-colonel. It just seemed logical to form the "D" (Delta) detachment commanded by a full colonel.

[2] Colonel Charlie A. Beckwith and Donald Knox, Delta Force: The U.S. Counter-Terrorist Unit and Iran Hostage Rescue Mission (New York: Harcourt, Brace, Jovanovich, 1983), p. 105.

[3] According to those same reports, appearing in the June 1990 edition of the Washington Monthly, a similar delay resulted in a Delta advisory team arriving late to the Egyptair hijacking later that year in Malta. The Egyptian operators, without any guidance from Delta, then assaulted the aircraft on their own, with the resulting carnage being horrific (See Egypt chapter).

[4] According to Delta operators, the best climbing tower that they have ever seen is the one in Wiener-Neusdtat, Austria, home to the Gendarmerie's Einsatzkommando Cobra.

[5] NAVSPECWARCOM also consists of the Naval Special Warfare Center, a school and think-tank of sorts in Coronado, and it has been reported, though not confirmed, that NAVSPECWARCOMDEVGROUP (or Development Group) is a semi-classified development unit that examines, test and procures equipment for the SEALs. According to several reports, NAVSPECWARCOMDEVGROUP is the bureaucratic structure that controls and commands SEAL Team SIX.

[6] According to reports, NSWU-10 in Rota was supposed to have been called NSWU-6, but it was thought that this would spark too much confusion with the "mysterious" SEAL Team SIX.

The tools of maritime special ops--Protec helmet, MP5, Kevlar gloves and about a year's worth of training. An operator from SEAL Team EIGHT races up a plank on board a U.S. Navy vessel honing his skills for actual ship-boardings in the Red Sea and Persian Gulf. (U.S. Navy)

# U.S.A. - Washington D.C.(ERT)

The Washington D.C. Metropolitan Police Department Emergency Response Team patch.

***April 19, 1995: At quarters, the unit was preparing itself for another day's work on the capital's mean streets--amid the halls of power and the pinnacle of American government are sidewalks paved with blood and spent shells and for years the nation's murder capital. It was just after 11:00 A.M. Officers were readying their gear, cleaning their weapons and monitoring the city's police frequencies for the job that would eventually involve them. Then, in a thunderous blast, came the news--the nine-story Alfred P. Murrah Federal Building in Oklahoma City, Oklahoma, had been devastated by an explosion. Although the blast could have been an accident or the results of a gas leak, federal buildings just don't explode and it was clear to the men of ERT that they would soon be called out to help secure the hundreds of sensitive federal targets in the D.C. area. The offices suiting up didn't know what terrorist group was involved, but knew that their services would be needed.***

Washington D.C. is a unique city. In addition to being the home of the President of the United States and a symbol of world power, it is the home of our federal government and houses numerous federal agencies. Aside from the 585,000 citizens who reside here, people from all walks of life and from all around the world flock to Washington D.C. Several hundred thousands persons are employed in the District and travel into the city daily from the surrounding jurisdictions. Tourism is the city's number one industry, which brings over twenty million others into the city to view the city's spectacular monuments and historical sites. In addition, because Washington, D.C. serves as the nation's capital, it has become a magnet for those who wish to demonstrate their beliefs, sometimes resulting in large scale civil disobedience.

Tactical training in the woods of Virginia with the MPD's ERT with the unit's Peacekeeper armored cars. (Courtesy: Lieutenant Larry D. McCoy/Washington D.C. Metropolitan Police Department Emergency Response Team)

In 1950, the Metropolitan Police Department established a Civil Disturbance Unit (CDU) within its uniform Patrol Bureau. This unit was comprised of officers who received additional training, which enabled them to better resolve those incidents involving barricaded criminals and hostage situations. They were also specially trained to deal with crowd control problems associated with demonstrations. In the event of a barricade situation, CDU members were pulled from their regular patrol duties and re-deployed to the incident site. There they formed two, three-man gas teams, and one, five-man search team. Additional teams were formed as needed. Although the ERT was not yet founded, the Hanafi Muslims take-over of three buildings in Washington, D.C. on Wednesday, March 7, 1977, proved there was an established need for such a unit. The incident lasted for thirty-nine hours, during which time one hundred forty-four people were taken hostage, one person was killed, and several others were wounded.

In April of 1984, the Metropolitan Police Department established its first full time unit dedicated to the resolution of incidents involving barricaded criminals, hostage situations, and acts of terrorism. In addition, the unit served those warrants deemed to be of a high risk nature, and intervened in suicide attempts. This unit was called the Emergency Response Team (ERT). The ERT and the Explosive Ordinance Unit (EOU) make up the Special Tactics Branch (STB), which is part of the Special Operations Division (SOD), all within the Patrol Services Bureau (PSB).

The Special Tactics Branch is currently commanded by Captain Rodney D. Monroe. At full strength, the unit is commanded by a Captain; the ERT-Negotiations Unit consists of one lieutenant, one sergeant and Officers; the EOU consists of one sergeant, five officer technicians, five K-9 handlers; ERT-Tactical Platoon One consists of one lieutenant with Team One commanded by one sergeant staffed by seven officers, and Team Two led by a sergeant and seven officers. ERT-Tactical Platoon Two is commanded by one lieutenant, with Team Three led by a sergeant and consisting of seven officers, and Team Four commanded by a sergeant and consisting of seven officers. One

An outdoor TAC house is assaulted by an ERT entry team performing a shooting drill during tactical training exercises in Virginia, as an instructor looks on pleased by the officer's abilities. (Courtesy: Lieutenant Larry D. McCoy/Washington D.C. Metropolitan Police Department Emergency Response Team)

Situated near many of the countries federal law enforcement agencies affords ERT officers the unique opportunity to train and hone their skills in the most state-of-the-art facilities in the world. Here, ERT officers train in gaining entry to a location using physical strength and teamwork. (Courtesy: Lieutenant Larry D. McCoy/Washington D.C. Metropolitan Police Department Emergency Response Team)

tactical platoon and half of the negotiators are scheduled to work the day tour of duty (7-to-3), while the other tactical platoon and negotiators work the evening tour of duty (3-to-11). Any calls for service that occur when personnel are not scheduled to work are handled by calling back those scheduled during the 3-to-11 tour first, then others as needed. A pager system is used for all call backs. To further expedite response the on-call team is provided with take home cruisers to respond directly to the scene.

Unlike many other units Washington D.C.'s ERT-Tactical officers, ERT-Negotiating officers, and EOU officers are all under the same command with the tactical officers and negotiators work side by side on a daily basis--not only during barricaded "perp" and hostage-taking situations, but also while performing other duties, such as assisting federal law enforcement and the U.S. Secret Service with presidential and VIP movements; crowd control and arrest situations during large-scale demonstrations outside of federal facilities; and, high visibility crime patrols in high crime areas of the city. Since tactical officers and negotiators know each other well and, on jobs, have developed a mutual respect for each other's assignment, friction that can sometimes exists at major crime incidents is replaced by cooperation.

One important factor in the ERT's unique and nationally renowned skills during crisis incident management is the direct chain of command which is clear and concise. When on the scene of an incident the SOD commander is the official in charge, with the commander of the STB running the operations. In the absence of the SOD commander, the senior ranking ERT official is in charge.

Assignment to òne of the tactical teams is the most sought after positions within the MPD and the selection process is rigorous and demanding. Candidates are first tested on their firearms proficiency and then subjected to a timed run through a grueling urban obstacle course (which was developed to duplicate those activities often encountered by ERT officers on the streets of D.C.), to test their agility and endurance. Finally, a panel of ERT officials evaluate and score each candidate's written essay and oral presentation. The four tactical teams are presently comprised of all male officers, although female officers have held these positions in the past and undoubtedly will hold

During the MPDC SWAT Competition, ERT officers (wearing their combination of Israeli-produced Kevlar infantry ballistic helmets and locally-produced Fritz variants) prepare their SIG-Sauer P226 pistols, Colt submachine guns and Body Bunkers prior to assaulting a "barricaded" location. (Courtesy: Lieutenant Larry D. McCoy/Washington D.C. Metropolitan Police Department Emergency Response Team)

them again in the future. Selection to one of the two negotiating teams is also a coveted assignment within the MPD. The selections process, however, does not include the physical or shooting requirements.

After initial selection, the ERT candidate must pass a six week basic ERT school. While this school is produced in house, it is offered to, and has been attended by, several other law enforcement agencies. Once assigned to a tactical team the members receive continuous training in order to perfect their skills and keep the edge. Officers are allotted two hours daily to conduct physical training. This helps to prepare them for a physical agility test, which they are required to pass three times a year.

In 1987 the unit established annual minimum training standards for the tactical officers. A wide range of training areas and disciplines pertaining to their specific duties are covered. Additional training is received through cross training with other law enforcement and military agencies such as the DEA, FBI, United States Secret Service, U.S. Marshals Service, Bureau of Alcohol, Tobacco and Firearms, Prince George County Police, Baltimore County Police, United States Capital Police, Metro Transit Police, United States Marine Corps and D.C. National Guard. ERT also receives additional tactical and weapons training from the Ashbury International Group, Inc., Colt, Armiger Police Training Inst., Heckler and Koch, Inc., Glock, the NRA, and the IACP training group. ERT training is augmented each year during the annual MPDC SWAT Competition. The competition is comprised of five events. Each incorporates a combination of thinking and physical skills such as; tactical shooting, rappelling, rescue, and deployment. The event is well attended by vendors displaying the latest tactical gear and technologies and SWAT teams from as far away as Canada and Florida.

Officer recovery exercises in the Virginia woods--After entering the TAC House during a shooting drill, ERT officers hone their skills in removing an injured officer or hostage once the smokes and bullets have cleared. (Courtesy: Lieutenant Larry D. McCoy/Washington D.C. Metropolitan Police Department Emergency Response Team)

It is interesting to note that the Washington D.C. Metropolitan Police ERT does not use the Heckler and Koch MP5 9mm submachine gun, instead opting for the American-made Colt 9mm submachine gun; the Israeli-produced Uzi 9mm submachine gun is also carried as a substitute for the Colt submachine gun. ERT officers carry the SIG-Sauer P-226 9mm semi-automatic with Sure-Fire 3-volt tactical light attachment; the 12-gauge shotgun of choice is the ever-reliable Remington 870; and, the Colt M-16A2 5.56mm assault rifle is also carried on tactical deployments. ERT snipers, among the nation's best, use the Remington 700 .308, bedded in a McMillan stock with Leupold 6.5x20 optics.

ERT officers undergo extensive firearms, tactical and physical training. Their minimum schedule includes:

***Firearms, Tear Gas and Diversionary Device Qualifications Yearly Totals***

| | | |
|---|---|---|
| • SIG-Sauer | (Quarterly) | 16 Hours |
| • Shotgun | (Quarterly) | 16 Hours |
| • Colt submachine gun | (Quarterly) | 16 Hours |
| • UZI | (Quarterly) | 16 Hours |
| • M-16 | (Quarterly) | 16 Hours |
| • 37mm | (Quarterly) | 16 Hours |
| • .308 rifle | (Bi-annual) | 16 Hours |
| • .22 rifle | (Bi-annual) | 8 Hours |
| • Diversionary Devices | (Bi-annual) | 8 Hours |

***Firearms, Tear Gas and Diversionary Device Classes***

| | | |
|---|---|---|
| • SIG-Sauer | (Quarterly) | 4 Hours |
| • Shotgun | (Quarterly) | 4 Hours |
| • Colt submachine gun | (Quarterly) | 4 Hours |
| • UZI | (Quarterly) | 4 Hours |
| • M-16 | (Quarterly) | 4 Hours |
| • 37mm | (Quarterly) | 4 Hours |
| • .308 rifle | (Bi-annual) | 2 Hours |
| • .22 rifle | (Bi-annual) | 2 Hours |
| • Diversionary Devices | (Bi-annual) | 2 Hours |
| • Taser (In House) | (Bi-annual) | 2 Hours |

***Tactical Training***

| | | |
|---|---|---|
| • Tactical Shooting | | 40 Hours |
| • Search and Containment | | 40 Hours |
| • Rappelling-Helicopter | (Quarterly) | 32 Hours |
| • Rappelling-Building | (Quarterly) | 32 Hours |
| • Air Bag Deployment | (Bi-annual) | 32 Hours |
| • Capture Net | (Bi-annual) | 8 Hours |
| • Taser | (Bi-annual) | 8 Hours |
| • Police Cam Acoustical Monitor | (Bi-annual) | 8 Hours |
| • Hand Signals | (Bi-annual) | 4 Hours |
| • Physical Training | | 240 Hours |
| • Physical Training Test | (Tri-annual) | 24 Hours |
| • First Aid | (Bi-annual) | 8 Hours |
| • CPR Certification | (Annual) | 8 Hours |
| • Fire Fighting | (Annual) | 4 Hours |
| • FTX | (Quarterly) | 32 Hours |

Throughout its history, from jobs a few blocks away from the Capital to the drug-infested streets of Anacostia, the ERT has been called out on hundreds of jobs. Some of their most notable "jobs" include:

• On Saturday, November 21, 1987, at 1:08 A.M., a suspect failed to stop for a routine sobriety check point and led police on a high speed vehicular chase. The vehicle pursuit ended when the suspect crashed into a light pole, but a foot pursuit was initiated when the suspect fled on foot. Two police officers located the suspect hiding under a nearby bush, but were both shot as they attempted to apprehend him. Although one officer was seriously hurt, the other was able to return fire and chased the subject to an area where he was contained until assistance arrived. Additional officers secured the area until ERT arrived to continue the search; they located the suspect in an outside basement stairwell. Attempts were made to negotiate with the suspect, but they failed. During the negotiations, the suspect, who already appeared to be high on drugs, was seen holding up a bag of white substance (cocaine). It was unknown if he was still is possession of his handgun. The suspect, who was out of view, remained hostile and continued to make threats against the police. Finally, to prevent the suspect from exiting the location, an attempt was made to subdue the suspect with tear gas. The tear gas failed and the suspect began firing his pistol at the police. An ERT sniper returned fire, as did an officer

ERT officers, many of them former U.S. Army and U.S. Marine Corps servicemen, undergo an obstacle course as part of the unit's demanding--through necessary--240 hours of annual physical training. (Courtesy: Lieutenant Larry D. McCoy/Washington D.C. Metropolitan Police Department Emergency Response Team)

on the containment team, mortally wounding the suspect. It was later determined that the suspect was wanted for Parole Violation in reference to a previous charges of Assault on a Police Officer. The two officers who were shot by the suspect recovered from their wounds and returned to duty.

- On Sunday, January 31, 1993, at 8:37 A.M., patrol officers responded to an apartment building to "investigate reports of trouble." On the scene, officers heard several gun shots and observed what appeared to be blood running from under the apartment's front door. As the officers prepared to make an emergency entry, a voice inside shouted, "Come on in, there's a girl in here with her brains blown out already and I'm going to kill you and them I'm going to kill myself. I have an AK-47 with forty-three rounds of ammunition and a .357 Magnum." While others were gearing up to watch the Super Bowl, ERT was called to resolve the most frustrating and deadly incident since its inception. Upon arrival, containment was immediately put in place and the scene was put under a total control of the ERT. Negotiations were established with the suspect. It was determined that there were two adult females and a seven week old infant being held hostage by a suspect possibly high on PCP. Negotiations continued for approximately twelve hours, during which time conversations were held with the suspect as well as with one of the adult females. Hearing of their son's involvement, the suspect's parents traveled to Washington, D.C. from North Carolina. With other negotiation and tactical attempts failing to resolve the incident, the suspect had exposed himself to one of the four ERT sniper teams that were deployed. Unfortunately, the green light, which had been on for the snipers throughout this ordeal, had been pulled off to allow the mother a chance to persuade her son to surrender. This negotiation attempt, however, was also to no avail. The infant child had been heard crying intermittently throughout the day and night. She was heard crying again at 7:55 P.M., at which time there was a gun shot followed by an ominous silence; seconds later, the female screamed that the child had, indeed, been shot. ERT officers had been waiting outside the door for nearly twelve hours, but did not attempt entry as the intelligence on the location was that the door was barricaded and it was feared that any attempt to "push" one's way in would result in additional hostages being harmed. Negotiations continued until 9:41 P.M. when someone attempted to exit the location. Once the door was unsecured, the ERT officers charged inside the apartment with shields held high and weapons at the ready. Passing two lifeless bodies in the living room, the point and cover officers reached a rear bedroom where they found

During tactical training, ERT officers negotiate an urban obstacle course--ideal preparations for the mean streets of Anacostia. (Courtesy: Lieutenant Larry D. McCoy/Washington D.C. Metropolitan Police Department Emergency Response Team)

ERT Sergeant Larry Scott (gazing at the blackboard) and Captain Rodney Monroe conduct a briefing at the ERT quarters prior to the unit serving a warrant. (Courtesy: Lieutenant Larry D. McCoy/Washington D.C. Metropolitan Police Department Emergency Response Team)

After their entry tools have done the trick, Kevlar-clad ERT officer serve a high-risk warrant in a public housing project. Note Israeli-produced Kevlar infantry-ballistic helmets, Body Bunker ballistic shields, and SIG-Sauer P226 9mm pistols poised for action. (Courtesy: Lieutenant Larry D. McCoy/Washington D.C. Metropolitan Police Department Emergency Response Team)

15. With a suspect "assuming the position" up against the wall under the watchful eyes of Officer Mangan, ERT Sergeant Robin Hoey enjoys a rewarding moment with a rescued child hostage. Note the specialized TAC-Vest worn by Officer David Taylor, center, including balaclava shooting mask. (Courtesy: Lieutenant Larry D. McCoy/Washington D.C. Metropolitan Police Department Emergency Response Team)

the suspect, who had raised his .357 Magnum and aimed the weapon at the two officers. Both officers reacted instantaneously and fired--killing the suspect in a hail of gunfire.

• On Thursday, August 11, 1994 at 2:00 A.M., patrol officers responded to a radio call assignment of a "Man With A Gun Holding A Female Hostage." Officers responding to the scene found a naked female running from the apartment who informed the responding units that a male armed with a weapon was holding a female and a four-month-old infant hostage inside a small apartment. ERT was immediately summoned and deployed around the building while negotiators attempted to forge a dialogue with the suspect. The perpetrator, believed to be high on crack, had already sexually assaulted the two women and had threatened to kill the child if the police made any attempt to arrest him. While the negotiating team maintained a contact, ERT initiated a full containment on the area and snipers carrying Remington 700 .308 rifles were deployed. As ERT tactical teams readied their Body Bunkers and prepared their final assault plan, the female hostage, clutching the baby, exited the apartment; the suspect, high on crack, had simply fallen asleep. Silently, the tactical team entered the apartment for the precarious task of apprehending the suspect. Securing each room slowly and methodically, they came upon the individual asleep on the floor holding a handgun to his chest. As the ERT officers approached, the suspect awoke and grabbed his weapon, only to be cut down by ERT 9mm fire.

• On Tuesday, October 11, 1994, at 2:45 A.M. the ERT was called to a row of houses in southern D.C. to deal with a man who had barricaded himself inside the attic and threatened to set his two children, ages eleven and thirteen on fire. An assault team was readied, an ERT sniper aimed his Remington 700 rifle at the attic and the entire block was contained by elements of ERT and the MPD. Unlike other barricaded situations, this one was the most volatile job the ERT had encountered in its ten-year history. The suspect, a child molester with a history of mental illness and incarceration to state asylums, had doused the room with gasoline, and a strong stench of flammable liquids emanated from the attic. An ERT operator, utilizing his rope skills, climbed to the roof where a trap door was uncovered. Negotiations continued for nearly five hours. Along with the Colt submachine guns and Remington 870 shotguns carried, a water-line was brought up to the tactical assault area just in case the suspect actually went through on his threat and lit a match. The preventative measures were, indeed, called for. At 7:05 A.M. the officers positioned outside the suspect's fortified door heard an ominous cry: "Put it out! Put it out!" The suspect, distraught and unwilling to surrender, had set the room on fire. One ERT entry team raced in from the roof, while the second burst through the front door--the point and cover officers went in behind a wall of water being poured on to the room--one child was rescued immediately, and the other was pursued by the perpetrator who was still attempting to light a match. An ERT officer shot the suspect in the head and rescued the second child while fire-fighters raced into the location to extinguish the flames. The suspect--miraculously--recovered from his gunshot wound and was incarcerated.

As the danger of narcotics-related violence increases in the nation's capital, so does the threat from both international terrorists and home-grown fanatics (such as those believed responsible for the Oklahoma City bombing) the ERT, and units like it throughout the United States, will be busier and more needed than ever.

In the shadows of the United States Capital building, the ERT (at the time of this book's writing) poses for a group portrait. (Courtesy: Lieutenant Larry D. McCoy/Washington D.C. Metropolitan Police Department Emergency Response Team)

Commander of the Washington D.C. Metropolitan Police Department's Emergency Response Team Captain Rodney Monroe and Lieutenant Larry D. McCoy pose with one of the unit's three Peacekeepers and the ERT equipment carrier vehicle. (Courtesy: Lieutenant Larry D. McCoy/Washington D.C. Metropolitan Police Department Emergency Response Team)

An ERT Tactical Team serves a high-risk warrant in Anacostia. Note officer (right) aiming his Colt 9mm submachine gun with flash-light attachment at a first-floor window as his fellow officers move in. (Courtesy: Lieutenant Larry D. McCoy/Washington D.C. Metropolitan Police Department Emergency Response Team)

## U.S.A. - New York City Police Department's Emergency Service Unit (ESU)

*Even by New York City standards, this was a big deal. Four men, immigrants to the United States from the Middle East, were about to be sentenced in Federal Court in downtown Manhattan to an incredible 240 years in prison. Their crime: the bombing of the World Trade Center on February 26, 1993, the murder of six people and the wounding of over 1,000 more; the bomb, a home-made device made of off-the-shelf fertilizers and chemicals, inflicted monetary damage of over $500 million and forever rocked a national sense of immunity and security. As the four stood in front of U.S. District Judge Kevin Duffy inside the courtroom, a flurry of activity surrounded the Athenian-styled courthouse. The four terrorists were security risks--another trial, of an additional cell charged with planning to bomb several city landmarks and assassinate Egyptian President Hosni Mubarak and U.S. senator Alfonse D'Amato was scheduled to begin in early 1995, and the thought of a bid to free the four, or even kill them before they could talk, did not escape the police hierarchy. As a result, hundreds of policemen ringed the building, supported by FBI agents and Federal Marshals. Yet the impervious ring of security, the one meant to deter any terrorist bid, belonged to a few dozen men, city cops, wearing Kevlar Fritz helmets and body armor, and cradling MP5s, Mini-14s and the ubiquitous 12-gauge pump action. Linked together by Motorola walkie-talkies and supervised by an NYPD chopper flying overhead, the officers were never more than a minute away from any*

The NYPD patch.

The NYPD Emergency Service Unit patch.

At the ESU training center at Floyd Bennet Field, Brooklyn, all the gear carried by the R.E.P (closest to camera) and the Truck is displayed. (Courtesy: New York City Police Department)

***trouble in lower Manhattan courtesy of their specially-designed trucks that doubled as mini-arsenals and mini-disaster relief stations. Overhead, snipers perched atop nearby buildings and skyscrapers peered through high-powered field glasses and the scopes of their M-24 sniper rifles. The officers providing this deterring gauntlet were members of an elite, all-volunteer, combined tactical assault and emergency rescue unit considered among the best and most unique not only in the United States but throughout the world. They are the officers of the New York City Police Department's Emergency Service Unit--the NYPD ESU.***

There is an old saying in the NYPD: "When a citizen needs help he calls a cop, when a cop needs help he calls Emergency Service. The men--and women--of ESU are ***the*** elite unit of the New York City Police Department and, in essence, the city's last resort in time of crisis. Some in the department call the ESU officers "super cops": they are SWAT operators capable of meeting and overcoming virtually any and all tactical situations, they are emergency medical technicians that can administer treatment and life-saving procedures to the victims of any and all disasters, and they are craftsman that can rescue trapped victims from overturned vehicles or blown up buildings with uncanny speed and remarkable resourcefulness. They are the best of the best that the city has to protect its citizens--and its cops. In the city that never sleeps where everything and anything can happen, this unit has seen and done it all.

The Emergency Service Unit traces its creation to 1925 and the formation of a reserve force of officers who could be called on to perform "extraordinary" rescue assignments; many of these volunteers were also part-time carpenters, welders, riggers and electricians and the trucks they rode, modified fire-trucks, soon carried larger and more specified emergency equipment; years later, life-saving gear was added to the trucks and the cops were sent to emergency medical training. The unit was also among the nation's first mobile tactical response force with what was once called the department's Firearms Battalion (as it was a force of officers armed with the old reliable Thompson submachine gun, the unit was also known by the nickname "Machine Gun Squad"). During the Second World War, it has been rumored, the unit stationed officers atop city bridges armed with elephant guns and binoculars to search for Italian and German midget subs attempting to enter New York City harbors. In the years to follow, the unit eventually developed into a force called the Mobile Security Unit (MSU) that would be tasked with responding with emergency situations such as wrecks and disasters, but also to meet dangerous tactical situations that the precinct officers were too lightly armed to meet; its personnel were drawn from the range and equipped with Suburban vehicles loaded with weapons. In the late 1960s, the unit included the legendary Stakeout Unit, a force of NYPD firearms instructors and officers who were concentrated into one effective squad tasked with combating a rash of murders and robberies, mainly of candy stores and liquor stores. The unit's counter-terrorist tactical role, especially involving hostage-rescue, developed in the early 1970s, specifically following the 1972 Munich Olympic Massacre. At the time, few police forces possessed a special tactics and weapons unit that could deal with a hostage crisis, and few police forces knew how to deal with the rising tide of criminals armed with heavier firepower than the cops on the beat. Virtually every police force in the world created a special hostage-rescue force following Munich, and virtually every police force in the United States created a SWAT unit. New York City already possessed such a unit, but it needed to be expanded.

ESU's order of battle consists of 400 officers (including bosses)--a small force considering the fact that with 38,300 men under uniform, the NYPD is the largest municipal police force in the United States, and the second largest in the world (next to the Tokyo Police). The Emergency Service Unit falls under the command of the NYPD's Special Operations Division (SOD), a command that also controls aviation, harbor, mounted, street crime and highway units. ESU is divided into ten trucks--or squads--spread out across the city's five boroughs, and the Emergency Service Squads are attached to regular neighborhood precincts: ESU One-Truck is based in Lower Manhattan; Two-Truck in Upper Manhattan; Three-Truck and Four-Truck are in the Bronx; Five-Truck is in Staten Island;[1] Six-Truck, Seven-Truck; and Eight-Truck are responsible for Brooklyn; and, Nine-Truck and Ten-Truck responsible for the borough of Queens. Although each "Truck" has a distinctive piece of territory carved out for itself, large-scale situation and city-wide emergencies many times warrant trucks to cross bridges and borough boundaries for back-up. This could range from a hostage situation in Queens requiring units from the Bronx and Manhattan, to city-wide disasters like the bombing of the World Trade Center on February 26, 1993, in which almost every unit in the city was rushed to lower Manhattan to search and rescue trapped victims.

In addition to the personnel in the ten trucks, the unit also boats the "A-Team," the nickname for the unit's "Apprehension Tactical Team." The "A-Team" dedicates itself to full-time tactical work and assisting the precinct captains (as well as federal agencies working in the city) in gaining a tactical entry to a location in order to serve a warrant; because ESU officers are only human and can only be in one place at one time, and because it is impossible to respond to a hostage situation when the officers on a truck are trying to separate a man from his over-turned truck, ESU has created tactical teams that are on permanent stand-by status. ESU is not a typical SWAT force sitting in quarters and working out while waiting for a job, it was decided that the unit's tactical capabilities would be markedly increased by the creation of such a team. In recent years, there has been an increase in the frequency in which ESU has been utilized in warrant enforcement, including felony arrest warrants and search warrants--especially in narcotics cases. While officers from various trucks will assist the local precincts with warrants and tactical jobs, the "A-Team" is a cohesive unit that utilizes and maximizes a tactical team concept in gaining entry to and securing a location. The "A-Team" also excels in reaching an objective discreetly, with unmarked vehicles, in order to arouse the minimum of attention and to prevent the escape of a suspect, the destruction of key evidence, and to prevent a suspect from barricading himself inside a particular location and seizing hostages.

Because ESU officers are trained tactically and equipped with heavy firepower and heavy protective vests and equipment, their role in these jobs has not only saved the lives of precinct officers and detectives, but suspects and perpetrators, as well, as they are less likely to resist against such a determined police assault. In cases of barricaded suspects and situations where hostages have been taken, ESU officers are also equipped with a variety of devices that not only afford entry--these include the rabbit tool, a hydraulic device that can open almost any door (even those locked to the hilt in New York City); a sledge-hammer; battering ram; the Hurst Tool, a hydraulic device for ripping through steel that its used mainly in automobile accidents and is more commonly known as the "Jaws of Life"; and, even a halligan tool that can slice through metal.

ESU's primary objective in all its tactical work--especially hostage situations--is that deadly force is a last resort. "We'd rather bore you to death than shoot you to death," boasts Lieutenant Bob Sobocienski, a twenty-six year veteran of the force, "the term acceptable casualties is not in our dictionary. Maybe its because we are also a rescue unit dedicated to saving lives, but we will do our utmost not to use deadly force." The unit deploys non-lethal weaponry (such as tasers) that are particularly effective against EDPs or emotionally disturbed persons, robotics, and each ESU officer possesses advanced training in a variety of specialized areas that can be decisively effective in diffusing a potentially lethal confrontation. It should be

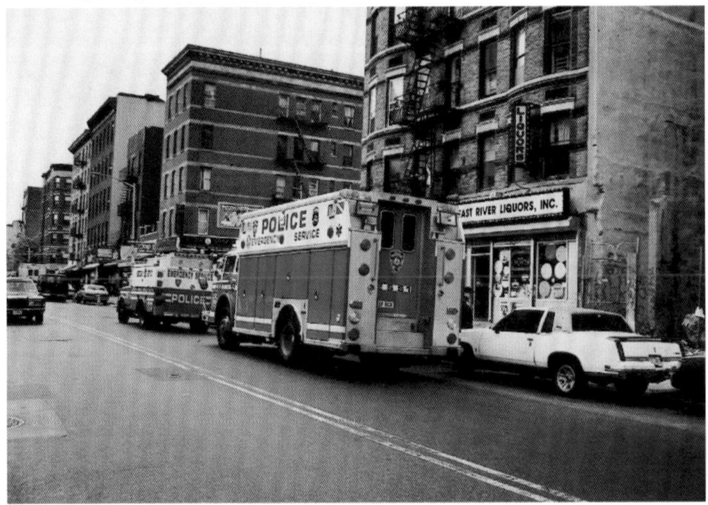


In lower Manhattan, an R.E.P. and Truck from One-Truck deploy for a "job." (Samuel M. Katz)

Attempting to maneuver its way through the labyrinth of Manhattan rush hour traffic, an R.E.P. attempts to reach a call for "officer needs assistance" several blocks away. (Samuel M. Katz)

Spent shells are kicked up as two ESU officers expend ammunition on the range at Camp Smith during a week of intensive tactical instruction and training. (Samuel M. Katz)

Lieutenant Bob Sobocienski fires his MP5 during a lengthy live-fire session on the range at Camp Smith. (Samuel M. Katz)

noted that all unit members are New York State Certified Emergency Medical Technicians (EMTs) and are trained as State Certified Psychological Technicians. There are jobs, however, where civilian and police lives are genuinely at risk and the officers afforded little choice but a tactical response.

In tactical terms, in addition to ESU's role as back-ups for precinct officers responding to gun jobs or tactical situations, and as an on-call tactical unit for warrants (or "hits" as they are known in the ESU vernacular), the Emergency Service Unit is also the department's primary force in providing dignitary protection and VIP security--a monstrous task in a city as large and diverse as New York City. This includes presidential visits, national political leaders, visits from foreign heads of state, religious leaders and other dignitaries that require special security details and consideration; as New York City is a truly an international city and headquarters to the United Nations and various international financial institutions, these details are carried out virtually all year round. In performing these duties, ESU interacts and operates with State and Federal agencies, such as the U.S. Secret Service, the FBI, the New York State Police, and foreign security agencies. ESU supervisors and officers will work together with representatives to develop and formulate escape and rescue routes. In their dignitary protection role, ESU utilizes all its vehicles and equipment, including a Counter-Assault Team Vehicle (or "C.A.T. Car") to follow motorcades, and observation teams and counter-sniper marksman. ESU also provides additional security assistance in bomb-sweeps and motorcade security--a precarious undertaking on New York's grid-lock plagued streets and thruways.

ESU is also responsible for assisting the NYPD Bomb Squad in the event a suspicious package or device is located. ESU units will secure a safe perimeter and follow the "I.C.E." doctrine--**I**solate, **C**ontain and **E**vacuate. ESU officers will assist in the search for any reported device, and will then assist the Bomb Squad in its removal in either the Bomb Truck, or a total containment vessel.

Should an aircraft be hijacked to either Kennedy International Airport or LaGuardia Airport, ESU will be the first unit to deploy on the scene and secure and isolate the aircraft, though a rescue operation might be executed only after the FBI's HRT can be flown in from Quantico, Virginia. Such was the case on February 11, 1993, when a Lufthansa jet was hijacked to New York by a Somali gunman and FBI personnel rushed to New York courtesy of a C-141 transport complete with their gear, vehicle and a bureau UH-60 Blackhawk.

A "truck" is the department vernacular for a squad's quarters and unit name and it is also the force's main work-stations, as the two types of vehicles the unit possesses are mini-command and rescue stations.

Live fire entry exercises at the outdoor TAC house--Camp Smith. After the Stun Device has detonated with a into a deafening blast and a blinding flash, the squad makes its move--while the officer with the Body Bunker races toward his objective, the MP5 of the team unleashes a quieting burst of 9mm fire. (Samuel M. Katz)

An officer practices firing his Glock pistol while holding the Body Bunker inside the TAC house. (Samuel M. Katz)

The smaller ESU vehicle is the R.E.P or **R**adio **E**mergency **P**atrol, a cabin of emergency gear loaded on a 4x4 pickup. Each ESU Truck usually maintains three R.E.P.s and two are usually on patrol through the Truck's area of responsibility; they are known as the "Adam," "Boy," and "Charlie" cars. By performing roving patrols, R.E.P.s are in an excellent position to respond to emergencies requiring ESU expertise, such as "pin jobs," and tactical support for precinct officers responding to confirmed reports of shots fired or robbery in progress. The R.E.P. carries a little bit of all the unit's emergency rescue equipment, protective body armor, though the heaviest bit of firepower carried is the 12-gauge shotgun. The larger of the two vehicles is the "Truck," a hulking $250,00 vehicle ($1,000,000 when fully equipped) the size of a garbage truck that possesses a mini-generator powerful enough to bring lights to a full city block; compressed oxygen; two sets of the jaws of life, hydraulic scissors that can bring 10,000 lb. of pressure to bear on a sheet of steel and cut out a passenger from the twisted ruins of a car with the speed and effectiveness of a sharpened scissors on a sheet of paper; special inflatable jacking bags to lift cars, trucks and even subway trains off of trapped victims and a lumber yard full of blocks to keep whatever has been inflated off the victim until emergency medical care has been issued; a hardware store full of sledge-hammers, axes, picks, and other entrance tools; and, a jet ski, a Zodiac inflatable boat, a wet suit and oxygen tanks.[2] Virtually all ESU personnel are SCUBA-qualified, making the unit the largest underwater rescue and tactical force outside the U.S. Navy. ESU officers also train in heliborne deployment, and train in rappelling and fast-roping from the NYPD's Aviation Unit's fleet of Bell-206 and Bell-412 choppers. During the World Trade Center bombing, for example, ESU officers were able to bring equipment to the roof of the tower, as well as evacuate civilians, courtesy of the choppers and steady flying capabilities of the Aviation Unit's flyers. With airborne support, an ESU team can be anywhere in the city in fifteen minutes. Other ESU vehicles include two M75 APCs known as E.R.Vs for **E**mergency **R**escue **V**ehicles, which are used primarily to evacuate a wounded officer or civilian in an areas under fire.

In 1993 alone, ESU performed a remarkable 1,200 room entry assault "jobs," the police term for a call, involving the breaking into a premises and either arresting a perpetrator, freeing a captive, or subduing an armed individual. This astounding number of jobs makes the unit among the busiest in the world, even more so than the busiest European forces (both the Italian GIS and NOCS), as well as the Israeli ***Ya'ma'm.*** These tactical jobs involved suiting up and deploying with heavy-firepower; some jobs lasted as little as thirty minutes, others have lasted up to sixteen hours. Tactically speaking, the NYPD ESU is as professional, skilled and battle-tested as they come. Although they have trained with a variety of law-enforcement and military agencies to develop and hone their skills, it is the lessons learned on the streets of the city that is the guiding force behind the tactics ESU uses on jobs.

The ESU training facility at Floyd Bennet Field, Brooklyn, is inside the spacious confines of an aircraft hanger. One portion houses many of the unit's vehicles and gear, as well as including a mock-up helicopter hanging five stories high that is used to teach officers to rappel and fast-rope. Another half of the hangar is a tactical classroom--a wooden mock-up of a perp's house where the officers perfect their skills to enter a house, search rooms, and take down perps, as well as a target firing range. Standing high-atop the wooden mock-up, on a precarious cat-walk, Detective Burke supervises as a team is taught the "proper" means of entering through a door. In a narrow hallway, nine men have assembled, all carrying the guns that a team would deploy on a job (MP5s and 9mm semi-automatics), and two officers are carrying bullet-proof Body Bunkers--ballistic shields that can stop most handgun and shotgun shells. The mock-up is meant to simulate realism--furniture is strewn about the mock-up to simulate realism--so that the officers, all with street experience, don't lose a sense of realism. "The rooms we enter have furniture," argues Detective Burke, "why shouldn't the mock-up?"

One instructor sits on a bed in the rear bedroom reading a copy of the Daily News--he's the bad guy in the exercise. Hopping atop the precarious boards of the cat-walk, Detective Burke shouts, "Get ready guys....anyone in the house is a perp! Start when you're ready." The officers assemble outside the door in a well-choreographed fashion. The shortest and fastest member of the team is the point man, and he will enter first--he is to hold the Body Bunker and, if necessary, serve as a target to draw the bad guy's fire, and pre-occupy the shooter while the ESU team handles the rest. The rest of the team will follow the point man throughout the apartment, constantly moving and never giving up the momentum and flow of their entry. If the point man stops, he bottles up everyone else and bunches the team into a big fat target for the bad guy. Each officer is also responsible for a room inside the targeted apartment which he must secure before allowing anyone in, and perform any secondary searches.

The assault begins. An officer with an MP5 shouts "POLICE" and

Detective Denis Burke, ESU tactical instructor, supervises his charges following an explosive entry--a critique follows each entry and corrected for the next time. (Samuel M. Katz)

The TAC house at Camp Smith. (Samuel M. Katz)

ESU officers train with the M75 APC, known in the ESU vernacular as the ERV or Emergency Rescue Vehicle. The lead officer carries the Ruger Mini-14 5.56mm assault rifle. (Samuel M. Katz)

Lieutenant Glen Panazzolo, commander of the ESU tactical training facility at Floyd Bennet Field, supervises training with the ERV. (Samuel M. Katz)

kicks open the door while the point man, 13 lb. Body Bunker and all, enters first--holding the shield with one hand and aiming his Glock 9mm automatic with the other. The other members of the team follow suit searching the confines of the apartment for bad guys and anything threatening--a perp hiding under a bed, inside a closet, or elsewhere. In the rear bedroom, the instructor is spotted, and apprehended with an MP5. A secondary search is ordered, and any place that might conceal a bad guy (closets, under beds, etc.) is searched carefully. Detective Burke is not satisfied, however. Several officers were tentative, a few stopped at a wall, and one officer moved too slowly around a wall rather than bursting straight into the kitchen. The officers are eager to do well, because the grade they are most concerned with is returning home after a job in one piece.

"Do it again," orders Burke, "this time with a Stun Device." As the choreographed ensemble sets up outside, one officer kicks open the door and hurls a Stun Device into the living room--the device, also known as a "flash bang," produces a blinding flash of light and a deafening blast. It will stun and immobilize an individual for a second or two, but that is all that's needed. The element of surprise allows the team to seize control of the situation without having to face a prepared opponent. On the streets, the team would have advanced intelligence on the target--blue-prints and reports of the position of furniture would have been obtained from the sniper who would perch himself across the street and serve as a marksman, as well as spotter and intelligence-gatherer. For the most part, however, the perps know not to mess with ESU, and ESU makes a point to announce their entry into any situation. According to Detective Brandt, "If we are going to surprise a drug house and not say its the police, the dealers, all heavily armed, will think that it is a rival drug gang out to rob and kill them, and they'll fight to the death to save their drugs and money. If they know it's us, they'll usually surrender and accept the time they'll need to serve." Training is fine, but it cannot replace the fear and anxiety that is felt on an ***actual*** job. According to one ESU officer, "Words could never describe the feeling of your heart pounding so hard that it is ready to burst through the confines of your body armor."

Live-fire tactical training is carried out at the NYPD range in Rodmen's Neck in the Bronx, and specialized tactical training is conducted annually (and sometimes three times a year) at Camp Smith, an army post and training camp along the Hudson River in upstate New York. At Camp Smith, ESU officers are able to practice their rappelling and fast-rope techniques (courtesy of a 300-foot high cliff); live fire TAC house where entry skills can be honed up and mastered anew; helicopters assault techniques; VIP protection exercises with the C.A.T. car; and, recovery exercises with the E.R.V.

ESU is the most exclusive unit in the entire department. Service in ESU is on a strictly volunteer basis, and the waiting list to get in or even be considered for the unit is 1,500 names long. To be eligible to volunteer, an officer must have five years on the job with an exemplary service record, pass a psychological and physical examination, as well as an extensive oral examination. ESU is primarily looking for officers with additional skills, such as carpenters, electricians and craftsman who can combine the tactical aspects of the job with the rescue role; officers with SCUBA or military skills are also recruited and sought. Much of the recruitment is done via word of mouth and recommendations. The actual training, called the Specialized Training School (STS), lasts sixteen weeks.

For years, the principal NYPD side-arm was the .38 police special revolver, though the department is now upgrading to 9mm semi-automatics--primarily the Glock Model 19. Most ESU officers are armed with Glocks, and Glocks and Beretta 92Ds fitted with flash-lights (for use by tactical point men carrying the Body Bunker) are carried on the truck. The unit's principal 9mm submachine gun is the Heckler and Koch MP5 A3 complete with HK94 tactical forearm with built-in light. The unit's primary assault rifle is the American-produced Ruger Mini-14 5.56mm assault rifle (an NYPD favorite), and the shotgun carried in R.E.P.s, patrol cars and supervisor vehicles is the Ithaca Model 37 12-gauge shotgun. The ESU sniper team used to carry the Austrian-produced Steyr Police Sniper weapon but has recently switched to Remington's M-24 7.62mm system.

[1] Five-Truck is the only ESU squad not under the control of the SOD, but rather the Borough Command.

[2] Besides being one of the world's largest single purchasers of rescue and life-saving gear, ESU's knowledge and expertise has been used around the globe. When Hurricane Hugo pummeled the island of Puerto Rico, an ESU team was en route to the battered island commonwealth, on a military transport, within hours of the devastating winds and waves. At their training facility inside a hangar at Floyd Bennet Field in Brooklyn, emergency medical, construction and recovery gear sits inside a sealed container awaiting deployment ANYWHERE in the world.

ESU officers are briefed prior to commencing ERV deployment training, at Camp Smith, New York. (Samuel M. Katz)

Simulating a rescue of a downed officer or civilian, an ESU takes aim with his Mini-14 behind the safe cover of the ERV. (Samuel M. Katz)

The ERV kicks up a cloud of dust as it races to its deployment with a full compliment of ESU officers safely inside the hulking vehicle. (Samuel M. Katz)

VIP security training with ESU's marked C.A.T. car. (Samuel M. Katz)

One of the NYPD Aviation Unit's Bell-412 rescue choppers--these aircraft can be used for reconnaissance, patrol, medevac and sea-rescue, and for the tactical deployment of ESU personnel. (Samuel M. Katz)

Prior to a "job" in Harlem, detectives, some undercover, brief officers from Two-Truck on the layout of an apartment about to be hit. (Samuel M. Katz)

After being briefed and gearing up, ESU awaits word from the precinct before beginning the motorcade toward the objective. Here, Sergeant Patrick Murphy clutches his Ruger Mini-14 as he stands in the doorway of a Truck. (Samuel M. Katz)

Prior to a hit in the Bronx of a known drug and weapons location (a drug and gun run), officers from Four-Truck prepare their weapons, including an Ithaca Model 37 12-gauge shotgun. (Samuel M. Katz)

Outside a Harlem precinct, ESU officers ready their equipment before entering the back of the Truck and making the short, though adrenaline-filled, journey toward the targeted location. (Samuel M. Katz)

The commander of the 30 Precinct, Deputy Inspector Thomas Sweeney, tells the men of Two-Truck to be safe and offers his best wishes prior to the hit of a known drug location. (Samuel M. Katz)

The entry--after racing out of the Truck, the officers climb up the stairs of a neglected building and prepare to gain entry. (Samuel M. Katz)

While entry is attempted with the Rabbit Tool, a Truck-Two sergeant brings up the "sledge" just in case its needed. (Samuel M. Katz)

A precinct officer places his hands over his ears, as a Stun Device is hurled inside the targeted apartment. ESU officers credit the incredible success of their work--the fact that so few of them have been hurt--by the effectiveness of these devices on hits. (Samuel M. Katz)

The A-Team in action. Officers stand poised and ready to move once entry into a Harlem drug location can be gained. (Samuel M. Katz)

A 12-gauge shotgun, "on-call," in its perch behind the driver's seat on a One-Truck vehicle. (Samuel M. Katz)

An ESU officer attached to the A-Team clutches his MP5 awaiting the choreographed charge inside the targeted location. (Samuel M. Katz)

Following a successful hit in the Bronx, an officer removes his heavy vest and rests his 12-gauge shotgun on the hood of a sector car as Lieutenant Bob Sobocienski, goes over the job with officers from Four-Truck. (Samuel M. Katz)

Officers from Two-Truck in Harlem engage in the relieved post-job critique following a successful hit in northern Manhattan. The officers have done this so many times, that each hit is part of their instinctive nature. Nevertheless, a discussion of the good and bad following a job guarantees that good points will be reinforced the next time, and any mistakes quickly corrected. (Samuel M. Katz)

An R.E.P. is parked, at the ready, outside Manhattan Federal Court during the trial of the World Trade Center bombers. (Samuel M. Katz)

Detective Kris Brandt displays the proper firing position when taking aim with a Beretta 9mm semi-automatic pistol. (Samuel M. Katz)

During a sea-rescue, ESU officers deploy from an Aviation Unit chopper in the waters off of Brooklyn. (Courtesy: New York City Police Department)

A-Team training at Floyd Bennet Field, Brooklyn. During hostage-training rescue classes at the indoor TAC house, Detective Denis Burke (center) plays hostage as his charges learn what they did right--and wrong--during a dry run. (Samuel M. Katz)

# U.S.A. - The Los Angeles Police Department SWAT Platoon

***As Italy and Brazil waged war on the soccer field amid the cries and cheers of the Rose Bowl, THEY stood at the ready, poised to strike. Clad in black fatigues and broiling in the Los Angeles heat underneath their Kevlar body armor, they clutched their MP5 9mm submachine guns and checked batteries on laser-aim devices awaiting that call on the emergency frequency that an incident was going down, that a terrorist group had struck, that a tactical response was required. They were the men of the Los Angeles Police Department SWAT unit, perhaps the nation's most famous, and they were tasked with making the world cup's final match, an event viewed by over a billion people around the world, a battle on the playing field and not a ripe target for a terrorist group eager to broadcast its gripes to a global television audience.***

The LAPD SWAT emblem.

Los Angeles is a city renown for being on the move, a conglomerate of diverse small communities connected by freeways and the fascination with motorcars and mobility rather than an urban patchwork of neighborhoods. The national (if not global) capital for the entertainment industry and for setting trends, Los Angeles has earned itself a reputation of being a bold and innovative town where ideas blossom into precedents borrowed the world over. Nowhere is this more accurate as in the city's law-enforcement abilities, and in its esteemed police force. For not only has the Los Angeles Police Department revolutionized many of the practices and tactics used by law-enforcement officers throughout the United States, but it created a small, highly mobile force of on-call tactical and weapons specialists long before any other force thought along similar lines. That unit would be tagged with the now ubiquitous tag of SWAT, for Special Weapons and Tactics, and the LAPD's was the nation's, and world's, first.

Long before the 1972 Munich Olympic Massacre, long before hostage-taking became a terrorist art form, the LAPD realized that certain outbreaks of public violence and certain criminal situations required more than an officer with his .38 in one hand and a bull horn in the other; in many of these high profile situations, even the police officer's old trusted 12-gauge shotgun just wouldn't do. The department required a small, though highly mobile, force of officers who would function as a group of virtual soldiers embedded in a civilian police agency. They would raid fortified locations, need to be expert in urban tactical situations, and be as proficient in a wide-assortment of large-caliber automatic weapons and firearms as a conventional combat soldier. It was the summer of 1965, Los Angeles had been rocked by the notorious and deadly Watts Riots, and police planners realized that the typical response to urban unrest in the 1960s, calling in the National Guard, took time and eventually cost civilians their lives. The man behind the notion of a police force SWAT unit was a young and innovative officer named Daryl Gates, a man who would later become one of the force's most aggressive and controversial commanders. Gates main concern back in 1965 was to be able to deploy a mobile force of officers who could deal ***tactically*** with snipers, a "riot phenomenon" that resulted in many casualties during the bloody Watts meleć, especially among the ranks of Los Angeles policemen. The unit was to be informal, officers patrolled their usual beats during normal shifts but could be summoned at a moment's notice to respond to any developing situation. Officers who volunteered for this new and mysterious unit got no extra pay, no special bonuses.

The LAPD SWAT unit was first trained in the art of tactical warfare by elements of the United States Marine Corps. The unit, fearing another large-scale riot, needed to acquaint itself with the "recapturing of the city" and the Marines, already owners of extensive combat experience from Vietnam, were ideal instructors. Yet the image that Hollywood has produced of the icon L.A. cop, spit and polish and polite in his black uniform and mirrored glasses, was far from the reality of the initial SWAT training. Armed with rifles, SWAT volunteers spent endless hours marching through the storm drains of the city practicing ways to move through the city undetected. That period was a time what many veterans call "Old SWAT," and although the unit never had to retake the city from the storm drains, two very violent incidents forever changed the scope, outlook and capabilities of LAPD SWAT.

On December 8, 1969, SWAT officers attempted to serve felony warrants at the party headquarters of the Black Panther Movement, a Black power group that had engaged in extremely aggressive and violent criminal activity peaked by the murders of police officers in several large cities. When the unit arrived at the fortified location at

Sergeant Al Preciado, one of the LAPD SWAT founding members, loads a fresh clip into his M-16 5.56mm assault rifle during the May 17, 1974, assault on the SLA building at 54th Street. (Mike Mullen)

The streets of L.A.--circa 1976. After robbing a supermarket and taking hostages once police units arrived, a suspect is hauled into custody courtesy of the SWAT unit. (Michael Haering/Los Angeles Herald-Examiner)

Dramatic sequence of photographs illustrating how the LAPD SWAT unit serves high-risk felony warrants. Note first photo as the door is yanked off its hinges courtesy of a Suburban, and then two SWAT elements move in for the arrest. (Courtesy: Sergeant Al Preciado/LAPD SWAT)

41st Street and Central Avenue, they were greeted by shotgun blasts and the explosions of automatic fire. For the next five hours, Black Panthers and LAPD units exchanged over 5,000 rounds of ammunition in a melee that resembled a battlefield rather than a city street. Eventually, the combination of the SWAT unit's dedicated firepower and the fact that the Panthers had virtually run out of ammunition, led to their surrender. Remarkably, nobody was killed in the battle, although three officers were hurt and ***one*** Panther received slight wounds.

Five years later, on May 17, 1974, the unit participated in the most notorious fire-fight in the city's history when nineteen SWAT officers descended on a house on 54th Street where they believed that kidnapped heiress Patricia Hearst was being held by the radical Symbionese Liberation Army (SLA). Three SWAT squads, armed with shotguns and M-16s, closed in on the residence and surrounded it, but the SLA terrorists inside did not respond to the bullhorn and plea to surrender, and when a tear-gas canister was fired into the house, the SLA responded with machine gun fire. For the next two hours, 54th Street was a war zone. Eventually, the house burned down to the ground with all six SLA gunmen dying in the blaze.

The two incidents were of tremendous significance to the SWAT unit.[1] They were ballistic wake-up calls as to how things should be done and proved that large-scale tactical incidents should not "go down" with a barrage of gunfire like a shoot-out in a B-movie Western, but rather a deliberate, precise and professional assault or response where the officer's training, equipment and abilities permit him to safely handle the situation with finesse rather than with massive firepower. The unit would have to become a cohesive squad of specialists, of special forces operators,[2] that believed that less was more, speed more important than brute force, and professionalism and training a religious and life-saving code that would personify every aspect of their job. As a result, admission standards to the unit were significantly raised and tightened, discipline enforced, and greater respect shown toward the community. It was not easy meshing these military and civilian law enforcement requirements into a viable entity, but LAPD was successful, and the SWAT unit became a national role model.

Following the Black Panther fire-fight in 1969, it was decided to centralize all SWAT personnel within the LAPD's Metropolitan Division where it is considered a "platoon." Remarkably, the unit is small by big city standards--only sixty-seven officers with the commanding officer being a lieutenant. A sergeant commands each squad which consists of two five-man elements, with each "element" commanded by a Senior Lead Officer. All element members are "operators," expertly trained assault specialists with several members cross-trained as snipers and observers--of the sixty SWAT operators, sixteen are snipers; of the six SWAT sergeants, two are snipers. When not on a tactical job, SWAT officers operate in uniform or plain clothes in unmarked police cars on anti-crime assignments. One of their busiest roles has been in issuing high-risk felony warrants to the city's most dangerous wanted men and women.

Also contained with the SWAT team are member of the LAPD's Crisis Negotiation Team (CT) who provide both verbal and tactical support to SWAT team elements during barricade and hostage incidents. For large-scale operation, a Tactical Operations Center (TOC) is called on to direct operations and deployments.

An assault team hones its skills in rescuing a bus hijacked by criminals or terrorists. (Courtesy: Sergeant Al Preciado/LAPD SWAT)

At the unit's training facility, snipers and observers perfect their skills with the Heckler and Koch GSG1 7.62mm police sniper rifle. (Courtesy: Sergeant Al Preciado/LAPD SWAT)

Yet the transformation of the "Old SWAT" born out of the ashes of Watts Riots into the modern and trailblazing unit of today was its preparations for the 1984 Summer Olympics. Confident in ***his*** unit's abilities, Los Angeles Police Chief Daryl Gates announced that the SWAT unit could handle any and all outbreaks of terrorism within the city limits even though a the SWAT unit commander, Lieutenant Jeff Rogers, told his commander that "we are a SWAT team, not an counter-terrorist outfit!" Gates quickly despatched his three most trusted officers--Lieutenant Rogers, Captain John Higgins and Sergeant Al Preciado--to embark on a globe-trotting counter-terrorist crash course studying the units tactics and equipment deployed by Israel's ***Ya'ma'm,*** Italy's GIS and NOCS, France's GIGN, a U.S. Army Special Forces counter-insurgency team operating in West Berlin, GSG-9 and other German state SEKs, and the British SAS, SO13 and SO19. The three Los Angeles officers returned from their trip full of ideas and a long wish list of equipment, gear and weapons that they would need should they truly be able to meet any terrorist attack launched during the Olympic games. The gear required included special tactical poles with mirrors on the ends for use in around-the-corner tactical situations inside or around buildings, and the pioneering the use of flash-lights attached to shotguns, assault rifles and automatic pistols. To prepare for the challenges of keeping the peace during the Olympics, as the fear from Munich twelve years earlier was still embedded in every officer's mind, the unit also entered into a joint training course with the U.S. Army's 1st SFOD-D at Fort Bragg. Much of this security instruction was also dedicated to VIP and dignitary security--both in plain clothes and in full tactical gear.

Prior to the 1984 Olympics, the SWAT unit generally trained with ***blanks*** in its then limited tactical assault course. Once counter-terrorism and hostage-rescue entered its vernacular, however, the unit began to use live rounds, and it used abandoned buildings as urban killing houses where they trained in the art of hostage-rescue by hitting mannequins substituting for terrorists while not hitting hostages and not getting hit in the crossfire of ***live ammunition***. In preparation for the 1984 games, the unit fired more rounds of ammunition and threw more diversionary devices (also known in the vernacular as "Flash Bang")in several months of instruction that they would have in twenty years of "regular" training. The games in Los Angeles went off without incident, partly due to the vast American law-enforcement and intelligence effort to locate and identify potential terrorist threats, and partly due to the deterring reputation of the unit.

The rigorous training (while preparing for the Olympics) has since become the unit's routine regimen. SWAT officers spend 240 hours a year honing their weapons skills, and perfecting their climbing and rappelling capabilities. Their heliborne skills are superb, even for a conventional or special forces military unit--LAPD SWAT officers, like their GSG-9 counterparts in Germany, are trained to fire from moving choppers; they are also trained to rappel and fast rope down lines thrown from choppers (or down the sides of buildings) during tactical situations. Most importantly, perhaps, the unit places

In the desert south of the city, SWAT members practice night-time firing with their .45 caliber automatics. Even though the advent of night-vision equipment has increased night-time marksmanship, an officer still needs to acclimate himself with weapons training in the dark. (Courtesy: Sergeant Al Preciado/LAPD SWAT)

Dramatic photograph of a high risk warrant being served in east Los Angeles by a SWAT element. Photograph shows to advantage the equipment worn and carried by SWAT personnel in the field during tactical jobs. (Courtesy: Sergeant Al Preciado/LAPD SWAT)

During hostage-rescue exercises held just before the 1984 Summer Olympics, SWAT personnel perform an explosive entry into a "shooting house" simulating a building where terrorists are holding hostages. Note officers armed with MP5s and carrying body bunker ballistic shields. (Courtesy: Sergeant Al Preciado/LAPD SWAT)

Wearing combat fatigues and Protec helmets, SWAT personnel prepare to fast rope from a LAPD Air Support Division Bell-212 chopper. (Courtesy: Sergeant Al Preciado/LAPD SWAT)

The use of the helicopter has had a tremendous impact on the SWAT unit's abilities to reach a scene in record time, as well as deploy against a target by fast roping from a hovering chopper. A chopper from the Air Support Division is assigned full time to the SWAT Platoon for training and tactical operations.

extraordinary emphasis on physical fitness. SWAT team members are expected to be able to run the most elaborate and exhaustive of close order drill military obstacles courses and must achieve a passing grade on the course on a quarterly basis. Even a volunteer to the unit must be in superb physical condition before the officer can even be considered for a spot on the force. All the volunteers must be from Metropolitan Division, must have a proficiency rating in the top twenty-five percentile within the entire force, and must have four years of experience on the force with a minimum two years of "field experience." The training course, which includes everything from small arms to the history of guerrilla warfare, lasts nearly six months.

Since their inception in 1966, the SWAT unit has been deployed over 1000 times in some of the meanest streets in America, where gang-bangers usually pack heavier firepower than the average officers. The principal side-arm carried by SWAT officers is an accurized Colt Government Model .45 ACP (modifications including fixed high-visibility sights, improved trigger, lowered ejection port, polished feed ramp, throated chamber and ambidextrous safety). The unit's submachine gun is, of course, the Heckler and Koch MP5 family of 9mm submachine guns issued to all operators Observers carry either the Heckler and Koch HK33K or CAR-15 5.56mm assault rifle, as well as a bolt action Remington Model 700 .308 sniper rifle with a 3x9 scope, and the primary sniper weapon is both the American-produced .308 and .223 "Special Marksman Scoped Bolt-Action Weapon" by

SWAT personnel fast rope down the sides of an Air Support Division chopper during counter-terrorist exercises. (Courtesy: Sergeant Al Preciado/LAPD SWAT)

Robar; the unit's former primary sniper weapon, the superb Heckler and Koch GSG1 7.62mm police sniper rifle, is now used primarily for night operations, and for fire-suppression missions. The primary shotgun carried by SWAT officers is the Italian-made Benelli 12-gauge M1 Super 90 shotgun (with a plastic stock and a forward pistol grip), as well the Benelli 121-M-1 recoil operation semi-automatic shotgun; it was during the 1969 encounter with the Black Panthers that SWAT officers found a pump-action weapon incompatible with firing from the prone position or one-handed. Each officer is issued with a two-piece Nomex flame-retardent combat suit, load bearing vest, and a set of Kevlar body armor with insertable ceramic plates to meet any high-velocity ballistic threat. Standard head-gear, in addition to the black balaclava, is a black Fritz-helmet equipped with an integrated Motorola personal radio earphone/microphone combination.

The unit's primary vehicles include unmarked police vehicles, and dark blue SWAT Trucks (GMC Step-Vans). In the mid-1980s the unit began using a pair of battering ram-equipped small armored cars, known as the V-100s, but their deployment stirred some controversy about a military vehicle being used in a civilian law enforcement situation. Although a court order is required for its deployment in a warrant-serving situation, the unit deploys it immediately and without question when shots are fired at either officers or civilians and mobile armored protection is required.

Today, SWAT officers train a small legion of SWAT and emergency response teams around the United States and Canada, and even in Central and South America. The unit also maintains close working links to most of the other SWAT units in the United States, as well as many of the world's top counter-terrorist units.

[1] The numbers "41" and "54" were even added to the unit patch and emblem.

[2] The unit would eventually train together with U.S. Army Special Forces and the U.S. Navy SEALs.

# U.S.A. - Seattle Police Department's Emergency Response Team (ERT)

The Seattle Police Department patch--worn on the shoulder of regular police uniforms.

The ERT patch--the unit motto is ***Fortuna Favet Fortibus,*** or "Fortune Favors The Bold."

The subdued Seattle Police Department patch--worn on the shoulder of the ERT uniforms during tactical operations.

"Deadly force is the absolute last choice." That motto is the catch-phrase of virtually all police SWAT and emergency response units. Unlike military counter-terrorist and hostage-rescue intervention squads, they do not enjoy the "luxury" of acceptable losses or casualty assessments. To these officers, ending an incident through peaceable means is the only policy that can guide their work; after all, these men--and women--must still police the streets of their cities, realizing that the smallest of tragic incidents leaves a residue of mistrust and hate for years to come. Bearing that in mind, they must be able to operate 365-days-a-year, in any and all geographic settings, and through any and all climactic conditions. They must be able to deal with a distraught substance abuser holding his family hostage at knife-point to a heavily armed gang of narco-terrorists establishing a foothold in a new neighborhood; the must also be able to hunt down a hostage in a mountain hideaway and free frightened schoolkids held captive on a schoolbus parked on an isolated bridge. If they succeed in performing their job with professionalism and skill, they are considered heroes--if they fail, their very existence as a unit, their careers as peace officers, is questioned. It is incredible pressure, and it is this tightrope that SWAT officers must endure in both large cities and sprawling rural suburbs. One unit which has managed to walk that tightrope with distinction has been the Seattle Police Department's Emergency Response Team--the ERT.

The death of a police officer and his assailant in 1984 brought the Seattle Police Department's Emergency Response Team to its present configuration. Until that time, the ERT consisted of one lieutenant, two sergeants, and twelve officers. Today, ERT falls under the command of the Special Patrol Unit and is headquartered in the Metropolitan Section, Special Operations Division of the Operations Bureau. Commanded by a lieutenant and staffed by four sergeants, each sergeant commanding a squad of six officers. The ERT is divided into two shifts, with two squads working each shift. Two squads work 1000 to 1800 Monday to Friday for one month and Tuesday to Saturday for the following month. The remaining two squads work form 1900-0300 with the same monthly rotation. The Day Team is responsible for ERT missions from 0300-1800 every day; the Night Team is responsible for missions between 1800-0300. Team members are assigned pagers and are responsible for "Call-Out Responses" twenty-four-hours a day, every day. Shift members are then assigned as either an Entry or Perimeter member with a sergeant serving as the Team Leader. There are eight Entry Team members and four Perimeter Team members for each shift.

Personnel selection receives high priority status in the Special Patrol Unit. Selection is based on experience, performance, integrity and motivation. Current assignments are not criterion for selection, and the Unit receives applicants from all units within the Department. Assignments are taken on a volunteer basis only. The selection process consists of the following:

- Applicants must have minimum of five years patrol experience.

Wearing hoods over the faces and Kevlar Fritz helmets, ERT officers are briefed on a job involving an explosive entry. (Courtesy: Seattle Police)

With the door kicked in courtesy of a ramming device, an officer aims his suppressed MP5 with attached flashlight at the "perp." (Courtesy: Seattle Police)

During counter-terrorist training, ERT officers, all armed with MP5s with double magazines, prepare to purify a building. (Courtesy: Seattle Police)

- Applicants must submit, through their current Supervisor, a request for a thirty day temporary assignment. Background investigation of the applicants will include, but not be limited to, a review of reports written sick time records, Internal Investigation records and Personnel records, Department shoot scores, Department Physical Fitness Test scores and an interview with their current and prior supervisors. Applicants must also pass the required obstacle course and a psychological interview. The Special Patrol Commander will then select from those officers.
- During the temporary assignment, the candidates' ability to work with little supervision, his/her dedication, aggressiveness, initiative and quality of arrests, and reports will be monitored. Performance during applicable ERT training will also be considered. At the completion of the assignment, Special Patrol Unit sergeants and officers will evaluate the candidate. The sergeants then conduct an oral interview with the candidate. The evaluation is then given to the unit commander.
- Those candidates with a positive recommendation are placed on a list for consideration for future assignments. Final selection is made by the unit Commander.

Team Members participate in four mandatory eight-hour training days per month, two of which are devoted solely to weapons proficiency. There are seven specialty weapons cadres in the ERT repertoire: (1) Benelli 12-gauge shotgun; (2) chemical agents; (3) Defensive Tactics; (4) Marksmen and Sniping, and counter-sniping; (5) The Heckler and Koch family of MP5 9mm submachine guns; (6) The M-16A2 and CAR-15 family of 5.56mm assault rifles; and, (7) The Colt .45 automatic. Each Cadre is assigned a Cadre sergeant and a Cadre Leader (Officer); sergeants and officers belong to at least two Cadres. Members are required to qualify quarterly with their specialty weapons along with the Unit's handgun, the Colt .45 automatic.

The final two days are devoted to tactical exercises: entering, clearing, building searches, hostage situations, down officer rescue and crisis entry. Four times a year the Team conducts a real time joint scenario with the Hostage Negotiation Team commanders from various precincts and divisions are invited to be the Field Commanders.

Officers are required to work out one hour at the beginning or end of each shift. Workouts are rotated between strength and aerobic. Physical fitness is a critical priority and members must be in top physical shape--those officers failing to pass their physical test and negotiate the SWAT obstacle course are bounced from the team.

Team members are sent to a multitude of specialty training courses from outside agencies and schools, including: the FBI Chemical Agent School, the FBI Sniper School, the BORTAC Drug Interdiction Course, the Heckler and Koch MP5 User/Instructor Courses, Phil Singleton's Dynamic Entry School, the Washington State Tactical Officers Association Quarterly Seminars, joint tactical training from U.S. Army Special Forces, including from 1st Special Forces Group (Airborne), based in Fort Lewis (and, it is believed, the U.S. Army's 1st SFOD-D), National Tactical Officers Seminars (annually), Los Angeles Police Department SWAT School, U.S. Secret Service tactical school, and the NTOA SWAT Supervisors Course.

Special Patrol Unit/ERT responsibilities include:

- Cases of barricaded persons, hostage situations and any incident that they feel requires the special training tactics and heavy firepower.
- Dignitary protection assignments, and the providing of protective details for international, national and local dignitaries, as well as security details for the City Council and other city agencies with special security concerns.
- Riot and crowd control.
- Saturation patrol, along with the Special Patrol Unit, at the request of other units the ERT will respond in squad or unit strength to ongoing or known problems throughout the city.
- Stake out assignments--ERT will, at the request from other units, stakeout areas for repeat/pattern offenses or wanted persons.

Due to the geographic location of Seattle, complete with eight square miles of water inside the city limits as well as a major port accessible to the Pacific Ocean, ERT conducts specialty training on all types of river and ocean-going vessels. ERT also trains on these vessels with the Seattle Police Harbor Unit in terms of reaching ships in midwater, as well as in deploying from speedboats and rubber dinghies; some ERT personnel are SCUBA qualified. ERT officers also train in rescuing hostages from Amtrak passenger trains, and buses and trams from the Seattle's Metro Bus System.

In August of 1989, ERT was given the primary responsibility for Hostage Rescue/Anti-Terrorist response for the Goodwill Games. Training was centered on this mission and several outside instructors from both law enforcement and military agencies came to Seattle to prepare the team. In January, the training accelerated to a daily basis; and in April, the team went on a full time alert status. During the games, the team was staged at a local airfield, with National Guard helicopters prepared to rush them to the scene of any incident.

After a job well done, the arrest of a "perp" without having to fire a shot, ERT officers remove their gear into the unit's Chevrolet Equipment truck. (Courtesy: Seattle Police)

Besides being able to deploy from any patrol car within the Seattle Police Department's vast motor pool, Special Patrol Unit/ERT vehicles include:

- Two 1992 GMC Econoline vans (extended series) with one "Bag Van"--shelved to carry personal ERT equipment bags, and the Special Patrol Unit Van--with seating capacity for 17 people
- Two 1992 Chevrolet Caprice 4-door sedans (unmarked with emergency equipment - lights, siren, radio, and mobile data terminal)
- One 1988 Chevrolet Equipment truck for AK 47 vests, ballistic helmets, shields, NFDD's, all Unit equipment that is not carried in personal bags.
- One 1979 Armored car (Loomis Style) complete with loudspeaker and emergency equipment.

Since the unit's inception, the ERT has responded to hundreds of "jobs" or incidents. Some of the largest and most important, include:

- In December of 1991, ERT responded to the scene of what was to be the longest call-out in the Team's history. A "recovering" heroin addict had shot his father with a shotgun and barricaded himself in his castle-style home. ERT and HNT responded to the scene but were unable to establish communications with the suspect. Day and Night teams began 12-hour shift rotations for three days while HNT attempted to establish a communications link. ERT was finally given permission to deliver chemical agents prior to making entry. Upon entering, ERT located the suspect and took him into custody.
- In March of 1993, an FBI Narcotics Task Force Surveillance Team spotted a multiple homicide suspect during their stakeout. The suspect was wanted for two murders, and for questioning in two more prior homicides. ERT was called and set up on the single bedroom apartment unit. The suspect refused to surrender and chemical agents were delivered. The delivery team received immediate gunfire from the residence, but were not hit. Negotiations continued for over 10 hours with frequent chemical agent deliveries. The suspect had barricaded the windows and stored water for relief from the chemicals. The order to make entry was given; and the team deployed NFDD's. However, immediately before entry, the suspect shot himself in the head. ERT recovered a fully auto Ingram Mac 10 and a Browning Hi Power 9mm at the suspect's side.
- In April of 1994, an ex-employee returned to his old office carrying a rifle and a satchel of explosives. The fifty-one-year-old male drove into the loading dock area and threw a flare into his front seat. The suspect had prepared several pipe bombs in his car, along with a canister of black powder and several different types of ammunition. The suspect then entered the office area and took five hostages. A distraction allowed the hostages to escape, but the suspect immediately found the manager and took him hostage. The suspect and hostage then went into the records storage vault. ERT responded and was on scene within twenty minutes. A Crisis Entry Team was deployed and plans for a Hostage Rescue were being made. Intelligence, gathered from HNT, revealed that the suspect had a sawed-off shotgun, a scoped rifle, a .357 revolver, several pipe bombs, and two fragmentation grenades. ERT delivered a phone and negotiations began. Negotiators were able to convince the suspect to release the hostage after about three hours. ERT continued fortifying their positions with equipment from the Bomb Squad and making contingency plans throughout the incident. After making several threats to take his own life the suspect surrendered, ending the 15 hour stand-off.

The Seattle Police Department's ERT can also respond at a moment's notice to assist the special weapon and tactics units from neighboring counties, including the Everett Washington Police "Tactical Team," the King County Police eighteen-member "TAC-30" unit, the Bellevue Police Department's "Tactical Arms Group" (TAG), and the South Snohomish County SWAT team.

Because of the heavy woods that dot much of the Seattle area, ERT officers are also expertly trained reconnaissance operators capable of invisibly moving through foliage and brush quickly and stealthily. (Courtesy: Seattle Police)

.An ERT sniper team--taking aim with a Heckler and Koch PSG-1 7.62mm sniper rifle. (Courtesy: Seattle Police)

# U.S.A .- City of Chicago Department of Police Hostage/Barricaded/Terrorist Team (HBT)

***There are some who say that TV is killing much of America. Sometimes, however, TV can even help keep bloodshed at a minimum.***

The Chicago P.D.'s lieutenant's patch.

Thursday April 3, 1986--Chicago, Illinois. In a dispute stemming from owed rent, a 6-foot-2-inch, 300-pound individual by the name of John Pasch fatally shot his landlord, Leslie Shearer, and then murdered a police officer, Richard Clark, as he stepped out of his patrol car while responding to the earlier shooting. With no place to run and with a TV-Guide full of entertainment to watch on the tube, Pasch locked himself inside his basement apartment while support police units raced to the scene. In Chicago, when the police require tactical back-up, there is one number the department dials--the department's elite Hostage-Barricade-Terrorist Squad. The HBT.

Led by unit commander Lieutenant John Kennedy, the HBT raced to the scene to try and convince Pasch to surrender without additional bloodshed. SWAT might mean special weapons and tactics but the dynamic entry and the pulling of a trigger is a final result. HBT officers donned their heavy flak vests and ballistic helmets, readied their Ruger Mini-14s, and secured a perimeter around the Pasch residence as virtually the entire neighborhood was evacuated. Floodlights were brought to the house, and snipers ringed the targeted location. There was one obstacles preventing the police from deploying tactically, however. Pasch was holding a seventy-four-year-old woman hostage.

The stand-off lasted a full thirty-six hours, the longest in Chicago history. During the ordeal, as police negotiators maintained constant telephone contact, Pasch only agreed to negotiate his surrender during commercial breaks from his favorite TV series, "Miami Vice," and an airing of the movie "The Battle of Bulge." At one point, as police feared the worst, Pasch ordered his hostage to witness him write his last will and testament. The HBT officers were eager to end the ordeal tactically, especially since Pasch was a cop killer; "The gut reaction of every cop is to waste the guy," HBT Sergeant Charles Springer told the Chicago Tribune, "but as long as he is not hurting anyone, the best thing we can do is wait." What eventually convinced Pasch to surrender were live news reports from the scene showing sharpshooters in position and tear gas ready to be deployed.

At 2:45 A.M. on the night of April 5, Pasch told police he was ready to give up. A bare-chested and defeated Pasch surrendered to police moments later.

The apprehension of John Pasch was a shining moment for the HBT--one of the nation's finest such units.

The Windy City, as Chicago is known, is also known as America's second city, and is the third largest city in the United States after New York and Los Angeles. The Chicago Police Department, one of the finest in the United States, consists of 13,000 sworn officers who patrol a city that the police have divided into five major areas and twenty-five districts. When a criminal or terrorist has taken a hostage, when an emotionally disturbed individual has barricaded himself inside a location, or when the P.D. is called upon to execute a counter-terrorist (VIP security, etc.) assignment, the HBT is summoned. The Chicago Police Department established the Hostage/Barricade/Terrorist Incident in 1979 incorporating aspects of the then current SWAT and negotiator models in existence throughout the country. The Chicago Model emphasizes proper command and

An HBT officer displays the gear worn for a inner perimeter/assault, including: tactical load bearing vest, spectra shield with pressure light mount, Kevlar shin protection, two 9mm semi-automatic pistols, and a Titanium helmet.(Courtesy: City of Chicago Department of Police)

The HBT sniper--here displaying night vision and regular binoculars, spotting scope, Ruger Mini-14 Ranch Model 5.56mm assault rifle with 4x scope. Remington Model 700, .308 caliber with 10x scope and bi-pod. (Courtesy: City of Chicago Department of Police)

control of tactical, negotiator, intelligence, and support elements at the scene of an HBT Incident. The Program consists of the HBT Incident Coordinator who is responsible for the selection of the tactical and negotiating teams--the HBT Coordinator responds to all such incidents and coordinates the overall operation in support of the officer-in-charge who would be the appropriate Deputy Chief of patrol for that area of the City. In this way, the final decision maker is insulated form natural competitive solution proposals form the tactical officers and negotiating teams. The HBT Program has resolved 235 hostage or barricaded gunmen incidents during the fifteen-years of its existence. Experience has shown that eighty-five percent of these incidents have been resolved through negotiations while fifteen-percent have necessitated tactical intervention. Throughout the 235 incidents all hostages have been safely released and those incidents where tactical intervention was necessary have been resolved safely.

Lieutenant John P. Kennedy, founder of the unit, is supported by an Auxiliary Coordinator, Lt. Fred Bosse, who assists in training and during operations and support sergeants and detectives. The HBT Program in Chicago consists of 100 containment officers and supervisors (inner perimeter, assault teams, observer/sniper, etc.) and seventy-five hostage negotiators. On duty personnel respond to the scene of an incident along with two Special Equipment Vehicles (SEVs) and the Mobile Command Post.

Various philosophies have been tried and developed in the law enforcement community in order to respond to and resolve hostage incidents and those involving barricaded offenders. Three basic models exist and they mirror the history of law enforcement's efforts to respond to these situations that have developed in three stages.

The first stage was the development of SWAT or Tactical Teams which began in the 1960s. This was in response to a real need in that law enforcement agencies were being confronted with events pre-planned by heavily armed offenders. The need to have a capability within a law enforcement agency to apply specialized tactics and equipment at these emergency scenes was recognized and met.

The second stage was initialed in the 1970s when it was realized that tactical resolution of hostage and barricaded situations was not only dangerous for the police officers involved but many times resulted in death or injury to the hostage. The concept of hostage negotiations, where pre-selected and trained officers engage an offender in a dialogue, was recognized as having the advantage of buying time for tactical capabilities to develop, but also resolved the majority of situations.

The third stage was initiated in the late 1970s by many law enforcement agencies based on the experience of resolving actual situations. It was recognized by many agencies that having highly proficient tactical personnel and equipment, and highly proficient negotiators would not, in and of itself, successfully resolve many situations. Upon critiquing instances which had gone bad or were perceived as having been quite difficult, it was determined that specialization without proper coordination and management could be counter-productive. This last and final stage concentrated on bringing together specially trained people in a manageable situation with a pre-determined officer in charge and an application of basic management principles such as unity of command, effective spans of control, division of labor by function, and pre-identification of proper staff support to the officer in charge.

An HBT officer displays the unit's heavy assaulted vest, titanium helmet with ballistic visor, and assault shotgun (extended magazine, collapsible stock and pressure light mounted.(Courtesy: City of Chicago Department of Police)

Interesting and detail photograph of the inner-perimeter gear worn and carried by an HBT officer, including: tactical load bearing vest, Ruger Mini-14 with collapsible stock with laser aiming system, and the ladders employed by the HBT for tactical entries.(Courtesy: City of Chicago Department of Police)

Some of the most important aspects of the Chicago Police Department's HBT program are:

- The utmost regard for the preservation of life and dominates any other consideration cannot overcome safety for all at the scene.
- Emphasis is placed on the negotiated resolution of these incidents. Neither the tactical commander nor the negotiation team leader makes the decision to tactically resolve an incident. That decision should rest only with the officer in charge.
- One individual must be in charge of a hostage or barricaded scene. Command by committee does not work. The individual pre-designated as the officer in charge of a hostage or barricaded scene must be of sufficient rank that he/she can mobilize police resources on their own authority. The rank must have the authority and ability to interact with other elements of government and the community, representing the police department, in order to facilitate the successful resolution of the incident.
- Tactical intervention is always an optional and functional alternative in the resolution of the situation.
- As suicide threats are a common element in many, if not the majority, of hostage and barricaded situation. As such, management guidelines, tactical training, and negotiations are targeted toward the recognition and diffusion of suicidal situation. The suicide diffusion concepts are based on the preservation of the subject's life but without the traditional stunts and bravado that have marked the traditional approach towards solving these situations.
- This model involves an emphasis on intelligence gathering and the management of the intelligence function. Intelligence is as important as the functions of inner perimeter, outer perimeter, and negotiations.

Service in the HBT is strictly voluntary and open to all officers who have served a minimum of four-years on the force and who pass a grueling examination, and an extensive ten week tactical and special operations course. The Chicago Police Department HBT Team maintains close contact with other SWAT units throughout the State of Illinois and the Midwest, and is in close contact with the FBI and other federal law enforcement agency tactical units.

The HBT Mobile Command Post/Negotiation Point, that includes: external/internal power sources with generator; multiple land-line or cellular phone systems; mobile data terminal; computer/word processor; cellular fax system, copier; two separate television systems, each incorporating 4 sets, VCRs and remote camera capability; extensive radio capability incorporating various local county, state and federal agency systems.; and, other miscellaneous equipment. (Courtesy: City of Chicago Department of Police)

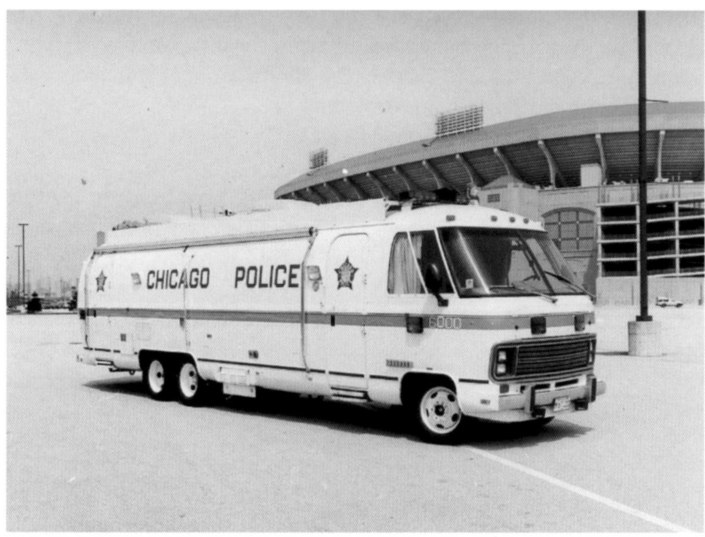


Gas delivery tools deployed by the HBT include: an Avon gas mask, Def-Tec .37 mm gas gun, .12 grenade launching system, and ISPRA tank dispenser (CS and OC). (Courtesy: City of Chicago Department of Police)

Five HBT officers display their gear in front of two of their specialized weapon carrier vehicles. Standing behind the ballistic shield, center, is Lieutenant John P. Kennedy/HBT Incident Coordinator. (Courtesy: City of Chicago Department of Police)

# U.S.A. - Portland Police Bureau Special Emergency Reaction Team

A line of MP5s in full auto during firearms training. (Courtesy: Officers Joe Savage and Mark Butler -- PPB TOD/SERT)

A good group from 7 yards on full auto. SERT uses the double tap method - two-round bursts, then an assessment of the target. (Courtesy: Officers Joe Savage and Mark Butler -- PPB TOD/SERT)

On the streets of America today, a new terrorist phenomenon has evolved--one where it is virtually impossible to differentiate between a street gang dealing narcotics and death to the Red Army Factions and Black Septembers of years past. Their motives might be different, control of a neighborhood's supply of crack cocaine or national liberation, but their results are identical--death, bloodshed, innocent loss of life and terror. Webster's Dictionary describes terrorism as the state of submission caused by an overwhelming fear of the presence of danger or evil.

It has been said that there stands a thin blue line of law enforcement between today's criminal element--the new form and breed of terrorism that has gripped is all--and the sheer fabric of law abiding society, but most police officers, by the very nature of their work, can only respond after the fact, to pick up the pieces and lay a yellow body bag over the latest crime scene. Yet in every military force or police unit, there is a small core of elite men and women who are tasked with the most dangerous, most desperate jobs meant to diffuse a potentially explosive situation, and provide a degree of professionalism, firepower and on-scene wisdom that will respond in kind when deadly force and tactical precision are the sole answers. These units are on-call in the course of their day-to-day activities, awaiting that call on the radio, the beeping rings on their pagers; as their skills are so unique and their numbers so small when compared to the rest of the forces or units they serve, that they in essence become on-call twenty-four hours a day. Most American municipal police forces have fostered and nourished such a unit to deal with hostages, high-risk criminal and potential terrorist attacks in their cities. In Portland, that task falls to the Police Bureau's elite Special Emergency Reaction Team (or "SERT"). When the street officer in the Portland, Oregon's Police Bureau calls for help, it is the Special Emergency Reaction Team that responds. It is a twenty-man force of volunteers that because of the nature of their work, intensity of their tactical training and weapon's proficiency, make them truly a unique and celebrated force not only in American circles, but also around the world.

The Portland Police Bureau's SERT has its origins in 1975 within the departments intelligence unit. A six man team consisting of five officers and one sergeant comprised the original group. Besides regular intelligence duties these officers would respond to crisis or tactical situations beyond the scope or logistical abilities of street officers in the Uniform Division with their personal equipment considerations based on a military style model. Team members were armed with revolvers as personal sidearm and shoulder weapons were 12-gauge shotguns or Armalite AR-18 assault rifles. Sniper weapons were limited to whatever bolt action rifle that became available through confiscation in the property room.

SERT's initial team structure, operational philosophy, member selection and physical assessment processes were patterned after the LAP SWAT Platoon after early SERT personnel attended an LAPD SWAT training class. In 1985 SERT members attended their first Los Angeles County Sheriff's Department Special Weapons Team basic SWAT school. SERT members left the school with a new understanding involving the principles and concepts of slow/covert clears. New SERT members continue to attend that school whenever possible as it is a Mecca of learning to develop proper attitudes about the ever-changing tactics and techniques required of municipal police tactical teams.

During this period a formal selection process for new members was implemented which utilized Bureau wide postings of orders from the Personnel Division announcing openings in the unit. Applicants for the team completed an arduous physical assessment as well as a formal oral board interview. In concert with these activities, an extensive in-house background investigation was completed on each applicant developing a summary of his performance as a police officer. That system of selection is continued today with tremendous success.

SERT currently consists of 20 members. One sergeant and one Officer serve full time with administrative and training issues and are also active members of the team. The remaining Sergeant and Officers work in Bureau wide assignments from Precinct Patrol to Gang Enforcement to Drug Interdiction. Each member is issued a pager and is on 24 hour emergency call up unless excused for other commitments.

The team consists of two elements. One sergeant and eight officers comprise the Assault Element and one sergeant and 10 members make up the Inner Perimeter Element. The Assault Element is responsible for planning and executing entry into hostile environs for hostage rescue, high risk warrant service and armed, barricaded suspects. The Inner Perimeter Element has as its duties the establishment of secure containment around a target location where the situation is occurring. Counter sniper/observer teams are deployed to use their skills to save lives and act as crucial intelligence gatherers to relay information to the Assault Element who will be busy planning rescue alternatives. In the event of a barricaded suspect the IP team will plan the delivery of tear-gas into the location to force the suspect out to an arrest team or inevitable showdown.

At every emergency occurrence SERT has a variety of Command and Support Staff available. The SERT Commander, a lieutenant, acts as a liaison between the team and the Incident Commander at the scene. The Incident Commander, depending on which Precinct the situation occurs in can be a different person from call to call. Having the same SERT Commander who is knowledgeable about the team's capabilities is vital for a successful resolution of any crisis.

In the event that SERT is called to a "job" (the now universal police term for an incident) the hostage negotiators, a group of specially trained detectives respond to the scene and attempt to talk to the suspect in an effort to resolve the situation peacefully.

The Portland Police Bureau's Explosive Disposal Unit (EDU) is also made available for counter-terrorist work. The EDU is responsible for making the charges that SERT will use for explosive entry whether it's a full scale door or wall entry or a smaller charge for blowing a lock or hinges. EDU also has a robot has many tactical uses. Not only does EDU use the robot for bomb manipulation and destruction but the tracked vehicle's claws and camera work very well in delivering gas and peering into dangerous places without risking the lives of the officers involved.

One of the many support units that SERT has access to is one deemed most important. A pool of 12 Fire/Medics from the Portland Fire Bureau is readily available at each emergency occurrence as well as high risk warrants. Also on the same pager system, these highly trained EMT's have spent considerable time training with SERT members and are familiar with the operations and weapons used by SERT. Four of them will respond to assist each time the pager goes off.

It has been said that "as you train, so will you fight" and the SERT's hallmark is detailed training, planning and preparation--before entering a structure, officers usually know every door, every room and every light switch. Often, the SERT rehearses every step of their planned tactical move on a chalked diagram on the floor.

Like a special forces military unit, weapons proficiency is stressed in the SERT. From the basics of stance, sight picture, and trigger control to the more advanced stages of peel shooting hostage/suspect targets on the move, SERT spends many hours a month on weapons training. The Assault Element uses as their primary weapon the Heckler and Koch MP5A2, A3, and SD models mounted with Surefire fore stock tactical lights. This 9mm automatic sub gun is perfect for maneuvering in all types of situations. All SERT members carry--as a weapon-back up the Glock 17 9mm automatic, many equipped with the Surefire Tactical light. Counter Snipers use the Remington Model 700 .308 caliber heavy barrel mounted with a Leopold 3.5 x 10 scope. Sniper Observers and other Inner Perimeter members carry a variety of assault rifles which include the M-16 and CAR-15 5.56mm assault rifles, or the Heckler and Koch 91 and 93 models. Most assault rifles are mounted with Pro Point illuminated dot scopes and lighting systems. A Litton Starlight scope is readily available for night time use. In certain tactical situations the use of the Benelli Super 90 semi-auto 12-gauge shotgun (considered the Rolls Royce of 12-gauge weapons) is handy, and (for barricaded subjects) a dandy door lock or hinge defeater is the Smith and Wesson in a shortened pump action version loaded with "Shok Lok" shells. For riot-control situations, the Portland SERT has a variety of less than lethal weapons on hand,

A light mounted Glock 17 is seen here during handgun training. The lighted Glocks are perfect for attics and crawl space clearing. (Courtesy: Officers Joe Savage and Mark Butler -- PPB TOD/SERT)

SERT uses both shouldered and CQB ( Close Quarter Battle) styles of MP5 shooting. Shown here is the CQB with tight sling and weapon shoved out and up. Sights are not used in CQB. (Courtesy: Officers Joe Savage and Mark Butler -- PPB TOD/SERT)

including the Royal Ordnance Arwen 37mm performs not only five shot capacity gas delivery but can be loaded with Kinetic energy batons to reach out and touch someone. Also available in 37mm are several Smith and Wesson gas guns that use the stingballs and wooden dowels loads. Smith and Wesson shotguns can disperse troublemakers with bean bag and stingball rounds.

The most dangerous of all tactical situations is the dynamic entry. Hostage situations and high-risk warrant service demand long and arduous hours of training to hone the skills necessary for this very demanding work. For covert/stealth entry, techniques are used to slowly and methodically enter and clear a location where an armed and dangerous felon is hidden. After time, talk, and tear gas have failed to extract a suspect, and it is time for the team to "go get 'em," covert/stealth entry techniques are deployed. Probably the second most used tactic by SERT, it takes many hours of training to learn and use properly and safely. Threat angles and assessment is continuous as the team moves in a coordinated effort to dominate the interior, room by room until the suspect is found and arrested.

The SERT has also practiced and perfected the art of assaulting vehicles that can be used by a suspect to take or move hostages--and these include trains, planes and buses. The SERT, like many SWAT units in the United States and counter-terrorist teams throughout the world, has also trained in rescuing hostages on board aircraft, such as a Boeing 737. Terrorist concerns have opened doors to allow SERT to train with Federal and state law enforcement agencies of all kinds to perfect the intricacies of aircraft entry and assault and rescue--both of military and civilian craft.

Other aspects of Portland Police Bureau SERT training, includes: dignitary protection, rappelling, explosive entries, wooded movement/searches, high risk vehicle stops, security site surveys, defensive tactics and intensified tactical training with outside agencies.

SERT deploys five standard Chevrolet Caprice Police cruisers, unmarked, that are used as first responder vehicles. The SERT van is a large Grumman van designed for equipment storage and as a mobile command post. This van is driven to the scene and SERT personnel gather their equipment from it. The two officers assigned to SERT as intelligence officers use the van as a command post. The BART (Bureau Armored Rescue Truck) is a refurbished and reworked armored transport vehicle. Used for a bank delivery truck, it was destined for destruction as law will not allow it to be sold. The armored BART is used for team delivery, hostage rescue, and as a very effective fortified door puller. Occasionally, when available for drug interdiction, the Oregon National Guard will deliver, complete with drivers, light armored vehicles (LAVs). These larger, faster vehicles are improved ballistically over BART and have great personnel delivery space and ability over rough terrain. Inside BART SERT carries a large assortment of breaching tools and body bunkers.

If future trends are an indication of the units operations, the SERT will be busier than ever in the years to come. In 1989, the unit was called to respond to an incident twelve times, in 1990 SERT was deployed twenty times, and twenty-two times in 1991. Since 1975, in fact, the unit has been involved in over 200 high-risk operations--ten times more than many of the best counter-terrorist units in Europe and Asia.

A counter sniper shoots a half face target--with live ammo!--in a window frame as the Assault Element readies for a hostage rescue. (Courtesy: Officers Joe Savage and Mark Butler -- PPB TOD/SERT)

Shooting on the move accurately is essential in hostage rescue techniques. SERT members practice shooting at targets moving in from fifteen yards. (Courtesy: Officers Joe Savage and Mark Butler -- PPB TOD/SERT)

Adding a little stress this officer moves through an obstacle course hitting small metal targets on a timed course. (Courtesy: Officers Joe Savage and Mark Butler -- PPB TOD/SERT)

Assault Element members practice a slow covert clearing technique. Note the rear guard. (Courtesy: Officers Joe Savage and Mark Butler -- PPB TOD/SERT)

Nice and tight boys. Members line up outside a doorway in preparation to practice a dynamic warrant service. Note the flash bang on the finger of the right hand of the first man. (Courtesy: Officers Joe Savage and Mark Butler -- PPB TOD/SERT)

An Oregon National Guard Light Armored Vehicle is used here for officer/citizen down rescue in a riot situation. Portland SERT assisted in training metropolitan Police SWAT teams in dealing with various riotous conditions. (Courtesy: Officers Joe Savage and Mark Butler -- PPB TOD/SERT)

Portland SERT directs local Metro SWAT teams in riot control training. Shown here are officer/citizen rescues using vehicles to surround victim, creating a pocket of protection. Note both lethal and less than lethal weapons, creating a 360° circle of coverage. (Courtesy: Officers Joe Savage and Mark Butler -- PPB TOD/SERT)

Using smoke to create a screen SERT officers move to rescue a downed person in front of a hostile residence. (Courtesy: Officers Joe Savage and Mark Butler -- PPB TOD/SERT)

Counter sniper and Observer teams work together as one unit to perfect their skills. Both members of each team trade off on their duties, especially throughout a long ordeal. (Courtesy: Officers Joe Savage and Mark Butler -- PPB TOD/SERT)

A counter sniper team prepares their equipment for a training exercise. These Inner perimeter members qualify quarterly with all weapons and must maintain peak performance and accuracy. (Courtesy: Officers Joe Savage and Mark Butler -- PPB TOD/SERT)

Inner Perimeter teams use camouflage techniques to their advantage even in the inner city. IP members sometimes have to stay in the same location unmoving for many hours and are exceptional masters of the art of camouflage--both urban and rural. (Courtesy: Officers Joe Savage and Mark Butler -- PPB TOD/SERT)

SERT members constantly challenge each other in timed obstacle courses to perform better than they had the previous time on the range, and also to persevere in any and all tactical situations where a little more speed and strength can mean the difference between life and death on the streets. (Courtesy: Officers Joe Savage and Mark Butler -- PPB TOD/SERT)

Rappelling is one of the more fun exercises that SERT must do. Both the Australian style (left) and the standard style must be mastered by all unit officers. (Courtesy: Officers Joe Savage and Mark Butler -- PPB TOD/SERT)

SERT has yet to have regular access to helicopters but a static helo body will do as members practice rappelling from the skids of a chopper. (Courtesy: Officers Joe Savage and Mark Butler -- PPB TOD/SERT)

Gas training can become painful when a member finds out the seal on his canister was leaking. SERT members constantly test their equipment to make sure it works when needed. (Courtesy: Officers Joe Savage and Mark Butler -- PPB TOD/SERT)

A Portland Explosive Disposal Unit officer explains how to properly place a charge onto a door's hinges and bolt areas. This field is constantly being updated with new techniques and devices. (Courtesy: Officers Joe Savage and Mark Butler -- PPB TOD/SERT)

The armored rescue truck (BART) and the SERT van provide a backdrop for some of the gear used by SERT. (Courtesy: Officers Joe Savage and Mark Butler -- PPB TOD/SERT)

The Bureau Armored Rescue Truck (BART) provides great cover and serves many purposes: team delivery, hostage rescue, and door pulls on warrants. (Courtesy: Officers Joe Savage and Mark Butler -- PPB TOD/SERT)

Members practice deployment for a door pull on a drug house using BART. Note hooks for fortified door. (Courtesy: Officers Joe Savage and Mark Butler -- PPB TOD/SERT)

Two of the first responder cars carry gear for SERT members. Having these cars assigned as "take home" insures that SERT officers will arrive with their equipment as soon as possible to deal with any crisis. (Courtesy: Officers Joe Savage and Mark Butler -- PPB TOD/SERT)

The SERT van is crammed with SERT equipment needed on a call out. The van also serves as a mobile command post. (Courtesy: Officers Joe Savage and Mark Butler -- PPB TOD/SERT)

The Bureau Armored Rescue Truck (BART). (Courtesy: Officers Joe Savage and Mark Butler -- PPB TOD/SERT)

SERT members relax for a photo shoot a few days before Christmas after a dynamic entry to serve a warrant on a dope house. Happy Holidays from SERT! (Courtesy: Officers Joe Savage and Mark Butler -- PPB TOD/SERT)

## U.S.A.- Metro-Dade Police Department Special Response Team (SRT)

*It begins as a routine balmy night on the streets, a cloud of humidity hangs over the city, as does the pounding rhythms of a Salsa beat and rap music pounding out of over-sized speakers crammed into jeeps and all-terrain vehicles cruising the boulevards. South Miami 1994. Car-jackings, drug deals and the unique brand of narco-terrorism that has gripped the United States. As the Cold War ends, the crime war, in all its violence and random death, enters its bloody fulcrum on the streets of American cities and towns.*

The Metro-Dade Police Department Patch.

*Outside a crack-house near Miami International Airport it is business as usual--lookouts, customers, and cash and weapons being flashed; the music from nearby stereos is interrupted by the beeping chime of pagers and the digital ring of cell phones. The house, a two-story wood structure, is reinforced inside by steel plates, bolts, and a small stable of angry pitbulls. The lookouts, youngsters carrying "9s" as 9mm automatics are known on the streets of the city, are expert in spotting patrol cars and unmarked police vehicles. Upon seeing "5-0," the street name for the police, the lookouts race to the house as all sales end, the product is immediately hidden, and weapons produced for an inevitable showdown.*

*The lookouts, however, are fooled by a decoy vehicle that looks more like it belongs to a rival dealer than to the department. By the time they understand what is happening, a green and white SRT truck has already raced down the narrow street and unloaded eight men, all wearing black Kevlar Fritz helmets, all wearing, body armor, and all wearing black "Metro-Dade Police Department" T-shirts. A sledgehammer is produced and the front door "forcibly opened" before it can be bolted shut. The lead assaulting officers carry ballistic shields and 9mm automatics fitted with aim-point lights; their support team carry MP5s and 12-gauge shotguns. The entry team purifies each room with split-second speed but with meticulous precision. A gun blast from a closet or under a bed can have lethal results and these officers are determined to subdue or neutralize the perpetrators on their terms, on their flash-of-an-eye timetable. Each room is secured by a pair of officers raising their MP5s and sawed-off 870 12-gaugers in ideal firing position. A loud bark of "SECURE" tells the team leader that one more room has been taken care of. The entry ends peacefully, though with arrests and the seizure of crack, cash and enough weaponry to equip a small army.*

*It is just another day for the men of SRT. Just another day on the streets of Dade County, Florida.*

A daunting and imposing sight to the bad guys--an SRT officer holds a Body Bunker ballistic shield and MP5 9mm submachine gun. (Richard Johnson, Courtesy Metro-Dade Police Department)

An SRT officer perfects an insertion technique courtesy of a fast rope high above a county parking lot. He is armed with a Mk. 870 12-gauge shotgun. (Courtesy: Metro-Dade Police Department/SRT)

For the men of the Metro-Dade Police Department's Special Response Team, it doesn't matter if the house they were assaulting was a terrorist hideout or a crack-house. "You know its bad going in if they call us, " claims SRT commander Captain Robert Hodges, "for us it's a gun drawn situation when we go in, therefore we know we are expecting trouble." Trouble in south Florida, unfortunately, comes frequently and it is unforgiving.

The Metro-Dade Police Department is the largest law-enforcement agency in the Southeastern United States with 2,7000 sworn officers and 1,300 civilian employees providing police services to over 1.9 million residents of south Florida in a geographic region of responsibility covering the 2,139 square miles of Dade County--which includes much of Miami. With the Metro-Dade Police Department also providing security functions to major county facilities such as Miami International Airport, the Port of Miami, and Jackson Memorial Hospital, the department's responsibility for combating the increasing forms of terrorism have increased ten-fold--especially when compared to many other United States municipal police departments and their special weapons and tactics units. But Miami, Dade County, is different. In terms of crime statistics, in can be considered a war zone. A homicide is committed every other day, there are twenty felonious incidents reported every hour, there is more narcotics roaming through the streets of Dade County than much of South America, and more weapons than Beirut and Sarajevo combined. More ominous than the dangers, cops are targeted in Dade County. Just as the Provisional IRA favors hitting members of the Royal Ulster Constabulary and just as Hamas takes a special pride in kidnapping and then assassinating Israeli soldiers and policemen, the bad guys in Dade take a special pride in aiming their weapons on police officers. Since 1980, twenty-seven police officers have been killed in the line of duty. Dozens others have been seriously wounded.

The Metro-Dade Special Response Team (SRT) was formed in 1977 to combat the growing tide of bombings, hijackings and heavy weapons assaults perpetrated on the streets of the county. Originally a "pool" of tactically trained officers and sergeants assigned to a district's uniform patrol, these specially trained "operators" were assembled from on duty units as situations necessitated--sometimes, an officer would be pulled off an ongoing arrest or investigation to head to an emergency requiring a tactical response. The officers selected for the "call out" would be drawn based on the individual's specific area of training. This concept, while a stop-gap, was not ideal as it provided poorly assembled and sporadic responses, and on many occasions resulted in an unbalanced teams composition. Over the ensuing two decades, a number of changes took place that led to the unit; quickly, however, the unit grew along with Dade County's dizzying growth and development during this time. With that growth and prosperity coupled with the County's proximity to South America, it was inevitable that criminality--especially narco-terrorism--would

H-Hour, Metro-Dade County. With their SRT truck in the rear, an SRT team prepares to assault a crack-house. Note lead officer with crowbar followed by the officer carrying sledge-hammer. (Courtesy: Metro-Dade Police Department/SRT)

Peering around a building's corner keeping out of sight from a "perp's" 9mm automatic, an SRT team prepares its assault on a block of flats while serving a high-risk warrant. (Courtesy: Metro-Dade Police Department/SRT)

rise geometrically.

Today, the SRT consists of one captain, two lieutenants, six sergeants and twenty-eight officers.

Making police work in Dade County more difficult and far more dangerous is the fact that Miami and its cluster of surrounding areas is a true melting pot of ethnic groups, races and cultures--African Americans, Hispanics, Haitians, displaced Nicaraguans and Hondurans, many of whom have extensive military training. Miami is also the funnel for the national drug trade, and it has made crime in the city and surrounding areas a focal point for the entire United States. The SRT is at the forefront, and the last line of defense against the most dangerous and most desperate criminal elements. It gets summoned on "call-outs" at least 400 times a year.

Initially, training consisted of one week focusing on firearms proficiency and chemical agent deployment. Currently, the basic school is three weeks of intensive training with a curriculum including: (a) Firearm qualification (hand gun, shotgun, assault rifle, and automatic weapons); (b) Chemical agents and their deployment; (c) Diversionary devices and their deployment; (d) Rappelling and fast rope insertion skills; (e) Building entries, including the use of explosive entry devices and battering rams; (f) Search techniques; (g) Hostage rescue, including assaulting buildings, automobiles, buses, boats, trains and planes where civilians are being held hostage by either emotionally disturbed people (EDPs), criminals or terrorists; (h) physical fitness; and, (i) First aid and trauma care to "combat" casualties. It should be noted that SRT instructors frown on classroom time, and instead emphasize maximum hands on candidate participation.

The Metro-Dade SRT provides services to all but five of the 28 municipalities and numerous state and federal agencies during circumstances which involve potentially life threatening situations. The prime objective of Special Response Teams is the resolution of high-risk police situations with a minimum of force, personal injury, and property damage. The SRT has highly trained supervisors and officers skilled in the use of special weapons, equipment, and techniques designed to reduce the risk to law enforcement personnel and innocent citizens in dangerous situations.

Usually, and the usual rarely holds the line in police work, situations that are likely to require a SRT response, include: (a) Barricaded subjects: including armed felony suspects and mentally unstable individuals; (b) Sniping incidents; (c) Hostage situations and scenarios; (d) Special security risk situations or protection of government officials when such is authorized, such as providing back-up to the U.S. Secret Service when the President visits, or backing up State Department security when a visiting head of state is in the Dade County area; (e) Search and Arrest Warrants, when considered high-risk (likelihood of armed subjects); (f) Riots, strikes, or civil disorder, to assist Mobile Field Forces (MFF); (g) Hijack Situations, including aircraft, boats, buses, trains and Metro-rail; and, (h) Major aircraft disasters, including those caused by terrorist attack.

The SRT is the most exclusive unit in the Metro-Dade Police Department with a long list of officers from the entire force submitting their requests to volunteer into the squad on a yearly basis. An initial announcement is published throughout the Department to all interested officers with an interest in becoming a member of the Special Response Team and once the applications are received, officers and sergeants are scheduled for a physical test. The test consists of cardio-vascular capacity, strength and a swim test. This must be successfully completed for the candidate to continue in the selection process.

After successful completion of a P/T test, an extensive background check is conducted on all candidates. This includes a review of his/her personnel and internal affairs jacket, along with interviews with previous supervisors in the candidates' chain-of-command. If no negative feedback is found, the candidates are administered a psychological exam and an oral interview with a panel of current Special Response Team members to assess their capabilities. Preferably, each candidate should have a minimum tenure of five years "on the job." After successful completion of all previous steps, the candidates are placed into the next available three week SRT Basic School. The candidate must complete all aspects of the school curriculum to become certified. They are then placed on a list and selected as vacancies occur.

Because of their tremendous operational activities, SRT members are equipped with a varied catalog of state-of-the-art equipment and gear. The principal SRT weapon is the entire Heckler and Koch MP5 family of 9mm submachine guns in all its variants. SRT members also deploy with the AR-15 5.56mm assault rifle (fitted with different sights and night-scopes) as well as the CAR-15 5.56mm carbine; the Remington M870 Mark 1 U.S. Marine Corps 12-gauge shotgun (many officers favor the sawed off version with an indigenously attached

An SRT squad undergoes a briefing prior to engaging an emotionally disturbed individual holding a hostage. Note unit emblem worn on the back of the team leader's T-shirt. (Courtesy: Metro-Dade Police Department/SRT)

The explosive entry--after deploying a CAP-STUN M-5G Gas Grenade, an SRT squad moves in for the precarious task of securing a house during the serving of a high-risk warrant. Note gas masks worn. (Courtesy: Metro-Dade Police Department/SRT)

flashlight); M9 Beretta 9mm automatics, and even the old standby, the policeman's favorite, the .38 caliber service revolver. Interestingly enough, the Metro-Dade SRT also deploys high-power crossbows in their SRT trucks. Body bunker ballistic shields are carried during most entries, and stun devices are also deployed regularly. A black Kevlar Fritz helmet is worn on all operations, as are fire-proof coveralls (though many officers wear T-shirts in the hot Florida sun), and gas masks are carried in special leg pouches just in case CS agents need to be deployed.

SRT trucks are also tactical tools--not only a means of carrying the gear and bringing the officers to a job. When an entry is hampered by a steel door or gate, a reinforced chain is attached to the rear of the truck and the door and, in the time it takes for the accelerator pedal to be pushed down, the steel gate or door is flung open like a beer can being popped. SRT also deploys Zodiac craft and speedboats for seaborne and even underwater tactical assignments. Trained by the U.S. Navy SEALs and Special Forces divers, SRT personnel are trained and equipped to end a hostage situation in mid-water, by reaching a boat or craft through SCUBA ***underwater***, and not having the bad guys know that they've deployed until the words "FREEZE: POLICE" are heard.

Metro-Dade Aviation Unit Bell 206L4 Jet Ranger choppers also support many SRT operations, and these choppers have recently been equipped with FLIR (Forward Looking Infra-Red) capabilities for night time assaults and chases.

"FREEZE, POLICE! GET YOUR HANDS IN THE AIR....NOW!" What an explosive entry looks like to the bad guy. Note officer carrying CAR-15 5.56mm assault rifle and other officer with Mk. 870 12-gauge shotgun fitted with high-powered flashlight. (Courtesy: Metro-Dade Police Department/SRT)

The results of the "job": rifles, handguns and drugs off the streets. (Courtesy: Metro-Dade Police Department/SRT)

Metro-Dade SRT is one of the busier special weapons and tactics units in the United States, and some "jobs" that personify its very nature, mandate and capabilities include:

- The Headquarters Special Investigations Division (HSID) -- Tactical Operations Section (TOS), was conducting a wire tap on a narcotics related kidnapping and discovered where the victim was being held. The victim was the five-year-old son of a narcotics importer who had not meet his financial obligations, so his son was being held for ransom. SRT was requested to make entry into the location and recover the victim before harm could come to him. The victim was being held inside a warehouse. He was being guarded by two armed subjects who commanded a view of the only access to the warehouse. A plan was developed to approach the door of the warehouse by rappelling from the roof to the parking area out of sight of the guard who was stationed inside looking through a mirrored window. During the approach, one subject exited the front door, crossed the parking lot, and left in a van. He failed to see the entry team poised above him. This subject was apprehended by detectives, as he drove out of the area. The detectives managed to obtain a key to the front door, and intelligence regarding the status of the other subject. The entry was initiated by rappelling down against the blind side wall, crawling under the mirrored window, and opening the front door with the key. During this approach, a dog confronted the entry team and became a nuisance by constantly licking the face of the lead officer as he crawled to the front door. The door opened to reveal a

SRT officers look on as an SRT instructor display his rappelling techniques. (Courtesy: Metro-Dade Police Department/SRT)

small office, unoccupied, with a shotgun leaning against the wall, and a close door that led to the storage area of the warehouse. The entry team immediately forced open this door with a sledge hammer, and confronted an unarmed adult male wearing a ski mask. This subject started to run into the storage area towards a 20' cabin cruiser on a trailer. He was stopped as he tried to enter the front of the boat. A sweep of the remainder of the structure revealed no other subjects. A sweep of the boat's forward storage space revealed a duffel bag containing the blind-folded and bound victim, who was unharmed. The scene was secured, and all persons were released to the detectives.

- A request was received from our Auto Theft Section (ATS), asking for SRT's assistance in serving an arrest warrant. The subject was known for his violent nature, and boasted that he would never be taken alive by the police and was known to be in possession of automatic weapons. As the residence was in a rural area of the county, a stealthy approach was mandated. The tactical plan called for members of the entry team to provide cover while other members worked to defeat a fortified door. The entry personnel were attempting their entry when the subject, armed with two .45 caliber pistols, fired through the door. The cover people returned fire, striking the subject once. The subject, then fled back into the house, barricading himself in the process. Chemical agents were introduced which caused the subject to flee out through the back door where he was taken into custody, without further incident.

- During the Christmas/New Year Holiday Season 1993, a depressed Vietnam War veteran, barricaded himself atop a housing project and began sniping with his rifle from this strategic position. SRT was summoned, and immediately upon arrival, began to assist uniform units in evacuating the complex and provide cover for those officers. During the evacuation process, one team sergeant was wounded by sniper fire, but the evacuation and tactical deployment continued. What followed was a fifteen-hour stand-off that included negotiations and the introduction of chemical agents. When these methods failed to have the desired effect another plan had to be developed. Because of the snipers position, he had advantage over any person or persons that might approach. Finally, it was agreed that the Fire Department was a resource, and a plan to assault the sniper with a water cannon was implemented. SRT personnel were able to work the equipment into position, and with a blast from the water hose, defeat the sniper and secure him without further injury.

There is only so much that the SRT can do--a fact not lost to political and police officials in Florida. In 1994, Florida Governor Bob Graham and other state officials concerned about the vulnerability of Florida's busy airports, seaports and tourist attractions (like Disney World) to terrorist attack considered a proposal to develop a statewide anti-terrorist squad within the Florida Department of Law Enforcement (FDLE). According to Graham, as quoted by the Fort-Lauderdale Sun-Sentinel, "We know on a daily basis our territory is invaded by small planes and boats bringing drugs and refugees. Those same planes and boats could bring terrorists and bombs. We have a special stake in being prepared." The understood threat in Florida is not from the Middle East, such as in the bombing of the World Trade Center or the Jewish Center in Buenos Aires, but from various Latin American and South American countries with unstable political situations. Under the proposed plan, the FDLE anti-terrorist squad would not solely be a counter-terrorist squad, but would also work hand-in-hand with other municipal and county SWAT units and police agencies in the execution of high-risk assignments (such as major arrests at drug stash houses and statewide manhunts for dangerous fugitives).

The planned FDLE unit would be trained and supported by the FBI HRT.

The SRT, it should be mentioned, has trained side-by-side with the FBI's HRT, the U.S. Secret Service, the Ohio State Police, the FDLE, and U.S. Army and U.S. Navy counter-terrorist units. The SRT has also trained foreign counter-terrorist units, including elements from the Royal Moroccan Intelligence Service, the Portuguese national police, and the Panamanian police, as well.

One of the vehicles deployed by SRT--especially useful in pulling the front door of a crack-house off its hinges. (Courtesy: Metro-Dade Police Department/SRT)

Preparing the assault, a reconnaissance officer returns from a roof-top surveillance stint. (Courtesy: Metro-Dade Police Department/SRT)

The Metro-Dade Police Department SRT truck. (Courtesy: Metro-Dade Police Department/SRT)

An SRT officer's personal gear. Note black Kevlar TAC-100R tactical face mask. (Courtesy: Metro-Dade Police Department/SRT)

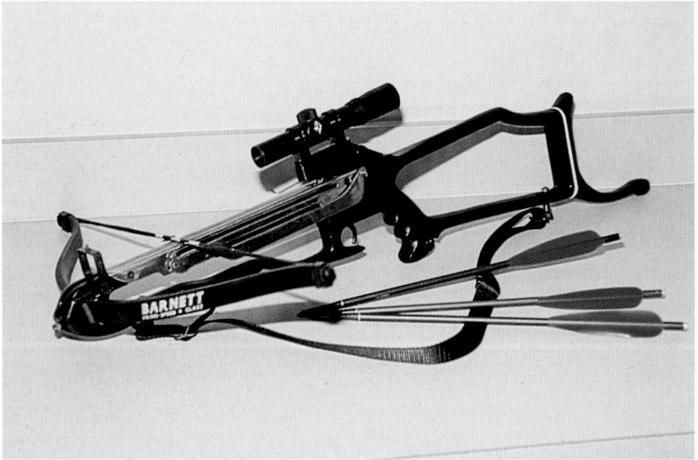


The power cross-bow used by the SRT during "special" jobs. (Courtesy: Metro-Dade Police Department/SRT)

One of the SRT's sniping weapons--the AR-15 5.56mm assault rifle fitted with a bi-pod and AN/PVS-4 second generation weapon sight. (Courtesy: Metro-Dade Police Department/SRT)

Mirrors, attached to poles, used during hostage-barricades and other tactical situations where peering around a corner can get the officer's head blown off. (Courtesy: Metro-Dade Police Department/SRT)

In full battle kit, and with his shotgun at the ready, an SRT officer prepares to follow the blows of the sledge-hammer and the door swinging open during a "job" near Miami International Airport. (Courtesy: Metro-Dade Police Department/SRT)

Also tasked with EOD assignments, SRT deploys an EOD robot sporting a 12-gauge shotgun to deal with a suspicious object left near a synagogue. (Courtesy: Metro-Dade Police Department/SRT)

Diversionary devices and gas grenades deployed by SRT. (Courtesy: Metro-Dade Police Department/SRT)

## U.S.A. - Las Vegas Metropolitan Police Department SWAT Section

In a city that truly never sleeps and where time pieces are a matter of luxurious obsolescence, the mesmerizing allure of millions of dollars changing hands every hour or so can be a dizzying experience. It can also be a tempting target for criminals and terrorists, and the potential for serious crime and violence is great in Las Vegas, Nevada: America's national playground. Las Vegas is a city like no other in the United States and the world, and its police department is considered among the nation's best. So, too, is their elite SWAT Section, a force of anti-crime officer and tactical operators who stand on alert all year round awaiting the call from command, the beeping noise from their pagers.

The Las Vegas Metropolitan Police Department's subdued patch--worn only by officers in the SWAT Section.

Las Vegas boasts a population of 854,780 residents, though the annual tourist volume to the miracle in the desert is nearly twenty-three million visitors a year. Keeping the peace is the Las Vegas Metropolitan Police Department (LVMPD) is a consolidated county police force with jurisdiction of Clark County and the City of Las Vegas; the department is responsible for 7,554 square miles. There are 1,435 officers on the job in Las Vegas and twenty-one officers serving in the department's SWAT Section; a unit assigned to the LVMPD's Organized Crime Bureau. According to the job definition, the Las Vegas Metropolitan Police Department's SWAT Section responsibilities are:

1. To provide support and protection for emergency units when under attack from sniper fire, assault fire, and when such force is anticipated.
2. To rescue officers and citizen captured, isolated or endangered by gunfire.
3. To perform fire control missions by securing a position of advantage and keeping the designated area clear of snipers.
4. To provide controlled assault firepower in non-riot police situations, such as barricaded subjects, and emotionally disturbed barricaded suspects and situations where non-lethal tactical force might be warranted.[1]
5. To provide anti-sniper and personal security arrangements for visiting dignitaries, and to work together with the U.S. Secret Service in coordinating security for presidential visits, and with the U.S. State Department Security Office for visiting foreign heads of state and VIPs.
6. To support units of the Department in planned or anticipated high risk arrests, and warrant situations.

In addition to their enforcement and response duties inside Las Vegas, the SWAT Section is also responsible for a large rural area--with a jurisdiction extending over 150 miles to the town of Laughlin and into the mountains of the Toyibe range. The large geographic area in the LVMPD's responsibility make the tactical work quite diverse--officers could be clearing a crack den in a three-story walk up in the morning, and hunting a sniper in the open desert a few hours later. The LVMPD SWAT Section owes its creation to the Los Angeles Police Department's SWAT Platoon and the lessons learned following the Watts riots, especially in regard to anti-sniper work. While an expensive endeavor for a small municipal department, creating a tactical answer to serious criminal or hostage incidents was viewed as "insurance for the unusual occurrence." From 1974 to 1976, the unit was known as the TRT--Tactical Response Team--and functioned mainly as a back-up squad unit for saturation patrols and robbery suppression. On July 4, 1976, the nation's bicentennial, the unit official became the SWAT Section.

The SWAT Section is the most prestigious unit within the LVMPD and the list of those wishing to volunteer into its ranks is a long one. Currently, in order to be considered for a spot on a team, an officer must service for at least three years in the patrol bureau before even being allowed to apply for the SWAT Section. Only officers with exemplary service records are considered, and those who pass a grueling pistol and shotgun qualification course, as well as pass an oral board made up of SWAT commanders and senior officers in the department are asked to join the unit. Upon acceptance into the unit, the officer receives an initial eighty hours of basic tactical training and is then assigned to a ten-man team; the team trains tactically for a minimum of four hours a day at the start of a shift. Training in the unit is intense, and consists of all aspects of tactical entries, live fire entries, vehicle assaults, tubular assaults and rescues, gas training, live fire skills and sniping, fast roping and helicopter deployments. As a result of Las Vegas being in the middle of a desert, officers are trained to function in a wide assortment of climactic conditions and hardships. During the day, the temperature on the strip can reach a scolding 115° (F) in the shade, while at night, temperatures in the desert can reach the freezing mark. Survival skills are taught for operations in the desert,

During assault entry training in the desert just outside Las Vegas, officers from the LVMPD's SWAT Section clutch their Beretta PM-12S submachine guns as a stun device is tossed in the door. (Courtesy: Sergeant Gary Schofield/LVMPD - SWAT Section)

One of the LVMPD's SWAT Section's most valuable tools--the aviation unit MD500 chopper. Here, in the desert just outside the entrance to the city, two operators deploy with weapons in hand during heliborne insertion exercises. (Courtesy: Sergeant Gary Schofield/LVMPD - SWAT Section)

and the unit works closely with the department's aviation unit in reconnaissance and observation, as well as in heliborne deployment.

The SWAT Section consists of twenty-one members; it is commanded by a lieutenant and divided into two ten-man teams. Each team is commanded by a sergeant, and consists of an assault team leader, two snipers, one pyrotechnics/gasman, and five assault entrymen. During a hostage situation or a barricaded job, tactical medics and electronic surveillance officers are pulled in from other units in the patrol division to augment the SWAT Section's capabilities.

Even though a small unit when compared to New York City, Miami and Los Angeles, the LVMPD's SWAT Section possesses a reputation as a second-to-none unit characterized by their intensive training and professional skills in dealing with the most adverse situations and scenarios. From the unit's inception in 1974 until 1994, the LVMPD SWAT Section has handled 204 hostage and barricaded incidents, and in the first half of 1994 alone the unit handled fourteen such incidents. During this brief period in 1994, the unit also handled over 100 high risk warrants for the LVMPD and other federal agencies, such as the FBI, Marshals Service, Drug Enforcement Agency and Secret Service--overall statistics for 1994 include forty-six tactical call-outs, 208 high risk warrants, and four VIP security jobs. It has been a busy squad and it only promises to be busier in the future.

While certainly among the more capable police tactical units in the United States, the LVMPD SWAT Section is also among the best equipped. SWAT officers are issued a 9mm Smith and Wesson 5906 semi-automatic pistols complete with light mounts, though officers can choose a wide variety of department approved weapons, including:

- 9mm pistols: Heckler and Koch P9s; Glock Model 17 and 19; Beretta 92F and 92SB; Smith and Wesson 3900 series, 5900 series, 6900 series and the 469 and 669 model; and, the SIG Sauer P226 and P225.
- .40 Caliber: Beretta 96; Glock 22 and 23; Smith and Wesson 4003 and 4006; and, SIG Sauer P229.
- .45 Caliber: Heckler and Koch P9s; Government Model Colt Commander; Glock 21; Smith and Wesson 645; and, SIG Sauer P220.

SWAT Section members display their heliborne skills during a display on the landing skids of a Bell-212 chopper. (Courtesy: Sergeant Gary Schofield/LVMPD - SWAT Section)

Unlike most military special forces units and police tactical outfits in the United States and throughout the world that swear by the Heckler and Koch MP5, the Las Vegas Metropolitan Police Department SWAT Section had gone against the tide and used the Beretta PM-12S 9mm submachine gun. Recently, however, the MP5 has become the section's primary tactical weapon. The SWAT Section's "stopper" of choice is the Remington Mk. 870 12-gauge shotgun, the CAR-15 and M-16 5.56mm assault rifle, and the .308 caliber Remington 700 BDL sniper weapon with a 3x9 scope and low-light capabilities. The unit also deploys Remington 37mm gas gun, and Def Tech, as well as FFE SF2 and SF7 distraction devices. While the unit possesses an equipment van, officers ride around in unmarked vehicles that carry bullet-resistant vests, gas masks, communications headsets, night-vision equipment, body bunkers, ballistic helmets, field uniforms and Nomex balaclavas and gloves, and cold-weather gear.

In addition, the unit also deploys two V-100 tactical armored vehicles and one Commando Peacekeeper.

[1] In order to ensure the safety of the SWAT and other uniformed members of the service during a barricaded situation, or an incident involving the taking of hostages, the Las Vegas Metropolitan Police Department relies heavily on hostage-negotiators. In a crisis situation where hostages are, indeed, seized, the function of the hostage-negotiators are as follows: (1) The Primary Negotiator will concentrate his entire attention on communicating with the subject; (2) The Secondary Negotiator will coach and support the primary, keep a log of significant points raised during any talks, and if the situation drags on into a multi-day scenario, relieve the primary; and, (3) The Intelligence Negotiator will assist the Primary and Secondary in evaluating the material discussed in negotiations, run errands, and act as a link between the negotiating team, the Command Post, and the SWAT Section commander.

Being able to fast-rope down the side of a casino during a hostage-taking situation is of paramount importance to SWAT Section officers--here, an officer armed with a 9mm pistol, lowers himself down toward a targeted floor on the exterior wall of a casino. (Courtesy: Sergeant Gary Schofield/LVMPD - SWAT Section)

## U.S.A. - Kansas City Police Department's Tactical Response Team (TRT)

The heartland of the United States of America was once thought of as immune from the scourge of violent crime and the urban terrorism plaguing so many larger cities, and the city of Kansas City, Missouri, is as heartland as one can find in the United States of America. Kansas City is the thirty-second most populous city in the United States--with a population of 435,146 and spread out over a sprawling 322 square miles, the city sits on the border between Missouri and Kansas and is connected and inter-connected by 2,200 miles of roadway. Tragically, Kansas City is listed by the Department of Justice as the eighth most dangerous city--with a crime per capita rate exceeding that of New York City, Los Angeles and Chicago. In 1993 alone, the Kansas City Police Department recorded an astounding 517,477 calls to 911. The American heartland has become a dangerous place.

The Kansas City Police Department Patches.

Protecting and serving the citizens of Kansas City is the city's Police Department, a sizable force served by 1,200 officers and 600 civilian employees that is divided into the Patrol Bureau with five Patrol Divisions, Investigative Bureau, the Administrative Bureau, Executive Services Bureau, and the Operations Support Bureau which encompasses the Special Operations Division. When the citizens of Kansas City need help, they call the cops--when the cops need help, they called the department's Tactical Response Team, or TRT, an elite group of officers that are the force's SWAT and special operations unit.

A Kansas City police tactical unit was created on February 1, 1966, as a response to the Los Angeles riots when most police departments around the United States evaluated their tactical assets and abilities; the unit was formed by Police Chief Clarence Kelly, the man who would succeed J. Edgar Hoover as FBI Director. It was known as the "Tac-Unit," and was a small force of tactically-trained officers divided into five squads. The unit's primary mission was anti-crime response and anti-sniper duty. In September 1974, Chief of Police Joseph MacNamara decentralized the unit, and placed a team at each of the city's three busiest stations in the mid-city area. Although the unit's mission hadn't changed much over the years, with the exception in the increase of barricaded jobs, their role and demand had expanded greatly. By 1990, the unit grew in size and was placed under the administrative command of the same body overseeing aviation and K-9, and by October 1993, combined with Traffic Division to form the Special Operations Division; the Tac-Unit became known as the Tactical Response Team, or TRT for short.

By its official mandate, the Tactical Response Team's missions include:

- "Operation 100"s
- Respond to radio calls
- Special Events
- Crowd Control (riots and demonstrations)
- Surveillance
- VIP Security

- Fugitive Apprehension
- Preventative Patrol
- Search Warrants
- Negotiator Response Situations
- Police Funeral Details

The true mission of the TRT is to save lives. SWAT may mean Special Weapons and Tactics to most laymen, but to police around the country the acronym stands for **S**it, **W**ait **A**nd **T**alk. Tactical force is a last resort but brought to bear to intimidate a suspect to surrender without the use of force. Studies have shown that law enforcement agencies that utilize highly trained tactical teams to perform high risk operations reduce their number of shooting incidents significantly. When the deployment of weapons is required, whether it be the serving of a high-risk warrant or the ending of a hostage-taking ordeal, it is the TRT that gets the job. They are Kansas City's first line of defense in situations of potential and actual violence.

The Special Operations Division is commanded by Major Gary Scherer, and the TRT is divided into three teams--each commanded by a captain. Each team consists of two squads commanded by a sergeant and consisting of six officers. TRT officers patrol in unmarked cars and are connected to division base by way of radio, beepers and cellular phones. A maximum response time to any situation developing in the city that requires TRT attention is one hour. Service in the unit is voluntary, and all wishing to try out for TRT must have three years of exemplary service on the job and pass a physical test and oral interview. TRT commanders seek stability in TRT operators, and the selection process is meant to weed out those officers who might be superb on patrol, but who just aren't tactical material. The responsibility of TRT officers is immense--they might be called to assault a schoolbus seized by a gunmen where their own personal stability and ability to cope with pressure can mean the difference between a peaceful resolution to a terrible scenario and tragedy. The selection process takes place at least once a year (or as needed), and, according to TRT commanding officer Captain William Massock, "The unit is looking for individuals displaying high motivation, self-discipline, and stability." Most importantly, perhaps, the unit demands a two-year TRT commitment from all those joining the unit.

Tactical training is carried out all year round for all TRT personnel--from those who are new to the unit to long-time veterans who have been in TRT for many years. Training is carried out five days per month, with half that time devoted to firearms and weapons proficiency; TRT sergeants are responsible for training the officers and often push their officers to hone their bodies and work out beyond the mandatory four hours per week of physical training required by unit standards. Tactical training consists of the basic SWAT assault and entry regimen, but the TRT devotes a great deal of attention to defensive tactics, anti-sniping training, as well as tubular assaults for freeing hostages held in trains, buses and buildings; the unit trains once every two years with the FBI's HRT at Kansas City International Airport learning how to assault a hijacked airliner. The unit also trains with SWAT and tactical units from departments throughout Kansas and the Midwest.

The bread and butter of the TRT's work is what is known in the Kansas City Police Department vernacular as "Operation 100s." Although a mysterious sounding code-name for jobs involving sniper attacks, armed and barricaded individuals and hostage situations, the situations are known as "Operation 100s" simply because the Chief of Police found out that such incidents usually end up with 100 officers on the scene--ranging from the TRT officers at a command post and in position, to traffic cops bringing in ambulances and additional emergency vehicles. When TRT personnel are summoned to an "Operation 100," whether they are on patrol in their unmarked police Crown Victorias or at home, they are ideally equipped and prepared to handle virtually any situation.

TRT officers wear "Trebark" BDU fatigues when responding to an "Operation 100"; the "Trebark" pattern was viewed as more effective that the Woodland pattern BDU and afforded unit snipers all-year weather camouflage capability. All officers wear their PBA Level III bullet-proof vest under their fatigues and uniforms, though they will wear the heavier Kevlar vests during tactical deployment. The basic TRT firearm is the Smith and Wesson 4026 .40 caliber semi-automatic pistol; the shotguns of choice are the Remington Mk. 870 (with flashlight attachment) and the Benelli M1 Super 90 semi-automatic 12-gauge shotgun also fitted with a flashlight attachment; the Heckler and Koch 94 9mm semi-automatic weapon is deployed (along with Pro-Point red dot aiming device); and, the Heckler and Koch 93 .223 assault rifle is also carried. Snipers with the Kansas City Police Department's Tactical Response Team use the Remington 700 PSS .308 caliber rifle fitted with either a 3x9 or 3x10 scope firing 168 grain hollow-point ammunition. It is interesting to note that TRT sergeants also bring Remington .22 caliber rifles to deployments for the specific purpose of removing street lights when it is tactically unsound to shut down power to a single home or even an entire block. For heavy-duty riot operations and crowd control, the unit deploys a 37mm Gas Gun and a 12-gauge tear-gas round. Devices carried by the TRT include Def-Tec diversionary grenades, as well as tear gas canisters, and smoke devices.

The Kansas City Police Department TRT's V-100 Armored Vehicle. (Courtesy: Captain William Massock/Kansas City Police Department)

The TRT's Equipment van, affectionately called the "Bread Truck," which carries the TRT's specialized equipment to "Operation 100" deployments. (Courtesy: Captain William Massock/Kansas City Police Department)

The TRT's "Peace-keeper" armored car. (Courtesy: Captain William Massock/Kansas City Police Department)

The most ubiquitous vehicle in American law enforcement today--the "Crown Vic" unmarked police vehicle--here in TRT use. (Courtesy: Captain William Massock/Kansas City Police Department)

Should the SWAT motto of Sit, Wait and Talk not be suitable and a tactical entry required, a TRT entry squad consists of one sergeant and six officers in the following configuration:

1. Point man with Smith and Wesson 4026 .40 caliber pistol and light along with Body Bunker ballistic shield
2. Officer with Benelli shotgun
3. Officer with HK94
4. Officer with Mk. 870 shotgun
5. Sergeant armed with Smith and Wesson 4026
6. Officer with HK94
7. Newest man to join the squad brings in the rear and he is armed with a Smith and Wesson 4026 .40 caliber pistol and/or the Remington Mk. 870 12-gauge shotgun.

A typical deployment will consist of one team, though many jobs have resulted in calling out a second and even third team. Officers are required to take their personal gear and weaponry with them in the Crown Victoria unmarked sedans, though much of the unit's specialized equipment is carried in the "Bread Truck," the square-shaped TRT supply vehicle. Some of the more specialized entry and control equipment carried by the TRT includes: night vision equipment; folding ladder, portable lights, special "around the corner" mirrors; bolt-cutters; battering rams; hydraulic door opening devices; sledge-hammers and crowbars; capture nets; hostage throw phones; fire extinguishers; magnum foggers; and, pepper foggers. Among the more interesting bits of equipment used in communications with a barricaded or hostage-holding subject is an indigenously produced steel cased "disjointed bull horn" complete with steel cables that cannot be cut; the device is thrown near the suspect and used to as a secure one-way communications system; since it can't be cut or shot and destroyed by the suspect, it is often used to annoy a suspect into giving up, with one example including playing a police siren through the device for hours on end.

Another specialized piece of equipment used by the Kansas City Tactical Response Team is armored vehicles, and the TRT deploy both the V-100 and the "Peace Keeper." TRT "Operation 100s" are supported by Schweizer 300 and Hughes OH6 choppers of the Kansas City Police Department, some fitted with FLIR forward looking infra-red.

The TRT is called to approximately fifteen "Operation 100"s a year involving an emotionally disturbed individual who has barricaded himself inside a building with hostages or with a gun to his head, or a situation where a perpetrator has taken hostages to facilitate an escape of some sort. In addition, the unit executes approximately fifty high-risk felony warrants a year.

Perhaps the unit's largest "Operation 100" came in 1984 when armed individuals ambushed a U.S. Marshals transporting a fugitive from Kansas City International Airport who had come from Denver to testify in open court; the Marshals were beaten and cuffed, and locked inside their car. A massive manhunt was carried out in Kansas City and throughout Missouri and Kansas, finally resulting in the location of the perpetrators--three males and a female--in a two-story house. A stand-off ensued and the Tactical Response Team called in. Negotiations and posturing went on all day and night, as snipers moved into position, officers established an inner perimeter with their assault weapons in hand, and the V-100 was called out in case a forcible entry under fire needed to transpire. The unit was prepared to move in when three perpetrators, the two men and one female who had ambushed the Marshals, fled the building and surrendered to police. TRT commanders on the scene realized that the fugitive, pronouncing that he would never go back to prison, was armed and likely to go out in a flurry of gunplay, and so decided to go in. The V-100 was pulled up against the garage door and a TRT entry team went in. The perpetrator had killed himself, but by his side officers found three handguns, one shotgun, a .30 caliber rifle and two Molotov cocktails; officers also found a police scanner.

In another large "Operation 100" at the end of 1991, TRT officers were summoned to search for a subject, wanted on a narcotics warrant, who had shot an officer during a traffic stop. TRT officers surrounded the targeted house and established a controlled perimeter. "Star," a K-9, a dog made famous by starring in the film K-9 with Jim Belushi, went in but was shot and killed by the perpetrator. Realizing a tactical response would be required, a TRT entry team made its assault. Room by room the house was cleared in meticulous fashion and deemed secure until a bedroom closet was encountered. From behind the closed doors of the closet the perpetrator opened fire with his AR-15 assault rifle and the cops responded with a flurry of fire; to the TRT's great surprise, the autopsy would reveal that the subject was not killed by police bullets but rather he had committed suicide--apparently, as the police were returning fire, the perpetrator shot himself in the head with his .45 caliber pistol. In the dead perpetrator's possession, TRT officers found the AR-15 assault rifle and .45, as well as a MAC-11 submachine gun.

If a special tactical unit can be judged by its professionalism and adherence to the principles of the job at hand, than the TRT is truly in a class of its own--in its history, they have only had to use firepower on three separate occasions.

The TRT "Bread Truck" and some of its equipment on display, including (left to right): weathered Body Bunker; heavy assault vest; TRT TAC vest; battering ram; and, door prying pole. (Courtesy: Captain William Massock/Kansas City Police Department)

TRT officer P.O. Mike Foster displays the proper position for firing the Heckler and Koch HK93 .223 assault rifle. (Courtesy: Captain William Massock/Kansas City Police Department)

A TRT sniper, P.O. Rick Smith, peers through the sights of his Remington 700 .308 sniper rifle. (Courtesy: Captain William Massock/Kansas City Police Department)

Dressed in the TRT's Trebark camouflage and Kevlar assault vest and body armor, TRT officers Jeff Emery, Rick Smith and Shawn Wadlé deploy from the back of the "Bread Truck." (Courtesy: Captain William Massock/Kansas City Police Department)

At Hogan's Alley, the TAC house at the Kansas City, Missouri Police Department's Pistol Range, P.O. Chris Bumpus and P.O. Shawn Wadle display what a "hit" is like with battering ram in hand. (Courtesy: Captain William Massock/Kansas City Police Department)

The weapons of the Kansas City, Missouri, Police Department Tactical Response Team (from top to bottom): the Remington 700 PPS, the HK 93 .223 assault rifle, the 37mm gas gun, the Benelli 12-gauge shotgun, a .22 rifle for street light duty, and the Smith and Wesson 4026 handgun with flashlight attachment. (Courtesy: Captain William Massock/Kansas City Police Department)

P.O. Jeff Emery (left with Smith and Wesson 4026 handgun) and P.O. Shawn Waddle (right, with HK 94), prepare to enter the bullet-scarred TAC House at Hogan's Alley. (Courtesy: Captain William Massock/Kansas City Police Department)

Excellent photograph of a tactical entry exercise--P.O. Shawn Wadle throws a distraction device through the door as his back-up, poised for action, stand at the ready for their entry. (Courtesy: Captain William Massock/Kansas City Police Department)

P.O. Shawn Wadle walks alongside the TAC house offering cover to the members of his assault team--note Trebark camouflage trousers, knee-pads, black Kevlar assault vest and Kevlar infantry ballistic helmet worn. (Courtesy: Captain William Massock/Kansas City Police Department)

P.O. Jeff Emery, the pointman, works Hogan's Alley with his Smith and Wesson 4026 with flashlight attachment. (Courtesy: Captain William Massock/Kansas City Police Department)

Freeze! Police! A perp's worst nightmare. The TRT, like most tactical police units, would rather bore an individual to death than shoot him. When firepower is the last remaining option, the unit hones its skills to be ready to face and persevere through any challenge. Here, during tactical assault entry training, P.O. Jeff Emery and P.O. Shawn Wadle aim their weapons through an opening in the TAC House. (Courtesy: Captain William Massock/Kansas City Police Department)

The moment of truth--a five-man TRT entry and the interior sweep of the target : P.O., Jeff Emery is the Bunker Man with ballistic shield and S&W 4026 with flashlight attachment and is covered by P.O. Rick Smith with Benelli 12-gauge shotgun and P.O. Shawn Wadle with HK 94, P.O. Mike Foster, also with HK 94 and Chris Bumps with 9mm pistol. (Courtesy: Captain William Massock/Kansas City Police Department)

The Kansas City, Missouri, Police Department's Tactical Response Team--one of the nation's finest. Major Gary Scherer, the department's Special Operations Division Commander, can be seen on the right. (Courtesy: Captain William Massock/Kansas City Police Department)

## Austria

The GEK Cobra wings, worn by unit ***Fallschirmspringer***s.

The GEK shoulder tag.

The Gendarmerie coat of arms.

The GEK Cobra patch.

The Gendarmerie nametape--worn over the left breast pocket.

A GEK NCO, armed with the Israeli-produced Uzi 9mm submachine gun, slinks through the woods around Schonau Castle during the Palestinian siege. (Courtesy: GEK Cobra)

***It is just before dawn over the picturesque suburbs of Vienna. The winter's haze has settled over the plush green plains, and the only sounds heard are the car engines of a few die hard workers determined to evade the morning's rush hour. The silence, however, is soon broken. The rotor blades of a Bell-206 Jet Ranger erupts over a row of snow dusted pines, and the royal blue chopper flies low, hugging the tree-line before lowering itself to twenty-feet above an empty rail line. Four men in black coveralls and black masks are hanging on to the landing skids of the Jet Ranger, they hold assault rifles and are poised to jump. The chopper reaches a lone rail car and strikes ten feet lower to perch the four men atop the rail car. A harness is produced and ropes lowered toward four large Plexiglas windows. A sniper's round cracks through the cabin's main window, shattering it into a connected maze of sliver, though allowing the operator to breech the window with a small C-4 charge. The four men throw themselves in the train while hanging from a rope in the wake of the C-4 blast while a dozen men, Glocks drawn, race through the entrance door facing the roadway. There are twenty cardboard cutouts simulating passengers and terrorists positioned throughout the seats of the inter-city rail car. By the time the forty-five seconds of explosions and crackling of automatic gunfire is complete, four of the cut-outs, looking like Middle Eastern terrorists, are peppered with dozens of 5.56mm and 9mm holes. The remaining sixteen cut-outs, painted to look like women, children and old men, are unscathed.***

***Outside the train, two officers in red berets and khaki drab fatigues look at their stopwatches and radio the helicopter and order it to come in one more time with the operators in tow. The raid had taken a full ninety seconds from deployment to the all's clear sign. GEK Cobra could do it in sixty.***

"If the Germans compliment your abilities," says one U.S. Special Forces counter-terrorist instructor, "then you are good." "If the Israelis consider you in an elite grouping," the officer continues, "then you are sure that you're good." "Finally, if the British say your among the best, then you know you are the best....the British compliment nobody." The unit that has warranted all this praise is the Austrian Gendarmerieeinsatzkommando (GEK) Cobra, a force of counter-terrorist operators that, through its unique and rigid training, meticulous execution of tactical operations and brilliant leadership, has become the vanguard of today's international intervention unit.

The forebear to Austria's GEK Cobra was formed in April of 1973, as every nation in Europe was determined to keep terrorists off its soil and be able to defeat them tactically should hostages be taken on their soil or on board their aircraft or ocean liners. The emphasis at the time was against Palestinian terrorists--it was the zenith of the Black September campaign throughout Europe, as well as business as usual for the litany of "Popular Fronts" for the Liberation of Palestine, Armenia, etc., who used the liberally exposed frontiers of Europe as convenient conduits for moving arms, money and manpower. Like West Germany, however, Austria had historic reasons to keep Palestinian terrorists at bay--the spilling of Jewish blood in Vienna (or elsewhere) constituted a public relations nightmare. As a neutral country, though, one not aligned to either the NATO alliance or the

Warsaw Pact, Austrian leaders thought that they could--through careful negotiations and secretive contacts--avoid the terrorist offensive taking its toll on human life and property in France, Holland, and the United Kingdom. Its intentions were to avoid violence and bloodshed, but in case diplomacy failed, the unit was to be a means of last resort. Austrian leaders would not have to wait long until it would learn that deals "cannot" be made with terrorists and the police would learn that terrorism can only be defeated when a government has the courage, coupled with good sense, to move.

Originally, the unit was known Gendarmeriekommando "Bad Vöslau" (GK Bad Vöslau) because the unit's headquarters was in Bad Vöslau, approximately twenty kilometer south of Vienna. Ironically, GK Bad Vöslau was signed into being as a result of a very precarious security situation being carried out on Austrian soil that had the potential for inviting a blood-bath. Since the emergence of détente

Oberst Johannes Pechter (left) salutes a wreath honoring the unit's fallen at the GEK Cobra's new base at Wiener Neustadt near Vienna. (Courtesy: Gendarmerieeinsatzkommando Cobra)

Wearing a black balaclava, Orlite Kevlar infantry-ballistic helmet (with integrated microphone and head-set), a Cobra operator prepares to fire his AUG carbine. (Courtesy: Gendarmerieeinsatzkommando Cobra)

A GEK operator, posing with a Heckler and Koch MP5 SD3 9mm submachine gun and newly developed ballistic operators helmet (with tinted visor). Most Cobra personnel use the Steyr 5.56mm AUG assault rifle, however. (Courtesy: Gendarmerieeinsatzkommando Cobra)

Stoic photograph of a GEK Cobra operator peering down the sights of Glock 9mm pistol with his Steyr 5.56mm AUG carbine at the ready. (Courtesy: Gendarmerieeinsatzkommando Cobra)

between the United States and the Soviet Union in 1971, more and more Soviet Jews were allowed to emigrate to Israel; Austria, the rail crossroads of Europe, was a convenient and logical transit point for the moving of so many refugees. Following the Munich Olympic Massacre, however, it became obvious that so many Jews in transit was too ripe a target for Palestinian terrorists ***not*** to attack. On September 28, 1973, Syrian-backed Palestinian terrorists from the ***as-Saiqa*** faction seized a train full of Soviet Jews using the Schonau castle facility as a staging point for their trips to Israel. What Austrian leaders had feared most was now transpiring, real-time, before their very eyes. The terrorists were heavily armed--complete with AK-47s, fragmentation grenades and automatic pistols--and demanded that the Austrian government shut down the facility or bear responsibility for the deaths of all the hostages.

The GK was immediately summoned, and even though it had been less than year since the unit was created, they had already formed the nucleus for a first-rate force. Operators wearing helmets and cradling Uzi submachine guns slinked their way around the besieged transit point, but the order to end the situation tactically was never given. The Pro-PLO Austrian Chancellor, Bruno Kriesky, ordered the facility closed days later and the crisis resolved with the terrorists allowed to return to Syria. For the GK it was a tell-tale sign that the political will was simply non-existent in the national resolve to fight terrorism. To many it appeared as if the government was willing to do lip service condemning terrorist violence but was willing to do little more. Nevertheless, in December 1973, the Ministry of the Interior initiated a deterrent to the hijacking of any El Al or other civilian aircraft in or out of the country--security at Vienna's Schwechat International

Fanatic about physical fitness, Cobra personnel undergo the weekly run at their training facility's obstacle course. (Courtesy: Gendarmerieeinsatzkommando Cobra)

At the GEK Cobra's state-of-the-art facility at Wiener Neustadt, operators endear themselves to the fine art of fast-roping down a 300-foot high tower. (Courtesy: Gendarmerieeinsatzkommando Cobra)

Preparing to assault a terrace--300 feet above the ground--Cobra gunners prepare to mount an Australian march downward with weapons ablaze. Trained to encounter and overcome any and all obstacles, there are very few targets--if any--that GEK Cobra cannot reach. (Courtesy: Gendarmerieeinsatzkommando Cobra)

Airport was taken out of the hands of the local police and handed to the GK.

The watershed year for Austria's fight against terrorism came, of course, in 1975 when the notorious Carlos,[1] led an international conglomerate of stars working for the Wadi Haddad Faction of the Popular Front for the Liberation of Palestine (PFLP) in the raid against the OPEC meetings in Vienna, and two people were killed and the ministers from the various OPEC nations taken hostage. The GK responded and quickly surrounded the building but they were not fully prepared tactically with the specific training required to initiate a rescue raid against such a determined force of heavy hitters. Even though the terrorists were under the watchful eyes of GK sharpshooters and riflemen for large segments of the ordeal, Bruno Kriesky's government authorized a hefty multi-million dollar ransom to Carlos and his gang, and allowed them safe passage out of Austria.

For Austria, it was the beginning of a chaotic wave of events that plunged Europe, especially Germany and Austria, into the grips of a major and unrelenting terrorist offensive. One year following the OPEC debacle, Baader-Meinhof Gang terrorists robbed a Vienna bank of several million marks, and later robbed a Ministry of the Interior printing plant where thousands of blank birth certificates, passports and drivers licenses were stolen--obviously for later use through the border crossings of Europe and beyond. In Vienna, the German Red Army Faction kidnapped Austrian industrialist Walter Michael Palmers and ransomed him off for a hefty fee, while in Germany, industrialist Hans Martin Schleyer was kidnapped and executed by the Red Army Faction. But there had been signs of hope on the international stage that sparked a change in Austria. Firstly, Israel's brilliant rescue raid in Entebbe had galvanized the world community into believing that special operations forces could do virtually anything should these units be equipped properly, be financed and supported properly, be instructed properly, and most importantly, receive the support form their governments to use them when warranted. Then, one year later, GSG-9 executed its now legendary assault on a hijacked airliner in Mogadishu. Once again, special operations forces had rescued hostages and had used skill, stealth and firepower to overcome seemingly insurmountable odds and obstacles. This new law-enforcement/military reality was not lost to the Austrian defense and interior ministries. The GK would be overhauled, revamped and trained to not only intervene, but deployed to deter, to confront and strike back. They would be responsible for fighting any terrorist threat to Austria and its citizens both at home and abroad. The unit was the ***Gendarmerieeinsatzkommando*** or GEK for short. Its emblem of a cobra would soon be adopted as the unit nickname and would hence be called GEK Cobra. It was signed into existence on January 1, 1978.

The man tasked with commanding GEK Cobra was Oberst Johannes Pechter--a Gendarmerie veteran and special operations genius who was an equal in insight, spirit and leadership charisma to the legendary Ulrich Wegener (the man who transformed GSG-9 from an idea on paper to one of the world's premier units). Like Wegener before him, Oberst Pechter sought the experience of nations and units that had successfully formed similar units and were engaged in similar struggles against equally violent terrorist threats. Pechter traveled to Germany where he formed extremely close ties with GSG-9 and he traveled to Israel where close ties were established with ***Sayeret Mat'kal*** and the newly formed ***Ya'ma'm***; similar foreign fact-finding forays were undertaken with the British SAS, Belgian ESI, Dutch BBE, and the French GIGN. A great admirer of the Germans and Israelis, he combined the virtues and attitudes of both units--mixing the absolute professionalism of GSG-9 and the German's meticulous adherence to details with the adventurous spirit and ***chutzpah*** of the Israelis. Perhaps most importantly, Oberst Pechter wanted to create a unit that would be the final answer to any contingency without having to rely on outside agencies or services to get the job done. Should terrorists have the gall--and stupidity--to operate on Austrian soil, then they would have to deal with GEK Cobra.

What Oberst Pechter would establish became one of the finest counter-terrorist and hostage-rescue forces in the world. Service in GEK Cobra is strictly voluntary--all applicants wishing to try out for the unit must be between the ages of twenty-two and thirty-five have at least three years of exemplary service with the Gendarmerie, possess a driver's license, and must sign a mandatory 36 months of service with the GEK should he pass the selection process and basic training to become a full-fledged operator. The selection process takes place twice a year and only those who score in the top twenty-percentile in the applied mental health, psychological, motivational, and physical examinations are permitted to begin GEK Cobra basic training--all three months of the instruction.

GEK training is long, arduous and dedicated to turning the volunteer into a precisioned tool capable of hitting his target--any target--with any of the weapons at his disposal. Special emphasis is placed on marksmanship skill. GEK operators are all expected to be master shots with anything from a .357 revolver to the 5.56mm Steyr AUG assault rifle. More than any other aspect of counter-terrorist work, Oberst Pechter has made sure that his unit is expert at explosive entry and any type of insertion. A student of history, Oberst Pechter was adamant not to repeat the mistakes of failed hostage-rescue raids in the past, especially such missions gone wrong as the May 1974 Ma'alot rescue. A great deal of the annual GEK training schedule would focus on entry--entering a bus, a train, a plane and, with the unit's ***Tauchschwimmer***s (frogman), even a boat. There would not be a building, structure or situation that the GEK couldn't get into--once in, the unit would have the skills to handle the situation tactically. GEK Cobra operators are expert ropesmen and can scale any building--from a Gothic cathedral in the center of Vienna, to an Alpine hideaway protected by trees and mountains in the snowy heights. After the OPEC seizure, GEK Cobra transformed the scaling up and down skyscrapers into an art form.

GEK Cobra is a force that consists of nearly 200 operators--including fifteen officers. Under the control of the Ministry of the Interior and the Directorate for State Security, the GEK is placed on alert at the signs of any potential terrorist threat or tactical situation that might develop involving hostages and heavily armed criminals. The unit participates in undercover counter-terrorist and counter-espionage operations in conjunction with the Directorate for State Security and GEK Cobra operators have also dressed as flight stewards and ground mechanics for Austrian Airlines to act as armed skymarshals on flights where a hijacking was threatened or perceived to be a possibility by Austrian intelligence, and they have also dressed as rail passengers and ticket agents on board Austrian Railways to be present in case of any terrorist attack.

GEK Cobra's principal means of transport is the unit's fleet of specially modified (details of which are not suitable for publication) Mercedes 300 SE sedans that are used for both transport and special undercover work. The GEK takes special care to train its drivers to be

A Ministry of the Interior Gendarmerie chopper hovers high above a rail car simulating a train seized by terrorists, as GEK Cobra operators fast rope down during the attempted rescue assault. (Courtesy: Gendarmerieeinsatzkommando Cobra)

As the chopper hovers as steady as it can in the sharp autumn windows of central Austria, a GEK gunner takes aim with his Steyr 5.56mm AUG assault rifle and places a full magazine well within the target. (Courtesy: Gendarmerieeinsatzkommando Cobra)

With one leg on a specially-modified landing skid perch and one eye peering through his AUG's sights, an operator prepares to unleash a full auto burst of 5.56mm fire. (Courtesy: Gendarmerieeinsatzkommando Cobra)

A GEK Cobra sniper awaits his order to unleash a single, well-placed, 7.62mm round from his Steyr 7.62mm police rifle. (Courtesy: Gendarmerieeinsatzkommando Cobra)

Wearing his Nomex balaclava hood and hooked into GEK central through several frequencies open solely to him, a GEK sniper prepares to fire his Steyr police rifle. (Courtesy: Gendarmerieeinsatzkommando Cobra)

A GEK sapper detonates a fire-bomb found at an undisclosed location in Vienna. Cobra personnel are also EOD trained. (Courtesy: Gendarmerieeinsatzkommando Cobra)

among the best in Europe and Cobra chauffeurs (as those tasked with driving the sedans are called) have been likened to "Formula One" racers for their skills at high speeds. GEK operators are also trained to fire--accurately--from speeding vehicles and expected to hit their targets through rolled down passenger windows as if they were in prone position on the range back at the unit's new training facility south of Vienna. Heavy transport and more arduous terrain vehicles are handled by a fleet of 4x4 Cachleitner all-terrain vehicles, and material and equipment is carried in 4x4 Steyr support vehicles. The Austrian national railway also provides for the GEK's disposal a special rail engine and car to transport the unit to the farthest stretches of the county at a half-hour's notice.

GEK Cobra can also rely upon a fleet of Gendarmerie and ***Bundesministerium f. Inneres*** (Ministry of the Interior) Bell-206 Jet Ranger and Austrian Army Bell-212 helicopters and Pilatus PC-7 transport planes. Besides being able to deploy and fast-rope from this fleet of aircraft, GEK Cobra operators are also trained to be high (and low) flying marksman and are tested for their skills in hitting targets at a hundred yards out from a fast moving chopper. If regular deployment or fast-roping is not suitable, there is a parachutist-qualified GEK Cobra unit--the ***Fallschirmspringer***s--that can deploy silently through free-fall from a chopper or a small piston-engine aircraft; around twenty men make up this unit and it jumps anywhere from 80-120 times a year. The GEK also possesses a frogman unit, the ***Tauchschwimmer***s, that can use the country's vast lakes and rivers as silent conduits to a destination. Just in case a river barge is seized by terrorists, GEK Cobra trains to reach the water target silently and then burst out of the water with weapons ablaze.

While most units carry the Heckler and Koch family of 9mm submachine guns,[2] GEK Cobra has opted to remain with a 5.56mm weapon, and the Steyr AUG is the unit's weapon of choice; in Austria, the weapon is simply known as the "77." Sturdy, robust and highly accurate, the indigenously-produced assault rifle has proved itself a handy long-range weapon as well as close-quarter mainstay. Again, with the indigenously-produced material being among the world's best, GEK Cobra's primary handgun is the Glock Model 17 9mm automatic, while the French MR 73 Manurhin .357 Magnum revolver is also carried and deployed for close-quarter fire-fights. The two shotguns carried by GEK Cobra are the Italian Franchi SPAS 12 12-gauge shotgun and the Remington Mk. 870 12-gauge masterpiece. The sniper weapon carried by GEK Cobra marksman in the Steyr police 7.62mm sniping weapon. GEK operators wear Israeli-produced Orlite Kevlar infantry-ballistic helmets and British-produced Kevlar body armor and assault vests.

Among GEK Cobra's international ties, the closest--obviously--exist with Germany's GSG-9 and the SEKs (and MEKs) from the state's closest to Austria. The units regularly visit one another and train together quite frequently, whether assaulting a speeding train seized by terrorists (exercises simulated in the Austrian Alps) or training at Düsseldorf (or Schwechat) International Airport to rescue hostages from a seized airliner. Since both nations share a common language and border, the relationship is not only an opportunity to see what the next door neighbor is doing--it also affords a face-to-face exchange of intelligence and problems that faxes, telexes and secure communications cannot replicate. GEK Cobra also has--for the obvious language and regional reasons--enjoyed extremely close ties to the various intervention squads in Switzerland--primarily those from the German-speaking portions of the country such as the Kantonpolizei Argau and the Stern units. The GEK has ventured to Switzerland for joint training, and Swiss units have traveled to Austria. Starting in 1980, the GEK participated in various CTCs where they not only won several competitions, but also established close ties with such units as the United Kingdom's 22nd Special Air Service (SAS) Regiment, the Italian GIS and NOCs, and close ties to the French GIGN. It was also during this period that GEK Cobra established its ties to the U.S. Army's 1st SFOD-Delta--the two units would soon exchange personnel and teams for joint-training. In 1986, the GEK established close ties to the Spanish National Police counter-terrorist, the GEO, and with its commander, Major Carlos Halgado, and also established ties with the People's Republic of China's police intervention squad, the Special Police Arms Unit. The GEK was also closely involved with joint training of the Jordanian Special Operation Unit and the Saudi Arabian Special Security Forces (SSF)

[1] At the time of this book's writing, Carlos is awaiting the commencement of his trial in Paris, France after being kidnapped from the Sudan by French GIGN commandos and DST counter-intelligence agents.

[2] It should be noted that several assault teams "are" issued with MP5s, and the unit often acquires new weapons--from the Israeli Mini-Galil to the Soviet AKS-74--in order to run test trials.

A cross-section of the Mercedes Benz 300 SE sedans used by GEK Cobra. (Courtesy: Gendarmerieeinsatzkommando Cobra)

A Gendarmerie Cachleitner 4x4 in use by the GEK Cobra. (Courtesy: Gendarmerieeinsatzkommando Cobra)

A Steyr 4x4 supply truck used by GEK Cobra for forward deployments. A traveling arsenal as well as logistics vehicle, featured here are roadblock material, generators, EOD lines, and illumination lights. (Courtesy: Gendarmerieeinsatzkommando Cobra)

Excellent photograph of GEK Cobra operators peering around a bush awaiting their order into action. Note Velcro patch on left shoulder to affix Austrian flag emblem usually worn by unit members on operations. (Courtesy: Gendarmerieeinsatzkommando Cobra)

During exercises meant to simulate assaulting a large estate seized by well-armed terrorists--the first photograph shows the operators rappelling toward the first floor windows and then the operators (next photograph) making their explosive entry. (Courtesy: Gendarmerieeinsatzkommando Cobra)

GEK Cobra operators deploy from a collapsible ladder during entry exercises--note Remington Mk. 870 12-gauge shotgun carried by gunner (left.) (Courtesy: Gendarmerieeinsatzkommando Cobra)

A Vienna transit bus is used to help train GEK Cobra operators in the fine art of assaulting a bus seized by terrorists. The sprint from cover position to the bus windows is to take less than 30 seconds, and the actual assault meant to be over before the terrorists have time to react properly. (Courtesy: Gendarmerieeinsatzkommando Cobra)

Revolvers, especially the French-produced MR 73 Manurhin .357 Magnum revolver, are the weapon of choice during close-quarter tactical situations. (Courtesy: Gendarmerieeinsatzkommando Cobra)

GEK Cobra ***Tauchschwimmer***s slink their way around a flotation device while preparing to assault their shoreline target. (Courtesy: Gendarmerieeinsatzkommando Cobra)

A GEK Cobra ***Tauchschwimmer*** team swims toward its target in the shallow waters of a lake. The GEK ***Tauchschwimmer***s train closely with German GSG-9 Section 2 operators, as well as German Navy ***Kamphschwimmer***s. (Courtesy: Gendarmerieeinsatzkommando Cobra)

Two ***Tauchschwimmer***s emerge from a lake after performing underwater reconnaissance on a potential target. (Courtesy: Gendarmerieeinsatzkommando Cobra)

Scouring the nearby lake-bed to see if his movements have been spotted, a GEK ***Tauchschwimmer*** moves cautiously through shallow waters before positioning himself for a tactical assault. He is armed with the Steyr AUG submachine gun. (Courtesy: Gendarmerieeinsatzkommando Cobra)

Abiding by the classic police technique of cover and concealment when engaging an armed subject, a GEK Cobra operator peers through the sights of his French-produced MR 73 Manurhin .357 Magnum revolver underneath a Mercedes Benz 300 SE sedan. (Courtesy: Gendarmerieeinsatzkommando Cobra)

GEK operators deploy for a fire-fight in the unit's outdoor TAC house during exercises. Note heavy Kevlar flak vests worn. (Courtesy: Gendarmerieeinsatzkommando Cobra)

GEK Cobra free-fall ***Fallschirmspringer***s line up to board an Austrian Army Pilatus PC-7 transport aircraft during large-scale insertion exercises. (Courtesy: Gendarmerieeinsatzkommando Cobra)

Free-fall GEK Cobra style. (Courtesy: Gendarmerieeinsatzkommando Cobra)

GENDARMERIEEINSATZKOMMANDO

EINSATZABTEILUNG

Einsatzabteilung

Kdt

KdoGr

TeGr

1. EE — Kdt — ZgTrp — Gr 1, Gr 2

2. EE — Kdt — ZgTrp — Gr 3, Gr 4

3. EE — Kdt — ZgTrp — Gr 5, Gr 6

4. EE — Kdt — ZgTrp — Gr 7, Gr 8

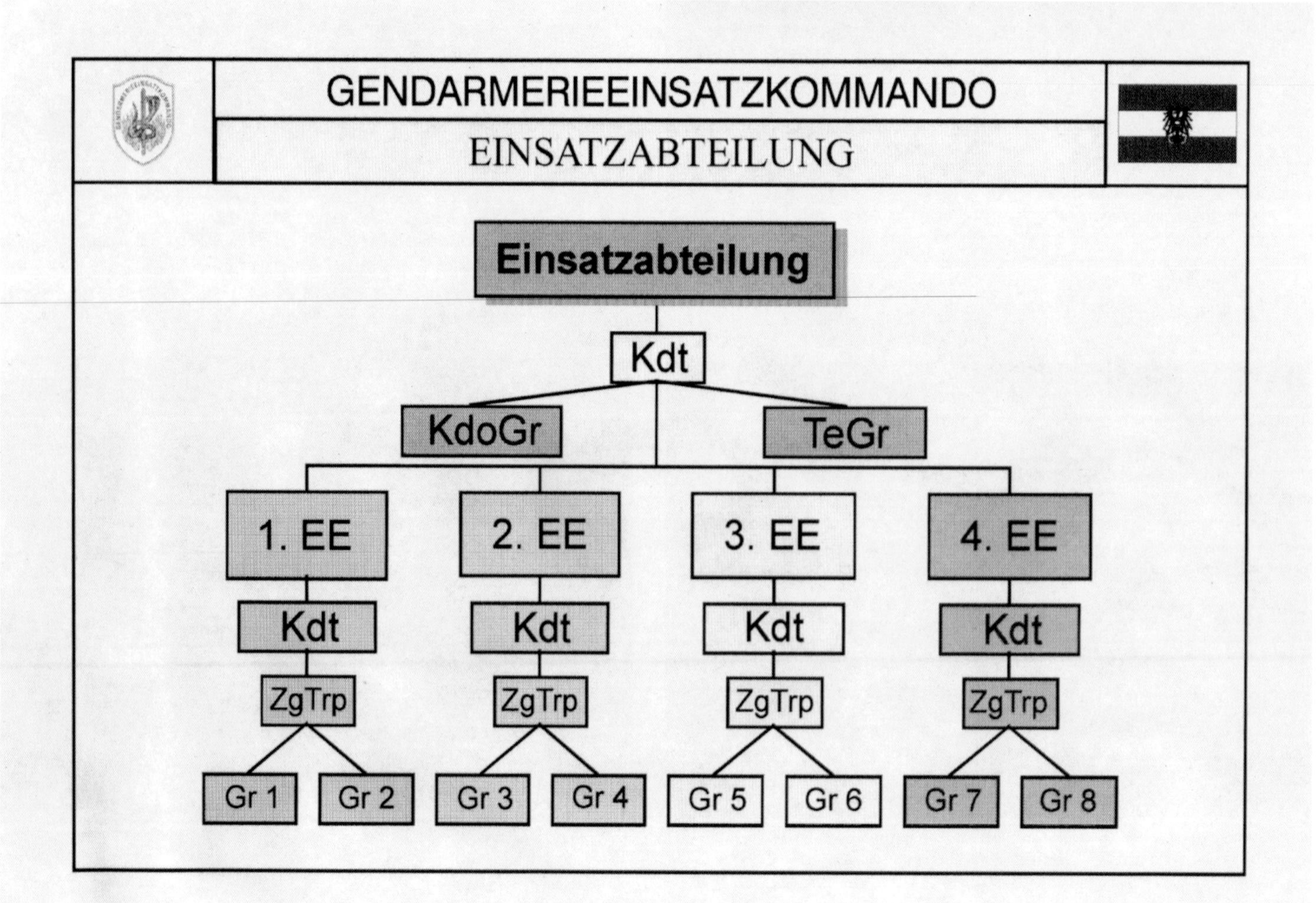

The GEK Cobra Order of Battle.

# Belgium

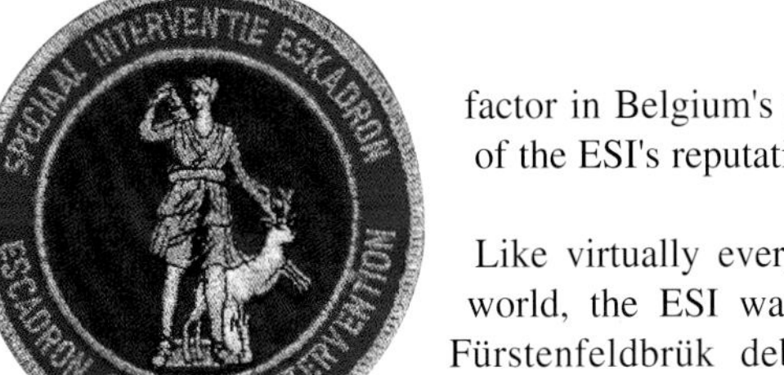

The ESI patch.

***April 24, 1994. It was a quiet night in the small port city of Zeebruge, Belgium, and the port--was quiet, too quiet. There wasn't the usual activity of vehicles, only a few boats were coming in and out of port even though shipments were expected and loads scheduled out; even the prostitutes outside the facility had been warned away by something. Strategically positioned throughout the coastal facility were 200 marines and 165 policemen from the Gendarmerie. The radio chatter was deafening and the sounds of the soldiers and policemen checking their weapons, banging against 30-round magazines and pulling on the slings of their assault rifles filled the frosty air. The soldiers and policemen didn't know for sure what they'd be up against but they were prepared for anything. Ready, in fact, for war.***

***In the early morning hours, a Gendarmerie Super Puma helicopter took off from a forward assault position and headed toward open water--toward the international border at sea several kilometers in the open Atlantic. On board the Puma were one dozen men wearing green Nomex coveralls and black balaclavas, and clutching their MP5s. As the Puma neared a small boat, a freighter heading for Zeebruge, the Puma hovered and lowered the operators down on a rope. Resistance was expected, and armed individuals on board the ship were, indeed, encountered, but not a shot fired in anger. The operators were able to seize the ship, its crew and, most importantly, its cargo. The ship carried ten tons of hashish and it was seized by the men of the ESI, the Special Intervention Squadron--Belgium's elite anti-terrorist and hostage-rescue unit.***

Belgium's ***Escadron Special D'Intervention*** (Special Intervention Squadron) is not among the most famous of the world's counter-terrorist and hostage-rescue units--their acronym title of ESI is not as famous as Germany's GSG-9 nor as mysterious as Britain's SAS. They do not evoke the same Hollywoodesque image of America's Delta Force and have not enjoyed the publicity and workload of Israel's various units. Yet the Belgian ESI is, perhaps, among the world's best units. It is a force ideally trained for intervention and hostage-rescue, and capable of handling just about any tactical situation and crisis imaginable. Among the world's best-trained specialists, they are also among the world's best-equipped. Terrorism has not been a major factor in Belgium's post-war history mainly as a result of the ESI's reputation as a second-to-none unit.

`One of the ESI's greatest skills is in reconnaissance and observation. Here, during an actual stake-out with the CBO, an ESI operator reports his findings to headquarters. (Courtesy: Lieutenant Eddy Huybens/Gendarmerie Public Relations Office)

Like virtually every other hostage-rescue unit in the world, the ESI was formed in the aftermath of the Fürstenfeldbrük debacle in October 1972. While Belgian police units were known throughout Europe for their tactical prowess--many of them being military veterans--it was decided that the task of rescuing hostages and being on call to respond to any extraordinary situation should be the Gendarmerie's responsibility. The Belgian Gendarmerie (or ***Rijkswacht*** in Flemish), like its counterpart in France, is drawn from the national militarized police. Like West Germany when it created GSG-9, Belgium looked to create a revolutionary force of specialists that would be a secretive element of the equation should an attack like the one perpetrated against the Olympic village ever be committed inside of Belgium.

Belgium's national counter-terrorist and hostage-rescue unit was officially formed on December 6, 1972, and was originally known as "***Le Groupe Diane***" (from the unit's symbol and the symbol of Belgian criminal justice system). The unit's first commander, Major Arsène Pint, was an Olympian who competed in the 1960 summer games in Rome and he actively recruited former members of the Para-Commandos who, like him, were athletic, wily, and superb fighters. Initially, ***Le Groupe Diane*** consisted of only a handful of men who

Freeze! ESI! Terrorists beware--during an exercise to free hostages from a safe-house in the Ardennes, ESI operators burst through the door of a one-story building as a cloud of tear gas engulfs the rural setting. (Courtesy: Lieutenant Eddy Huybens/Gendarmerie Public Relations Office)

"Subject in the cross-hairs, awaiting further orders!" Hooked into three separate police frequencies and ultimately controlling the action, an ESI sniper awaits his order to fire. His weapon is the Finnish Sako Ltd. 7.62mm sniper rifle. (suppressed). (Courtesy: Lieutenant Eddy Huybens/Gendarmerie Public Relations Office)

Rear-view of an ESI sniper's position--both operators are equipped with the self-produced 7.62mm police rifle. (Courtesy: Lieutenant Eddy Huybens/Gendarmerie Public Relations Office)

formed six mobile squads of Gendarmes, "on-call" to respond to any terrorist incident inside Belgium. Although still a fledgling unit, they were there and could rely on Gendarmerie aircraft and vehicles to transport them to any spot in the country at a moment's notice. More than anything else, "Diane Group" was a stop-gap measure until the full potential of a national hostage-rescue unit could be realized. In 1973, a year after the Munich Massacre, ***Le Groupe Diane*** sent several of its officers to Europe, Israel, Asia and the United States to visit with the special forces and counter-terrorist units established (or being established) in Germany, France, Switzerland, Denmark, Norway, Italy, Austria, Israel, The United States, Indonesia and Hong Kong. More of a fact-finding mission than anything connected to joint-training, the venture was an intelligence-gathering foray to prepare for the future. In 1974 the unit would officially change its name to the ***Escadron Special D'Intervention*** (***Speciaal Interventie Eskadron*** in Flemish) though the title of "Diane Group" would stay with the force for many years--to this day, the Belgian press refers to the units as Diane rather than ESI; in 1980, after a major reorganization, the unit was brought to full strength of approximately 200 operators. As its catch-phrase, the ESI would adopt ***l'Intervention, l'Observation et l'Appui***--Intervention, Observation and Support.

From its inception and then through its manifestation as the ESI, the unit assumed a far-reaching, active, and sensitive security role inside Belgium. ESI operators were immediately despatched to Brussels International Airport to secure incoming and outgoing El Al flights, forward bases were set up around embassies and other sensitive installations belonging to foreign governments and agencies--especially those belonging to the Japanese (target of the Red Army), Germans (targets of the Baader-Meinhof Gang), British (the Irish Republican Army), and, of course, Israeli and Jewish facilities. As the home seat to the North Atlantic Treaty Organization (NATO), Brussels was also at the epicenter of the Warsaw Pact's espionage campaign against the west and, as a result, state-sponsored terrorist activity as well. The Ministry of Defense, at the time in command of the ESI, opted to take an aggressive approach to counter-terrorism--almost an offensive stance. The ESI would not sit in its barracks and react like many of the other units throughout Europe. It would initiate and orchestrate. It would let the bad guy know they were out there and if "they" wanted an engagement they would get it.

By its very mandate, the ESI is the national hostage-rescue unit tasked with all such situations, and all heavy tactical situations inside the country and outside, as well. Although several reports list the nation's special forces element, the 1st Para-Commando Regiment, as the unit that would be tasked to liberate hostages abroad should a Belgian aircraft or ship be seized, it is believed that this army force is only deployed to rescue and evacuate large numbers of Belgian nationals overseas. If a Sabena aircraft should be hijacked, for example, to a Middle East nation or somewhere in Africa, the Para-Commandos might secure the airfield or an operational perimeter, but the actual entry and rescue would belong to the ESI; the Para-Commandos are not believed trained in this aspect of special warfare. Although not specifically trained in bomb-disposal and other EOD work (there is a national bomb disposal unit, the ***Service d'Enlevement et de Destruction des Engins Explosifs***) the ESI is called to supervise and secure bomb sites. The ESI also works very closely with the national domestic counter-terrorist and counter-espionage service, the CBO, as well as with other Belgian intelligence and security organizations.[1]

Over the last twenty years, since their inception, the ESI has performed hundreds (if not thousands) of jobs--ranging from the routine (such as intelligence and reconnaissance) to pro-active (assaulting terrorist safe-houses). While security restrictions prevent the publication of many of its missions against a whole host of terrorist groups using Belgium as either a staging point for attacks in Western Europe, or preparing to attack targets inside Belgium, there is one classic example of the ESI putting to practice its motto of ***l'Intervention, l'Observation et l'Appui.*** In December 1990, a week before Princess Diana of Great Britain was scheduled to arrive in Brussels, the ESI, operating together with Great Britain's Scotland Yard Special Branch and MI5, assaulted an Provisional IRA safe-house in Antwerp. The house was well fortified and patrolled by the terrorists, but the ESI task force was able to slink its way into the area unnoticed and then assault the safe-house in a split-second raid. Four terrorists were apprehended and several dozen kilograms of high-explosives, AK-47s, sniper weapons, shotguns, pistols and revolvers, and hundreds of rounds of ammunition. Undoubtedly, the life of the princess was saved.

Although trained to encounter, defeat and overcome all odds against the most determined, vicious and heavily armed terrorists, increasingly the ESI has found too many of its work combating the rising tide of violent crime sweeping through much of Europe--much it originating in the shambles of the former Soviet Union. In 1993 alone, the ESI spent nearly 20,000 man hours involved in combating organized crime; nearly 7,000 man hours in fighting narcotics trafficking; nearly 2,000 man hours in fighting kidnapping, hostage-taking and extortion; 1,500 man hours in transferring dangerous criminals and terrorists (including dangerous criminals who have escaped to the four corners of the globe, such as the notorious--and extremely dangerous--Patrick Haemers, brought back to Belgium from Brazil in a complex and very sensitive military operation); and, only 1,000 hours on true counter-terrorism work.

Some anti-crime operations are routine--supporting the police on dangerous warrants being served and safe-guarding a prisoner (one deemed highly sensitive either due to the nature of his crime or chances that he will either be attacked or even be an escape risk). Other ESI anti-crime operations aren't so ordinary. One "job," typical of the mission, the mandate and the unit, took place in Morstel, near Antwerp, on April 30, 1990. At 8:40 A.M., two armed men, with enough ammunition to wage a small war, entered a bank in the center of town and announced a holdup--anyone who resisted would be shot dead. A silent alarm alerted police units who, by 10:00 A.M. had already requested assistance from the ESI. Within an hour, an assault team had arrived from Brussels complete with electronic monitoring equipment, the tools to make a forced entry and the usual tools of the trade--MP5s, 12-gauge shotguns and sniper weapons. A collapsible ballistic shield was removed from the supply truck and assembled outside the rear-door. Through a small slot (usually used for aiming one's MP5), the ESI commander on the scene, a lieutenant, attempted to negotiate with the gunmen, though the perpetrators were not in a talking mood. At 2:45 P.M. the ESI struck. Explosives were used to blow the door off their hinges and through a cloud of blinding smoke, entry afforded into the building. Within seconds, the failed bank robbers were isolated, subdued and handcuffed. Mission accomplished.

Perhaps more than any other counter-terrorist and hostage-rescue force in the world, the ESI makes ***maximum*** use of its K-9 force. Here, during a search for a violent perpetrator, an ESI operator in full kit prepares to unleash his partner--a Belgian Malinois. (Courtesy: Lieutenant Eddy Huybens/Gendarmerie Public Relations Office)

The ESI's Order of Battle is as follows:

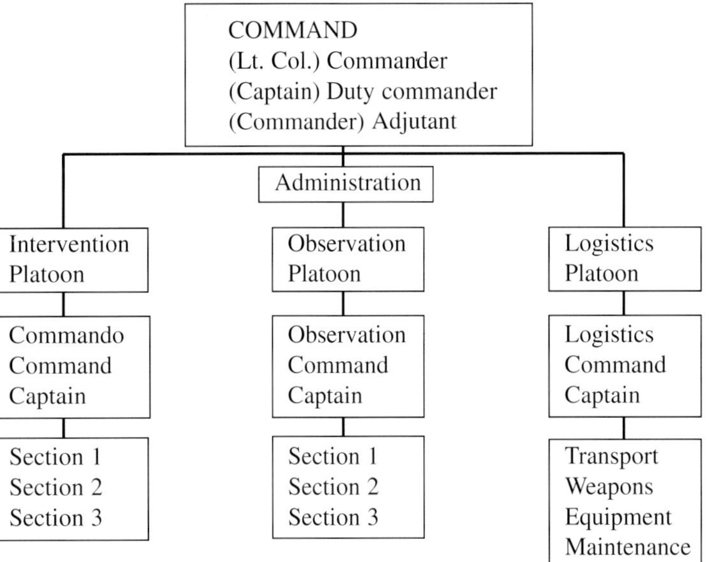


In the late 1980s, however, the need came about to expand the ESI--it was overworked and unable to meet the intense workload

During actual "jobs," under the most difficult entry conditions, dogs (Belgian Malinois) accompany ESI operators everywhere. Here, during an actual entry into a second-story window, an operator prepares to fire his Browning 9mm automatic while carrying his Belgian Malinois secured on a back harness. (Courtesy: Lieutenant Eddy Huybens/Gendarmerie Public Relations Office)

caused by its increasing involvement in the rising tide of crime sweeping across Belgium and Western Europe. As a result, the Gendarmerie created five territorial units that can best be likened to an American SWAT and tactical narcotics unit. Called POSAs (the French acronym for **P**rotection, **O**bservation, **S**outien and **A**rrestion), the units were stationed among the five Gendarmerie headquarters in Brussels, Liège, Charleroi, Gand, and Anvers.

Service in the ESI is considered a privilege and is strictly voluntary. Those wishing to become operators must first endure the tortures of a lengthy qualification course where they are subjected to a grueling physical and psychological examination. The purpose of the torture, as operators call the period, is not to see who runs the fastest, carries the most and can endure the most, but those who can translate mind over pain, and will over physical limitations. Counter-terrorist skills can be learned, bodies honed up and abilities improved--mental capacities, however, attitude and motivation cannot be taught in the classroom, on the rifle range or in the field. The selection process lasts two weeks with an attrition rate of nearly 50%. ESI training, the course that transforms the volunteer into a full-fledged operator lasts three months. Among the specialist qualifications and course available for ESI operators are: (1) combat medic; (2) explosives; (3) marksmanship shooting; (4) operational--combat--shooting; (5) weapons instructor; (6) negotiator; (7) bodyguard and VIP protection; (8) oxygen intervention diver; (9) B-Class parachutist [taught with Para-Commando regiment]; (10) B-Class Commando [taught with Para-Commando regiment]; (11) Alpine-qualified operational climber; (12) Master ropesman; (13) Defense and Evasive driving; (14) radioman; (15) combat fitness; (16) motorcyclist; (17) camouflage and concealment. Females are permitted to be operating members of ESI, but are used solely for observation and undercover work.

Taking aim behind a tree-trunk, an ESI operator peers down the sights to his Remington 870 12-gauge shotgun fitted with flash-light. (Courtesy: Lieutenant Eddy Huybens/Gendarmerie Public Relations Office)

ESI's closest foreign contact, in terms of exchanging ideas and personnel as well as joint and cross training, is obviously in France and the GIGN and RAID units. Since the language barrier is non-existent, both units are allowed to cooperate freely and unhindered. To the same extent, the ESI enjoys a unique close working relationship with the Dutch BBE. The ESI also maintains close working ties to Germany's GSG-9 and various SEKs, as well Spain's GEO, Italy's GIS and NOCs, and the Moroccan secret service. Ties have also been established with American units, including the FBI HRT, and the U.S. Army's 1st SFOD; in fact, Delta has visited with the ESI on numerous occasions--especially during annual CTCs (counter-terrorist competitions).

The primary weapon deployed by ESI operators is, of course, the Heckler and Koch family of MP5 9mm submachine guns, and FN 9mm automatics; interestingly enough, the unit has begun to use the Glock Model 17 9mm automatic as well as a special--and quite mysterious--Glock underwater naval special warfare pistol. The sniper rifles include a self-designed 7.62mm police sniper rifle, and the Finnish Sako TRG-21 7.62mm sniping rifle.

ESI vehicles include 4x4 Range Rovers; armored intervention trucks; a special SCUBA equipment truck; unmarked sedans and vans for use in undercover work, armored sedans and CAT cars for VIP work; tracking and pursuit vehicles (mainly Mercedes sedans); observation vehicles and electronic surveillance vans; various types of motorcycles; and, for naval special warfare tasks, Zodiac rubber inflatable crafts. It should be noted that ESI personnel are trained to carry out daring high-speed pursuits and chases, as well as taught how to drive at extremely high-speeds and through adverse road and climactic conditions in order to reach an incident quickly. ESI personnel are also taught how to use their vehicles as ramming devices and how to break through a roadblock of other vehicles or obstacles and inflict the "least" amount of damage as possible to their vehicles. According to one French GIGN officer, "The best drivers in Europe can be found in Belgium and in the ESI."

[1] Some written accounts have claimed that the ESI is backed by the GRT (***Grupe de Repression du Terrorisme***) of the "so-called" Judiciary Police; the GRT, it is alleged, is a plain-clothed anti-terrorist unit coordinating all anti-terrorist activities in Belgium. ESI and CBO officials claim such accounts to be nothing more than the figment of one's imagination.

Wearing civilian mountain hiking boots and carrying powerful portable flash-light devices, a four-man ESI assault troop prepares to storm a suspected terrorist safe-house near Brussels. (Courtesy: Lieutenant Eddy Huybens/Gendarmerie Public Relations Office)

Surrender is a good idea! Once the door is breached, the awaiting sight of ESI operators holding weapons drawn and a "hungry" Belgian Malinois is enough to convince even the most fanatic terrorist that the only option is unconditional surrender. (Courtesy: Lieutenant Eddy Huybens/Gendarmerie Public Relations Office)

Excellent close-up view of the ESI battle-harness as worn by an operators leading an assault with his Remington 870 12-gauge shotgun. Note mid-section holster for 9mm Browning automatic. (Courtesy: Lieutenant Eddy Huybens/Gendarmerie Public Relations Office)

During an impromptu live-fire practice, ESI operators take aim with their Heckler and Koch MP5 A2 9mm submachine guns fitted with optical sights. (Courtesy: Lieutenant Eddy Huybens/Gendarmerie Public Relations Office)

.A group photograph of an eight man ESI section along with their faithful K-9 support. Photograph shows, to advantage, the ESI service uniform, load bearing equipment, and black nylon balaclava. (Courtesy: Lieutenant Eddy Huybens/Gendarmerie Public Relations Office)

Also SCUBA trained and as proficient a naval special warfare force as can be found anywhere in Europe, a four-man ESI team races toward a riverine objective near Antwerp courtesy of a Zodiac rubber inflatable. Note special CT scuba suits worn. (Courtesy: Lieutenant Eddy Huybens/Gendarmerie Public Relations Office)

During riverine insertion exercises, ESI operators are lowered down to a small river boat courtesy of a Gendarmerie Aérospatiale SA.330 Puma helicopter. Many ESI operators are airborne qualified, as well. (Courtesy: Lieutenant Eddy Huybens/Gendarmerie Public Relations Office)

.Experts in VIP security, ESI operators are thanked by one of their charges--his holiness, Pope John Paul II. (Courtesy: Lieutenant Eddy Huybens/Gendarmerie Public Relations Office)

.ESI operators engage in cross-country skiing--the unit is expert in all forms of winter warfare and mountain warfare. (Courtesy: Lieutenant Eddy Huybens/Gendarmerie Public Relations Office)

During open-sea exercises, an ESI operator is lowered to the deck of a Belgian Navy ship during exercises in the Atlantic. Increasingly, the ESI has been used against heavy armed narcotics smugglers who uses Antwerp as a gateway for all of northern Europe. (Courtesy: Lieutenant Eddy Huybens/Gendarmerie Public Relations Office)

The long barrel Smith and Wesson .38 special revolver--a favorite close-quarter ESI personal side-arm. (Courtesy: Lieutenant Eddy Huybens/Gendarmerie Public Relations Office)

The Heckler and Koch 9mm Model 94 submachine gun. (Courtesy: Lieutenant Eddy Huybens/Gendarmerie Public Relations Office)

The ESI's "flash bang." (Courtesy: Lieutenant Eddy Huybens/Gendarmerie Public Relations Office)

A modified "flash bang" with the added CN tear-gas element. (Courtesy: Lieutenant Eddy Huybens/Gendarmerie Public Relations Office)

Another ESI favorite--the Heckler and Koch MZP-1 40mm multi-purpose pistol. (Courtesy: Lieutenant Eddy Huybens/Gendarmerie Public Relations Office)

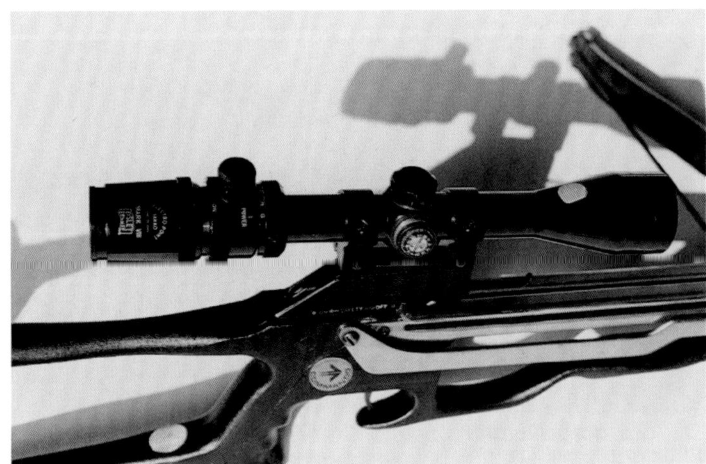

A Commando crossbow--used by the ESI in special cases. (Courtesy: Lieutenant Eddy Huybens/Gendarmerie Public Relations Office)

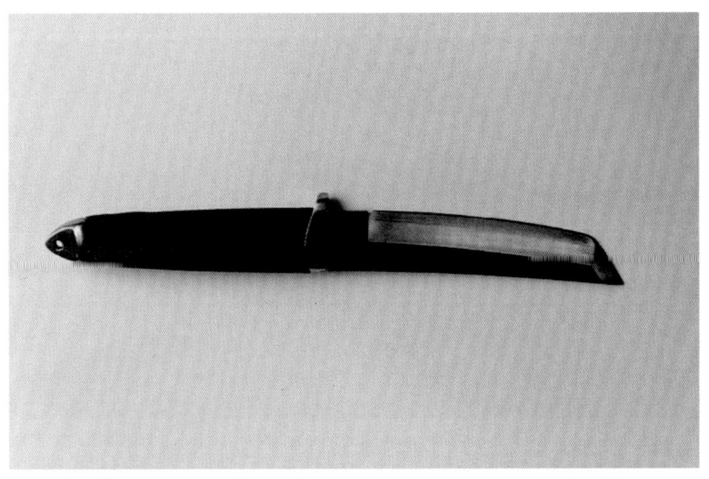

The Tanto razor knife, a Japanese-made close-quarter killing tool ordered by the ESI from a company in California. (Courtesy: Lieutenant Eddy Huybens/Gendarmerie Public Relations Office)

# Denmark

Since the outbreak of the great international terrorist revolution in 1968, many terrorists organizations, from Ahmed Jibril's Popular Front for the Liberation of Palestine General Command (PFLP-GC) to the Red Army Faction in Germany, have used Scandinavia as a convenient staging ground for mounting their operations and attacks against northwestern Europe. Scandinavia, with its liberal societies, was an easy place for a terrorist cell to operate in, as well as for wanted operatives to disappear by blending into immigrant communities; some Western intelligence officials have even said that because of Scandinavian women owning a reputation as being liberal, left-wing and sexually attracted to Middle Easterners, the region has been a fertile recruiting ground for unwitting terrorist operatives. Denmark, considered one of the strictest Scandinavian governments in terms of law-enforcement and internal security, has been spared much of the terrorist activity that plagued Norway in the 1970's and Sweden in the late 1980's[1] with very few reported incidents. Part of this "hands-off" policy is as a result of the reputation of Danish special forces, and its police counter-terrorist unit.

The ***Rigspolitichefen***, or national police, created a national counter-terrorist hostage rescue unit in 1973 in the wake of the disastrous attempt by the Bavarian police to rescue the Israeli athletes at Fürstenfeldbrük Airport. Called the ***Politiets Efterretningstjeneste***, or PET as it is affectionately known in Denmark, the unit is a small force of approximately 100 operators dispersed throughout the nation and is responsible for most police "heavy action" tactical situations, most counter-terrorist assaults (attacking safe-houses or executing warrants on dangerous criminals or terrorists) and most hostage-rescue scenarios. Because the Danes are extremely security conscience, very little information has been released on the unit, including its exact size, true mandate, and its weapons and equipment. It is known from German, Norwegian and British sources that the unit has trained with GSG-9 and various other German SEKs, as well as Norway's Deltatroppen and Scotland Yard's SO13 counter-terrorist unit and its SO19 heavy firearms squad. It is known that their principal weapon is the Heckler and Koch MP5A3 9m submachine gun and the Austrian Glock 19 9mm pistol.

The handling of very sensitive terrorist incidents, including (it is believed), hijackings of SAS flights at Copenhagen's Kastrup International Airport (as well as hijacking of SAS aircraft originating out of Denmark with primarily Danish hostages) would fall with the Danish Army's elite Ranger element--the ***Jægerkorpset***. For years, Denmark enjoyed a unique strategic importance to NATO's overall defensive plans for safeguarding western Europe from Soviet attack--especially in controlling the strategic waterways connecting the Baltic to the North Sea and its ocean junctions--and the ***Jægerkorpset*** was an instrumental element of that defensive--and offensive--capability. Expert in small unit reconnaissance assignments and airborne infiltration, ***Jægerkorpset*** operators are also trained in urban combat and hostage-rescue assignments; much of this training is conducted with GSG-9, the 22nd Special Air Service Regiment, Swedish Rangers, Norwegian Jäegers and U.S. Special Forces (including the 1st Special Forces Operation Detachment-Delta). The unit's main weapons are the Heckler and Koch MP5 (primarily the MP5SD2 and the MP5SD3) and the Swedish "K" 9mm submachine gun--the primary sniper weapon being the PSG-1 7.62mm rifle. During counter-terrorist operation exercises, ***Jægerkorpset*** teams are known to parachute (both static line and HALO) toward the objective courtesy of Royal Danish Air Force C-130s or CH-47s, to establish immediate perimeters around an objective, and then attack it with stealth and single-shot accuracy.

Maritime counter-terrorism is believed to be the responsibility of the Royal Danish Navy's special warfare unit, the ***Frømandskorpsets***. As Denmark's sea-faring heritage is a rich one, and the nation's many islands and inlets surrounded by water, it is highly probable that any potential terrorist strike would be one targeting a Danish ship, ferry or oil rig. The ***Frømandskorpsets***, considered to be one of the final naval special warfare units in Europe, has trained since the early 1980s to counter any terrorist strike along the Danish coast or to rescue hostages aboard any seaborne vessel or platform. Considered highly effective ground warriors, ***Frømandskorpsets*** combat swimmers are able to reach their objectives via Klepper canoes, motorized inflatables, submarine and via airborne means, such as modified MD500 special operations choppers and CH-47s; once on the ground, the unit is more than capable to meet any challenge and quickly neutralize all opposition. ***Frømandskorpsets*** combat swimmers have studied past

A two-man ***Jægerkorpset*** sniper team, both armed with the reliable Heckler and Koch PSG-1 7.62mm sniper rifle, select targets during hostage-rescue maneuvers near Copenhagen's Kastrup International Airport. (Courtesy: Headquarters, Chief of Defense--Denmark)

Two ***Jægerkorpset*** operators, wearing their "uncharacteristic" black coveralls, Protec helmet and gas mask/visor combination, prepare to deploy from MD500 modified special operations choppers during hostage-rescue exercises in the northern part of the country. (Courtesy: Headquarters, Chief of Defense--Denmark)

maritime incidents, such as the October 1985 ***Achille Lauro*** seajacking, and have trained together with SEAL Team SIX, SBS "M" Squadron and "Black" Troop, and Norway's ***Marinejegerlags***.

Recent reports indicate that the Royal Danish Ministry of Defense is considering the creation of a special military anti-terrorist force, similar in scope to the U.S. Army's 1st SFOD-D that would assume sole responsibility for handling all major terrorist incidents against Danish soil and Danish citizens.

[1] For many years, from 1980-92, Stockholm was considered the "Palestinian Station" in northern Europe.

A two-man ***Jægerkorpset*** team displays its insertion and extraction skills and capabilities on the landing skids of a MD500 Little Bird. During demonstrations for visiting special forces units, ***Jægerkorpset*** personnel have been known to cling from a MD500 while firing their MP5s at moving targets--scoring virtual bulls-eyes on all shots! (Courtesy: Headquarters, Chief of Defense--Denmark)

A ***Frømandskorpsets*** operator, emerges from the sea to slowly climb aboard a freighter harboring--for the sake of the photographed exercises--terrorists attempting to land illegally from the Middle East. Note the Swedish "K" special operations 9mm submachine gun. (Courtesy: Headquarters, Chief of Defense--Denmark)

Slicing their way through the North Sea surf, two ***Frømandskorpsets*** combat swimmers approach a target courtesy of a Klepper canoe. The ***Frømandskorpsets***' legendary infiltration capabilities make their counter-terrorist capabilities, especially in stealth-like surprise assaults, most effective. (Courtesy: Headquarters, Chief of Defense--Denmark)

# Finland

***A terrible blizzard has engulfed Helsinki's Helsinki-Vantaa International Airport, and air traffic has been brought to a halt. Activity on the runway, however, is brisk and running at a fever's pace. Terrorists on board a Finnair DC-10 are threatening to kill all 200 men, women and children on board unless their demands are met. The Finnish authorities commence negotiations, but the "A" Plan is about to be executed. Under the guise of preparing the aircraft for imminent flight--a hint that the government will capitulate--floodlights are brought to the remote corner of the tarmac in order to allow the crews to fill the tanks with jet fuel, and perform routine maintenance. The lights blind all those inside, and is the cover needed for twenty men, all wearing white coveralls and clutching Glock 17 9mm automatics, to ski in sprinter's speed to the aircraft. In a well-choreographed display of synchronization, they remove their skis and gain entry into the aircraft courtesy of a trap door worked open; white balaclavas are drawn across the faces protecting their identities and faces from detection and the sub-zero chill. Within thirty-five seconds ten men are inside, ten waiting under the aircraft with ladders, rubberized so they won't go clank when placed against the fuselage and painted white to blend in with the snowy surroundings. Power is turned off and the signal to attack is given. There are four terrorists in all, and within forty seconds, there are four dead terrorists. Ambulances race toward the aircraft and chutes bring the frightened hostages to their freedom.***

At the "Bear Force" training facility near Helsinki Airport, operators endure the daily menace of the obstacle course. (***Helsingen Poliisilaitos***)

***This bone-chilling display was just that--a show: the dead terrorists were mannequins, though they were peppered with live ammunition (the hostages were Helsinki cops). It was an exercise meant to show Finland's readiness in meeting any terrorist threat. And, the onlooking government officials looking would observe, the men of "Bear Force, "put on a damn impressive show.***

In 1972 and in response to the Munich Olympic debacle, the Helsinki Police (***Helsingen Poliisilaitos***) created an intervention squad known by the acronym of ETY. The force was a small unit, twelve officers in all, and centered on marksman as opposed to strike squads capable of storming a particular location. Under control of the Ministry of the Interior, the unit was under the command of an officer attached to headquarters and who could summon the volunteers from their routine police duties throughout the city--and the country--whenever needed. In 1975, however, as terrorist attacks throughout Europe escalated at an alarming rate, the ***Helsingen Poliisilaitos*** opted to created a fully mobilized force whose sole task was counter-terrorism and rescue. It would adopt the name ***Osasto Karhusta*** ("Bear Force") and would be officially sanctioned in 1978 and include approximately forty policemen; the unit was divided into three ten-man teams and commanded by a police inspector.

Known for their expert wilderness and cold-weather skills, the "Bear Force" would obviously draw officers with varied military and outdoorsman skills; virtually all officers who have served in the unit are expert skiers, skaters, and swimmers and the "Bear Force," with its limited means and size when compared to other units, is a truly all-weather all-terrain intervention force. "Bear Force" is a purely volunteer unit, with a stringent selection process and training that lasts for fifteen weeks. The unit deploys primarily from Swedish-built Saab 900 sedans and Volkswagen mini-vans, although a Finnish Air Force Bell-212 chopper stands at the ready on on-call status twenty-four-hours-a-day, seven days a week, 365 days a year.

"Bear Force" operators carry either the Smith and Wesson .357 Magnum revolver or the Glock Model 17 9mm automatic as the personal side-arm, and the primary assault weapon is the Heckler and Koch MP5 family of 9mm submachine guns. The unit carries indigenous 12-gauge shotguns and the primary sniper weapon is the Heckler and Koch PSG-1 7.62mm rifle, though officers have been known to bring their own hunting rifles to the range and request to deploy them in the field.

"Bear Force" maintains it closest links to the newly created intervention units in Latvia, Lithuania and Estonia (units which are now trained by the Israelis), though has trained with GSG-9, Norway's ***Deltatroppen***, and the Russian Spetsnaz. Senior Finnish police officers, including commanders of the "Bear Force," have visited the United States and toured several large municipal SWAT and Emergency Response units.

A "Bear Force" instructor prepares to rappel down a menacing 200-foot high tower. Expert ropesmen and climbers, "Bear Force" operators like to boast that there isn't a hill, valley, building or obstacle that they cannot overcome. (***Helsingen Poliisilaitos***)

During tactical training, a "Bear Force" point-man carrying a Body Bunker shield prepares to toss a flash-bang grenade into a room. Note bright blue wind-breaker coveralls, and indigenously produced body armor worn. (***Helsingen Poliisilaitos***)

Explosive entry--"Bear Force" style. (***Helsingen Poliisilaitos***)

"Bear Force" personnel take great pride in their martial arts skills and prowess, and enjoy breaking it up with fists and clubs wherever and whenever possible. (***Helsingen Poliisilaitos***)

The back-to-back approach of purifying a room. A two-man assault team, one carrying a Glock and the other a .357 Magnum, take aim in full battle kit. (***Helsingen Poliisilaitos***)

During snow condition maneuvers (a nearly year round occurrence in Finland), operators fast-rope from a Bell-212. (***Helsingen Poliisilaitos***)

# France

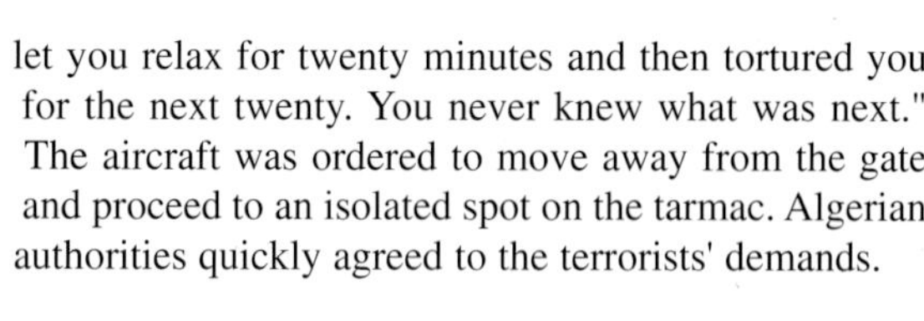

The GIGN patch.

It was supposed to have been a quiet Christmas for the men of the ***Groupe d'Intervention Gendarmerie Nationale***, the elite French counter-terrorist unit better known by the acronym of GIGN. Saturday morning, December 24, 1994, brought cool weather to the town of Satory, just south of Paris and home to the GIGN, and the operators spent the early morning hours attending to last minute shopping, and packing their gear for the holiday leave. The barracks were decorated in an elaborate Christmas array of lights, though the glitter could not hide the military atmosphere that permeated throughout the facility. The commander of the unit, Major Denis Favier, looked through his roster to keep on hand a skeleton staff and everyone else would be allowed to go home; after all, every operator carried electronic pagers and in case of emergency could be summoned back to base in a matter of hour. There was also always a fifteen-man force ready, geared up and available for any emergency. The thoughts at Satory centered more on Christmas dinner than any new developments in the Middle East or Bosnia, but one ear was always glued to the radio. The call to cancel holiday leaves and assemble the unit came at 11:30 A.M.

Thirty minutes earlier, on the tarmac at Algiers Houari-Boumediene International Airport, Air France flight 8969, was about to commence its taxi from the gate toward its take-off position on the runway, and the two hour flight to Orly Airport in Paris. The A300 Airbus was full this Saturday morning, loaded with 227 passengers and twelve crewpersons; many of the passengers were women and children, French nationals, ordered by their husbands to escape the Algerian civil strife. At 11:00 A.M., four young men wearing blue coveralls with Air Algérie identification badges boarded the aircraft. They told the bewildered flight crew that they were security, and proceeded to check the passports of the passengers already secure in their seatbelts. The inspection proceeded quickly, but brusquely ended when they closed the cabin's doors and shouted ***"Allahu Akbar!"*** They produced AK-47 assault rifles and pistols and indicated that the aircraft was being hijacked by the "GIA," the Armed Islamic Group--Algeria's most militant fundamentalist guerrilla organization. The four gunmen, proudly proclaiming to their hostages that they were ready to die, began to terrorizing the passengers, promising that anyone who didn't cooperate would be killed instantly. "The terrorists had a sadistic art form to their madness", claimed one hostage to French TV, "they let you relax for twenty minutes and then tortured you for the next twenty. You never knew what was next." The aircraft was ordered to move away from the gate and proceed to an isolated spot on the tarmac. Algerian authorities quickly agreed to the terrorists' demands.

Already by 12:00 A.M. that Saturday morning, Major Denis Favier had spoken to the French Defense Minister and Transportation Minister. He had summoned all of his men who were on leave, and ordered those still in barracks to ready their gear for a quick ride to a military airfield outside of Paris. It was obvious to Major Favier and his command staff that this hijacking would end violently and probably with GIGN intervention. After all, the unit had studied the internal strife inside Algeria with great interest, they had read about the tremendous death toll inflicted against the secular and foreign population by Moslem radicals, and they had read intelligence reports warning about a possible spill over of Islamic violence into France; they had already encountered elements of this underground in Paris a month earlier during a massive police sweep. Most importantly, they knew only too well that these men were fanatics, eager to kill and willing to die.

Leaving a skeleton staff inside France, Major Favier assembled his best operators and quickly arranged for Air France to avail an Airbus A300 aircraft that would fly the unit to the Spanish island of Palma de Mallorca, within earshot of Algiers, just in case immediate GIGN response was required. While on the aircraft, also ferrying DST agents to Palma de Mallorca, the GIGN operators studied the blueprints of the aircraft, its unique characteristics, possible locations where the terrorists might hide explosives, and possible places where terrorists might hide aboard the aircraft once stormed. Throughout the ninety minute flight to the sunny shores of Palma de Mallorca, the

A GIGN sniper team gazes across a valley during take-down exercises in southern France. The sniper is armed with the FR-F2 7.62mm sniping weapon--the mainstay of French military and police marksmen. (Courtesy: SIRPA Gendarmerie)

A GIGN operator poses with his "puppy" outside the unit's home base of Satory, near Paris prior to an exercise. Note the unit's renown blue overalls, indigenously produced assault vest and Kevlar ballistic helmet with visor. Note parachutist wings worn proudly above right breast pocket in typical French manner. (Courtesy: SIRPA Gendarmerie)

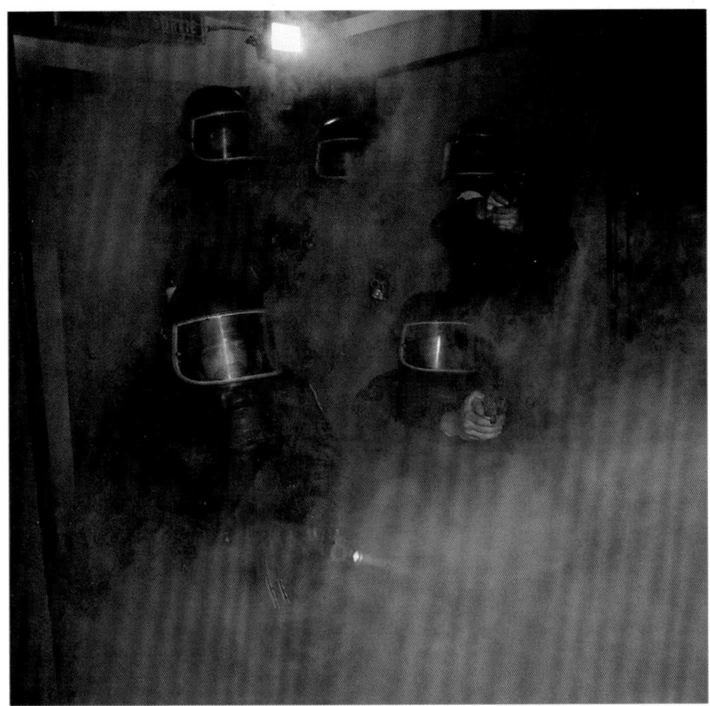

During live-fire exercises inside the GIGN "Shooting House" in Satory, operators storm a room after hurling in three Type 46 flash bang grenades. They are armed with MP5s and MR 73 .357 revolvers--all equipped with laser aim-point devices. (Courtesy: SIRPA Gendarmerie)

Two GIGN operators prepare to fast rope down the side of a three-story building during exterior entry exercises. Note black balaclavas worn for identity concealment. (Courtesy: SIRPA Gendarmerie)

GIGN operators studied intelligence reports faxed to them in mid-air, listened to the ongoing events via radio from Algiers, and checked their gear time and time again, careful not to forget any bit of their equipment and weaponry.

On the tarmac at a military section of Palma de Mallorca airport the GIGN operators established a secluded command post and deployment staging area. Most of the operators had a gut feeling that the Algerian authorities did not want to act militarily against the aircraft, or unleash Algerian special forces in a rescue bid. The GIGN officers believed that the Algerians were hoping that the incident would either end peacefully (nineteen people had already been released, after all) or move to another jurisdiction. In the meantime, the operators trained and honed their tubular assault skills. Vehicles with built-in ramps were raced toward the fuselage away from view, and then operators raced up the improvised stairways with Matra Defense .357 MR 73 Manurhin Type Gendarmerie pistols in hand. During the exercises, as Major Favier stood on the tarmac with a digital stopwatch in one hand and a cellular phone in the other, he received word that the terrorists had killed two hostages and dumped their bodies on the runway--one of the murdered hostages was an off-duty Algerian policeman on the flight, and the other was a Vietnamese national. The GIGN task force trained harder after learning of the sobering developments. It was certain to virtually every operator in the field that they would be the ones that would bring about a resolution to the crisis; after all, it was a French aircraft that had been seized. Most thought that the rescue would take place in Algiers, and specs on Houari-Boumediene International Airport were rushed to Palma de Mallorca.

Christmas day, December 25, brought hope and heartache. At 02:00 hours, the terrorists released more women and children, and at 08:15 hours they issued demands--the release of two leaders from the banned Islamic Salvation Front--but over twelve hours later they shot and killed a French embassy staffer and his body, too, was thrown on the tarmac in a gruesome act of indignity. The killing of the French citizen was the straw that broke the camel's back for the Ministry of Defense in Paris--if something wasn't done soon, the hijackers were likely to blow up the aircraft and everyone on board. The French informed the Algerians that they were preparing to deploy their commandos for a rescue raid no matter what the status of the negotiations, but Algerian authorities resisted. The Armed Islamic Group, the most militant of the Algerian fundamentalists, had been waging a war since 1992 to eliminate foreign and non-Islamic influence from Algerian society. Should the French, with their historic ties to local hatred and resentment, send soldiers to Algerian soil and be permitted to kill Algerian "holy warriors," a new age of explosive Islamic nationalism would engulf an already volatile situation. Algerian authorities, looking for an exit, offered the hijackers permission to fly the aircraft out of the country. The hijackers chose France as their destination. The GIGN was relieved. At 02:00 hours on the morning of December 26, 1994, AF 8969 took off from Algiers destined for Marignane airport twenty-five miles north of Marseilles, ostensibly for a refueling stop, with 172 hostages on board.

An aircraft hijacking is a remarkable phenomenon in its ability to bring about a mobilized emergency response army awaiting a peaceful conclusion or a bloody mess. Hospitals in Marseilles were readied for combat conditions, fire engines surrounded the aircraft fearing a dynamite blast and possible run-off to other aircraft at the field, and hostage negotiators were called upon to open a dialog and line of trust with the hijackers, trying to stall and comfort, while attempting to gain the release of as many hostages as they could possibly bargain for. More hostages were released--mainly elderly women--and food was brought on board, but the young hijackers were erratic in their demands and uncannily brutal in their treatment of the hostages. They rambled about the Armed Islamic Group, and about the joys of paradise. Ominously, they also demanded that the aircraft be fueled so that they could fly to Paris. This demand was the red flag the French authorities feared and that the GIGN knew would bring them into action. In a hijacking, a group whose demands are not precise or attainable will usually settle for the promise of safe passage or a few

A GIGN sniper poses for the camera wearing his specially-constructed black sniper coverall, French-built assault vest and pouch, and harness for fast-roping to his perch. He carries the FR-F1 sniper rifle. (Courtesy: SIRPA Gendarmerie)

During heliborne insertion training, a GIGN operator fast-ropes from an Army Aérospatiale SA319B Alouette III chopper. (Courtesy: SIRPA Gendarmerie)

token political gestures in exchange for the release of the hostages. They rarely ask for permission to refuel in order to fly to another destination in the same country--its an act of desperation and delay that simply means that the hijackers or suicidal zealots have yet to reach their final and ultimate objective. French counter-intelligence and counter-terrorist officials, realizing that the terrorists had explosives rigged to the cockpit, now feared that the hijackers were planning to crash the aircraft into Paris. AF 8969 would not be allowed to take-off.

From the moment the airbus touched-down at Marseilles, French authorities had succeeded in maintaining a dialog with the terrorists (via the pilot and co-pilot acting as intermediaries), but as timed dragged on the communications became less substantive and highly erratic. Twelve hours after the aircraft touched down on French soil, at 15:30 hours, the hijackers released two additional elderly hostages, but then stopped communicating altogether. The last radio contact was at 16:50 hours. Ten minutes later, GIGN was authorized to move in. "Assaulting a hijacked airliner is an art form," claims one German GSG-9 officer who had literally wrote the manual in aircraft assaults, "the greater the rescue the more the masterpiece will be appreciated in the years to follow." Units like GIGN train for this scenario for years without ever having the chance to pull it off. Major Denis Favier now had ten minutes to ready his men for their assault and opportunity to make history. Forty men would carry out the assault. A sniper team was positioned in the control tower peering directly inside the cockpit.

Reaching the aircraft was not the difficulty for the GIGN operators--entering it was. In fact, they had been in and around the aircraft all day. It is believed that a GIGN operator had managed to slink his way on board the aircraft courtesy of the front landing gear and had planted eaves-dropping devices so that officers in the CP could monitor developments inside the aircraft. During the day, as the negotiations continued, GIGN operators donned airport uniforms to gain closer access to the aircraft--they posed as caterers to bring food on board the plane, and as mechanics to check on the plane's fuel and hydraulic levels; GIGN operators even cleaned out the overstuffed toilets and vacuum the carpeted floor. They planted microphones and high-tech monitoring devices to track the terrorists throughout the aircraft. These were small necessary steps to lay the groundwork for a rescue assault. When it was time to go, the effort would be a massive one. Pulling down the black balaclavas over their heads, the assault force split into two approaching the A300 Airbus from the tail section. Twenty-five operators positioned themselves on the tarmac underneath the aircraft, and fifteen slowly began climbing a mobile staircase that had been left near the front right door of the aircraft. The plan called for the operators to slowly open the door and then hurl a stun device inside the passageway leading to the cockpit. Once the device would detonate, half the operators would move in for the assault on the terrorists inside the cockpit, while the remaining commandos would purify the aircraft of any potential terrorists lingering in the rear of the plane, initiate activation of the aircraft's emergency chutes, and evacuate the hostages. In maneuvers, when such assaults were practiced on "borrowed" aircraft from Air France or Air Inter, the assault should take no longer than ninety seconds from moment of entry until the aircraft is deemed secured. Training is often realistic but never mirrored accurately in the field under a hail of gunfire. Training is never carried live on French TV (on channels TF1 and LCI) as this drama was, and innocent lives are never at risk during an exercise.

"DO NOT CARJACK IN FRANCE!" At the Les Mans speedway, GIGN operators train in deploying tactically from a speeding vehicle and motorcycle to thwart a kidnapping or car-jacking; or, to apprehend a terrorist suspect. (Courtesy: SIRPA Gendarmerie)

As the operators moved in for the assault awaiting Major Denis Favier's signal to attack, one of the hijackers slid open a cockpit window and began firing upon the control tower with a full auto burst from his AK-47 7.62mm assault rifle shattering the tower's windows. Interior Minister Pasqua gave the GIGN a green light, and Major Favier ordered the operators inside after receiving a signal from the pilot that all four terrorists, known by the coded term "Tangos," were in or around the cockpit. The open cockpit window afforded the point operator an interesting option. Instead of losing the element of surprise by forcing the door open, charging in and hurling a stun device inside, the officer tried to pitch the flash bang through the open window. His throwing arm was not as accurate as he had hoped and the grenade mixed its mark--it bounced off the windshield and detonated on the tarmac below. The operator then grabbed another flash bang from his assault vest and this time managed to place in squarely through the open pane of glass. A bright orange glow, followed by a thud, indicated that the device had detonated properly. With the terrorists now alerted to the raid, the operators faced little choice but to move on in. Another device was hurled inside the aircraft and following the blinding flash and deafening explosion, the GIGN rescue force made its explosive entry but, at first had difficulty in opening up the aircraft door due to a miscalculation. They were met by a hail of lethal AK-47 fire fired from the cockpit and forced to race through the ricocheting rounds and bits of flying shrapnel. According to Captain Favier, "It was really hell. Six of the eight men by the cockpit were wounded by gun and grenade fire." They raced down the aisles of the A300 with their .357 revolvers cocked and ready for action, and yelling, "Keep your heads down and do not move!" Captain Favier's men used an emergency plan that they had rehearsed twenty times in the previous hours entering the aircraft at three points moving from front to back and then from back to front. The operators had to move quickly and make sure that no terrorists were masquerading as hostages and hiding out in a row of seats, and they had to get everybody off the aircraft immediately just in case the terrorists in the cockpit succeeded in detonating the explosives they boasted were in their possession. They didn't know where the terrorists were until they realized that they weren't in the main cabin area; all that the operators heard was screaming, crying and issuing pleas for help. Bullets, fired from the cockpit, were still flying through the aircraft hitting some passengers and operators in the ballistic melee exacerbated by a choking cloud of smoke.

Securing the aircraft took less than a minute, and the passengers were ordered told to stay still and not move by the operators, though once the aircraft was secured, the GIGN commander yelled for the hostages to crawl along the aisle-way and not stand up under any circumstance. As operators on the ground aimed their weapons on the opening doors, the emergency chutes were inflated and the hostages rushed off the plane. A fleet of fifty ambulances rushed the hostages to safety. Nearly a dozen had been wounded by stray bullets and by the stampede toward the emergency exits.

Stoic portrait of a GIGN three-man assault team. Note operator (bottom, right) carrying MP5 SD3 9mm submachine gun equipped with SOPELEM PS 2 spotlight projector and OB-50 SOPELEM night firing scope; he is also wearing the SOPELEM TN2-1 night observation and driving sight. The operator (standing) is carrying the Matra Defense .357 MR 73 Manurhin Type Gendarmerie pistol with laser aim-point device. (Courtesy: SIRPA Gendarmerie)

With the hostages secure, the remaining force of GIGN operators raced into the aircraft and assumed firing positions facing the cockpit. The co-pilot, Jean-Paul Borderie, the only hostage still held by the terrorists, took advantage of a secondary lapse in attention by the gunmen and jumped through the open window to the tarmac below. He broke his leg during the fall but also removed the last obstacle the GIGN faced in ending the ordeal. With the terrorist alone and cornered in the cockpit, the true assault began. Additional stun devices were tossed by the cockpit door and the level of GIGN fire increased. A GIGN sniper in the control tower, monitoring the silhouettes through the Modéle 53 bis scope of his FR-F2 7.62mm sniper rifle, unleashed two rounds killing one of the terrorists, and within minutes the level of French fire overwhelmed the terrorists. All four were killed inside the cockpit without having detonated the dynamite they had prepared and put in place near the pilot's compartment. The battle developed into a fire-fight with high-power sniper rifles.

At 17:35, Major Favier sent a message to the control tower signaling the end to the ordeal. "The operation is terminated," Major Favier reported, "damage limited."

The entire rescue operation took twenty minutes. In all twenty-five people were injured--thirteen passengers, three crewmembers, and nine GIGN operators including one who lost his hand when the terrorists tossed a fragmentation grenade from the cockpit. The following day, eighty hostages, as well as the GIGN operators, arrived at Orly Airport in Paris to tumultuous applause and cries of "Viva La France." President Francois Mitterrand personally congratulated each one of the GIGN rescue force, and Prime Minister Edouard Balludar proudly boasted how the operation had been carried out with "exemplary courage and efficiency." In hindsight, however, the French were extremely fortunate that the hijackers were as inexperienced as they were. By flying to France, they guaranteed that the authorities would have a free hand in moving operationally--negotiations and any decision to react tactically would come on the scene from government authorities. The terrorists didn't object to the plane being parked at a remote stretch of the airport directly in front of the main control tower. Most importantly, when the assault began, they bunched up in the cockpit where they lost control overt the one commodity that kept them alive--the hostages--and made it easier for the GIGN operators to terminate them.[1]

French Interior Minister Charles Pasqua, a known hard-liner on Islamic militants operating in France, told reporters that he ordered the rescue attempt only when it was apparent that no other action would save the lives of the hostages. In retrospect, in light of information confirming France's worst fears that the hijackers wanted to crash the aircraft into Paris, Minister Pasqua's decision shows unique boldness and insight in the preservation of many more lives than those held captive. But the hijacking was the first terrorist spillover from the war in Algeria to erupt in France. With GIA spokesmen in Algiers vowing revenge for the rescue operation in Marseilles, it appears as if the GIGN's campaign against the Islamic terrorists has only just begun.

For most in France and around the world, the brilliant and daring rescue of AF8969 was the first time that they had ever heard of the GIGN--certainly one of Europe's best and oldest counter-terrorist units. The ***Groupe d'Intervention Gendarmerie Nationale*** was created on March 10, 1974, as a national response to any terrorist incident involving hostages. The GIGN was formed in direct response to the Bavarian police's failure in Munich, in 1972, yet France had much to be concerned with on its own soil. With a liberal pro-Arab policy in the early 1970s, France was home and European station to many of the Middle East's most notorious terrorist groups--from Fatah's covert Black September Organization to Dr. George Habash's Popular Front for the Liberation of Palestine. The KGB was strong in France, particularly in Paris, as was a small army of Third World activists who were on Moscow's payroll. Some intelligence experts compare Paris of the 1970s to Vienna after the Second World War and Beirut of the mid-1950s. It was a wild and chaotic time in the French capital, especially since counter-terrorist agents from Israel and about half a dozen other nations used Paris as a convenient extension of their own battlefields. Into this violent and combustible scene came the likes of French counter-terrorist and counter-intelligence agencies, the DST, and notorious figures like the infamous Carlos the Jackal.

The GIGN was designed to be a fast response force that could intervene decisively to any large-scale terrorist incident; as a law-enforcement agency the GIGN would also be called to fight dangerous criminals or emotionally disturbed people holding hostages, but counter-terrorism was its bread and butter. The Ministry of Defense is the body that commands the Gendarmerie, and, indeed, it was decided that France's hostage-rescue unit would adapt a uniquely militaristic philosophy and appearance. From its inception, Ministry of Defense officials did not want a force larger than 100 men, and it wanted its ranks drawn solely from the 60,000 men currently serving in the force; it was thought that should parachutists or Foreign Legion officers or NCOs be included, that certain police character required in a unit of this nature and caliber would be lost.

At first the GIGN was divided into two separate though equal entities--GIGN I, responsible for northern France and based just outside of Paris at Maisons-Alfort, and GIGN IV, response for southern France, based at Mont-de-Marsan in the south, but in essence GIGN I controlled the shots. In 1976, both GIGN elements were combined to become one cohesive force. The unit was divided into four brigades of fifteen operators each, assisted by administrative staff, medical and ordnance specialists, and intelligence officers as well. In total, GIGN's strength never surpassed ninety men, though at the time of the AF 8969, its order of battle boasted eighty-seven operators, nine of whom were officers.

Although it hadn't received the international accolades of GSG-9, the SAS or even Delta (even though it has been far more operational), from its inception in 1974 to the time of this book's writing, the GIGN has executed over 650 operations against terrorists, armed guerrillas, criminals, emotionally disturbed individuals holed up with weapons, and hardened convicts during bloody prison riots. In these operations, they have set free over 500 hostages and killed dozens of terrorists and "bad guys" and arrested nearly 1,000 of them; to date, the unit has suffered five dead and dozens seriously wounded in action.

Their first major operation was the now legendary February 1976 rescue in Djibouti. Early, on the morning of February 3, 1976,

During a counter-terrorist sweep of a sensitive communications facility, a GIGN patrol makes a low-level search of a perimeter courtesy of a Army Aérospatiale SA319B Alouette III chopper. (Courtesy: SIRPA Gendarmerie)

Having learned much about winter-time security operations during the 1992 Albertville Winter Olympics, the GIGN trains throughout the winter to hone its Alpine rescue (tactical) skills. Here, an operator is lowered down into a ravine courtesy of a French Army Aérospatiale SA319B Alouette III chopper. (Courtesy: SIRPA Gendarmerie)

terrorists from the Front for the Liberation of the Coast of Somalia (FLCS) hijacked a schoolbus carrying thirty students, the small children of French Air Force personnel stationed in country. French Foreign Legion units quickly surrounded the bus, though it was clear that this was just the sort of "job" that the GIGN was created for. The unit's legendary first commander, Lieutenant Prouteau, flew to Djibouti with nine men, all sharpshooters, to execute the rescue. There were six terrorists in all, armed with AK-47s, and they were receiving some assistance from local Somali policemen, but the GIGN attended to the matter with a level of professionalism and decisiveness that has since come to personify the unit. Each sniper received one terrorist to "handle," and when the order to assault the bus would be given, it was hoped that the six rounds to be fired from strategically positioned perches would end the ordeal without actually having to assault the bus with weapons ablaze. When the terrorists agreed to allow food to be brought on the bus, GIGN operators permitted the sandwiches to be doped up with tranquilizers, thus putting the children to sleep and removing possibly confusing silhouettes from view. Once the snipers went to work, the operators would then charge the bus and secure the area before Somali border policemen could intervene; the Legionnaires were instructed to keep the Somalis busy during the rescue operation. The plan worked. After a ten hour standoff, Lieutenant Prouteau issued the order to fire. Each sniper placed a 7.5mm French service round through the head of one terrorist, but they only hit five of them; one was off the bus. As the operators began their 200 meter charge toward the bus, they came under heavy fire from the Somali police positions and a fierce fire-fight broke out in the orange glow of a Red Sea dusk. GIGN snipers killed ten Somali policemen, and the Legionnaires took care of the rest. But amid the chaos of the fire-fight, the sixth terrorist had reboarded the bus and killed, in cold-blood, a five-year-old girl before he was cut down with a thunderous volley of GIGN fire. Twenty-nine school kids were rescued in an operation that history, as a result of Entebbe and Mogadishu happening so soon after, has virtually forgotten.

One year later the unit participated in a highly successful rescue operation of a prison warden and his deputy held at Clairvaux Prison by rioting inmates. Interestingly enough, however, perhaps the GIGN's most successful operation and certainly its largest was its still never admitted to role in ending the siege of the Great Mosque (***Kabaa***) in Mecca in 1979. Muslim pilgrims who had made the ***Haj*** to Mecca, armed and believed to be inspired by the Iranian Revolutionary Guard, seized the holiest shrine in Islam and challenged Saudi forces to dislodge them. The fighting between the zealots and Saudi National Guardsmen was fierce and bloody and is believed to have resulted in hundreds of dead and scores more wounded. Exasperated and failing to make any headway against the insurgents, the Saudi government turned to the GIGN (at the time considered to be Europe's finest counter-terrorist unit) for help. GIGN officers advised the Saudis and helped lay the groundwork for an indigenous hostage-rescue squad (the Special Security Force), and also participated in much of the fighting; as the GIGN has never admitted it was in Saudi Arabia, a casualty count is impossible to come by but reports claim that the operators exacted a heavy toll on the insurgents and ended the siege days after their arrival. Rumor also has it that upon their arrival in Mecca, the entire unit was "quickly" converted to Islam so that they could legally enter the holy city.

In the coming years, the GIGN would display its skill and professional prowess rescuing hostages on board an Iran Air jet at Orly Airport in Paris in July 1983, and at Marseilles Airport in 1984 when, ominously, an Algerian hijacker attempted to seize an Air France cargo plane. They have ventured to Ouvea, New Caledonia, to rescue hostages from island extremists and have arrested Basque ETA terrorists in the wild wilderness of the border region with Spain. As VIP protection and embassy security is one of the GIGN's secondary functions, the unit has seen extensive action in Lebanon, first as security detail for French diplomats during and after the Lebanese Civil War, and as bodyguards to French go-betweens attempting to secure the release of French citizens being held hostage in Lebanon. In fact, the GIGN owns a fierce reputation in Lebanon. According to Middle East insiders, the GIGN is as rough, and tough, and "no nonsense" a counter-terrorist force as they come. Legend has it that when chief French negotiator for the release of the French hostages being held in Lebanon by Hizbollah, Jean-Charles Marciani (a former DST officer) went to Beirut with a Lebanese to guide him through the labyrinth of local politics, militias and hostage-takers, he traveled with a twelve-man team of GIGN operators, all fellow Corsicans, and all cradling suppressed MP5 submachine guns. When he met with high-ranking Hizbollah leaders to discuss the fate of French hostages, Mr. Marciani went to his face-to-face encounter with his entourage, and with the GIGN officers looking on, reeled off the names of the brothers, cousins and friends of those with whom he was meeting who

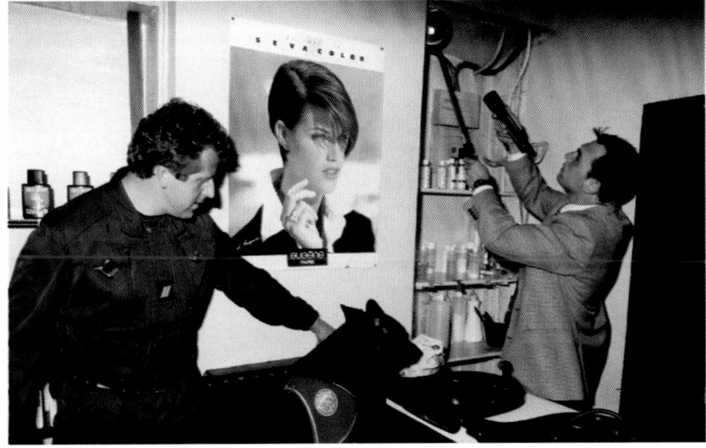
A GIGN EOD officer and his faithful bomb-sniffing dog assist a plainclothes detective in search of explosive material during a raid on a beauty salon in a Parisian suburb believed to be a terrorist arms cache. (Courtesy: SIRPA Gendarmerie)

A building search in Basque country. During a sweep of possible ETA hide-outs near the Spanish border, a GIGN task force searches a village with weapons at the ready and with finger's on the trigger. (Courtesy: SIRPA Gendarmerie)

An EPIGN sniper in full jump kit awaits his turn on line to board a French Air Force C-130 prior to an early morning line jump in the south of France. Note red jump helmet and FR-F1 7.62mm sniper weapon carried. He wears the EPIGN patch on his right shoulder. (Courtesy: SIRPA Gendarmerie)

were living in France. As his GIGN escorts cocked their weapons and cleaned their nails with their razor sharp daggers, Mr. Marciani is reported to have told his Hizbollah hosts, "If anything goes wrong with the hostages in Lebanon, my Corsican friends will look after all your relatives and friends."

Perhaps the GIGN's most internationally covered operation, prior to the rescue of Air France flight 8969, was its role in assisting the DST agents in the capture and successful transport back to France of the infamous Carlos the Jackal from his apparent hide-away in the Sudan on August 15, 1994.

Indeed, many of the GIGN's eighty-seven operators are Corsicans--tough, no-nonsense individuals who are expert soldiers. The GIGN recruits ***exclusively*** from the ranks of the Gendarmerie, and in order to volunteer a Gendarme must have five years on the job and possess an exemplary service record. The GIGN selection process is legendary throughout Europe for its brutal toughness and high standards, and according to reports, an acceptance rate of seven-percent is standard for the unit. That small percentage of volunteers which are able to pass the three weeks of intellectual, physical and psychological entry exams are then subjected to a grueling ten month basic training and special operations instruction regimen considered among the finest in Europe and the world. Even though the Gendarme is acquainted with weaponry and police procedure, GIGN instructors attempt to break the volunteer down to his most basic component and then build him back up again along GIGN lines. GIGN training lasts ten months and includes basic firearms proficiency with not only the weaponry and tactical equipment to be deployed by the unit, but with just about any weapon that terrorists could get their hands on. GIGN trainees are also taught the martial arts and the secrets of unarmed combat and cold-killing; communications is taught on anything from the basic Motorola radio to a SATCOM system and the most advanced and secure cellular phones; EOD training is provided; and, the trainees receive an in-depth history in the who's-who of the world's major terrorist organizations. Because France is a nation of enormous geographic diversity (large urban metropolises, scenic rural areas, agricultural zones, mountains, the Alps, and a near tropical shoreline in the south) GIGN training must prepare the operator to function in a wide array of geographic and climactic areas. As a result, all GIGN operators are SCUBA-trained and qualified, taught by France's best naval special warfare instructors from the Army's combat swimmers. Unlike the United States and Great Britain, nations that possess underwater counter-terrorist units, France relies upon the GIGN should a boat or ferry be seized by terrorists, or should a chalet or riverside hotel by taken over by heavily armed individuals. GIGN operators also receive extensive mountain warfare instruction and are all trained in tactical skiing and cold-weather operations; during the 1992 Winter Olympics in Albertville, GIGN personnel in white coveralls provided an invisible, though closely guarded ring of security to the Olympic village. Should hostages be held in the French Alps, GIGN is more than able to not only reach even the most secluded of mountain-top targets, but to function tactically, as well. GIGN operators are also provided with an intensive high-speed driving course at Les Mans.

All GIGN operators are parachutist-qualified (taught at the legendary French Jump School at Pau) and they proudly wear their gold parachutist wings proudly on their coveralls. Even though the unit is a police force, the creators of the GIGN thought it imperative to have the national counter-terrorist entity able to perform any and all types of insertions. GIGN operators are reported to jump five times a year from a variety of French Air Force and Gendarmerie aircraft and helicopters, and have also been reported to execute at least one "wet jump" in full SCUBA gear per year.

Although French police and special forces units are as chauvinistic as they come when it comes to equipment, not carrying anything unless it was made in France, the GIGN prefers quality over national pride and deploys what ***it*** feels are the world's finest pieces of weaponry and combat gear. Unlike other counter-terrorist units around the world, the GIGN considers its principal assault weapon to be not a 9mm submachine gun or even a 5.56mm assault rifle or carbine, but rather the Matra Defense .357 MR 73 Manurhin Type Gendarmerie revolver. Reliable, sturdy and lethal in proper hands, the weapon is ideal for close-quarter combat. It should be noted that when Major Favier's task force assaulted Air France flight 8969 at Marseilles, the operators storming the aircraft were ***all*** armed with the Matra Defense .357 MR 73 Manurhin Type Gendarmerie revolver; even those operators on the ground, covering the entry force, were armed with the revolver.[2] The GIGN's 9mm submachine gun of choice is, of course, the Heckler and Koch family of MP5s. While the unit began its operational service in 1974 carrying the "legendary" MAT 49 9mm submachine gun, even hard-core French chauvinists admit that the MP5 family of 9mm submachine gun is undoubtedly the world's finest. The favored MP5s carried by the GIGN are the MP5A3, the MP5A5E, MP5SD3 and MP5K A5; though for certain assignments, it has been reported that operators will also carry the Israeli Mini-Uzi 9mm submachine gun. While shotguns are not carried as a rule by the GIGN, the riot gun of choice is the French-produced SNPE 12-gauge Type APAE shotgun. Virtually all GIGN operators are trained as marksman, though only those displaying the highest shooting scores are selected to serve as snipers on a particular job. The GIGN sniper weapon is both the ***Groupement Industriel des Armements Terrestres*** FR-F1 and FR-F2 family of 7.62mm rifle--a ten-shot, manually-operated bolt action rifle based on the now obsolete 7.5mm Model 1936. Originally, the FR-F1 was manufactured in the French 7.5mm caliber, but was also produced in a NATO 7.62mm caliber. The FR-F1, though still in service, was gradually replaced by the FR-F2, a similar weapon by design but produced with a smaller barrel solely in 7.62mm with basic design improvements over its predecessor. The GIGN also considers its vast arsenal of pyrotechnics and explosive devices as important to its operational abilities, as it does its assault weapon and gear. The rescue of Air France flight 8969 was a testimony to the unit's reliance on flash-bang stun devices, and the unit will employ whatever non-lethal diversionary means are in its disposal during an assault.

Prior to the rescue of Air France flight 8969, the GIGN had established close operational ties with many of the world's top units--from Australia to the United States. The GIGN has trained many counter-terrorist units around the world, especially those in the Third World from former French colonies; the unit has also assumed an instructor role to units in Saudi Arabia, the Persian Gulf, and the former East Bloc--primarily with Polish police units and the army's ***Grom*** hostage-rescue force, and new units being established in the Czech Republic, Slovakia, and Romania. GIGN's closest operational and training relationship is with the Belgian ESI, as both nations share a common frontier and language; the units train together and exchange officers on long exercises and even on some lengthy operational assignments. The GIGN also maintains close ties to the British SAS, Germany's GSG-9 and the SEKs from Frankfurt and Munich, Swiss police units, the Italian GIS, the Spanish GEO and UEI, and Israel's ***Ya'ma'm***. The GIGN has established ties to American counter-terrorist units, such as the U.S. Army's 1st SFOD-D and the U.S. Navy's SEAL Team SIX, as well as the FBI's HRT; the GIGN has also had contact with municipal SWAT units, primarily the esteemed Los Angeles Police Department SWAT Platoon.

There are three other French counter-terrorist and hostage-rescue units of note that (although are not as well known as the GIGN and certainly not as famous as the unit in light of the Marseilles operation) they are uniquely skilled and experienced and on par operationally with any of the world's finest intervention squads.

The unit most similar to the GIGN in history, mandate and training is the EPIGN--the ***Escadron Parachutiste d'Intervention de la Gendarmerie Nationale***, the Parachutist Intervention Squadron of the National Gendarmerie. The unit, created on January 1, 1984, by ministerial decree originated from the EPGM (***Escadron Parachutiste de Gendarmerie Mobile***), an airborne element of the National Gendarmerie. Until the creation of the GIGN in 1974, the EPGM was the nation's sole on-call intervention unit and, in 1975, had deployed against Corsican separatists from the FLNC. In the years to follow, EPGM units were sent to Chad, Beirut and other international hot-spots where French diplomats and civilians required evacuation or additional security. More a military police unit than a militarized law-enforcement force, the EPIGN was created to provide the Gendarmerie with an airborne-qualified force of special forces capable of responding at a moment's notice to an crisis abroad--and even inside France. Trained as counter-terrorist operators, the unit was to have deployed in situations that required additional tactical muscle, though which had yet to reach the point of no return where the GIGN would need to be deployed. Both units, in fact, work side-by-side with one another. In the case where an Air France aircraft might be hijacked to an unfriendly nation, EPIGN units might be called upon to secure the airport while the GIGN executes a rescue.

In 1985, the EPIGN was deployed along the Spanish frontier to help local Gendarmerie units to keep peace in the volatile Basque-country against ETA terrorists; in 1986, the unit was called into to round up hundreds of violent criminals in Aix-en-Provence; and, in July 1987, the unit was deployed to New Caledonia.

A EPIGN jumper puts on a display of "come down to earth accuracy" during a "dog and pony" show for visiting German ***Bundesgrenzschutz*** officers at Satory. (Courtesy: SIRPA Gendarmerie)

The EPIGN is considerably larger than the GIGN--it consists of 160 men divided into four thirty-five man platoons reinforced by a free-fall platoon; the unit is commanded by a Captain, and has four officers in its command cadre. One platoon is on permanent on-call status for immediate deployment to any location in the world, and one platoon specializes in dignitary protection (one of the EPIGN's tasks since 1986). The EPIGN is a volunteer force made up solely of policemen with a minimum of five-years experience in the Mobile Gendarmerie. Interestingly enough, the EPIGN selection process is identical to that employed by French Airborne and special forces as opposed to the GIGN's method of selecting its trainees.

The EPIGN does not carry the MP5 family of 9mm submachine gun, and deploys only French-produced weapons and equipment. Its weapon of choice is the Famas 5.56mm assault rifle.

The French National Police also possesses its own elite intervention unit, a force of skilled and well-trained operators known as RAID--if the GIGN can be compared to the U.S. Army's 1st SFOD-D or the British SAS (since its responsibilities stretch from the French interior to just about any spot in the world where French hostages are being held), then the RAID unit is similar to the FBI's HRT or the Italian NOCS as a force purely supplemental to tactical emergencies developing inside the country. RAID stands for **R**eaction, **A**ssistance, **I**ntervention, **D**issuasion (***Réaction, Assistance, Intervention, Dissauder***), and is answerable to the Ministry of the Interior as opposed to the GIGN subordinate to the French Ministry of Defense. Formed in 1985 to meet the ever growing wave of violent crime and terrorism sweeping through France, especially involving Middle Eastern immigrant groups settled in France as well as right-wing groups known for carrying out violent attacks, RAID has quickly developed a reputation for itself as a second-to-none police intervention unit not only performing at a professional level equal to the world's best police special units, but setting a trend for excellence and innovation that other units around the globe are now emulating.

RAID, also known as the Black Panthers as a result of the "sinister" black overalls and black silk jackets worn, is a small unit, consisting of eighty officers--like the GIGN, sixty RAID operators form four assault groups, and ten officers and NCOs form the command cadre; ten officers serve as specialists (hostage-negotiators, dog-handlers, and EOD personnel). The unit, based in Bievres on the outskirts of Paris, accepts volunteers from all over France, but applicants wishing to try out for a spot on the next RAID training class

During training with the French Foreign Legion in Corsica, an EPIGN operator is lowered down to a platform from a French Navy Aérospatiale SA 321G Super Frelon. (Courtesy: Yves Debay)

must be between the ages of twenty-five and thirty-five, and have at least five years experience on the job; volunteers must also be in excellent physical shape, and trainees (as well as operators already inside the unit) are expected to engage in at least six hours of physical fitness training per day. The selection process is incredibly prejudicial--only ten applicants are usually selected from a list of 600 vying for a spot on the force. RAID training is equally difficult. It lasts nearly nine months, and involves every aspect of counter-terrorism and hostage rescue; many RAID members are former servicemen and many are airborne qualified, but parachuting is not in the unit curriculum. Like the GIGN, RAID carries similar weapons and equipment, and the Matra Defense .357 MR 73 Manurhin Type Gendarmerie revolver is the weapon of choice along with the MP5. RAID officers, unlike the GIGN, are permitted to select whatever weapon they feel most comfortable with, and many officers in the unit now sport of the Glock Model 19. Because (among the unit's many responsibilities) RAID groups are responsible for providing dignitary protection, the unit has been known to operate undercover and in plain clothes.

There is no special high-risk pay for RAID officers--operators received the standard 8,000 Francs (approximately US$1,500) per month. Since 1985, two RAID officers have been killed in action and dozens of others wounded. The unit has been deployed nearly 100 times in some of the meanest stretches of France--from the narcotic dens of Marseilles to the Algerian slums around Paris. Their first operation was in December 1985, shortly after their creation, when the unit captured four leaders of the Action Directe terrorist group holding hostages in a courthouse in Nantes. The unit's finest moment, however, would come eight years later.

At 9:30 A.M. on the morning of Thursday May 13, 1993, a man wearing a ski mask over his face walked into a nursery school in the affluent Parisian suburb of Neuilly-sur-Seine, burst into a classroom and took twenty-one children and a teacher hostage. The individual, an Algerian named Eric Schmit, had sixteen sticks of dynamite strapped to his body and was brandishing a revolver; he demanded that the government pay him 100 million francs in exchange for the safe release of the children. Police units raced to the scene, but found that they were not dealing with the "average" psychopath. He was intelligent, knowledgeable of police procedure, and apparently quite willing to die should his demands not be met; he demanded that the negotiators refer to him as the "Human Bomb."

The GIGN was placed on alert, but this was a job for RAID and a fifteen-man assault team was rushed to the besieged schoolhouse. Snipers set up positions around the schoolhouse, and an assault element, later reinforced by additional RAID personnel, studied the blueprints of the building in order to lay the groundwork for the assault plan. At first, however, the police negotiators were making some headway. On Thursday, at 13:30 hours, the "Human Bomb" released nine children, and at 18:00 he released four more; after allowing a French TV correspondent to interview him, Mr. Schmit released two more children. On Friday, for nearly eighteen hours, the police engaged in an endless and tiresome negotiations session. The details of the demanded payment were set forth, as were the details of his getaway. It was hoped that the police would succeed in ending the ordeal peacefully; making a tactical move when the hostages are small children is perhaps the most difficult dilemma facing any police official. At 00:40 hours on Saturday May 15, 1993, Eric Schmit called off the negotiations. The police feared he was growing tired and despondent. They would make their move at dawn.

At 07:25 hours on the morning of May 15, special audio devices planted around the school by RAID personnel indicated that Mr. Schmit was snoring. Having him asleep was an opportunity too good not to take advantage of. One force of RAID officers, all volunteers forming a human shield to evacuate the hostages and protect them should the dynamite go off, entered the building and quickly rushed the children to safety while a second adjacent force raced toward where intelligence reported Schmit to be held up. The sounds of the escaping children and the stomping boots of the RAID officers woke Mr. Schmit up, and he grabbed his gun and began making menacing moves in the direction of the approaching policemen. Three .357 rounds put an end to the ordeal. The entire operation took thirty seconds.

In, perhaps, its largest deployment ever, RAID personnel assisted French police and DST agents on November 8, 1994, in an unprecedented sweep of Islamic militants and fundamentalists guerrillas suspected of having set up shop in France. Approximately 1,000 French police officers participated in the nation-wide operation, including officers from RAID, the GIGN and the EPIGN. The group targeted during the operation were members of the Armed Islamic Group, and police arrested ninety-five senior GIA activists and cell commander. During the nationwide sweep, police captured dozens of AK-47 assault rifles, shotguns, pistols, grenades, ammunition and sophisticated detonators.

One month later, at Christmas, the same group targeted in the French dragnet hijacked Air France flight 8969.

RAID maintains close ties to several police tactical units throughout Europe, and is reported to be close with the Swiss Enzian unit, the Italian NOCS, Great Britain's SO-19, the Israeli ***Ya'ma'm*** and the SEK from Baden-Württemberg.

One last French unit involved solely in VIP protection, security and presidential protection is the GSPR--***Groupe de Sécurité du Président de la République***--and is similar in mandate and function to the U.S. Secret Service.

[1] The terrorists did employ certain "tricks of the trade" indicating that they had received certain professional training. To counteract the effects and skills of the hostage-negotiators, the terrorists used the pilot as the "cut-out, relaying their demands and communications through him as to avoid being drawn into any personal contact with French authorities; this also prevented the hijackers from having their voices taped and analyzed for stress levels.

[2] In certain situations, GIGN will also carry the ***Manfacture d'Armes Automatiques*** (MAB) 9mm PA15 pistol.

## Germany

The GSG-9 patch.

*It is just after dawn on a crisp winter's morning near Bonn and already the thumping sounds of low-flying helicopters and the crackling blasts of automatic weapons fire has been heard for hours. A light blue, though badly tattered Mercedes, powered by remote control and ferrying five "passengers," is being driven across a clearing surrounded by a snow frosted Pine forest, when the roar of its diesel engine is suddenly muffled by the sound of a Bell-212's beating rotor blades. The chopper, adorned in the green scheme and markings of the Bundesgrenzschutz, comes in from the east flying so close to the tree tops that its landing skids almost touch the crisp lime colored leaves. At the clearing, the chopper swoops down sharply behind the Mercedes and four men, wearing green overalls, black face masks and camouflaged helmets produce assault rifles swing open the side door and prepare their weapons. As the Bell-212 makes a low-level pass at the Mercedes, sharp red laser beams emerge from the chopper's cargo hold and the ear-piercing sounds of gunfire is heard. Nearly a dozen bullets are launched at the Mercedes, but only two of the passengers (actually mannequins) are hit. One, simulating a terrorist holding a gun on the driver from the passenger side, is hit by six rounds of 7.62mm fire--all the rounds enter his upper torso or head. The plastic head of the second mannequin, also simulated to be holding a gun on two hostages in the rear seats, has been obliterated by the high-powered rounds.*

The GSG-9 wings.

*From a command post, the unit commander, a rugged looking officer wearing an Israeli-made green parka and a bright green berets, is not impressed by the display. The Mercedes was only traveling at a speed of 40 kilometers per hour and a car seized by terrorists would be traveling at a minimum speed of 90. "Have the chopper fly by again and have the car go to 60," the officer snaps at his deputy as he lights his tenth cigarette of the morning, "have the chopper fly lower and faster. If we are going to do this for real on the autobahn we'll have to do it for real here." Once again the Mercedes is readied, the dummies set in place and the chopper flown. It is, after all, just another day at the office for Grenzschutzgruppe-9.*

*As the Polizeioberrat spoke on a flip-phone to a liaison in the BKA, discussing an ongoing terrorist investigation that could likely involve the unit before the end of the week, the seasoned counter-terrorist veteran could not help but be taken aback by how very far the unit had actually come in the twenty years since it was created. The twenty years have seen incredible days and bloody nights. They have been truly historic.*

GSG-9 was born out of history. It was the direct result of one the most promising moments in modern German history and one of its most tragic: one fateful--and failed--ambush at Fürstenfeldbrük airport

Bavarian police display the sniper rifle used by marksman during the ill-fated rescue bid at Fürstenfeldbrük. (U.S. Army)

Visiting Italian GIS operators observe the GSG-9 obstacle course at the unit's headquarters in St. Augustin. (Samuel M. Katz)

During helicopter insertion exercises, GSG-9 operators perfect immediate deployment from a Bell-212 chopper. (Courtesy: BGS/GSG-9)

GSG-9 officers display thorough rope traversing skills at the St. Augustin obstacle course. (Courtesy: BGS/GSG-9)

Carrying their full compliment of MP5 SD3, MP5K and Heckler and Koch HK512 12-gauge shotgun, GSG-9/1 operators pose for the camera following the successful completion of combat exercises. (Courtesy: BGS/GSG-9)

near Munich in September 1972 during the Olympic games when terrorism changed the ante of global violence and tolerance to a higher more explosive level. Had German police been better, more prepared, readier to meet the challenge at hand, or as one SAS officer states, "Perhaps the way the world now fights terrorism would have remained in the dark ages."

It was known as "Operation Berim and Ikrit," named so in memory of two Arab Christian villages that had treacherously surrendered to Israel in 1948 without even putting up a fight. The names Berim and Ikrit had become Palestinian terms for defeat and surrender. Now it was the world's turn to buckle its knees and grab at its insides. Fear and terror would soon be felt whenever the word "Munich" was uttered. On September 5, 1972, eight terrorists from Fatah's Black September Organization snuck into Munich's Olympic Village amid one of the most exciting and historic Olympiads in recent memory and proceeded toward 31 Connolly Strasse--the living quarters of the Israeli Olympic team. The eight men were all athletically fit, wearing blue Adidas track suits, and carried large sporting bags--not an uncommon sight in the village. Security was non-existent in Munich's village of peace. A few lightly armed police officers were on hand but they basically were entrusted with keeping drunken athletes and spectators from engaging in beer room brawls. In retrospect, the terrorists couldn't have chosen an easier mark.[1]

Operators from GSG-9/2 deploy from a BGS Bell-212 atop an oil-rig during hostage-rescue exercises in the North Sea. (Courtesy: BGS/GSG-9)

A GSG-9/3 operator glides to earth after jumping from a German Air Force C-130 over St. Augustin. (Courtesy: BGS/GSG-9)

Once the terrorists reached 31 Connolly Strasse, they pulled wool caps and masks over their faces, produced AK-47 assault rifles from their bags and entered the living quarters where the small twenty-two man Israeli Olympic team was based. The terrorists tried to kick down the two doors to the Israeli dorm, but the heavy doors were locked and the ruckus awoke several of the athletes. Two Israeli wrestlers, Joseph Romano and his coach Moshe Weinberg, reacted quickly and barricaded the door with their towering bodies; they also helped organize an escape of eleven athletes through a broken glass door facing the street. Romano and Weinberg held out just long enough for half their comrades to escape and call for help. The terrorists burst through the door and killed both wrestlers with point-blank 7.62mm fire. Nine Israeli athletes did not escape, however, and, after a complimentary beating at the hands of the terrorists, they were bound and gagged. Within minutes of the attack, Bavarian police rushed to the scene, as did a small army of reporters and newscasters. Black September was now playing to a global audience--an event of truly epic proportions covered by 6,000 journalists and broadcast to an audience of a billion people.

For the next twenty-one hours, the world watched as the terrorists held the German government at bay. The terrorists were demanding the release of over 200 of their jailed comrades from European, Israeli and Jordanian jails, as well as safe passage for themselves and the hostages to Cairo or Tripoli. The governor of Bavaria, and the government of Bonn contemplated acquiescing to the terrorists, while in Jerusalem, Prime Minister Golda Meir and her cabinet realized that there would be no negotiating with Black September. They had resigned themselves to the knowledge that only a military strike could free the hostages, but they knew the Germans were unwilling and incapable of mounting such a move. The Israelis offered to send ***Sayeret Mat'kal*** to Munich to attempt the rescue, but the Germans did not want Israeli soldiers on their soil, though they agreed to allow the head of the Mossad, Major-General (Res.) Tzvi Zamir and a ***Shin Bet*** officer to supervise and advise on any rescue mission to be attempted.

Bavarian authorities did not want the matter to become a federal one, and promised Bonn that its police units could handle the situation; they, too, had come to realize that a tactical assault was the only solution. But the policemen ringing Connolly Strasse were lightly armed and not trained in close quarter combat--even the submachine gun toting cops in track suits that had surrounded the besieged building that wanted to go in and "kill the bastards" realized that they were not suited for such an assault and any attempt would likely result in the deaths of all the hostages as well as the terrorists, the policemen and a good many other innocents. Bavarian police officials wanted to avoid any head on attack and instead they opted on an ambush--an engagement on their own terms--when the Palestinians would be vulnerable, exposed, and incapable of killing the hostages. The killing zone chosen was the NATO airfield at Fürstenfeldbrük Airport.

Negotiators informed the terrorists that the governments of German, Israel and Jordan had agreed to their demands and that safe passage would be made courtesy of a Lufthansa Boeing 707 standing ready at the NATO airfield. The terrorists and their hostages were ferried to Fürstenfeldbrük in two West German Army Bell-205 choppers piloted by volunteer airmen. The aerial taxi from the Olympic Village to the airfield took ten minutes and by the time the two birds touched down, the Bavarian police snipers were firmly in place atop the control tower roof and prepared their gauntlet. Bavarian police commanders were confident that their sharpshooters would terminate the ordeal positively; the Israelis on hand, exasperated in their pleas to modify the ambush, knew that disaster was about to strike. The German snipers, armed with single-shot bolt-action rifles, had insufficiently prepared for the ambush; they had failed to secure proper illumination and emergency illumination for their barrage, they failed to establish lines of fire and they were told that there were only four Palestinian terrorists when, in fact, there were eight. The police snipers were it, and had requested no back-up--in retrospect a tragic shortcoming when encountering an adversary armed with AK-47 assault rifles and Soviet-produced F-1 fragmentation grenades. The snipers had no night-fighting equipment available to them.

The snipers had planned to snare the terrorists at that one moment when they'd be most vulnerable--walking on the tarmac after inspecting the Lufthansa Boeing 707 several hundred feet away on a secluded stretch of the runway. Gazing through their field glasses, the snipers and the Israelis could see the hostages sitting in their two choppers bound and gagged and under guard; they couldn't see all the terrorists, however. As the lead terrorist emerged from the jet waving a "V" for victory sign, the snipers removed their safeties and began breathing in the meticulous fashion in which they were trained in order to have just enough air in their lungs when the time came to squeeze the trigger. The lead terrorist was halfway between the jet and the

Known as trailblazers in the counter-terrorist industry, GSG-9 officers and planners have virtually invented the art of tubular rescues. here, aboard a German Rail inter-city train moving at high-speeds, GSG-9 operators prepare to mount an explosive entry into a car being held, in these exercises, by Red Army Faction terrorists. (Courtesy: BGS/GSG-9)

GSG-9 operators prepare for the anti-Nazi task with some riot-busting training on the parade grounds at St. Augustin. (Courtesy: BGS/GSG-9)

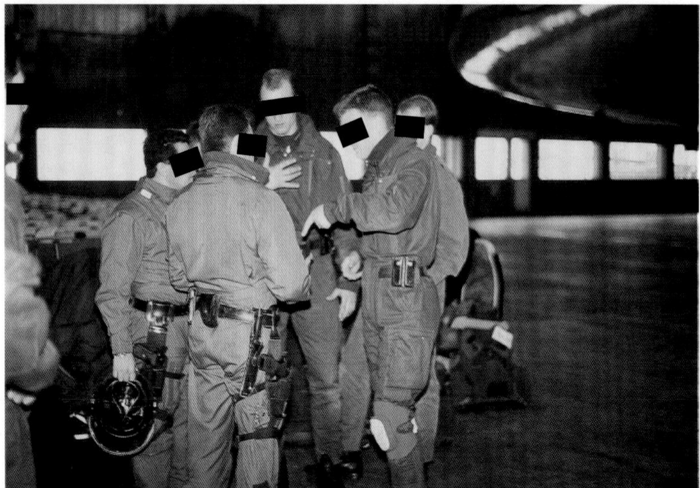

Inside a hangar at Dusseldorf International Airport, GSG-9/3 operators confer with a visiting contingent of Italian GIS operators after training in the art of aircraft rescues. (Samuel M. Katz)

An airborne GSG-9/2 SET, their underwater comrades have already reached their target, prepare to deploy on a ferry in the North Sea during maritime rescue exercises with Danish and Norwegian frogmen. (Courtesy: BGS/GSG-9)

choppers talking to his lieutenant when the first 7.62mm round cracked through the air; three additional shots rang out milli-seconds later. The snipers had been off. The lead shot missed the lead terrorist and instead blew open the head of his lieutenant. The terrorist commander then grabbed his AK-47, slid into the shadows and began firing back at the control tower where the snipers and Israelis were perched. Eight terrorists armed with automatic weapons and grenades were now battling four German snipers armed with bolt-action rifles and Heckler and Koch pistols. A stray bullet sliced through an electrical transformer and plunged the airport into complete darkness. For the next ninety minutes, a "quiet chaos" engulfed Fürstenfeldbrük; a few lone shots rang out as did the barking of orders in Arabic shouted by one terrorist to the rest. Bavarian reinforcements had yet to make an appearance. Suddenly, and without warning, the terrorists emerged from their darkened cover and raked the two helicopters with magazine-emptying bursts of AK-47 fire; for good measure, grenades were tossed into the helicopters and they erupted into orange fireballs. The Bavarians looked on dumbfounded as Mossad chief Zamir and his ***Shin Bet*** liaison openly wept.

West German soldiers, brought into the fray far too late, engaged the surviving terrorists in a three hour fire-fight; the German soldiers, supported by armored cars, succeeded in killing four additional terrorists and captured three other. But terrorism scored an incredible victory. They had reached their ultimate objective--terrorizing not only their targets but virtually the entire world by attacking such a institution as the Olympic Games. They succeeded in tugging at the world's gut with the blood of the dead Israeli athletes and at the expense of modern Germany, a Germany hoping to pull itself out of its violent past.

For Germany, more than any other country, the debacle at Fürstenfeldbrük was a symbolic tragedy of true national significance. Olympic games meant to erase images of the old Germany now would be forever linked to new Germany's inability--or indifference--to the saving of Jewish lives. German police and military officials were embarrassed by the showing at Fürstenfeldbrük and were outraged by the fact that the terrorists actually captured on the tarmac would not be punished for their heinous crimes. On October 29, 1972, Black September hijacked a Lufthansa airliner flying from Beirut to Ankara in order to secure the release of the three incarcerated terrorists. Germany, have been taught its impatience in fighting terrorism, was forced to succumb, and the three men flown to Libya.

German officials had to move quickly in order to ensure that future Munichs would never happen again. The German Army wanted responsibility for fighting terrorism, but creating an elite military unit that might have to turn its weapons on its own citizens was too reminiscent of the SS for the government to stomach; terrorism, it was argued, was a police matter to be dealt with by law enforcement. On September 8, 1972, following the funeral of the Bavarian officer killed in the Fürstenfeldbrük melee, German Interior Minister Hans-Dietricht Genscher was given permission to form a special group, within the Federal Border Police (***Bundesgrenzschutz***), to combat terrorism. The unit would be para-military and had complete national authority and international responsibility for safe-guarding German diplomats--and installations--in trouble-spots. The man tasked with getting this notion off the ground was Ulrich Wegener, a counter-terrorist expert and fifteen-year veteran of the ***Bundesgrenzschutz*** who had built extremely close-links to Israeli special forces,[2] National Police and ***Shin Bet*** (General Security Services) during his years of service, as well as police forces in Switzerland, Austria, Belgium, Holland and France. Using ***Sayeret Mat'kal***, the Israel Defense Forces' elite General Staff Reconnaissance Unit, as his working model, Wegener called his unit ***Grenzschutzgruppe Neun,*** or Border Protection Group Nine, though the world would soon come to know it simply as GSG-9. Through an energetic and fast-paced recruitment and training regimen, Wegener was able to make GSG-9 operational in less than a year. Although odd for an Israeli unit to be the inspiration behind a force of German commandos, Wegener realized the significance of this new force if Germany was ever to erase her violent and savage past.

GSG-9/3 operators climb up an indigenous BGS rubber-coated ladder during anti-hijack exercises at Dusseldorf International Airport, courtesy of LTU airlines. (Samuel M. Katz)

A mobile GSG-9 arsenal and equipment store--all inside the confines of a BGS truck. A highly mobile force, GSG-9 can be deployed--fully equipped--anywhere in Germany in a matter of hours. (Samuel M. Katz)

During a raid of suspected R.A.F. safe-house in Bremen, GSG-9/1 operators support a BKA criminal investigation team in entering an as of yet unsecured room. Note GSG-9's unique camouflage helmet and sage green coveralls, and specially produced load-bearing gear--designed by a returned unit operator. (Courtesy: BGS/GSG-9)

In October 1972, Wegener and his skeleton staff conducted their first recruitment drive at the ***Bundesgrenzschutz*** headquarters and garrison at St. Augustin, near the federal capital of Bonn. Volunteers were offered a chance to join a new and revolutionary unit the likes of which had never before been seen in the new Germany; Wegener interviewed each applicant personally, and promised challenge, excitement and the opportunity to make history. Wegener was looking for a specific breed of man to join the new and fledgling force--he didn't want the volunteer to be a superhuman commando type nor was he looking for the ***average*** police officer--he was looking for a man who had yet to reach his full potential, though one who could be pushed and molded to achieve the impossible. He was looking for an operator, one to function and perform as told but who was independent, innovative and capable of just about anything. The force was to be a significant one--numbering close to 300 operators, and would be divided into three Combat Units. It would be equipped with the most advanced equipment available and be afforded the most lavish training and instruction. There was to be no expense spared in ensuring that the Munich massacres would never be repeated on German soil.

On April 17, 1973, Wegener informed Interior Minister Hans-Dietricht Genscher that two units were ready for action and deployable from their headquarters at St. Augustin.[3] Already, even though they had yet to deploy on a job, GSG-9 had developed a second-to-none reputation in the blossoming community of world counter-terrorist units. Around Europe, and around the world, Wegener's reputation as a genius for recruitment and training became legendary; he also was a skillful diplomat and lobbyist and obtained virtually an unlimited budget for his men from the federal government. Under Wegener's tutelage, GSG-9 trained in mountain warfare at the mountaineering center at Kührointhaus; they learned the art of surveillance and reconnaissance at the I-LRRPS NATO school near Munich; driving at the Porsche and Daimler Benz factories; and, shooting from retired British and Israeli snipers and weapons experts. One GSG-9 Combat Unit, GSG-9/2, would be tasked with maritime counter-terrorism and hostage-rescue and was SCUBA trained by the West German Navy, while GSG-9/3 would be parachutist-qualified and capable of mounting silent airborne insertions. Throughout this period, GSG-9 was also solidifying its ties to other German police units and municipalities, and, as a result of its ties to the German ***Bundeskriminalt*** (BKA), the Federal Office of Criminal Investigation, GSG-9 soon assumed responsibility for VIP security.

From 1973-77 GSG-9 trained and prepared for what most knew was the inevitable--the chance to intervene in a terrorist incident and excise the ghosts of Munich. Their first chance came in June 1974 when GSG-9 teams assisted police in providing security to the World Cup games being held in Germany; organizers feared that terrorists would want to once again disrupt a global event in Germany, but the sight of the green berets walking their post with sniper rifles and G3 assault rifles proved to be an effective deterrent. Many GSG-9 operators had joined the unit to prove that Germans, too, could fight terrorism, others joined because they wanted to be part of something quite special. The security precautions at the World Cup were most successful, even though intelligence reported that the Baader-Meinhoff Gang was planning some sort of attack: the operation was the unit's first step toward proving their worth. Over the next few years, GSG-9 was deployed outside Germany on several occasions to provide security details or two provide assistance to foreign units; these missions including assisting the Austrians in securing the 1976 Winter Olympics at Innsbruck, assisting the Royal Canadian Mounted Police in performing security operations prior to the 1976 Summer Olympics in Montreal, and advising Dutch police and military officials during the Moluccan attacks in December 1976. According to several reports, GSG-9 officers had visited the British 22nd Special Air Service Regiment on operations in Northern Ireland and had observed first-hand the ugliness and ruthlessness required on a professional level to defeat--or at least contain--a determined terrorist threat.

International recognition was nice, and the close-knit relationship with Britain's SAS had shown how a unit tasked with counter-terrorist and special operations assignments functions on a year-round basis; albeit the SAS policy of "shoot first, ask questions later" was something that the Germans could not replicate at home. Wegener was pleased by the progress of his unit on paper and by their growing international ties, but he was waiting for history to invite GSG-9 into its embrace. GSG-9's shining moment, the operation that cemented its elite reputation, came on October 17-18, 1977.

On October 13, 1977, a Lufthansa jet was hijacked by four Arab terrorists--two men and two women--seeking the release of Baader-Meinhof terrorists jailed in Germany. After criss-crossing the Middle East for several days, the aircraft was finally ordered to fly to the Somali capital of Mogadishu and was rushed to a secluded stretch of the desert airstrip. The German government at first hoped to end the hijacking through negotiations, but the terrorist leader, a madman known as "Captain Mahmud," executed the plane's pilot after irresponsible press reports indicated that he had been assisting authorities by conveying valuable information on the terrorist to the German authorities via his radio. The killing of the pilot was a point of no return to officials in Bonn, and they ordered GSG-9 deployed to Somalia; the moment the aircraft was hijacked, it should be pointed out, a GSG-9 SET was placed on high alert and had all its gear loaded onto a special Lufthansa Boeing 707 that would fly them to Somalia should the need arise. The unit arrived in Mogadishu at 17:30 hours on October 17. On board the special aircraft, "the Stuttgart," they had prepared their weapons and gear and were ready, should the situation require, to storm the hijacked aircraft the moment they touched down in Mogadishu. Also on board the "Stuttgart" were two British SAS officers, invited by Ulrich Wegener to Somalia to observe the rescue assault. Lieutenant-Colonel Wegener's immediate objective once in Mogadishu was to isolate the hijacked aircraft, reconnoiter it and cover it with GSG-9 snipers, and then ready his men for the rescue. Unlike

Wearing heavy Kevlar body armor, GSG-9 operators gingerly secure a rear stairwell during a tactical deployment with the BKA in northern Germany. While once viewed with disdain, shotguns are now quite popular in SET philosophy and deployed as much for their tactical benefits as they are for the psychological deterrent presence. (Courtesy: BGS/GSG-9)

Although not as popular as the Glock or even the SIG, GSG-9 swears by the Heckler and Koch P7 and P9. Here, during fast-rope insertion exercises, operators aim their P7s at a possible target after having been deployed by a BGS chopper. (Courtesy: BGS/GSG-9)

The Heckler and Koch P7K3--a new generation of pistol available in either a .380 or .22LR caliber. (Heckler and Koch)

The Heckler and Koch P9S--a weapon being slowly incorporated into GSG-9 holsters. The weapon is available in either a 9mm or .45 caliber. (Heckler and Koch)

the French rescue mission to Djibouti a year earlier, Somali authorities were not acting in concert with the terrorists and instead had pledged their support to the GSG-9 operators. Somali special forces ringed the hijacked Lufthansa jet and they even offered their services in helping set up a diversion--their efforts would be needed.

An hour after landing in Somalia, Wegener was meeting with his twenty-man assault and command staff to finalize the assault plan; the snipers, already in position around the aircraft, were peering through the sights of the Mauser 66 and G3 SG1 weapons and relaying back their observations to Wegener and his deputies. At 23:15 hours, the assault teams, led personally by Wegener, made their slow approach toward the aircraft from the rear; the SAS officers, bringing with them special "flash-bang" diversionary grenades also followed the GSG-9 commander en route to the aircraft. The operators brought with them specially-produced rubber-coated ladders to bring up the aircraft's emergency exists, as well as Smith and Wesson .38 specials. H-Hour is set for 00:00 on October 18.

At 23:50 hours, the terrorists received word that their demands had been met and the Red Army Faction terrorists, whose release they requested, were en route to Mogadishu. A false sense of security engulfed the hijackers in the cockpit, as did a sense of mystery. Approximately 100 yards in front of the cockpit, Somali special forces set a huge bonfire. Its a diversion meant to bring the terrorists into the cockpit. At 00:05, the assault begins. The operators moved out of their crouch underneath the right wing, and placed their rubberized ladders against the aircraft frame; Wegener was among the first up the ladder. As the "flash bang" grenades were removed from the operators pouches, Wegener uttered the code-word ***Zauber-Feuer*** ("Magic Fire") indicating the commencement of the assault. The emergency doors were forced open and the operators entered the aircraft tossing the flash bangs toward to the cockpit, The grenades, special operations marvels, blinded the terrorists with a 50,000-watt brilliance and a deafening explosion. They permitted the twenty operators to enter the narrow passageways unhindered by fire. Half the force split toward the rear of the aircraft while Wegener and his group headed toward the cockpit. A female terrorists was encountered immediately and terminated by a .38 round between her eyes. A second female terrorist raced to the rear of the aircraft and engaged the GSG-9 force from a toilet. She was critically wounded by a full auto blast of 9mm fire from an operator's MP5 and taken out of action; she would also survive the ordeal.

At 00:07 hours, with the rear of the aircraft secure, the operators initiated the aircraft's emergency chutes and saw to evacuation of the hostages. The battle for the cockpit still raged. Although peppered with numerous .38 rounds, "Captain Mahmud" managed to toss two fragmentation grenades at the rescuers; the grenades exploded under a row of seats and did little damage. "Captain Mahmud" was terminated by a full auto burst of 9mm fire from an MP5 and then Lieutenant-Colonel Wegener saw to the termination of the mission when the he personally placed several .38 rounds through the head of the fourth hijacker. By 00:16 hours, all the hostages had been evacuated, all the terrorists had been killed or neutralized and Wegener was able to contact Bonn and tell them that the mission was a complete success.

In Mogadishu, Wegener had gotten his wish. GSG-9 had made history. In a few minutes, eighty-six hostages were freed unharmed and GSG-9 became a force of national heroes to a nation devoid of such figures since the end of the Second World War. For GSG-9, Mogadishu was a baptism of fire for the unit and a rite of passage. For the next fifteen years, being a member of GSG-9 was just about the most prestigious thing a German could achieve. Many volunteers into the ***Bundesgrenzschutz*** joined the force specifically for the chance to volunteer into the ranks of GSG-9; the thought of being one of Germany's best was the driving source of inspiration for the men in the midst of their two plus years worth of instruction needed to transform

Considered among the world's most disciplined and capable marksmen, GSG-9 snipers have literally written the book in the art of precision long-range shooting. Here, during an actual deployment, a GSG-9 sniper and his observer peer through the sights of their Heckler and Koch PSG-1 7.62mm sniping weapon. ((Courtesy: BGS/GSG-9))

Having secured the roof with a few sniper rounds and a quick climb up courtesy of a chimney, a building deemed "***Sicher***" (secure) is the invitation to an awaiting BGS chopper to enter the fray and ferry in an SET of operators. (Courtesy: BGS/GSG-9)

The GSG-9 killing house, St. Augustin. Carrying ballistic body bunkers and heavy Kevlar vests, operators assault a room held by terrorists (actually fellow operators in civilian dress). (Courtesy: BGS/GSG-9)

The Heckler and Koch MP5 A3 9mm submachine gun--the GSG-9 mainstay. (Heckler and Koch)

With GSG-9 turning to a 5.56mm caliber, the Heckler and Koch HK33E is seeing additional use by GSG-9 on exercises and on "jobs." (Heckler and Koch)

During maritime counter-terrorist training, a four-man Germany Navy ***Kampfschwimmer*** team prepares to assault a seaside shack held, in these exercises, by terrorists. (Courtesy: German Navy)

A GSG-9 operator prepares to test-fire a Swiss-produced SIG 550/551 SP at the range at St. Augustin. (Samuel M. Katz)

a Border Guard into an operator. Being part of GSG-9 was having proven one's self worth beyond what could be achieved in conscripted military service or climbing up one of the many corporate ladders in the private sector.

For the next fifteen years, GSG-9 could do no wrong. It was untouched by criticism or scrutiny until a fusillade of gunfire erupted on a darkened train track in the rural town of Bad Kleinen. On the night of June 27, 1993, approximately thirty GSG-9 operators found themselves in a stake-out operation, along with BKA agents, at the train station of the eastern village of Bad Kleinen in an attempt to arrest Birgit Hogefeld, thirty-seven-years-old, and Wolfgang Grams, forty-years-old, two of the most wanted members of the renegade Red Army Faction (R.A.F.). Because of the typical German bureaucracy involved in such undercover operations, officers from several federal, state and local police agencies were involved in the operation and it went bad--very bad: Grams managed to kill one GSG-9 operator and wound another before he was gunned down on Track 4 of the poorly lit station. The incident might have ended there, were it not for a series of investigative leaks to the vibrant--and hungry--German tabloid press, and the statements of an eyewitness who swore that a member of GSG-9 had shot Grams in cold-blood as he lay still on the tracks. The ensuing scandal exposed the inner workings of the BKA's campaign against the almost dormant R.A.F., as well as providing an inner-glimpse into the workings of GSG-9. Officials resigned, and the very fate of GSG-9 as the nation's cutting edge were jeopardized in the charges of police brutality, a cover-up and ineffectiveness even though an official investigative committee would find that Grams had shot himself.

GSG-9 returned to the spotlight shortly after the murders in Bad Kleinen. On August 17, 1993, a KLM flight from Tunis to Amsterdam was hijacked to Düsseldorf by a lone Egyptian, a follower of fire-brand Egyptian Sheikh Omar Abdel Rahman, who demanded the cleric's release from his incarceration in New York. GSG-9 was called to the scene and an assault squad of operators gained entrance to the aircraft and subdued the hijacker without firing a shot. The "rescue" in Düsseldorf was a fitting footnote to the Bad Kleinen controversy. Even the German press, which had a field day with the death of Wolfgang Grams and the resulting scandal, applauded GSG-9's skill and restraint in dealing with the KLM hijacking. An editorial in the usually critical ***Aachener Volkszeitung*** stated, "The incident at Düsseldorf proved that the men of GSG-9 know their craft and are not blood-thirsty or trigger happy." The full page editorial went on to profess, "What will happen tomorrow if a madman, a fanatic, or serious terrorist challenges our state? Will our politicians take on the work of GSG-9? Every civilized country needs an elite unit like this. When a fire is put out badly, no one talks about eliminating the fire department."

Even though the threats to German internal security have increased remarkably and ironically since reunification, GSG-9's strength remains the same--approximately 250 operators, with a support technical staff; the unit is divided into three operational sections or "Combat Units" and one combat unit made up of technicians, communications specialists and armament experts. Combat Unit 1, believed to consist of approximately 100 men, is a fire-team, a conventional, counter-terrorist hostage rescue assault unit, divided into ten, five-man ***Sonder-Einsatztrupp*** or SETs (Special Combat Teams), the smallest operational detachment in GSG-9. Commanders deploy their units in terms of combat teams, which consist of machine gunners, riflemen and a sniper. Of the three operational Combat Units, Unit 1 is the conventional force. Unit 2 is the same size as the a regular unit and capable of mounting similar missions as Unit 1, but is also trained in naval special warfare and

A portion of the GSG-9 motor-pool's compliment of Mercedes sedans awaits a call to action for the boys from St. Augustin. (Samuel M. Katz)

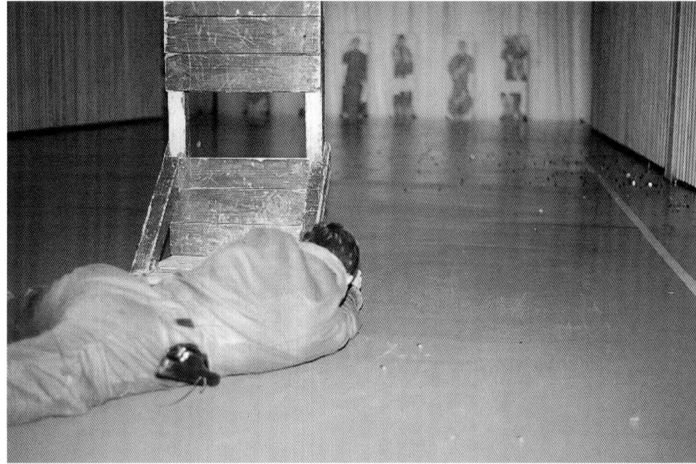

An operator, his Heckler and Koch P7 9mm pistol in firing position, prepares to pepper a target for his commandant's inspection on a floor already decorated with the refuse of a busy morning on the range. (Samuel M. Katz)

The cap and emblem of the ***Spezialeinsatzkommano Rheinland-Pfalz,*** seen inside the car of a senior SEK commander. (Samuel M. Katz)

maritime counter-terrorism. Trained by the Germany Navy's elite naval commando forces, the ***Kampfschwimmers***, many are also EOD-qualified. If a river barge on the Rhine or Elbe would be hijacked, if a dangerous smuggling gang would be operating along one of Germany's waterways, or if a dangerous hostage or criminal situation developed in the North Sea, Unit 2 would get the call. Although many in the German military (or in Coronado, California or Poole, United Kingdom for that matter) would not admit it publicly, GSG-9/Combat Unit 2 (GSG-9/2) is considered one of the world's best naval special warfare units, expert in surprise assaults and underwater demolitions; the unit has developed a virtual armory of special underwater combat gear and equipment--from underwater flash bang grenades to special body armor. Trained in a full array of underwater swimming and delivery techniques by ***Kampfschwimmer*** instructors, the operators are as capable a naval special warfare "commando" as are the men of the SBS or the SEALs; in fact, GSG-9/2 and SEAL Team SIX regularly train together (as do GSG-9 Section 2 operators with members of the SBS counter-terrorist community, Italian Navy ***Incurso***s, Danish ***Frømandkorpset***, and the Australian Special Air Service's Tactical Assault Group). In order to make the transition from stealth-like swimmer to counter-terrorist commando a safe one, GSG-9/Section swimmers are issued with specially-designed underwater body armor, made of Kevlar, that can be fitted with up to several inches of additional steel plating for added protection. Although GSG-9 is close-mouthed about operations in which underwater means of insertion or extraction are used, according to GSG-9 officers such operations are "routine," especially against kidnappers held out on a Rhine or Ruhr boat, or against heavily armed smugglers. Like the SBS's "M" Squadron, GSG-9 has also begun operations against drug smugglers entering Germany (often, it has been suggested, in international waters).

Training for GSG-9/2 begins with a volunteer in the ***BGS*** (Federal Border Guard) opting to try out for GSG-9. From the time a volunteer joins the selection process to the time his GSG-9 wings are "sewn" to his chest, the operator hopeful has undergone a good eighteen months of training. For those who will serve as GSG-9/2 operators, an additional twelve months of instruction (much of it at the hands of ***Kampfschwimmer*** officers and NCOs) is routine.

Unit 3, the smaller of the three combat units, is the free-fall parachutist qualified GSG-9 combat unit. Trained in both free-fall and HALO parachuting techniques, this unit is specially trained to infiltrate into a hotly contested, or ground secured location through airborne means. Most jumps are conducted from light aircraft, although many helicopter jumps are also practiced.

Although all the Combat Units have their own unique specialty, each are capable in the "basics" of hostage-rescue and combat assaults. All train to assault a building where hostages are held, a bus or train where hostages are held, and, of course, a hijacked aircraft--a GSG-9 calling card. To carry out these, and other more specialized, tasks, GSG-9's weaponry includes the German-made Heckler and Koch family of MP5 9mm submachine guns, including the standard MP5, the MP5 SD1, SD2, and SD3 suppressed (as well as the newer MP5 SD4 with three-round burst capability and fifteen-round magazine) and the MP5 K A5 (short). Always looking for the ultimate firing machine, GSG-9 is now experimenting with the Swiss-made SIG SG 551-1P 5.56mm special operations assault rifle and the new SIG SWAT sniper rifle. The sole assault rifle currently in service is the Heckler and Koch 7.62mm G8 special rifle, and precision shooting rifles deployed by GSG-9 include the old standard (and favored by many) Mauser Model SP66 7.62mm sniper rifle (as well as the Mauser Model SP86 7.62mm sniper rifle), and the Heckler and Koch PSG-1 7.62mm sniper rifle. Although the unit is considering changing its personal side-arm to the Austrian-made Glock 19 9mm pistol, the old--if not sentimental--favorite personal side-arm, although the Smith and Wesson .357 Magnum revolver is still the old standard (as it is with the SAS, the SBS' "M" Squadron, SEAL Team SIX and Delta Force) for indoor shoot-ups. Yet because of the changing face of terrorism much of GSG-9's heavy firepower is kept locked up in the unit's armory. Much of their work, especially undercover operations with the BKA, involves nothing more than their P7s and their instincts and policeman's sixth sense.

GSG-9 also deploys a small fleet of vehicles that transport them to targets or operations close to their home base at St. Augustin consisting primarily of the Mercedes Benz 280 SE high-performance passenger car, a Mercedes Benz 280 GE cross-country personnel vehicle (as well as a specially armored version of the 280 GE that is equipped with firing slots for the passenger seat next to the driver), and a mini-fleet of Volkswagen mini-buses. Other vehicles include trailers for equipment and specialized EOD gear and illumination material, Volkswagen VW 281 CH equipment carrier for diving unit and unit equipment base car.

Supporting virtually all GSG-9 deployments are the aircraft, all helicopters, of the ***Bundesgrenzschutz'***s ***Grenzschutz-Fliegergruppe***, or flight group. Stationed a few hundred meters away from the unit's barracks, the flight group is formally the property of the ***Bundesgrenzschutz***, and fulfills all duties required by the Federal Border Police. In time of emergency, however, these are the aerial taxis that GSG-9 uses to reach their objectives. ***Grenzschutz-Fliegergruppe*** pilots are considered among Germany's best--even better chopper drivers than exist in the German Air Force. Trained to land on a dime and fly through the most harrowing of urban and rural obstacles, the pilots realize that when they ferry in a SET or even elements of a Combat Unit toward an objective, the elements of time and surprise are crucial. Lives hang in the balance--the lives of hostages and the lives of the operators--and each moment in the air is attended to with the finesse of a surgeon. Bundesgrenzschutz aircraft include the Bell-212 (UH-1D) and Aérospatiale SA.332 Super Puma, and Aérospatiale Alouette (mainly for one-man insertion and reconnaissance).

Although the ***Grenzschutz-Fliegergruppe*** is a federal police aviation unit, it ranks high among the world's special operations aviation units in terms of pilot skill, daredevil low-level flight and the ability to ferry in a force of operators. GSG-9 makes the maximum use of its aerial assets for insertion, diversion and extraction. Unlike the aviators from the U.S. Army's 160th Special Operations Aviation Regiment, the legendary "Night Stalkers" with whom GSG-9 has trained, and unlike the U.S. Air Force's Special Operations Wings, the ***Grenzschutz-Fliegergruppe*** doesn't have to concern itself with evading enemy radar when attempting to reach an objective, nor must it evade multi-barreled 23mm anti-aircraft guns. The only defenses built in to the choppers are minor infra-red deflectors to deter the path of a SA-7 (which many terrorist groups carry as frequently as 9mm pistols) and modified low-noise engines. "The most effective weapon that these aircraft are equipped with," states a GSG-9 officer, "is the skill, courage and daring of the pilots behind the throttle." Over the course of GSG-9's history, the pilots of the ***Grenzschutz-Fliegergruppe*** based at St. Augustin, GSG-9's principal source of aerial transport, have developed a reputation as the finest helicopter pilots in Germany. Many of the pilots are veterans chopper drivers from the German Air Force, others volunteer directly into police service and the ***Bundesgrenzschutz*** flight school. Before they get their BGS wings, and before they are permitted to transport a team into action (or even on maneuvers)

The GSG-9 barracks at St. Augustin, near Bonn, is considered a Mecca to the world's counter-terrorist forces. In the good old days, when funds were endless, GSG-9 was a "have submachine gun, will travel" organization. They regularly visited units all over the world and there was a time when the unit's favorite destination was Israel. For years a special relationship, almost a brotherhood, existed between GSG-9 and ***Sayeret Mat'kal***, and later the Border Guard's ***Ya'ma'm*** hostage-rescue unit Because of a lack of funds that every government body is enduring since re-unification, GSG-9 has put its travel bags away. The travelers have become the hosts as any unit worth its salt sends some of its men to St. Augustin for a visit, a peek, and a chance for joint-training. The walls of the command center and barracks compound are adorned with plaques and souvenirs from these contacts--framed offerings of thanks, appreciation and friendship from Britain's SAS, the Australian and New Zealand SAS, the Spanish

A Rheinland-Pfalz SEK officer displays his utilities and protective body armor--note modified Heckler and Koch 12-gauge shotgun: enough firepower to stop even the most determined criminal. (Author's collection)

Interesting photograph of a Rheinland-Pfalz SEK policeman demonstrating his specialized gear, including indigenously produced Kevlar policeman's tactical helmet and protective visor. Note Heckler and Koch MP5 SD2 9mm submachine gun. (Author's collection)

A Rheinland-Pfalz SEK sniper, armed with a Heckler and Koch PSG-1 7.62mm sniper rifle displays his coveted weapon. Along with the Mauser SP 66 system, German snipers swear by the effectiveness and ease of operating the PSG-1. (Author's collection)

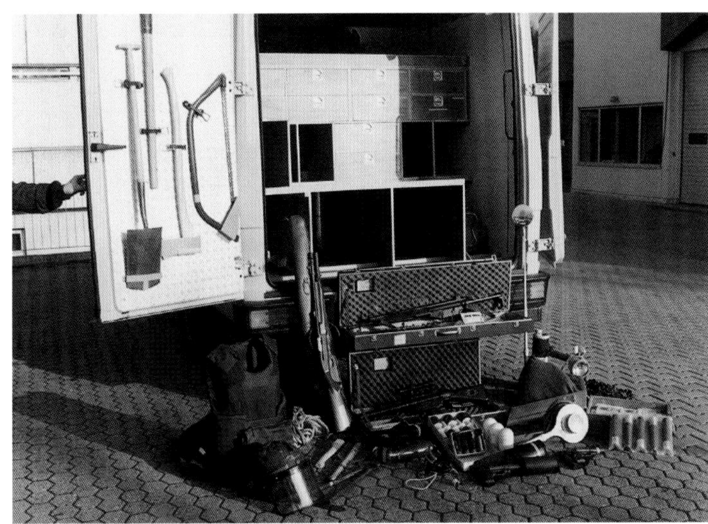

Officers from the Rheinland-Pfalz SEK display the gear stowed in the back of the Volkswagen mobile command center vans. Like their SWAT counterparts in the United States, SEK units throughout Germany have learned that the more equipment carried inside a vehicle affords the responding officers greater flexibility in handling a job on the spot, rather than being forced it to the point of escalation. (Author's collection)

GEO, the Italian Carabinieri's GIS, Norway's ***Deltatroppen***, France's GIGN, and, of course, Austria's ***Gendarmerieeinsatzkommando*** Cobra--one of GSG-9's closest allies. Although a distraction to the day-to-day rigors of training and preparation, these contacts are invaluable tools for gathering intelligence, sharing techniques and finding out what is new and different in the world of counter-terrorism. Operators always like to know what the next guy is doing, carrying and deploying, whether it be what communications device the ***Duvdevan*** (Cherry) commandos are using in the West Bank, to the new entry device used by officers in the Spanish GEO or Hong Kong's Special Duties Unit. For the obvious reasons, GSG-9's close international ties have been with Austria's Gendarmerieeinsatzkommando Cobra and the Swiss Enzian and Stern units. GSG-9 instruction has assisted the Dutch in the creation of the BSB, formed from a cadre of officers serving in the ***Königlichen Marechausse***. Over the past ten years, however, GSG-9's closest contacts are with the Americans--the men of the Army's Delta Force and the Navy's SEAL Team SIX. The units train together on a regular basis, share intelligence, tactics, and new bits of equipment they have developed. GSG-9 has also trained U.S. Marine Corps FAST units, as well as U.S. Military Police units in Germany, teaching the MPs the art of cold-killing and tactical intuition in their role in safe-guarding U.S. military installations. GSG-9 has also trained with several large municipal American SWAT units, including the Los Angeles SWAT Platoon.

Mostly, however, units venture to Germany to watch and learn how GSG-9 infiltrates its operators into an operational zone, and how they rescue an aircraft crammed with hostages--GSG-9 is considered the world's premier aircraft rescue unit and it trains and conducts exercises on all types of aircraft, in all of Germany's airports, throughout the year, as well as trains and buses perfecting the art of tubular assaults.

Perhaps more important than the history of its operation, GSG-9 has become world renowned as a result of the way in which it selects, trains and sculpts its operators--from volunteer policemen to counter-terrorist dynamos. One cannot simply volunteer into ***Grenzschutzgruppe 9***--not regular local municipal or state policemen, not military personnel or even agents in the BKA. Only serving policemen in the BGS (the affectionate acronym for the

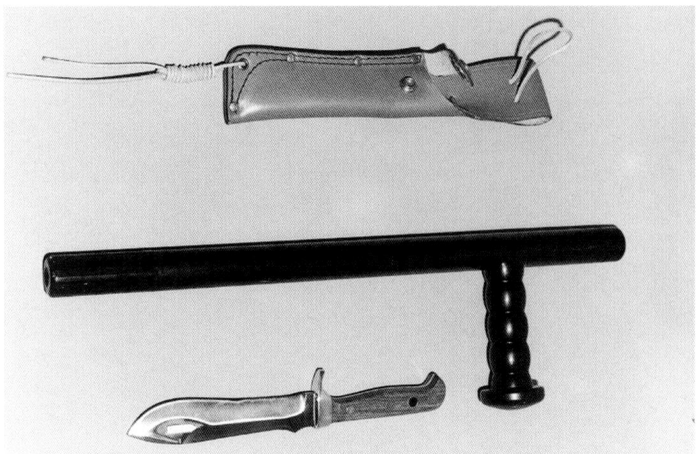

A "commando-like" dagger and the club--some of the more basic of equipment carried by each SEK officer in the field. (Author's collection)

A Heckler and Koch MP5 SD3, used by most of Germany's SEKs, seen here with a unique mini-tripod attachment for those long hours on stake-out or poised against a hostage-taker. (Author's collection)

***Bundesgrenzschutz)*** are allowed to submit their paperwork, and only those who have undergone an exhaustive security examination and psychological testing are even allowed into the selection process. The selection process, from the physical trials to the psychological examinations, takes nearly six months. Basic GSG-9 training, from basic weapons and endurance instructions to the very basics of counter-terrorism and combat assaults last nearly a year, and until the candidate is finally "ordained" an operator and awarded the GSG-9 wings. Following completion of the basic training, the operators go on to more specialized instruction, including undercover work, disguise, SCUBA or jump training, advanced language skills, ordnance and demolition, and high-speed driving skills. During the course of the instruction, a candidate can be dropped from the unit at any time.

Much has been said about GSG-9's status as legends, but in reality their future is somewhat in jeopardy. The very fact that they were so good and effective as a unit virtually guaranteed that they would have less work in the years to come. The fact that they existed as a unit was in itself a deterrent factor for terrorists planning to hijack a plane or train, so terrorists resorted to delay action bombing and selective assassinations instead of taking hostages. On a federal level, the terrorist statistics in Germany fell dramatically over the last few years and GSG-9 found itself being deployed less and less in its traditional role, and more and more as a federal tactical force combating the rise of violent right-wing neo-Nazi groups, organized crime from Eastern Europe, and working in an undercover capacity with the BKA on large-scale federal criminal investigations. In fact, GSG-9's status in the new and subsequently unified Germany has decreased in favor of

Rheinland-Pfalz SEK policemen sit on the landing skids of a MBB BO 105 transport shopper during insertion exercises in a forest near Frankfurt. (Author's collection)

a type of state and municipal special police units that has not only been much busier in the day-to-day tactical work that a counter-terrorist unit requires in order to keep its edge, but have since developed tactics and training methods which have surpassed those taught at St. Augustin. These units are the SEKs--Germany's SWAT units.

Law enforcement in Germany is similar to the United States, and is handled at a federal level (cases that could eventually involve GSG-9 deployment), and at the state and local level. For years, when it was thought that urban terrorism wouldn't come to West Germany, there was no push to prepare a domestic counter-terrorist policy or to prepare local law-enforcement to handle any terrorist emergency--a shortcoming made fatally clear during the Munich Olympics. This shouldn't be translated to mean that German police were primitive in their investigative or law-enforcement abilities, just ill-equipped and not trained to meet any terrorist incident. In this regard, the debacle at Fürstenfeldbrük wiped the slate clean.

Prior to the reunification of Germany, the Federal Republic consisted of ten ***Leander*** (states) and the city state of West Berlin.[4] Each state, with the exception of the ***Stadtstaaten*** (city state) of Hamburg and Bremen, and with the exception of the Saarland, a comparatively small state, is divided into several ***Regierungsbezirke*** (governmental districts) which are divided into ***Landkresie*** (counties) and ***Kreisfreie Staadte***. The organizational structure, mission and functions of the police in Germany are divided per state (the administrative political body that overseas police activities) and consist of ***Schutzpolizei*** (uniformed police), ***Kriminalpolizei*** (criminal police, or detectives), and ***Wasserschutzpolizei*** (Water Police). From 1977 onward, the BKA has also been involved in combating terrorism, but more in the coordination of state and local police in the administration and tactical execution of investigations and activities; typically the BKA would assume the responsibility for much of the investigative work and the state police units would provide back-up and tactical support.

Following Munich, when the inadequacies of the Bavarian police response was made so clear, it was decided to create tactical teams within each state and city police force. This decision met with stiff resistance in Germany, a nation where the police have developed from the military and been centralized and government orientated. The liberal left in Germany warned that tactically capable police would amount to a "back door capital punishment policy" in Germany, and result in the deaths of hundreds of innocent people on the streets of

A barge on the Rhine is boarded during maritime hostage-rescue exercises with a MBB BO 105 chopper. Many city and state SEKs are assuming responsibilities for counter-terrorism and high-crime incidents that were once the sole domain of GSG-9. (Author's collection)

Germany. At the time, however, it was the policeman who was under the gun. Policemen, armed with PPK 7.65mm automatics and obsolete body armor, were facing terrorists armed with RPGs and AK-47s, and some tactical shoring up was desperately required. The answer was a two-fold response--first was the ***Mobile Einsatzkommandos***, or MEKs, special observation and arrest teams subjugated to the investigation department of a district or city, and the second was the ***Spezialeinsatzkommandos***, or SEKs, a special task force drawn from members of the patrol division or the tactical riot response forces, and most similar in make-up and mandate to U.S. municipal SWAT teams.

Although SEKs vary in size depending on location and organizational set-up, most teams consist of anywhere between ten and twenty-four police officers, with a reserve strength of an equal number of policemen, and can field approximately fifty officers in a matter of an hour to meet any terrorist incident. Some SEKs have integral sniper teams, called PSKs, and others have their own special operations elements that allow them to perform extraordinary surveillance and reconnaissance tasks. Like GSG-9, the most basic element of the SEK is the SET, the three-four man cell which work together as a team and uses one vehicle to approach a scene. SET members are usually armed with nothing heavier than a 9mm pistol, but have specialized gear in their vehicles, such as MP5s and shotguns; should a situation develop and require calling out several SETs or even the entire SEK, then specially-produced unmarked vans and trucks can ferry emergency tactical gear such as sniper weapons, other EOD material, and entry devices. It should be noted that virtually all SEKs carry weaponry and equipment identical to GSG-9--the entire MP5 family of 9mm submachine guns, G3 assault rifles, PSG-1 sniper weapons and Heckler and Koch shotguns.[5]

SEKs throughout Germany are voluntary forces made up of officers between the ages of twenty-five and thirty who pass a lengthy series of psychological, and physical fitness examinations. The training regimen varies from department to department; smaller SEKs, for example, do not train in rescuing hostages from airliners or river barges, while larger SEKs train and practice in all types of tubular assaults and even send contingencies abroad for advanced instruction. Other aspects of SEK training include combat shooting; assault equipment; legal procedure and considerations; radio procedure; observation, reconnaissance and surveillance techniques; defensive driving skills; rappelling; door entry techniques; and marksmanship and sniping. The mold which all these units use as the basis for their instruction and operational procedure is, of course, GSG-9's. Over the years, however, there has been a high-level of competition between the various SEKs and GSG-9 over not only work, but bragging rights as being Germany's premier tactical response unit. Unlike GSG-9 which might have to wait years until it is called out on a large-scale mission, the state and city SEKs are constantly "on the job." While their daily patrol and investigative tasks might not involve fast-roping down the side of an office tower in order to perform an assault into an office besieged by Red Army gunmen, their police functions do provide these tactical officers with street smarts that GSG-9 officers simply do not have. Some SEKs are only involved in a few dozen calls a year, while others have participated in thousands of jobs. From their inception in June 1973 until 1985 the West Berlin SEK, for example, made 1295 arrests, captured thirty-five terrorists of various nationalities, as well as thirty extremely violent criminals. Throughout this period of non-stop activity, they peacefully ended fourteen hostage/barricaded situations, confiscated 300 handguns, twenty-two assault rifles and several hundred pounds of ammunitions and explosives.

Today, many of the SEKs are considered either equal to GSG-9 in skill and experience or even better. At a recent CTC (Combat Team Competition) in St. Augustin, where thirty-nine counter-terrorist and special forces units from thirteen nations participated, GSG-9 didn't even make it in the top ten of qualifying unit, though five SEKs did make the cut.[6] The competition tested the operators shooting, driving, and obstacle course skills and was something of an anomaly because the Delta team won; for several years earlier, SEK Munich had walked off with the championship. SEK Munich, it should be noted, is considered among one of the world's finest counter-terrorist and hostage-rescue units, and has trained in Israel with the ***Ya'ma'm***, in Italy with the NOCS, and in France with the RAID unit.

On purely military terms, should terrorists strike at a German ship or maritime target, more likely than not it will be the German Navy's frogman unit that will be called to execute the rescue raid, or set-up the scene allowing GSG-9 to move in. According to many naval commando officers from all over the world who were interviewed for this book, from British SBS operators to U.S. Navy SEALs, few naval special warfare forces in the world own such a professional and elite status for the combat and diving proficiency as do the German Navy ***Kampfschwimmer***s, or combat swimmers. A throwback to the World War II-era combat divers and swimmers of the legendary K-Flotilla, the "new" German Navy's Combat Swimmer force was created shortly after the Second World War when K-Flotilla veterans (those with clean slates and no Nazi party affiliations) were remaindered into the Federal Germany Navy in the early 1950s. With the creation of NATO and the Federal Republic of Germany's strategic role in the Cold War, this small cadre of combat swimmers were sent to France, and Corsica, to train with the combat swimmers of the Jaubert Commandos in 1959. This joint French-German naval special warfare training was at first difficult for the two former enemies, but the French found the Germans

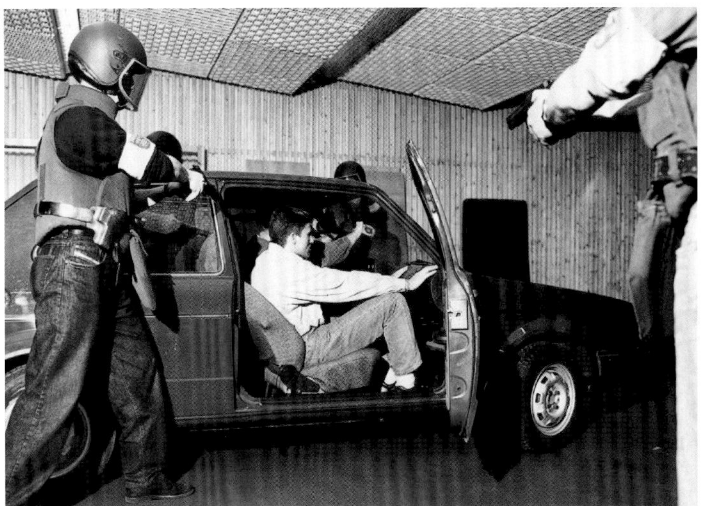

Stopping a fleeing terrorist in a speeding vehicle, whether he is escaping from an airport where he just perpetrated a massacre or is heading to a safe-house with hostage in tow, has proven to be one of the most difficult operations in counter-terrorist measures; in Germany, such "attempted" car stops have resulted in the deaths of numerous police officers. As a result, SEK police officers train incessantly in the art of stopping a vehicle and safely removing its armed passengers. Here, in this sequence of photographs, SEK officers armed with Browning Hi-Power automatics practice (1) stopping a vehicle and covering a passenger exiting the car; (2) subduing the subject; and, (3) searching him for weapons. (Author's collection)

to be professional, highly capable, and innovative in the art of naval sabotage and assault. From the creation of the modern, or post-war, German naval commando entity, the ***Kampfschwimmer*** companies were to play an instrumental, albeit still classified, role in the covert war against the Warsaw Pact. With an order of battle consisting of three platoons, a support platoon and a training platoon, the ***Kampfschwimmer*** Company was based at Eckernfoerde, along the Baltic coast. Although never believed to have numbered over 100 combat swimmers throughout their strongest days, the ***Kampfschwimmer*** was considered to be one of the most potent such forces in the world. Trained in all aspects of combat diving and underwater assault, the ***Kampfschwimmer*** units were also parachutist and heliborne qualified, as well as superior "land commandos" in essence, they were among the world's first SEAL teams incorporating the inclusive elements of sea and land. Expert shots with their coveted Israeli-produced Uzi 9mm submachine guns, ***Kampfschwimmer*** squads trained for assaulting Warsaw Pact harbors and coastal fortifications; unconfirmed reports indicate that the ***Kampfschwimmer***s were extremely active throughout the 1960s and 1970s conducting intelligence-gathering (and even sabotage) forays against the Warsaw Pact's Baltic fleet. The ***Kampfschwimmer***s were tasked with coastal and inshore harbor reconnaissance, intelligence-gathering and covert work with the German BND, the foreign espionage service, as well as sabotage strikes against harbors and enemy shipping, and beach reconnaissance and clearance. The ***Kampfschwimmer***s deploy from a wide variety of means, including German Air Force transport aircraft and helicopters, submarines (employing "lock out" and "lock in" extractions and insertion through sub torpedo tubes), surface craft, naval vessels, and SDVs. Interestingly enough, ***Kampfschwimmer*** operators are expert canoeists, employing the silent and effective delivery means favored by the NATO counterparts the British (and Dutch) SBS and the French Jaubert commandos.

Although the German Navy will not confirm the true training paths of their combat swimmers, instruction for a German Navy divers lasts over one full year.

[1] In light of documentation that has been released following the collapse of the former Soviet Union and reunification of Germany, it is now believed the East German intelligence was instrumental in the Black September execution of the operation--from the pre-planning reconnaissance, intelligence and logistic assistance to the actually smuggling of the weaponry and ammunition to Munich.

[2] Legend has it that Wegener was an invited guest of the Israelis to witness and participate in the rescue raid on Entebbe on July 3-4, 1976, though this rumor has since been denied by several sources including Wegener.

[3] The third SET, GSG-9/3, became operational on September 21, 1973.

[4] The states include Berlin, Schleswig-Holstein,. Hamburg, Bremen, Niedersachsen, Nordrhein-Westfalen, Hessen, Bayern, Baden-Würtemberg, Saarland, and Rheinland-Pfalz.

[5] SEK personnel are given a bit more freedom in terms of the side-arms they are allowed to carry, with many opting for Glocks, some opting for SIGs and officers in the Munich SEK, the unit with ties to both Israel and Italy, carry Jerichos, Desert Eagles or even Berettas.

[6] In the 1993 competition, the U.S. Army's 1st SFOD-D finished first; GEK Cobra from Austria finished in second place; SEK Rheinland-Pfalz finished third; the U.S. Navy's SEAL Team SIX finished fourth; SEK Südbayern finished fifth; SEK Baden-Würtemberg finished sixth; the Swiss ***Kantonpolizei*** Aaragu, Team Argus, finished seventh; SEK Nordbayern finished eight; SEK Niedersachsen finished ninth; and, the Swiss ***Kantonpolizei*** Bern, Team Enzian, finished tenth.

SEK officers perfect the art of the tactical car stop outdoors as they race to a stopped vehicles with guns drawn and trigger fingers poised to unload a 9mm barrage onto its target.

Always experimenting, always trying to stay one step ahead of the bad guy, an SEK squad employs a pyrotechnic device as a diversionary tool while the officers move in for the apprehension.

## Greece

Greece, an aquatic crossroads between the Near East and Europe, has managed to walk a tightrope in the international struggle against terrorism--because it is a member of NATO it has been the target of indigenous groups as well as foreign terrorist factions, yet it has always managed to maintain close ties to Arab states, especially the Palestinians and radical states such as Libya, Syria and Iraq, in the attempt to keep terrorist acts from being perpetrated on Greek soil. The arrangement has worked, though as a result of the close knit relationship between Greece and the Arabs, many Western security officials view Greece as a security basket case. Athens International Airport, it should be noted, has been referred to by many security officials around the world as a "Terrorist Grand Central Station," and many of the world's most notorious hijackings and aircraft seizures, including those leading to the Entebbe rescue and the now infamous hijackings of Egyptair 648 and TWA 847, all emanated from Athens.

In the event that a hostage situation is perpetrated on Greek soil or involves a Greek ship or Olympic Airways aircraft, Greek police units are responsible for handling the matter, although military units are also tasked and prepared for carrying out such work. In Athens, for example, the city's SWAT unit, the "Special Mission Platoon," is the principal hostage-rescue and heavy-duty tactical force. They are trained like most municipal American SWAT units, and is believed to number fifty officers. Little is known of their cross-training, although it is believed that they have had American assistance and training. They are armed with MP5s and Browning Hi-Power 9mm pistols, and their snipers are believed to carry PSG-1s, as well as the American M24 system. They have had very little operational experience, and it is not known how effective they would be in handling a terrorist or hostage-taking situation involving numerous individuals and hostile firepower.

Because Greece is virtually surrounded by water and consists of hundreds of islands, the Greek Navy's naval special warfare unit has increasingly trained in the art of hostage-rescue. Like many nations that have had close military ties with the United States, Greece has emulated the U.S. Navy's special warfare assets with the creation of the Greek SEALs. Greece's naval special warfare unit, however, is not a mere Cold War creation mean to shore up a NATO flank. It is a highly professional combat unit drawing on Greece's unique sea-faring and diving history. The Greek Navy's special warfare unit, created in 1957, ***Monas Ymourhon Katastpofon***, known also as the MYK, meaning underwater destruction unit. The MYK is divided into four OYKs (***Omada Ymourhon Katastpofon***) or "Underwater Destruction Detachments;" basically, they are teams built along the line of the U.S. Navy SEALs, though there isn't a specific team tasked with counter-terrorism work with all units expected to be able to carry out a selective maritime rescue operation. The MYK's three primary missions are: infiltration, sabotage and attacking enemy shipping; reconnaissance and pre-landing beach clearance and designation, and ordnance disposal, though maritime counter-terrorism is now a serious operational necessity. Considered an elite special operations force within the NATO ORBAT, they are superb ground operators, as well. Armed with sophisticated individual firepower (MP5s, MP 11s, M16A2s and MG-3 7.62mm light machine guns), the MYK divers are a lethal assault force. During the Gulf War, MYK operators saw action enforcing the United Nations blockade against Iraq; two OYK teams sent to the Red Sea and the Indian Ocean and Persian Gulf to enforce the embargo actually boarded an astounding 217 freighters.

## Hungary

Before the collapse of the Berlin Wall and communism as a political force in Eastern Europe, many of the world's most notorious terrorist groups found sanctuary, operational bases and overt military and irregular warfare training in the capitals of Poland, Czechoslovakia and the Soviet Union. Hungary was unique, in as much as it never participated in the active irregular warfare training of major terrorist organization personnel,[1] yet until 1988, Hungary served as the European headquarters for perhaps the most fanatic Palestinian terrorist group, and the most violent--the Abu Nidal Faction (also known as "Black June").

In 1990, with the Cold War over and Hungary eager to shed its former ties (forged under the stranglehold of Moscow), ties to all terrorist faction were terminated. One year later, on May 1, 1991, the Hungarian Minister of the Interior ordered the creation of a national counter-terrorist force to meet any terrorist threat and challenge, as well as counter the threat of heavily armed criminal gangs operating inside the republic. The unit was the Police Special Force, or PSF.

Because of its former ties to terrorist

A PSF officer, displays the proper firing stance with his Israeli Mini-Uzi 9mm submachine gun. Note Israeli Kevlar infantry ballistic helmet worn, as well as Israeli special operations assault ***Ephod***, or vest. (courtesy: PSF)

`The full kit of a PSF officer, seen to advantage here in this posed shot. Note balaclava worn as cap, Israel-made assault vest, and dagger hanging from scabbard. Missing is the unit's now characteristic claret beret. (Courtesy: PSF)

Actual photograph of a PSF raid on a criminal hide-out near Budapest, early 1994--operations that displays the PSF ability in handling incidents involving either heavily armed criminals (such as those featured here) or heavily armed terrorists. (Courtesy: PSF)

PSF officers, their faces camouflaged with black paint, stand at the ready while civilians (in a poor neighborhood of Budapest) are evacuated from the potential scene of a fire-fight. Note PSF officer carrying what appears to be a Beretta RS200P 12-gauge shotgun, and other officers carrying body bunkers and Mini-Uzi 9mm submachine guns. (Courtesy: PSF)

The explosive entry--holding a small mini aim-light device, a PSF officers clutches his Mini-Uzi with one hand, ordering all suspects to raise their hands and drop to the ground while his exposed activity is covered by two assault team-mates. (Courtesy: PSF)

outfits, the Hungarian Police and the Hungarian counter-intelligence services were quite familiar with terrorist tactics and capabilities. As a result, the PSF began it operational existence one step above many similar units formed following the 1972 Munich Massacre--the Hungarians knew exactly what they were up against. PSF officers studied former intelligence material, manuals and intelligence reports provided by other former Warsaw Pact police agencies, and trained to not only aggressively meet any terrorist threat, but to act aggressively and offensively against locations where intelligence reports suggested terrorists had established safe houses or transit points; like an elite military unit, the PSF's operating guidelines stipulated that "defense" meant a good and heavy fire-power offense. Since the winter of 1991, when the first PSF class graduated, to the winter of 1994, the unit has participated in over 100 successful operations, and three hostage-rescue assaults.

Like many SWAT teams in the United States, only serving officers with the National Police force are allowed to volunteer into the PSF's selection process. Only those officers with a minimum of three years outstanding service on the job, as well as those who pass stringent medical, psychological and physical examinations are allowed to begin training; because of Hungary's former ties to terrorist groups, PSF volunteers undergo exhaustive and grueling security checks as well. Acceptance into the unit, certainly the most selective "combat" force in all of Hungary (including the Hungarian military), secures absolutely nothing. The founders of their unit were determined to make each operator work as hard to get into the force as he would work to stay in the PSF, and all officers, from deputy commanders to the newest member, are subject to performance revues and possible termination from the force each and every year.

Although the exact number of officers serving on the PSF is classified, the standby unit, on call 24-hours-a-day, is known to consist of twenty officers.

As a former Warsaw Pact satellite eager to shed its links to the east bloc, the Hungarian police quickly and enthusiastically set up close ties to various Western police forces. The PSF, in turn, quickly established close working ties to the French Police RAID unit, the Louisiana State Police SWAT unit,[2] and has participated in the U.S. State Department's anti-terrorist programs and seminars. Oddly enough, for a nation that was once the prime European headquarters for Abu Nidal terrorist operations, the PSF has forged its closest

In search of suspects seen loitering around the area by intelligence spotters before their assault, a PSF assault squads cleans out a garage and out-house during an operation. (Courtesy: PSF)

Assaulted, neutralized and apprehended in a matter of seconds, a criminal gang, with known connections to narco-terrorists from the Middle East, are readied for a trip to a police interrogation--courtesy the men of Hungary's PSF. (Courtesy: PSF)

Operating undercover, a PSF "operator: takes cover behind a recently pulled up squad car in apprehending a wanted terrorist suspect. (Courtesy: PSF)

alliance with Israel and Israeli police special units, primarily the ***Ya'ma'm.*** The PSF has trained with the ***Ya'ma'm*** and has used the Israeli Special Police Unit as its role model both in structure, doctrine, operational expectations, organization, as well as in the procurement of equipment; the PSF believes that if weaponry and equipment is good enough for the Israelis then it's good enough for them. The PSF, unlike many of its European counterparts has shied away from the Heckler and Koch family of weapons and has instead opted to use the Israeli Mini-Uzi 9mm submachine gun, Israeli .357 Magnum Desert Eagles, and foreign-made (primarily Belgian, Italian and American) 12-gauge shotguns and sniper rifles.

[1] While terrorists from the various Palestinian groups or other European forces of revolution (such as the Red Army Faction and Provisional Irish Republican Army) did not learn the art of blowing up airliners or hijacking trains in Hungarian facilities, Hungarian military officers ***did*** provide conventional military instruction to "conventional" elements of ***Fatah,*** Yasir Arafat's military wing of the PLO, namely the Kastel, Karameh and Yarmouk Brigade prior to Israel's 1982 invasion of Lebanon. This instruction primarily consisted of armored warfare training, and specifically training PLO recruits in the A-Zs of operating antiquated T-34 tanks that the Hungarian military sold to the PLO in 1981.

[2] It is believed that the PSF has also trained with the U.S. Marshals Service's elite counter-terrorist force, the Special Operations Group (SOG), at Camp Beauregard, in Louisiana.

Following a successful mission--one where all the bad guys were seized and one when not a shot needed to be fired in anger--two PSF officers stand on a just secured balcony and offer a brief, though deserved, smile. (Courtesy: PSF)

# Ireland

***It was too early for a raid, but in order to surprise a few "bad guys" hopefully a bit dazed after a night in the pub it was really the perfect time. The neat red brick houses were quiet, the inhabitants of the alley road fast asleep in the early morning hours, and only the distant mufflers of car engines on the roadway to Dun Laoghaire could be heard in the distance. Two white Fiat vans had wisely stopped a block down the road and the sixteen officers they carried slowly hugged the walls of the targeted house. They were prepared to meet any weapon threat, all were wearing Level-III body armor vests, and all clutched their Austrian-produced Steyr AUG 5.56mm assault rifles. Two officers stood outside the targeted door with their weapons pointed straight at the rusty metal number, while four others covered the windows peering through the sights of the space-age looking assault rifles. A sledge-hammer was brought along "just in case," but the rear kitchen door was open. A slow twist of the knob and then the flash-bang was thrown in. It took all of four seconds for the diversionary device to detonate and worked as planned--it blew out the kitchen window, and two others in an adjacent bedroom. Before the smoke could clear, the operators went in shouting "Garda, Stay Down and put your hands up!!!!" There was no one in the house, however. Special Branch had received a bad tip. There were no terrorists inside this Dublin house.***

Fighting terrorism in the Republic of Ireland is the responsibility of the ***Garda Siochana*** (Gaelic for Irish Police) and the Irish Defense Forces. Throughout the history of the Irish conflict, the south has been a safe haven for Republican terrorists, though the Irish government has attempted to limit the movement of known IRA operatives and their field soldiers. The Irish government has made a determined effort to combat northern terrorists on Irish soil, and has cooperated with British authorities, although there have been problems. The Garda has, on several occasions, arrested marauding SAS teams who have crossed into the south in pursuit of PIRA squads, and official difficulties have arisen over the extradition of fugitives back to the north. On the whole, however, the arrangement has worked out well and with the signing of the 1985 Anglo-Irish Agreement, cooperation between the RUC and the Garda has proved most effective. On the intelligence front, cooperation between the Garda Special Branch and the RUC Special Branch and MI5 has been smooth.

The 11,000-man Garda is, on the whole, an unarmed police force policing Ireland in the same way it has done for generations--stopping petty thefts, rural and farm crime, and upholding the public order. The Garda's Special Branch is the entity in the police force tasked with tactical police work, and in many cases apprehending terrorists inside Ireland. Trained primarily by the Dutch and French police, though maintaining close ties to SO19, the unit is primarily equipped with Austrian-produced Steyr AUG 5.56mm assault rifles, Glock Model 19 pistols and Israeli-produced Kevlar body armor and infantry ballistic gear. Special Branch units have been instrumental in serving warrants of known PIRA and IRA terrorists inside Ireland, as well as securing the often porous frontier with the north. In their stake-outs and search operations, Garda Special Branch units have scored considerable successes, including uncovering a 4,200lb bomb plus mortars and other weapons in Letterkenny, County Donnegal on March 10, 1992. Frequently, the RUC and the British Army will conduct operations in the Armagh which are often conducted in direct liaison with the Garda Special Branch.

Supplementing the Garda in an internal security mandate is the Irish Defense Forces, and several infantry battalions and a cavalry squadron permanently function with the Garda along the border. Yet true hostage-rescue work in the Republic of Ireland is the domain of the Irish military, and the ARW--the Army Ranger Wing. Created in 1980 with the U.S. Army's 1st SFOD-D as its role model, the ARW was established as a permanent on-call force of operators tasked with handling hostage-rescues (including rescuing hostages from planes, trains, buses and boats) and VIP-security. Believed to number around 100 operators, the ARW is an elite force that trains incessantly for that one late night phone call when they are summoned to Dublin or Shannon to rescue passengers from a hijacked aircraft, or to Cork, Limerick, Galway or anywhere else to respond to heavily armed individuals holding hostages.

The ARW is armed with Steyr AUG 5.56mm assault rifles, Steyr Police sniping 7.62mm rifles, and Glock 9mm pistols; recently, however, the ARW, as well as the Special Branch, have begun carrying MP5s, primarily the MP5 A3, on assignment. They have trained with the U.S. Army's 75th Ranger Regiment (Airborne) and the 1st SFOD-D, the French GIGN and the Dutch BBE.

Acting on an RUC tip, Garda Special Branch officers engage in searching for an IRA fugitive in a Dublin slum. Note Israeli-produced Kevlar infantry ballistic helmets and Austrian-produced Steyr AUG 5.56mm assault rifles. (Courtesy: Steyr)

An Army Ranger Wing NCO poses for the cameras prior to an exercise with the Garda near Dublin. Note heavy-duty Kevlar protective body armor, helmet with plexi-glass visor, and Austrian-produced Steyr AUG 5.56mm assault rifle. (Courtesy: Steyr)

# Italy

***A light snow had begun to fall on the tarmac at Dusseldorf's sprawling international airport. A row of Lockheed jets belonging to LTU were getting dusted by the flakes and readied for flights to the Greek Isles, Majorca, and the golden coast of Morocco. Inside the main hangar, however, work of another kind was underway. Operators from GSG-9 were practicing taking down a hijacked airliner but this was no ordinary exercise--it was more of a display. Visiting Germany this frigid February morning was a squad of operators from Italy, from the Gruppo di Intervento Speciale (GIS), the elite counter-terrorist unit of the Carabinieri.***

***From the dawn's first light to the midday snow, both units had worked at perfecting the proper entry into an aircraft, the proper assault technique and the proper firing position for firing an MP5 while racing down a narrow aisle. For much of the morning, inside the hangar, it was the German's show but when the training was taken outside, when the blinding snow would keep these activities far from the eyes of curious travelers looking outside the terminal windows, it was the Italians' time to show and tell. Dressed in their olive Nomex coveralls and wearing black cap/balaclava combinations, the Italians studied the scenario (three terrorists, two men and a woman) of the hijacked craft and then readied their Beretta 9mm automatics and protective body armor. Deploying from their Fiat mini-vans they had driven from Italy to St. Augustin, Germany, the Italians raced along the snow covered runway at speeds near 70mph in evasive maneuvers to simulate an assault and to impress their hosts. The two vans screeched to a halt underneath the L-1011's right wing and the operators emerged in a sprint to their positions. A rubberized ladder was produced and placed near the pilot's door--entry would be from the cockpit, though two operators armed with MP5s, found a secret entrance near the landing gear and would act as the cover force. Inside the aircraft, cardboard cutouts simulated the terrorists and GSG-9 operators would play the hostages. The assault took all of fifty-seven seconds.***

***The Germans were impressed, and proceeded to storm the aircraft and rescue the hostages (this time GIS troopers) in sixty-five seconds. The competitive spirit being what it is among these units, the GSG-9 operators looked forward to "impress" the Italians later in the year during a courtesy return visit at Rome's Leonardo Da Vinci International Airport.***

The Italians had come to Germany to learn and to teach. GSG-9 had the reputation, but the GIS had the experience. "One of the world's best counter-terrorist units because of their experience," according to the Israelis, Italy's counter-terrorist and hostage rescue units have had nearly twenty years of irregular warfare combat battling a violent and ruthless litany of enemies--from the Red Brigade to the Sicilian Mafia. Few democratic countries in Europe--and in the world--have been able to assemble as talented a group of counter-terrorist policemen and soldiers as has Italy, and few countries have been as courageous in the decision to deploy these units decisively and often in order to defeat the terrorist and criminal groups that not only threatened the lives of innocent civilians, but the very fabric of government, as well.

The principal Italian counter-terrorist and hostage-rescue unit, the one called to execute the most dangerous and nationally important operations, is the Carabinieri's ***Gruppo di Intervento Speciale*** (GIS). The GIS consists of approximately 100 operators and is drawn from the airborne parachutist-qualified element within the Carabinieri; the unit is based in the picturesque town of Livorno, north of Rome. The GIS approach to counter-terrorism is purely military--offense and initiative breeds results. If they are assaulting a safe-house harboring Red Brigade terrorists, a narcotics den where the Mafia is storing hundreds of pounds of heroin, or if they are rescuing a hostage being held by a crazed gunman, they do so as if they are encountering a military problem--a quick and decisive solution to any scenario. Known for their courage almost as much as for their skills and professionalism. Formed in 1978, in the wake of the explosive and violent eruption of the narcotics trade emanating from Sicily, as well as the introduction of the Red Brigade as a serious security threat, the GIS soon became one of the world's premier intervention units.

Soldiers and military policemen serving in the Carabinieri are allowed to volunteer for consideration into the ranks of the GIS if they have an exemplary military service record, if they have passed an exhaustive and grueling security check, and if they are able to pass a board of military psychiatrists, physicians and senior GIS officers who attempt to dissuade the potential volunteer; "the pay is not great and the workload immense," officers have been known to tell candidates. For those who have made it past obstacle number one, a stumbling block that accounts for a forty-percent attrition rate, a difficult and physically intensive two-week selection process is entered. Here,

A GIS operator places a C-4 charge to a window frame at a "shooting house" during explosive entry exercises. Note Model 12 Beretta with Italian-produced forward pistol grip/flashlight attachment. (Courtesy: Carabinieri)

A two-man GIS entry team, wearing black coveralls, gas masks and Nomex hoods, await a C-4 charge to allow them entry into a suspected terrorist safe-house during exercises in northern Italy. Note Italian-produced forward pistol grip/flash-light attachment to grip of MP5 (right) and Beretta Model 12 (left). (Courtesy: Carabinieri)

During forced entry exercises in their home base, GIS operators lower themselves down on a fast rope. Note operator (left) who is covering the assault team with his MP5--should a terrorist stick his head or weapon out, it will quickly be taken out. (Courtesy: Carabinieri)

Excellent close-up photograph of a GIS officer, wearing his Nomex hood/balaclava combination, as he peers through the sights of his Heckler and Koch MP5 A3 9mm submachine gun. (Courtesy: Carabinieri)

volunteers are forced to endure countless forced marches, long combat swims, endless drills, and a host of torturous exercises meant to convince those who are not GIS material that it is time to quit (no black mark is held against a Carabinieri soldier or officer who fails this process), and convince those motivated by the challenge--and capable of meeting it--that this is a home for them.

GIS training lasts, it has been reported, nearly ten months and runs the entire gamut of the special operations and counter-terrorist curriculum and more. The course consists of the following: terrorist ideology (where operators are taught to behave, think and act instinctively as Red Brigade terrorists); combat shooting and marksmanship; explosives and EOD; hand-to-hand combat and unarmed and cold-killing (GIS operators are considered to be among the best martial-artists in all of Europe, second only to, some have said, the Russian Spetsnaz and their Alpha-Team counter-terrorist unit); rappelling and fast-rope techniques; advanced combat medics courses; advanced intelligence-gathering and reconnaissance courses; advanced communications and radio instruction; and, basic hostage-negotiations. Of course, as Italian drivers are known throughout the world for their skill (as well as reckless daring) and "Formula One-type" evasive driving skills are taught to all GIS candidates, including, it has been reported, a week of instruction at the famed Ferrari factory and speed roadway. As the Italian armed forces are among the most specialized in all of Europe, the GIS also trains with Italian special forces--including advanced mountain and alpine warfare skills from the ***Alpini*** Brigade in the Italian Alps, and combat swimming from the famed--and among the world's best--naval special warfare unit in the world, the ***Incursori.*** In fact, the GIS maintains a twenty-man frogman unit on constant alert for possible maritime operations. In October 1985, after Palestinian terrorists from the Abu Abbass Faction of the Palestine Liberation Front (PLF) seajacked the Italian-registered ocean liner S.S. ***Achille Lauro***, the GIS frogmen were poised to launch a rescue raid; interestingly enough, so too were operators from the U.S. Navy's SEAL Team SIX, as most of the hostages were American citizens. Why the GIS wasn't actually deployed in a bid to rescue the ***Achille Lauro*** remains a mystery to this day, though it appears as if the Italian government of then Premier Benito Craxi was unwilling to anger the PLO by having some of their men killed by Italian commandos.

Italy's, and the GIS's, most serious threat has been from the ***Brigate Rosse*** (or Red Brigades), an ultra-left wing movement

A huge military force, the Carabinieri can provide the GIS with its vast national resources, including its air-wing. Here, six GIS operators cling to the landing skids of a Carabinieri Bell 412 during fast-rope exercises. (Courtesy: Carabinieri)

spawned by the ultra-radical wings of the Italian labor movement. Formed in 1970 with a direct and clear objective of destroying the Italian establishment, the Red Brigades soon expanded their scope to include attacks on NATO personnel, and carrying out attacks against "imperialist multinational corporations" based in or operating out of Italy. Supported by the various Marxist Palestinian organizations, liberation armies and popular fronts that had set up shop in Europe, the Red Brigade was also well entrenched with the German Red Army Faction and the French Direct Action (AD); supported by Eastern-bloc intelligence, the group was lavishly armed with everything from 9mm ammunition stolen from Italian Army barracks and grenades seized from NATO caches, to RPG-7s from Soviet-bloc diplomatic pouches. Many GIS operations against the Red Brigades, carried out with other Italian intelligence and police agencies, were lightning fast middle of the night raids against safe-houses and weapons stores. The GIS would isolate and secure a target and then perform an explosive entry. Securing and apprehending all inside, the GIS would then leave and allow intelligence and law-enforcement personnel to conduct interrogations and gather evidence for trial.

While the threat from the Red Brigades has diminished considerably in the last few years and much of the counter-terrorist work that the GIS is involved in now deals with outside elements and narco-terrorists, it should be noted that between 1973 and 1983, the Red Brigades mounted a remarkable 9,361 attacks resulting in the deaths of 116 individuals and the wounding of hundreds more.

In July 1992, the GIS was in the vanguard as the Italian military declared war against the Sicilian Mafia in what many saw as a return to Mussolini-era tactics. Over 3,000 Italian airborne troopers and special forces operators, led by GIS action teams, were flown to Sicily and tasked with seizing known drug and criminal locations. Most importantly, they were tasked with the safe-guarding of government facilities and figures. While troops from the Friuli Motorized Regiment and the red-beret paratroopers from the Folgore Regiment secured key installations and roadways, the GIS and other elite forces ventured into the countryside to seek out, hunt, and apprehend or eliminate key Mafia officers and soldiers; much of these operations are classified and top-secret, as Italian emergency laws and counter-terrorist regulations The soldiers had the status of special constables, taking over routine duties to allow the specialized police units and the Carabinieri to concentrate on the manhunt aspect of the anti-Mafia work.

The GIS is among the best equipped counter-terrorist units in Europe--lavishly funded and able to purchase the finest weapons and gear on the market in Europe, as well as the multitude of material produced in Italy. The premier weapon used by the GIS is the Beretta Model 12S 9mm submachine gun--especially variants equipped with silencers, scopes and laser aim-point devices. Recently, the GIS has begun to carry and try out the MP5 family of weapons, and operators have been most pleased with the MP5's performance--especially the MP5 A3 and the MP5 SD 3. For more conventional deployments, especially against the Mafia in Sicily, the weapon of choice is the Beretta SC70/90 5.56mm assault rifle. The unit's primary side-arm is the Beretta Model 92 SB 9mm automatic (modified from the 92F variant by being equipped with the safety lever on both sides for truly ambidextrous firing, and by having the magazine release button placed underneath the trigger guard), though the favored revolver carried, especially for close-quarter combat, is the Smith and Wesson "Patrolman" .357 Magnum, and the Smith and Wesson .38 caliber "Bodyguard." Sniper weapons deployed by GIS snipers including the Heckler and Koch PSG-1 7.62mm rifle, as well as the Mauser SP86 7.62mm rifle; the unit has also just begun the deployment of the Barett M82 12.7mm sniper rifle--a piece of devastating hardware that has proven itself to be more of an intimidating deterrent (especially in Sicily) rather than a tactical piece of equipment. The GIS is also very fond of shotguns, both pump-action and automatic--especially for entries and intimidation. The unit's primary shotguns include the Franchi 12-gauge SPAS 12 shotgun, the SPAS-15 12-gauge shotgun, and the 12-gauge PA3 riot shotgun.

GIS immediate deployment. Armed with a combination of MP5s and Model 12 Berettas, a GIS strike detachment races toward its target from a Carabinieri air wing Bell-412. Note black Kevlar infantry ballistic helmets, and black balaclavas. (Courtesy: Carabinieri)

In Germany, GIS operators (wearing helmets with visors) confer with GSG-9 officers during anti-hijacking exercises. (Samuel M. Katz)

In May 1994, back in Rome, at Leonardo da Vinci International Airport, the chaos near the Alitalia hangar mounts as mechanics and supervisors ready the day's flights to and from the Middle East, Europe and North America. One aircraft, a Boeing 747-Combi, is parked to a remote corner of the tarmac where only a few can gaze upon its shimmering white fuselage. Underneath the left wing, twenty men wearing black Nomex coveralls and green Kevlar flak vests stand around a ladder. The commander of the team, wearing his red beret and clutching a Beretta 92F with an aim-point device attached, speaks in a soft voice as he tells those assembled the time that he deems proper to rescue the simulated 300 hostages on board the aircraft. This exercise will be difficult, the commander explains, as the terrorists have wired explosives to the two main exits located by row at the end of the

During joint aircraft rescue exercises with GSG-9, a GIS officer reaches for his Beretta 92F SB 9mm automatic on a rubber-coated ladder placed alongside the aircraft fuselage. (Samuel M. Katz)

A GIS operator secures his bullet-proof helmet prior to engaging in anti-hijack exercises in Germany. Note close-up view of GIS holster set-up and new Kevlar protective vests. (Samuel M. Katz)

GIS and GSG-9 officers confer in a hangar at Dusseldorf International Airport prior to commencing large-scale anti-hijack exercises. (Samuel M. Katz)

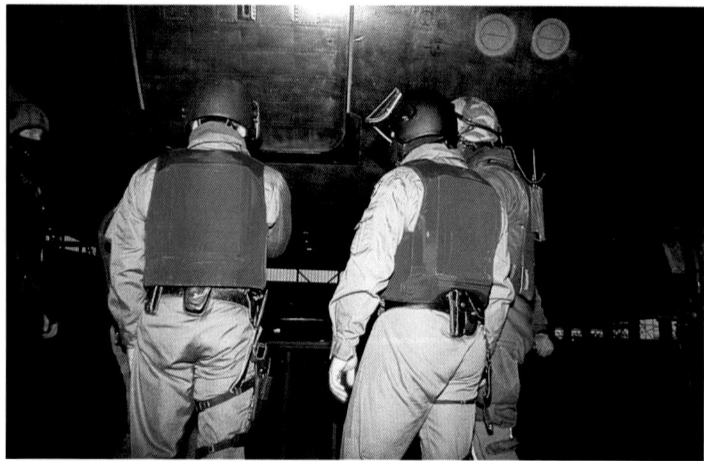

Excellent rear-view of the GIS protective vest and their holster system. Here, two GIS operators confer with a GSG-9 officer. (Samuel M. Katz)

second-level stairway. It is decided to try something different this time. The operators would make their entry through the hump; no hostages were held in the additional seating compartment, but it was believed no explosives were in place, either. A few extra sections were added to the ladders and the drill commenced.

The operators perform one last, final, weapons and equipment check, black balaclavas are placed over heads already engulfed by a shiny cover of perspiration. Over the communications frequency reserved for the operators and scrambled against any outside eavesdropping, the commander, clutching the ladder and ready to race forward, orders the support crew to assume their defensive positions; six gunners, all carrying MP5s, race underneath the aircraft and point their barrels upward. Hiding behind an Alitalia food truck, the operators await the signal from the cover team before beginning their charge with ladder is hand. The operators positioned the now elongated piece so that it just reached the hump's exit and it reached it at an angle that the terrorists couldn't see what was going on. Entry into the aircraft was made quietly and quickly--rescuers function with the premise that the terrorists have eyes-on intelligence working with them from a terminal or a distant vantage point somewhere along the runway. Within ninety-nine seconds, and after twenty rounds of blanks are fired, the plane is declared secured.

Watching the exercise at Leornado da Vinci International Airport that cool spring's morning is a liaison officer from the NOCS. The NOCS, the affectionate nickname for the ***Nucleo Operativo Centrale di Sicurezza***, is the counter-terrorist and hostage rescue unit of the national state police. There has always been a fierce competition between the GIS and the NOCS over who is the true national counter-terrorist and hostage-rescue unit, and there has also been much confusion in this matter, as well. The NOCS consists of approximately 100 agents, all hand-picked volunteers, who have excelled in their police work; while the ranks consist of officers from the national police, officers from municipal agencies are also allowed to volunteer. The unit, based at a state-of-the-art facility on the island of Sardinia, is trained in virtually the same fashion and regimen as the men of the GIS, though they engage in far more police work, and many of their "jobs" are against armed criminals as well as terrorists.

The NOCS were formed following the 1978 kidnapping and murder of Aldo Morro, the Christian Democrat and former Prime Minister (and, it should be noted, a man expected to one day be the Italian President). On March 16, 1988, a well-train team of Red Brigades operatives ambushed Aldo Morro's car, killed his five bodyguards and abducted the elderly politician. Aldo Morro was held for fifty-four days by the terrorists, but their demands that the Italian government release hundreds of political prisoners were never heeded and he was killed with a shot to the head by a Skorpion machine pistol. The kidnapping of Aldo Morro was a watershed turning point in Italy's history of battling terrorism--much as the Munich Olympic Massacre and the killing of Hans-Martin Schleyer had changed the rules for combating terrorism in Germany. Immediately following the discovery of Ado Morro's bullet-ridden corpse on in the trunk of an abandoned car parked on a Rome street, Prime Minister Giulio Andreotti summoned his top military and police officials and proposed special emergency laws permitting preventative arrests, and bugging prison cells. He also attempted to bring together Italian military and law-enforcement units to mount a coordinated and unified campaign against this seemingly unstoppable force.

The three main agencies involved in fighting terrorism in Italy were the Public Security Guard (PSG), the national police, which consisted of 50,000 officers throughout the country and was under the control of the Ministry of the Interior; the para-military Carabinieri, a force of 85,000 men controlled by the Ministry of Defense that performed rural police work and frontier protection; and, the Italian Finance Police, the ***Guardia di Finanza***, a 42,000-man national force responsible for financial crimes, such as tax evasion, money laundering and arms and narcotics smuggling, and an agency that maintains its own counter-terrorist unit and intervention squad.[1] The triumvirate, working in the other jurisdictions and on identical cases, was ineffective. In 1974, the government tried to coordinate the Carabinieri and the police by creating the Inspectorate for Action Against Terrorism, but it was a bureaucratic title for a working relationship that never worked. As a result, the Italian government authorized the creation of a national police counter-terrorist force--if the different services were going to fight and bicker, it was argued, then at least each force should possess a special force of its own capable of meeting any terrorist challenge. That force was the NOCS.

Interestingly enough, the NOCS' most famous operation was the January 1982 rescue of kidnapped American Brigadier General James Dozier from a Padua safe house where the terrorists were planning to execute him. Using the noise of an outside construction site for camouflage, a ten-man NOCS squad entered the flat using might (a kick through the front door) rather than any type of exotic explosive charge or a shotgun blast to the hinge and lock. In a matter of seconds, the ten men were in the apartment and had subdued the Red Brigade terrorists; including one with a M12 Beretta to General Dozier's head.

Although separate entities with very distinctive objectives and budgetary considerations, both the NOCS and the GIS maintain similar relations with other units around the world, though, for example, the GIS might be closer to the U.S. Army's 1st SFOD-Delta than the NOCS, and the NOCS might enjoy a closer working relationship with the FBI's HRT. The GIS, for example maintains extremely close-ties with the French GIGN, the U.S. Army's 1st SFOD-D (and SEAL Team SIX), the Belgian ESI, GSG-9, the British SAS and the Israeli ***Sayeret Mat'kal.*** The NOCS maintain closer ties to the Paris RAIDS unit, the German SEKs (especially SEK-Munich), and the Austrian GEK Cobra; the NOCS closest ties are with Israel's ***Ya'ma'm***, and the two units routinely exchange officers and personnel for joint-training.

Italy's counter-terrorist capabilities, it should be noted, are greatly enhanced by the efforts and skills of the SISDE, Italy's foreign intelligence-gathering agency, the SISME, Italian military intelligence and counter-intelligence,[2] and the ***Ufficio Centrale per le Investigazioni Generale e per le Operazioni Speciali*** (UGICOS), the Italian police intelligence unit under the control of the Ministry of the Interior. On the same note, it should be added, Italy's counter-terrorist abilities have been hampered by a series of sweeping scandals that have rocked the intelligence community leading President Scalfaro to order a purge of the intelligence services.

[1] Remarkably, this force is heavily armed, trained in aspects of covert and guerrilla warfare, and even is airborne qualified; in June 1990, weeks before Italy hosted the World Cup, the unit conducted an airborne exercise on the beach near Pomezia, south of Rome, where they entered a "Shooting House" after landing on the beach and rescued hostages. The unit is armed primarily with Beretta 92F 9mm automatics, Model 12S Beretta 9mm submachine guns, and SPAS Franchi 12-gauge shotguns.

[2] In October 1993, 300 military intelligence agents, instructors for a unit named ***Gladio*** that was designed to act as a guerrilla force in case of a Warsaw Pact invasion, were laid off and not assigned new positions in the war against terrorism and organized crime.

Excellent side-view of GIS operators, seen here near their Fiat van, at Dusseldorf International Airport; note the Carabinieri/GIS airborne red beret tucked into the leg pocket of their Nomex coveralls. (Samuel M. Katz)

An international counter-terrorist exchange of ideas and information--on the tarmac in Germany, GSG-9, GIS and Belgian Gendarmerie office talk about the problems of their special trade. (Samuel M. Katz)

Having just completed rescuing an LTU jet loaded with hostages, GIS officers deplane the aircraft to do it one more time. (Samuel M. Katz)

At St. Augustin, GIS officers look over the GSG-9 obstacle course. (Samuel M. Katz)

## Netherlands

***"In the early morning hours of a frigid winter's day, a call comes through to Royal Netherlands Marine Corps headquarters in Rotterdam with a desperate message--a North Sea ferry has been seized by ten terrorists, all heavily armed, willing to kill themselves and their hundred hostages, unless five hundred jailed "freedom fighters"--spread out in prisons from Berlin to Jerusalem--are freed within twelve hours. The cross channel ferry has been booby-trapped and until the demands are met, the terrorists will begin executing their hostages at a rate of five an hour. With no time to lose, the duty officer contacts two men who never stray far away from the cellular phones and beepers--the commander of the 7 NL SBS and the commander of the BBE. They are The Netherlands double-edged sword in the fight against terrorism.***

The BBE emblem.

The above listed scenario, among those that are on the contingency books of the Dutch Ministry of Defense, illustrates the vulnerability of a democratic nation, especially a liberal and small state like Holland. The existence of two elite fighting forces like the 7 NL SBS and the BBE illustrates the steps such a nation is willing--and capable to take--to combat any potential terrorist threat.

As a result of Holland's one-time dominance of the world's shipping lanes, the motto of the Royal Netherlands's Marine Corps is "***Qua Pater Orbis***," or "Wherever The World Extends." Although a force of just over 3,000 men, the RNLMC has developed into one of the world's truly elite amphibious combat units. Beyond being known for their unique raiding skills, and recceing abilities, the Dutch Marines are, perhaps, best known for the close-knit alliance they have developed with their green beret counterparts in Great Britain. Few military forces from two separate nations have succeeded in forging such intimate ties, and such an effective working relationship; the relationship dates back to 1702 when 400 Dutch Marines participated

The side-lined train at de Pont, hijacked by South Moluccan terrorists on May 23, 1977, hours before the rescue assault by Dutch forces. (Courtesy: *Audio Visuele Dienst Koninklijke Marine)*

One of the South Moluccan terrorists, who would later die in the assault, presents a list of demands to anxious Dutch authorities. While snipers were able to monitor the movement of many of the terrorists, the great equalizer in the assault was the fly-pass of the Royal Dutch Air Force F-104 Starfighters. (Courtesy: *Audio Visuele Dienst Koninklijke Marine*)

The aftermath of the assault. (Courtesy: *Audio Visuele Dienst Koninklijke Marine*)

in the capture of Gibraltar. Under NATO, the Dutch Marines are under the command Supreme Allied Commander Europe, as part of the ACE Mobile Force (AMF) and also under the command of the Supreme Allied Commander Atlantic, as joint UK/Netherlands Landing Force.[1] Under mobilization, the 1st Royal Netherlands Marine Corps Battalion is incorporated into the 3 Commando Brigade Royal Marines, and the RNLMC's Combat Boat Company, with its fleet of landing craft and inflatable and rigid raiding craft modified for assault operations in the Arctic, becomes an element of the Royal Marines' 539 Assault Squadron. Like the Royal Marines, the RNLMC enjoys a unique, and close-knit esprit de corps particular of a soldier who is "the thinking man's infantry." Like the Royal Marines, the RNLMC "does the Norway," conducting its Arctic training on the frozen mountains of NATO's northern flank. Like the Royal Marines, the Isle of Sky in Scotland is the sight of the RNLMC's nine weeks of cold-weather, wet and slippery mountain warfare instruction and like the Royal Marines, the RNLMC, too, has its own force of underwater special warfare operators, and they too are known as the SBS--the 7 NL Special Boat Section.

The men of 7 NL SBS are parachutist-trained combat swimmers considered among the world's best. In many ways, through their training, mandate, and sub-units, the Dutch SBS and British SBS are virtually indistinguishable. A Dutch SBS operator must first complete his service with the RNLMC before being able to volunteer into 7 NL SBS; even though there is one-year of mandatory military service in the Netherlands, all marines in the RNLMC are volunteers, and volunteers that must prove their worth before being allowed to enter through the gates of the RNLMC's training center. Upon completion of a successful stint in the RNLMC, a marine is entitled to submit a formal request to volunteer into the 7 NL SBS. Like the British SBS, a marine wishing to become a combat swimmer must first pass a grueling and extremely arduous selection process, and then (after only about thirty-percent pass this 1st stage) endure a year long training regimen; like his counter-part in the British SBS, the candidate can be removed from the course at any time. Phases of the training include: tactical swimming; SCUBA (7 NL SBS personnel deploy the Dräger LAR V re-breather); advanced combat jungle training (Martinique), advanced combat desert training (Curaçao); sabotage and explosives; sniping; parachuting; intelligence-gathering, tactical photography and beach recceing (including a few weeks of infamous beach crawling in mud that feels like quicksand); counter-terrorist training; and, most importantly, canoeing. In terms of the 7 NL SBS's infatuation with the Klepper canoe, the unit is virtually indistinguishable from their British counter-parts. The 7 NL SBS has also joined a long line of other naval commando units around the world (SEAL Team Six, SBS "M" Squadron, element of Israel's Flotilla 13, and the Tactical Assault Group, or TAG, of the Australian 1st SAS) who have dedicated resources to executing maritime and seaborne hostage-rescue assaults. 7 NL SBS maintains a small force of combat divers tasked with maritime security tasks on board liners and passenger ferries (should another Achille Lauro scenario arise in Dutch waters or with a Dutch ship), as well as North Sea oil rigs. According to a retired SEALs officer who had spent many years operating with "NAVSOCWARCOM DEV GROUP" and JSOC, "The Dutch are among the most innovative and imaginative of maritime counter-terrorist operators."

While 7 NL SBS is the Royal Netherlands Marine Corps' elite force of amphibious explorers and combat divers, counter-terrorist duty inside Holland is reserved for a very special force, drawn too from the RNLMC, and made up mostly of 7 NL SBS operators. Known by the acronym of BBE (for ***Bijzondere Bijstands Eenheid,*** or special intervention force), the unit answers to the Dutch Ministry of Justice and has established a reputation for itself as one of the finest intervention and rescue squads in all of Europe. The BBE was formed in the aftermath of the 1972 Munich Olympic Massacre when virtually ***every*** European Ministry of Defense and Justice laid the groundwork for the establishment of a nation-wide counter-terrorist unit. The BBE's first operation was the retaking of the Scheveningen jail in October 1974 during an insurrection by interned Palestinian terrorists. Using stun grenades, the BBE operators were able to storm the prison and subdue the prisoners in hand-to-hand combat; the unit was reluctant to use deadly force (even though the prisoners were armed) making them one of the world's most humane hostage-rescue forces.

Their most famous operation was the force's 1977 rescue of a schoolhouse and train seized by Moluccan terrorists. On the morning of May 23, 1977, nine young South Moluccan men, all heavily armed with submachine guns and grenades, seized control of a passenger train at de Punt with ninety-four people on board. Simultaneously, four other Moluccan terrorists took over a schoolhouse at Bovensmilde, and took 105 children and four teachers hostage. The Dutch government, still immune to the terrorist onslaught that overtook much of Europe in the years 1972-77, entered into negotiations with the terrorists confident that diplomacy and good will would end the ordeal. They were wrong. The ordeal dragged on for three weeks, with little progress made in releasing the hostages. Finally, on June 11, the Dutch government ordered the BBE into action. At Bovensmilde, the BBE was deployed behind a protective shield of Dutch Military Police M113 APCs, and the assault on the schoolhouse succeeded without bloodshed. The train at de Punt was a different story. Dutch Marine officers realized that the BBE would need help to handle the situation, and behind the scenes the BBE rigged a duplicate version of the train and spent the three weeks of the stand-off to hone their skills for the one chance at assaulting the train. Finally, the order to attack was issued. A pair of Royal Netherlands Air Force F-104 Starfighters made a low-level pass over the train, its atmospheric blast so powerful that it shocked and surprised even those terrorists expecting an assault. The BBE's entrance into the train was lightning fast--within seconds, doors had been kicked open, and six of the nine terrorists were killed; tragically, two hostages were also killed in the melee.

The BBE is unique among many of the world's counter-terrorist units in as much as it is part military, part police, part covert action team. Much of the groundwork that proceeds a BBE operation is done by the local police and Gendarmerie forces, while the BBE also operates jointly with Dutch military units--including covert reconnaissance and direct action work with a mysterious unit believed to be known as "104 ROS," a force that is the Dutch Army's equivalent of the U.S. Delta Force. Legally, the BBE answers to the Ministry of Justice even though much of its work falls under the boundaries of the Ministry of Defense.

The BBE is made up of approximately 100 men, commanded by a Marine major, and divided into two operational sections that are each divided into five man fire teams. Each team consists of gunners, a sniper and a trained medic; team members are also trained in EOD assignments, communications and intelligence work. Because The Netherlands is a relatively small nation, the BBE prides itself on its ability to reach any incident in what is (in operational terms) split-second timing--ninety minutes from first call to deployment ***anywhere*** in the country. When there are areas of The Netherlands that the unit cannot reach with its fleet of Mercedes 280 cross-country vehicles, Dutch military and police helicopters, such as the Lynx HAS.8, are deployed, as are Zodiac inflatables, Klepper canoes and even jet skis for canals and other areas only accessible by boat. Should a KLM aircraft be seized and held at either Amsterdam's Schiphol International Airport or at another location in The Netherlands, somewhere in Europe (or even in African and Asia) it would be the BBE that would get the call.

What makes the BBE such an elite fighting force, many have said, is the fact that the unit selection process is but just one arduous step along a long list of grueling rites of passage that each volunteer has already endured. First, potential BBE volunteers have endured the rigorous selection process employed by the parent force--the Royal Netherlands Marine Corps; BBE volunteers must also maintain a spotless two-year service record in the Corps before even being able to contemplate ever being accepted into the BBE selection process.[2] The BBE selection, while scrutinizing a candidate's physical abilities, pays special attention to the psychological make-up of each volunteer. BBE commanders must make sure if a potential member of an assault team can withstand the immense pressure of handling a hostage scenario, and, indeed, restrain himself from acting independently even when a hostage has been killed. According to one BBE officer, "We look for men with iron bodies, nerves of steel, bionic legs, and the judgment and wisdom of Solomon!"

BBE equipment is standard special operations fare, and all operators carry the entire and all-inclusive MP5 family of 9mm submachine guns.[3] Side-arms include the Glock 17 (favored during maritime operations) though the side-arm now being used most by BBE operators is the Swiss SIG-Sauer P-226 (a weapon that one U.S. Special Forces operator calls the "best automatic ever made"). Sniper rifles include the Austrian Steyr Police sniper rifle fitted with the 6x Kähle ZF scope, and the Heckler and Koch PSG-1 7.62mm rifle fitted with the 6x42 Zeiss Diaviri scope.

Although renowned in the international counter-terrorist community for their marksmanship and assault skills, the BBE maintains close-links and conducts joint-training with GSG-9 and northern German SEK units, the Belgian ESI (with whom the Dutch maintain very close ties), the Spanish GEO, and the French GIGN and

During maritime rescue maneuvers, a joint-force of 7 NL SBS operators and BBE rescuers assault a North Sea oil seized by terrorists. Note operators wearing water-proof neoprene overalls (believed to be lined with Nomex), and wearing Nomex hoods, and carrying SIG-Sauer pistols and MP5s. (Courtesy: *Audio Visuele Dienst Koninklijke Marine*)

During maneuvers in which BBE operators rescue a seajacked ferry, an operator stands cautiously on the deck of a Royal Netherlands Navy warship. The BBE is fortunate to have such close-links to the Navy and Marine Corps, as its eliminates any bureaucracy during seaborne operations. Note improvised sling for the MP5A2. (Courtesy: *Audio Visuele Dienst Koninklijke Marine)*

***"One bad guy neutralized.......seven to go!"*** After climbing on board a seajacked ferry during maneuvers in the North Sea, a sailor playing a terrorist is neutralized and taken into custody. Note body armor worn beneath assault vest and over green Nomex coveralls (used only during seaborne, non-amphibious operations). (Courtesy: *Audio Visuele Dienst Koninklijke Marine)*

RAID units. The BBE also maintains close ties to the British SBS "M" Squadron, Danish P.E.T. and ***Jægerkorpset***, Norway's Deltatroppen, and several Italian units. Little information is available on the ties between the BBE and U.S. units.

There are also several Dutch police units tasked with counter-terrorist work. The Federal Police (***Rijkspolitie***) have merged with the County Police (***Gemeentepolitie***) into what is now called Regional Police (***Regionale Politie***). One of its responsibilities is the training of the Police BBE (***Bijzondere Bijstandseenheid***) or "Special Assistance Unit," a nationally mandated SWAT and special investigative force. This unit consists specifically of marksmen who are capable of dropping a terrorist with one shot in hostage situations. The BBEK (the K stands for ***Krijgsmacht***, or Armed Forces) is identical to the Police BBE and tasked with the same assignment, though is under the command of the Military Police and has wider responsibilities including attacks against armed forces units both in The Netherlands and throughout NATO.

The BSB (***Brigade Speciale Beveiligingsopdrachten***), or "Unit for the Special Security Assignments" is not a counter-terrorist outfit in the true sense of the word, but more of a counter-terrorist deterrent squad. During the turbulent times of the Red Army Faction in Germany killing NATO officers and planting explosives in and around NATO facilities, as well as the times of Provisional IRA hitmen roaming northern Europe in search of British officers to assassinate, the BSB was tasked with protecting visiting military VIPs, foreign dignitaries and high-risked political figures targeted for politically inspired terrorism. Since then, however, the emphasis has moved to observation and arresting teams, charged with the surveillance and apprehension of dangerous criminals. The BSB is part of the ***Koninklijke Marechaussee*** (Royal Mounted Police); founded in 1814,

During seaborne rescue exercises, a BBE operator assumes proper firing position with his MP5A2 securing an area. Linked to one another by sophisticated Philips communications devices and closely "watched" by the unit operations officer (who is a master at monitoring the position of every one of his men during every phase of an operation), coordination is perhaps the most powerful weapon used by BBE operators in any built-up area, close-quarter assault. (Courtesy: *Audio Visuele Dienst Koninklijke Marine)*

the ***Koninklijke Marechaussee***, or KMar for short, was originally tasked with maintaining peace in the southern provinces and policing the army. Today, the KMar is responsible for guarding the borders and frontiers (they garrison the sprawling Schiphol International Airport, for example and provide additional security for sensitive flights entering the country, such as those of El Al and KLM flights to and from Israel), policing the armed forces, and assisting the city police forces when the need arises.

[1] This joint-force served together in Kurdistan in "Operation Safe Haven."

[2] Many B.B.E. volunteers are drawn from the 7 NL SBS who endure highly selective selection processes of their own.

[3] During the unit's early days, including at the time of the 1977 Moluccan hijacking, the unit used the RNLMC's standard submachine gun, the 9mm Uzi.

Fascinating photograph of a BBE squad preparing for an assault--courtesy of a Lynx chopper and the old reliable fast rope. Note operators sliding in his trusted Mossberg 12-gauge Cruiser 500 shotgun into an indigenous leather holster. The photograph shows to advantage the load bearing and assault gear carried by a BBE operator on maritime operations, including Eagle industries pouches. *(Courtesy: Audio Visuele Dienst Koninklijke Marine)*

BBE operators fast rope down a Lynx chopper during maritime exercises, and assume a defensive firing ring securing the chopper until its departure from the fire zone. (Courtesy: *Audio Visuele Dienst Koninklijke Marine)*

Two 7 NL SBS operators participate in counter-terrorist exercises by infiltrating a waterway courtesy of the Klepper canoe, and then establishing an intelligence OP before the BBE is called in. *(Courtesy: Audio Visuele Dienst Koninklijke Marine)*

Two BBE operators pose for cameras and display their MP5SD3 fitted with laser scopes. Note life-vests and British Mk. 6 helmets worn. (Courtesy: *Audio Visuele Dienst Koninklijke Marine)*

BBE operates perfect their urban assault course while a no-nonsense training officer looks on. Note officer wearing the BBE's calling card navy blue fatigues and navy blue Royal Netherlands Marine Corps beret and badge. (Courtesy: *Audio Visuele Dienst Koninklijke Marine)*

As other specialists make use of their time (background) for some open air shooting, a BBE assault team fast ropes down the side of a Lynx chopper during exercises and then race toward their objective--today a bus hijacked by terrorists. Several RNLMC Lynx choppers remain on call, 24-hours-a-day, for possible deployment by the BBE. (Courtesy: *Audio Visuele Dienst Koninklijke Marine)*

Perhaps having used ***too*** much C-4 to blow open a door, BBE specialists practice their entry techniques in an outdoor killing house at the unit's home base near Rotterdam. (Courtesy: *Audio Visuele Dienst Koninklijke Marine)*

The BSB of the KMar in action--using a portable entry device, like the rabbit tool used with such perfection by the NYPD ESU, to enter a suspected terrorist safe-house near Amsterdam. (Courtesy: *Information Department of the Koninklijke Marechaussee)*

Excellent close-up view of a BBE operator as he readies himself to fire a SIG-Sauer P226 9mm automatic. Note navy blue coveralls, navy blue Mk. 6 helmet and black balaclava, and MP5 slung over shoulder. (Courtesy: *Audio Visuele Dienst Koninklijke Marine)*

During a hostage-rescue simulation in an Amsterdam park, BBE operators race to a restaurant where local police officers (playing terrorists) have seized a tour group. (Courtesy: *Audio Visuele Dienst Koninklijke Marine)*

## Norway

***The scenario was burned into the minds of virtually every police and security officer charged with safeguarding the 1994 Winter Olympics in Lillehammer, a picturesque winter resort village in central Norway. Amid the performances of world class athletes and breaking of world records was the possibility of a different sort of excitement--one of a more explosive variety. A dozen men--and women--armed with assault rifle and fragmentation grenades breech the perimeter of the Olympic Village and proceed toward the living quarters of the American, Israeli and French teams. In an explosive few seconds, several hundred rounds of ammunition are fired and several grenades hurled into rooms where athletes sleep. Games of peace and international competition are reduced to a desperate war of nerves as hostages are killed and further bloodshed threatened. Determined not to have Lillehammer associated with the debacle of Munich twenty-two years earlier, Norwegian police units seal off the entire village to athletes and the media. "Hunters," from the army's elite Jager battalion, secure the perimeter to the village ready to support any tactical operation while snipers have placed their cross-hairs on the heads of several terrorists visible from 500 meters out. As negotiators attempt to placate the terrorists , a force of men, clad in black Nomex fatigues and wearing face masks, slink their way in the village and poise for a strike. They are the operators from the Beredskapstroppen or "Readiness Troop," Norway's response to terrorism.***

The ***Beredskapstroppen*** shoulder patch.

Norway was fortunate that the only controversy surrounding the 1994 Lillehammer games was on the figure skating ring, but the ***Beredskapstroppen*** was ready, positioned at strategic points around the Olympic Village.

The ***Beredskapstroppen***[1] was created in 1975 to shore up Norway's limited, virtually non-existent, response to a terrorist attack and hostage taking. Following Munich, the Palestinians had established Oslo as one of Black September's northern European bases of operations and the Palestinians and the Israeli Mossad had used the picturesque Scandinavian country as a battleground for their covert attacks and hit operations; one of the Mossad's famed bungled hit operations, in fact, the wrongful murder of a Moroccan waiter, took place on a secluded road in Lillehammer. As a result of the potential for terrorist violence on its shores, the Ministry of Justice required a special on-call force, made up of the best policemen inside the national force, who could be on alert status, 24-hours-a-day all year round, to intervene in any terrorist or hostage-taking scenarios.[2] That assignment fell to the ***Politikammer*** (National Police), who quickly sought out officers, with military experience in elite units, to establish the command and training cadre required for the creation of a national rescue and intervention squad. Under its legal mandate, the ***Beredskapstroppen*** provides assistance to the chiefs of police from all over Norway and the district of Svalbard, though administratively they are under the command of the Oslo Police Department.

What makes the ***Beredskapstroppen*** so unique is that Norwegian policemen are forbidden by law from carrying firearms--the permission to carry a weapon is granted by the chief of police only on special occasions. Officers wishing to volunteer into the ranks of ***Beredskapstroppen***, a force that carries out 150 armed missions a year, must be active duty policemen with a minimum of two-years on the job. Volunteers are remanded to a exhaustive and arduous selection process where their physical and psychological strengths are judged and scrutinized. All those passing this stage are admitted to a training class that usually lasts as long as three months.

According to published accounts, there are approximately fifty officers serving in the ***Beredskapstroppen***. Like an American SWAT unit, the officers of the ***Beredskapstroppen*** divide their time between day-to-day duty as "regular" policemen, and their special operations counter-terrorist training--***Beredskapstroppen*** operators undergo a mandatory 900 hours a year of tactical training (physical and close quarter combat, weapons and tactics). Some of the operators are parachutist and HALO qualified, and some are SCUBA qualified, as well; all are expert boatmen and sailors. Once summoned to an incident, the unit can rely on its fleet of Volvo 940 Turbo sedans and Chevy Blazer and Mercedes 280 GE all-terrain vehicles; the unit can also summon a ***Politikammer*** or Norwegian military helicopter--even call upon a Royal Norwegian navy warship in order to reach its destination.

***Beredskapstroppen*** operators prepare to fast rope down the side of a ***Politikammer*** Bell-212 chopper. (Courtesy: Oslo Politikammer)

During exercises simulating a seizure of a fjord pleasure boat, ***Beredskapstroppen*** operators race toward their objective courtesy of a large Zodiac inflatable. Situations and jurisdictions decide whether or not the ***Beredskapstroppen*** or ***Marinejägers*** would get the call to any maritime assignment. (Courtesy: Oslo Politikammer)

The standard ***Beredskapstroppen*** weapon is the Heckler and Koch family of MP5 9m submachine guns, Glock 17 9mm automatics (as well as Heckler and Koch P7s), and the .357 Magnum revolver. The unit's primary sniper weapon is the indigenous NM-142 7.62mm high-powered rifle.

Obviously, ***Beredskapstroppen*** maintains close ties to the other Scandinavian and European police agencies and hostage-rescue units, such as Britain's SO19, Germany's GSG-9 and the various state SEKs, and the Dutch B.B.E.

Also tasked with counter-terrorist operations, primarily in the maritime arena, is the Norwegian Navy's elite ***Marinejägerlag*** (MJL), a title which loosely translated means Navy Hunter Platoon, and, in war-time, is tasked with reconnaissance, intelligence-gathering and lightning strikes as ***far as fifty kilometers behind enemy lines***. Their primary function was to be the army's eyes and ears during riverine and amphibious operations; if the army needs to deploy to greater ranges behind enemy lines, they will call on Special Forces units like the para-rangers. From their creation to the present day, the ***Marinejäger***s were trained to be part U.S. Navy SEALs (to function in an offensive land and sea role), part guerrilla force like U.S. Special Forces groups (capable of surviving in the wilderness for a month while raiding and striking against enemy forces, or "occupation troops"), and part Arctic warfare specialists (much like elements of the Soviet Spetsnaz). The ***Marinejäger***s operate in small units consisting of anywhere from two men, to twelve "operators;" the mission decides the size of the deployment group. The entire ***Marinejäger*** unit consist of nearly 200 men.[3]

In his full maritime gear, a ***Beredskapstroppen*** officer scales up a ladder toward a ferry during hostage-rescue exercises in the North Sea. (Courtesy: Oslo Politikammer)

Like SEAL Team SIX (NAVSPECWARCOM DEV GROUP), and similar rescue units found in virtually every naval special warfare unit around the world--from Great Britain's Special Boat Service to Israel's Flotilla 13. They are primarily to be deployed in hostage-rescue scenarios involving the seajacking of vessels on the open seas, or incidents beyond the legal jurisdiction or operational range of the ***Beredskapstroppen***.

Weapons and equipment deployed by the ***Marinejäger*** includes the H&K G7 7.62mm NATO assault rifle, H&K P7 9mm pistol, and the special operations H&K MP5 9mm submachine gun. The ***Marinejäger***'s principal sniping rifle is the Norwegian-produced NM-142 7.62mm high-powered rifle--for a heavy duty counter-terrorist assignments the unit deploys M72 66mm LAW rockets and even the M-2GC Carl Gustav 84mm recoilless rifle.

[1] ***Beredskapstroppen*** is also known as ***Deltatroppen*** ("Delta Troop") because of its Delta call sign.

[2] Recently, however, that mandate has been expanded to also include fighting heavily armed criminal gangs, primarily from the east, in a plague that has struck virtually every western European nation since the end of communism.

[3] Interview, senior officer Norwegian Defense HQ, November 5, 1993.

Not allowing the snow or cold weather to limit their mobility or the scope of their reach, a fire-team of ***Beredskapstroppen*** operators cling to the sides of their modified Chevrolet all-terrain "Blazer" vehicle followed by a police armored snow-mobile and a Norwegian security service Mercedes sedan. (Courtesy: Oslo Politikammer)

With the safeties removed from their MP5s, a ***Beredskapstroppen*** fire-team demonstrates its agility using their special Chevrolet vehicle--especially when assaulting second story rooms. (Courtesy: Oslo Politikammer)

Dramatic photograph of the ***Beredskapstroppen*** at work. While a fire-team abseils down the side of a building, a second assault squad, standing atop their heavily modified Chevrolet and Mercedes all-terrain vehicles, assault a second-story terrace with weapons ablaze. (Courtesy: Oslo Politikammer)

During counter-insurgency maneuvers in the northern part of the country, a ***Marinejäger*** emerges from behind a large rock as he makes a cautious advance while clutching his Finnish M1931 9mm submachine gun (one of the unit's favorite and most reliable weapons). ***Beredskapstroppen*** and Norwegian special forces often train together for any and all contingencies. (Courtesy: HQ Defense Command Norway)

A *Marinejäger* "naval hunter" emerges from the depths with his MP5 at the ready during hostage-rescue operations in the North Sea. (Courtesy: HQ Defense Command Norway)

A group of *Marinejägers* prepare to parachute in the vicinity of a secluded shoreline villa during joint *Marinejäger/Beredskapstroppen* exercises. (Courtesy: HQ Defense Command Norway)

## Poland

***For an operator, no matter from what unit he is from, knowing that there is a $150,000 price on your head leads one to clutch his weapon's trigger housing ever so tighter and to keep one's eyes wide open--especially when that bounty is posted in one of the world's poorest countries. All it takes is the pull of the trigger for a major international incident and some men returning home in body bags. This place was so different than their homeland. For the men on patrol, the climate and terrain wasn't anything like home. Hot and humid, rolling hills and the sounds of French Creole spoken in the countryside, as well as the beating rhythm of UH-60 rotors and the roar of HUMVEE engines. The operators, used to the snowy peaks of the Carpathian Mountains and the plush green plains of the west country, were physically out of place but part of a very special and very precarious mission in a place "lovingly" referred to as "The Hell Hole." Clutching their MP5 9mm submachine guns, the patrol was hooked together by Motorola walkie-talkies with small ear-pieces and microphones and they were tasked with safeguarding one of the most sensitive of targets--American generals, United Nations representatives and visiting international monitors and dignitaries--and protecting them from gunmen and fanatics eager to turn an international mission of national preservation into a quagmire. These soldiers weren't American, however; most didn't even speak English.***

The place was Haiti, half an island of hell and hostility, and the operators were soldiers and officers of the Polish Army, volunteers to Operation Uphold Democracy, a multi-national peace-keeping effort sanctioned by the United Nations to restore--initiate--democratic rule to Haiti. When the Republic of Poland decided to contribute troops to this international effort, it opted to send its best--operators who had trained for four years in the art of counter-terrorist warfare and hostage-rescue assignments. They were the men of the ***Grupa Reagowania Operacyjno Mobilnego*** (Operational Mobile Response Group), known in Polish by the acronym of GROM, or "Thunder." A new entity in the post-Warsaw Pact era of Polish special forces, GROM was founded and commanded by fire-branding special operations veteran officer named Colonel Slawomir Petelicki. A professional soldier from a long line of decorated officers in the Polish military, Colonel Petelicki envisioned himself as a Polish Colonel Wegener, a man who had it within his mandate and ability to revolutionize the art of counter-terrorist warfare. He vowed to make GROM one of the world's best units.

President Lech Walesa, the president of Poland, issues the Officers Cross of Poland Renaissance Order to the commander of GROM, Colonel Sławomir Petelicki, November 1992. (Courtesy: GROM)

There was a time in the not so distant past when the mere thought of a Eastern European counter-terrorist unit was absurd. At the height of the Cold War, many of the revolutionary organizations that are now considered "terrorist," "subversive," and "politically and criminally threatening" were not only the recipients of military and irregular warfare instruction at the hands of the Polish Army, but were also supported covertly by Polish intelligence. Like most former members of the Warsaw Pact, Poland has released itself from the yoke of Soviet-rule and has entered a democratic future and free-market economy, including impending membership in NATO. With democracy comes the underground forces of terrorism and crime, as well as the military and police forces a nation requires to field in order to combat it.

For years counter-terrorist operations in Poland was the responsibility of the Polish Capital Police Command Counter-Terrorist Division (PCCTC). Tasked with combating both criminal and political violence, the unit was believed to number approximately 100 officer, and the Polish Capital Police Command Counter-Terrorist Division worked closely with the Bureau of State Security, the UOP, as well as with the national Border Guard Forces, the WOP.

The Polish Capital Police Command Counter-Terrorist Division (PCCTC) was equipped with a combination of Polish and Soviet-produced weaponry: shock troopers armed with AKSU-74 5.45mm submachine guns, AKS-74 5.45mm assault rifles, and 7.62mm Dragunov sniper rifles (SVD) issued to snipers. Operators carry Polish-produced P-64 9mm pistols, while officers, interestingly enough, are known to carry Wz63 (PM-63) 9mm submachine guns, the preferred weapon of many of the world's most notorious terrorist groups, including the Abu Nidal Black June Faction.

Polish Capital Police Command Counter-Terrorist Division and police prevention units (lightly armed SWAT formations) deployed from indigenously-produced ***Polonez*** five-door sedans (local copies of the Fiat 125), a Polish-produced ***Nysa*** mini-van with room for seven police officers and their equipment; Russian-produced ***Uaz*** all-terrain vehicles, and locally produced ***Star*** trucks and special vehicles.

The unit was responsible for protecting Polish political and military leaders, as well as visiting foreign dignitaries. As the Polish nation airline, LOT, has established dozens of new routes throughout Europe, the Middle East and North America since the collapse of the Soviet Union, the Polish Capital Police Command Counter-Terrorist Division has begun feverish training in counter-hijacking assault operations, as well as rescuing hostages from trains, buses and passenger ships--even river ferries. Much of the units most recent training and actual operations have targeted the exploding organized crime phenomenon, virtually all of it originating in the former Soviet Union, that has swept through Eastern Europe and is now laying its roots in the NATO nations. The crime gangs, dealing in everything from heroin to stolen Levis, are known to be ruthless, willing to kill, and armed with just about any and every weapon that they were able to buy or steal from the Russian military--from AK-47s to RPGs. They are considered by police officials as dangerous as the most dedicated and suicidal Middle East terrorist factions.

Most of the Polish Capital Police Command Counter-Terrorist Division personnel had military experience--most from elite units in the Polish airborne and marines. Polish Capital Police Command Counter-Terrorist Division accept only volunteers, only highly intelligent personnel with officer potential and those with "politically correct" backgrounds. Training included parachuting, alpine skiing, SCUBA operations cold-killing and martial arts, sniper skills and typical special forces type weapons proficiency.

On September 27, 1990, the Polish Police rejoined Interpol, and since 1992, the Polish Capital Police Command Counter-Terrorist

GROM operators, all fully SCUBA-qualified, take part in maritime hostage-rescue drills on a borrowed ocean liner in Gdansk harbor. (Courtesy: GROM)

A GROM operator takes part in free-fall training during the annual winter jump season. Note indigenous GROM camouflage pattern. (Courtesy: GROM)

Colonel Slawomir Petelicki poses with GSG-9 commander "J." during a visit by GROM to the GSG-9 compound at St. Augustin. (Courtesy: GROM)

Division has forged working ties with other former East-bloc police and military units that have been quickly established since the end of Soviet control of Eastern Europe, and good relations and joint-training exists with the Czech and Hungarian forces. Recently, however, the Polish Capital Police Command Counter-Terrorist Division has looked west, and has sent officers to study and observe the training, tactics and equipment of German units and the French GIGN; Polish police officers have also forged ties with the Israeli police and counter-terrorist community.

In 1990, however, the need to create a larger counter-terrorist force--one along the lines of Western units--became evident in Poland. The collapse of the Soviet Union saw massive migration of Jews to Israel--Poland was often a transit point and, as a result, a sensitive target to terrorist attack. Arab military and guerrilla officers had once trained in Poland, and Polish intelligence had a good line into many of the most fanatical Palestinian groups. Intelligence emanating into Warsaw was foreboding--there were planned strikes against Jewish émigrés, attacks involving bombings and the taking of hostages; as a harbinger of things to come, Polish diplomats were attacked in Beirut. The government of Polish Prime Minister Tadeuz Mazowiecki opted to act fast and seek the military's assistance.[1]

At the same time as Polish security officials reinforced their watch over sensitive targets, the United States Special Operations Command (USSOCOM) and the British Directorate of Special Forces (DSF) offered counter-terrorist fighting assistance to the Polish armed forces. Officers from the U.S. Army's 1st SFOD-Delta and the British Army's 22nd Special Air Service Regiment ventured to Warsaw to meet with military officers in setting up an indigenous ***military*** counter-terrorist and hostage-rescue unit. For the first time in Poland's history, the prospect of Polish nationals being held hostage abroad became a likely scenario and a solution--if not deterrent--was required.

Tasked with creating the Polish military counter-terrorist unit, Colonel Slawomir Petelicki faced two choices---rescue missions could be tasked to several smaller units, such as those involving maritime rescue ops, or one force could be trained and sufficiently equipped to carry out any rescue or any task no matter where or when. Having had his initial contact with USSOCOM and the British DSF, Colonel Petelicki was also determined to avoid jurisdictional in-fighting that had plagued both the United States (in fights between the Army's 1st SFOD-D and the Navy's SEAL Team SIX and with the British, between the 22nd SAS Regiment's SP Teams and the Special Boat Service's "M Squadron"). The Polish unit would have a 360° spectrum in which to operate and be open to all personnel serving in Polish elite forces--be it airborne or naval. One thing that Colonel Petelicki was determined to foster in this new unit were strong international ties in Europe and North America--the Middle East and Asia. In laying the groundwork for GROM Colonel Petelicki would enjoy bureaucratic leeway--as terrorism was the responsibility of the Ministry of the Interior, not the Ministry of Defense, defense policy and budgetary constraints would not inhibit the requirements and needs of the unit.

Colonel Petelicki GROM's founding threads on the model of the U.S. Army's 1st SFOD-D and the SAS--combining the best attributes of both these units, though the selection process was copied straight from GSG-9. When the unit was sanctioned, word spread throughout the Polish special operations community that this new and revolutionary unit was being formed. Prior to the collapse of the Soviet

GROM operators train in the firing of their Heckler and Koch MZP-1 multi-purpose 40mm pistol. (Courtesy: GROM)

Wearing their characteristic Protec helmets, GROM operators storm a LOT airliner at Warsaw International Airport during a hostage-rescue training exercise. Trained by the best in the business, GROM is now considered a world-class hostage-rescue unit. (Courtesy: GROM)

Under the light of a full moon, a Polish Army Sokol-Anakonda chopper hovers above a rooftop while GROM operators fast-rope down. Beside being airborne qualified, GROM operators are expert at heliborne insertions. (Courtesy: GROM)

Union and the political liberation of Eastern Europe, Poland was unique among the Warsaw Pact as possessing a large array of elite units, some division size in strength, that were considered among the best of the alliance, including the ***6 Pomorska Dywizya Powietrzna-Desantowa*** (6th Pomeranian Air Assault Division); a marine assault division known as ***7 Luzycka Dywizya Desantnoa-Morska*** (7th Luzycka Naval Assault Division); and, several frogmen and reconnaissance units, including the elite ***Grupa Rozpoznawco Naprowadzajaca*** (assault divers from the GRN Scouting and Reconnaissance Group). Volunteers responding to the GROM call-out were first subjected to a grueling psychological examination meant to search for confident and innovative soldiers, as well as those who might be lacking supreme physical strength though in possession of that rare gift--internal iron will. Because GROM functions in small-man trams, sometimes numbering only a handful of operators, the unit was looking for operators who could act as individuals as well as members of an integral machine. All those who then passed the psychological barrier were presented with a week-long physical exercise meant to display their very basic skills and abilities; since all the volunteers were serving in Polish elite units, physical ability was not a major factor. All those who had survived the first selection process for GROM in 1991 were the founding cadre for the unit and immediately sent to Germany, to GSG-9's home base St. Augustin, for some urgent basic skills in order to be ready with advanced training should a terrorist act be perpetrated on Polish soil.

Today, the final aspect of the GROM physical selection process closely resembles the British SAS "Test of Truth." Taken to the most inhospitable stretches of the Carpathian Mountains, the volunteers are forced march with a load of up to forty kilometers on their back for anywhere between fifty and eighty kilos. The exhausted--and sometimes physically broken men--were met by a GROM officer at the end of their prescribed march only to be told the following, "What are you slowing down for, DON'T REMOVE YOUR PACKS, you have another twenty kilometers to go!!" At this stage, those who are about to break do just that--collapse under the weight of their pack and the psychological burden of knowing that they can traverse no additional ground, and realize that they have failed the selection process and will be returning to their parent unit. Those who will persevere this challenge and proceed to the real finish line will earn their GROM wings and take their spot in the unit.

Since that first selection and training program, GROM has grown and expanded--yet its exact order of battle, including actual strength, remains classified top-secret. The ***Grupa Reagowania Operacyjno Mobilnego*** is divided into several combat sections which are divided into four-man assault teams. In the field, the four-man team is taught--and expected--to act as a single organism. Each operator moving into position must know--instinctively--what his three comrades are doing and where they are positioned. All operators in the unit are trained as full-fledged combat assault personnel, but it is interesting to note that seventy-five per-cent of the unit are certified as paramedics and male nurses, and several doctors, certified M.D.s, are also in the unit. In the team, the medics and doctors function as combat assault troops in full kit, though should a member be hit and require medical attention, they will attend to the casualty. To hone their abilities to treat gunshot and trauma injuries, the operators ***routinely*** ride in Warsaw ambulances in some of the more dangerous sections of the city.

Unlike virtually all other counter-terrorist units around the world, the ***Grupa Reagowania Operacyjno Mobilnego*** possesses a combat reconnaissance group that consists of ***female*** personnel--professional soldiers, warrant officers and officers trained in the entire gamut of counter-terrorist fare. Although much of what these female operators do falls under the provision of classified top-secret, they are believed to be heavily involved in stake-outs and intelligence-gathering and allow for GROM officers to obtain suitable covers when working undercover in civilian dress in Poland and abroad. ***All*** GROM personnel speak at least two languages--and many have had intelligence and counter-espionage instruction.

Unlike the members of the PCCTC, GROM has abandoned Eastern-bloc weaponry for the standard Western fare used by most of the world's top units. The personal weapon of choice is the Heckler and Koch MP5 family of 9mm submachine guns. Operators are offered an option of choosing their own 9mm sidearm, and most choose either the Browning HP, CZ-85, Glock Model 19, and SIG-Sauer P228s. Shotguns are not used in any great frequency by GROM, though the unit does still carry the ***Tantal***, the Polish-produced version of the Soviet AK-74 5.45mm assault rifles, as well as some exotic bits of equipment, including crossbows, regular bows and even hatchets. All GROM personnel are expertly trained in cold-killing and the martial arts.

Assault teams are never sent into action alone--they are always the spearhead of a much larger GROM deployment. GROM snipers, the best in the entire Polish military (as well as Eastern Europe) belong to Observation Formations that supervise and reconnoiter unit deployments. The snipers, all former sharpshooters with their parent units and trained with SVDs, are equipped with German-produced

An interesting and improvised GROM tubular assault "Tac House." Empty crates simulate passenger seats on an inter-city bus, as GROM operators practice liberating a hijacked bus from terrorists. (Courtesy: GROM)

Lurking silently in the snow, a GROM sniper peers through the sights of his Dragunov SVD 7.62mm marksman's rifle and stalks his target. (Courtesy: GROM)

Heckler and Koch PSG-1 7.62mm sniper rifles, as well as German-produced Mauser 86 7.62mm sniper rifles. GROM snipers, sometimes forced to lay in ambush and position for days on end, are also expertly trained survivalists.

GROM Support Formations consist of technicians and analysts, support staff and EOD operatives. Many of the Support Formation personnel are former commandos and operators who are either too old for participation in Assault Teams, or who have endured injuries prohibiting them from full assault duties.

When Colonel Petelicki received the governmental mandate to command this new unit, he was adamant that its training be as realistic as possible and held all year round. ***All*** training is carried out with live ammunition, including "Killing House" entries; while dangerous, this is the only possible means to introduce an operator to the realistic danger and terror of ballistic ordnance flying through a room close to one's head. Training with live fire also teaches the operator the important skill of pulling the trigger only when the target is clearly in the weapon's sights. GROM operators are noted for their expert marksmanship. Like the SAS and the U.S. Army's 1st SFOD-D, GROM operators fire thousands of rounds of ammunition a week on countless ranges and built-up firing scenarios. Fighting terrorists is far more complex than just being able to hit your target. GROM operators train in virtually all forms of insertion, including heliborne techniques (fast-roping and rappelling), as well as through underwater means. GROM operators are all airborne and SCUBA qualified, and undergo extensive instruction at the hands of 6th Pomeranian Air Assault Division officers, as well as instructors from the 7th Luzycka Naval Assault Division and the GRN Scouting and Reconnaissance Group. It has also been reported that GROM operators receive advanced communications training, as well as courses in high-speed and evasive driving, and rudimentary EOD instruction.

Because of Poland's vast size and diverse range of topography, GROM personnel are trained to operate in virtually all types of terrain and scenarios. With the cooperation of LOT Polish Airlines, GROM personnel routinely train in assaulting a hijacked airliner and rescuing passengers; as the LOT fleet is now a combination of Soviet-built aircraft and American-built Boeing, their airline assault instruction has become more specialized. Having learned the art of storming aircraft from GSG-9, SAS and the U.S. Army's 1st SFOD-D--as well as, now from the French following the Marseilles operation in December 1994--GROM personnel are uniquely equipped with the skills and experience needed to gain entry into a besieged aircraft and terminate a hostage-taking situation without unnecessary loss of life. Because of Poland's vast network of ports and shipping lines, the operators are trained in maritime counter-terrorism and undergo regular and frequent exercises in assaulting seized ferries, oil rigs and large vessels. GROM operators are also trained in mountain warfare, as well as operations in Alpine-like conditions.

Although much of their covert work remains classified, GROM teams have been active ***inside*** Poland--primarily against heavily-armed organized crime gangs from the former Soviet Union. They were also deployed with great success in Haiti during "Operation Restore Democracy." Following the creation of GROM in 1991 and the initial contact between Colonel Petelicki and his American and British advisors, foreign observers looking at the unit in the field were, perhaps, most impressed by GROM's ability in VIP-protection. When GROM was selected to participate in the Haiti mission in October 1994, the unit arrived in the Caribbean asked to fill very large shoes--they were to be reinforcements and replacements for operators from the U.S. Army's 1st SFOD-D and the Navy's SEAL Team SIX who had been protecting American generals and State Department officials in Port-au-Prince and throughout the countryside. Being selected for such a sensitive mission was a tremendous boost in morale for GROM, as American USSOCOM commanders on the scene were quick to point out that the Poles received the mission solely on the ground of merit. They had trained for years to gel as a unit and their first international show was a unique testing ground.

Initially, GROM was selected to take part in the American-led effort because it was feared--and expected--that heavy firepower would be needed. Since the Haitian Army was virtually non-existent, it was expected the lethal firepower would have to be directed in small units, in a lengthy and tedious counter-insurgency campaign. It was just the type of warfare that GROM excelled in, and the Polish President was quick to despatch them to the Caribbean. Even though the American-led invasion of Haiti was a peaceful one, security operations in Haiti were difficult. A nation beset by violence and terrorism, albeit at the hands of the police and state security officials, Haiti was a powder-keg. Militiamen from FRAPH, the armed group opposed to return of President Jean-Bertrand Aristede, vowed to kill American soldiers and officials and, with little knowledge of the political landscape or French Creole, GROM officers set forth to safeguard the architects and guardians of this international mission. First, the GROM operators were despatched to Camp Santiago, the Puerto Rican highlands to acquaint themselves with the U.S. Army's special forces means of doing things. For GROM, it was "Trust and

On the airport tarmac at Port-au-Prince, Colonel Petelicki and his junior officers confer with their U.S. Army 1st SFOD-Delta liaison (right). (Courtesy: GROM)

During a tactical insertion, GROM operators secure a U.S. Army MH-60 Pave Hawk. Note MP5 carried by operators and red and white POLAND patch. (Courtesy: GROM)

Check" time--operators from the U.S. Army's 3rd Special Forces Group (Airborne) watched as the GROM personnel displayed their shooting skills, and their high-speed and evasive driving skills 3rd Group instructors taught the Poles the A-Zs of Haitian politics and socio-economic intricacies, as well as an indoctrination of the type of resistance (from voodoo priests with machetes to booby-trapped explosive devices) bound to be encountered on the island. The Poles, and the Americans, knew that the majority of hostile operations would be mob assaults against fixed targets (such as relief centers) and VIPs and dignitaries.

Once in Haiti, GROM took over security duties from Delta and SEAL Team SIX operators, and their Polish-speaking liaison personnel from the U.S. Army's 10th Special Forces Group (Airborne),[2] (the group responsible for Europe), the fifty GROM operators were stationed twenty miles from the Haitian capital; from the American point-of-view, it was crucial that the Poles be able to establish their own base and safe-guard it. Taking the threat-factor very seriously, Colonel Petelicki and his men attended to their task with dire seriousness. Armed with their MP5s and 9mm sidearms, the operators guaranteed the security of Major-General David C. Meade and his staff. With their faces concealed by camouflage paint and balaclavas, GROM operators presented a formidable appearance backed by true professionalism.

Among the VIPs that GROM operators provided security for were General Secretary of the United Nations Buthros Buthros Ghali; Anthony Lake, advisor to President Clinton for national security affairs; Secretary of Defense William Perry; Secretary of the Army Togo D West; the chiefs of the delegations of seven chiefs of staff from the Caribbean armies despatched to the international operation in Haiti; U.S. senators; and, various American generals. The most dangerous task that GROM received was safeguarding the special representative for the General Secretary of the United Nations Lalhdar Brahimi. Opponents of the Aristede return to power had posted a $150,000 bounty for Brahimi's murder and on an island where $100 is an annual income, there were hundreds of trained killers eager to cash in on the offer. To protect Brahimi, GROM personnel were on guard twenty-four hours a day, seven days a week, making sure that any sign of threat was handled both tactically and immediately.

GROM operators on patrol on the streets of Port-au-Prince. Note GROM insignia. (Courtesy: GROM)

In addition to safeguarding high-ranking American officers and visiting VIPs, GROM's primary role was that of a lightning reactionary force to intervene at a moment's notice at the signs of any potential trouble. In several incidents near the International HQ in Port-au-Prince, GROM operators intervened saving the lives of over a dozen Haitians, and several foreigners. On November 25, 1994, GROM participated in its largest tactical response when, en route back to their base north of Port-au-Prince, they were stopped by a mob of slum dwellers under fire from heavily armed militiamen holding a boy hostage; the building where the child was held was set afire and a volatile situation developed. With the help of U.S. Army MPs, GROM operators extinguished their fire and made tactical entry to the building--freeing the boy and putting an end to a situation that could have cost countless lives.

When the unit departed Haiti on December 12, 1994, their role was so appreciated that U.S. commander Major-General David C. Meade awarded Colonel Slawomir Petelicki the "Army Commendation Medal"--the first time in American military history that a foreign unit was awarded such a medal. Although awarded with the Officers Cross of the Renaissance of Poland medal in 1992 by President Lech Walesa, to Colonel Petelicki and the men--and women--of GROM, Major-General Meade's medal was the most poignant recognition of their worth as a unit and an official statement of ***Dziekuje*** (Thank You); General Meade was so impressed by the Pole's ability that he even requested that they stay in country for an extended tour of duty.

GROM returned to Poland on December 15, 1994, and returned to its counter-terrorist mandate shortly thereafter. In January 1995, Polish officials received word that Pope John Paul II would be visiting his homeland later in the year. For Poles, the return of the Holy Father was a source of pride and rejoicing. For Colonel Petelicki and GROM, it meant business as usual. Pope John Paul II was a target and GROM was determined to safeguard the pontiff at all costs.

[1] It is believed that the Polish Capital Police Command Counter-Terrorist Division is now a national SWAT unit, tasked with handling low-level criminal situations requiring a tactical solution.

[2] Until the arrival of GROM, the U.S. Special Forces contingent in Haiti was spearheaded by 3rd Special Forces Group (Airborne) out of Fort Bragg, North Carolina, the unit responsible for the Caribbean and Latin America.

In Port-au-Prince, Colonel Petelicki is greeted by U.S. Secretary of Defense William Perry and thanked for a job well done. (Courtesy: GROM)

# Portugal

They are, according to the unit commander, "the last resort." They are a force of specialists, trained by Britain's SAS, whose presence on any scene, during any crisis, is meant to be a conclusion to any incident. They are, according to one marine officer, the finest commandos in all of Portugal. They are the operators of the ***Grupo De Operaçoes Especiais***, or GOE, the Portuguese national police's counter-terrorist and hostage rescue unit, and they are considered among the best in all of Europe.

By emergency government decree, the Portuguese Home Ministry created the GOE on December 24, 1979, following the course set by most European nations in the wake of the 1972 Munich Olympic Massacre; Lisbon had been a center of international espionage and intrigue during the Second World War and Portuguese security officials were adamant not to have the trappings of geography repeat itself during the terrorist wars of the late 1970s. Portugal, a country with rich history of elite fighting forces and military "specialists" (as they are known in the local slang), possessed a vast talent pool from which to draw the founding cadre for its national counter-terrorist and hostage-rescue force--the ***Fuzileiros*** or Marine Corps. Under the command of the ***Policia de Seguranca Publica*** (Public Security Police), the first GOE officers were de-activated ***Fuzileiros*** commandos, primarily from its elite special warfare unit the Special Missions Detachment, who were expert in fast strike missions and who had trained with foreign elite units, such as the U.S. Marine Corps and British and Dutch Royal Marines. These officers, with lavish funding and a blank page, began the first GOE course for the several hundred volunteers who made their way to the units base near Lisbon on March 29, 1982. That first course, considered the most grueling by many GOE and intelligence service insiders, had an attrition rate of 90%--most of the volunteers, military veterans, were unable to withstand, the intensive medical, physical, and psychological examinations. In early 1983, the 150 or so operators who survived the selection process and the nearly twelve-month long training regimen were formally sworn in as the nation's first intervention unit. As part of that first training course, the volunteers were flown to Hereford, United Kingdom, where they trained together with the SAS--including the "Pagoda

GOE intervention squad operators partake in the unit's now legendary "face-to-face" daily target practice. (Courtesy: GOE)

Dressed as Ninjas and as agile and lethal in combat, GOE operators negotiate a live-fire obstacle course at the unit's base near Lisbon. (Courtesy: GOE)

Two GOE operators display their varied uniforms and gear--the sniper (left) carries a Mauser 666 and is dressed for field and rural operations in the indigenous Portuguese diagonal lizard pattern scheme, and the intervention squad striker (right) wears the now standard urban counter-terrorist black outfit with assault vest and balaclava face mask. Note operator armed with MP5A3 with laser designator. (Courtesy: GOE)

Troop" which had just completed its successful Iranian embassy operation. The GOE, as a result of its close ties to the boys from Hereford, opted to base their unit along SAS lines, both in its command and control structure, and in how future operators would be trained.

By its mandate, the GOE was responsible for crisis international ***throughout*** Portugal, including Portuguese interests (such as TAP airlines flights and shipping lines,), and VIP protection of Portuguese diplomats and ministers both at home and abroad; the GOE was also to assume responsibility for handling the security and potential intervention in any terrorist incidents involving foreign embassies and installations in Portugal. The first incident to which the GOE was summoned to intervene was the July 27, 1983, suicide assault by Armenian ASALA terrorists on the Turkish Embassy in Lisbon. The six man squad, who had reached the embassy compound in a van hired by men with Libyan passports, had quickly eliminated the security guard with a point-blank 9mm round to the head, but encountered determined resistance at the hands of armed Turkish secret service officers (one terrorist was killed in the fusillade of gunfire) and were unable to breech their way into the chancery building; instead, they took control of the ambassador's residence instead. Upon word of the terrorist attack, the GOE was immediately summoned to the scene and within thirty minutes of the first shot being fired the unit had deployed around the embassy, securing a defensive perimeter. GOE doctrine called for the unit psychologist to begin a dialog with the terrorists and attempt to end any such incident peacefully. The terrorists, however, showed no signs of wanting to talk and the GOE squad prepared to storm the building. Just as the GOE commander, Intendente M.,[1] was poised to order the assault, a powerful explosion rocked the ambassador's residence; the terrorists, preparing a booby-trap explosive device by the main door had inadvertently detonated their bomb. In the ensuing fire, all five terrorists were killed as were a Turkish diplomat and his wife.

"Hijackers beware!" GOE operators execute an early morning anti-hijacking exercise at Lisbon International Airport courtesy of a TAP Tristar. (Courtesy: GOE)

Under the official guidelines of the operational mandate, the GOE's missions are as follows:

- Execute, and be equipped to execute, independent offensive actions--in which speed and surprise are of paramount importance--to isolate and attack known locations where terrorists and armed criminal have been identified as holding out.
- In the cases of kidnappings and hostage-taking scenarios:

(1) Participate in negotiations to try and secure the release of the hostages or victims.

(2) Gathering, analyzing and interpreting intelligence and reconnaissance from an incident site, and preparing assault--and defensive--contingency plans.

(3) Neutralize the terrorists and liberate the hostages from ***any*** type of installation or building, or vehicle, aircraft or sea-faring vessel.

(4) Pursue escaping criminals/terrorists from the scene of terrorist or criminal incidents, intercept them, and overcome any forms of armed resistance. This mandate also calls for the unit to operate abroad in the apprehension and abduction of known terrorists/criminals who have perpetrated acts in Portugal or against Portuguese interests or individuals abroad.

- Cooperating with the Portuguese intelligence service, through the office of the commanding general, Public Security Police, in investigating law-enforcement efforts against terrorists and heavily armed criminals.
- The GOE, a ***reserve*** unit under the direct command of the General Commander of the Public Security Police.

The GOE is divided into the following order of battle:

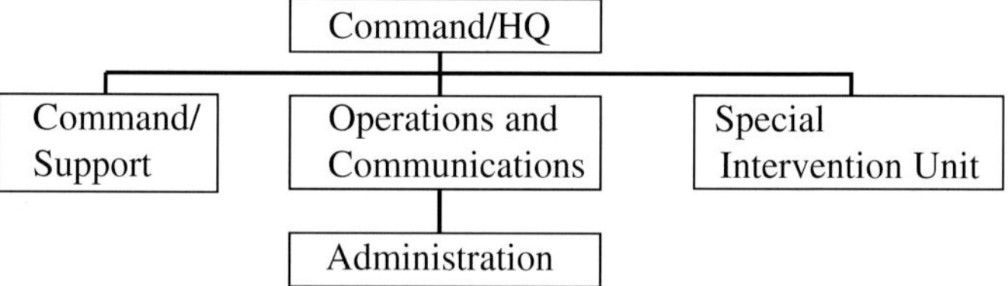


As a result of their national "on-call" status, the Public Security Police has availed to the GOE a lavish pool of vehicles and transport by which the unit can reach virtually every potential incident inside the country in the shortest possible time. These means range from specially modified Range Rovers and Mercedes all-terrain vehicles (many fitted with special hoists to allow operators to climb up and assault moving targets such as buses and aircraft), to access to police and military aircraft, helicopters and naval vessels.

Following a forced entry into a TAP Boeing 707, GOE operators bring a "suspect" into custody. The GOE has honed its skills to where it can neutralize a hijacked airliner in a matter of seconds. (Courtesy: GOE)

The unit's principal weapon is the Heckler and Koch MP5 family of 9mm submachine gun, including the MP5A1, MP5A2, MP5A3, and MP5SD-1. GOE operators are particularly fond of shotguns, and the standard unit 12-gauge piece of artillery is the Heckler and Koch 502. GOE unit members are offered a liberal policy as far as personal side-arms are concerned, and pistols in GOE service range from 9mm Brownings to SIG Sauer P228 and, recently, both 9mm Glocks and .357 Magnum Israeli-made Desert Eagles. Considered among the finest marksmen in Europe, GOE snipers favor the Mauser 666 7.62mm rifle for training, and the Heckler and Koch PSG-1 7.62mm rifle in the field; because of their recently established close-ties to Israeli units, the GOE is evaluating the Galil 7.62mm sniper rifle as well as the SIG SG 550. The GOE has also toyed with exotic weapons, including crossbows fitted with laser designators; in fact, during anti-hijack exercises with TAP aircraft, GOE operators have been seen firing arrows at dummies simulating terrorists holding hostages on the tarmac.

The GOE green beret, beret badge, and chest insignia displayed alongside the Heckler and Koch MP5 9mm submachine gun (seen here with laser designator). (Courtesy: GOE)

In a recent CTC (Counter-Terrorist Competition) held in Europe where the competition included the likes of the U.S. Army's 1st SFOD-D and the FBI HRT, GSG-9 and other German SEKs, the Dutch BBE, the Belgian ESI, the Italian GIS, and the Spanish GEO, the GOE finished fourth overall in the competition. Its reputation as one of the finest intervention squads in the world stems from the brutal training volunteers must undergo, and their incessant training once inside the unit. Virtually every GOE volunteer is a veteran of either Portuguese special forces or marine or paratroop units and is expert with small arms and rifles. Once inside the unit, target practice is a daily occurrence. GOE operators also train in undercover work and high-profile security assignments for deployment abroad securing Portuguese embassies and consulates in trouble spots around the world, as well as protecting TAP installations and "sensitive" airports.

The GOE maintains obvious close ties to the Spanish GEO, but also maintains close ties to units in Germany, France, Italy and Israel; the GOE also maintains close ties with Brazilian police intervention squads. The GOE's closest ties, however, are with the British Special Air Service. The last two months of the GOE's training eight-month long instruction, in fact, the segment dedicated to VIP protection, is taught by SAS officers on loan to the unit. It should also be added that the GOE obtains much of its special operations expertise and proficiency from within the Portuguese military, and in particular from the ***Instruçäo de Operaçöes Especiais***, the JFKSWCS of Portugal.

[1] Identity withheld for security reasons.

A portion of the unit's fleet of modified Range Rovers is displayed with GOE operators poised for an assault. Note hoist system built atop the roof of the vehicle and ladder fastened to the hoist base. Note Heckler and Koch Type 502 12-gauge shotgun nestled against ladder. (Courtesy: GOE)

The ingenious aspect of the ladder modified to the Range Rover is seen here to advantage as GOE operators assault a split-level house, and enter a second floor window with virtual ease. (Courtesy: GOE)

Virtually invisible to terrorists manning a sentry around a safe house, a GOE sniper becomes one with the terrain and keep a close eye on his target. (Courtesy: GOE)

Still wearing their fast-rope harnesses, a GOE assault team enters a "killing house" with MP5s at the ready and aim-lights on full blast. (Courtesy: GOE)

GOE marksmanship weapons: the Mauser 666, a PSG-1, and two Heckler and Koch G3 SG/1 7.62mm police sniping rifle. (Courtesy: GOE)

Having pursued a minibus traveling in excess of 100 miles per hour, GOE pursuit squads outmaneuver the fleeing terrorists and engineer a ballistic roadblock. (Courtesy: GOE)

GOE riot-gear and special gear, including (left to right) Heckler and Koch G3 A3 FZ (without scope) sniping 7.62mm rifle, Italian-made Franchi SPAS 12 shotgun, and Heckler and Koch 502 shotgun. (Courtesy: GOE)

GOE night-vision and side-arms on display--weapons featured include all variants of the MP5, a Browning 9mm automatic, and a SIG-Sauer P230. (Courtesy: GOE)

The GOE crossbow--now a staple of the unit's operations and legend. (Courtesy: GOE)

# Russia

There was a time in the early 1970s, when terrorism was rampant in Western Europe, that the mere thought of a Soviet counter-terrorist team seemed completely absurd--after all, virtually all of the world's terrorist groups, from the Provisional IRA to the Armenian ASALA, were supported and directed by Moscow in one way or another. Moscow owned these groups, knew the operators (they had trained most of them, paid their bosses and after all), knew where they were hiding and operating from, and had such a tight grip over their actions that no major terrorist strikes could be perpetrated, virtually anywhere in the world, without some KGB liaison officer learning of it and ultimately approving it.

During the late 1970s, however, home-grown terrorism began to appear inside the confines of the Soviet Union--mainly aircraft hijackings (by individuals, mainly Jewish dissidents, seeking to escape the USSR) or violent cases of kidnappings and extortion (especially in the Asian republics). By 1991, in fact, at the crossroads of the end of the Soviet Empire, there had been an astounding 103 hijackings and attempts resulting in 120 deaths and over 200 seriously wounded. Soviet authorities weren't as concerned as by the rise in air piracy and violent crime, as they were by the international perception that law and order inside the USSR at collapsed. Steps needed to be taken. The first military effort to create a national counter-terrorist strike unit and hostage-rescue force came in 1978 when the MVD, the Ministry of Interior, in preparation for the 1980 Summer Olympics to be hosted in Moscow, sanctioned the creation of a special counter-terrorist company. The unit was known by the acronym of ***OMON*** (Special Operations State Militia) and drawn of former Spetsnaz, paratroop and Marine veterans who were both physically fit and politically reliable. Armed with the basic Soviet small arms hardware (AKMS assault rifles and 9mm Tokarovs) the unit trained in the traditional SWAT-like room and building entries using speed, minimum lethal force and expert combat shooting skills to rescue hostages; as a force used to massive assaults, refining the combat skills was of paramount importance. The unit, to considerable press at the time, vowed that no repeat of the 1972 Munich Olympic Massacre would be permitted to transpire on Soviet soil during the games;[1] ***OMON*** snipers, armed with 7.62mm SVDs and hooded faces, were shown firing live rounds at an urban training center outside of Moscow, and operators were filmed fast-roping down from hovering Mi-8 choppers above dormitory-like structures. The Olympics, of course, American boycott and all, went off without a hitch, and the ***OMON*** displays were so successful that similar units to the Moscow militia were formed in each major Soviet city. Today, it has been reported, a special MVD unit exists consisting of over 300 officers exists to deal specifically with aircraft hijackings, bus seizures and terrorist assaults on trains.

When the Soviet Union first became interested in counter-terrorist operations, the KGB, too, began creating units under ***its*** control that could be called upon to rescue hostages inside the boundaries of the Soviet Union and Warsaw Pact, as well as anywhere else in the world should an Aeroflot aircraft be hijacked, or Soviet dignitaries be kidnapped or attacked. For years, the KGB possessed special operations squads that could be called upon to execute "nasty" covert operations, and these "operators" were primarily under the control and command of the organization's 1st Directorate. In 1974, however, the KGB's Department 7, replacing the 1st Directorate as the body in charge of foreign operations, created "Alpha Group," to respond to terrorist operations inside the Warsaw Pact, and "Beta Group," a Delta-Force of sorts to be despatched across international boundaries for special preemptive counter-terrorist strikes. Many in the Western media have confused these units with the Spetsnaz commandos, but their missions, training and mandates are quite different--opposite in many regards.

Both the activities of "Alpha" and "Beta" Groups have been shrouded in tremendous secrecy by Russian officials, as these units are extremely sensitive in these tense political times for the Federation. They have been quite active in attempting to rescue hostages on board the multitude of aerial platforms that criminals, freedom seekers and extortionists have hijacked to get hefty ransoms from Moscow, including Aeroflot jets, shuttle helicopters and military transports. The true sensitive nature of the "Alpha Group" operations has been their strikes against Russian organized crime.

"Beta Group," it is believed, has been just as busy as "Alpha" in tactical operations, though under greater scrutiny. A rumored "Beta Group" operation involved the 1985 kidnapping of four Soviet diplomats in Beirut by Iranian-backed Shiite guerrillas who demanded that a multi-million dollar ransom be paid. Acting as a rogue force despatched into the Beka'a Valley, the "Beta Group" operators, individuals who had trained Syrian special forces and intelligence agents, kidnapped twelve hostages of their own--all close relations of the kidnappers. One of those seized by the "Beta Group" officers was killed and his genitals hacked off; the removed bits of flesh were sent via courier to the kidnappers, instead of the expected ransom, along with a simple note: ***"This will happen to you unless our people are let go!"*** Less than twelve hours later, the four Soviet diplomats were freed in front of the Soviet Embassy in West Beirut.

Recently, it is believed that "Beta Group" has been active in the Chechen civil war as a forward special operations and assassination unit.

It is believed that "Alpha" and "Beta" Group operators are selected from a Spetsnaz volunteer pool, and subjected to a lengthy selection process as well as nearly nine months of basic infantry and combat training; additional training includes: cold-killing and the martial arts; language skills; high-speed driving; reconnaissance and intelligence-gathering techniques; sharp-shooting and sniping skills; tracking; heliborne insertion and extraction as well as airborne skills (line and HALO); and, negotiations skills.

In terms of maritime counter-terrorism, the Russian Republic has prepared for all contingencies and has been reported trained a company of ***Voyska Spetsial' Nogo Nazrachenniya*** (Naval Spetsnaz) for any ferry or boat seizures.

One additional unit known to exist (they've been seen raiding criminal locations on the streets of Moscow) is a squad drawn from the FSK--the Federal Counterintelligence Service and the successor to the KGB. The unit, a part of President Boris Yeltsin's personal security service, is renowned in Moscow for its violent operations against organized crime factions and its penchant for exotic form KGB weapons.

Following the break-up of the Soviet Union and its disintegration into separate republics, many of the ***OMON*** units were simply incorporated into the various new national counter-terrorist units. According to noted Soviet military author Steven J. Zaloga, the five ***OMON*** units that had been set up in the Ukraine, for example, created the cadre for the new Ukrainian national unit, known as the ***Berkut***, or

Golden Eagle. Similar ***OMON***-inspired units exist in the other republics, with the better squads being in the former Baltic states. Israeli advisors have trained small police units in Estonia and Latvia as have police SEKs from Germany and, it has been reported, French personnel from both RAID and the GIGN. The best of the Baltic units is believed to be the Lithuanian Police ***Aras*** unit--trained by the Israelis and GSG-9. ***Aras*** personnel are armed with AK-74 5.45mm assault rifles and Israel Military Industries (Ta'as) Mini-Uzi 9mm submachine guns.

[1] This, of course, was an interesting statement considering that the Black September terrorists who perpetrated the atrocity were supported by the East German Stasi.

## Spain

During cold-killing training, a GEO operatives displays his cold-killing techniques on a "terrorist" carrying a Model Z-70/B Star 9mm submachine gun. (Courtesy: Spanish Embassy, Office of the Military Attaché, Washington D.C.)

While an operator scales the wall of a fortified target, a GEO NCO aims his MP5 toward the "about-to-be-entered" window. (Courtesy: Spanish Embassy, Office of the Military Attaché, Washington D.C.)

***Peering into the sights of his PSG-1 rifle, the sniper breathed slowly and caressed the trigger with his right index finger. This was an impressive day, and he wanted to be sure he got the job done. Perched on a fourth floor ledge, the sniper had a grand view of the avenida below with an unobstructed view of all movements to the north and south as well as a good chunk of Madrid. He could not have been in a better position, nor could his subjects. Centered through his PSG-1's red centering dot was the head of Israeli Prime Minister Yitzhak Shamir, moving to his left he observed the Spanish Prime Minister and his aide-de-camp. "Alpha-Seven to Base," the sniper reported to his boss, "targets in sight and awaiting instructions."***

***Fortunately for the course of Middle East peace, the sniper perched atop a roof in the Spanish capital was an officer with the GEO, the Grupo Especial de Operaciones, Spain's national counter-terrorist force and one of the world's best. November 1, 1991: the Gulf War had just ended and the Americans had taken advantage of the post-war victory to bring the odd assortment of its coalition to the peace talks; Spain graciously extended an invitation for the enemies to meet in Spain's capital. Spanish intelligence received reports that Hizbollah, the Iranian-backed terrorist group had infiltrated several hit teams into Spain to disrupt the peace conference. According to the intelligence data, the terrorists would either try to detonate a high-explosive device near the outdoor gathering or mount a suicidal automatic weapon barrage, similar to the Abu Nidal attack at Rome and Vienna's airports in 1985. The GEO, sniper teams, TAC teams with MP5s and EOD officers were determined that the conference go off without incident.***

***The 1991 Madrid Middle East Peace Conference would be good practice for the GEO. A year later they would be safeguarding the Olympic Games in Barcelona.***

Spain has endured one of the most brutal and hard-fought terrorism campaigns in modern European history, a two-fold assault from the Basque ETA and foreign terrorists using Spanish territory as a battlefield, and it has persevered through this challenge with a three-tier approach. Counter-terrorist responsibilities inside Spain fall on three separate, though highly capable, entities, that are specifically trained to meet the most dedicated terrorist threat and challenge--from bombings and random machine gun attacks to aircraft hijackings and high-level assassinations.

The primary Spanish counter-terrorist unit and hostage-rescue, is the National Police's ***Grupo Especial de Operaciones***, the Special Operations Group known internationally by its acronym calling-card, the GEO. Mandated with all major hostage-rescue work throughout Spain, the GEO is a force of 150 operators permanently on call to respond to any incident involving terrorists and heavily armed criminals. For years, terrorism in Spain was non-existent; the dictatorship of Generalisimo Fransisco Franco eliminated most forms of political oppositions and the secret police, with their harsh and unforgiving methods, took care of the rest. When Franco died and a constitutional monarchy evolved into a vibrant democracy, Spain soon began to suffer from many of the problems that had plagued Western Europe for the previous decade--most notably of which was international terrorism. Because of its proximity to North Africa and political proximity to the turbulent politics of the Middle East, Spain became a national extension of the Arab-Israeli conflict; as far back as 1973, the Mossad and Black September had fought it out on the streets of Madrid and Barcelona, but now terrorist groups were establishing safe-houses and arms caches, targeting Israeli and Spanish targets, and preparing for the type of bloodshed and carnage that was previously seen on the streets of Belfast, London, Paris and Munich.

Yet the most pressing terrorist threat was from within. The ***Euzkadi ta Askatasuna,*** the Basque Fatherland and Liberty group better known throughout the world as the ETA, is among the oldest European terrorist factions; formed in 1959, the group maintains a Marxist ideology but its sole objective is the liberation of Basque country from Spanish (and to a lesser extent French) occupation. Highly sophisticated and compartmentalized like no other terrorist outfit in the world, ETA has proven an effective and lethal foe--they have killed over 500 individuals since 1968 when the group, following the Palestinian example, began a military uprising. Their primary targets for the ETA have been Spanish government officials, officers in the military and security forces, and moderate Basque politicians for assassination. Kidnapping and extortion are the major ETA means for raising funds, and these acts of human bartering has been transformed into an art form by ETA squads. ETA assault squads are also among Europe's most capable bank robbers, and have perfected hitting banks, especially on days when large sums of cash are being moved about, into a major source of fund-raising. Finally, ETA bombers are considered to be the world's most innovative and capable and the ETA philosophy has been "if you can't shoot it and kill it, then blow it up and obliterate it." Another terrorist faction that the GEO has been active against is GRAPO, a ultra-left wing communist faction that had a penchant for kidnappings and assassinations.

The ETA has kept the GEO ***extremely*** busy since the unit was sanctioned in 1978, and its level of operations in Basque country has made the GEO one of the world's most operationally experienced counter-terrorist units, as well as one of the world's best. When the Spanish Ministry of Defense authorized the creation of a national hostage-rescue unit, remarkably six years after most other European nations created their own intervention squads, the man selected to create this new and revolutionary unit was Commandante Quijada, a police superstar who perceived his unit to be the nation's elite and enacted a stringent, almost impossible-to-pass selection process for the GEO's first cadre of operators--all volunteers had to be physically fit and psychologically sound, but the principal requirement was three-years on the job with the police and owners of an exemplary service record. Of the initial call-out for 1,000 volunteers, only fifty made it through the first grueling selection phase--involving nearly two-weeks of physical and psychological examinations. Eventually, the unit accepted nearly 100 applicants; Commandante Quijada was specifically looking for psychologically sound applicants from the ranks of the national police. The objective of the unit was the apprehension of terrorists, no matter how horrendous the act they might have perpetrated, not their wholesale murder. GEO operators would have to be able to make that distinction in the field, Quijada told each volunteer: those who knew that not pulling the trigger would be a problem were disqualified, while those who understood the need for a national police unit, such as the GEO, that played by very specific legal rules were looked upon favorably. The value of taking suspects into custody is all-important. It deprives a hostile terrorist outfit of a martyr and also unnerves his/her comrades who have eluded capture. Needless to say, the intelligence reward that could be gained by a good dose of secret service interrogation is sometimes more valuable than a justified sense of revenge that counter-terrorist operators might occasionally seek. It is important to note than in the hundreds of operations that the GEO has participated in, it has had to use deadly force on only three occasions.

A GEO operator is hurled to the ground during martial-arts training with a Spanish Army special forces personnel. (Courtesy: Spanish Embassy, Office of the Military Attaché, Washington D.C.)

GEO operators jump from a Spanish Air Force Puma during static-line jump training. (Courtesy: Spanish Embassy, Office of the Military Attaché, Washington D.C.)

GEO free-fallers hone their stealth-like infiltration skills above the plains of central Spain. (Courtesy: Spanish Embassy, Office of the Military Attaché, Washington D.C.)

By its mandate, the GEO is responsible for most major counter-terrorist and rescue operations inside Spain, as well as involved in the rescue of Spanish citizens held abroad. At its vast training center on the Castillian plain near Guadalajara, the unit trains for every possible scenario to which they might be called to. Every type of possible building entry is practiced at the training facility, from using Goma 2 plastique explosives on a front door to fast-roping down a building's exterior to blow in a window. GEO officers like to boast that there isn't a building anywhere in Spain that the unit can't make it inside, secure or terminate the opposition, and rescue hostages from within. GEO operators regularly train at various airports throughout the country in rescuing hostages from hijacked Iberia airliners, as well as from trains and buses seized by terrorists. Virtually all of the GEO's training is carried out with live ammunition, especially tactical assault exercises. GEO operators are taught to experience the danger of live fire, feel its power and absorb all its sensations. When going through a door in order to free a hostage or engage a suicidal terrorist, the operator can display or possess no apprehension--no doubt. According to a German SEK officer who had his assault team visit with the GEO, "The Spaniards are as cocky, confident and capable as they come."

Their largest and certainly most intensive period of training came in the months before the 1992 Summer Olympics in Barcelona. Terrorists tend to manipulate symbolic dates and locations and nothing could have been more tempting than a strike at the twentieth anniversary of the Munich bloodletting. Spanish intelligence reported that Hizbollah was possibly planning a massive bombing campaign at an Olympic event, while other intelligence sources reported that an Abu Nidal suicide squad was already in Spain laying the groundwork for a massive hostage-taking endeavor. To ensure that the most serious incident at the games was a drunken brawl outside a Tapas Bar, a massive force of 45,000 police officers and soldiers secured the Olympic Villages and outlying areas. The GEO was in the vanguard. The unit was reportedly firing nearly 2,500 rounds of ammunition a day during the six months preceding the games, and several televised "run throughs" of a GEO tactical assault were aired on Spanish television. The news clips showed a squad of operators, wearing their leaf-pattern camouflage fatigues and faces hidden behind helmets and balaclavas, using significant C-4 charges to gain entry into a building. Once inside, the operators went through the rehearsed and meticulous choreography of securing room after room after room. The use of the explosives for gaining entry into a locked room was not just good TV--it was a ballistic message. Unlike Munich, the GEO would not be

GEO operators practice their underwater infiltration techniques in the Mediterranean during training with Spanish naval frogmen. (Courtesy: Spanish Embassy, Office of the Military Attaché, Washington D.C.)

intimated by any obstacle separating them from the rescue of their charges. The deterrent worked. The games at Barcelona were a brilliant success.

Throughout their nearly twenty years as a unit, the GEO has participated in hundreds of operations against the ETA, GRAPO, and groups as diverse and as dangerous as Hizbollah and the Provisional IRA. Some operations have been "typical" counter-terrorist fare--assaults on safe-houses, high-level security for terrorist trials. GEO operators have rescued hostages, including the kidnapped father of singer Julio Iglesias, and have rescued hostages from besieged buildings such as banks and government offices. Another GEO role is VIP security, and this includes foreign dignitaries visiting Spain or Spanish territory, as well as Spanish officials traveling abroad. The GEO has been deployed to Lebanon, El Salvador, Cuba and Egypt.

Among noted GEO operations are the rescue of kidnapped individuals, such as Dr. Julio Iglesias Puga in 1982, industrial magnate Guzmán Uribe in 1986, and Niña Melodie Nackachian in 1987; hostage-rescue operations include the assault on the terrorist-held Banco Central de Barcelona in 1981, the Banco de Vizcaya in Bilbao in 1982, and the Banco de Sabadell in Barcelona in 1987; and the GEO has also rescued wardens and guards from prison riots, including the two in the Carabnachel Prison in 1983 and 1985 and an uprising in the infamous Basauri Prison in 1986.

The greatest single influence on the GEO was a visit to St. Augustin Germany in 1978 and a chance to meet Colonel Wegener and the men of GSG-9. GSG-9 had just come off its ultra-successful rescue at Mogadishu, and the Spanish were eager students and prized graduates. Following the visit to Germany, the GEO would adopt GSG-9 training and selection techniques, as well as an almost

UEI operators, armed with a Empressa Nacional "Santa Bárbara" de Industrias Militares SA 9mm C2 submachine gun, depart the safety of their Klepper canoe while practicing amphibious assault techniques. (Courtesy: Spanish Embassy, Office of the Military Attaché, Washington D.C.)

exclusive line of German weaponry and equipment. Like GSG-9, the GEO has sections that are specifically trained for maritime counter-terrorist and hostage-rescue operations (trained by Spanish navy frogmen at Cartagena), as well as by Spanish Marines,[1] a section that is airborne qualified and trained for parachute (both static line and HALO) insertions; this section is trained by seasoned GEO officers, as well as by operators from the ***Unidad De Operaciones Especiales***, Spanish Army Special Forces, and the Spanish Air Force Jump School instructors. From its initial creation, the GEO has used the German example as law and the unit has favored German equipment and weaponry over anything else available from Spanish-produced rifles and pistols to vehicles and assault equipment. The principal weaponry carried by a GEO operator is a Heckler and Koch MP5A2 9mm submachine worn over the shoulder courtesy of a canvas sling and a Heckler and Koch P-9S 9mm semi-automatic pistol worn on a waist holster. Other variants of the MP5 carried by GEO personnel include the MP5 PT for the dispensing of plastic munitions, the suppressed MP5 SD, and the MP5K for use by close-protection detachments. GEO snipers use both the Heckler and Koch PSG-1 7.62mm system, and the Mauser SP 66--Spanish snipers are considered among Europe's best and routinely finish in first place in European CTCs--as well as the Swiss SIG-Sauer SSG 2000 7.62mm sniping rifle. The GEO also deploys the Heckler and Koch HK33E 5.56mm assault rifle as well as a long line of 12-gauge shotguns, including the Franchi 12-gauge SPAS 12, the Heckler and Koch HK512, and the Remington Mk. 870--favored among operators who have trained with American units, such as Delta and the FBI's HRT. The GEO deploys an extensive fleet of vehicles, ranging from patrol cars, vans and motorbikes, to BLR (***Blindado Ligero de Ruedas***) armored personnel carriers and BMR ***(Blindado Medio de Ruedas)*** 600 infantry fighting vehicles. The GEO also has at its disposal a fleet of National Police MBB/Kawasaki BK117 multi-purpose helicopters. GEO supply trucks, mobile armories that follow the unit's deployments throughout Spain, are also equipped with SCUBA gear and Zodiac craft for any potential underwater and amphibious work.

The GEO maintains very close ties to GSG-9 and various State-SEKs, as well as with Portugal's GOE, Austria's Gendarmerie Einsatzkommando Cobra, France's GIGN and RAID units, Great Britain's 22nd Special Air Service Regiment, Italy's GIS, and Israel's ***Ya'ma'm***.

During training for operations in Basque country, Spanish Army special forces personnel practice cold-killing sentry removal techniques. (Courtesy: Spanish Embassy, Office of the Military Attaché, Washington D.C.)

Also in 1978, the national ***Guardia Civil***, sanctioned the creation of its own counter-terrorist and hostage-rescue unit. The ***Guardia Civil*** and the National Police, to which the GEO is a part, share an operational relationship similar to the one shared in Italy by the National Police and the Carabinieri. The ***Guardia Civil*** is a militarized force under the command of the Ministry of the Interior, though under the overall control of the Ministry of Defense; in a certain sense of law-enforcement comparisons, they are similar to U.S. State Troopers. Although a nationwide force, their primary area of responsibility is the country-side and rural areas and are a staple of Spanish rural life; as a result, they have also been most active in the war against ETA in the three Basque provinces in the north.

The ***Guardia Civil*** possesses two specialized anti-terrorist and hostage-rescue units that some in Spain consider equal to the GEO--some say that they are even better. The larger unit is the ***Unidad Especial de Intervencion***, known throughout the world by its acronym of UEI. The UEI is an elite force of volunteers made up of individuals with at least ***five*** years of experience with the ***Guardia Civil***, and pass a grueling selection process where an applicant's undergoes a rigid security check, as well as a stringent physical and psychological examinations. The UEI prides itself as a truly elite fighting force, and the selection process is such that less than five per cent of the total applicants are ever allowed to commence its year long training. UEI instruction is similar to GEO instruction, though geared more toward conventional combat skills as opposed to specialized VIP security work. Because they operate in the mountains of Spain, along the coastal plains and inside inhospitable forest areas, UEI operators undergo an exhaustive combat course designed to prepare the unit for operations in all terrain and all climates. "They are like regular army commandos," claims a Spanish naval officer who has observed UEI training, "they are special forces material and as good as anything in the regular army and as good as anything in the NATO order of battle." UEI operators have visited the I-LRRPS school in Germany, as well as the German Army's Mountain Warfare School at 1st Mountain Division's home base at Garmisch-Partenkirchen. The UEI has trained with the Spanish Marine's reconnaissance battalion (the ***Unidad Especial Buceadores De Combate***), as well as with the Spanish Navy's naval special warfare unit.

Because they are in the countryside, in contact on a daily basis with high-risk criminal elements in the heart of Basque country, the UEI gets less high-profile assault and rescue operations, instead deploying virtually daily as a mobile SWAT force.

The ***Guardia Civil***'s second counter-terrorist unit is the ***Grupos Antiterroristas Rurales*** (Rural Anti-Terrorist Group), known by its acronym of GAR. The GAR is also a volunteer force made up of ***Guardia Civil*** officers who are stationed in the most remote stretches of Spain, and as a result they are trained to operate in smaller forces against, sometimes, the most violent and heavily armed elements of the ETA. Their training is similar to the UEI, though they are more of a patrol presence in the rural areas and call the UEI for tactical back-up during large-scale jobs. Like the GEO and UEI, the GAR is armed completely by Heckler and Koch--carrying the full-line of MP5 9mm submachine guns, as well as Spanish-produced CETME 5.56mm assault rifles. Like the ETA operatives they face in the confused battlefield of counter-insurgency, GAR operators are trained as lethal guerrilla fighters capable of living--and operating--in the bush for considerable stretches of time.

The GAR is a large force by counter-terrorist unit standards, consisting of nearly 600 policemen. The unit is commanded by a lieutenant-colonel (***teniente coronel***), two commandantes, five captains, twelve lieutenants, seventeen sergeants, thirty-seven corporals and 510 guards.

Spanish military special forces also undergo rudimentary counter-terrorist and hostage-rescue training. Spanish Army units from the ***Unidad De Operaciones Especiales*** are known throughout Europe as superb fighters and expert shots with their CETME 5.56mm assault rifles. The Spanish Navy possesses a naval special warfare unit, the ***Unidad Especial de Bueadores de Combate*** (Special Combat Divers' Unit) and the Air Force's EZAPAC, the ***Escuadrilla de Zapadores Paracaidistas***, Parachutist Engineer Squadron.

While preparing for the security arrangements for the 1992 Madrid Olympic games, naval operators from the ***Unidad Especial de Bueadores de Combate*** deploy for additional security/counter-terrorist assignments. (Courtesy: Spanish Embassy, Office of the Military Attaché, Washington D.C.)

A footnote: Recently, in the winter of 1994-1995, there has been great controversy in Spain concerning the activities of a mysterious group known as the Anti-Terrorist Liberations Group (GAL). Spanish authorities claimed that GAL operated death squads that secretly hunted down Basque operatives in Basque provinces and in southwestern France between 1983 and 1986, resulting in the deaths of over twenty individuals. It is not known if GEO, UEI or GAR operators have been implicated in the hit squads, but Ministry of Interior officials have been subsequently jailed.

[1] This unit of marines also trains for counter-terrorist missions and has been operational against ETA targets in Basque-country.

During training for operations in the heart of ETA-Basque country, a Spanish Army ***Unidad De Operaciones Especiales*** "Alpha Team" peer through their weapon sights. (Courtesy: Spanish Embassy, Office of the Military Attaché, Washington D.C.)

## Switzerland

In a country run on the premise of neatness and order, the potential for disaster required the "Swiss touch." October, 1972. Thirty days after the killings in Munich, high-ranking officers in the Swiss military and police began the intensive lobbying effort among the politicians to authorize the creation of a national hostage-rescue entity. The officers didn't care who would get the calling--the army or the police--but something had to be done before the blood of innocent civilians were caught in the crossfire of an attack inside Switzerland. The Swiss parliament, a conglomerate of independent-minded Cantons (states) covering a multitude of interests, ethnic groups and languages, mulled over the notion for nearly six years. Military commanders of Switzerland's vast citizen army were, on one hand, eager to have their specialized forces play some sort of role in hostage-rescue operations against sensitive targets such as aircraft, ferries and trains, though they did not want to enter the tactical minefield of operating inside cities and towns in the hunting and pursuit of international terrorist groups. The Swiss Police realized that counter-terrorism was a police matter and a national matter, but also knew that the public would have to get used to heavily armed police officers entering into the murky and sometimes bloody world of hostage-takers, bombers and master terrorists.

The ***Kantonspolizei Zürich*** patch, worn by all FLUSIPO operators.

Swiss lawmakers were unsuccessful in forming a national response unit, and it was decided that each Canton, or State, would be responsible for ending terrorist incidents inside its regional confines. The federal authorities, the security services and the border police would be responsible for keeping outside trouble from entering Switzerland, local units would be tasked with cleaning up the mess of what managed to slip through.

The trend-setter of Swiss counter-terrorism was the ***Kantonspolizei Zürich*** and its ***Flughafenpolizei Sicherheitsabteilung Einsatzgruppen--***a unit known by its acronym of FLUSIPO. On February 18, 1969, terrorists from the Popular Front for the Liberation of Palestine (PFLP) attacked an El Al Israel Airlines DC-8 at Zurich airport; the terrorists assaulted the passenger lounge with machine gun and grenade fire and killed an El Al stewardess and wounded several passengers. Airport police, at the time armed with nothing more than SIG pistols, were grossly under armed, and poorly trained to counter any determined terrorist threat; they were capable of deterring pickpockets and thefts, not men and women firing indiscriminate bursts from AK-47s.

The airport police began a recruitment drive seeking volunteers who were both physically and psychologically able to meet the challenges of counter-terrorist duty, and those who had exemplary service records. Officers were drawn from the airport detail and rushed into a protective security and tactical assault course. Their main objective was deterrence and to serve as a reaction force to any indiscriminate attack that would be perpetrated at the Zurich airport. They were taught to secure perimeter grounds with armored cars and bullet-proof vehicles and the skills of close-quarter combat that would be needed should they have to respond to a suicide-squad of gunmen opening up on a departure lounge crowded with travelers. FLUSIPO officers were trained in the martial arts, underwent a commando's course by the Swiss Army, and were even trained in rudimentary EOD work in case explosives were found and time did not permit waiting for the bomb squad. Although specifically trained and certified in tubular assaults, FLUSIPO officers are not expected to assault hijacked aircraft forced down in Switzerland. Their task is to cordon off the aircraft, position snipers around the inner-perimeter, and assist the hostage-rescue force sanctioned for the mission.

Although Swiss sources are, naturally, close-mouthed concerning the actual size of the Zurich Police's special airport anti-terrorist unit, the unit is believed to number over 100 officers. They are armed with SIG Sauer P228 9mm pistols, Heckler and Koch MP5 9mm submachine guns and Heckler and Koch HK 33E 5.56mm assault rifle. The unit's principal sniper weapon is the SIG-Sauer SSG 2000 7.62mm marksman's weapon, along with the SIG-Sauer SG550 Sniper. FLUSIPO squads secure sensitive aircraft, such as those belonging to El Al, with MOWAG Piranha 6x6 armored cars.

FLUSIPO was a responsive measure by the Swiss authorities in

FLUSIPO officers, armed with Heckler and Koch 33E 5.56mm assault rifles, race across the grassy inner-perimeter at Zurich International Airport during an infiltration drill. (Courtesy: Kantonspolizei Zürich Public Affairs Office)

FLUSIPO officers engage in the martial arts, during close-contact training at the unit headquarters in Zurich International Airport. (Courtesy: Kantonspolizei Zürich Public Affairs Office)

the early 1970s to counter the trend, at the time, in international terrorism--aircraft hijackings and indiscriminate attacks against airports. Once, following the 1972 Munich Olympic Massacre, hostages were taken for political gain and for the purpose of barter, a new type of police entity needed to be formed inside the various Swiss Cantons. The true genesis in Swiss counter-terrorist units came in January 1975 with the formation of the ***Stadtpolizei Bern***'s "Enzian Group," the capital city's counter-terrorist unit, and the "Stern Group," the ***Kantonspolizei Bern***'s canton-wide counter-terrorist team. The units accepted volunteers from the "regular" police who had at least five-years on the job, and who possessed an exemplary service record. Volunteers had to pass a grueling physical and psychological test, and endure an additional six months of tactical training, including heavy weapons and tactics (MP5s, 12-gauge shotguns, and sniper weapons), EOD basics, SCUBA and mountaineering, high-speed driving, and be certified as emergency medical technicians. Officers in both the "Stern" and "Enzian" groups are trained in the martial arts, and are expert shots--most of their instruction is live-fire. The "Enzian Group"'s baptism of fire was the take-over of the Polish embassy in Bern in 1984 where the hostage-takers were successfully subdued by the officers carrying water-cannons (Swiss police prefer non-lethal means, if possible).

Because of the success of the "Stern" and "Enzian Groups, all the cantons formed their own "ATs," or assault teams, as they are known. In 1984, for example, the Geneva AT rescued sixty-two hostages on board of a hijacked Air France jet when its officers posed as groundscrewmen.

Although the "Stern" and "Enzian" units have warranted the most attention and press, the best Swiss counter-terrorist and hostage-rescue unit is undoubtedly the ***Kantonspolizei Aargau Grenadierzug Argus***. Routinely finishing at the top of European CTCs (Combat Team Competitions), even beating out GSG-9 and the U.S. Army's 1st SFOD-Delta (Airborne) ***Kantonspolizei Aargau Grenadierzug Argus*** is a force of sixty-five officers specifically trained for counter-terrorist and heavy crime-fighting duties in Canton Aargau, a 1,403.63 square kilometer patch of territory which is home to 524,000 people.

***Kantonspolizei Aargau Grenadierzug Argus***, like the other Swiss AT teams and units, deploys the Heckler and Koch family of MP5 9mm submachine guns, SIG-Sauer 9mm and .40 caliber handguns, Heckler and Koch and Remington 12-gauge shotguns, and the SIG-Sauer family of tactical sniping rifles. Swiss units maintain their closest ties to one another, GSG-9, German SEKs, and the Austria's GEK Cobra, while the Geneva AT maintains close ties to the French GIGN.

A FLUSIPO EOD expert maneuvers his EOD robot out of the response van during a bomb-scare outside an El Al aircraft about to take-off for the daily flight to Tel Aviv. (Courtesy: Kantonspolizei Zürich Public Affairs Office)

An abandoned briefcase sitting on the tarmac at Zurich International Airport exacts the attention of a FLUSIPO robot and some tense nerves. (Courtesy: Kantonspolizei Zürich Public Affairs Office)

After receiving intelligence that terrorists were planning a suicide attack against an Israeli "target" in Zurich, a FLUSIPO Mowag Pirhana armored car protects an El Al jet that just landed. (Courtesy: Kantonspolizei Zürich Public Affairs Office)

At Geneva International Airport, a Geneva Airport Security Detachment police M113 APC stands guard in front of a Swissair jet during a prisoner exchange between the Popular Front for the Liberation of Palestine General Command (PFLP-GC) and Israel in May 1985. (IDF Spokesman)

The SIG-Sauer SSG-3000 .308 Winchester precision rifle--viewed by many to be the best marksman rifle in the world and the mainstay of all Swiss police and military special operations units. (Courtesy: SIG-Sauer)

The SIG-Sauer SG550 Sniper 5.56mm police sniping rifle--a semi-automatic precision weapon favored by many Swiss tactical units for its ballistic properties and ease of use. (Courtesy: SIG-Sauer)

Peering through his SIG-Sauer SSG3000 7.62mm precision weapon, a ***Kantonspolizei Zürich*** sniper peers through his Hensoldt telescopic 1.5 - 6 x 42 BL sight during a hostage-taking drama. (Courtesy: SIG-Sauer)

Positioned conveniently across the street from an ongoing hostage-taking situation involving an emotionally disturbed male with a gun, a ***Kantonspolizei Zürich*** sniper peers through his SIG-Sauer SG 550 Sniper awaiting the call take down his target. (Courtesy: SIG-Sauer)

Armed with the latest version of the SSG550, the SIG-Sauer SSG 551-1P with Hensoldt scope, a ***Kantonspolizei Zürich*** sniper carefully keeps tracks of his target inside his sights. (Courtesy: SIG-Sauer)

Wearing his sniper's mesh mask and hooked to his observer by remote radio, a ***Kantonspolizei Zürich*** sniper uses the foliage outside a Zurich park as cover to monitor a terrorist suspect. He is armed with the SIG-Sauer SG 55 Sniper 5.56mm assault/sniping weapon. (Courtesy: SIG-Sauer)

The SIG-Sauer P228 9mm semi-automatic pistol: Considered by special forces personnel--from the Sultanate of Oman to the U.S. Army's 1st SFOD-Delta (Airborne)--to be among the finest 9mm handguns in existence. The P228 is in use by virtually all Swiss counter-terrorist teams. (Courtesy: SIG-Sauer)

The SIG-Sauer .40 Smith and Wesson caliber power handgun--the newest sidearm to enter Swiss police service. (Courtesy: SIG-Sauer)

Two officers from the "Enzian Group" use a water cannon on an emotionally disturbed individual during hostage-rescue exercises in a Bern forest. (Courtesy: Eugen Egli)

In the frost of a winter's morning in Bern, two officers from the "Enzian Group" clutch their Heckler and Koch MP5s awaiting word from a hostage-taker. Note bullhorn loudspeaker in the officer's hand. (Courtesy: Eugen Egli)

***"Polizei! Still stehen, sich nicht bewegen!"*** "Enzian Group" officers practice the art of a road stop and subduing and neutralizing a fleeing terrorist. Note photograph offers an excellent view of the ***Bern Stadtpolizei*** police cruiser. (Courtesy: Eugen Egli)

Because of the altitudes in which they must function (the Alps) and because of the many skyscrapers inside the Bern city limits, "Enzian Group" operators are among the best in Europe with rope work--many are trained in Austria by the world's true rope masters--Austria's Gendarmerieeinsatzkommando Cobra. (Courtesy: Eugen Egli)

A "Stern Group" sniper, armed with the SIG-Sauer SG 550 Sniper 5.56mm assault/sniper rifle, peers through the cross-hairs of his weapon's sight at a target several hundred yards away. (Courtesy: Eugen Egli)

"Stern Group" officers gingerly pepper their pop-up targets with well-placed 9mm holes during the unit's daily tour at the indoor firing range. (Courtesy: Eugen Egli)

Utilizing their unique rope skills, "Enzian Unit" officers cling to their line while at the same time poised to strike through a plate-glass window into a room where "terrorists" are holding an office staff hostage. (Courtesy: Eugen Egli)

During tactical assault training at a Bern high-rise, "Enzian Group" officers slowly slink down a six-story facade of a building as they train their weapons on a window where an armed "terrorist" is holding a room full of people hostage. (Courtesy: Eugen Egli)

Two "Enzian Group" officers, wearing black fish-net masks display their technique for entering a room in which the location of the terrorist/criminal/hostage-taker is NOT known. (Courtesy: Eugen Egli)

Wearing their dark blue overalls and Kevlar ballistic vests, "Enzian Group" officers move through a hallway with weapons at hand while securing the rooms of an office building during counter-terrorist warfare training. (Courtesy: Eugen Egli)

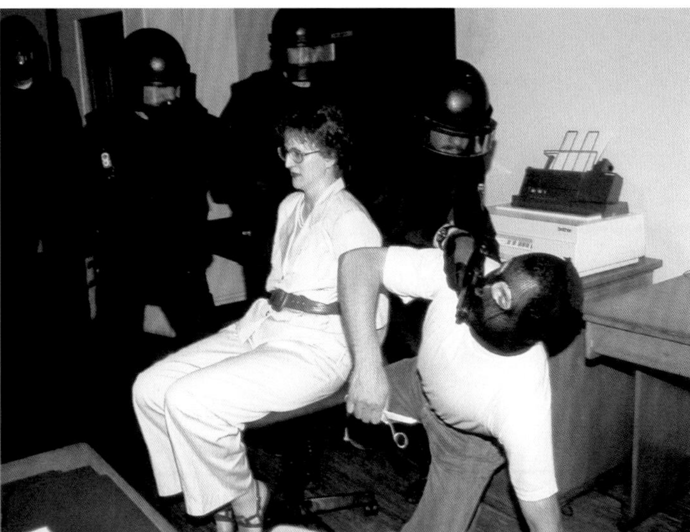

In a brief second, "Enzian Group" officers burst through a door and rush to a hostage-taker and his prisoner--first the officers must subdue the hostage-taker and then deal with the relieved, though shocked, victim. (Courtesy: Eugen Egli)

An intimidating scene to stop even the most hardened international terrorist--the rescuer's gun barrel piercing into the back of the criminal's head. (Courtesy: Eugen Egli)

Unarmed combat training with the Enzian Group--Swiss police AT unit officers are all expected to be deadly with their 9mm SIG-Sauers as well as with their bare hands. (Courtesy: Eugen Egli)

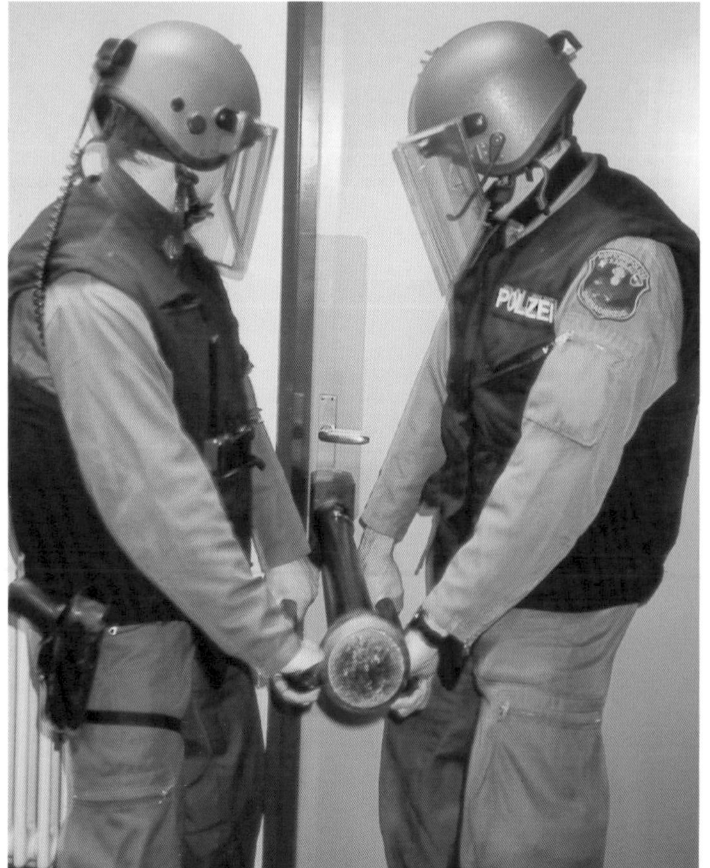

While ***Kantonspolizei Aargau Grenadierzug Argus*** officers train their P228 pistols and Remington 870 12-gauge shotguns at a door, the entry team, deploying the battering ram, prepare to gain entry to a barricaded location. (Courtesy: ***Kantonspolizei Aargau Grenadierzug Argus***)

A police officer from ***Kantonspolizei Aargau Grenadierzug Argus*** slowly lowers himself down the side of a building aiming his SIG-Sauer P228 9mm pistol at a suspected window. (Courtesy: ***Kantonspolizei Aargau Grenadierzug Argus***)

A ***Kantonspolizei Aargau Grenadierzug Argus*** group photo--next to their all-terrain deployment vehicle. (Courtesy: ***Kantonspolizei Aargau Grenadierzug Argus***)

A ***Kantonspolizei Aargau Grenadierzug Argus*** assault team uses a battering ram to gain entry into a barricaded room. (Courtesy: ***Kantonspolizei Aargau Grenadierzug Argus***)

A ***Kantonspolizei Aargau Grenadierzug Argus*** officer aims his Remington 870 12-gauge shotgun during live-fire exercises. Note Kevlar body-armor adorned with reflective ***POLIZEI*** patch. (Courtesy: ***Kantonspolizei Aargau Grenadierzug Argus***)

During a visit to St. Augustin, Germany, ***Kantonspolizei Aargau Grenadierzug Argus*** officers pose by the now legendary unit sign. (Courtesy: ***Kantonspolizei Aargau Grenadierzug Argus***)

A ***Kantonspolizei Aargau Grenadierzug Argus*** assault team practices assaulting a bus hijacked by terrorists. (Courtesy: ***Kantonspolizei Aargau Grenadierzug Argus***)

***Kantonspolizei Aargau Grenadierzug Argus*** officers fast rope down a Swiss police chopper during infiltration exercises. Note ski blades on the Allouette's landing wheels. (Courtesy: ***Kantonspolizei Aargau Grenadierzug Argus***)

The patch from the *Kantonspolizei Aargau.*

The patch from the ***Kantonspolizei Aargau***'s counter-terrorist unit--the ***Grenadierzug Argus***.

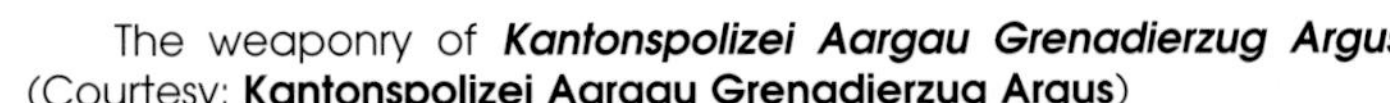

The weaponry of ***Kantonspolizei Aargau Grenadierzug Argus***. (Courtesy: **Kantonspolizei Aargau Grenadierzug Argus**)

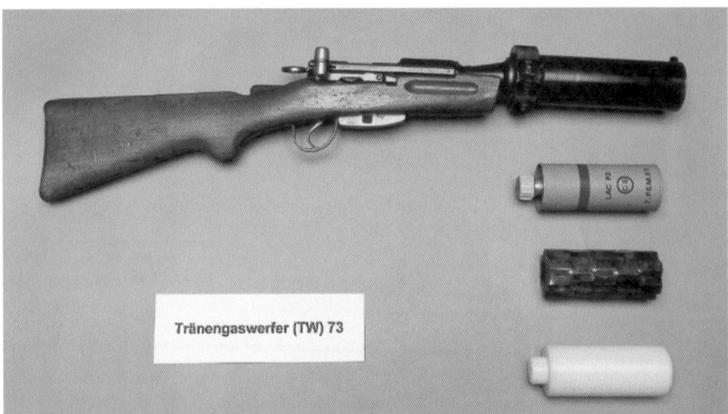

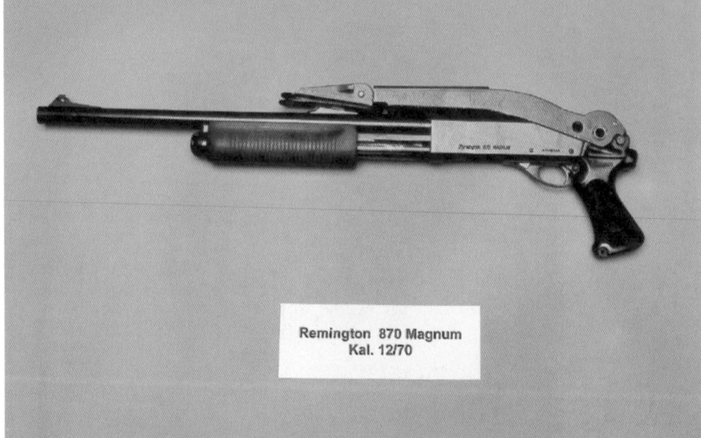

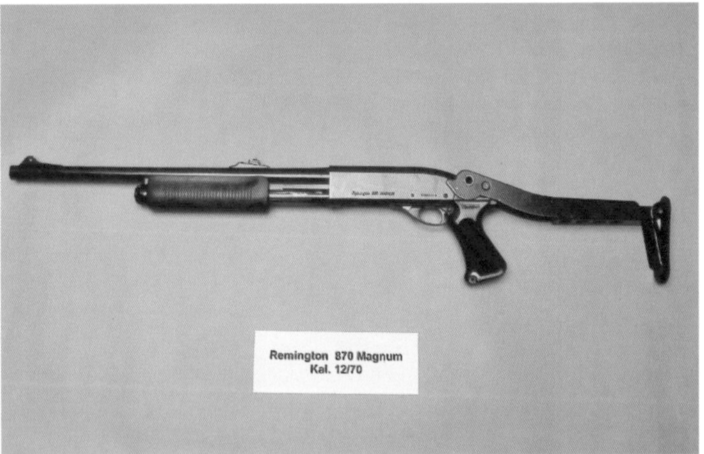


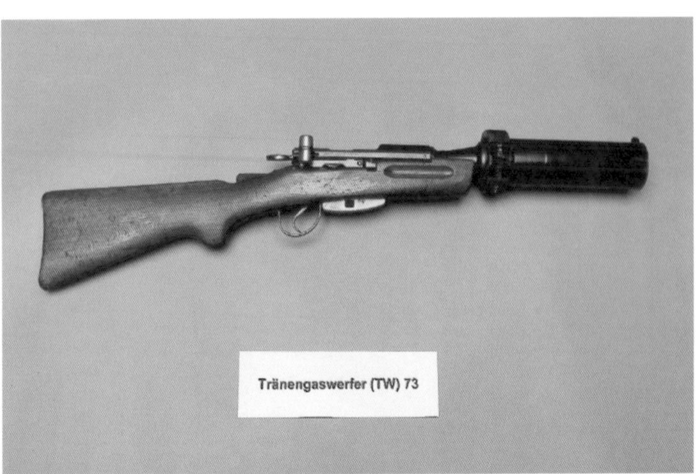


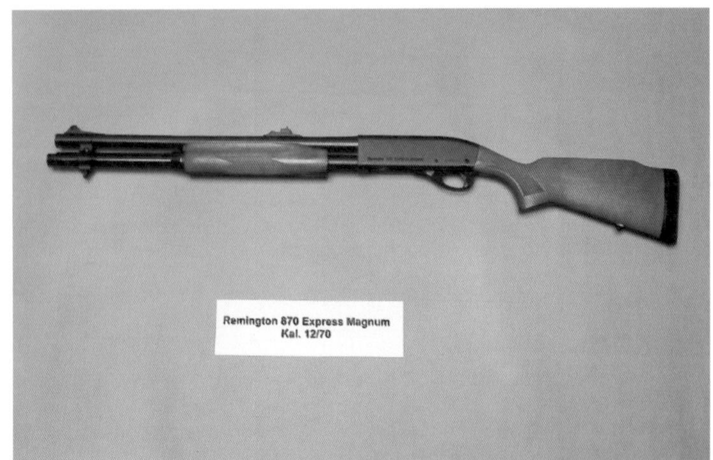

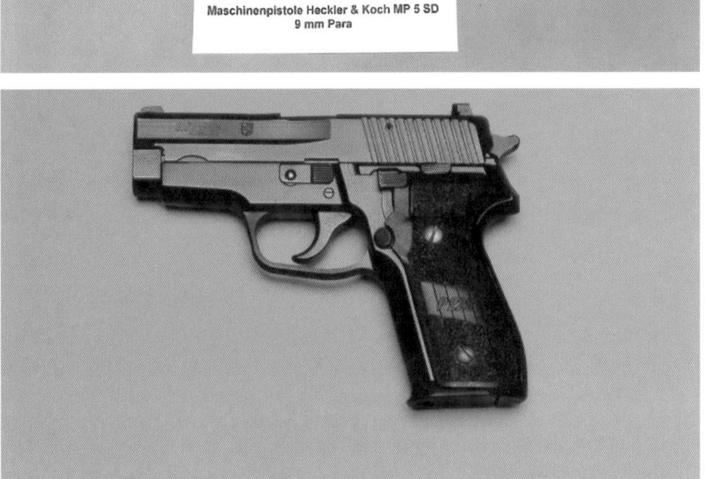

The weaponry of ***Kantonspolizei Aargau Grenadierzug Argus***. (Courtesy: ***Kantonspolizei Aargau Grenadierzug Argu)***

## UNITED KINGDOM - SAS, SBS

To one of the operators, it looked like a scene from a James Bond movie. Inside a cleared cut-out in picturesque jungle setting, complete with swinging palms and howling cockatoos, a British soldier with a North London accent removed a Browning Hi-Power 9mm from a custom made leather holster and proceeded to walk through a live-fire obstacle course, simulating a room, complete with cardboard cutouts of hostages, terrorists, old women and even booby-trapped explosives. "Always know what you are looking for," the NCO barked in his distinctive voice, "and kill it." After receiving the OK from the safety officer, the trooper entered the house and in fifteen seconds raced through the plywood room firing all thirteen rounds from his well-maintained weapon in a well rehearsed symphony of 9mm ballistics. As the assembled look on in awe, they pass through the course to see that the cutouts simulating terrorists, six in all, each received two 9mm holes in their heads and hearts; only the female terrorist cutout, carrying what appeared to be a detonator, was shot three times in the head. The audience was impressed, but they spoke Spanish among one another and many were jotting down notes.

This was not the average jungle training class in Borneo or Brunei where British soldiers have traditionally gone to learn the art of jungle warfare. This was Colombia, in the heart of cocaine country, and the British instructors were operators from the 22nd Special Air Service Regiment of Hereford, England, perhaps the world's most famous special operations unit and clearly among the world's best. The SAS, as the "Hereford Boys" are known throughout the world, were not in the Colombian jungles to engage the Colombian cartels personally, nor had the Irish problem disappeared to the point where narco-terrorism

"An SAS Target": A PIRA gunman, armed with an Armalite rifle, poses for the camera in a Belfast safe-house. (Courtesy: Photo Press UK Defence)

"Operation Nimrod": The May 5, 1980 assault into the Iranian Embassy at Princess Gate. (Courtesy: U.S. Army Special Operations Command)

was the next order of the day. The SAS were in Colombia to act as advisors, instructors, and examples. If Colombia was to fight the drug barons with the counter-insurgency strategy that made the SAS both famous and infamous in Northern Ireland, then the SAS were as good as one could find in the classroom. As a result of its operations in Northern Ireland against the Provisional Irish Republican Army, a lawless fight where the term "Big Boys' Rule" was born, the SAS has literally written the book on fighting a guerrilla and counter-terrorist campaigns. They penned the rules and then broke them with cunning guile, 9mm flurries, and unforgiving ruthlessness. Tales of the Armagh, Belfast and Loughgall soon overshadowed the Princess Gate. Similar special operations units around the world envied them, terrorists were scared to death of them.

The SAS exchange program in Colombia began in 1989 with a small advisory team of SAS officers, operators from the Special Boat Service (SBS) and the Royal Military Police Close Protection Squad (CPS), and has now become an annual exercise. Colombian special forces and counter-terrorist units have since become better, wiser and bolder. Who Dares Wins, after all.

The SAS possesses a reputation in the international special forces community that is beyond elite, beyond exclusive and beyond question. In the words of the late Colonel Charles Beckwith, the founder of the U.S. Army's 1st SFOD-D, "There is the SAS and there is everyone else." But unlike many of the world's top counter-terrorist and hostage-rescue units, the SAS was not born out of the charred remains of two ***Bundesgrenzschutz*** choppers smoldering on the runway at Fürstenfeldbrük. The Special Air Service inherited the role of British national counter-terrorist force because innovation, incredible courage and the willingness and ability to use lethal firepower is the only way to defeat a terrorist threat--the British government simply realized far sooner and far blunter than most other governments.

The Special Air Service was created by a military genius named David Stirling, a man who revolutionized warfare in the Second World War, by inserting small highly-trained and heavily armed units deep behind enemy lines for intelligence-gathering forays, sabotage strikes and even assassination assignments. Stirling's "Aberdeen Testing Ground" for this small unit special warfare was the Western Desert, with the Long Range Desert Group and similar "commandos" who functioned as private armies against the better judgments of such staff officers as Wavell, Ritchie, Auchinleck, and Montgomery. Stirling

During survival training in the Scottish highlands, an SAS operator scans his map and operational orders. Note sand beret, "Who Dares Wins" winged dagger badge, and DPM camouflage jacket. (Courtesy: Photo Press UK Defence)

wasn't a soldier by profession, he was a student at Cambridge and a mountain climber, and his irreverent view of the trappings of conventional soldiering created an upstart image of daring souls eager to prove the impossible which attracted the unique and bizarre throughout the British Army. If you could march until you dropped and then farther, if you were fond of climbing and parachuting, and if you could kill with unrelenting ferocity, you were Stirling material. After their now legendary forays in the Western Desert, where the commandos were keen to ride about the desert wasteland in full beard and Arab headdress, the unit adopted a trademark: A winged dagger device representing Excalibur and motto "Who Dares Wins."

Throughout their service in the Second World War, the soon-to-be accorded 1st Special Air Service Regiment served as a covert operations entity in virtually every campaign theater. "The Boys Stirling" fought in North Africa, the Aegean, Italy, and Northwest Europe. Following the war, SAS officers had hoped to have the unit expanded, but the regiment was disbanded[1] and in 1947 a Territorial Army (reserve) unit known as the 21st Special Air Service Regiment (Artists Rifles) was formed; the London-based TA or reservist unit dated back to 1860 as a mean of setting aside officer material for military service in time of emergency.[2]

The SAS disappearance from the British Army's active duty order of battle lasted until 1951 when the Malayan Emergency came about and the SAS became a full-time regiment. The SAS operated as a covert counter-insurgency force for seven years in the Communist insurgency in Malaya where they became known as the Malayan Scouts and eventually as the 22 Special Air Service Regiment. In the bitter and difficult combat in Malaya, the SAS proved that Western troops could indeed operate in an inhospitable territory behind enemy lines for months at a time. They also proved the value of behind-the-lines reconnaissance and intelligence-gathering, and how harassing an enemy in his secure rear could strike a devastating blow to morale, even among indoctrinated ideologs fighting for a cause rather than a nation. Malaya also proved to the Ministry of Defense the need for a full-time special operations regiment to be on-call for service in many of the former empire's trouble-spots. Over the next ten years, the SAS saw action in Borneo and Oman. In 1974, the SAS saw action for the time in the land of the troubles--Northern Ireland.

"The troubles" came at a time when much of Western Europe was discovering that the Middle Eastern battlefield had washed up on the continent and war by proxy was being waged on its city streets and in the countryside. In September 1970, following the hijacking of a BOAC jet to Jordan by Black September, officials in Whitehall responsible for SAS deployments and operations began to ponder what steps could be taken to not only retrieve a hijacked aircraft but rescue those passengers on board. Great Britain was emerging as a primary terrorist target, and with a dire political stake in Northern Ireland and interests in the Arab-Israeli conflict, Whitehall and the security services were concerned about an explosion of terrorism on the streets of London and against British aircraft and shipping interests. When Israeli commandos from ***Sayeret Mat'kal*** stormed the Sabena Belgian Airlines Boeing 707 on the tarmac at Lod Airport in May 1972, the SAS took notice. A military response to terrorist incidents was not only possible, it could be brilliantly successful. The regiment's commanding officer at the time, legendary Lieutenant-Colonel John Waddy, prepared a status report for the MoD suggesting three roles for 22 SAS in this new and uncharted form of warfare: intelligence-gathering, preempting planned terrorists actions, and responding to specific terrorist attacks. Whitehall was impressed. The word soon came to Hereford--the last stop for any terrorist would be the SAS.

Trained to live in the bush and survive amid a hostile population, the SAS soon developed innovative techniques in training for hostage-rescue work. One squadron dedicated solely to counter-terrorist work was established, and CT training evolved into two primary fields of expertise: Entry and Shooting. When preparing their manual for rescue assignments, SAS officers viewed entering a seized location--be it a plane, train, boat or building--to be among the most serious challenge. Entry meant showing one's hand and, as a result, had to be done quickly and effectively: to counteract the booby-trapped doors of a hijacked aircraft, the SAS developed a technique where the roof or undercarriage of the aircraft could be blown "out" with a unique explosive charge; to counteract sentries and observers in a seized building, the SAS developed tactics for having operators cling to a heliborne line and swinging into action; and, most significantly, in order to gain a few precious seconds of surprise once a door was kicked in or a panel blown out, SAS ordnance officers developed a special "flash bang" grenade that produced a deafening blast and blinding flash generated by a 50,000 candlepower illumination meant to incapacitate a target for a number of seconds. In terms of shooting and weapons proficiency, nothing would be spared in preparing the operators for a potential close-quarter fire-fight. The sounds of automatic fire filled the Stirling Lines Barracks in Hereford--virtually twenty-four hours a day. Operators were taught to become one with their side-arms, their submachine guns and their M-16 assault rifles. The number of rounds fired in Hereford in one month equaled the annual allotment for many armies. "We don't count spent ammo so we won't have to count dead hostages," quipped an SAS NCO to a visiting German GSG-9 officer in 1975. The Germans would soon thereafter become less frugal when counting their bullets, too.

Wearing oxygen masks for a 25,000 foot HALO parachute drop, SAS operators pose for the camera carrying FN MAG 7.62mm light machine guns, and CAR-15 5.56mm assault rifles. HALO jumps are but one means of SAS stealth insertion behind enemy lines. (Courtesy: Photo Press UK Defence)

SAS operators were also afforded incredible leeway in selecting weaponry and equipment that they were comfortable with as opposed to materials, that Whitehall had procured for them. The pistol of choice became the Belgian-produced Browning Hi-Power 9mm; the suppressed Sterling L34A1 9mm submachine gun was chosen, as was the Accuracy International sniper weapons for the marksman.

The regiment commander created a Counter-Revolutionary Wing (CRW) that would be tasked with primarily VIP security and intelligence-gathering, but would serve as the primary logistic body in the regiment tasked with counter-terrorism. The CRW School at Hereford specialized in teaching Close-Quarter Battle (CQB) and Fighting In Built-Up Area (FIBUA) skills. A sophisticated live-fire range was built at Hereford, where an operators skills and instincts could be developed, refined and perfected. Pop-up targets, simulating a terrorist clutching a hostage or an innocent child would simply appear throughout the course, and the operator would be expected to hit the center of his target and nothing else. Ridiculous time frames

An RAF Chinook CH-47 special ops chopper from 47 Squadron--the special operations aviation unit trained and sanctioned to fly SP Teams in support of their counter-terrorist or combat operations. (Courtesy: Photo Press UK Defence)

were awarded to each participant on the course forcing them to push their bodies through the hundred yard long obstacles, as well as their minds and trigger fingers. Once CQB became a SAS mandate, operators were ordered to refrain from pumping up their bodies and upper body strength with weight training, and coerced into running and aerobic exercises dedicated to increasing speed and endurance.

To replicate the reality of entering a confined space and rescuing a hostage held by gun-toting professionals and fanatics, the now legendary and infamous "Killing House" was built at Stirling Lines. The Killing House, a mock-up of a room that could be configured with different furnishings and wall structures, was meant to be a reusable training ground designed to prepare the operator for the thrill, terror and requirement of hostage-rescue work. Live ammunition could be used in the Killing House, as could flash-bangs and even smoke and fragmentation grenades. Special hinges simulated real doors that would blown off before each assault with a 12-gauge shotgun blast and then the operators in the assault teams would enter the room and proceed to fire at mannequins simulating the hostages while at the same time avoiding fellow SAS troopers sitting in chairs or standing in corners simulating "very live" hostages. In a matter of seconds, the assault force had to distinguish between bad guy and hostage, and kill the bad guy. Video-cameras and instructors monitored each assault and the lessons learned were studied and incorporated into the next, and the next entry into the Killing House. SAS doctrine suggested that a competent pair of operators, armed with pistols and submachine guns, should be able to neutralize a seized room in five seconds. The use of live subjects in a room where 9mm rounds were flying fast and furious was a bold statement--it was meant to instill a sense of ballistic discipline into the minds and trigger fingers of the operators, as well as instill courage and bravado into the minds of the entire troop. As one SAS officer would say, "Terrorists train with live fire in their obstacles courses in Lebanon, why shouldn't we!"[3]

Careful not to slip on the spent 9mm shells littering the floor, an SAS SP trooper fires his Heckler and Koch MP5 A3 9mm submachine gun inside the now legendary SAS Killing House at Hereford. (Courtesy: Photo Press UK Defence)

A "Killing Commercial Jet," a mock-up of an airliner, is also operational at Hereford. Several British airlines, including British Airways, have made their aircraft and facilities available to the SAS for hostage-rescue training. SAS operators have trained in freeing hostages seized on board a subway train courtesy of the London Underground, and British Rail has made available their high-speed inter-city trains for use by SAS troopers during late-night hours.

The CRW would also be responsible for what would become known in the Hereford vernacular as the SP Teams, the "Special Project Teams," a rotating on-call squadron permanently on alert force responsible for responding to any terrorist incident inside Great Britain or anywhere in the world. When deployed, SP Teams are divided into two distinctive force: outer perimeter and assault. Operators responsible for the outer perimeter include marksman and EOD officers, and operators maintaining a secure perimeter for the operation while on call for action as reinforcements should additional firepower be required. The assault team consists of the operators who actually enter the house and execute the rescue or hit.

SP Teams are known in Hereford slang as "Old Women" because they are reduced, in one sense of the word, to sitting by the phone awaiting a call to action. From 1976 to 1980, SP Teams received several calls, but they were mainly requests by friendly governments to help out with their own hostage situations. In 1976, SAS officers served as advisors to the Royal Netherlands Marines Corps in the Du Pont train seizure; according to reports, the SAS offered the Dutch use of the flash bang, but Dutch officials refused, as they feared the loud blast of the device would permanently damage the hearing of the small children held hostage on board the train. Clearly the most famous SAS advisory role came in Mogadishu, with the GSG-9 rescue. One of the first units that GSG-9 founder Ulrich Wegener visited when creating the GSG-9 was the SAS; their reputation, even in 1972, was strong, and Wegener had seen them in action in West Germany. Wegener was impressed by SAS training methods, and their irreverent brand of discipline that prompted the arrogance and confidence needed in this line of work. When GSG-9 was summoned to Mogadishu, Wegener

SAS tactics call for entries to be a "two-man affair," illustrated here by two operators unleashing 9mm rounds into the center of their targets. The lead operator, wearing the now characteristic gas mask, is firing his Heckler and Koch MP5K 9mm submachine gun with thirty-round magazine, and his partner is about to unleash to the hammer on his Browning Hi-Power pistol. (Courtesy: Photo Press UK Defence)

Side-view of an SP Team MP5 gunner walking through the indoor obstacle course of the Hereford Killing House. Note personal gear strapped to the operator's legs including rappelling hooks. Of interest is the fact that the MP5 A3's two thirty-round magazines are held together courtesy of a magnetic clip--not tape. (Courtesy: Photo Press UK Defence)

offered SAS personnel, Major Alastair Morrison and Sergeant Barry Davis, the chance to come along, and allowed them to participate in the rescue operation of the Lufthansa jet. The rescue at Mogadishu, one of the most successful hostage-rescue raids ever, was made possible in many ways due to GSG-9's use of the flash-bang grenade.

The SAS, too, was influenced by outside sources. Following Mogadishu, they replaced their suppressed Sterling 9mm submachine guns in favor of the Heckler and Koch family of 9mm submachine guns--regarded as the Rolls Royce of ballistic firepower. Mogadishu also presented an operational challenge to the SAS--the German government had made available a specially equipped Boeing 707 aircraft to take the GSG-9 operators anywhere in the world in order to see to an end to the Lufthansa hijacking. While the SAS could rely on the RAF for transport, it was decided to create a special operations aviation entity within the RAF that would also be on year-round alert status. Special Forces Flight of 47 Squadron would be responsible for making available C-130s, Lynx and Puma choppers, while special communications officers from the 264 Signal Squadron (SAS) would facilitate communications to Whitehall or Hereford from any SAS deployment anywhere in the world.

Following the Israeli rescue at Lod in 1972, the SAS realized that such work could truly be accomplished; following Entebbe and Mogadishu, the unit realized that such operations could be executed far from home. The Israelis, the Dutch and the Germans all had their moment in the spotlight, and even though a unit like the SAS considers attention an operational threat as lethal as a terrorist round, the chance

During the Killing House obstacle course, operators routinely assume different firing positions to test their skills and reactions to different scenarios. Here, an operator fires his Browning Hi-Power 9mm semi-automatic at a target of a busty female clutching an AK-47. The coil attachment to his utility belt is an innovation of the Italian GIS. (Courtesy: Photo Press UK Defence)

to prove their capabilities was, after all, the true reason behind the countless hours of training, hard work, blood and sweat. The SAS moment in the sun came in the spring of 1980.

On Wednesday, April 30, 1980, word filtered to Hereford that a hostage-taking situation was ongoing in London that might require regimental participation. Five heavily armed terrorists from the Libyan-based and Iraqi-supported Democratic Front for the Liberation of Arabistan (DFLA), a Marxist group seeking autonomy for the Arabic-speaking region of Iran, walked into the Iranian Embassy and took twenty-two people hostage, including Scotland Yard constable Trevor Lock and a BBC reporter seeking a visa to Iran. Although Prime Minister Thatcher and her cabinet ordered the SAS on standby-status, the SP Team, "B Squadron," had already driven its fleet of Range Rovers from Hereford to London and were in the capital for six hours assessing the situation and preparing assault plans when official orders came down for them to deploy to London. The MoD's Joint Operations Center, the body that overseas SAS operations, worked on a contingency plan while everyone waited for the terrorists to make demands and a move of some sort.

For the next four days, Scotland Yard negotiators dragged the talks out as best they could--gaining the release of an ill female hostage and the removal of two dead bodies, Iranian diplomats, killed by the terrorists. While police cordoned off the area and police and SAS observers began sketching the plans for their assault, MI5 technicians succeeded in slinking into the building and planting eavesdropping devices so that the terrorists' movements could be monitored. Scotland Yard negotiators had studied the skills and tactics of the best such team in the world, the NYPD's Hostage Negotiation Team, and opted for a strategy of "boring the terrorists to death." On Wednesday May 5, however, the terrorists began to lose their patience. Their initial demand that the Iranians release ninety-one prisoners was ignored, as were their demands that they be provided with a plane and safe passage out of the United Kingdom. Exasperated, the terrorists' patience ran out. On Monday May 5, they shot Abbas Lavasani, a member of the embassy staff. Prime Minister Thatcher ordered the SAS into action.

Assaulting the building on Princess Gate was an operation quite easier than the multi-faceted missions trained for in Hereford and in

While one SAS operator opts to forgo use of his MP5 A3 in favor of his trusted Browning Hi-Power pistol, his partner fires a brief burst of 9mm fire from his MP5. (Courtesy: Photo Press UK Defence)

AN MP5 entry team fire in unison toward several different targets upon entry into a Killing House room. Note "target" of innocent woman clutching child perched against the wall, and rear wall peppered with 9mm holes. (Courtesy: Photo Press UK Defence)

Side-view of an SAS SP Team operator in firing position with his MP5 A3. Note hip magazine pouch for MP5 9mm thirty-round magazines. (Courtesy: Photo Press UK Defence)

British training grounds throughout the United Kingdom and, indeed, throughout the world. The assault plan was simple--Two four-man teams (Red Team) would abseil down the roof of the embassy to the first floor and ground floor balconies of the building and burst through the windows and begin their assault. Another team (Blue Team) would enter the building from a font balcony on No. 16 Princess Gate. The SAS operators had learned some lessons from previous operations--the need for contained breathing apparatus, the need for fire-retardent clothing and the need for body harness and equipment rigs to enable easy rope work. This was all evident in the now legendary black garb worn by the operators at "Princess Gate." The operators carried MP5s,, Browning Hi-Power 9mm pistols and the knowledge that their operation was to be filmed--not by the Ministry of Defense, but by British television. At 19:26 hours on May 5, the assault began.

As an assembled crowd looked on in awe, the operators began their rope journey to their targeted windows. Deploying frame charges, shotguns and sledgehammers, the operators used guile and brute force in breaking through the embassy's fortified windows and to force their way into embassy; once a breech was made, dozens of stun grenades were hurled into the building. The breach explosion was significant, and besides blowing out the embassy's windows and quite a few ear drums, caused part of the building to catch on fire. One operator, in one of the memorable images of the assault, was nearly burnt to death when his abseil rope got tangled amid the flames. With surgical precision and well-rehearsed skill, the operators moved throughout the embassy neutralizing the facility room by room, floor by floor. The terrorists, busy with the building on fire and the sounds of gunfire were no match for the approaching operators. One terrorist, holding fifteen hostages captive in the embassy's telex room foolishly walked to the window to see what the commotion was about, and he was cut down with a single shot by an SAS sniper, Sgt. S., who had seen the terrorist through his sights and took advantage of the one or two seconds of opportunity afforded by being able to strike "his" target down. The SAS assault was a manifestation of the years spent inside the Hereford Killing House as the room-by-room entry was quick, thorough and decisive. In a matter of minutes, five of the six DFLA terrorists had been obliterated by 9mm fire; the final terrorist, attempting to pass himself off as one of the hostages, was dully arrested by Special Branch officers waiting outside. The spectacle in central London was known as "Operation Nimrod."

The SAS was finally on the map--there was Sabena, Entebbe, Du Pont, Djibouti, Mogadishu and now Princess Gate. The rescue at the Iranian Embassy was a public relations bonanza for the SAS and this once anonymous force of covert warriors became celebrities not only in Great Britain, but throughout the world, as well. A major film, "Who Dares Wins," was made exalting the SAS as the world's most professional counter-terrorist unit, and a library of books would soon be published on this mysterious and sought after unit. Princess Gate was the shinning moment in the sun for the SAS but Northern Ireland would be its bread and butter. It would be a secretive and deadly campaign where TV cameras would not follow the unit into battle, and where, indeed, "Big Boys' Rules" would certainly apply.

In dealing with operational terrorist units in Ulster, the British realized that when the IRA loses key members in becomes a great setback to the organization, as they do not have an endless supply of highly trained and motivated individuals; each terrorist is the sum of a considerable investment for the masters, and potential recruits are easily deterred when they see those who have preceded them laying sprawled out on a West Belfast road pummeled with several dozen rounds of ammunition. The Ministry of Defense understood that the Royal Ulster Constabulary (RUC) could contain the terrorists, the British military--the Ulster Defense Regiment, the Paras, Royal Marine Commandos and Guards--could defeat the terrorists in an open confrontation, but only special forces could hunt the terrorists down, capture them or kill them. Northern Ireland--and, indeed, the Republic of Ireland in the south--would become a SAS battlefield.

The SAS was deployed to Ulster in 1969 at the commencement of the "troubles" when "D Squadron" of 22 SAS was despatched across the water, though primarily in the war against Protestant gun-runners in County Down. At first, the SAS deployed considerable forces to Ulster, mainly in the South Armagh to hunt for Provisional IRA.[4] ASUs (Active Service Units), who had been most successful in their attacks against RUC and British military positions; in January 1976, the PIRA had killed twenty-one individuals and overrun several army OPs (Observation Posts). The deployment of the SAS was both tactically necessary and a terrific brand of psychological warfare; the

British Army publicized false and ultra-violent tales of the SAS to deify them as some sort of sadistic supernatural soldiers. Indeed, SAS operations in particular stretches of bandit country were highly successful in obtaining intelligence on known PIRA activists, but also successful in bringing these operatives to justice or to a grave in late-night fire-fights. Much of the SAS work was reconnaissance, observation and intelligence-gathering. Trained to move about silently and for prolonged stretches of time in the bush, SAS OPs proved to be invisible to most of the locals, even those who were quick to boast about their intimacy with the hills and countryside when sitting in "safe" PIRA pubs. Yet SAS operations in the southern portion of Northern Ireland were beginning to hurt the regiment and Hereford demanded changes.

At the time, the SAS routinely deployed one full squadron, consisting of approximately seventy operators, for tours that lasted as long as four months. With one squadron of the unit always in Ulster, one squadron having just returned and on leave, and one squadron preparing to go to Northern Ireland, virtually the entire SAS order of battle was involved in one way or another in the "Irish Troubles." With only four squadrons at its disposal, this deployment severely strained the unit's capabilities around the world. The Northern Ireland deployments were also hurting the unit's operational skills and annual program. The SAS was not created for duty in the north, and had a regimen of training in Brunei, the Arctic, Oman and Kuwait, and Hereford to contend with on a daily basis. The British Army's HQ in Northern Ireland, situated in a ***heavily*** fortified base at Lisburn, also wanted to expand the SAS role in country while reducing the number of operators posted to the command. Lisburn wanted the SAS to operate closer with another secretive military unit--even more secretive than the SAS: the 14 Intelligence Company.

14 Intelligence Company was--and is--perhaps the most secretive unit within the British military. Part super-sleuths, part super soldiers, 14 Intelligence Company is a force of deep-cover operatives who could make themselves invisible for long stretches of time, as well as fight it out with the best of them. Formed in 1973, the unit was a volunteer force and those wishing to join its rank had to endure a grueling and highly rigorous selection process. Many members of this newly formed unit were former SAS; others could have been SAS had they chosen to head to Hereford. Like the SAS, 14 Intelligence Company ran a selection course twice a year, and looked for a soldier's intelligence, resourcefulness and psychological strength as opposed to the physical stamina and endurance for pain so useful in the regiment. Volunteers are usually young, unattached, officer material, and deemed suited for the long-term assignment of surveillance work. Like the SAS, 14 Intelligence Company recruits from all branches of the British military, though unlike the SAS, the unit also recruits from the Royal Marines. Much of the work is undercover, in civilian dress, amid the terrorist population.

In 1980, as the level of armaments reaching the six counties of Ulster grew in alarming numbers, it was decided to draw the SAS and the 14 Intelligence Company closer together. The new operative group combining the efforts of these two forces was called the Intelligence and Security Group Northern Ireland, though would be known in the vernacular as "Int & Sy Group," or simply "The Group." Once combined with the intel troops, SAS deployments to Northern Ireland shrank from a full squadron to a strengthened troop consisting of twenty operators; and the personnel were drawn from SP Teams already on alert status and could conceivably be pulled back to Hereford should there be a hijacking or hostage-taking incident in Britain, or anywhere else in the world.

"Group" operations were highly professional exercises in counter-intelligence and counter-terrorist grit. 14 Intelligence Company personnel would monitor and observe PIRA terrorists, gather information and evidence, and then the SAS (often operating in civilian dress) would be called in for the capture or the kill. Between 1976 and 1987, the SAS killed twenty-five PIRA terrorists in ambushes and operations, while the entire British Army in Ulster only managed to kill nine during the same period. The most spectacular SAS ambush was the May 8, 1987, ambush and killing of eight PIRA operatives en route to blow up the Loughgall Police station. Because of their penchant for using firepower, the SAS developed a fierce reputation among the locals that helped the British efforts by terrorizing those who might find themselves in the sights of an operator's MP5. In early 1985, for example, three IRA terrorists were killed by three SAS operators who had fired a total of 117 rounds into the "bad guys"; each terrorist was then shot once in the head.

The SAS and 14 Intelligence Company operations were characterized by shrewd undercover work and beyond reproach professionalism. Each "op," as the assignments were known, was carried out with meticulous planning, intelligence and execution no independent of whether a team was after a suspected terrorist agent believed to be carrying nothing heavier than a switchblade, or a PIRA ASU armed with Armalite rifles, M-60 machines and even RPGs. The

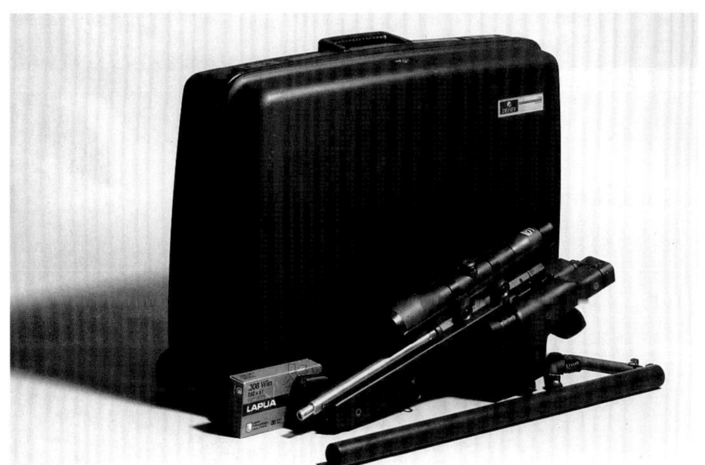


The Accuracy International 7.62mm Covert sniping weapon system--used by the SAS during deployments to Northern Ireland and in hostage-rescue missions. Note special carrying case for "covert" carrying and concealment. (Courtesy: Accurancy International)

The Accuracy International 7.62mm AWP suppressed counter-terrorist sniping rifle--the SAS mainstay--a silenced version of the standard British Army L96A1 rifle. (Courtesy: Accuracy International)

undercover work suited the SAS perfectly--they liked being able to deploy in jeans and leather jackets, and SP Teams deployed to Northern Ireland considered the tours to be the greatest counter-terrorist learning experience available. Other operators have returned to Hereford somewhat disillusioned by the process. They view the situation in Ulster as one better served by the police, and find the legal restrictions that they are forced to live under, the same legal rules of force by which the uniformed troops and police are governed by, too confining for their brand of counter-insurgency warfare. Like the brave and dedicated policemen of the RUC, the SAS has taken casualties in Northern Ireland--and several have been killed in fire-fights with ASU operatives armed with heavy weapons or a terrorist's determination to die and take as many of the enemy down with him.

SAS operations against the IRA were two-fold. In pursuit of the IRA, the SAS has not restricted itself to the bogs of the Armagh and corners of the Falls Road. They have operated against the IRA in northern Europe, in Germany and in The Netherlands; they have followed IRA operations throughout Europe, even to locations as remote as Malmo, Sweden. Although in 1976 eight heavily armed SAS troopers were arrested by the Irish Garda after accidentally entering the Republic in pursuit of PIRA operatives that had fled across the frontier into the south, the most notorious SAS operation against the IRA outside of the confines of Northern Ireland was undoubtedly "Operation Flavius": the March 6, 1988, SAS killing of three IRA terrorists in Gibraltar. It is an incident still causing tremors through the hallways of Whitehall.

In early 1988, British intelligence learned of an IRA plan to detonate a powerful bomb along the parade route for the ceremonial guard on Gibraltar, a popular tourist attraction usually crowded with overseas visitors and schoolchildren. The IRA had, in the past, displayed a penchant for using powerful explosives to hit British forces in Northern Ireland, at sea (the assassination of Lord Mountbatten), in London (the Horse Guard parade), and Brighton (the attempted assassination of Prime Minister Margaret Thatcher). Because of the sophistication and ingenuity that the terrorists had displayed in building its bombs and in planting the means for their detonation, it was feared that the device in Gibraltar could be triggered by a radio signal emanating outside Gibraltar from Spain. As a result, the bomb and those planning it had to be stopped before the device could be parked along a Gibraltar thoroughfare and before a high-frequency radio signal could result in the deaths of dozens, and the maiming of hundreds.

The operation to apprehend and stop the terrorist plan involved a coordinated effort by the British security apparatus. A British intelligence team, including MI5 and MI6 agents, along with Special Branch officers and eight SAS operators[5] was assembled in Gibraltar and briefed on an operational plan. According to reports, Spanish intelligence officers and operators from the GEO monitored the three IRA heavy-hitters-Daniel McCann, Sean Savage and Mairead Farrel--in Spain across the frontier. After close-surveillance in Gibraltar involving a roaming stake-out, four SAS operators confronted the three IRA terrorists and ordered them to surrender. All three were killed in a flurry of gunfire in front of witnesses and on camera. Many said that the SAS had simply executed the three Irish terrorists, but instead of retreating into the anonymous world of covert operations in Northern Ireland, the SAS troopers were questioned about their actions at a Gibraltar inquest court; in the court proceedings, the SAS officers in charge of the mission claimed the operation was what the unit calls a "hard arrest" and not a classic ambush. Nevertheless, the unit suffered irreparable harm as a result of "Operation Flavius." The British press had a field day with the incident, with one British cartoon showing two SAS operators and one saying to the other, "Why'd you shoot him sixteen times?" A pause, and then the reply, "I ran out of bullets!" Even the regiment suffered, as the MoD criticized the SAS and their rules of engagement. As with many of its fatal operations in Northern Ireland in which terrorists, innocent bystanders and operators are killed, the senior SAS supervisors in Gibraltar were not in the field with the men but rather in the operations room monitoring the transpiring events on radio. Some attribute this lack of leadership by example as a symptom of having leaders serve in the unit as temporary fixtures, where, in the course of the command structure and rise up the ranks, they don't attend the courses required to lead with the "follow me" ethic of command.

Although "Operation Flavius" had, in hindsight, probably saved countless lives, it was a public relations nightmare for the regiment. Interestingly enough, only six months earlier the SAS had participated in a brilliant hostage-rescue operation, on British soil, that received absolutely no public attention. In October 1987, fifty dangerous prisoners in Scotland's Peterhead Prison, men convicted on multiple counts of murder and rape, staged an uprising in the prison's notorious "D Block" and seized a hostage, a fifty-six-year-old prison guard with a kidney condition. Prison officials tried to end the ordeal for a week, but they were ill-equipped and ill-trained to mount a rescue. Under the Military Aid to the Civil Powers Act (MAC-P), the SAS was called in for assistance. Using explosives to gain entry into the barricaded block, the operators used staves, not MP5s, to engage the prisoners barricaded and rescue the hostage. The entire operation took all of six minutes.

In the post-cold war era, even with an Irish problem still not (as of yet) fully resolved, the SAS finds itself in search of a new counter-terrorist and special ops assignment, and it has brought them into the arena of crime-fighting. The details of this work has remained quite secret, even after the efforts of the vibrant British media to seek out

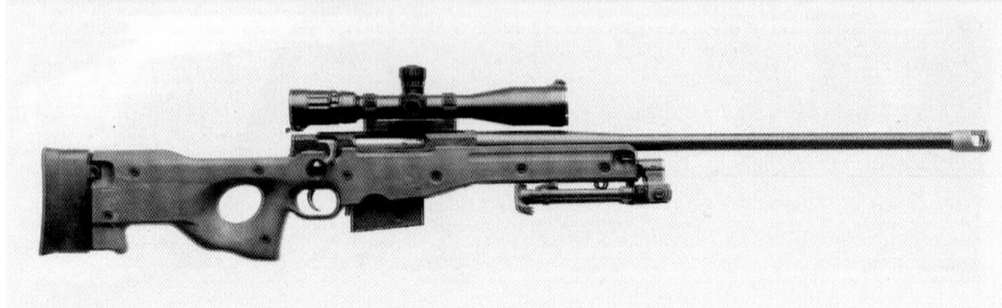
The Accuracy International Super Magnum .338--a weapon favored by some SAS sniper teams. (Courtesy: Accuracy International)

An SAS operator "on the ground" (or in the water) in Northern Ireland observes a terrorist target with MP5 A3 in hand. (Courtesy: Photo Press UK Defence)

During the SBS selection week, a Royal Marine commando displays his rope climbing skills. (Courtesy: Royal Marines Public Relations)

any facts, though it is known that heavily armed SAS teams have accompanied officers from SO19, Scotland Yard's firearms unit, on operations to arrest armed criminals and to end domestic hostage-taking incidents and armed barricades. Although SO19 officers are armed with shotguns and MP5s, criminals in the United Kingdom, especially implanted thugs from Sicily, Colombia and the former Soviet Union, are heavily armed, ruthless and all too willing to use guns in their operations. Operators used on covert operations in the Middle East, Asia or the Armagh are pleased with the work in the civilian sector; SAS teams are reported to rotate on two-week shifts to SO19, also known as the "blue berets," and operate throughout the United Kingdom, including Scotland and Wales. Scotland Yard officials are wary about publicizing the operations of this military elite on the streets of London, Manchester or Birmingham--even though such news would certainly act as a significant point of deterrence to most "sane" criminals. According to one DSF officer, "The liberal left would have a field day with the news of 'roaming hit squads' prowling through the city streets," and the once civil image of the polite bobby would forever be destroyed if bad guys confronting the police wound up dead. In an article written in the London Sunday Times, a Home Office spokesman said, "There are contingency plans for the use of special forces by the police, but these operations are never discussed." Indeed, under existing legal arrangements, a chief constable of a police force can summon the DSF and request the SAS "in aid of the civil power" by signing a document which hands control of an emergency, such as a barricaded siege with hostages, temporarily to the military.

Beyond the scope of their counter-terrorist and counter-insurgency work, as well as in addition to the new status as super crime busters, the SAS is still a conventional special forces unit. During the Gulf War, the SAS achieved notable success in hunting SCUDs and operating deep behind enemy lines. As a result of U.S. commander General Schwarzkopf's refusal to deploy U.S. special forces to the region in order to not rob the conventional limelight, it was British

"M Squadron" operators pose inside the bowels of a North Sea oil rig after successfully capturing it from terrorists (actually Royal Marines) during maneuvers. Note variants of the MP5 9mm submachine gun carried by assault team members. (Courtesy: Royal Marines Public Relations)

special forces who were responsible for much of the special ops assignments against the Iraqis in the days preceding the ground assault. The SAS, and British special forces, were awarded an astounding fifty-two decorations for valor. Four SAS operators were killed in the war, several from mishaps as a result of their desert patrol vehicles and several at the hands of the Iraqis.

The 22 Special Air Service Regiment is open to volunteers from all branches from the British Army and the Royal Air Force, but the Paras are undoubtedly the feeder regiment for the 22nd Special Air Service Regiment. "The Paras," according to a Special Boat Service officer, "are a rough and tumble lot eager for action and capable of the less gentle aspects of military service." Many volunteers into the Paras come from the tougher stretches of Britain--the East end of London, the North Country, and the poor coal regions of Scotland. In the Paras, they are offered training, discipline and operational experience in a tour of Ulster. Para dominance of SAS ranks and mentality is absolute. By 1987, over half of the operators in 22 SAS were originally in the Paras, and some say the percentages have only increased in recent years. By the nature of their assault work, Paras are known to be of a more violent and aggressive nature than soldiers from other units; "they would rather punch you out than suss you out," claims one SBS veteran. Many in the regiment, however, agree, and claim the influx of red berets has decreased the regiment's capabilities.

SAS selection courses are held twice a year for aspiring volunteers wishing to prove their worth and learn the extent of their physical and psychological envelopes of pain and suffering. The initial selection process into the unit is open to all members of the British armed forces with a minimum of two-years of service and a spotless service record. Soldiers are subjected to a now legendary (and much copied) torture process meant to weed out all those who think that they are SAS material, and those who will never wear the sand color beret and winged dagger badge. Among the trials in the selection process are "Resistance to Interrogation" session where candidates are interrogated, subjected to sensory deprivation and often beaten quite severely, and the back-breaking forty-five mile endurance march across the Brecon Beacons. Veteran SAS officers and NCOs sit on the board of the selection committee, and as a result have tremendous influence on the makeup of the regiment for some time to come. SAS training, for those worthy enough to have made it through the selection, lasts a full year and includes: advanced weapons and assault

During maritime rescue exercises, when operators are tasked with assaulting an English Channel ferry seized by terrorists, operators from "M Squadron" deploy from a rubberized inflatable craft. (Courtesy: Royal Marines Public Relations)

training; courses in mobile special warfare with Pink Panther land rovers, DPVs and specially-modified motorcycles; Arctic warfare training in Norway; desert warfare training in Oman; jungle warfare training in Brunei and Belize; mountain warfare in Bavaria; high-speed driving; EOD and explosives; unarmed warfare and cold-killing; and, parachute-training and HALO insertion techniques.

Although the SAS is now immortalized with images of the Princess Gate operation with the operators wearing black gear and clutching MP5s, the American-made M-16 and CAR-15 5.56mm is the favored weapon of SAS operators in the field, either in the wind swept mountains of western Iraq or the plush green fields of County Antrim. The MP5 is the 9mm submachine gun, of course, and it is reported that SAS officers were instrumental in the designs of countless improvements made to the MP5 in the past few years. The SAS 9mm pistol of choice is the Browning Hi-Power, though several special operations sidearms are produced in the United Kingdom, including .22 caliber silenced pistols, and Spitfire 9mm pistols built to operators specifications. Although the unit once carried and experimented with the Heckler and Koch 512 12-gauge shotgun, the "door-blaster" of choice is the American-produced Ithaca 37 12-gauge shotgun; SAS operators also carry the Arwen Ace single-shot weapon firing 37mm anti-riot munitions, as well as the Arwen 37 multi-shot, self-loading semi-automatic anti-riot weapon with a five round magazine. The primary SAS sniper weapon is the Accuracy International family of sniper weapons, including the PM 7.62mm weapon (designated by the British Army as the L96A1), the Covert folding-PM, and the .338 Super Magnum. Some SAS operators are reported to use Parker-Hale rifles, as well as foreign systems, as well.

According to one NCO in the U.S. Army's 1st SFOD-D, "The SAS doesn't maintain links to foreign units, foreign units maintain ties to the SAS." The SAS is, perhaps, the most sought after of the world's counter-terrorist units for their expertise and skills, and the regiment has trained units the world over. The SAS maintains its closest training and working relationship with the Australian and New Zealand SAS--the units routinely train together on various tours throughout Asia. A close working relationship is nurtured with U.S. Special Forces and the 1st SFOD-D; an SAS officer is on permanent attachment to Fort Bragg, and the liaison is frequently "over the fence" at the Delta compound. The SAS and Delta have trained together, worked together, and succeeded in forging a friendly and close-knit relationship. The SAS also maintains ties to the Dutch BBE, GSG-9 and the Munich SEK; Belgium's ESI; France's GIGN; Spain's GEO; Portugal's GOE; the Italian GIS; Jordan's SOU; the Saudi SSF; India's Black Cats; Pakistan's SSG; Singapore's Police Tactical Team and 1st Commando Battalion; and, the Hong Kong Police Special Duties Unit. The SAS does not maintain formal ties to Israeli counter-terrorist and hostage-rescue units, even though police ties between the two nations are strong--especially on counter-terrorist cooperation. Informal ties do exist, however, between ***Sayeret Mat'kal*** and ***Ya'ma'm*** senior officers and SAS commanders, though these are maintained on personal levels and not officially.

In Hereford, the operators know that even if peace comes to Ulster and smaller wars no longer involve NATO or the United Kingdom, there will still be work for them. After the GIGN stormed Air France 8969 at Marseilles, one of the first things the SAS commander did was call Paris to compare notes. It is virtually impossible to predict when the next time an aircraft, train or embassy will be seized and that is why the unit stands at the ready twenty-four hours a day, seven days a week, 365 days a year.

The SAS is not the sole British military special operations unit tasked with counter-terrorism and hostage-rescue operations. The Special Boat Service (SBS) is the second-half of the British special forces order of battle, and since 1987 a full-fledged--although overshadowed--partner with their comrades at Hereford in a command structure known as the DSF--Director of Special Forces. Under the designation of the DSF (comparable in structure and purpose to the United States Special Operations Command, or USSOCOM in the

Training for maritime rescues, whether it be on board a passenger ferry or oil platform, is conducted year round during all weather conditions. Here, during a blinding fog spell, "M Squadron" operators move about the narrow passageways of an oil rig to practice an assault and rescue. Note operator gingerly clutching his MP5 A3 with gloved finger gently caressing the trigger housing. (Courtesy: Royal Marines Public Relations)

inescapable military vernacular), the DSF commander is an SAS officer and his deputy is an SBS senior rank. Under the command of the Director of Special Forces both the SAS and SBS are the cutting edge in Britain's ability to conduct special operations, on a global level, at any time and any place--from the Falls Road of Belfast to more precarious locations in the Middle East and Asia.

The dividing line between those missions tasked to the SAS or SBS is the "high water mark!". Above water goes to Hereford and on water or below goes to Poole--home to the SBS. As the water mark goes in distinguishing which unit is assigned which task, so too does it divide counter-terrorist duties. Like the SAS and the entity of the SP Team, the SBS has developed unique counter-terrorist and hostage-rescue skills, and like the U.S. Navy's elite SEAL Team SIX, the SBS has created its own counter-terrorist force: the mysterious "M Squadron."

Operators in the SBS do not volunteer into the service in order to serve in any particular sub-unit. All SBS personnel are drawn ***solely*** from the ranks of the Royal Marines. During the 30-weeks of Royal Marines basic training, SBS officers are already monitoring those exceptional marines that they feel have the potential of becoming an operator. While a Royal Marine cannot volunteer into the SBS until he has racked up two year's worth of service, he can submit his specialization request after only one year. Those who can march the fastest, endure the obstacle courses in the best time, and attain the highest marksmanship scores with the SA-80 5.56mm assault rifle have their personal records noted, but the most important recommendations come from their direct unit commanders. Following the training at Lympstone, the marine is assigned to a "Commando" or other support unit, and despatched to advanced training. First comes winter warfare training in Norway (or "do the Norway" in the RM vernacular), and then several months of mountain training in the inhospitable confines of the Isle of Sky and the Scottish highlands. Next, the commandos undergo amphibious training with small craft, landing vessels, and Rigid Raiders; this period is concluded with complete 3 Commando Brigade exercises, conducted on many occasions with American, Norwegian, and Dutch and marines. Next comes counter-insurgency 101: a six month operational tour in Northern Ireland. Just like the winter warfare training, where the marine learns invaluable special warfare skills such as sniping and deception (laying false tracks, for example), Northern Ireland prepares the future SBS operators for operations deep behind enemy lines. It is here that Royal Marines refine their overall combat skills; according to Lieutenant "M,"[6] an SBS operator and instructor, "There is no better school for irregular warfare than in the narrow streets of West Belfast or in the green hills of the South Armagh." Although jungle and anti-drug training in the Caribbean follows Ulster (termed "fun in the sun" by the green berets) Northern Ireland rocks the thinking process of most marines. They are now ready to choose their specialist classification. Some become radiomen, others weapons specialists, others even cooks and drivers. A select few, however, feel an itch to test their worth, they want to see if they have what it takes to leave the task of soldiering on planet earth for life in a completely different world. This is the time to volunteer into the SBS, even though most marines, even after two years of service with the green berets, still know very little of what the SBS is all about.

An "M Squadron" operator uses the muscles and grit in him to climb up an oil platform and secure a rope line, as a comrade awaits his ascent in their Zodiac rigid hull inflatable boat. Note operator wearing Protec assault helmet. (Courtesy: Royal Marines Public Relations)

The point man of a six-man "M Squadron" assault team moves slowly and cautiously down the staircase of a passenger ferry used as a training platform for counter-terrorist training. Note point operator's MP5 SD3 9mm submachine gun, and the operators' special wet-suit assault uniforms. (Courtesy: Royal Marines Public Relations)

Even before the formal request is made to be accepted into an SBS selection process, the marine has acquired a thick personnel file compiled by his senior officers. His performance in the field is measured, judged and noted. It is just as important how he functions with a Goretex pack on his back slicing his way through the jungle, as it is to know how he got along with his mates behind the fortifications, isolation and corrugated tin of their barracks near the Falls Road in Belfast. The SBS functions in small squadrons and teams and the ability to get along with others in an operational setting is absolutely essential. Since the Royal Marines is a small and self-contained community, numbering only 6,800, it is quite easy to monitor the development of one of their own.

Several months before the actual SBS course begins, those who volunteer (and whose military profiles indicate potential) participate in a two-week long selection process that will test, to the outer envelope, the volunteers physical and psychological frontiers of tolerance and suffering. The two-week test period takes place at Poole, one of the largest Royal Marine and SBS facilities in Great Britain, and is designed to weed out nearly 90% of those brave--or foolish--enough to volunteer. For all those who make the cut, SBS training lasts approximately twelve months, and is a full year of intense "slogging." Much of the SBS training is, naturally, classified top-secret by the British Ministry of Defense, and not suitable for publication, but includes: signals, explosives, driving (both high-speed and evasive), weapons, sniping, parachutist, swimming, diving (SCUBA), boating, and, of course, intelligence-gathering and reconnaissance. The first phase of SBS training is a two-week canoeing phase, designed to begin the attrition process that will slowly whittle down the number of volunteers in the course; attrition, in fact, is the course's calling card as each day the number of candidates shrink. The training on the Kleppers is incessant, grueling, and it requires not only a sharp intellect and physical stamina, but the where-with-all to function operationally in a two-man system; there are numerous multi-mile "paddles," including a thirty-mile race in choppy waters, and a ten-mile portage over inhospitable terrain that must be completed in a prescribed time period. In the hours that are not spent in the water fisting it out with the paddles, the volunteer is subjected to intensive classroom study. If, for example, sixty volunteers begin the course, it is hoped that only forty will remain once the canoeing phase is complete. This is done for a simple and practical purpose. Sixty volunteers are too many for the second phase--jungle training--and there must come a point when the numbers worn on the DPM smocks can be replaced by the instructors calling the marines by their real names.

With the flames of the oil rig shooting up toward the sky, an "M Squadron" operator pulls himself up toward a perch from where he can act as an observer for the assault team sniper. (Courtesy: Royal Marines Public Relations)

During assault maneuvers on a North Sea oil rig, operators rappel down toward the targeted area where hostages are being held. Note civilian-purchased hiking boots preferred by many "M Squadron" operators. (Courtesy: Royal Marines Public Relations)

The jungle phase of the training is considered by many to be the most physically grueling, and to make sure that the marine volunteers are up to the task, they are flown up to Stirling Lines in Hereford for some toughening up and the very basics of survival training with the SAS. The SAS tend not to treat their Royal Marine comrades with the greatest of gentility and, in fact, resentment between the two special forces units is quite pronounced. The SBS take offense to the SAS's penchant for a sophisticated headline grabbing PR apparatus, and the gray berets making unwelcome inferences to the marines about their resemblance to the SBS's frog emblem. The SAS, of course, are not amused by SBS operators taking liberties with the sanctified "Who Dares Win" motto by altering it to "Who Cares Wins!" All that

"M Squadron/Black Troop" operators abseil down a Sea King chopper during counter-terrorist maneuvers on a North Sea oil rig clutching his MP5 A3 9mm submachine gun. (Courtesy: Royal Marines Public Relations)

considered, Hereford is a vacation compared to the jungle. The two month jungle training is carried out in Brunei, a rain forest training ground considered by senior SBS officers to be a "Good clean jungle." After several weeks of patrolling, and ambushing in the jungle, the candidates learn the ballistic secrets of a few of the SBS's most favored weapons, such as the Heckler and Koch MP5 9mm submachine gun and the M16A2 5.56mm assault rifle. They also learn reconnaissance, communications, surveillance, photography, sabotage (blowing up bridges and fortifications), and other basics of special forces. A full week is usually dedicated to each specialty: for example, there is "OP Week" to learn how to man and camouflage an intelligence-gathering observation post.

Following the jungle, the volunteers return to Hereford for a more intense and serious survival training. Here, the volunteers learn field medicine, what to eat--and not to--in the bush, and the trials and tribulation of escape and evasion. For about ten days, the SBS volunteers are run along through an obstacle course In some of the most difficult terrain to be found in Britain. It is a demanding period when the candidate is constantly on the run, evading "enemy" patrols, and living off the land. The SAS patrols are relentless and the SBS hopefuls are captured (they are always captured), and interrogated in sometimes brutal fashion. They must not disclose any information other than the obligatory name, rank and serial number, but they are subjected to, in the words of Lieutenant "M," "Soft-core suffering." Unofficial beatings (the kind that don't leave marks!) are administered, and burlap bags are tightly noosed around the poor victim's head. The longer one can hold out--naturally--the better one's grades. The entire process is carefully modified by both SAS and SBS medical officers and psychiatrists. Basically the aim of the exercise is to determine if, under true interrogation conditions, the prisoner can hold out for two days; it is the SBS's belief that information older than 48 hours old is no longer of any use to the enemy. It is also during this period, military intelligence and other investigate services (including, it is believed, MI5) conduct a grueling security check on those applicants still in the training; naturally, as the SBS is a covert force conducting many of its operations under the auspices of Britain's intelligence services, security is of the utmost importance.

The following phases of training include, a two week boating phase (Zodiacs and Rigid Raiders, and deployment and extraction from submarines) in the frigid waters off of Scotland, advanced combat courses with an enormous variety of weapons (everything from the old silenced L34A1 Sterling 9mm submachine gun, a weapon termed as "British ballistic plumbing" by senior ranking SBS officer to the Parker Hale and Accuracy International family of sniping rifles and other exotic, and top-secret James Bond-like killing tools are also included), cold-killing, explosives (the SBS is considered among the world's most capable saboteurs) advanced underwater and tactical swimming, and intelligence instruction. Throughout the training, the emphasis of the SBS instruction is to hone the volunteers' mental strength in order to allow him to absorb the instructional material, as well as to allow his body to persevere through the trying physical tests. Professionalism, in every aspect of the training and subsequent operational service, is stressed to all as the most important aspect of being an SBS operator. Instructors like to tell stories from the Falklands, and stress the ability of training and conditioning to allow a mere man to overcome ice water, sub-freezing temperatures, and very lonely recces deep behind enemy lines.

The final phase of an "operators" training is a four-week

The SBS emblem and coat of arms. (Sigalit Katz)

A PIRA gunman walks through a Belfast slum clutching his M3 Grease-gun. (Courtesy: U.S. Army Special Operations Command)

parachutist course, from C-130s, run by the Royal Air Force at Brize Norton. Following the hell of the jungle and the deserts in which they have been trained and examined, and following the endless hours of having their flesh soaked to the bone in frigid waters, the RAF Jump Course is considered "R and R." Nevertheless, jump school is serious business (and jump wings are coveted). It is here that the operators learn how to jump into water, jump with their canoes, and function in a truly airborne manner. Even though the marine has already been in the course for over a year at this point, he can still be dropped should he not make the grade.

Less than thirty-percent of those who started the course at Poole are around at its completion to qualify for the rating "swimmer canoeist" grade 3, and be designated as an "operator." SBS operators must sign on an additional thirty six months of service following the completion of the course; most sign on for many more. Few naval special warfare forces in the world can boast such long term commitments from its covert warriors, and very few can boast such a professional combat cadre. Even operators from the U.S. Navy SEALs, a force that likes to boast itself as being the world's best, grudgingly admit that the SBS is unique for its professionalism and combat ability. The SEALs should know. They train with the SBS regularly--a SEAL officer is permanently assigned to the Special Boat Service, and an SBS operator is permanently assigned to the headquarters of Naval Special Warfare Group Two at Little Creek, Virginia.

Once a full-fledged operator, there is more specialist training so that he join one of the SBS operational squadrons. According to published sources, the swimmer canoeists are usually incorporated into "C" Squadron, where the underwater and Klepper canoe talents are maximized; those expert in small craft, mini-subs and delivery vehicles, as well as long-range insertion craft (civilian-bought power speed boats, for example) are assigned to "S" Squadrons, while others to be trained specifically in anti-terrorist duties are assigned to "M Squadron." The squadron is similar, in many ways, to SEAL Team SIX in its function and training--both are maritime rescuers and it is considered the cream of the entire SBS in terms of the individuals asked to join its ranks, as well as those officers and NCOs already serving in the unit. "Maritime counter-terrorism is a far different ballgame than ***conventional*** kicking in doors rescue work," claims on SBS officer, "getting there, to your target, is half the fun, half the torture and the difference between getting yourselves and hostages killed and pulling off a successful mission." Indeed, unlike an SAS SP Team tasked with rescuing hostages held in a foreign embassy near Hyde Park in London, "M Squadron" operators are not afforded the luxury of driving to the scene, using basements or rooftops for observation posts, and of taking cover a block away while the secondary team's sniper pin down the bad guys. Reaching the target, be it an ocean liner or North Sea oil platform, requires stealth, speed and surprise; reaching a target, sometimes platforms and vessels the size of a football arena, is half the challenge and the effort can exhaust a troop of operators who must then engage in an exhaustive and systematic purification of the target. Most of the targets that would be "M Squadron" responsibility are platforms filled with fuel and other flammable material, and the possibility of a breaching charge detonating a ship or setting fire to it are very real. Unlike the SAS, or the American Delta Force, these men are denied the ease of bursting through wooden doors to reach and rescue hostages, instead they must blow their way through several feet of steel on an oil rig or inside a secured compartment of a passenger ship.

A "Commachio Group" EOD officer searches a vessel for explosives with his trusted bomb-sniffing dog near a Royal Navy sub base. (Courtesy: Royal Marines Public Relations)

Because of the specialized nature of their work, the troopers of "M" Squadron engage in far more room-to-room combat training than their colleagues at Hereford. Since the unit is so small and reinforcements not always available--depending on how many can actually reach a target--assaults need to succeed on the first try. When reaching a target via underwater means is deemed impractical, the "M Squadron" order of battle consists of a troop of Royal Marines, known as "Black Troop," whose sole military function is to fast-rope and rappel down a Sea King chopper onto a ship or oil platform and engage the terrorists in a gun-fight. "Black Troop" operators are trained in the same counter-terrorist techniques as their comrades in "M Squadron" (and at Hereford, for that matter) with the exception of underwater work.

"M Squadron" has been operational in, along and underneath, the endless waterways and lochs of Northern Ireland. Yet these operations tend to focus more on intelligence-gathering and observation work, as compared to the ambush ops of the SP Team working side-by-side with 14 Intelligence Company; most of these assignments are still classified top-secret by the British MoD and not suitable for publication. One of the most famous "M Squadron" operations was not executed on the waterways of Northern Ireland but rather in the port of Woolwich--like the SAS, the SBS has been recruited by the Home Office to participate in Britain's ever growing and increasingly violent war on serious crime and narco-terrorism. On November 23, 1992, a task force of SBS "M Squadron" operators, SO19 armed policemen and customs agents executed "Operation Emerge," the seizure of a ton of cocaine brought into the United Kingdom on a Panamanian-registered tug whose journey originated in Venezuela. The raid involved twenty "M Squadron" operators, all armed with MP5s and wearing black balaclavas, who reached the ship courtesy of high-speed rubber inflatable boats and then boarded the vessel and arrested everyone on board. A year later, "M Squadron" once again was involved in a major anti-drug operation in the waters of Ireland. Acting on a tip, "M

Squadron" operators abseiled from a Sea King helicopter onto a ship bringing drugs into the United Kingdom and seized the ship for police. Wearing wet suits and camouflage paint on their faces, the operators landed on the main deck of the boat and neutralized the crew; "Apparently," claimed one police officer, "there was resistance on board but the SBS beat the hell out of them." Unlike a counter-terrorist strike, lethal force was to be avoided in order to execute an arrest and gain intelligence, so SBS operators used their hand-to-hand combat skills to maximum advantage. During the operation, the SBS was responsible in seizing three tons of marijuana worth an estimated £6.5 million on the streets.

SBS, "M Squadron" and "Black Troop" operators all carry the MP5 family of 9m submachine gun--the favored variants being the MP5 SD2, the MP5A3 and the MP5 SD6. Although operators carry a wide assortment of 9mm handguns, from the Browning Hi-Power to the SIG P228, the handgun of choice is the American-produced Smith and Wesson .357 Magnum revolver, a weapon deemed as "ideal" for clearing the passageways of a ship or oil platform; the .357, in fact, is carried by most operators for most assignments as it is sturdy, reliable and an ideal augmentation to the MP5. For heavy duty counter-terrorist operations, "M Squadron" operators carry the American-made M-60 7.62mm light machine gun, and the Remington Mk. 870 12-gauge shotgun. Like the SAS, the SBS and "M Squadron" use Accuracy International sniper weapons, especially the L96A1.

The SBS is perhaps one of the most exclusive combat units anywhere in the world, and it is certainly one of the most professional, and many units around the world are eager to gains contacts and forge ties with it. Obviously, SEAL Team SIX is "M Squadron's" closest international partner, but the unit also maintains close ties to the Australian SAS TAG, the Dutch 7 NL SBS and the BBE, the French GIGN, and GSG-9/2.

The "regular" Royal Marines also possess units specifically tasked with counter-terrorist work worthy of mention. In the mid 1970s, there was increased awareness of the vulnerability of Great Britain's North Sea oil installations and rigs to sabotage or seizure by terrorist factions. The Ministry of Defense, along with the oil companies, feared the potential for a massive strike against a rig that could not only lead to a major geological disaster, but severe economic loss, as well. The prospect of a terrorist seizing a platform and then holding it and the crew hostage in exchange for a hefty ransom or the release of several hundred "Provos" from the Kesh was one that needed to be acknowledged. Also one of the Ministry of Defense's greatest fears in its brutal and nasty war against terrorism, caused primarily by active brigades in the PIRA, was that one of Britain's nuclear facilities would be targeted for attack. As a result, the MoD authorized the Royal Marines to select a unique force of commandos who would function solely as a protection group for the Royal Navy's fleet of Polaris and Trident-class nuclear submarines and their nuclear ballistic missiles, as well as Royal Air Force nuclear weapons and bombers, and the army's Lance nuclear missile warheads and 155mm M109 nuclear projectiles. The unit entrusted with this sensitive role was the "Commachio Group." Originally, on July 20, 1977, L Company of 42 Commando was deployed to the North Sea as part of the MoD's "Operation Oilsafe," but when "Commachio Group" was formed in 1980, the ranks were expanded to included seven rifle troops plus ancillaries. Named after the lake in Italy where 43 Commando fought a gallant battle against the Germans in 1943, the group was formed in 1980 and consists of over 300 commandos. Much of their work is at the Clyde Submarine Base near Helensborough, but the Group is based at Arbroath in Angus. Among safeguarding the countries nuclear deterrent, "Commachio Group" is also the principal force tasked with carrying out waterborne patrols of Northern Ireland. The unit is virtually self-sufficient, and as a result "Commachio Group" commandos are equipped with motorized rubberized inflatables, special vehicles for shore patrols, and a whole range of night-vision equipment that allows them to safeguard their posts in optimum form twenty-four-hours-a-day. "Commachio Group is known for their assault techniques--especially in beating back an attack during perimeter defense--and Group snipers are legendary throughout the Royal Marines. "Commachio Group" commandos are equipped with standard Royal Marine kit, gear and equipment, and carry the SA-80 5.56mm assault rifle.

The Royal Marines 3 Commando Brigade is also one of the world's most experienced conventional counter-terrorist unit, and certainly among the most capable for security duty in the British Army. A brief description of the responsibilities and day-to-day existence in Northern Ireland is worthy of mention, even though at the time of this book's writing peace talks between the British government and Sinn Fein, the political arm of the IRA, are proceeding.

For the Royal Marines, the training that each commando undergoes before crossing the water into Northern Ireland sends a surge of adrenaline into every green beret. They are pumped for action, geared both physically and mentally for the coming daily grind ahead of them. As per their briefings, all marines expect to be attacked at any moment and they behave accordingly. The now famous Northern Ireland choreographed patrol dance of a trooper walking a post, and then stopping to take aim with his SA-80, is attended to in fastidious fashion. A month or two into the tour, however, and monotony threatens to maintain his awareness levels to complacency and the urge to go back to the mainland, or to do a jungle training or a Norway. Complacency is an Ulster catchword for dead marine. Ninety-nine times out of one hundred the patrol will be routine, quiet, and without incident. It is that one milli-second when a marine's (or paratroopers'

A "Commachio Group" EOD officer searches a vessel for explosives along a waterway in Northern Ireland. (Courtesy: Royal Marines Public Relations)

A Royal Navy patrol boat coordinates its patrol of an inlet near Derry with a squad of "Commachio Group" commandos on a motorized rubber dinghy. (Courtesy: Royal Marines Public Relations)

Royal Marines from 45 Commando patrol a stretch of roadway in the Armagh on the lookout for a terrorist ambush or hidden booby-trapped device. (Courtesy: Royal Marines Public Relations)

or RUC policeman's) guard is down that the Provos strike. Each Royal Marine heading for a tour of Ulster is asked to repeat the following phrase by his commander: "A single shot and the daydreamer gets it!"

It is, in fact, the way the IRA work to find the daydreamer. IRA operatives observe everything and report everything. The terrorist intelligence-gathering infrastructure in Northern Ireland is fantastic. Although the Provisional IRA is believed to be no stronger than a few hundred strong, and the "regular" IRA a few hundred more than them, they are supported by an army of a hundred thousand sympathizers and passive supporters. This support could be passive intelligence-gathering (a bloke in a pub telling a brigade intelligence officer that “there is this marine patrolling our street who fancies the young O'Donnell woman”, for example) to overt fugitive hiding. "The IRA are patient little buggers," claims Captain "B."[7] a veteran of many marine tours of Ulster, they wait, wait, and wait, until they see the opposing forces as vulnerable. If they want to strike at a particular unit, if the orders from the south or Derry are to hit 40 Commando, for example, then they will wait for months until they can formulate a plan that will allow for maximum destruction and their minimum chance of apprehension--they will do nothing if there is a chance that they can get caught."

There are several aspects of life in Ulster that are routine for servicemen keeping the peace: checkpoints, stops and searches, and house searches. The aim of the checkpoint, both temporary and permanent, is to deter and disrupt the movement of terrorists and their arms and ammunition. Marines hate checkpoint duty--it is dangerous, and they are exposed to a drive-by shooting or being run down by an "SS"--an individual with a stop and search police warrant. House-searches are another unpleasant, though highly necessary element of duty in Ulster. As per Emergency Regulations, a member of the RUC (Royal Ulster Constabulary) is always present during the operations. Although such raids usually embitter the local populace, they sometime yield arms caches and invaluable intelligence. It should be remembered that between 1985 and 1986 the IRA took delivery of nearly 120 tons of arms and explosives from Libya, including a full ton of Grade-A Czechoslovak Semtex, and 12 SA-7 "Strella" hand-held surface-to-air missiles; this is in addition to the tons of equipment and ordnance obtained from the United States such as Armalite rifles and C-4. That material is out there, and the security forces need to locate the caches and confiscate them if they don't want them used against them.

Much of a marine's life in Northern Ireland is self-preservation--keeping one's self from harm--making sure his equipment is operational, and staying alert. Marine's don't get a lot of rest in Northern Ireland--especially a particular unit's corporals and second-lieutenants. Either they are out on patrol, coming back from a patrol, or getting their men ready for yet another patrol. Although Ulster has never reached the body counts of other terrorist-plagued areas (Beirut, for example), much of the law and order maintained throughout the six counties is as a result of the absolutely professional means of soldiering the British military has executed in the north.

Life for a marine in Ulster is a tireless and protected existence--their barracks are hardened fortifications protected against Provo commando assault, or mortar and rocket attack. There is no "in town" leave during emergency tours, marines cannot go out of their barracks in civvies for a pint of Guinness or Murphy's stout at the local pub. His off hours from patrolling and counter-terrorist work is inside the barbed wired confines of his quarters, cleaning his SA-80, readying his gear, and enjoying the three cans of beer a day that every British servicemen in Ulster is allotted.

Belfast is an easier area to police than the rural Armagh. Although there are more terrorists per capita in Belfast, and bombs blowing up on a Belfast main thoroughfare makes the news around the globe, the patrols are in armored cars for the most part (Saracens, Humber one-tons 4x4s, and Shortland SB 501s), and within a rifle shot of reinforcements. The terrain in Belfast is easier. Foot slogging the pavement is not a difficult task for men capable of "yomping" thirty miles in the Scottish highlands. There are less dangers of an ambush in an urban environment, although the threat from car-bombs and snipers is very real; most marines wear visors on their helmets in case they should be sprayed by pellets, attacked by rocks, and assaulted with hot cooking oil or bleach hurled from a window. Although one of the missions of the British military is to win the hearts and minds in order to win the peace, fraternization is strictly forbidden. A resident seen speaking to a British soldier, especially a Royal Marine commando, might be mistaken for a "tout" or informer, and end up with a .38 round fired through his mouth by a Provo counter-intelligence team.

The Armagh is the most difficult to patrol, simply because the terrain is rural and rough, and there are more places for the terrorists to hide bombs, perpetrate an ambush, or let loose one sniper round. There are also virtually no vehicle patrols of the Armagh as all roads

A marine from 40 Commando checks the identity of a married couple along the Falls Road in West Belfast during a routine patrol. He is armed with the British-produced SA-80 5.56mm assault rifle. (Courtesy: Royal Marines Public Relations)

are mined, and if a vehicle attempts to pass a country road ***it will be blown up***! This leaves only two means for patrol: on foot and by air. Foot patrols are, of course, dangerous and difficult. Slugging it through pastures, valleys and farms, the marines are under constant danger of pulling a trip wire or finding themselves in a volley of Armalite fire. No matter how quick they move carrying their eighty or so pounds of gear, there is no stealth movement in the Armagh. Villagers and town folks inform the next village or town of the impending arrival of a marine patrol--this is done through telephone call or, remarkably, smoke signal. A home in a village, for example, will burn their garbage in the fireplace once a patrol walks by; the smoke, seen for miles, alerts the next village of the marines imminent arrival. In order for the movements of a marine force to remain unknown, the force must stay out in the bush, in the bogs and impassable forests, for days on end in ambush. The Provos fear the marines for their tenacious and extremely lethal ambushing capabilities, and the marines respect the Provos' tenacious and deadly instincts. The Armagh is, indeed, Bandit Country.

The helicopter is, obviously, the quickest and most potent means of movement in the Armagh. "Desperate Mill," the main RAF facility and military headquarters in the Armagh, is the busiest heliport in the world. Hopping through the Armagh by air is not safe, either. A terrific bounty is placed on RAF, Army and Marine choppers, and several transport helicopters ferrying troops have come under automatic, and even .50 caliber fire. The helicopter is used for insertion and extraction for day and night patrols, as well as surprise assaults on villages where, intelligence has learned, Provo ambushes are laying in wait at roadside entrances. An heliborne average patrol of the Armagh consists of twelve men, led by an officer, equipped with SA-80s and a few FN

Fearing an engagement with a group of men who could be PIRA terrorists, a Royal Marine commando takes cover behind some enemy graffiti and peers through the sights of this SA-80 assault rifle.(Courtesy: Royal Marines Public Relations)

MAGs brought along for good measure; radios are brought along, as are smoke grenades, flares, and even some stun grenades in case a house with civilians needs to be entered before the SAS can be called in. Patrols cannot walk on the roads, since they are mined. They must negotiate the bush and the hillside. They can last for a minimum of eight hours, and sometimes extend into several days. While on patrol, they must stick to a rigid timetable. Helicopter pick-ups and supply flights are at pre-designated times in order to avoid having the exposed chopper out in the open for too long. Marine patrols MUST make these rendezvous. The most valuable element of any patrol is the pre-mission intelligence and preparation. It is here that Commando intelligence officers come into their own as handlers and analysts, and they bear a tremendous responsibility over the fate of their men. Good intelligence can save lives. A bad piece of data or tainted information from a tout can result in dead marines. It is here that the marines come into contact with "The Group" and the Special Air Service.

[1] Interestingly enough, the French created their own SAS following the end of the war, the ***2e*** and ***3e Regiments Chasseurs Parachutistes***, and the Belgian created the 1st Para-Commando Battalion.

[2] Years later, a second SAS TA regiment, the 23rd, would be formed.

[3] The Killing House remained a staple at Hereford until the fall of 1988, when an SAS sergeant accidentally moved his head during a drill and was rewarded with a 9mm round between his eyes. The death of the sergeant was a tragic loss and led to immediate safety improvements in the Killing House. A new design was subsequently designed, using filmed images projected on the wall. Interestingly enough, the tragic death of the SAS sergeant led to more stringent safety measures inside the "House." The average SAS operator entering a week of training at the Killing House will fire a minimum of 5,000 rounds of ammunition most of which end up embedded in the bullet-proof walls; instructors, therefore, working in the room are exposed to airborne lead poisoning. As a result, a new type of wall has been put into the Killing House, one composed of angled rubber baffles the absorb the impact of each bullet, slows it down and directs it to the floor where the spent rounds can be swept up and properly disposed of.

[4] In addition to the Provisional Irish Republican Army (PIRA), Republic terrorist groups functioning in Ulster include the Irish National Liberation Army (INLA), the Irish People's Liberation Organization (IPLO), Official Irish Republican Army (OIRA), ***Cumann na nBan*** (the female branch of the IRA), and ***Fianna na hEireann*** (the youth wing of the IRA). Loyalist terrorist factions include, the Ulster Defense Association (UDA), the Ulster Volunteer Force (UVF), the Ulster Freedom Fighters (UFF), the Protestant Action Force (PAF), and Red Hand Commandos. All groups are heavily armed, loyal to their goals and views and considered most dangerous.

[5] In order to preserve their anonymity during operations, SAS operators are known by letter titles: "Soldier A," "B," and so on. At Gibraltar, the SP Team entity was commanded by "Soldier F."

[6] Identity withheld for security considerations.

[7] Identity withheld for security considerations.

# UNITED KINGDOM - POLICE UNITS

***Terminal One--Heathrow Airport, London: At 9:30 P.M. the bustle around Gate 21 picked up as El Al Flight 318 to Tel Aviv was boarding. A long line of passengers had gathered to enter the secure gate after having had their check-in baggage X-rayed and questions asked as to how their luggage was packed and how they got to the airport. Security was tight at Heathrow--especially for flights coming from and going to Israel; in 1986, a Palestinian-born Jordanian working for Syrian Air Force Intelligence almost succeeded in planting a bomb on board an El Al flight from New York continuing on to Tel Aviv using his unknowing pregnant Irish girlfriend as a "mule" or smuggler. Most of the passengers on the flight were Israeli tourists heading home from a brief visit; Britons, used to a more refined modes of air travel, prefer British Airways to the hustle and chaos of El Al. Most of the travelers were laden down with heavy shopping bags and gifts from the city's endless shops and attractions. The tourists had seen it all--Big Ben, Buckingham Palace and London Bridge. Now, at Gate 21, they were to see a sight once thought of as unheard of--two Bobbies walking their beat carrying Glock pistols and cradling a Heckler and Koch MP5 9mm submachine guns.***

Could there be a time when police officers, with little or no training, could pick up a firearm and take it on patrol, just because it was night time and they felt the need to carry a "comforter?" Could the House of Commons voice their concern over the number of cases involving police use of guns. These measures raised eyebrows in London at the turn of the century, and many people then regarded police carrying firearms as a modern "evil', at odds with the fine tradition of an unarmed police service. Incredibly, the public voice has changed very little in the past century and, in fact, the Metropolitan Police issued instructions for the carriage and use of firearms more than 100 years ago--instructions that were to remain largely unaltered until very recently. Armed British policemen were once thought of as impossible in the United Kingdom, and many stalwarts believed that the day British policemen formed SWAT units was the day the nation was doomed. Increasingly, however, the street terrorism of violent crime, once thought the sole domain of large American cities, has invaded the United Kingdom with a vengeance. Hostages are no longer seized solely by heavily armed terrorists trained, but by emotionally disturbed persons--some armed, some not. Criminals in the United Kingdom no longer use their fists, truncheons and blades to terrorize their victims, but they now rob and steal with snubnose revolvers and protect drug turf with shotguns and 9mm pistols. For most people the traditional image of the British police officer comes

Two Metropolitan police officers stand their post near the Horse Guard parade on Whitehall. As a result of the fact that the officers do not carry their firearms openly, the Home Office wants terrorists and criminals never to know when an officer will be able to remove a Glock from his coat and handle a situation tactically. (Sigalit Katz)

A Metropolitan Police ARV. (Sigalit Katz)

The effects of an IRA bomb on the streets of central London. (Courtesy: Photo Press UK Defence)

During the visit of a dignitary to London's Heathrow Airport, a SO19 sniper keeps a faithful watch from a protected perch. He is armed with the Steyr SSG 69 7.62mm sniping rifle. (Courtesy: Steyr)

An RUC Hotspur Landrover fitted with specialist roof boxing to negate the effects of drogue bombs thrown at the vehicle. It is reported that the MHSU's and SSUs deploy from such vehicles. (Courtesy: RUC)

from the "Bobby" image of the early 1950's, best embodied in the character of PC George Dixon in the film "The Blue Lamp." This was an image that the police service itself felt (and still feels) illustrated all that is good about the British police. It is an image that is obsolete and has forever changed.

However, one day in 1966, something happened that was to horrify the public and cause the police to examine its approach to firearms. On August 12, 1966, the three police officers crewing "Foxtrot 11" an unmarked police car, challenged a gang of armed robbers. The entire crew were gunned down and murdered by the gang. The manhunt that was to follow exposed how unprepared police were to deal with serious armed crimes. Firearms training was virtually non existent, weapons inadequate, and tactics unheard of. The Metropolitan Police turned to the FBI academy and several other police agencies for advice and shortly after, in December 1966, the Firearms Unit was formed.

At first, the Firearms Unit (now called SO19) was responsible for training police officers in the use of firearms. But, more recently, to meet the changing needs of the police service, the unit has grown and its expertise is used operationally. For example, the unit was a key player in the Balcombe Street Siege of IRA terrorists, the Spaghetti House restaurant siege of armed robbers, and the Iranian Embassy siege where it secured an outer perimeter and put snipers in place until the boys from Hereford could take control of the situation. The unit steadily expanded to provide teams of officers, highly trained and specially equipped, to deal with serious armed crime, hostage rescue, and terrorists seizing key installations and captives. The Firearms Unit was also tasked in deterring a terrorist act--a Bobby walking his post armed with nothing more than a truncheon and Motorola did little by way of intimidation when facing a squad of terrorists armed with AK-47s and fragmentation grenades. The police required a tactical edge, a high-profile intimacy with weapons and the means to respond to a "job" with this firepower quickly and, on many occasions, unobtrusively. In the early 1980s, it was considered a busy year if the unit received two or three calls outs; now, in 1995, the unit responds to that many calls each day. This dramatic increase in work is due partly to changing crime patterns, and partly to the need for a highly professional approach in dealing with armed crime and terrorist offenses serious enough to involve weaponry, yet not beyond that invisible border when the MoD would assume control of the situation and call in a Special Air Service SP Team.

Police officers who make up the teams are selected on the basis of experience, marksmanship skills, tactical ability and physical fitness. They have to pass a demanding course of instruction and achieve a high standard of excellence in order to earn the title "Specialist Firearms Officer." The training responsibility of the unit has, like the operational side, grown and developed. In the early 1980s as many as 4,800 Metropolitan Police officers were trained and authorized to carry firearms. Their training, although an improvement over the pre-1968 era, was basic and limited in scope. An initial training course lasted only four days and further training was limited to only two days a year. Many of the officers trained were never required to carry firearms operationally and there was no team structure for the bulk of them, who were based at police stations. It should be noted that an astounding seventy-percent of the applicants to the unit fail the selection and training process. "Applicants aren't selected in," claimed on SO19 instructor, "they are selected out!"

The unit has its main training establishment at Lippits Hill in North London and six training ranges located in police buildings throughout the Metropolitan Police District. The unit also uses a number of military facilities and temporary tactical training sites. This allows for a range of thirty-five different courses to take place constantly throughout the year. Similar training installations exist throughout the country handling the requirements of various regional constabularies.

Beyond the officer actually removing his Glock from his leather holster, the most important asset of the unit are its fleet of vehicles. Rapid response to armed incidents is of paramount importance in order to support unarmed officers and improve the service to the public. To do this, the Metropolitan Police Service introduced Armed Response Vehicles (ARVs) in 1991. These vehicles, Ford pickups and vans in typical police markings, are crewed by uniformed officers who have been selected and trained to stabilize and control armed incidents, stop and search suspect vehicles, and search premises. These officers are the first armed officers to arrive on the scene and, in serious cases, will support and prepare the ground for the specialist firearms teams. Each ARV is crewed by three officers in ordinary police uniform, who patrol specific areas to ensure the fastest possible response to armed incidents. The rapid response, combined with the high standards demanded of them, has proved the value of the units, whose workload has increased to an average of twenty-five calls a day. The Home Office then introduced new recommendations relating to firearms nationally and the Service immediately set about restructuring the numbers and displacement of armed officers. The main responsibility for carrying firearms went to specialist units, such as Royalty and Diplomatic Protection, Airport Security, Robbery Squad and of course the Firearms Unit itself. As a result, the number of authorized firearms officers has fallen to under 2,000, only a few of whom are based at police stations.

Each ARV is equipped with a formidable armory: Glock semi-automatic 9mm pistols (including those with light-attachments); Heckler and Koch MP5 9mm submachine guns; ballistic infantry helmets with protective visors; body bunkers; Dragon lights; visual probes and listening devices; entry tools; emergency medical equipment; and, voice projection equipment. Most ARVs are bullet-proof.

To draw their weapons, ARV officers must be authorized by an assistant chief constable or, in a matter of immediate emergency, a superintendent. Only a small number of officers, those trained by the SAS as close protection personnel and snipers, carry their weapons with them at all times, and these include officers on Royal Family protection details, as well as those protecting ministers and VIPs, as well as safeguarding sensitive targets and transferring terrorists to and from trial and prison.

They are many in the United Kingdom who fear the introduction of tactical police units is a sad sign that Britain is following the American example. But there are stretches of Manchester, Liverpool, Glasgow and London that make the most dangerous stretches of the Bronx, Miami and Watts look like secure holiday areas, and the police need superior firepower. Of the 137,000 police officers in the United Kingdom, only 5.5% of them (approximately 7,700) are authorized to draw firearms and only a small percentage of these officers are considered "Level 1 Officers," trained in every aspect of weaponry and their tactical use.

It is a combination of experience and training which has given the Metropolitan Police Service Firearms Unit a unique responsibility to respond effectively to many thousands of armed operations while rarely having to resort to the use of their firearms. Like most municipal police forces in Canada, the United States and throughout Europe, negotiators are preferred over 9mm gunfire; the men--and women--of SO10, the police negotiating team, are among the world's best.

A bright red Ford Sierra and RUC armored "saloon" vehicle used for surveillance and special operations by specialized units of the Royal Ulster Constabulary. (Courtesy: RUC)

On the mainland, British police can preach restraint and use deadly firepower only as a last resort. Ulster is a different story.

No discussion of the United Kingdom's specialized tactical police units could be complete with looking at two distinctive units within the Royal Ulster Constabulary (RUC). All officers serving in the RUC are authorized to carry weapons, though RUC officers routinely carry MP5s, CAR-15s and M-16A2s on their daily patrols; all RUC officers on patrol wear heavy ballistic vests. The RUC is divided into twelve divisions, two for each of the province's six counties, and maintains several specialist units and both are based at the force's Knock headquarters just outside East Belfast. The specialist covert operations unit, one of the five divisions of E Department,[1] is known as E4A, and it is responsible for intelligence-gathering, observation and ambushes. Its officers are all volunteers, screened thoroughly for their loyalty, service record and reliability, and are tactically trained by the Special Air Service. E4A is commanded by a Superintendent or Chief Superintendent and is considered among the "plum" assignments in the RUC.

The RUC's special tactical unit and the one called for special ambushes and the recovery of hostages is the SSU--the Special Support Unit. Divisional Mobile Support Units (DMSUs) are used for anti-riot duty and Headquarters Mobile Support Units (HMSUs) are used outside Belfast, and the SSUs are basically the RUC's SWAT unit. Trained by the Paras and the SAS at Hereford, Aldershot and Ballykinlar, the unit is trained in assaults, room entries, VIP and dignitary protection and ambushes. They operate in urban OPs, in civilian dress and in uniform, and are often deployed in armored cars and specially-designed bullet-proof sedans. They are armed with MP5s, Heckler and Koch HK 33 5.56mm assault rifles, Smith and Wesson Model 59 revolvers, and Steyr 7.62mm police sniping weapons.

[1] In addition to the Army's 14 Intelligence Company and SAS combination ("Int and Sy Group") and the RUC's E Department, the final portion of the intelligence-gathering triumvirate in Northern Ireland is the seventy-man MI5 contingent in Ulster known as the Security Liaison Offices (SLOs).

An RUC sniper and his observer peer through their scopes and field glasses during protective security duty. The sniper is armed with the Steyr Police rifle with silencer. (Courtesy: Steyr)

# Egypt

According to one officer in the British Special Boat Service (SBS), upon returning to England after a covert tour of duty in Northern Ireland, "Fighting terrorism isn't a matter of skill as much as a matter of courage to first encounter the bastards and then luck when assaulting a schoolhouse held by suicidal crazies." Luck is an integral element of any military operations. The most cunning planners, the most methodological officers and the bravest of soldiers can make even the most complex and impossible plans look easy on paper but when the bullets start flying and lives--especially innocent lives--are on the line, the unknown element of fate and luck does, indeed, play a significant role. Luck is even a greater factor in counter-terrorist operations--but foresight and logic are also important elements, as important as a soldiers' weapon and the intelligence obtained on a target. Around the world, Egypt's Unit 777 is a counter-terrorist force that has lacked both luck and foresight and has been involved in some of the most significant hostage-rescue screw ups in modern military history. In the counter-terrorist community they have been the brunt of many jokes and have been known as "the unit who rescues the terrorists and kills the hostages." They are, however, an elite force of operators who personify the true difficulties of an hostage-rescue work and how the best intentions and most heroic assaults are sometimes simply not enough.

There was a time, in the early 1970s, when Egypt didn't require a hostage-rescue commando unit. Egyptian special forces and the Egyptian intelligence service, the ***Muchabarat***, were responsible in training aspects and elements of virtually every major Palestinian terrorist faction, as well as terrorists leaders from many European and Asian groups--from the Provisional IRA to the African National Congress. Egypt was a dictatorship, albeit under the guise of a democracy, it was the leader of the Arab world and a nation firmly entrenched in the Soviet orbit. The 1973 War changed everything. The initial surprise scored against Israeli forces and the initial good showing by Egyptian forces was viewed in Cairo as a victory, and one needed in order to not only return pride to the nation, taken following the 1967 War, but also a step in the diplomatic process that would return the Sinai peninsula to Egyptian control and help forge close ties between Egypt and the United States of American and West and all its billions of dollars in monetary aid. The Egyptian government officially left the Soviet camp in 1972 when President Anwar as-Sadat kicked out 30,000 Soviet advisors from his country, but his move toward the West became reality in 1974 and 1975 when disengagement talks between Egypt and Israel developed into a groundwork for peace. Palestinian groups, especially pro-Syrian factions determined not to permit any negotiations with the Jewish State, vowed violence. For the first time, Egyptian intelligence received word from such groups as the Abu Nidal faction and the Popular Front for the Liberation of Palestine that Egyptian targets and individuals would be targeted. The Egyptian military was tasked with creating a force of counter-terrorist and hostage-rescue operators that could respond to any such situation.

Egyptian special forces had performed well since the 1967-70 War of Attrition against Israeli forces along the Suez Canal and during the 1973 War; in raids meant to kill and capture soldiers, as well as sabotage installations deep behind enemy lines, the units displayed impressive courage and operational professionalism. When the Egyptian government and defense ministry realized the necessity to create a counter-terrorist entity, it was firstly decided that the unit would not be a police force, like GSG-9, but rather a purely military operation run by the special forces command. Special forces in Egypt, the units that include frogmen, shock troopers and reconnaissance rangers, are known as ***As-Saiqa*** (Lighting) commandos. The ***As-Saiqa*** headquarters is situated adjacent to the Ministry of Defense in Cairo, and their training facility is in the backdrop of the pyramids approximately an hour out of the Egyptian capital. Egyptian military planners had to be careful when selecting a cadre to form the core of this new unit--volunteers had to be not only perfect soldiers, highly intelligent and motivated, but they needed to be politically reliable. Operators for this unit could not have ties to radical Palestinian groups or have had contact with any individuals belonging to these organizations, and soldiers volunteering could not have ties to the secretive and underground Muslim Brotherhood that, although inactive, was always a thorn in the side of the Egyptian security apparatus. Most importantly, the unit commanders realized that they needed a force of men who would have no hesitation in firing upon Arabs or Europeans, Egyptians or Palestinians, when the green light for an assault was issued.

Egypt's special forces counter-terrorist entity was formally sanctioned in July 1977 and adopted the name of Force 777. At first,

As-Saiqa commanders move about near Israeli positions along the canal in 1973--the surviving members of the unit provided an experienced focus when Force 777 was formed in 1977. (UN)

Egyptian reconnaissance paratroopers line up for inspection prior to maneuvers in the desert near Cairo--Force 777 recruits solely from the paratroops and special forces. (U.S. Department of Defense)

Egyptian special forces pose with their AKMS 7.62mm assault rifles and RPG-7 grenade launchers. Even though Egypt has been in the Western (American) fold for nearly twenty years, the armed forces still carry Soviet-produced weaponry. (U.S. Department of Defense)

the unit consisted of three officers, four NCOs and forty operators. They began pretty much from scratch, and relied on advise from a few private consultants and international contacts. The unit wouldn't have long to wait, however, until it would receive its baptism of fire. Through the latter portion of 1977 and early 1978, tensions between Egypt and Libya bordered on the escalation of full-scale war; Egypt's peace overtures to Israel and moderation toward the west--particular the United States. The Egyptians feared that the Libyans would launch terrorists strikes from the border desert area into Egypt proper, and as a result Force 777 was despatched into Libya on intelligence-gathering sorties and hit-and-run strikes against suspected terrorist training bases in the Libyan desert from which (Egyptian military intelligence had gathered) operators were preparing for forays into Egypt. In terms of an operational existence, Force 777 was still in its infancy when the Libyan troubles began--the unit had no firm order of battle, no formal rescue experience and little by way of organization. It was still referred to as a section of the ***as-Saiqa*** commandos.

On February 18, 1978, in the wake of Egyptian President Sadat's historic peace pilgrimage to Jerusalem, terrorists from Dr. George Habash's Popular Front for the Liberation of Palestine (PFLP) murdered a prominent Egyptian newspaper editor and confidante of Sadat, and then hijacked a Cyprus Airways jet in Nicosia that was scheduled to take-off for Cairo. The plane took off, but returned to Cyprus hours later to be positioned at a remote stretch of the airfield under the guard of Cypriot National Guardsmen. In Cairo, the murder of Sadat's close friend and the holding of a few dozen Egyptian nationals on board the aircraft was viewed as an act requiring immediate response. Sadat ordered the ***as-Saiqa***/Force 777 commandos to resolve the matter immediately. The flight time from Cairo to Nicosia lasted only an hour on board the Antonov transport, and the commandos went over their assault plan in mid-air: they were to land and before the aircraft would roll to a complete stop they would race toward the hijacked aircraft and assault it in a semi-copy of the Entebbe operation two years earlier. The only problem was the fact that the Egyptian Ministry of Defense failed to secure the permission of the Cypriot authorities; in fact, they hadn't even informed them of the impending military action. When the commandos landed and began their sprint on the runway toward the surrounded aircraft, Cypriot police and Guardsmen units, thinking the men carrying AK-47s in fatigues and tracksuits to be additional terrorists, opened fire. In an amazing and tragic scene, the Egyptian commandos and Cypriot soldiers engaged in a ferocious eighty-minute fire-fight on the runway, all the time as the terrorists, who must have certainly been confused, looked on from the aircraft. In the end, fifteen Egyptians and several Cypriots were killed in the fiasco.

The Nicosia disaster led to many changes in how Egyptian soldiers and counter-terrorist operators would be deployed outside the national boundaries, and policy statements concerning a chain of command and international liaisons. The next time Force 777 would be deployed outside Egypt, the necessities of authorizations and liaisons would be handled smoothly--it would be the operation itself that would end disastrously.

On September 25, 1985, Israeli warplanes launched a surprise attack against PLO headquarters in Tunis; the F-15s and F-16s destroyed the facility and killed dozens. The Abu Abbass Faction of the Palestine Liberation Front, a faction within the PLO, retaliated for the Israeli operation on October 3, 1985, when four PLF terrorists hijacked the Italian cruise ship, the S.S. ***Achille Lauro*** in the middle of a pleasure cruise of Egypt, Israel and the Mediterranean; the terrorists, had, in fact, been on the boat as a means of entering Israel, but were discovered by a crewmember and subsequently seized the ship. After an ordeal at sea during which the terrorists brutally murdered a wheel-chair bound American-Jewish passenger, sixty-nine-year-old Leon Klinghoffer, they agreed to surrender to Egyptian authorities in Alexandria in exchange for safe passage out of Egypt. In a controver-sial move, Egyptian-President Hosni Mubarak acquiesced to the demands a desire to move the ugly incident away from his area of attention, and in fact ordered an Egyptair 737 along with four secret service agents and Abu Abbass himself to take the terrorists back to Tunis. The Americans, upon learning of the murder of Leon Klinghoffer, decided to act decisively and, with Israeli assistance, they launched a naval operation that would capture the terrorists and bring them to justice. As most of the hostages on board the ***Achille Lauro*** were Americans from the New York and New Jersey area, a significant American naval presence had been in the area anyway just in case a rescue would have been authorized, and elements from SEAL Team SIX and Delta were in position in the region. The Egyptian Boeing 737 was intercepted by U.S. Navy F-14 Tomcats and diverted to the NATO air station at Sigonella, Sicily. In the now famous story, Delta and Team SIX operators surrounded the aircraft and took the four terrorists into custody. Abu Abbass was permitted to escape via Yugoslavia courtesy of the Italian government (not wanting to have a rash of terrorist attacks and bombings perpetrated on the streets of Rome, Florence and Milan) and the Egyptians allowed to take their aircraft back to Cairo.

For the United States, the operation was viewed as a victory. Palestinian radicals, however, were angered at the Egyptians for not safeguarding Abu Abbas and the ***Achille Lauro*** hijackers and they now vowed revenge. On November 24, 1985, terrorists from the Abu Nidal faction boarded Egyptair Flight 648 at Athens International Airport and subsequently hijacked it to Luga International Airport in Malta. The terrorists were demanding the release of the jailed ***Achille Lauro*** terrorists, along with other demands. They had already shot five hostages, include two Egyptian secret service security sky marshals flying shotgun and three female hostages, including two Israelis travelers heading to the Far East; the bodies of the shot hostages were thrown on the tarmac, although some miraculously lived. In an ironic twist of fate, the Flight 648 was the same aircraft as the one seized and forced down at Sigonella several weeks earlier.

Upon learning of the hijacking, the Egyptian Ministry of Defense immediately summoned Force 777 to a secure portion of Cairo International Airport where they boarded a fully prepared Egyptian Air Force C-130 transport; Ministry of Defense officials had, in the interim, secured support from Maltese officials. Upon landing in Luga, the Egyptian operators immediately braced for an assault, though when it did begin the mission would become a disaster; in fact, according to a retired high-ranking American military counter-terrorist officer, "It proved to be a classic example as to how not to mount a rescue mission." Egyptian military officials on the ground at Luga failed to used any surveillance devices or equipment to find the location of the hijackers inside the aircraft, and they failed to even bother to interview and debrief hostages released. In essence, they were to assault the aircraft blindly without knowing the best location to enter and exactly what they were up against. Against better logic, the commander opted to forgo a door assault and, instead, blow a hole through the ceiling of the luggage hold while others would then assault through doors that would be blown open. The operators did not carry stun grenades, nor did they carry with them a blueprint of the Boeing 737 aircraft.

Maltese police and military units secured the aircraft and the airfield, and entered into negotiations with the terrorists while the Egyptians were left to their own devices to prepare the assault. In all, Mubarak had sent eighty Force 777 operators to Malta on board an Egyptian Air Force C-130 transport kept on alert status all year round for such an eventuality, and the commander on the scene, a colonel, opted to use about forty in the initial assault. Snipers ringed the aircraft and covered any possible target with the Drugenov 7.62mm sniper rifles, as the operators moved in closer for the assault. Although five passengers had already been shot and two murdered, it had been nearly six hours since the last eruption of gunfire on board the aircraft. Negotiators urged the Egyptians to wait and use restraint, but at 23:15 hours the assault was poised to commence.

"The difficulty in entering an aircraft through the bottom or top with explosives," according to one German SEK officer, "is that you lose the element of surprise since you must wait for the dust and smoke to clear before then negotiating your way through the slots into the main cabin. By losing the surprise, you lose time and ultimately the lives of the hostages." The Force 777 commander opted to gain some of the time back by using a larger portion of explosives than recommended when blowing off the ceiling; this, he thought, would stun the terrorists and buy a momentary diversion. It didn't. When the operators assaulted the aircraft, the blast was so powerful that the force of the explosion blew six rows of seats off their hinges and subsequently crushed to death nearly twenty hostages. Additional teams of operators then entered the aircraft through the emergency exits, but for some inexplicable reason, they began hurling "smoke" grenades inside the fuselage and firing at any target they thought of as justified inside the chaotic and smoke-filled interior of the aircraft. Amid the terrorist gunfire, the operator's rounds and the smoke and flames, the botched operation resulted in fifty-seven dead hostages; it is believed that the snipers positioned atop rescue vehicles actually shot hostages being evacuated on the emergency chutes.

Following the fiasco at Luga, Force 777 retreated into the abyss of anonymity and little mention of the unit has been made since--both in the West and in Egypt. It is known that they have been active in Egypt's

Force 777 hopefuls abseil down a Mi-8 choppers during training and selection exercises near Cairo. (U.S. Department of Defense)

bloody civil war against Muslim fundamentalists from the "Brotherhood," and have participated in hundreds of ops against Brotherhood strongholds in the slums of Cairo, as well as in the south where gun-running from the Sudan has been problematic. The war against the Brotherhood is, perhaps, the opposite end of the counter-terrorist spectrum--it is full-scale bloody combat not so much a selective type of warfare meant to save hostages, but a method of laying down intense firepower in order to save the lives of the attacking policemen and soldiers. It is believed that in this war, hundreds of Egyptian policemen have been killed along with a dozen or so Force 777 operators.

The unit is headquartered near Cairo at the main facility housing Egyptian special forces. A fleet of Soviet-built Mi-8 and Westland Command 1 choppers are maintained and ready around the clock for any possible deployment, as are several Egyptian Air Force C-130s. All pilots connected to Force 777 are volunteers, specifically trained in special operations, and among the best in the entire air force.

As a result of the secrecy in which they function, it is difficult to confirm accurate details as to the equipment and weaponry carried by Force 777 operators. It is known that in Larnaca, for example, unit members carried AKMS 7.62mm assault rifles, Port Said 9mm submachine guns and Egyptian-produced ***Helwan*** 9mm pistols--local copies of the Beretta 951. At Luga, however, it is believed that the operators--or at least snipers--carried Belgian FAL 7.62mm assault rifles. It is not known if the unit has switched to the MP5 family of 9mm submachine guns. The extent of Force 777's foreign contacts are also somewhat unclear, though it is known that they have had extensive dealings and instructional seminars from the U.S. Army's 1st SFOD-Delta, the U.S. Navy's SEAL Team SIX, and France's GIGN; Force 777 is also believed to have had some contacts with GSG-9. Because of the unit's close contacts with the U.S. military, it is believed that now much of the gear carried and deployed by Force 777 is now American produced.

# *Israel - Israel Defense Forces Units*

April 9, 1973. Sitting in their Opel Sedan, rented courtesy of the ***Mossad***, outside the luxury block of flats on Rue Verdun in fashionable West Beirut, the operators nervously clutched their Ingram Mac-10 .45 caliber submachine guns outside the luxury block of flats on Rue Verdun in fashionable West Beirut. The Mac-10s weren't very accurate, but they weren't issue, and they weren't traceable either; the only thing linking these weapons to the State of Israel were the fingers that caressed the triggers. Other operators clutched the sleek AK-47 Kalashnikov assault rifle, weapons which only a few years ago belong to the Syrian Army. Waiting nervously as a Lebanese Gendarme armored car rolled slowly down the boulevard away from view, four men, dressed as hippies, emerged from the vehicle with suitcases in hand. Two other rented cars had pulled up behind the Opel, and their passengers emerged from the vehicles whose engines continued to run, and they assumed positions around the block; some of the people looked like flower children from Woodstock, others were seemingly attractive blondes with stunning figures and heavy blue hand bags. There was no time for anyone to be scared this evening--they were too busy living off of the adrenaline of anxious hearts, and the arrogance of knowing that they belonged to the most elite fighting unit in modern military history. The hippies and the "women" crossed the street toward the entrance to the building and walked up to two black Mercedes staffed by three PLO "Force 17" bodyguards smoking cigarettes and listening to the energetic songs of a Lebanese diva on Beirut radio. The guards paid little notice to the hippies, Beirut was crammed with hashish-followers from Europe, but the women were sexy and one of the men even offered a brief smile of approval. His lust was terminated by a point-blank .22 round to the temple; the two other men were cut down with silenced fire in a matter of seconds, and the guards in the second car were also hammered with volleys of fire, but not before a stray round sliced through the hood, igniting the horn in an endless assault on the eardrums. A stumbling block had been eliminated, but the authorities might have been alerted. The operation was now entering its critical phase.

Quickly, four men raced into the entrance of the building, and sprinted up the brightly lit stairway to the sixth floor. Their first stop was at the door of Abu Yusef, the Black September operational genius who had planned the Munich Olympic Massacre. The team leader, Major Yoni Netanyahu, produced plastic explosives from the brown leather suitcase he carried, and quickly blew the front door off its hinges. The four men burst through the apartment and found Abu Yusef desperately searching for the AK-47 assault rifle that Yasir Arafat had presented to him personally. He never made it to his trusted AK-47. He was killed by a thirty-round burst of fire from Yoni's Mac-10; his wife and son, also in the apartment, observed the hit in horror, while the remaining operators gathered papers and personal files from the apartment and raced down stairs to the awaiting cars below.

Simultaneously, two other teams entered an adjacent building on Rue Verdun and visited the apartments of Kamal A'dwan, a Black September terrorist mastermind running operations in Europe and Israel, and Kamal Nasser, the Black September spokesman and operations officer. Both men would join Abu Yusef in terrorist hell.

By the time the operators made it downstairs, they found their comrades engaged in a desperate close-quarter gun fight with a few dozen Lebanese Gendarmes. The Mossad drivers performed some race-car stunts, reversed into the intersection of Ibn Walid Street, and headed for the Mediterranean at top speed. There, the operators and the espionage agents abandoned their vehicles, grabbed their suitcases loaded to capacity with intelligence material, and headed to sea on rubber dinghies courtesy of Israeli frogmen.

This episode was the lead chapter in a larger raid known as "Operation Spring of Youth." It was a remarkable success and the largest counter-terrorist raid ever mounted by a nation against the guerrilla armies sworn to destroy her. The operators also knew that the results would be controversial, but political mayhem was something they liked to inflict on those sitting behind their locked doors and mahogany desks; after all, one of the unit's favorite sayings, paraphrasing Josephus Flavious, stated "There are no big victories without taking big chances." These men were the best of the best, and a statement of a nation's ability to produce--and despatch--men courageous and intelligent enough to be despatched deep behind enemy lines to mount missions with seemingly impossible chances of success. These men were operators in ***Sayeret Mat'kal,*** Israel's General Staff Reconnaissance Unit--the toughest fighting force ever assembled. It is a unit that has captured the world's imagination--from the heart of Beirut to the darkened tarmac at Entebbe airport--even though the vast majority of its operations are state secrets of the

Lieutenant Meir Har-Zion (standing, holding MP40) instructs his group of Unit 101 veterans prior to a retaliatory raid, circa 1953. (IDF Archives)

"Operation Gift," December 28, 1968: Amid the flaming skeletons of Middle East Airlines (MEA) aircraft, ***Sayeret Mat'kal*** operators take cover en route to their next targeted aircraft. (IDF Archives)

May 8, 1972: Border Guard policemen patrol the outer-reaches of Lod Airport with the hijacked Sabena 707 in the background. (IGPO)

highest order that might never be released to the public. One of the unit's nicknames is "The Chief of Staff's Boys," a not so subtle reference to the fact that the IDF's Chief of Staff knows all the operators personally, and has a list of their names inside his desk. Others in the Israeli special operations community call them a "Covert Alarm Clock," since they serve as a wake-up call to the various heads of the Palestinian terrorist organizations, to sit up and take notice that they, too, are vulnerable. They are the world's most experienced, busiest and undoubtedly most famous counter-terrorist units.

***Sayeret Mat'kal*** was created in 1957 not as a counter-terrorist and counter-insurgency force but rather as a covert special operations intelligence-gathering unit--they were sanctioned as a result of some very serious shortcomings in Israel's ability to spy on its Arab neighbors. The brainchild of one Major Avraham Arnan, a legendary intelligence officer who ran ***Shtinkerim*** (or informers) in Jordanian-held East Jerusalem, ***Sayeret Mat'kal*** was to be an ultra-secretive intelligence-gathering force to conduct "deniable" mission-impossible type forays deep behind enemy lines throughout the entire Middle East, and parts beyond as well. Until Arnan battled the narrow-minded bureaucracy and blazed a trail for the creation of this unit among the halls of the IDF General Staff, the army relied on outside elements, mainly agents and "sympathetic friends" to obtain its intelligence data; often, the material was tainted and late. The IDF desperately needed and ***internal*** and ***reliable*** force to get its information. It would be no easy task, and this force would have to be made up of the toughest, most intelligent and innovative conscripted sons of the state. The success of ***Sayeret Mat'kal*** as a unit depended on it being a "deniable" intelligence-gathering entity that could venture out into the deepest reaches of enemy territory and perform its top-secret missions without getting caught, embroiling the national into a sticky political and military predicament. One of the primary reasons behind the unit's creation was the 1954 capture of four Israeli paratroopers seized behind Syrian lines as they were replacing a battery on a listening device atop the Golan Heights; the four were imprisoned--one eventually committing suicide--and tortured in embarrassing incident for Israel's intelligence.

Arnan first recruited veterans from the infamous Unit 101, the retaliatory commando force that a young and upstart major named "Arik" Sharon formed in 1953, and urban kids, especially those young Israelis whose parents came from the Arabic Diaspora. Although discriminated against in the European-dominated Labor-led Israel of the late 1950s and early 1960s, and usually excluded by the air force and the other elite reconnaissance commandos units, these kids (whom the state had labeled as disadvantaged) understood the Arab mentality,

IDF Chief of Staff, Lieutenant-General David Elazar walks nervously among a squad of ***Sayeret Mat'kal*** operators, already in their white airline mechanic coveralls, as they prepare to mount their daring rescue raid aboard the hijacked Sabena Boeing 707. (IDF Spokesman)

knew Arabic, and, most importantly, had chips on their shoulders that translated into a competitive edge that the other Sabras, or native born Israelis, would have been hard pressed to emulate. Arnan was dedicated to "Arabize" his men--European Jews, or ***Ashkenazim,*** were sent to the desert for some instruction by Bedouin tribal chiefs.

Finally, Arnan ventured to the country's Kibbutzim--Israel's nationwide well for pilots, commandos and combat officers; the Kibbutzim are a special forces talent pool that the SAS, Delta Force and the SEALs all envy. Kibbutznikim tended to be healthy, physically fit, and used to living in a society with a firm bureaucracy (like the military); this trait also ensured that they knew how to bend the rules when required to, something that would definitely be needed in a unit like ***Sayeret Mat'kal***. Perhaps most importantly, Kibbutznikim are subjected to competitive peer pressure that exists in no other civilization on earth. In 1959 Avraham Arnan found one such competitive and capable Kibbutzniks--a soldier around whom he would shape his unit. That soldier was a young conscript named Ehud Barak.

Arnan modeled ***Sayeret Mat'kal*** along the lines of the British Special Air Service (SAS), Captain David Stirling's legendary band of rogue warriors of the Second World War; in fact, a plaque with the SAS motto "Who Dares Wins" hangs above the main table at the ***Sayeret Mat'kal*** mess at their base "somewhere" in central Israel. As a rogue force, ***Sayeret Mat'kal*** was separate from the regular IDF and, in many ways, those serving in the unit (for all purposes), were released from regular active service. They were the best of the best, and had to earn that reputation behind enemy lines. ***Sayeret Mat'kal*** operates in small bands called a ***Tzevet*** or "team"; squads of a handful of men who are trained in virtually every facet of ground combat, expert in every weapon to be found in the Middle East, and capable of acting independent of the larger formation. "One of the truly remarkable aspects about ***Sayeret Mat'kal***," according to a former naval commando officer who worked with the unit on a very frequent basis many miles behind enemy lines, was how they prepared for an operation. It didn't matter how big their target was or how small, they studied it exhaustively. Each soldier knew his task, as well as that of the others on the mission. Every contingency was thought of and responses prepared--if a million things could go wrong with an operation, they would plan and be prepared for a million and one things to go wrong." ***Sayeret Mat'kal***'s absolute professional in the field and behind enemy lines brought results--that as a result of intelligence work they do, remain classified to this day. "If you don't hear about their exploits in the headlines," confides an officer in the IDF field security division, "it means that its business as usual with the unit."

When Arnan envisioned this force, he did not design a formation of robots and supermen--he knew that the men who would carry out such work and survive it all needed to be part war hero, part spy, part bastard and ten parts individualist! Discipline is high, but the unit tends to have its own book of rules. There are endless tales roaming through the IDF rumor mill of ***Mat'kal*** exploits--from beating up military policemen to stealing jeeps from generals. They are a confident and cocky bunch, and seem to operate in a universe different than the average soldier.

Virtually all of ***Sayeret Mat'kal***'s intelligence-gathering operations remain state secrets of the highest orders, although reports in non-Israeli publications have hinted that the unit "routinely" reconnoiters enemy lands--from Syria to Tunisia and Libya. One aspect--albeit an extremely limited one--of ***Sayeret Mat'kal***'s work that has reached the boundaries of public knowledge has been their anti-terrorist operations. Although not a part of their mandate, ***Sayeret Mat'kal*** inherited the role as the nation's primary hostage-rescue and retaliatory force when the hijackings and bombings entered the international vernacular following the 1967 Six Day War simply because there were no other units in either the army or national police force trained or sanctioned for hostage-rescue work. When Palestinian terrorists began hijacking first El Al aircraft, then the aircraft of other carriers flying to and from Israel, and taking the passengers hostage in exchange for the release of jailed comrades, the IDF General Staff could not send a force of eighteen-year-old infantrymen armed with FAL rifles and straight out of basic training to attempt a rescue, nor could it send older, more experienced, reservists--even if they were from airborne or reconnaissance units. Mossad or General Security Service agents might have been cunning, ultra-intelligent spies and counter-sleuths that could blend in as natives in the Arab or Warsaw Pact capitals, but could they kick down a door and shoot half a dozen terrorists before hostages were butchered? The men of ***Sayeret Mat'kal***, by the mandate of their specialized training, their meticulous professionalism, and the cold gut courage required for cross-border intelligence-gathering missions, had the metal required for hostage-rescue work. They were the IDF's best, could fire any weapon in the world, and were all airborne-qualified. By simply being who they were they won the job.

When Palestinian terrorists hijacked El Al flight 426 from Rome to Tel Aviv and diverted it to Algeria on July 22, 1968, the IDF General Staff prepared a contingency rescue operation similar to the rescue at Entebbe which would capture the world's imagination years later. According to the proposals, the IAF would land transport aircraft on the tarmac at Algiers Airport and unload a force of paratroopers and reconnaissance infantrymen; the soldiers would occupy the entire airport, destroy key communications facilities and the few MiG fighters of the Algerian Air Force stationed at the airport. Commandos from ***Sayeret Mat'kal*** were to then locate the terminal building where the hostages were being held, secure their release, and fly back to Israel on the lead transport aircraft. The mission, in its blue-print code-name form, was known as "Operation Ruth." It was considered too risky to try, too close to a tantamount invasion of Algeria for Israel's volatile political stature to survive.

***Sayeret Mat'kal***'s first "known" counter-terrorist operation was

A ***Sayeret Mat'kal*** operator removes one of the female hijackers, shot in the side by a .22 round, off of the hijacked Sabena 707 during the first moments of "Operation Isotope 1," May 9,1972. (IDF Spokesman)

Still wearing his white coveralls, ***Sayeret Mat'kal*** commander Lieutenant-Colonel Ehud Barak (until December 31, 1994 the IDF's fourteenth chief of staff) stands by the body of a dead terrorist, as other operators removed frightened and shaken former hostages to safety. (IDF Spokesman)

More hostages are evacuated from the rear door of the hijacked Sabena Boeing 707; the evacuation covered by a ***Sayeret Mat'kal*** operator carrying a Beretta .22 pistol. (IDF Spokesman)

May 15, 1974: Ma'alot, northern Israel. ***Sayeret Mat'kal*** operators assault the besieged schoolhouse in the attempt to rescue the 100 hostages held by three DFLP gunmen. (IGPO)

not a hostage-rescue but rather a measure of retaliation and deterrence. On December 26, 1968, Palestinian terrorists attacked an El Al jet at Athens International Airport. They attempted to seize the aircraft but when confronted by authorities simply sprayed it with machine gun and grenade fire killing one and wounding dozens. Israel had reached its limit with terrorist attacks launched against El Al, and it decided to act militarily--the when, who and how was not hard to find. Since most of the Arab terrorists attacking El Al aircraft in southern Europe had reached the continent via Beirut and Lebanon's Middle East Airlines, the target and the opportunity to exact a just revenge and a stirring warning could be fit into one neat and very symbolic operation. On the night of December 27, 1968, a heliborne force of ***Sayeret Mat'kal*** operators, along with a task force from the IDF's paratroop brigade's reconnaissance force (***Sayeret Tzanhanim***), ventured to Beirut International Airport and proceeded to blow up thirteen airliners belonging to Lebanon's Middle east Airlines (MEA); the Israelis took great pains not to kill anyone that night, but their destructive raid was felt throughout the Arab world. The raid was a retaliatory strike meant to punish and warn.

Other ***Sayeret Mat'kal*** missions with a message haven't been as benign. They have been spectacular and violent, lethal and historic. The most known spectacular ***Sayeret Mat'kal*** retaliatory and proactive counter-terrorist operations ever mounted include:

- "Operation Basket", the June 21, 1972, kidnapping of five Syrian General Staff officers who were supervising terrorist attacks along Israel's northern frontier. Although not an attack that made many headlines, it was as if, according to Colonel (Res.) Y., a retired special operations officer, "The Germans had kidnapped Eisenhower's staff prior to D-Day." The officers were later released in exchange for two Israeli pilots shot down over Syria months earlier.
- "Operation Spring of Youth", the April 9-10, 1973, raid against Black September in Beirut. "Operation Spring of Youth" was the culmination of Israel's covert war of elimination and revenge Black September for perpetrating the Munich Olympic Massacre, and according to foreign reports, ***Mat'kal*** operators were part of the infamous Mossad hit teams that roamed Europe and killed the three top leaders of Black September in their luxurious West Beirut apartments.
- According to published accounts, the Mossad and ***Sayeret Mat'kal*** ventured to Tunisia on April 16, 1988, to assassinate PLO deputy commander Abu Jihad in his Tunis home. In the true definition of Byzantine justice and coincidence, the man who Abu Jihad replaced as PLO military commander was Abu Yusef, killed in Beirut nearly fifteen years before to the day.
- ***Sayeret Mat'kal*** was also behind the July 31, 1989, kidnapping of ***Hizbollah*** commander Sheikh Abdel Karim Obeid from his lair of Jibchit in southern Lebanon, a move that eventually secured the released of all Western hostages from Lebanon several years later, as well as, four years later, the kidnapping of senior ***Hizbollah*** commander Mustafa Dirani, from his southern Lebanese lair. For these operations, ***Sayeret Mat'kal*** is issued with the most technologically advanced and superior equipment--from weapons to communications devices. According to one retired special operations officer, "They are years ahead of the Americans and Germans in their gear."
- Nineteen years after Operation Spring of Youth, many of those who were in Beirut that cool spring night, Mac-10s and Kalashnikovs in hand, were on a training ground in southern Israel. Although these men were older, more reserved and experienced then when they landed in Beirut, their connection to ***Sayeret Mat'kal*** and Israeli special operations were as intimate as ever. These former Chief of Staff's Boys were now, themselves, serving officers on the General's Staff--all were major-generals in charge of territorial commands, or corps, except for Lieutenant-General Ehud Barak, he was the IDF Chief of Staff. Israel's most decorated soldier (the true stories behind most of his medals for valor remain classified top-secret) Ehud Barak is a remarkable officer and gentlemen considered by many to be part "Rambo" and part James Bond; through his abilities behind enemy lines on a dark night, courage and uncanny charisma, Ehud Barak had personally guided ***Sayeret Mat'kal*** to excellence during the 1960s and 1970s, and had risen through the ranks to assume command of Israel's military. Former top-secret operatives now controlled the IDF, and it seemed obvious that ***Sayeret Mat'kal*** would be in the vanguard of Israel's secret campaign. On this November morning, ***Sayeret Mat'kal*** was once again attempting to breech the envelope of the imagination by taking enormous risks. In the late afternoon hours of Thursday, November 5, 1992, Israeli commuters heading home for the start of the Sabbath weekend found nothing but sad songs of mourning playing on their car radios. No explanation was given for the removal of folk tunes and rock ballads from the airwaves, but none was really needed--somber music on every station on the dial meant only one thing in a nation where soldiers died on an all too regular basis. Earlier that day, in the sandy hills of the Negev Desert training base called Tze'elim, five soldiers, all twenty-year-old conscripts, had been killed in a training accident and six others seriously hurt; "somebody" received the order to fire a live warhead it is believed, a secretly modified wire-guided antitank guided projectile, when the exercises were still in their dry stage. It was a horrendous error leading to tragic loss of life. All armies train with live ammunition, and accidents will happen, but this accident, according to foreign reports,[1] occurred during no ordinary maneuvers, and it happened to no ordinary unit--it happened to ***Sayeret Mat'kal***! At first, the army tried to hush up the incident and

Under incredible small arms and grenade fire, ***Sayeret Mat'kal*** operators evacuate wounded students as additional units enter the battle. (IDF Spokesman)

Stretcher bearers bring in a wounded ***Sayeret Mat'kal*** operator to an aid station following the bloody and still controversial rescue bid at the Ma'alot schoolhouse, May 15, 1974. (IDF Spokesman)

downplay the exercises as "routine," yet the words "***Sayeret Mat'kal***" were in a headline, and it meant serious news. ***"Who was really there?" "What were they training for?" "What was the unit preparing to do?"*** The following day, the Miami Herald and London's Guardian reported that the training maneuvers in Tze'elim was a dry run for a ***Sayeret Mat'kal*** operation to be mounted later that night, in conjunction with the Israeli Air Force and the Mossad in Beirut whose objective was the kidnapping or assassination of Sheikh Hassan Nasrallah, the man who succeeded Sheikh Abbas Musawi as ***Hizbollah*** commander when Musawi was killed by Israel Air Force (IAF) helicopter gunships in February 1992. The subsequent controversy resulted in the censure of several foreign journalists and a re-examination of Israel's censorship laws; ***Sayeret Mat'kal*** is a unit that by its very nature survives off of its absolute anonymity and the public scrutiny was most unwelcome. The controversy wasn't over, however. According to reports leaked to the London Sunday Times, the ***Sayeret Mat'kal*** team training in the desert that crisp November morning was performing a dress-rehearsal dry run for an operation that was even bolder and more audacious than a venture into ***Hizbollah***-controlled West Beirut. This raid would make history, and perhaps change the political map of the region forever: ***Sayeret Mat'kal*** was heading to Baghdad in an operation that would have targeted Iraqi strongman Saddam Hussein himself. The State of Israel was about to exact payback for the thirty-nine SCUD missiles that landed in Israel during the 1991 Gulf War and ***Sayeret Mat'kal*** was to be its messengers of vengeance. According to headlines in the London Sunday Times, operators were to be transported into Baghdad with the support of Mossad agents, and target Saddam Hussein with a "newly developed body-heat seeking missile" that the Israelis had developed; in fact, according to the report, it was this missile that fatally slammed into the team of operators. "The accident saved Saddam's life," a senior Israeli official was quoted in the Sunday Times, because chances of success hinged on one, ***very specific opportunity***, to get Saddam.

***Sayeret Mat'kal*** is a national enigma. It is such a mystery, shrouded in secrecy, myth and folklore. The unit is considered a cut above the norm of human behavior, and even regulation military behavior--according to one junior ***Mat'kal*** officer, "The army hasn't even written manuals or regulations for what we do!" They do the work, sometimes spectacular and sometimes unsavory, that no other unit in the IDF can perform. Interestingly enough, it was hostage-rescue operations that would separate ***Sayeret Mat'kal*** from the special forces of its time and even the specialized counter-terrorist units of today. Because they are a military unit, one with acceptable casualties and an offensive strategy behind their operational doctrine, they have entered situations that most units would shy away from or wouldn't even be tasked to execute in the first place. Among their most spectacular operations are:

- "Operation Isotope 1", the May 9, 1972 rescue of nearly 100 passengers on board a hijacked Sabena Belgian Airlines Boeing 707 at Lod Airport by ***Mat'kal*** commandos who, dressed in white coveralls, stormed the aircraft masquerading as airline mechanics--one ***Mat'kal*** commando wounded in this ground-breaking hostage-rescue mission was a young lieutenant named Benjamin "Bibi" Netanyahu, today the leader of the Likud. In the operation, two terrorists were killed by the commandos, including the PFLP gunman who hijacked El Al 426 back in July 1968, and two female terrorists were seriously wounded and taken into custody. "Operation Isotope 1" was the world's first commando rescue of passengers trapped on board a hijacked airliner and would set the precedent-emulated later in Mogadishu, in Thailand and in Marseilles.
- The rescue attempt of 100 hostages, mainly schoolchildren, being held at a schoolhouse in the northern Israeli town of Ma'alot on May 14, 1974. Three Palestinian terrorists from Nayif Hawatmeh's Democratic Front for the Liberation of Palestine (DFLP) seized a schoolhouse in Ma'alot and 100 students hostage, and threatened to kill the children unless hundreds of Palestinians in Israeli jails were released. The Israeli government of Prime Minister Golda Meir, unflinching in the national stance to negotiate with terrorists, ordered ***Sayeret Mat'kal*** to attempt a rescue. The attack met with stiff resistance and difficulties and several ***Mat'kal*** mistakes--the assault used overbearing firepower instead of selective tactical prowess, the attack force miscalculated the proper hiding place of the terrorists, and the terrorists turned their weapons on the hostages instead of the oncoming ***Sayeret Mat'kal*** operators. In the ensuing bloodbath, twenty-six hostages were killed and over sixty critically wounded. The failed raid resulted in the Israeli government turning internal security and counter-terrorism over to the National Police and saw to the creation of the police hostage-rescue force, the ***Ya'ma'm***.
- The March 7, 1975, assault on Tel Aviv's seaside Savoy Hotel, seized by Black September terrorists. A ***Sayeret Mat'kal*** rescue raid was successful, but a former unit commander leading the assault, Colonel Uzi Ya'iri, was killed in the raid, and the terrorists succeeded in detonating explosive booby-traps they had hidden throughout the building.
- The July 3-4, 1976, "Operation Thunderball", of course, is the most famous commando raid in history--the substance of legend, mystique and endless Hollywood treatment. On June 27, 1976, an Air France flight from Tel Aviv to Paris via Athens was hijacked to Entebbe, Uganda, by a mixed force of German and Palestinian terrorists acting with the full collusion of Ugandan strongman Idi Amin and his military. When the terrorists performed their symbolic

March 7, 1975: The Tel Aviv shorefront, Savoy Hotel. ***Sayeret Mat'kal*** operators inch their way closer to the besieged hotel hours before the rescue attempt was mounted. (IGPO)

July 3, 1976: Israeli Prime Minister Yitzhak Rabin (center) talks to the ***Sayeret Mat'kal*** operators who are about to embark on history and attempt the rescue of the 103 Israeli and Jewish hostages held by the PFLP in Entebbe. (IDF Spokesman)

***Selektion***, separation of the 103 Jewish and Israeli hostages from those that were eventually released, Israel had to react; the ***Selektion*** brought back images of the Holocaust and Israel had to act decisively before Jews were once again readied for the slaughter. In a courageous decision, the Israeli government despatched ***Sayeret Mat'kal*** (along with several other commando units) to Africa. Following a brutal eight hour flight inside the bellies of an armada of Hercules transport aircraft, the Israelis landed undetected at Entebbe. The ***Mat'kal*** commandos, masquerading as Idi Amin's bodyguards (Black Mercedes and all) managed to eliminate the terrorists and rescue the hostages. Typifying the "follow me" ethic of command that was perfected in ***Sayeret Mat'kal*** and similar units, ***Mat'kal*** commander Lieutenant-Colonel Jonathan "Yoni" Netanyahu, Benjamin Netanyahu's brother, was killed leading the task force. He was the sole Israeli combat fatality.

- The April 6, 1980 rescue of over twenty schoolchildren from a nursery in Kibbutz Misgav Am in northern Israel along the Lebanese frontier; the Kibbutz was raided by terrorists from the Iraqi-based Arab Liberation Front. A combined force of commandos from ***Sayeret Golani*** (the reconnaissance force from the 1st ***Golani*** Infantry Brigade) and ***Sayeret Mat'kal*** stormed the nursery where the terrorists were held up and killed them; tragically, a two-year-old girl was killed by the terrorists, as was a Kibbutz worker and a ***Golani*** soldier.
- On April 12, 1984, three Palestinian terrorists hijacked a bus traveling from Tel Aviv's central bus station to the southern coastal city of Ashdod. Just outside the Gaza Strip, the bus was stopped by police and a stand-off ensued. Although the ***Ya'ma'm*** was summoned to the scene and readied for action, the OC IDF Southern Command wanted ***Sayeret Mat'kal*** to handle the incident. At 04:43 hours on the morning of April 13, the assault began with a multitude of 7.62mm sniper rounds killing one terrorist; the subsequent storming of the bus resulted in the capture of two terrorists and the death of one hostage, a female Israeli soldier named Irit Portugez. A footnote to the operation: the two captured terrorists were later taken to a secluded citrus grove by ***Shin Bet*** (General Security Service) agents and subsequently murdered.

***Sayeret Mat'kal***'s impact on the entire Israel Defense Forces has been profound--they have served as a beacon of excellence which the remainder of the army has emulated. This is, perhaps, best expressed by the fact that Lieutenant-General Ehud Barak, a former Chief of Staff's Boy, was the commander of the IDF from 1991-1995; when he assumed the post in April 1991, he quickly appointed his fellow ***Sayeret Mat'kal*** comrades, such as Major-General Danny Yatom, and Major-General Amiram Levine, all men with extraordinary ability and decorated--albeit top-secret--pasts, to General Staff posts. Like Ehud Barak, Major-General Levine spent virtually his entire military career in ***Sayeret Mat'kal***, not leaving the unit until he concluded a most distinguished tour as the unit commander. Like Barak, Levine was also in Beirut that April night in 1973, dressed in drag as a blonde bombshell, with his Mac-10. Levine, like many those who are part of the ***Sayeret Mat'kal*** mystique, was considered one of the nation's finest. Wounded four times in action and decorated, he participated in countless operations with the unit, including the victorious rescue of the passengers on the hijacked Sabena aircraft in 1972, as well as the tragic rescue attempt of the Ma'alot schoolhouse in 1974; in March 1975, he saw one of his best friends, former unit commander Uzi Ya'iri, killed in Tel Aviv's Savoy Hotel, seized by a Black September suicide squad, and assaulted by ***Sayeret Mat'kal***. He was the man who replaced "Yoni" as ***Sayeret*** commander following Entebbe, and was, in fact, given Yoni's helmet and web gear to carry on the mantle.

Among the world's counter-terrorist and special operations units, few have been clouded in secrecy as have ***Sayeret Mat'kal***. Little is known of the weaponry they carry, other than the unit prefers the Soviet-built AK-47 7.62mm assault rifle, and the Mini-Uzi 9m submachine gun. Little information is available on the unit's foreign contacts, though it is known, through foreign sources, that the unit does maintain contacts with the U.S. Army's 1st SFOD-D.

When an Israeli adolescent turns seventeen, he is sent to a military center to undergo a series of physical and psycho-technical examinations. The data will determine which teenagers-soon-to-be-conscripts will be allowed to volunteer for pilot courses or an elite reconnaissance units. Upon conscription, those with special skills or talents are allowed to volunteer for various elite units--many dream of becoming F-15 pilots, others can taste becoming a ***Sayeret Mat'kal*** operator and are determined to make the most of this once in a lifetime chance.

At first, all volunteers participate in a ***Gibush,*** or test period, where for a period of one week they are subjected to incredible hardships and challenges. Those who show potential, leadership and charisma, as well as those who display determination and grittiness, are allowed to begin their lengthy and arduous training. Being accepted into the ***Mat'kal*** program does not guarantee earning their reconnaissance wings; the attrition rate is believed to be beyond 90%. The training includes the basic paratroopers basic training, jump school, and then a classified period of (according to foreign reports) highly specialized instruction in all aspects of weaponry, reconnaissance, communications, surveillance, and other "black" aspects of special warfare. ***Sayeret Mat'kal*** operators are expected to be able to march for hundreds of kilometers, know how to operate virtually every weapon to be found, and be expert cold-killers.

As a result of the prestige and status involved in being a ***Sayeret Mat'kal*** operator, many teenagers begin their physical conditioning in body-building programs when they are fifteen and sixteen. "It is all a waste of time," quips one former ***Mat'kal*** officer, "what the unit is looking for is a mental strength, not bulging biceps. What we want you are born with--pure and simple!"

The IDF's other counter-terrorist unit is the ***Mista'arvim,*** or Undercover Arabists--a lethal force of undercover commandos who masquerade as Arabs to infiltrate towns and villages in order to capture wanted terrorists, and assault their known strongholds. These undercover units were the byproduct of the Palestinian Intifadah, the extremely violent--and ongoing--popular uprising that erupted in December 1987, and resulted in the deaths of over one thousand Arabs and several hundred Israelis. Israel attempted conventional, albeit violent, means to suppress the Intifadah although these strong arm tactics proved ineffective against mob rule, and ended up gaining the Palestinians incredible press and worldwide sympathy and support. The Intifadah was a public relations nightmare for Israel and especially its army, the Israel Defense Forces (IDF), and it needed to be stopped. Then Defense Minister Rabin allowed the IDF to use deadly force against rock-throwing demonstrators and even ordered Israeli soldiers to "break their bones," but the mightiest army in the region couldn't break the will of the uprising. A year into the struggle of stone-throwing youths against tear-gas and rubber-bullet firing soldiers, the IDF General Staff realized unconventional means were required to restore law and order and two Arabist undercover units were eventually sanctioned: one known as ***Duvdevan***, or "Cherry," was responsible for the West Bank, and ***Shimshon***, "Samson," would ply its trade in the crowded squalor of the Gaza Strip. To the Israeli leadership, the Arabists, or undercover units, were a vital strike force that worked hand-in-hand with agents from the GSS in defeating the unstoppable terror. Because of their tactics, and because of the close-knit relationship with the GSS, they are undoubtedly Israel's most controversial military unit. Their tactics are, indeed, unconventional but their results in the field have been irrefutably decisive. Many observers, both Palestinian and Israeli, credit the Arabist units with breaking the back of the uprising by compromising the Palestinian's sense of security among their own. The undercover units first broke the back of Fatah, the military wing of Arafat's PLO and the Popular Front for the Liberation of Palestine (PFLP) by capturing known commanders, and then humbled the Islamic fundamentalists of Hamas by identifying, locating and either apprehending or killing most of the organization's leadership. The undercover units were not thrown into the chaotic mix of the Intifadah--they were never meant to chase down stone throwing kids into secluded alleyways or apprehend masked youths spray-painting political slogans on a wall. These commandos were to target the men who ran the uprising--the faction commanders, those who carried weapons, and those who killed. Those known to have killed Israelis or Palestinians accused of collaborating with the Israeli security forces received priority attention; in the six years of uprising over 1,000 Arabs were murdered by other Arabs on suspicion of cooperation with the Israeli authorities. The undercover units do not fire rubber bullets or hurl tear gas canisters. Their firepower is lethal: 9mm automatics, Uzi submachine guns, and CAR-15 5.56mm assault rifles. If they produce their weapons, they intend to use them with devastating and deadly accuracy. Over the course of the Intifadah, they have arrested hundreds of known gunmen, and killed several dozens foolish enough to resist.

Lieutenant-Colonel Yonatan "Yoni" Netanyahu, ***Sayeret Mat'kal*** commander and the lone IDF fatality of Entebbe. (IDF Spokesman)

July, 4, 1976: At Tel Aviv's Bet Sokolov Press Center, IDF Chief Paratroop and Infantry Officer Brigadier-General Dan Shomron briefs an amazed press corps as to the details that can be released on the just completed "Operational Thunderball" rescue. (IDF Spokesman)

One such man was twenty-four-year-old Imad Aqal--truly Israel's most wanted fugitive. A commander of the ***Izzadine al-Qassam*** Brigade, the military arm of the fundamentalist Hamas**,** Aqal was a legendary figure in Gaza for his role in the murder of eleven Israeli soldiers, one Israeli civilian and the brutal butchery of four Palestinians suspected of collaborating. Known to march around the side-streets of Gaza with the Galil assault rifle he lifted from the bleeding corpse of a dying Israeli servicemen, Aqal was what both the Israelis and PLO considered a threat to the peace-process. To D. and his comrades in the Samson unit, Aqal was a target that everyone knew would not allow himself to be taken alive. On a cool windswept morning, on November 24, 1993, Aqal was killed in a shoot-out with a Samson unit fire team. He had once said that he hoped to go to paradise after a shoot-out with Israeli forces. His wish came true, and days of subsequent violence followed. Peace in Gaza was in desperate peril.

The undercover units' penchant for firepower and being the judge, jury and executioner of many of the men they seek has prompted many to label them a covert force of cold-blooded assassins; Palestinians and international human rights groups have labeled the units as nothing more than "costumed hit men." Various Israeli political parties--including Knesset members, parents of soldiers serving in these units, and human rights organizations active in Israel--have long since called for the disbanding of these covert forces. Yet it can be argued, however, that by humbling the brain and the brawn of the Intifadah by targeting--***and hitting***--its leadership and henchmen (killing the snake by chopping off its head and removing its fangs), the undercover units actually won the Intifadah for Israel and convinced the PLO that uncontrolled mob violence would not win a homeland for the Palestinian people.

For years, the existence of the undercover units was probably the worst kept secrets of the Intifadah. The Palestinians had known about the existence of these units because they saw them operate on a daily

The IAF C-130 ferrying home the ***Sayeret Mat'kal*** operators touches down at Lod Airport, July 4, 1976. (IDF Spokesman)

Idi Amin's black Mercedes is off-loaded in Israel by victorious ***Sayeret Mat'kal*** operators. Note operators wearing Syrian-pattern lizard pattern camouflage used to impersonate the PFLP terrorists. (IDF Spokesman)

basis. Israeli censors tried to stop reports of these units from being publishing, but slowly news stories about their activities were leaked by the foreign media. The Israeli public, in fact, only learned of the existence of the units one Friday night in June 1991, when Israeli television, with the blessing of IDF Chief of Staff Lieutenant-General Ehud Barak, aired a thirty-minute documentary on the Samson and Cherry units, disclosing for the first time the fact that such units actually existed, as well as showing the incredible tactics employed by these masquerading commandos. Young men were shown dressing as women and as farmers and producing high-powered submachine guns from beneath their robes, and then unleashing accurate 9mm bursts into the centers of cardboard targets. The documentary showed actual footage of undercover unit members making arrests, and openly and candidly discussing their roles in this covert and nasty little war. Perhaps, in retrospect, airing the show may have been part of an exercise in psychological warfare intended to induce feelings of high uncertainty among wanted Palestinians; for fugitives, the knowledge than an old woman--***any*** old woman--moving slowly through the village alleyways might be a heavily armed Israeli commando was daunting. Lieutenant-General Barak, himself Israel's most decorated soldier and former commander of the ultra top-secret ***Sayeret Mat'kal*** General Staff Reconnaissance Unit, commented on the exposure and contended that "there is no room in the army for units that have denied existence, when the adversary knows what they do. The very existence of this denial combined with their shrouded operations might create a situation very detrimental to the soldiers themselves and might effect their service in the field." Following the televised report, Israeli intelligence officers were shocked to find an increasing number of wanted Palestinians turning themselves in to security forces out of fear that they would become the target of the undercover units.

Although made famous, or infamous as some claim, as a result of their operations in the Intifadah, Israelis have been disguising themselves as Arabs for nearly a hundred years in the unstoppable cycle of violence of the Arab-Israeli conflict. A ***Mista'arev*** is someone who isn't an Arab by origin, but due to various reasons dresses in Arab garb, acts in accordance with Arab manners and customs, speaks Arabic, and lives where most of the population is Arab. The term ***Mista'arvim*** is derived from the Arabic expression of ***Musta'arvim***, meaning "intervening." Jewish ***Mista'arvim*** date back to 1909 and the "***Shomer***," an organization designed to provide security to the first Jewish settlements in Palestine. Shomer guards rode Arabian horses, dressed in traditional Arab garments, and learned to speak fluent Arabic to not only gain the respect of their neighbors, but also gather intelligence. The Haganah, the primary military arm of the Jewish settlements in pre-independence Israel, created its own Arabist intelligence unit during the bloody Arab revolt of 1936-39, when agents in Arab garb were despatched to infiltrate local Arab villages. During the Second World War, a Haganah ***Mista'arvim*** platoon called "the Syrian Company" was set up with British support to carry out sabotage missions deep behind Vichy lines in Syria and Lebanon. Most of the volunteers to this small, though unique unit, were of Oriental descent--men whose families had come from the Arab Diaspora and who were fluent in Arabic and Arab customs. Commanded by Captain N. N. Hammond, an eccentric British intelligence officer and professor of Greek history at Cambridge, the Syrian Company received extensive small arms, sharp-shooting, demolition, communications, and hand-to-hand combat training, as well intensive Arab language, customs and culture instructions. The cadets were also taught how to assimilate in Arab populations; many practiced in the Arab town of Jaffa, a suburb south of Tel Aviv. Another ***Mista'arvim*** company was "***Shachar,***" or "Dawn," more a force of intelligence plants than commandos, who penetrated large work sites; they also opened small cover businesses and peddler stands in Arab markets to camouflage their activities. Many of these agents transferred to the GSS and the Mossad, to carry out intelligence-gathering and special operations.

Yet until the eruption of the Intifadah, the unit that wrote the rule book for undercover tactics was a small and unheralded entity known as ***Rimon*** or "Pomegranate." Created in 1970 by the rambunctious and controversial O/C Southern Command at the time, Major-General Ariel "Arik" Sharon, "Pomegranate" would prove to be as revolutionary as they were decisively effective. For three years following the 1967 Six Day War victory and capture of the Gaza Strip from Egypt, Israel ruled the densely populated squalor in name only. Heavily armed terrorists openly carried their weapons through the streets and alleyways of the strip and its refugee camps, and bloody attacks against Israeli soldiers and civilians were daily occurrences. The mighty IDF, an army that only a few years back humbled the entire Arab world, could not conquer a few hundred hard core terrorists. "Pomegranate Recon" was formed to change the equation. A small force of only a few dozen men, Pomegranate Recon was commanded by a visionary special operations officer named Captain Meir Dagan, who realized that conventional means could never defeat an unconventional army. Together with a concentrated effort by the GSS, Captain Dagan and his men became what they hunted--"When you are in Gaza act like you are from Gaza" was a unit catch phrase. Unit operators not only dressed as local Arabs, but even disguised

Jubilant former hostages emerge from the cargo hold of an IAF C-130 after their epic and truly remarkable rescue raid at Entebbe. (IDF Spokesman)

themselves as terrorists, moving through populated areas clutching Soviet-made assault rifles. They infiltrated the terrorists' world by eating in their restaurants, shopping in their markets, even staking out their whore houses. They made the terrorists uneasy and unsure of their own backyard--never to know who to trust, where to walk, and when they'd be attacked. In one year, "Pomegranate Recon" crushed the terrorist uprising in Gaza. They killed those who were armed (and some who weren't), destroyed intelligence networks, and blew up terrorist safe houses and arms caches; they even blew up caves and left terrorists trapped inside for eternity. As a result of many operations that remain classified even to this day, Pomegranate Recon brought a subdued peace to Gaza that lasted until the eruption of the Intifadah. Their operations were effective without being controversial; in the days before CNN and satellite links, few people around the world cared about what went on in the strip. The burly and rambunctious "Arik" Sharon is reported to have led many "Pomegranate" missions personally. Arab sources claim that the unit killed hundreds.

When the Intifadah erupted in December 1987, the IDF hoped to replicate this unit's success by creating two new undercover units employing similar tactics.

Even before the Palestinian uprising began, then O/C Central Command and today's Chief of Staff, Ehud Barak, felt that the IDF needed a special operations element inside the territories. In early 1987, months before the world knew what an Intifadah was, he decided to establish an undercover ***Mista'arvim*** unit that would operate in the West Bank as a covert intelligence and reconnaissance entity; this unit would be known as "Cherry." The first soldiers in the unit, all volunteers, were graduates of the Paratrooper Brigade's squad commanders' course, and were later given a complete undercover instruction regimen including a "disguise course," counter-terrorist training, and intensive instruction in Arabic and Palestinian customs. A second undercover unit, responsible for the Gaza Strip, was formed a year later at the height of the uprising. Because of the difficulty in apprehending known and wanted terrorists in an area as dense and ripe for violence as the Gaza Strip, a struggle of what was considered biblical proportions, that ***Mista'arvim*** unit would be known as ***Shimshon*** or "Samson," after the biblical hero who fought the Philistines in Gaza. The unit was nurtured by Major-General Yitzhak Mordechai, a legendary and highly decorated no-nonsense paratroop officer, who was the O/C Southern Command at the time.

Contrary to public conception, the men who volunteer into Israel's three undercover units are not bloodthirsty killers looking to avenge any past Palestinian act of terrorism, but rather ordinary eighteen year old conscripts looking for a challenge in their three years of mandatory military service. Extensive psychological profiles are compiled on all volunteers, and anyone not deemed 100% stable is prohibited from even trying out for the units. According to an interview on Israeli Army radio, senior Samson unit commanders admitted that they also screen out volunteers who might have strong right-wing political beliefs. In fact, any soldier who has had a family member hurt or killed in the Intifadah is automatically disqualified from volunteering into the unit. Much like the eager conscripts who want to prove their worth when entering the IDF by trying out for pilot's course, or volunteering to join one of the many elite reconnaissance units, volunteering for an undercover unit is also a measure of one's capabilities. Most of the volunteers come from the country's Kibbutzim and Moshavim collective farms. The qualities sought after in a ***Mista'arvim*** candidate are more mental than physical, explains one Israeli special operations officer. "Any number of young kids have the physical where-with-all to parachute out of an airplane, run for twenty kilometers at a stretch, or march up a mountain with fifty kilograms on his back, but only a small minority of men have the mental stamina to learn to how assume a foreign identity, cultivate it into a believable act, and then combine these acting and intelligence skills with that of a proficient special operations commando." "Being a ***Mista'arev*** is a state of mind", claims Sergeant Y., a Samson unit team leader. "Sure I am trained to leap out of a vehicle and in a split second have my weapon trained on a wanted terrorist, but if I cannot pass myself as one of them, I am not worth the costume I am issued with. I have to know how to talk like them, look like them, eat like them, laugh like them and even smell like them. I must know that if an old women passes me in street I must respectfully move to the left, and if an old man passes me, I should greet him with the words '***Salaam, Aleikum***.' I must think in Arabic, react in Arabic, and ensure that the masquerade remains strong until the green light is given, my weapon is produced, and my true identity is finally compromised to the locals. If I get out of character for even one small second before the mission begins, I not only endanger myself and my team, but the back-up force and a lot of innocent Palestinians who could wind up in the middle of a fire fight. My acting abilities won't earn my an Academy award, but it will save lives and reduce the need for firepower to its absolute minimum." A good undercover unit mission is one where no shots are fired!

The training course for a ***Mista'arev*** is extremely lengthy, and is dedicated to intelligence work, the art of masquerading, the "Arabization" of the fighter (from learning traditional customs and culture to intensive language instruction). The undercover candidates are immersed in everything and anything Palestinian--from the slang used by common laborers to the words to nationalistic songs broadcast on the PLO's Radio Monte Carlo. Arabic cannot be second nature, it must be a primary persona. They must think in Arabic, react in Arabic, and functions as Arabs; many trainees return home on leave only to find themselves talking to parents and friends in Arabic. Only once the operator has mastered his new identity can intensive close-quarter combat instruction commence. Soldiers are taught to burst into buildings or vehicle, and to overcome armed individuals with speed rather than firepower, surprise rather than brute force. All undercover unit operators are expert marksman, proficient in the martial arts, and recipients of advanced medical and communications training; all undercover operators are equipped with sophisticated communications equipment in various sizes which enable the soldiers to maintain communication links among themselves and with backup forces and command centers, even at long ranges.

A reconnaissance trooper peers through the sights of his Glilon 5.56mm SAR equipped with a laser-aim point device, a piece of equipment used, according to foreign reports, by ***Sayeret Mat'kal*** during the April 16, 1988, assassination of Abu Jihad in Tunis. (Courtesy: IT Lasers)

Before every operation, from an assault on a targeted home to a simple reconnaissance assignment, the undercover team always meet the regular soldiers of the rescue force face to face. The rescue force, heavily armed and wearing body armor, is briefed, and told when to and not open fire. Bitter experience has shown that being mistaken as a Palestinian can have tragic consequences. Many ***Mista'arvim*** operators have been too good at their trade for their own good. On July 10th 1992, a "Cherry" team went into action in the evening, to capture a gang of armed wanted men in the village Barta'a, in north Samaria. According to intelligence provided by the GSS, the wanted men, all ranking members of Hamas, gathered nightly in the village mosque for prayers. Lieutenant-Colonel A., the commander of the unit and a former commander of the IDF's Counter-Terrorist School, led the operation personally. Reaching the mosque in several vehicles with Palestinian license plates, the operators approached the mosque from different directions in order to block all possible escape routes. In the middle of the operation, Lieutenant-Colonel A. improvised his assault plan, and without informing the remainder of the assault squad ordered Sergeant Eli Isha, dressed as an Arab teenager, to move away from his original position to a spot several yards closer to the mosque entrance. Moments later, Sergeant Isha was cut down by fellow undercover soldiers who mistook the "armed Arab teenager" inside their fire zone as a justified target. "We thought that one of the wanted men identified us and was going to open fire on us," said N., a unit team leader, in a broken voice to investigating officers following the incident, "and we were horrified to find one of our own laying dead." Lieutenant-Colonel A. was brought up on charges following the incident in a closed-door proceeding.

The very sensitive national and military mandate that these young men--as well as their experienced commanding officers--are entrusted to execute takes its inevitable and sometimes tragic human toll. Casualties in the units have been considerable. The fact that soldiers are killed in action by terrorists, as well as in tragic friendly fire incidents compounds a sense of isolation and danger among the operators. Unlike "regular army" combat troops who train for war and only occasionally are rotated to the territories for Intifadah duty, the undercover soldiers risk it on the line day after day in a never-ending war, and they constantly find themselves under the enemy's gun, the media's scrutiny, and the contempt of many politicians.

From early 1988 to the September 13, 1993 signing of the peace accords between Yasir Arafat and Israeli Prime Minister Yitzhak Rabin, the effectiveness of the undercover units is unparalleled. The list of fugitive and known terrorists wanted in 1990, for example,

***Sayeret Mat'kal*** operators re-enact the rescue of the children hostages from the nursery at Kibbutz Misgav Am, April 6, 1980, after an attack by terrorists from the Iraqi-based Arab Liberation Front. (IDF Spokesman)

included hundreds of names in the West Bank alone--by 1993, only a few dozen names remained on "West Bank's Most Wanted." Many terrorists preferred to surrender to security forces, or escape to Jordan and Egypt rather than find themselves behind the cross-hairs of an undercover soldier's weapon. The peace accords signed in Washington, however, promise to realign the equation one final and bloody time. As the fundamentalists regroup for the eruption of a holy war against both the Israelis and Palestinians allied to Yasir Arafat, terrorism and bloodshed is likely to increase dramatically. If the peace process should progress as expected, and Palestinian self-rule come to the territories, it is logical to assume that the ***Mista'arvim*** units would disband. Logic, however, has never been a currency of reliable value in the Middle East.

Other IDF units that have also participated in counter-terrorist operations, especially preventative measures and retaliatory strikes, include Flotilla 13, the IDF/Navy's naval special warfare unit; ***Sayeret Tzanhanim***, the conscript paratroop brigade's reconnaissance unit; ***Sayeret Golani***, the 1st Golani Infantry Brigade's reconnaissance force; ***Sayeret Giva'ati***, the Giva'ati Brigade's reconnaissance unit; and, ***Yechidat Shaldag,*** a special operations aviation unit that is considered top-secret, but whose activities resemble those of the U.S. Army's 160th Special Operations Aviation Regiment (Airborne).

[1] Like many ***Mat'kal*** operations, Israel has never acknowledged that the unit involved in the accident in Tze'elim was, indeed, ***Sayeret Mat'kal***, even though a storm of foreign reports--and leaked quotes from anonymous Israeli officers--confirm this speculation to be fact.

# Israel - Border Guard and Police Units

The Israeli Police patch.

The Israeli Police Border Guard patch.

The *Ya'ma'm* wings.

The Israeli Police headgear badge.

Few nations on earth have endured the bloody wrath of the modern phenomenon known as terrorism as has the State of Israel. The Jewish State has been ***the*** principal target for every existing Palestinian and Islamic fundamentalist terrorist organization, not to mention the likes of the Provisional IRA, the German Red Army Faction, the Japanese Red Army and Italy's Red Brigades. This multi-national terrorist army has struck on the four corners of the globe, from the West Bank town of Ramallah to the Eucalyptus tree-lined streets of Tel Aviv, from Munich and Manhattan, to Buenos Aires and Bangkok. These irregular warfare specialists, state-sponsored mercenaries for causes, religions or national ambitions, have declared the entire world their battlefield, and so, too, have the Israelis. Few nations on earth have invested as heavily, or have become as expert, in the art of counter-terrorism and hostage-rescue as have the special forces of the Israel Defense Forces (IDF) and the Israel National Police. Many experts in the world consider them to be the world's finest. These units have been both offensive and reactive in nature, and have written the book on how a nation can develop and foster military and police units into a cohesive anvil through which to strike at and defeat terrorism.

Being among the world's best and most experienced units doesn't take into consideration the risk of such work. The true invariable of Murphy's Law that takes over the most ingenious rescue plan, the uncontrollable phenomenon that allows the unexpected and the bizarre to destroy the most meticulously planned and executed plan to go wrong, is a fundamental reality to the very risk of counter-terrorist and hostage-rescue operations. Sometimes, such as in the Sabena rescue of 1972, all the phases of the operation "gel" together in such a way that the mission, from beginning to end, is executed perfectly with the terrorists being either killed or captured and the hostages freed; casualties, if kept to an absolute minimum in both innocent dead and wounded, can still be considered a victory. In Entebbe, the most meticulous of preparation, innovation and actual execution allowed for the rescue for over 100 hostages, but also resulted in hostages suffering casualties and the commander of the mission, Lieutenant-Colonel

A *Ya'ma'm* superintendent, identity still withheld for security reasons, removes the web gear from dead female terrorist Dalal Mughrabi, after the deadly Country Club Massacre on March 11, 1978. (IGPO)

Yonatan "Yoni" Netanyahu, being killed. Then, there are operations like the October 14, 1994, raid to rescue Corporal Nachshon Waxman, an Israeli soldier kidnapped by Hamas terrorists. Sometimes, operations characterized by the best of intentions and most remarkable displays of heroism are thwarted by fate and bad luck.

Nineteen-year-old Corporal Nachshon was kidnapped by Hamas terrorists while hitch-hiking on October 9, 1994, as he headed toward his girlfriend's home near Jerusalem from his basic training base in the West Bank; the kidnappers, it had been reported were dressed as Hasidic Jews. In a gruesome video-tape released two days after the abduction, the kidnappers (masked in kefiyeh headdress and brandishing weapons) demanded the released of Sheikh Ahmed Yassin, the paralyzed spiritual leader of Hamas jailed since 1989 for planning the kidnapping and murder of two Israeli soldiers, and 200 other Palestinian and Lebanese prisoners. Then, the kidnappers put the camera on a dazed and frightened Waxman, and allowed him to read from a prepared statement. As if speaking to Prime Minister Yitzhak Rabin personally, Nachshon said, "I ask you to do all you can do so I can get out of here alive." If the terrorists' demands were not met by Friday night October 14, at 21:00 hours, Waxman would be executed.

Soldiers had been kidnapped by terrorists before and they had

***Ya'ma'm*** personnel hone their climbing skills at a tower at the unit's home base in central Israel. (Courtesy: Israel Police)

***Ya'ma'm*** instructors and officers engage in ***Krav Maga*** training. Great emphasis is placed on martial arts and cold-killing. (Courtesy: Israel Police)

been murdered in cold blood. But this case was difference. The release of the video-tape struck at the very soul of the Israeli conscience; all Israelis, after all, serve in the military, and this could have been anyone of them--their fathers, brothers, and sons. Politically, the kidnapping was a volatile tripwire that threatened to end the peace deal between Israel and the PLO. At first, all eyes turned to the Gaza Strip and the spiritual Mecca for Hamas and its followers. The Israelis, already launching a massive intelligence effort by themselves, warned that they might just invade the Strip--again--in order to look for Corporal Waxman and his abductors. With little choice, PLO Chairman Yasir Arafat unleashed virtually the entire 9,500-man Palestinian Police force in a dragnet against Hamas; 300 militants were subsequently arrested and interrogated. The mood in Israel, meanwhile, was turning from grim to desperate. Corporal Waxman's parents had issued heart-wrenching pleas to his kidnappers, and on a cool and somber Thursday night, 50,000 worshippers prayed at the Wailing Wall in Jerusalem for Waxman's safe release.

On Friday October 19, as the deadline neared, the Israelis received intelligence that Corporal Waxman was not being held in the Gaza Strip, but rather in the ***Israeli-controlled*** West Bank, in a safe-house in the village of Bir Nabal,[1] near Jerusalem. Prime Minister Rabin, also the Defense Minister, ordered the security forces to prepare contingency plans and to rescue the kidnapped soldier before the Hamas-deadline went into effect. The Israeli National Police Border Guard hostage-rescue unit, the ***Ya'ma'm***, prepared for a raid, as did ***Sayeret Mat'kal.*** Both units offered a detailed plan as to how they would rescue the hostage, but the commander of the ***Ya'ma'm***, Commander David Tzur, was abroad, and with the Israeli Chief-of-Staff and most of the generals on the General Staff former ***Mat'kal*** operators, the General Staff Reconnaissance Unit was chosen to execute the mission. At 14:00 hours, the ***Mat'kal*** force that would attempt to rescue Waxman, led by Captain Nir Poraz, arrived at an anonymous military base in Jerusalem for a briefing by Chief of Staff Lieutenant-General Ehud Barak and his intelligence staff who were monitoring events outside the safe-house in Bir Nabala. As the rescue force was en route to the village, ***Shin Bet*** agents informed the task force that a black Mercedes, driven by known Hamas terrorists, had pulled up to the house and the fear that Waxman would be moved promoted the operation to be accelerated.

By 17:15 the ***Mat'kal*** operators were in place. At a CP set-up in the base in northern Jerusalem, Chief of Staff Barak, his deputy Major-General Amnon Shahak, Military Intelligence commander Major-General Uri Saguy, O/C Central Command Major-General Ilan Biran, West Bank commander Major-General Shaul Mofez, O/C Manpower Branch Major-General Yoram Yair, ***Shin Bet*** deputy commander Y.,[2] and Police commander of the Autonomous Region Major-General (Chief) Alik Ron monitored the transpiring events on a series of radios; all the officers, except Major-General Yair, were undercover, wearing civilian clothes. In the event of an emergency, two IAF transport choppers were on immediate stand-by alert status moments from the action.

At 19:15 hours, as the sun began to set over the hills into the Mediterranean, the ***Mat'kal*** operators began to slowly crawl and slink their way to the safe-house, moving silently though quickly the village, still alive with worshipers returning from the mosque's evening prayers, until the walls of the house were reached. One force climbed the building's walls and reached the roof where they waited in ambush for the terrorists to escape, and also as an auxiliary entry team; other teams, including the lead assault element led by Captain Poraz, moved into and through the main and western entrances. Once word was received that a roof-assault was impossible, Captain Poraz ordered his sappers into action--silently and methodically, explosive charges were placed on three doors where the ***Mat'kal*** were to attempt entry: two doors on the ground floor, in the northern approach including the main entrance; and, an entrance on the western side of the house leading into the kitchen, a porch and the living room.

At 19:47 hours, the three explosive charges were detonated, but only one worked and exploded properly; additional charges were immediately brought up and quickly detonated. From the main northern doorway, a dozen ***Mat'kal*** operators quickly raced into the house, up a flight of stairs, and quickly into the living room; a terrorist, perched on the sofa in firing position, was killed immediately by a burst of gunfire. But Nachshon Waxman, bound and gagged, was held in a small room inside the flat by two abductors--the room was barricaded and fortified; the only door into the small room, a heavy steel plate, was bolstered by a additional steel bolts.

The operators attempted to breech the doorway with explosives, but the charges mangled the steel into a twisted barrier even more formidable that the locked door. Upon hearing the commandos at the door, the terrorists fired seven rounds from their AK-47 into Corporal Waxman's neck, chest and stomach, killing their hostage after brutally torturing him for nearly a week; according to foreign reports, Waxman's body was badly bruised and he was missing his finger-nails and toe-nails (he was also reported to have been savagely bitten by one of his kidnappers). The terrorists then began firing their weapons through the walls at the oncoming commandos. "Surrender," Captain Poraz shouted in Arabic, but the terrorists responded with a chilling reply of their own in Hebrew, "We'll kill Nachshon and then die!" They then began hurling grenades and explosive charges at the Israelis, as well as firing in all directions. In the charge to enter the room, Captain Poraz, the first in, was hit in the head by a 7.62mm round and killed instantly. An additional twelve operators were also seriously wounded. In the end, after seventeen minutes of gunfire, the two surviving kidnappers were killed.[3]

What had begun as a hope for salvation had ended in a myriad of blood and death. Major-General Yoram Yair headed to Corporal Nachshon Waxman's home to break the news to his parents, while Prime Minister Rabin and Chief of Staff Barak addressed a stunned and heartbroken Israeli public. "This sort of operation is very complicated and involved, and the unit carrying it out acted in a very determined way under difficult conditions, facing serious opposition during the implementation," stated Barak; "it was the right thing to do." Other Israelis, including police operators, were quoted in wire news service reports, maintained that the delays in breaching the door left the raid with little chance for success. One was quoted as saying, "Rescuing a hostage is a matter of seconds. It took minutes because they weren't prepared."

Hindsight in any operation of this sort is always 20-20! And, indeed, many in Israel asked why the police special anti-terrorist unit, one specifically maintained and exhaustively prepared and trained for such eventualities, wasn't permitted to rescue the kidnapped corporal. In true Israeli fashion, a bitter war of words soon developed between the IDF and the police over the handling of the raid; the Israeli press, as vibrant and sometime ruthless as they come, also entered the mix printing stories that many claimed were inaccurate and only added fuel to the fire of the tragedy. Major-General Mofez, defending ***Sayeret Mat'kal***, proclaimed, "The ***Ya'ma'm*** doesn't hold any advantage over the General Staff Reconnaissance Unit, even in this [hostage-rescue] work." An Israeli TV news report even claimed that the ***Ya'ma'm*** wasn't selected because a proposed plan they had offered failed in an exercise. The crisis was averted when the IDF and police spokesmen issued a joint statement refuting the bad blood between the units, and attempting to once and for all to extinguish the controversy, but questions remained. After all, didn't the ***Ya'ma'm*** possessed uniquely trained and equipped sappers and entry specialists that were in the unit precisely for the scenario as the house in Bir Nabala? Even when ***Sayeret Mat'kal*** was selected over the ***Ya'ma'm***, police officers offered the services of the ***Ya'ma'm*** specialists for the raid, but Chief of Staff Barak refused to attach ***Ya'ma'm*** operators to the raid. Why? many in Israel still ask, "why wasn't the ***Ya'ma'm*** called into the house in Bir Nabala?"

***Sayeret Mat'kal*** is not the sole Israeli counter-terrorist unit, and it is not the sole national hostage-rescue force; in fact, according to an act of the Israeli Knesset (Parliament), it is not even supposed to participate in counter-terrorist operations ***inside*** the Israeli Green Line. That awesome responsibility is the domain of the Israel National Police Border Guard's ***Ya'ma'm***, the Hebrew acronym for ***Yechida Mishtartit Meyuchedet***, or Special Police Unit, which (since 1973) has become one the finest--and busiest--counter-terrorist unit in the world.

Until 1972, when Black September hijacked the Sabena Belgian Airlines Boeing 707, terrorists didn't take hostages in Israel. The State of Israel's policy that any citizen taken hostage was a soldier in the national struggle meant that some sort of military response would definitely be taken against the terrorists, and most terrorists were quite content to take their chances in Europe rather than against the IDF. In 1972, however, after Lod Airport and after the Munich debacle, Israeli security officials became aware of an alarming trend among terrorist attacks: they were bolder, larger in scale than before, and virtually always involving hostages. Inside the halls of the Israeli Ministry of Defense and National Police HQ, contingency plans were drawn up to prepare the nation for an expected increase in terrorist strikes inside Israel where vulnerable citizens would be seized and possibly killed. In early 1973, the Israeli National Police Border Guards (***Mishmar Ha'Gvul***) ordered the creation of the ***Yechida Mishtartit Meyuchedet*** (Special Police Unit), or the ***Ya'ma'm*** as it became known. The ***Ya'ma'm*** was formed as a special assault unit of the Border Guard to help terminate a potential hostage situation along the frontiers by simply striking the terrorists from the time their cross-border foray was detected until they reached their target. The similarities between the

With Jerichos in hand, a ***Ya'ma'm*** unit trains in the art of taking down a hijacked bus. (Courtesy: Israel Police)

Following a terrorist hostage-taking incident at a Kibbutz in southern Israel, ***Ya'ma'm*** officers (note "regular" Uzis) stand-down after an engagement. (IDF Spokesman)

creation of an Israeli Border Guard unit and the German GSG-9 are quite interesting, but the ***Ya'ma'm*** wasn't intended to be a national hostage-rescue force. Instead, it was to be an intervention unit of operators to augment the joint-security arrangement along Israel's frontiers with Lebanon, Syria and Lebanon.

In May 1974, however, on Israeli independence day, a three-man suicide squad from Nayif Hawatmeh's Democratic Front for the Liberation of Palestine (DFLP) crossed the Lebanese border into Israel and seized nearly 100 students on a field trip inside a schoolhouse in the border town of Ma'alot. The terrorists booby-trapped the building with explosives, and then threatened to kill the children off one by one unless Israel released hundreds of Palestinian terrorists languishing in prison. Army units were summoned and immediately surrounded the building, and elements of ***Sayeret Mat'kal*** gathered and prepared their assault. When the situation permitted, the operators struck but the rescue raid was not the clean and synchronized personification of precision that was displayed during the rescue of the Sabena aircraft. The terrorists turned their weapons on the hostages instead of the assaulting commandos, and the ***Mat'kal*** operators had used improper explosive breaching tools to gain entry into the school. In the end, the three terrorists were killed, but they had managed to kill twenty-four Israeli children and wound dozens more. It was, many would say, the Israeli Munich. A disaster.

Israeli Prime Minister Golda Meir authorized the formation of a governmental commission to investigate the Ma'alot Massacre and to not only examine the nature of post-Munich terrorist attacks, but to also define the areas of responsibility between the Police and the IDF in handling terrorist attacks; specialized rescue units were popping up all over Europe, many would argue, Israel needed one as well. The Horev Commission's findings were substantial. The Israeli National Police would assume responsibility for all internal security and terrorist matters inside the Green Line (the pre-1967 borders) and the IDF (and its elite reconnaissance units) would be responsible for the West Bank and Gaza Strip, not to mention cross-border forays and possible international rescue assignments; it was realized that a gray murky area of jurisdiction would sometimes cause problems as to who would be deployed to a mission, but it was hoped that bickering and problems would not develop. As a result of the 1976 Government Resolution No. 411, the ***Ya'ma'm*** was placed under the special administrative command of National Police HQ in Jerusalem (even though it was still logistically a Border Guard unit). Consequently, the unit was first staffed by professional Border Guard officers and volunteers from the pool of conscripts that the Border Guards received. For an elite unit tasked with such daunting responsibilities, the ***Ya'ma'm***'s first commanders realized that this selection process was incompatible with the requirements of hostage-rescue work. Slowly, the conscripts were phased out and professionals incorporated into this unit. The ***Ya'ma'm*** began recruiting IDF special operations officers about to be released from active duty who they felt would be suited to this kind of work; adds were placed in major dailies with the following sales pitch:

***THE SPECIAL POLICE ANTI-TERRORIST UNIT IS LOOKING FOR OFFICERS AND COMBATANTS***

***If you are from a field unit, a graduate of squad commanders course or above, with a high-school education, twenty-five-years-old and healthy, we are offering interesting work with a young cadre. Good salary and work benefits, and potential for advancement. All those interested please apply to..........***

By 1980, the ***Ya'ma'm*** was made up solely of professional officers. Most of the operators were veterans of either the Paratroops or Golani Infantry Brigade, or veterans of various reconnaissance formations. Many were sergeants and officers who had extensive special operations experience behind enemy lines in southern Lebanon, and in the territories.

The ***Ya'ma'm***'s first call to action--in the criminal arena--came about in 1977, when a large group of prisoners, hard-core criminals incarcerated for the most violent and heinous crimes, managed to escape from prison and terrorize much of central Israel. As if it were hunting out terrorists, the ***Ya'ma'm*** was called into action and quickly rounded up the fugitives. The ***Ya'ma'm***'s first true counter-terrorist

As a German BKA agent once said in a now famous instruction to a squad of GSG-9 operators, "Shoot the women first!" At the ***Ya'ma'm*** training base in central Israel, a plain-clothed operator aims his Mini-Uzi at a peppered female target. (Courtesy: Israel Police)

During a night-time deployment, an IAF helicopter hovers overhead as ***Ya'ma'm*** personnel execute a search mission. (Courtesy: Israel Police)

operation came on March 11, 1978, when terrorists from Force 17, the elite strike force of Yasir Arafat's ***Fatah*** faction, landed on Israel's Mediterranean coast halfway between Tel Aviv and Haifa and commandeered a bus full of hostages headed toward Tel Aviv; the terrorist task force, interestingly enough, was commanded by a female. At the Country Club Junction, just due north of the city along the bustling coastal highway, Israeli police and military units, including the ***Ya'ma'm***, had set up a roadblock. As the ***Ya'ma'm*** readied itself for a rescue assault, one of the hostages attempted to overpower a terrorist by seizing his gun; shots soon rang out and a grenade detonated prematurely. Fearing that the terrorists had begun executing the hostages, the ***Ya'ma'm***, which was still deploying to the scene, made its move. Before the melee was over, thirty-seven hostages were killed and nearly fifty seriously wounded. All the terrorists were either killed or captured. Several ***Ya'ma'm*** operators were also wounded in the battle, including the unit commander, Inspector Asaf Hefetz. Today, at the time of this book's writing, Asaf Hefetz is the Israeli Police Commissioner.

While the first ***Ya'ma'm*** unit was being trained--and bloodied--senior commanders in the Israeli Police were studying developments far from the Middle East and Europe, when set in order to the guidelines for the ***Ya'ma'm***'s areas of responsibilities. The unit's secondary mission, the police hierarchy decided, was the tactical support of the "regular" police in the fight against crime, essentially violent and organized crime, and the restoration of public order in the case of a national breakdown or crisis. The ***Ya'ma'm*** would also assume responsibility for rescuing hostages held by criminals (such as from a bank robbery gone bad) to rescuing hostages held by emotionally disturbed persons (EDPs); in essence, they would become a national counter-terrorist force combined with the tasks of a municipal SWAT team.

In the early 1980s, when the ***Ya'ma'm*** truly and slowly developed into a top-notch fighting force, it cemented its operational principals as: (1) quick reaction to any situation to which they are called, and, upon arrival, and (2) the highest level of professionalism displayed in the preparation for, and execution of, any tactical situation. Reaction with speed was most important. Although Israel did not cover far-reaching stretches of territory, and it was possible to get from the northern most point to the southern most point in a ten hour ride, most cities and towns were separated by no more than a one hour drive at high speeds. Equipment and devices would have to stand at the ready in place ready to deploy at a moments notice, ***Ya'ma'm*** drivers were trained in the art of high-speed driving to overcome the narrow and congested roadways and to reach a crisis scene in no more than an hour; augmenting this ability was the IAF--a chopper was always on-call at the ***Ya'ma'm***'s main base in central Israel, and in an emergency additional helicopter transports would be made available. The second principle to be adhered to religiously was professionalism--absolute professionalism. IDF special forces adhere to the ideals of ***Dvika Be'Matara*** (Sticking to the Target)--a job is always handled professionally with everyone doing his utmost in order to hit the target as effectively and quickly as possible. All ***Ya'ma'm*** exercises and subsequent operational deployments are based upon the unit's SOPs (Standard Operational Procedure), pre-rehearsed plans and contingency functions that are adhered to religiously. SOPs, and the different scenarios presented in training and in the field, also require a certain bit of innovation and improvisation--from the CO level down to the operator hurling the Stun Device into a room full of terrorists.

"There is nothing like close-quarter accuracy!" A ***Ya'ma'm*** officers plugs a cardboard cut-out of a female terrorist full of neat, well-placed 9mm holes during a run on the live-fire IFF (Identification Friend or Foe) range. (Courtesy: Israel Police)

From 1980 onward, the ***Ya'ma'm*** recruited only the most capable, intelligent and motivated personnel, eager to prove their worth as the national cutting edge in the fight against terrorism. Already, and not coincidentally, the ***Ya'ma'm*** had trained extensively with GSG-9 both in St. Augustin and in Israel--a special bond, in fact, had developed between the two national "Border Guard" hostage-rescue units. The ***Ya'ma'm*** training facility in central Israel had slowly built a reputation for itself as a state-of-the-art counter-terrorist learning center, with the finest instructors, most intensive course, and the best firing range in the world. In Israel, however, the unit was not truly appreciated. In situations where a ***Ya'ma'm*** deployment was warranted, the IDF, and namely ***Sayeret Mat'kal***, assumed command and control of the situation. On March 6, 1975, when ***Fatah*** terrorists seized the Savoy Hotel along the Mediterranean beach in Tel Aviv, it was ***Sayeret Mat'kal*** that got the call; when the assault began, the terrorists blew the hotel up with the attack force inside, and mission commander

A ***Ya'ma'm*** operator practices roof entry and exiting techniques during a training mission on the West Bank. (Courtesy: Israel Police)

Two ***Ya'ma'm*** squads deploy atop a typical West Bank structure during training exercises. The unit's access to both police choppers and IAF transport allows the ***Ya'ma'm*** to deploy anywhere in Israel within an hour no matter where in the country a crisis develops. (Courtesy: Israel Police)

During an operation "somewhere" in the West Bank, ***Ya'ma'm*** operatives head into action courtesy of an IAF Bell-212 chopper. (Courtesy: Israel Police)

Colonel Uzi Yairi was killed. On April 7, 1980, when a three-man Arab Liberation Front suicide squad crossed into Israel from southern Lebanon and seized the nursery at Kibbutz Misgav Am, again it was ***Sayeret Mat'kal*** to the rescue; this time, the operation was a complete success. On April 14, 1984, terrorists seized the No. 300 bus traveling from Tel Aviv to the southern coastal city of Ashqelon. This time the ***Ya'ma'm*** was deployed and readied for a rescue assault but ***Sayeret Mat'kal,*** also summoned to the scene, was eventually tasked with the rescue; in the rescue assault the terrorists were killed, but the operators had inadvertently killed one of the hostages, a female soldier named Irit Portugez. After the raid, ***Shin Bet*** agents took the two surviving terrorists to a citrus grove and without authorization, executed them, commencing one of the most divisive cover-ups and political scandals in Israeli history.

It was only in Lebanon, during the 1982 Israeli invasion, that the ***Ya'ma'm*** was able to truly prove what it was capable of doing. Supporting the operations of Border Guard companies 20 and 21 (mainly policing and terrorist round-ups), the ***Ya'ma'm*** was brought into southern Lebanon as a tactical supplement. In Lebanon, in executing counter-terrorist ambushes and dragnets, they operated ideally in the lawless and chaotic labyrinth of danger that existed in the wake of the Israeli advance, and functioned in most of their missions side-by-side with the ***Shin Bet***; in fact, many Israeli military personnel stationed in Lebanon called the ***Ya'ma'm*** the ***Shin Bet's*** private army. The ***Ya'ma'm*** was behind the seizure of many of the most wanted and notorious Palestinian terrorists, including Azmi Zerayer, the butcher of Tyre, who was one of the most brutal PLO chieftains.

Lebanon had opened the eyes of many IDF officials who were wary of the ***Ya'ma'm***, the debacle that followed the Bus No. 300 hijacking convinced many that perhaps ***Sayeret Mat'kal*** was better suited to the cross-border mission impossibles that weren't released to news wire services, and that the police anti-terrorist unit be given its fair due. In December 1987, the Intifadah erupted--already, in the first days of the uprising, the ***Ya'ma'm*** found itself deployed to the territories as tactical augmentation to conscript IDF units and Border Guard patrols. In March 1988, the unit would finally be given its chance to make a mark for itself; to prove to itself and to the Israeli leadership that it was an elite counter-terrorist hostage-rescue force to be trusted and deployed. The ***Ya'ma'm***'s opportunity would come in the Negev Desert, on a shady stretch of road one winter's day.

Since the signing of the Camp David Peace Accords between the late Anwar es-Sadat and Menachem Begin in 1978, the Egyptian-Israeli frontier has largely been peaceful and tranquil. With the exception of Bedouin hashish smugglers, lost camel herds and tourists gone astray, the border has been a placid sea of calm in a very turbulent area. A multi-national peace-keeping force patrolled the once heated battlefields of Sinai and feelings of good will and cooperation were prevalent on both sides. Both Egypt and Israel were intent on maintaining the very acceptable status quo, but the PLO, eager to raise the ante of violence at the height of the uprising, had other plans.

In the early morning hours of March 7, 1988, three heavily armed members of Force 17 crossed the Egyptian-Israeli and cut through the fortified border fence; at 0630 hours they stopped an IDF-issue Renault 4 on the mountain road three kilometers north of Nafkha Prison in the southern Negev Desert. The car was driven by four unarmed officers from the IDF's officer academy, and the terrorists with their AK-47 assault rifles and Carl Gustav submachine-guns had little difficulty in seizing it. Foolishly, the terrorists allowed the Israelis to escape and they immediately ran towards the nearby prison to inform the authorities. The efficient Israeli internal security apparatus went into swift full gear. The isolated desert Kibbutzim and Moshavim were notified of the terrorist infiltration by telephone short-wave radio and their gates were sealed. Air-raid sirens ordered the women and children into the shelters and the men into defensive positions with weapons to hand. Throughout the Negev Desert, dozens of sleepy-eyed policemen rushed to their vehicles to patrol and set up road-blocks. Heavily armed policemen were stationed at key intersections from the Egyptian frontier to the outskirts of Tel Aviv. As a colossal police pursuit of the white Renault 4 commenced in the beautiful sandy wilderness of southern Israel, a call went through from the National Police operations center in Jerusalem ordering the Border Guard anti-terrorist commandos to be placed on a full alert.

By 0715 hours the terrorists had reached their first road-block at the Yerucham-Dimona Junction. It failed to stop them; they swerved around the obstacles and sped on their way. A half-hour chase now ensued with the police shooting unsuccessfully at the terrorist's tires and receiving return fire. IDF forces on maneuvers nearby joined in the fray, firing unsuccessfully upon the Renault as it passed by. Along the road to Dimona the terrorists ditched their listing, bullet-riddled car and tried but failed to commandeer a semi-trailer. They then set up an

ימ"מ

היחידה המיוחדת ללוחמה בטרור

דרושים

# קצינים ולוחמים

אם אתה יוצא יחידת שדה, בוגר קורס פיקודי (מ"כים ומעלה), בעל השכלה תיכונית, גיל עד 25 ובריאות תקינה.
אנו מציעים לך עבודה מעניינת עם צוות צעיר, שכר ותנאי שירות טובים, אפשרויות קידום וקביעות בעבודה.
מועמדים העונים לכל הדרישות מוזמנים לוועדות קבלה בלשכת הגיוס של המשטרה בת"א, רח' הרכבת 14, בתאריכים הר"מ:
יום ב', 28.3.88, בשעה 16.00.
יום ג', 29.3.88, בשעה 9.00 .

סודיות מובטחת

A ***Ya'ma'm*** want ad from the IDF magazine asking for "Officers and combat personnel looking for interesting work."

The Bus of Mothers rescue March 7, 1988--***Ya'ma'm*** officers race to the bus hijacked by Force 17 terrorists and end the ordeal with an explosive fury of firepower. (IDF Spokesman)

During an operation "somewhere" in the West Bank, ***Ya'ma'm*** operatives a briefed before heading into action courtesy of an IAF Bell-212 chopper. (Courtesy: Israel Police)

ambush, hoping to snare their next means of transportation before the Israelis arrives.

Soon, an inter-city bus carrying workers from their homes in Be'ersheba to the Nuclear Research Center in Dimona appeared. The driver managed to identify the three figures racing towards his Volvo bus as terrorists and screeched to a hasty stop. He opened his doors and ordered the passengers to leave, but eight women and one male were trapped when the three Palestinians assumed control of the stopped bus. Seconds later the vanguard of the police pursuit force reached the scene, as did OC Southern Command, Major-General Yitzhak Mordechai, and his advanced command team. A stand-off ensued.

In the Renault, IDF officers found a rucksack full of grenades which the terrorists had apparently forgotten, and the semi-trailer's driver was questioned in order to gather some "impromptu field intelligence." While the bus was gingerly surrounded by ad hoc response teams consisting of dozens of police officers and hastily summoned IDF soldiers, the district police commander, Chaim Ben Oyen, commenced the negotiations in fluent Arabic, hoping to gain some time and invaluable psychological insight.

Within minutes the area had become the busiest location in the country. Scores of men in the Israeli defense community's "Who's Who?" reached the scene, including Defence Minister Lieutenant-General (Res.) Yitzhak Rabin, Police Minister Lieutenant-General (Res.) Chaim Bar-Lev, the National Police inspector General, Chief of Staff Lieutenant-General Dan Shomron, Deputy C-o-S Major -General Ehud Barak and dozens of lesser known though highly experienced generals. Helicopters overhead kicked up a sandy cyclone, while the dust thrown up by the dozens of army cars, trucks and ambulances made visual command and control difficult. ***Sayeret Mat'kal*** prepared a defensive perimeter surrounding the bus, as well as preparing for an assault, and were later reinforced by ***Ya'ma'm*** elements. For many of the assembled the incident was a repeat of the No. 300 bus hijacking, although its politically damaging by-products were to be avoided at all costs! This time it would be the ***Ya'ma'm*** who would be given the job of rescuing the hostages and killing the terrorists.

Unlike the hijackers of the No. 300 bus in 1984, the terrorists holding the Be'ersheba-Dimona bus were well-trained professionals armed with numerous automatic weapons and grenades. Their determination to have a bloody fire-fight was expressed numerous times from 09:00 to 10: 00 hours when they fired bursts of 7.62mm fire at the surrounding crowds and threw fragmentation grenades at encroaching security personnel. Through the hails of gunfire, Ben Oyen attempted a sporadic dialogue with the three Palestinians. They demanded the release of Palestinian prisoners from Israeli jails and

The ***Ya'ma'm*** IFF firing range. (Courtesy: Israel Police)

The Ta'as Jericho 941 9mm pistol--a ***Ya'ma'm*** staple. (Ta'as)

Ta'as No.21 Stun Grenades. (Ta'as)

safe passage to a friendly Arab nation. Ben Oyen pleaded with the terrorists to stop the gunfire, but his anguished appeals for calm were ignored with the promise to throw a body out of the bus every thirty minutes.

The decision to act was forced on the rescuers when gunfire was heard from inside the bus at 10:00 hours. Dissatisfied with the Israeli response to their demands, the terrorists opted to strengthen their position by killing a hostage in cold blood. As Chief of Staff Shomron and OC Southern Command Mordechai (a man already quite intimate with such situations) retreated to a command post in a small sand-hill yards away, the ***Ya'ma'm*** was ordered to prepare its gear and its final assault plan. For the Border Guard anti-terrorist commandos, wearing bullet-proof vests and carrying the ultra-compact and deadly Mini-Uzi 9mm submachine-gun, this was to be their moment of truth as policemen and as a unit.

As the operators moved in and prepared for what many knew would be the inevitable assault, the ***Ya'ma'm*** hostage-negotiating team, a mini-army of psychoanalysts and psychologists, attempted to establish and build a dialog between the terrorists and the authorities. Although military trained and made up exclusively of military veterans, the ***Ya'ma'm*** is, after all, a police unit and a force that does not believe in "acceptable casualties." Interestingly enough, given their backgrounds, the hostage-negotiators, too, were not strangers to participation at the cutting-edge of combat operations. Even as a unit, the ***Ya'ma'm*** had seen action in Lebanon with the Border Guards; they had also been used inside Israel in support of ***Shin Bet*** during delicate security operations, and in August 1985 had helped seize a crazed escaped criminal who was holding hostages in a block of flats.[4] But this was to be their first leading role in the task for which they were created. When the decision was issued ordering them into action, it would be a moment of anxious fear each fighter would remember for years to come, especially for the ***Ya'ma'm***'s commanding officer, Commander Alek Ron, a veteran of ***Sayeret Mat'kal*** and the 1976 Entebbe rescue, and a man who lobbied long and hard for the ***Ya'ma'm*** to be given a fair chance.

Through eavesdropping means, the commanders at the ***Ya'ma'm*** CP understood that a volatile situation was becoming chaotic. The terrorists were not only adamant in not surrendering but had begun to fight and bicker among themselves. At 10:15 hours, after shots were once again heard from inside the bus, the ***Ya'ma'm*** burst into action in an explosive manner. Sniper rounds shattered the windows of the bus, and in a blaze of between-the-eyes accuracy, the three terrorists, wearing T-shirts with the word "Palestine" emblazoned across the chest, were killed. Just seconds prior to the rescue assault, however, the terrorists managed to kill two more hostages, adding a tragic end to a brilliant and decisive operation for the operators.

Because the Be'ersheba-Dimona bus was carrying women laborers to their jobs, the incident has become known as the "Bus of Mothers." The entire episode was a stark reminder of the horror and bloodshed a resolute and well-trained terrorist force could still inflict on an unsuspecting civilian population. Abu Jihad would pay for the crime a month later in Tunis with seventy-five bullets to his body. The ***Ya'ma'm***, finally permitted to prove their worth, would soon find itself involved in more work than they could handle. They would enter the very thick of the Intifadah fires. According to David Tzur, the former unit commander, "The incident put the ***Ya'ma'm*** on the map."

Indeed, many of the young IDF special operations officer who advanced up the chain of command in units that trained with the ***Ya'ma'm***, were now in positions of authority. These operators, not burdened with the anti-police prejudice that used to afflict many in the General Staff, knew the ***Ya'ma'm***'s capabilities, respected the unit's officers and combatants, and considered the unit not as a separate entity under the command of a separate agency, but rather as an integral tool that the IDF could ***rely*** upon in special situations. The Intifadah brought about an immense workload for the ***Ya'ma'm***, as well as for other IDF and police elite units. By the third year of the Palestinian uprising and the eruption of the Hamas-inspired Holy War, the ***Ya'ma'm***'s approximate 300 operators were performing over 250 tactical missions annually--making them on par, per capita, along with the New York City Police Department's Emergency Service Unit as the busiest police special unit in the world. As was the case in Lebanon, the ***Ya'ma'm*** found itself working very close with the ***Shin Bet*** General Security Service and most of its operations, those that were

***Ya'ma'm*** officers survey the equipment carried by an Abu Abbas Faction of the Palestine Liberation Front suicide squad after they were captured in a gun fight south of Tel Aviv on the Nitzanim beach, May 30, 1990. (IDF Spokesman)

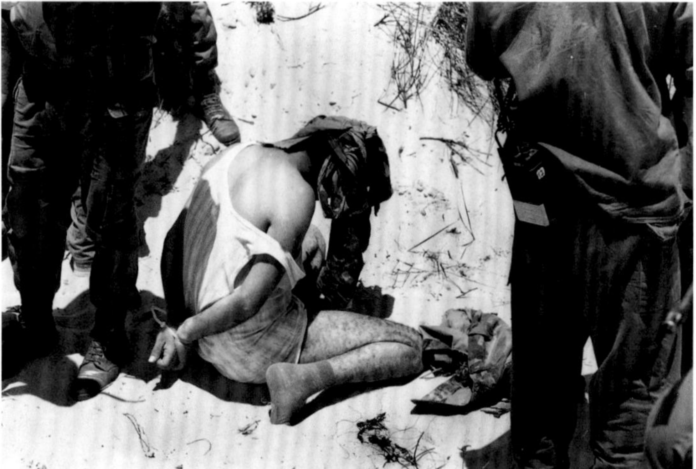

One of the captured Abu Abbas Faction of the Palestine Liberation Front terrorists in ***Ya'ma'm*** custody. (IDF Spokesman)

published and those that are still classified top-secret, were carried in conjunction with the counter-terrorist agents of the ***Shin Bet.*** Among the ***Ya'ma'm***'s more recent operations (those that are suitable for publication) are:

- The May 22, 1992, ambush and killing of the most notorious Hamas terrorist in the Gaza Strip: Marwun Za'iya, a "terrorist engineer" who personally killed twenty-four Israelis and Palestinians, including the stabbing deaths of three Israeli factory workers in the Tel Aviv suburb of Jaffa. The ambush to "get" Za'iya was a most difficult and complicated operation. His home was in the center of an overcrowded complex of connecting flats, congested areas where children played and women cooked and hung their washing. Any tactical deployment amid a civilian population is difficult and precarious; any tactical deployment in a hostile civilian population is deadly. The terrorists know that Israeli units like the ***Ya'ma'm***, who operate under strict guidelines in the use of deadly force, will not fire at women and children, and use the civilians, their own people, as human shields. When the ***Ya'ma'm*** task force reached the building early on the morning of May 21, the terrorists saw what was coming and quickly escaped up the building's stairs. One ***Ya'ma'm*** unit, led by Sergeant-Major Eran Sobelman, followed the terrorist up the staircase but hesitated momentarily when he saw the area crowded with old women and small children. Sergeant-Major Sobelman was killed by a gunshot to the head fired by one of the terrorists taking advantage of his human shields. The building was quickly surrounded as reinforcements raced to the scene; with the building neutralized, the terrorists were killed in a furious fire-fight. At the funeral for Inspector Sobelemen (posthumously promoted), ***Ya'ma'm*** Commander Tzur said, "This case, like many others before it, prove that Eran, like many others like him, are not a part of units who deal with hunting wanted people, but he is the best of our youth who exposes himself to everyday danger of fighting terrorists who are acting without any law or limits from within their population, who operate out of buildings filled with women and children, and they force us to adapt the fighting to this jungle in which we find ourselves operating."

The Ta'as Mini-Uzi 9mm submachine gun--the ***Ya'ma'm*** favorite. (Ta'as)

- On August 26, 1992, the ***Ya'ma'm*** was summoned to a most delicate and desperate operation. Superintendent Eli Avraham, a former ***Ya'ma'm*** officer, was the commander of the Border Guard's undercover unit, known by the acronym of ***Ya'mas***, and had composed a force of men that managed to capture or kill the most wanted terrorists in the West Bank city of Jenin without making too much noise--either among the local Palestinians or in the media. His men were such expert undercover operatives that they managed to get close enough to the targeted men to make small talk with them before pulling out their weapons and capturing them; the disguises were so good that many times Avraham's men were warned about Israeli army undercover unit activity in the area by concerned Palestinians. On August 26, Superintendent Avraham led a force of operators from the ***Ya'mas*** to capture an armed terrorist unit from the notorious Black Panthers, an enforcer unit from Yasir Arafat's Fatah, in the city of Jenin. Patience, tenacity and the ability to hold one's self back are some of the qualities required by an undercover officer in it for the long haul. But Superintendent Avraham strayed from the safety parameters that guide such dangerous work. He improvised from the blue-prints of the operation and charged the building, already under heavy fire, from the roof instead of as part of a coordinated frontal assault. He was killed by a shot to the head. The operators on the scene faced a dilemma, not only were the terrorists returning fire, but their commander's mortally wounded body was, in essence, being held hostage. The ***Ya'ma'm*** force that was on-call immediately suited up and raced toward the embattled house in the town of Jenin, and other teams, including the unit commander, was summoned to action. ***Ya'ma'm*** operators quickly established an inner and outer perimeter and prepared for the assault. Under heavy point-blank fire, the operators moved in. The assault was lightning quick and the rescue operation over in a minute. The operators had killed both terrorists, but tragically Superintendant Avraham was dead, too.
- On September 8, 1992, Eitan Mor, a deranged Israeli psychopath who managed to get his hands on an Uzi submachine gun, entered a mental health clinic in the Jerusalem neighborhood of Kiryat Yuval and without reason or warning, began shooting. Before he emptied two full magazines of 9mm ammunition, Mr. Mor killed four women, including two who were pregnant, and wounded two others. He then raced through the streets of the neighborhood, followed by

patrolmen, to the roof of a nearby building. He had fired an additional thirty rounds of 9mm ammunition from his Uzi, and had also emptied the magazine of his Beretta M1951 pistol. Atop the roof, he dared the police to take him down. A stand-off ensued, and finally Mor was taken-down by two 7.62mm rounds from a ***Ya'ma'm*** sniper. Israeli police officials had long boasted that this sort of random violence only plagued America and isolated parts of Europe, but here the bloodshed was being seen on the streets of the Israeli capital. The incident, however, one of the most tragic cases of criminal violence in Israel, sparked severe debate on the allocation of pistol and gun permits.

- On December 11, 1992, in a coordinated ***Shin Bet/Ya'ma'm*** operation, a group of intelligence operatives and operators cornered the house of wanted Islamic Jihad terrorist, I'sam Barhami, in the village of A'nza, near Jenin; he was charged with multiple homicides, and considered to be one of the most lethal terrorists in the West Bank. Barhami and two bodyguards were located and identified outside their home. The ***Ya'ma'm*** launched its assault, killing the two bodyguards, but a critically wounded Barhami raced inside the building--now engulfed by flames. Instead of letting the building burn to the ground, the IDF, responsible for the area, ordered in the fire brigade. When the ***Ya'ma'm*** entered the building two hours later, a recon force encountered a wounded Barhami, burnt over most of his body though still alive and still clutching both Uzi and Carl Gustav submachine guns. Barhami succeeded in killing Inspector Sasson Mordoch, and wounding three others; an additional ***Ya'ma'm*** operator was severely wounded during the rescue bid. Over 100 kilograms of TNT were then placed around the pillars of the building still sheltering a defiant Barhami, and the structure evaporated into a thunderous blasts. Inspector Mordoch, thirty-years-old, was the fourth ***Ya'ma'm*** operator killed in the line of duty in 1992, and at his funeral the ***Ya'ma'm*** CO, Commander Tzur, said the following, "We stand here shocked and pained by the loss, and we are unwilling to accept it."

The loss of so many operators in one year was a bitter loss for a small and cohesive unit such as the ***Ya'ma'm***, and it proved to many in the police hierarchy, especially the unit commander, that something had to be done. These selective operations, as rewarding as they were in bringing to justice--or extreme vengeance termination--many of the most notorious terrorists running about, were simply too dangerous, too risky, and far too costly. Soon after, the IDF and the ***Ya'ma'm*** adapted a different policy whereby, if a location was found to be void of any innocent civilians, extreme firepower, often anti-tank missiles, would be deployed as a safeguarding tool.

Other ***Ya'ma'm*** operations, include:

- In the spring of 1994, in what promised to be the Israeli-version of the Waco, Texas, Branch-Davidian stand-off, a crazed rabbi, Amit Meshulam, and a group of heavily armed followers opened fire on a police unit attempting to investigate the group in the town of Yahud, in central Israel; several officers were hit though not fatally wounded. Although the ***Ya'ma'm*** was poised to act tactically (and most certainly would have had the Rabbi's followers been Arabs, many have since argued), it was decided to use the ***Ya'ma'm*** negotiators and to resolve the situation through peaceful means; the rabbi's followers had barricaded the house and planted booby-trap devices throughout the facility. The rabbi was cut off from his followers while engaging in the dialog and subsequently apprehended without additional firepower being brought to bare.
- The June 1994 ambush and killing of Abdel al-Muna'am Muhammed Yusuf Naji, a Hamas terrorist responsible for the assassination of a ***Shin Bet*** agent near Ramallah, in the village of al-Ram near Jerusalem. The ***Ya'ma'm*** operators, equipped in heavy ballistic vests and high-caliber weaponry, had received accurate intelligence that the terrorist and his bodyguard would be in the village and set-up a text-book interception operation.
- An October 17, 1994, assault on a four-story block of flats in the southern frontier town of Dimona, when a known drug user and criminal threatened to kill himself and his daughter by detonating a propane gas tank in his apartment. The stand-off ensued for seven hours until the ***Ya'ma'm*** was called in. Operators, dressed as cable-TV installers, fast-roped down the side of the building and burst through his window. The perpetrator was apprehended before he could detonate his propane device and kill several dozen civilians and policemen.

The ***Ya'ma'm*** today, consists of approximately 300 operators,[5] and although its exact order of battle and sub-division of units remains classified top-secret, it has been reported to be built along the lines of GSG-9 in three primary section. It is obviously on-call twenty-four-hours a day, 365 days a year, with at least thirty operators, according to Commander Tzur, always on suit-up standby status. The unit also possesses its own sappers and hostage-negotiators who in the field are fighters tried and true, but bring their own unique skills to any situation.

A "professional" force, service in the ***Ya'ma'm*** is obviously voluntary and subject to a lengthy process of selection, security checks, training and instruction that lasts approximately one full year, including seven months of intensive tactical and weapons training. Although much of the ***Ya'ma'm***'s instruction is classified top-secret, it is known that the training consists of basic knowledge of police organization, Israeli law and police procedure; after all, while in the

A police sniper, with a Galil 7.62mm sniper weapon, peers through his scope onto his target. (Ta'as)

The Galil 7.62mm sniper weapon. (Ta'as)

A ***Ya'ma'm*** EOD officer searches the parade ground outside the Wailing Wall for explosives prior to a ceremony attended by politicians and VIPs. (Samuel M. Katz)

Following the call of a possible terrorist attack, a Border Guard jeep races through the streets of Jerusalem. (Samuel M. Katz)

***Ya'ma'm*** these soldiers turned operators are also police officers. Another all-important element of ***Ya'ma'm*** instruction is physical training--all operators are expected to be in top-notch physical shape. The men of the hostage-rescue unit were keen to prove their worth. Composed entirely of veterans from the IDF's elite combat units (such as the paratroops, and other reconnaissance and commando formations), those volunteering into the ***Ya'ma'm*** are trained in a brutally-paced regime of hand-to-hand combat, cold weapon killing, marksmanship, judo, ***Krav Maga*** (an Israeli-inspired form of intuitive martial arts) and split-second synchronized assaults on terrorist/enemy-held targets. Each ***Ya'ma'm*** operator is trained to proficiency in every type of infantry weapon imaginable: from a K-Bar knife to a hand-gun, from an assault rifle to an RPG-7. Special emphasis is given to urban combat training, by day or night, and to eliminating the terrorists in the first burst of gunfire so that hostages can be rescued unharmed. As a result, each member of a squad is expert in any task he might be called on to perform.

What makes the ***Ya'ma'm*** quite unique, especially as an Israeli unit, is the fact that it is a "rich" force in a poor country. The ***Ya'ma'm*** is equipped with the finest equipment in the world--both material designed and produced in Israel often to ***Ya'ma'm*** specifications, as well as the best "bought-off-the-shelf" gear available in Asia, Europe and the United States; the procurement limitations and bureaucracy that exists for the IDF or even other police units does not exist in the ***Ya'ma'm***. Much of the equipment purchased abroad is returned the unit's laboratory and, in the unit's terms, "converted to Judaism" with modifications and upgrades mandated by ***Ya'ma'm*** specifications.

Unlike virtually every other counter-terrorist and hostage-rescue unit in the world today, the ***Ya'ma'm*** does not deploy the Heckler and Koch family of 9mm submachine guns, nor the Glock Model 19 9mm pistol. The unit's primary personal weapon is the Ta'as (formerly Israel Military Industries) Mini-Uzi 9mm submachine gun; most fitted with various laser aim points, mag-lites and other illumination and targeting devices. The primary ***Ya'ma'm*** handgun is a specially designed, almost sportsman, Ta'as Jericho 9mm 941ME, which come complete with compensators and are designed personally for each operator. The ***Ya'ma'm*** places supreme importance on sharp-shooting, and a wide variety of sniping rifles are carried by the unit, including the Ta'as 7.62mm Galil sniping rifle; the joint Israeli-Austrian Sirkis M36 7.62mm sniping rifle;[6] American-made Macmillan rifles; American-made Remington M24 and M40 7.62mm sniping systems; the Robar Co. family of 5.56mm, 7mm, 7.62mm and .300 caliber weapons; and, the 7.62mm RAI convertible long range rifle Model 300, and the .50 in (12.7mm) RAI long-range rifle Model 500. The unit also deploys the Ta'as No. 21 Stun Hand Grenade (producing a flash of approximately 1,500,000 candela and a stunning bang of about 140 decibels), though fragmentation devices are often used inside the territories during non-hostage-rescue assignments. Tactical and protective gear, from infantry ballistic helmets to flak vests and load bearing equipment, are Israeli produced, and are modified variants of the standard gear issued to front-line IDF units.

The unit trains on a year-round basis in the art of tactical assaults, in rescuing hostages and handling any situation in built-up areas, desert and mountainous terrain, inside hijacked aircraft buses, or trains, and just about any other contingency--both terrorist-related and criminal--that could be encountered within the boundaries of the State of Israel and its immediate surroundings. The ***Ya'ma'm*** trains regularly with other IDF elite units, including ***Sayeret Mat'kal,*** and Flotilla 13, the IDF/Navy's naval special warfare unit. Though the ***Ya'ma'm*** maintains very close contacts with the U.S. Army's 1st SFOD-D and the FBI's HRT, (and in the past has trained (and trained with) several American units, including officers from the LAPD SWAT Platoon, the Metro-Dade SRT, and, in the months prior to the 1994 World Cup in the United States, the New Jersey State Police SWAT team), the ***Ya'ma'm*** has also enjoyed a close-knit relationship with the RCMP's ERT (and now the military force tasked with counter-terrorist work in Canada), as well as with Great Britain's SO-13 counter-terrorist unit, and SO-19 tactical firearms unit. The ***Ya'ma'm***'s closest foreign contacts, including overseas visits and training, is with the Italian NOCS (a relationship that has lasted now for nearly twenty years), the Austrian GEK Cobra, and the Munich SEK. Many smaller units around the world, especially those in the former Warsaw Pact have turned to the Israelis for tactical instruction and assistance, especially the Hungarians, Poles, Czechs, Latvians and Estonians. The close-knit ties that the ***Ya'ma'm*** once enjoyed with GSG-9 are still strong, but no longer as close as before, mainly because of the drop-off in operations assigned to GSG-9; as Commander Tzur was quoted as saying, "A unit is not measured by its training or equipment, but by ***Tachlis*** (the Hebrew slang for action and reality), by its operations, the amount of their operations and the type of operations they execute." Although official ties between the ***Ya'ma'm*** and the British SAS have not truly been realized[7], terrorism conferences do lead to contacts and friendships that inturn lead to inter-service cooperation. "After all," as Commander Tzur pointed

Two ***Ya'ma'm*** officers walk a beat during an IDF display in the town of Ramat Gan. (Samuel M. Katz)

Border Guard policemen brace themselves for an entry into a suspected terrorist arms cache in East Jerusalem. (Samuel M. Katz)

out, the British problems with the Provos in Ulster is quite similar to the problem we have [had] in Gaza with Hamas, and similar to the problem that still exists in the West Bank.

In the first years of the Palestinian uprising, the ***Ya'ma'm*** found itself functioning virtually exclusively in Arab East Jerusalem, primarily in the Old City of Jerusalem in the confines of the el-Aqsas mosque. Demonstrations by fundamentalists, often where weapons were deployed, characterized the Jerusalem front of the uprising. The ***Ya'ma'm***, trained in lightning fast assaults, now found itself containing massive demonstrations and riots--often through non-lethal means. In one instance, a ***Ya'ma'm*** operator was kidnapped by a mob of worshippers and brought inside the mosque where he was savagely beaten and robbed of his weapon and radio. A stand-off ensued and with the media watching, ***Ya'ma'm*** officers were able to convince the cleric of the mosque that it was in the best interest of the faithful to return the officer and his weapon immediately. The "Battle for Jerusalem," as many police officer called it, was difficult and tense, and resulted in the formation of a special police unit to deal with volatile riot and mob situations. That unit was the ***Ya'sa'm*** (Hebrew acronym for Special Patrol Unit)--unit attached to city and regional commands that initiated tactical patrols through volatile areas in order to quell the seeds of disturbance. Should a demonstration be out of control (be it in a hotbed neighborhood for Hamas or in an ultra-Orthodox Jewish neighborhood), the ***Ya'sa'm*** would be called in to end matters through non-lethal means if possible, and lethal means if required. Characteristic in their khaki fatigues and blue baseball caps, ***Ya'sa'm*** officers carry heavy weapons (Uzis and CAR-15) and are expert shots.

Another specialized Israeli "police" counter-terrorist unit is the ***Yechidat Ha'Mista'arvim Shel Mishmar Ha'Gvul*** (Border Guard Undercover Unit), better known by its acronym of ***Ya'mas***. Created in 1990 to supplement the over-burdened IDF undercover units (Cherry and Samson), the ***Ya'mas*** soon developed into the premier IDF undercover unit meant to seize, and apprehend, if necessary, the most dangerous terrorist fugitives. Initially made up of ***Ya'ma'm*** volunteers (as was the case of the unit's first commander, Superintendant Eli Avraham whose killing was listed in the text), the ***Ya'mas*** operated throughout the Occupied Territories with ease and complete cover; they dressed as old men, old women, young girls and Hamas fire-branding marchers. According to their commander, Superintendent 'N.'[8] "These men feel as comfortable walking around the casbah of Nablus as they do strolling in Tel Aviv." Superintendent 'N.' knows of what he speaks. The thirty-seven-year old operator assumed command of the unit following the death of Superintendent Avraham, and before his undercover duties he served for twelve years as an officer in the ***Ya'ma'm.***

In the operational assignments, the men of the ***Ya'mas*** are faced with a variety of tactical situations that few units of a similar make-up ever encounter--they must sometimes apprehend and subdue a suspect in the middle of an uncontrollable flow of civilians (some of whom are sometimes armed); know how to fire accurately while on the run or from a moving vehicle; and, display unquestioned courage in light of overwhelming numeric odds. Between 1990-1994, the ***Ya'mas*** was responsible for the apprehension of seventy wanted terrorist fugitives, and the killings of fifty of the most violent and most defiant Hamas terrorists. Trained to be remarkable shots, ***Ya'mas*** undercover operators favor the Ta'as Mini-Uzi 9mm submachine gun and the CAR-15 5.56mm assault rifle--often an Israeli-modified variant with attached forward pistol grip and attached flashlight.

The ***Ya'mas*** is ***not*** a professional police unit like the ***Ya'ma'm***, and different from IDF elite units who draw their personnel from volunteers who strive to be in the unit and often work hard before conscription to hone their minds and bodies to meet such a unit's exacting standards. ***Ya'mas*** officers, instead, begin to monitor candidates they feel comfortable with at the Border Guards basic training base, while most eighteen-year-old Israelis are conscripted into the IDF, others are taken directly into the Border Guard and serve their three years of mandatory service in the ***Mishmar Ha'Gvul.*** During Border Guards basic training, which lasts six months and is an infantry and police regimen, ***Ya'mas*** commanders begin to monitor the developments of those individuals who are from Middle East backgrounds, who look like Arabs, and who can converse freely in Arabic. If that policeman is a good "soldier," disciplined though showing initiative, special attention is placed on that individual once the training is complete and they are despatched into the field--primarily for security details in the West Bank and Jerusalem. If he's very good, he is ordered to attend a roundtable of Border Guard officers who, for lack of a better word, volunteer the unknowing policeman into the unit. Most, honored for the privilege, gladly accept, and head to a secret training course that lasts three additional months.

Also supplementing the efforts of the Israeli Police to keep the streets of the cities (as well as the West Bank) free from terrorist attack, are police sappers, or bomb-disposal experts, who are also among the most experienced in the world. They respond to literally tens of thousands of calls a year throughout the country, handling calls of suspicious packages that sometimes turn out to be nothing but discarded or lost items, but sometimes turn out to be massive explosive devices. A special sapper unit exists in the West Bank, under Border Guard command, that deals with this problem on a slightly larger scale, at a more fanatic pace, with far more actual devices discovered and handled than the false alarms found inside the Green Line.

The high regard in which the ***Ya'ma'm*** is now held is personified by the fact that much as the army is now dominated by ***Sayeret Mat'kal*** veterans, the hierarchy of the Israeli police is now dominated by veteran ***Ya'ma'm*** officers and commanders, such as Commissioner Asaf Hefetz and Major-General (Chief) Alek Ron, and a special operations atmosphere has overtaken the Israeli police. That mind-set will be needed. Following the announcement of peace between Jordan and Israel, both nations announced what was rumored to have been in existence for many years--close cooperation on the counter-terrorist front between the two nations. In late October 1994, IDF Military Intelligence commander Major-General Uri Saguy met with his Jordanian counter-part, General Tachsin Shurdom, to solidify the counter-terrorist front. Intelligence will most certainly be shared and perhaps units will visit one another, and the ***Ya'ma'm*** might even train alongside the Jordanian SOU. In the wake of the kidnapping and killing of Corporal Nachshon Waxman, and the October 26, 1994, suicide-bombing of the No. 5 bus in Tel Aviv in which twenty-one were killed, Israel will need all the help it can get in once and for all combating and eradicating the last hard-core ring of terrorists still opposed to peace.

***Ya'sa'm*** policemen confer with Border Guard units during offensive patrols of Arab East Jerusalem. (Samuel M. Katz)

[1] According to Israeli security sources, they were not surprised when the word was received of Waxman being held in Bir Nabal, a village of 6,000 inhabitants a few miles north of the Jerusalem city limits. Known in ***Shin Bet*** computers as a Hamas hot-bed, nearly half of the village's residents are American citizens who reside most of the year in the United States. The Hamas safe-house where Corporal Waxman was held, interestingly enough, was built and owned by a Palestinian-American living in Virginia, believed to be the American epicenter of Hamas.

[2] Identity withheld for security reasons.

[3] The three kidnappers were identified by the Israelis as "Hamas heavy hitters": and included Abdel Karim Badr, Taysir el-Natsheh, and Tsalah Hassan Jedala, better known in Hamas circles as the "Jerusalem Gang." All had been wanted by the Israeli authorities for several years.

[4] The ***Ya'ma'm***'s anti-terrorist role does not restrict them from executing their police duties; in many cases to exciting and spectacular extremes. In February 1990, for example, a ***Ya'ma'm*** task force left their anti-Intifadah and anti-terrorist duties in Israel proper to hinder the lucrative drug-smuggling routes which have sprouted from Lebanon since 1982, when, in many ways, the fates of the two nations became forever intertwined. The ***Ya'ma'm*** force, heavily armed and disguised as Lebanese fisherman, raided the Christian port of Junieh, north of Beirut, not only to destroy a drug pipeline but gain intelligence as to their connection back in Israel.

[5] The exact number of personnel remains classified.

[6] Until recently, the ***Ya'ma'm*** also deployed the Austrian Steyr Police 7.62mm sniping weapon.

[7] According to reports, the ***Ya'ma'm*** would like to establish closer ties to British units, and indeed, gestures have been made by both sides, but it is reported that the British Home Office, still staffed by Arabists and those unwilling to include Israel in any long-term policy plans, have canceled any joint fact-finding missions by the two units.

[8] Identity withheld for security reasons.

A ***Ya'sa'm*** chief inspector stands at the ready in the narrow streets of East Jerusalem searching for possible snipers or youths hurling Molotov cocktails. (Samuel M. Katz)

Supporting Border Guard units, ***Ya'sa'm*** officers deploy for action in East Jerusalem right outside the Old City. (Samuel M. Katz)

A Jerusalem ***Ya'sa'm*** officer stands his post by a wall decorated with the latest Hamas graffiti. (Samuel M. Katz)

A checkpoint into the main approach into Jerusalem, ***Ya'sa'm*** officers search vehicles from the West Bank attempting to enter into Israel. (Samuel M. Katz)

A Police Bomb-Disposal Unit truck races to the sighting of a suspicious package abandoned near a Tel Aviv bus. (Samuel M. Katz)

Inside a Hamas stronghold, on the streets of Ramallah, a Border Guard bomb-disposal officer returns to his jeep after neutralizing a terrorist device. (Samuel M. Katz)

With his partner coordinating the "Bambi" robot, a Border Guard sapper disarms a device with a robotics tool. (Samuel M. Katz)

זהירות! ! !
אזרח נכבד, למען בטחונך!
• אל תפתח את החבילה לפני שבדקת: האם אתה מצפה לחבילה ממען זה?
• אם יש לך חשד כלשהו, אנא הודע לפקיד אשר יפנה לעזרת המשטרה.
משרד התקשורת

BE CAREFUL! ! !
Dear Citizen – for your security!
Don't open the parcel before checking.
Are you expecting a parcel from this address? If you have any doubt, please advise the employee who will call the Police for aid.
The Ministry of Communications

تنبيـــه !
لا تفتح العلبه قبل ان تحقق !
هل تتوقع العلبه من هذا العنوان ؟
اذ لديك اي شك الرجاء اخبار الموظف ليتوجه الى الشرطة .
توقيـع وزارة الاتصـال
3-2412/7

An Israeli-police warning placed on all packages delivered by the postal authority.(Sigalit Katz)

The police bomb-disposal unit wings. (Samuel M. Katz)

A Ta'as TSR robot opens the door of a suspected car bomb in Jerusalem. (Ta'as)

A Hamas bomb, hidden inside a book, on display at the sapper's base in Ramallah. (Samuel M. Katz)

# Jordan

One of the most experienced and battle ready counter-terrorist and hostage-rescue units in the Middle East is Jordan's Special Operation Unit or (SOU). Throughout its history, Jordan has been a nation caught in the explosive middle of the Arab-Israeli conflict--at war with Israel, attempting to maintain a delicate balance with its large Palestinian refugee population, and criticized by many in the Arab world for not being forceful enough in the struggle against Israel, Jordan and Jordanian interests have always been under the gun by a host of enemies. No more acute was this problem than in September 1970, when the very sovereignty of the Hashemite Kingdom was threatened. Following the 1967 War, Palestinian guerrillas had transformed the Hashemite Kingdom into a large desert terrorist and training and staging facility for launching their war against the State of Israel from across the Jordan River and for waging their international terrorist revolution in the capitals of Europe. Tension between the government of King Hussein and these guerrilla factions operating in Jordan soon escalated into fire-fights and skirmishes, but a showdown was inevitable. On September 6, 1970, the Popular Front for the Liberation of Palestine (PFLP) hijacked three airliners, two of them to Dawson's Field in the Jordanian desert, and declared war on Jordanian sovereignty over her own territory. The date was known as "Skyjack Sunday" and it was also the first day of the Jordanian civil war. In the next two weeks, the Jordanian military fought a very bloody civil war on the streets of Amman, inside the alleyways of the squalor refugee camps, and in the mountains near the Israeli and Syrian frontiers. The fight was bitter and close-quarter, but one that the Jordanian military won decisively. The majority of Palestinian terrorist forces ousted during the fighting soon set up shop in Lebanon, but the enormous death toll and unbearable fact that Arab fought Arab caused Palestinians to call the period ***Ailul al-Aswad***--"Black September."

To avenge the ***Ailul al-Aswad***, Yasir Arafat's ***Fatah*** faction of the PLO created a covert and deniable special operations unit that would perpetrate the most aggressive and imaginative of terrorist outrages to strike at Israel and its supporters, but to most importantly punish the Jordanian ruling circle. The first victim of Black September was Wasfi at-Tal, the Jordanian premier, killed as he left a reception at the Cairo Hotel on November 28, 1971; less than two weeks later, the Jordanian ambassador to Great Britain was shot, and the Jordanian embassy in Geneva bombed. The Jordanian response to this new threat was one with its intelligence service, the ***Muchabarat***, in the vanguard; Black September was to be defeated in a covert war of espionage, not a military campaign. Yet following the Munich Olympic Massacre, most nations realized that they were negligently lacking in possession of a force of operators capable of entering a hostage-taking situation with any serious hope of retrieving any innocents alive from a forced entry and inevitable fire-fight. The Royal Jordanian Army's commando element, the 101st Special Forces Battalion, created a small, though highly cohesive force of operators who would train specifically for the fight against terrorism and hostage-rescue. These were the best fighters in the elite Jordanian military--the smartest and toughest soldiers, those with the strongest elements of command and those with the natural skills of innovation and improvisation that are a must in the world of a special forces operators. When a hostage situation transpired in Amman, the Jordanian capital, the unit went into action.

Special Operations Unit team members display their skill at assaulting a bus--here a borrowed Amman cross-town carrier--during maneuvers just outside the Jordanian capital. Note special leather leg holsters for Browning 9mm automatics. (Courtesy: Royal Jordanian Special Forces Command)

At 09:40 hours on the morning of March 26, 1976, four terrorists from Dr. George Habash's Popular Front for the Liberation of Palestine (PFLP) burst into the Intercontinental Hotel in downtown Amman in the attempt to seize hostages and publicize the PFLP's opposition to the discussions at the ongoing Rabat Summit; they were armed with automatic weapons, fragmentation grenades and side-arms. The terrorists, however, were eager for a fight and instead of securing all the civilians in the lobby and taking them hostage, they threw grenades and sprayed the room with gunfire--killing two employees and injuring dozens of guests. Panicking, the terrorists then fired at responding police units before holding up on the roof. The Special Forces unit was rushed to the scene and, once it was established that there were no hostages on the roof of the hotel, commenced their assault began. The battle was fierce and close-quarter. Two special forces operators had been killed, as had seven civilians killed in the terrorists' initial assault. Three of the four terrorists were also killed.

With his MP5 in hand, a Special Operations Unit point man guides his assault team (carrying collapsible ladder) along the side of a building, before attempting a forceful entry. Note K-Bar knife strapped to scabbard in operators leg; Jordanian special forces personnel are renowned throughout the Middle East for their martial arts and close-quarter combat skill. (Courtesy: Royal Jordanian Special Forces Command)

Interesting view of a four-man team preparing to storm a building simulating where hostages are held. Note balaclavas and MP5s carried. (Courtesy: Royal Jordanian Special Forces Command)

In technical terms, the termination of the terrorist squad was a victory, but in realistic terms the death of two of their own and the seven civilians[1] was proof that the unit was not yet ready for full-scale hostage-rescue work. The Jordanian General Staff ordered the 101st Special Forces Battalion to create a CT team that, while being an integral element of the parent unit, would be assigned specific counter-terrorist operations with the security services, as well as all rescue work inside and outside the country. In the early 1990s, the counter-terrorist team was removed from the battalion and upgraded to a national force, under the command and control of the Ministry of Defense and General Staff. Virtually all the unit's operations are classified, especially those involving preventative measures taken against armed terrorists operating in Jordan or using Jordan as a transit point for staging attacks against Israel. Nevertheless, the very fact that so few attacks are actually perpetrated is a testament to the unit's activities and professional level. As one senior SBS officer once stated when talking about counter-terrorist operations, "It's when nobody hears about what we do that the public can rest assured that we are doing our jobs well."

The unit is believed to consist of between 100-200 operators (divided into 30-40 man teams). The force is made up solely of volunteers, virtually 100% Bedouin, whose backgrounds and loyalties are without questions and who have accumulated a positive service record within the battalion. Before a commando can volunteer into the unit, he is (of course) special forces qualified, having undergone basic training and more likely than not training at the hands of U.S. Special Forces or British Special Air Service instructors. Yet before being allowed to join a training class, the volunteer must first pass a special unit medical examination, IQ test, Physical Training test, Endurance Test, and Psychological Test. The actual training regimen for the "Special Operations Unit" consists of (1) physical fitness training; (2) sharp-shooting skills; (3) explosives and EOD; (4) first aid and emergency medical technician training; (5) climbing, and rappelling; (6) heliborne insertion and extraction; (7) assault training--performing rescues against targets like aircraft, buildings, vehicles and ships; (8) special night assault training; and, (9) sniper training. Known for their BDU fatigues and British DPM pattern bullet-proof vests, the unit's equipment consists of the ubiquitous Heckler and Koch MP5 family of 9mm submachine guns, Steyr special police sniper rifles, 12-gauge shotguns, and Browning Hi-Power automatics. Recent reports indicate that the unit will soon replace its MP5s with a 5.56mm weapon--believed to be the SIG SG550/SG551 SP assault rifles.

The Special Operations Unit has had quite a lucrative cooperative history with many of the world's anti-terrorist units, and has trained with the U.S. Army's 1st Special Forces Operations Detachment-Delta

Seconds before the entry, a 12-gauge shotgun (with folding stock) is aimed at a locked door before the force makes its ballistic entry. Note Kevlar ballistic helmet with gas mask, and combination of U.S. and British pattern flak vests. (Courtesy: Royal Jordanian Special Forces Command)

(as well as the FBI's HRT) and other U.S. military special forces, Britain's 22nd Special Air Service Regiment, France's GIGN, and Oman's "Special Force."

It should be noted that, according to published accounts, the Jordanian secret service is reported to deploy an airborne army of sky marshals on board Alia flights to deter in-flight hijackings. Believed to be based at Amman's Queen Alia International Airport, the unit is based loosely along the lines of the Israeli ***Shin Bet*** sky marshals who safeguard El Al, and they are even reported to use suppressed .22 Beretta automatics.[2] The unit only accepts former special forces or combat unit veterans. After a series of terrorist attacks against Jordanian embassies, consulates and installations around Europe and the Middle East, it is believed that this unit expanded its mandate to such security details as well.

A positive and encouraging footnote should be the fact that both Jordan and Israel, as part of the Washington Accords concluding on July 25, 1994, between King Hussein and Israeli Prime Minister Yitzhak Rabin, both countries have pledged to form a joint anti-terrorism task force. As relations between Jordan and Israel improve and the proponents of peace mobilize to counter its enemies, it is not inconceivable that the Special Operation Unit will soon participate in joint maneuvers with Israel's ***Ya'ma'm***.

[1] The seven civilian dead had been killed in the initial terrorist attack.

[2] Although impossible to confirm at this point and time, it has been suggested that the ***Shin Bet*** might have even assisted the Jordanians at setting up this unit.

The ubiquitous killing house--during stopwatch trials, an assault team prepares to enter the wooden and rubber mock-up of a house where hostages are held. (Courtesy: Royal Jordanian Special Forces Command)

A Royal Jordanian Air Force Bell-212 prepares to unload a squad of Rangers during the live-fire exercise at Zarqa. (Samuel M. Katz)

Jordanian special forces offers look on as troops engage in a live-fire exercise. (Samuel M. Katz)

Rangers from the Royal Jordanian Special Forces demonstrate their skills with Khukri. (Samual M. Katz)

Operatiors from the Royal Jordanian Special Forces Ranger Battalion provide the Operation Wings for Peace participants with a high-pitched martial arts display. (Samuel M. Katz)

## South Africa

***There was blood on the tarmac at Johannesburg's sprawling airport, and it was the kind of incident that could ruin the months of prosperity and good will that had overtaken the new South Africa. No longer in the grips of Apartheid, no longer the international Pariah, the new democracy had emerged on the world stage as a nation of reconciliation to be honored and respected throughout the world. White separatists, heavily armed Afrikaners, had hijacked a South African Airways Boeing 747 en route to London and brought it back to Jo'Burg. They demanded the release of 200 fellow white separatists in prisons throughout South Africa in exchange for not killing a hostage every hour--with 300 people on board, the potential for horrific carnage was all too real. The government was not going to acquiesce to the terrorist demands, but they had already killed five hostages and thrown their bodies onto the tarmac. The next hostage was scheduled to die in forty-minutes.***

South African Police Special Task Force cloth hat insignia. (Courtesy: Robert Pitta)

South African Police Special Task Force qualification badge. (Courtesy: Robert Pitta)

South African Police Special Task Force cloth wings. (Courtesy: Robert Pitta)

***In a move meant to convince the hijackers that the demands were to be met, a South African Puma helicopter was flown to their airport and landed in front of the hijacked 747. The landing helicopter kicked up a cloud of dust and made an enormous racket, and it was just the diversion needed. As the hijackers peered out the cockpit window to see if they could identify the man in the suit who had just gotten off the chopper, two dozen men, all wearing civilian dress, produced Armscor BXP 9mm submachine guns from their leather jackets and climbed atop the wing. The lead man set a small explosive charge on the exit door, and then radioed the control tower that the assault was ready. He pulled out a Armscor Z-88 9mm pistol, and then awaited his invitation to the mix--a sniper's round that would take out at least one "tango" in the cockpit. A second after the crack of the 7.62mm round shattered the cockpit glass, the small explosive charge popped the door off its hinge allowing the operators entry into the aircraft. Six men raced toward the cockpit, the remaining eighteen split into two rows of nine and raced toward the rear of the plane in each aisle. Purifying the aircraft took one minute***

***and fifty-three seconds; the emergency chutes were inflated signaling the end of the ordeal. The show at Jo'Burg airport at 5:00 A.M. was just that--a show. On hand were police officials, South African Airway executives, and military and counter-terrorist intelligence officials wishing to see for themselves just how good the STF were. They weren't disappointed.***

Counter-terrorism and hostage-rescue in South Africa is the responsibility of the Police, not the army, and of the Police Special Task Force, or STF, in particular. For years, it was thought that the repressive police measures meant to enforce Apartheid would exclude any possibility for terrorist attack and hostage-taking inside the white areas of South Africa's cities and towns. The Munich Olympics shattered senses of security around the globe, but the call to create a national hostage-rescue force, similar to units being formed throughout Europe, came on April 28, 1974 in what would become known as the "Fox Street Incident." A disgruntled security guard at the Israeli consulate on Fox Street who had headed to the consular offices to kill his supervisor began an ordeal of hostage-taking, wild bursts of automatic fire into the street, and kidnapping that would take the better part of the day to terminate with the suspects capture. Police units from the Flying Squad had cordoned off Fox Street and snipers were in place to take the suspect and his accomplice down, but the incident displayed some serious shortcomings of the ability of the police to respond forcibly and tactically to what could have been--and what sounded like--a terrorist incident. As a result of this incident, it was decided to establish a unit that would specialize in the handling of hostage and similar situations. The Special Task Force was established in January 1976.

Faced with tribal discord, the African National Congress and a whole host of mercenaries, white separatists and criminal gangs, the STF found itself to be a very busy unit. Much of their work in the early years was as a tactical back-up to the operations of the notorious Bureau of State Security, the much dreaded counter-intelligence agency known by the acronym of "BOSS." The unit, commanded by a combination of police veterans and army special forces commandos, primarily from the legendary Reconnaissance Regiment, proved to be a formidable unit; an initial training stint in Israel helped set a course that would be followed to this day. The unit adopted the Israeli-method of ***Gibush*** or selection period for pre-screening volunteers, and then applying stringent acceptance standards throughout the unit's six month training. At present, applicants must be permanent members of the South African Police, at least twenty-one years of age, have performed at least two years of practical police service and be physically and mentally suited to rigorous training. Such an applicant must be mature, have sound judgment and display definite leadership qualities.

The applicant is subjected to a Task Force selection course which involves, among other things, psychological aptitudes tests, a selection course, a basic training course of approximately six months and specialized training for a period of approximately one year. On successful completion of the selection course, members must undertake to serve in the unit for at least two years. The training involves counter insurgency (bush warfare), anti-urban terrorism (dealing with hostage situations and take-over dramas), tactical rescue operations, long-range rescue operations (mountaineering and other rescue techniques to recover hostages stashed in the bush or wilderness), handling of weapons (all locally made as well as terrorist weapons), the handling and identification of explosives, home-made explosive devices and weapons, the guarding of very important persons, parachuting and diving, the training of other special units, the combating of unrest, marksmanship and evaluation of new equipment.

A scene from the Silverton Bank Siege--the first deployment of the STF during a hostage-rescue scenario. (Paratus Magazine courtesy of Robert Pitta)

A STF sniper peers through the scope of his weapon before unleashing a 7.62mm round into the target's epicenter. (Paratus Magazine courtesy of Robert Pitta)

STF operators in training. (Paratus Magazine courtesy of Robert Pitta)

A South African Police counter-insurgency unit in action during the 1976 riots--the inability of the police to deal with selective terrorists incidents led to the creation of the STF. (Paratus Magazine courtesy of Robert Pitta)

STF operators training in house entries and assaults. Because of South Africa's diverse geographic landscape, STF operators must train in an enormous variety of settings--from assaulting a cave in the bush to rappelling down the side of a skyscraper in cosmopolitan Johannesburg. (Paratus Magazine courtesy of Robert Pitta)

The training is conducted approximately 230 kilometers from Pretoria at the Task Force's training center. On average only twenty-five percent of the applicants pass the selection test. The training techniques employed by the unit are techniques developed and perfected locally as well as techniques used by special units abroad and adapted to South African conditions. Most details of the training are classified top-secret.

Since its inception the Task Force has been used in numerous operations. These operations were, among others, the tracing and elimination of terrorists, terrorist bases and arms caches, the rescue of hostages, underwater searches for bodies and evidence, and rescue work (mountain rescue). Their most famous--and most publicized--operation was the January 25, 1980 siege outside the Silverton Branch of the Volkskas Bank in the capital of Pretoria. Three ANC terrorists, armed with grenades and AK-47 assault rifles took the customers and employees of the branch hostage and the STF was immediately summoned to the scene; the terrorists demanded the release of ANC leader Nelson Mandela and others from custody. The STF deployed for action, but the first plan was to eliminate the terrorists with sniper rounds, thereby reducing risk of any hostages being killed or wounded in a frontal assault. Captain De Swardt of the STF carried out negotiations with the gunmen, but they were in no mood to talk and refused to leave their secure positions inside the bank; snipers, situated on nearby rooftops reported that they had no shots. Fearing that the hostages were about to be executed, Captain De Swardt ordered the STF inside. Following the detonation of several flash bang grenades, the STF assault force stormed the bank branch and split into two groups: the first group engaged the terrorists and immediately killed two of them, while the second squad supervised and covered the evacuation of the hostages. Before the third terrorist could be killed he managed to squeeze off twenty-seven rounds from his AK-47 into the fleeing and panicking hostages; one was killed and nine injured before a point blank full-auto burst of 9mm fire ended the third terrorists' life. The entire assault took all of 100 seconds.

Other STF operations include:

- The July 30, 1988 hostage situation at Goedemoed Prison, where twenty-two prisoners attacked the prison guards and took one hostage. Although armed with nothing more than "shanks" (sharpened objects), the prisoners repeatedly stabbed their hostage and threatened to slash his throat unless they were released. The SAP Special Task Force was summoned and nine operators flown to Goedemoed Prison. In a joint operation with a prison negotiator, one of the prisoners was killed and another wounded by STF fire and the hostage freed.
- The September 14, 1988, bus hijacking at Lesotho, where terrorists from the Lesotho Freedom Alliance hijacked a bus transporting seventy-four passengers outside the British embassy who were en route to hear the Pope speak, who at the time was visiting Maseru. The Special Task Forces was summoned to intervene and immediately surrounded the bus and commenced negotiations. When the terrorists began firing at the British embassy and attempting to use the bus as a battering ram to get inside the embassy grounds, the STF responded tactically. The operators stormed the bus and killed three terrorists and captured one more; seventeen hostages were injured in the melee.
- On July 4, 1993, an emotionally unstable individual brandishing a weapon hijacked a Fokker FU28 aircraft of the Royal Swazi Airlines to Jan Smuts Airport near Johannesburg; twenty-one crew and passengers were taken hostages. The STF was summoned and twenty-two operators despatched the airport to ready a rescue operation. With only one hijacker on board, the operators were able to gain access to the aircraft without difficulty and the storming of the airliner achieved in a matter of seconds; the hijacker was shot in the head (though lived) in the assault, one hostage was wounded in the shoulder and the pilot was shot in the leg in the gun battle.

Members of the Task Force continually undergo retraining to ensure that the standard of fitness and expertise is kept at a high level. Members must be ready at all times to leave for any place in the country. The nature of the activities of the Task Force means, almost without exception, that the members must leave at short notice; police helicopters, as well as choppers belonging to the army, air force and navy, are made available to the unit at all times and without the bureaucratic difficulties usually encountered in police or military operations. Some of the policemen are parachutist-qualified and are veterans of reconnaissance units, and as a result could be parachuted into a targeted area.

Beyond their role in defeating terrorism, members of the Special Task Force play an important role in combating serious crimes and criminals as well, including heavily armed organized gangs, narcotics smuggling groups, and tribal criminal gangs that are heavily armed and ruthless.

Little information is available on the weaponry carried by STF personnel, and about their foreign contacts and cross-training. It is known that virtually all their gear and weaponry is produced in South Africa, including the X-88 9mm pistols, the BXP 9m submachine gun and the R4 and R5 5.56mm assault rifles (copies of the Israeli Galil). It is known that the STF has trained in Israel and has been trained by Israeli instructors, and is also believed to have trained with Taiwanese counter-terrorist units. Now that apartheid has ended and South Africa has returned to the "family of nations," it is believed that the STF will expand on its foreign contacts and begin making the "circuit" tour of similar police units in Africa, the Middle East and Europe.

Another South African counter-terrorist that is no longer in service but is still worthy of mention was the South African Railway Police Special Task Force. The South African Railway Police (SARP) traces its roots to 1867 and is one of the oldest police organizations in the world. Its Special Task Force (SARP STF) was formed on October 24, 1975, as the force specifically mandated with hostage rescue on board ships, aircraft, trains and buses throughout South Africa. Like its regular police counterpart, the SARP STF was tasked with a wide geographic diversity, from stalking a hijacked bus traveling on a dirt road in the bush, to assaulting a hijacked airliner. SARP STF personnel were trained at South African Defense Force reconnaissance bases, and its operators armed with Israeli-produced Uzi 9mm submachine guns. The unit was feared by most blacks and Asians, and their special camouflage uniforms and camouflage berets became notorious. The unit was disbanded on October 1, 1986, and its personnel incorporated into the STF where their tubular assault expertise was immediately put into the unit's books.

Two STF officers slowly approach a targeted house during an exercise. The FN rifle was used until the early 1990s, as operators found the 7.62mm round suitable for their tasks. The primary weapon of choice is now the Mini-Uzi or BXP 9mm submachine gun and the R4 and R5 5.56mm assault rifles. (Paratus Magazine courtesy of Robert Pitta)

The Israeli-produced 7.62mm Galil sniper rifle--used for nearly ten years by STF snipers. (IMI-Ta'as)

Instruction at the STF training facility near Pretoria. The distinctive Maleoskop emblem can be clearly seen in the background. (Paratus Magazine courtesy of Robert Pitta)

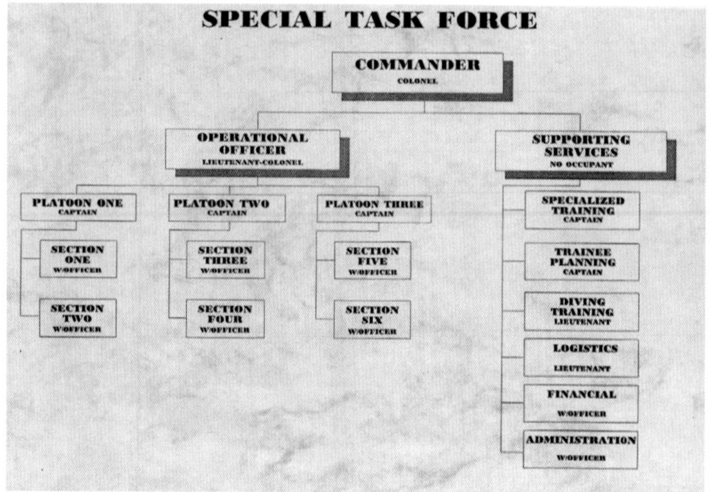


The Special Task Force Organizational Chart.

# Australia

***January 16, 1995, Kingsford-Smith International Airport; Sydney, Australia:** The face of one Ramzi Ahmed Yousef, a twenty-seven-year old Kuwaiti-born terrorist, was engraved in the minds of several dozen men, all wearing black Nomex coveralls, as they sat inside the hold of their S-70-9 chopper circling the airport arrivals terminal. Ramzi Yousef, wanted by the American FBI for his role in masterminding the February 26, 1993, bombing of the World Trade Center in New York City, had been on the run for nearly two years—with a $2,000,000 price on his head, and he was reported to have been seen in Iraq and Iran. In January 1995, however, he was sighted in Manila, "PI," at a very inconvenient time for law enforcement officials—coinciding with a visit to The Philippines by Pope John Paul II. On January 7, 1995, Philippine Police raided an apartment suspected of being a terrorist safe-house—in the flat, authorities uncovered itineraries of American airlines, material on the Pope, explosives, and Ramzi Yousef's fingerprints. The raided apartment was within 100 meters of where the pontiff was to have stayed during his four day visit to the islands and Philippine authorities were concerned that a major terrorist network, one that had already shown its penchant for setting off bombs, was about to strike against a most sensitive of targets. The raid in Manila also set off buzzers in Canberra, the capital of Australia. Following his visit to The Philippines, Pope John Paul II was due in Sydney for a whirlwind thirty-nine hour visit to Australia. Police officials in Sydney mobilized their forces, as did the Defense Ministry. The phone also rang at Campbell Barracks, Swanbourne—home of the Australian Army's 1st Special Air Service Regiment (SASR) and its elite hand-picked group of counter-terrorist operators, the Tactical Assault Group (TAG).*

The Regimental beret badge—"Who Dares Wins."

***Just the thought of Pope John Paul II visiting Australia being pursued and targeted by Mr. Yousef caused tremendous concern in the halls of the Ministry of Defense, and in the secret halls of the Australian Security and Intelligence Organization (ASIO). Australian officials didn't know what they were up against and weren't in the mood to take any chances. Pope John Paul II would be protected—the police would see to it, so would the TAG. Airborne over Sydney's airport, the choppers ferrying the TAG's A-Team was preparing for any and all contingencies—an attempted assassination, a bombing, a random automatic fire assault or, worse, the taking of hostages. The operators in the chopper had been through it all and had trained for any contingency imaginable in the CO's wicked and sadistic mind. Now they realized why that had been forced to do what it took to earn their wings and badge, and what it took to stay in the regiment. Honing their minds and bodies guaranteed that they'd be focused and attentive. As the S-70-9 made one more fly-over of the airport, the operators clutched their MP5s ever so tighter and pulled their balaclavas down over their faces with a bit more determination.***

***When the chopper landed and the operators raced out to a briefing at a secluded stretch of the airfield, the operators were covered by two TAG sniper teams, men peering through field glasses and the sights of a PSG-1 7.62mm sniper rifle, as well as a Tikka Finlander .22-250 suppressed precision weapon. The Pope would not be harmed this day in Australia.***

Counter-terrorism in Australia, like any tactical scenario requiring the work of the specialists, is the primary domain of the Australian Army's 1st Special Air Service Regiment (1 SASR).[1] One of the most romanticized military units in existence anywhere in the world, the Australian branch of the "Who Dares Wins" motto, has become legendary as one of the world's finest special operations forces, as well as certainly among the most professional.

The Australian SAS dates back to the Second World War when the Australian Army raised and operated a number of independent companies and commando squadrons to wreak havoc behind Japanese lines. With its aggressive raids and innovative sabotage strikes—the now legendary "Z Force" was respected by both the Allied Command and the Japanese who engaged them in the jungle. Australian special forces, known for their intuitive skill and unquestionable courage under fire, operated in small groups of specially trained men and organized personnel, operating independently or in concert with conventional or indigenous forces. They exerted disproportionate influence to their numbers on the battlefield. The 250 men of 2/2nd Independent Commando Company, for example, conducted behind-enemy-line sabotage and harassment operations on the island of Timor in 1942. While losing forty men in engagements with Japanese forces,

An SASR operator training at Fort Bragg, North Carolina, with fellow operators from the U.S. Army's 1st SFOD-Delta (Courtesy: Hans Halberstadt/Arms Communications)

A painting at the Killing House at Campbell Barracks, Swanbourne. (Courtesy: Australian Special Forces)

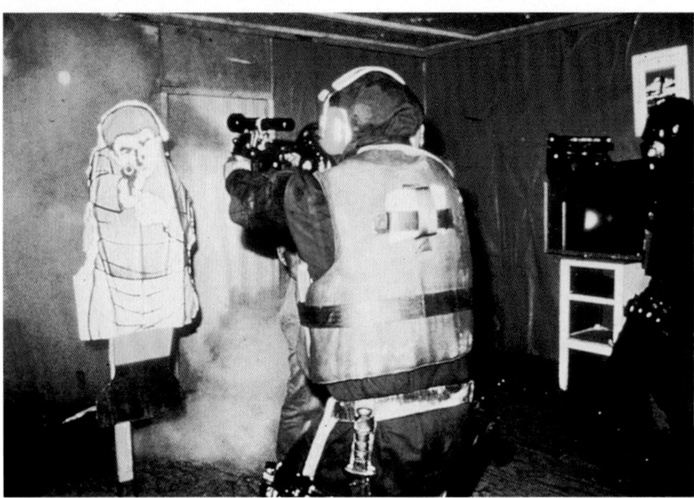

A TAG fire team engages a target inside the unit Killing House—the MP5K is the favorite weapon of Australia's counter-terrorist operators. (Courtesy: Australian Special Forces)

they successfully tied down 30,000 Japanese soldiers for nearly a year. In August 1943, a handful of men from Special Operations Australia (SOA) conducted a covert raid on Singapore harbor in which they sank 39,000 tons of enemy shipping in a single raid. Few Allied soldiers who saw the Australian special forces in action could have imagined there being any better soldiers. In fact, one British Special Air Service officer wrote of his Australian counterparts, "By temperament and environment and quick wits, I have always imagined that the Australian soldier would provide the ideal SAS material."

Following the war most of the regular army units were demobilized, though on October 23, 1951, an airborne platoon of the Royal Australian Regiment (RAR) was created, followed, in 1955, by two Commando Companies that were part of the Citizen's Military Force. Having studied the British experience—and success—in special operations warfare in Malaya, the Australian 1st Special Air Service Company (RAR) was created in early 1957—completely along British lines. The primary role of this new unit was medium-range reconnaissance, long-range intelligence-gathering, and specified military tasks. The Australian Directorate of Military Operations, a body known for thinking camouflage paint was revolutionary, was naturally suspicious of this new elite entity—especially since its equipment requisition list included everything from plastic explosives to Klepper canoes. Until 1964, when the unit was deployed to Borneo to participate in the counter-insurgency campaign alongside the British SAS and SBS, the 1st Special Air Service Company trained incessantly in the hostile and treacherous terrain of northwestern Australia. Following its successful counter-insurgency operations in Borneo, a mission that earned them the respect of their brethren from Hereford, the unit severed its linked to the Royal Australian Regiment and developed into its own special operations regiment, the SASR, consisting of two field squadrons and a HQ Squadron. The Australian SASR was deployed to Borneo alongside British and New Zealand Special Air Service squadrons in the fight against Indonesian insurgents. At the same time, the SASR was posted to South Vietnam where their efforts earned them the name of ***Ma Rung***, or "Jungle Ghosts." During their ten years of service in Vietnam, the Australian SASR (alongside the New Zealand SAS) killed over 500 of the enemy while suffering one combat fatality.

Following Vietnam, the unit returned to Australia in 1972 more professional and battle-ready than an Australian combat unit had ever been. In Vietnam the SASR worked side-by-side with American special forces and a unique relationship between the SASR and the U.S. Army Special Forces exists to this day. Following Vietnam, the list of names wishing to volunteer into the SASR swelled far beyond what the regiment had room—or desire—to accept. Today, the regiment is open to all active duty personnel who have been in the military for at least two years, and the average age of the volunteer for NCOs is twenty-five, and for officers records indicate that the average age is twenty-seven. To hone the regiment into a highly selective special forces entity, an extremely stringent selection process was soon developed—a three week exercise in torture that is considered by many to be the toughest in the world. Before a soldier is allowed to volunteer into the SASR, he must pass a grueling three week process of elimination meant to prove if he is, indeed, Special Air Service material. Among the noted aspects of this test period, conducted at the legendary Stirling Ranges in southwestern Australia, include a five-day navigation's course requiring each man carry more than fifty kilograms of equipment and rations over some of the most inhospitable terrain on the planet; a three-day exercise on one day's rations; and, daily twenty-kilometer runs with a rifle (no slings, of course) and a forty-kilo load. The purpose of the selection of process is simple—to determine which candidates, called "Rangers" have the physical metal and the mental will to persevere and overcome and challenge and hardship. According to a SASR lieutenant-colonel at Stirling Lines, "Physical toughness is important, but that is more easily achieved and measured than is the mental side which is a combination of maturity, confidence, intelligence and motivation." While SASR selection courses are slightly different from year to year. Each year, approximately 400 soldiers in various branches of the Australian military place their names on the list applying for a spot on the SASR's bi-annual selection process with most of the NCOs and officers working out a full-year before even thinking of volunteering. The usual "survival" rate for the selection process is less than ten percent. many of those who fail the selection process end up in hospital, as do several candidates who pass the process, as well. It is that grueling.

According to Lieutenant-Colonel David G. Christie, the Australian SAS Regiment Liaison Officer to the United States Army Special Operations Command assigned to the JFK Special Warfare Center and School, "The selection course is approximately three weeks in duration but it is not meant to teach. It is designed to identify those applicants best equipped to be able to assimilate the demanding year of training that will follow the selection course and then use that training to accomplish assigned tasks. Motivation plays a very big part in success on the selection course and in service in the regiment." The selection course was designed to make the volunteer ready for the nearly year-long training regiment meant to earn the sand-colored beret; the training is meant to prepare the operator for any mission he might encounter—even counter-terrorism and hostage-rescue.

Following the Vietnam War, the SASR was immediately given a new roles inside Australia, conducting regional long-range surveillance patrols (LRSPs) in the vast northwestern deserts, and training for war-time missions—no matter who the enemy. From 1957 to 1978, however, the thought of deploying the 1st SASR in a counter-terrorist role was considerable "unthinkable." At 00:40 Hours on the morning of February 13, 1978, a powerful bomb ripped through the entrance of the Hilton Hotel, on George Street, in central Sydney; two persons were killed and six seriously hurt. A major international conference was set to commence at the hotel the next morning and the Indian Prime Minister, Moraji Desai, was asleep in his suite when the blast went off (the attack was allegedly carried out by the extremist Ananda Marga religious sect). Terrorism was something that happened in Belfast, Beirut, Jerusalem and Munich—not New South Wales. Australia had been immune to the horror of terrorism, but its physical isolation in the south Pacific was no guarantee that terrorists wouldn't use the continent as an extended battleground, nor could it guarantee that Australian aircraft wouldn't be hijacked and its government officials kidnapped or assassinated. Ten days following the Hilton Hotel bombing, the government of Prime Minster Malcolm Fraser announced immediate measures meant to safeguard the nation against terrorist attack and establish a security infrastructure designed to counter, thwart and deter terrorist strikes against Australia proper and against Australian interests around the world. With examples of Entebbe and Mogadishu fresh in everyone's mind, it was clear that Australia's principal response to terrorism would come from the 1st SASR. A newly formed 1 Squadron would be the CT Force, while 2 and 3 Squadrons would train for the Regiment's wartime role and were subdivided into a headquarters, free-fall troop, water operations troop and a vehicle-mounted troop. Operationally, four- to six-man patrols are deployed depending on the task and manning levels. Radio communications are maintained by "152 Signals Squadron." A signal troop is attached to the headquarters of each "Sabre Squadron." "Base Squadron" is responsible for local administration and logistical support. It has the capacity to detach medical, mechanical, transport and catering specialists to the "Sabre" Squadrons when they are deployed independently form the Regiment. Training Squadron is responsible for SASR selection and advanced training and is decided into six wings: Water Operations Wing conducts specialist courses for combat divers and small marine operation; Climbing/Survival Wing teaches basic survival skills and roping/abseiling techniques; Demolition Wing teaches all aspects of explosives and sabotage; Vehicle-Mounted Wing teaches navigation, maintenance and all other aspects of long-range vehicle patrols; and Reinforcement Wing conducts SAS selection and coordinates the reinforcement training cycle.

Australia has a federal system of government with administrative responsibilities divided between Federal and State Governments. Under the Australian Constitution, the Federal Government has responsibility for such matters as national defense, foreign relations, aviation, trade and immigration, to mention just a few. The six States, the Northern Territory and the Australian Capital Territory Government are responsible, amongst other things, for law enforcement. The Federal Government has no power to over-ride the States/Territory Governments and must therefore rely on cooperation where law enforcement matters extend beyond State/Territory boundaries. As a result the Australian Governments have established a national committee to oversight counter terrorism arrangements. That committee, known as the Standing Advisory Committee on Commonwealth/State Cooperation for Protection Against Violence or SAC PAV, is administered by the Protective Security Coordination Center, part of the Federal Attorney General's Department. The SAC-PAV maintains a national anti terrorist plan and facilitates the development and maintenance of capabilities on a nation-wide basis which are required to prevent and respond to acts of politically motivated violence, including terrorism. In relation to assault capabilities each State police service maintains a police assault group which is used for both serious criminal incidents and counter terrorism. These groups would be backed up by the SASR.

Even before the Hilton Hotel bombing, the SASR had trained in the art of close-quarter battle, including the A-Zs of house-to-house combat, but its training regimen did not focus on assaulting fortified targets seized by terrorists where hostages were held and required rescue. The regiment did not train in assaulting passenger aircraft, ferries or ships, nor did its operators train to operate in civilian dress in undercover work. Most importantly, there wasn't a single specific unit within the regiment tasked with dealing with irregular warfare or counter-terrorist work. Following the Israeli rescue at Entebbe, officers in the SASR began to take the matter of counter-terrorism potential far more seriously as this was the first known example of a special operations military unit being called upon to rescue hostages from terrorists; subsequently, the 1977 rescue at Mogadishu had similar effects of sparking interest in the regiment as to a potential course of action. In 1977, Colonel John Essex-Clark, commander of the Infantry Center, ventured to the United Kingdom, the Netherlands, the Federal Republic of Germany and the United States to view how other nations around the world were gearing their own special operations units for the fight against terrorism. In August 1978, a formal plan to create an army counter-terrorist unit was accepted by SO1 (Joint and Special Warfare section) and the Chief of the Defense Force Staff. Provisionally, it was to be called the "Tactical Assault Group" (TAG) and it was suggested that the unit be a part of the SASR. At Campbell Barracks, Swanbourne, the decision was met by cheers and energetic enthusiasm at the home of the regiment. Even before the first dollar headed toward the unit to establish the TAG unit, NCOs and junior officers began constructing urban training simulators and scouring the junkyards of Australia for buses and discarded train carriages that could be used for tubular assault practice. Until the government approved funding, in fact, the Killing House was nothing more than thousands of sandbags, sheets of plywood and galvanized iron; the unit's financial problems in establishing the unit were so dire, that gas masks had to be borrowed from the Western Australia Police Department.

An OAT team races to a rig being used as a training field in the Bass Straits. (Courtesy: Australian Special Forces)

From the onset SASR officers knew that the TAG entity would have to be an on-call force, as well as one that could be completely mobile and have all its gear packed and stored on palettes ready for transport to anywhere in Australia, and the world—much like the British 22 Special Air Service and its SP Teams. Traditionally, each "troop" had its own specialty: "A Troop" had been the free-fall troop, "B Troop" was the naval special warfare entity of the regiment, and "C Troop" had specialized in vehicle operations and long-range reconnaissance in the bush. Now, with a new mandate, "B Troop" became the TAG and "C Troop" was absorbed into "A Troop" which continued its training and operations in preparations for any wartime tasks it might be called up to perform. With governmental funding, the unit was allowed to hone its skills in order to be able respond to any terrorist-attack scenario. The TAG's facilities at Campbell Barracks, Swanbourne were reported to have cost A$22 million and include advanced electronic outdoor close quarter battle ranges, an outdoor snipers' range and numerous urban training scenarios at Swanbourne; a special urban CT complex and vertical snipers' range at Bindoon; and aircraft mock-ups at Gin Gin airfield, Western Australia. The unit had extraordinary influence from the British 22 SAS, as TAG officers were frequent students and visitors at Hereford. With a budget permitting overseas travel, TAG personnel also visited St. Augustin, Germany, and GSG-9, as well as the newly formed U.S. Army's 1st SFOD-Delta at Fort Bragg, North Carolina.

TAG training became incessant and highly ballistic; "You'd need a calculator and an army of cleaning men to figure out how many rounds we fire a week," boasted one TAG veteran visiting Fort Bragg. The 1st SASR TAG philosophy behind training its operators for the "real thing" was to acquaint them with the very feel of firepower so that it became second nature. By just being in the regiment the men had proven that they could march faster and farther than anyone else in the Australian Army, and they new how to conceal themselves better than most creatures in the bush, and they could sabotage the most heavily guarded of enemy installations. But bursting into the lobby of a Sydney hotel and rescuing scores of hostages from the gun sights of suicidal fanatics required more than good soldiering—it demanded instincts and a second-nature feel for the work.

The incredible training regimen TAG operators were subjected to began to drain the overall capabilities of the regiment, including its conventional tasks. But before additional funds and personnel could be channeled into the unit, Canberra came up with yet another role for the regiment's counter-terrorist capabilities—maritime hostage-rescue. In July 1980, the regiment received a directive from the Ministry of Defense that it needed to develop capabilities to retake offshore oil platforms in Bass Strait. The code-word BURSA was to be used when referring to any such incident and the maritime unit was to be called the Offshore Installations Assault Group (OAG); several instructors from the SBS arrived in Australia to help set up the unit. As this new unit presented an incredible manpower drain on the unit. According to reports, the Australian Ministry of Defense at first wanted the TAG to consist of two operational teams with no more than forty operators. Since the unit also had to have a support team in training, the OAG's and the required support and logistic staff would have warranted that the unit exceed 200 operators. As a result, the TAG and the OAG enlisted the support of the Royal Australian Navy's Clearance Diving Teams with over twenty operators changing their branch of service to join the SASR.[2]

SASR officers were determined to make the OAG a separate but equal element of the TAG and were adamant about staying clear from the competition and bitterness that not only existed between the British SAS and SBS, but among Delta and SEAL Team SIX in the United States. Eventually, the OAG had its calling card change to the Offshore Assault Team (OAT) and sent its personnel for training assignments in Great Britain, West Germany, the United States, and Thailand. For months after the decision to create the OAG, oil rig workers were perplexed by the sight of Sea King choppers hovering over abandoned rigs engulfed by white and red smoke, and immersed in the sounds of automatic gun fire.

A TAG/OAT diver awaits his summon to action. (Courtesy: Australian Special Forces)

The CT Force provides routine security for VIPs and at important public events, for example the Commonwealth Games, and has been placed on Special CT Alert three times: after the bombing of the Israeli consulate in Sydney (December 1982); after a threat to blow up TAA aircraft (January 1983); and when the Australian Security and Intelligence Organization (ASIO) reported the likelihood of Armenian terrorist attacks in Australia (August 1983).

The Group was kitted out with tried and tested equipment from Britain's 22 SAS and was trained in close quarter battle and hostage-rescue techniques. Virtually every fact of the Hereford philosophy, from training to actual assault courses, were replicated in the Campbell Barracks, Swanbourne, along with the meticulous adherence toward professionalism. While the TAG assault course is equipped with the obligatory Killing House; the SASR specialty is low-light encounters where operators burst into a dark room and at the commander's barking are ordered to turn on their weapon's flashlights and fire at the targets—all which must be hit within seconds. Much of its training is carried out late at night in various towns and cities on actual structures. Although the Australian deny this practice, the unit has been seen performing mock assaults on high-rise buildings, emphasizing portals of entry such as air-conditioning ducts and lift shafts, as well as on actual aircraft and ships in airports and harbors.

The SASR wears standard Australian Army uniforms with the distinctive sand colored beret and the famous winged dagger SAS badge. British Special Air Service-type straight-topped parachute wings are usually worn on the right upper sleeve. The principal weapon carried by the Regiment is the M16A2 5.56mm assault rifle and the Australian-produced F88 5.56mm assault rifle (the indigenous copy of the Austrian-produced Steyr), though the TAG operators are firm believers in the MP5 family of 9mm submachine guns. Virtually ever variant of the MP5 is carried by the unit, including an indigenously-modified MP5 SD4 fitted with an elongated silencer and a forward attached pistol grip. The favored MP5 submachine, however, is the MP5K, usually carried by operators also packing a Beretta 12-gauge RS202 M1-M2 shotgun in a side-pouch. SASR/TAG/OAT sniper rifles include the Ta'as 7.62mm Israeli-produced Galil rifle, the Heckler and Koch PSG-1 7.62mm rifle, the Finnish Tikka Finlander .223, and the Parker Hale Model 82 sniper rifle—favored by many of the old timer TAG snipers. Australians are particularly fond of handguns, and the favored SASR weapon is the Browning HP 9mm, though quite a few SIG-Sauer P228s are being carried out in the field.

All SASR TAG and OAT personnel are airborne qualified, and parachute quite frequently in both static-line and HALO techniques—most regiment personnel are as familiar with the insides of a C-130 Hercules as they are with their own pickup trucks. SASR TAG operators are also among the world's best at heliborne insertions, fast-roping and rappelling down lines into jungle clearings and atop city skyscrapers. A SASR TAG specialty is deploying from F-100 counter-terrorist vehicles—stopping short before a target and then assaulting a building or a fortification with blinding speed and lethal firepower.

Overall policy, planning, liaison and coordination of SAS operations is handled by the Director of Special Action Forces at the

Army Office in Canberra. Perhaps the glue, or intelligence bond, that coordinates, directs and sometimes participates in Australian counter-terrorist operations is the much vaunted Australian Security and Intelligence Organization (ASIO), the Australian intelligence-gathering and counter-intelligence service formed in 1950. While a tight, and seemingly hermetic, veil of secrecy surrounds the ASIO, they have been involved in several operations where they have exceeded their authority and professional guidelines in zealous behavior including staging (while most of the agents were drunk) a mock hostage-rescue operation in the lobby of the Melbourne Sheraton Hotel.

The TAG and OAT units frequently train with foreign units, especially the U.S. Army's 1st SFOD-Delta and the U.S. Navy's SEAL Team SIX; Australian officers are permanently assigned to both Fort Bragg and Little Creek, NAB. The unit also cross-trains with the SAS and SBS in Great Britain, GSG-9 in Germany, and most of the hostage-rescue units in southeast Asia.

On a local level, as per the individual Australian states, "routine" terrorist/hard-core criminal situations, including those where hostages are being held, are the responsibility of the local state SWAT units. All of these units are trained by the Australian SAS, as well as other counter-terrorist units around the world (from local Asian units, like the national police hostage-rescue team in New Zealand to similar units in Singapore, to such international units as GSG-9 and the FBI's HRT). Considering the vast stretches of territories that must be covered to reach Police SWAT units are provided with a wide assortment of transport—from all -terrain Rovers and carriers to the service of police, and even Army Bell-212 choppers usually on stand-by status for the SASR. One recent example of one of these SWAT units action came on December 5, 1994, when a tactical unit in Melbourne shot and killed a deranged gunmen who had gone on a shooting rampage in a northern suburb. The primary policy of the state SWAT units in Australia is "Containment and Negotiations." Virtually all SWAT members are full-time tactical cops and, as a result, their down time is spent training and honing their skills. The state of New South Wales, for example, possesses a sixty-man SWAT unit known as the State Protection Group (SPG), all equipped with Heckler and Koch MP5s and Glock 17s. The SPG also possesses fifteen snipers, all expertly trained, all dead-on shots with their Remington 700 .308 rifles; the rifles are all fitted with carbon fiber stocks and re-barreled with a fluted stainless steel barrel produced in Australia by Tobler Barrels. The Remington's are fitted with 6 x 42 Leupold scopes and US 168 grain hollow point Winchester rounds.

Other Australian police SWAT units, using Uzi 9mm submachine guns and M16A2s and CAR-15 5.56mm assault rifles, and MP5s, include The Tasmanian Police's Special Operations Group (SOG); the Victoria Police's SOG; the Queensland's Police Special Emergency Response Team (SERT); Western Australian Police's Tactical Response Group (TRG); Northwest Territory Police's Task Force (TF); and South Australia Police's Special Tasks and Rescue Force (STAR Force).

[1] The Special Forces community in Australia consists of Headquarters Special Forces; the 1st Special Air Service Regiments; and, the 1st Commando Regiment.

[2] These divers, as a result of a protest by SASR personnel unwilling to have their ranks diluted with "unworthy sailors," had to endure and pass the SASR Selection Course as well as jump training.

A TAG operator, perfecting all forms of stealth-like insertion, engages in a free-fall jump from a Royal Australian Air Force C-130 Hercules. (Courtesy: Australian Special Forces)

## China

Although the Chinese have always had some form of para-military response to terrorist attack--should such an unlikely scenario transpire--it has been organized very much along as hoc People's Liberation Army (PLA) lines. The Tiananmen incident showed a glaring weakness in the Chinese Government's ability and spectrum of response to instantaneous acts of rebellion, armed opposition and conceivably terrorist attack. As illustrated by the Tiananmen Square massacre, the PLA had no means of combating a minor civil insurrections with anything other than tanks!

The Public Security Bureau (PSB), which is organized on a provincial basis, was tasked to address this both from the tactical and equipment standpoint. A force of approximately 6,000 was organized to deal with civil insurrection and more specialist incidents--the Shenzen Stock Exchange riots showed their ability to use CS and other riot control tools.

In the late 1980s, a unit was formed in Peking to deal, specifically, with counter-terrorist operations. The unit is small and consists of approximately forty operators; the unit is believed to have grown in size in 1993, following Beijing's attempts to be awarded host city for the 2000 Olympics and, in fact, is believed to have been formed as a direct response to the People's Republic of China's desire to host an Olympic game and lessen the edge of its sharpened image following the Tiananmen Square massacre.

The unit's ethos is very much along "Kung Fu" lines and any and all demos provided to members of the media (although they have been very few in nature) depict their ability to withstand spear attacks, dagger assaults to the throat, and all the good Shaolin material of a bad B martial arts film rather than demonstrating their skills and prowess in a CQB warfare. Although their budget is endless and they've sought Western equipment and weaponry, the unit has had to make do with the procurement of MP5 imitations of Pakistan origin. The unit is undoubtedly very fit and motivated. Strategically and tactically for the CT role they have not been tested, although there are one or two western security firms with the background in CT operations, including Israeli and French companies, vying to teach them or at least get contracts to do so.

## Hong Kong

The SDU emblem.

In 1974, two years following the Munich Olympic Massacre, the Hong Kong government recognized the need for a well equipped and professionally trained counter-terrorist unit in order to provide an effective response to the ever increasing threat of international terrorism; in late 1972, Black September terrorists seized the Israeli embassy in Bangkok, Thailand, and the possibility of such an attack in Hong Kong was very real. Along with most other governments at the time, the Hong Kong Government took the policy line that perpetrators of terrorist acts would not be provided with sanctuary or immunity and that all efforts would be made to bring them to trial, or, in scenarios where terrorists choose to end a situation with gunfire, take them down.

With such a policy it was obvious that a military response capability was necessary in order to provide credibility to the firm stance the government was prepared to take. The Royal Hong Kong Police was tasked with setting up such a Unit and in mid-1974 a small team was established from within Royal Hong Kong Police resources and using existing police weaponry. This team then set about equipping itself with the skills and techniques required to provide an armed response, and with the tools, equipment, weaponry and modes of transportation to reach and deal with virtually any terrorist scenario. The force was called the Special Duties Unit, but now more commonly known by its SDU acronym.

In early 1978, a supervisory team from the British 22nd Special Air Service Regiment was invited to Hong Kong, initially to evaluate the team and then subsequently to train a land assault team based on their own order of battle, as well as instruct the Hong Kong police unit in SAS doctrine, training techniques, and tactical deployment. This advisory group, consisting of over twenty men, trained two police assault teams. In 1982, in an incident still considered classified, the possibility of a maritime terrorist threat was realized and an advisory team from the British Special Boat Service (SBS) counter-terrorism unit, "M Squadron," ventured to the Far East to help the Hong Kong Police SDU establish a special, SCUBA-trained water team.

Twenty years ago, the SDU was a small force of volunteers. Today, it consists of over 100 officers and is growing annually. The SDU a solid international reputation and is held in high regard by its overseas counterparts (especially with Singapore, Thai, Australian, New Zealand and, of course, UK units, as well as American SWAT units and Germany's GSG-9) with whom it conducts regular joint exchange both locally and overseas. Because of the financial stability of the government the unit has always received state-of-the-art equipment and training facilities. As an example of recent procurements to improve overall efficiency the unit now boasts:

1) Two S-70 Blackhawk helicopters with logistical support

Operators from an assault team climb up the stairs of a "shooting house," their MP5s in hand, during urban assault exercises in the New Territories. (Courtesy: Royal Hong Kong Police)

An all-out assault by the SDU during a training exercise. While one fire team deploys from the top of a vehicle courtesy of a modified ladder, another team fast ropes down the side of a S-70. (Courtesy: Royal Hong Kong Police)

from the Government Flying Service (GFS).

2) Six purpose built MCT vessels capable of tactical deployment at high speed deployed by a specially trained boat team attached to the Water Unit.

3) An on camp range facility which includes a 100 meter range, an indoor 25 meter range, eight computerized mini-ranges, and a multi-million dollar close quarter battle house which is widely believed to be one of the most advanced in the world.

In addition the SDU enjoys access to a number of commercial facilities that assist the unit in training, and prove crucial in the execution of operational deployments. The SDU, for example, maintains an excellent relationship with several airlines serving Hong Kong, so the unit is provided almost unlimited access to aircraft for hostage-rescue training. On the maritime counter-terrorist (MCT) side, the SDU has fostered close relations with the major shipping companies allowing ample training on ships entering or leaving Hong Kong as well as ships at anchor. The same can be said of both the overland and underground train services.

The SDU ORBAT consists of the following:

1. The training team which is responsible for instructing new members to the unit and also continuation training for the operational teams.
2. The medical support team who are all highly trained combat medics responsible for providing immediate first aid at the scene.
3. The headquarters section which is mainly responsible for unit administration but who also form the intelligence cell in operations.
4. The boat team who run and maintain the MCT vessels.
5. The close quarter battle team who set up and maintain the CQB house.
6. The operational (tactical) teams which are further split into three.
   a. The land assault.
   b. The water assault who are primarily concerned with the MCT role but also perform on land.
   c. The sniper team. Half of the unit marksman are also fully trained divers who can support the water team on MCT operations.

Apart from the obvious role as a CT team, the SDU is also tasked with serious criminal cases involving firearms and/or hostages. This role is brought about by the fact that SDU officers are all members of the Royal Hong Kong Police Force and as such are still required to discharge their constabulary duties. It is in this role that the Unit is able to implement first hand theories and practices learned in a training environment. This experience is considered vital particularly when the unit has yet to be involved in a terrorist case. Having said that, the SDU has been deployed against highly motivated criminal gangs who have resorted to the use of hand grenades and AK-47 assault rifles, such as in an incident on February 12, 1992, when several SDU operators were seriously wounded in a fire-fight.

Like many Asian units, the SDU cherishes the veil of secrecy which keeps its operations, deployments, training patterns and equipment secret. It is known, however, that SDU operators carry Heckler and Koch MP5 9mm submachine guns and Browning 9mm Hi-Power. It is ***believed*** that unit sniper weapons include the Heckler and Koch PSG-1 and the 7.62mm British-produced Model 87 Parker-Hale Police Sniper Rifle.

SDU team members fast-rope toward an objective during tactical training courtesy of a Government Flying Service S-70 Blackhawk. (Courtesy: Royal Hong Kong Police)

## India

***The captain, wearing his characteristic black--special operations--turban, looked on from a scaffold perch with walkie-talkie and clipboard in hand, as the training exercise commenced. A shiny black Cadillac limousine, adorned with the Indian flag, drove slowly down an asphalt parade ground followed by three jeeps and a white, nondescript van, all traveling at a steady, though controlled, 30-mph. At the captain's signal, three snipers from a nearby rooftop began to fire live 7.62mm rounds just in front of the Cadillac--the ricocheting rounds bounced around the asphalt floor in a whining sound of a ballistic near miss. As Indian secret service bodyguards leapt from the vehicle and secured the vehicle's immediate departure away from the fire zone, a dozen men, all clad in black Nomex coveralls, leapt out of the van. They were armed with Heckler and Koch MP5A2 9mm submachine guns and Heckler and Koch PSG-1 sniper's rifles; black balaclava hoods covered their faces. The operators had 100 - yards to traverse in order to reach the building from where the hostile sniper emanated from--they were 100 precarious yards where they had to criss-cross and race in obscene motions in order to avoid being placed through the sights of the assassin's weapon. The gauntlet of deadly--live--fire was crossed in a little over one minute; operators fired as they ran, some tossed smoke grenades. The building was reached and the stairs climbed in a three minute dash of well-choreographed version of the Tactical 3-Cs--COVER, CONCEALMENT AND CONTINUE! Exactly four minutes and thirty-seven seconds after the first 7.62mm round had landed four feet in front of the Cadillac, the operators had reached the ledge and, in a simulated barrage, killed "or" captured the assassins. The lieutenant on the rooftop supervising the events, pressed his stopwatch and radioed the unit commander. "Good job men," the lieutenant offered the perspiring men, "now let's do it***

*from 200 yards away!"*

***These black-clad operators are known simply as the "Black Cats," and for them crossing a parade ground under fire, or assaulting an Air India jumbo jet seized by suicidal fanatics is just business as usual. They are considered among the finest special operations units in all of south Asia.***

The Indian military has a long tradition and history of professional military service and the fostering of ultra-professional, highly skilled, superbly trained and courageously commanded special forces entities. Dating back to the 50 Indian Parachute Brigade, formed in October 1941, and to the elite 44 Indian Airborne Division (complete with its own reconnaissance element) Indian special forces units have distinguished themselves in the 1947 War for Indian independence, the 1961 China War, the 1965 Indo-Pakistani War, the 1971 Indo-Pakistani War and operations in Sri Lanka in 1987. Indian Army special forces have also been active in internal-security operations, primarily in the Punjab against Sikh militants and terrorists. The largest such operation came on the night of May 30, 1984, in Amristar, in what became known as "Operation Bluestar" when the army, led by plain-clothed elements of the 1st Para Commando Battalion, assaulted the Sikh's Golden Temple.

One of the earliest units tasked with counter-terrorism during the late 1970s was the Special Frontier Force (SFF), a Tibetan para-commando outfit originally formed with the help of the CIA and India's Research and Analysis Wing (RAW), the Indian foreign intelligence-gathering espionage service. Formed in 1962 following the end of the Sino-Indian War. the SFF became an elite indigenous force of Tibetan operators trained to function in a counter-insurgency role possible, Chinese-infiltration and subversive operation. At its peak, in 1968, the unit was commanded by a lieutenant-colonel and consisted of nearly 12,000 men divided into six battalions with each battalion divided into six companies. In the late 1970s, the SFF was issued with a new mandate--counter-terrorism and hostage-rescue--and a Special Group formed. The Tibetans made ideal counter-terrorist operators for the volatile and precarious Indian political landscape; because they weren't Indian, just professional soldiers, their loyalties did not hinge on sects, parties or other incidentals that plagued the Indian police and military. Although parachute-qualified and an elite formation, the SFF Special Group failed on June 5, 1984, to enter the Golden Temple in Punjab and found itself pinned down by a motley group of militants armed with home-made rifles.

As a result of the SFF Special Group fiasco at the Golden Temple,[1] the Indian Home Ministry realized that India was twelve years behind the times in counter-terrorist and hostage-rescue capabilities and sanctioned the creation of a new unit based along the lines of Germany's GSG-9, the U.S. Army's 1st SFOD-Delta (Airborne) and the British 22 Special Air Service Regiment. The unit, called the National Security Guard (NSG) soon developed the nickname of "Black Cats" because of the black Nomex coveralls they favored, and the black balaclavas they tended to wear while in the field and on parade; many have publicly said, however, that the black balaclavas are worn because of its spotty success record (despite its large budget), the unit has been the target of much public criticism!

The NSG is divided into two formations--the 4,000-man Special Action Group (SAG) consisting of army personnel, mainly jumpers from the Para regiment and the Special Ranger Group (SRG), a 2,000-man detachment of para-military officers. The NSG's largest deployment came on May 12, 1988, in "Operation Black Thunder II," when the Sikh Golden Temple was once again assaulted by Indian forces following increased acts of Sikh-separatist terrorism--including the shooting of a police inspector general. In a six-day pitched battle involving gunfire, rockets and sniper fire, NSG operators were able to break through Sikh defenses and crush resistance.

The Black Cat's last known operation was in September 1993, when they successfully stormed an Indian Airlines jet in Amristar seized by Muslim Hizbul Islami terrorists.

Besides their internal security duty, it has been reported that an NSG contingent is ***permanently*** stationed at New Delhi's Indira Ghandi International Airport for any hijacking scenarios. It has also been reported that the Black Cats have received foreign instruction at the hands of GSG-9, the British SAS, and, in 1992, it was quietly acknowledged in the publication ***India Times*** (the Time Magazine of India) that a handful of NSG personnel were trained in Israel by military and police counter-terrorist special operations units. The NSG weapon of choice is the Heckler and Koch family of 9mm submachine guns (the MP5 SD3 is favored), the PSG-1 7.62mm sniper weapon, and the Heckler and Koch 512 12-gauge shotgun.

Maritime counter-terrorism and hostage-rescue is the domain of the Indian Marine Special Forces (IMSF), a naval special warfare entity formed in 1987 and tasked, among other duties, with rescuing hostages held on seaborne platforms or ships. Trained by the U.S. Navy SEALs and British SBS, the IMSF is an elite formation made up of 300 volunteers, all airborne qualified, based at Bombay.

[1] In late 1984, SFF Special Group was temporarily used for VIP security work around the time of the assassination of Prime Minister Indira Ghandi. In 1985, the Home Ministry created the Special Protection Group (SPG), a force of bodyguards, modeled along the lines of the U.S. Secret Service, to protect Indian politicians and visiting dignitaries.

## Indonesia

On March 28, 1981, five Muslim fundamentalists of the Indonesian ***Imran*** (Jihad Command) hijacked a domestic Garuda (Indonesia's flag-carrier) flight on its way from Jakarta to the city of Medan in north Sumatra; as is the case with many Asian airlines, each plane is given its own name; in this case, the aircraft was named the "Woyla." The hijackers demanded a ransom, the release of other ***Imran*** fundamentalists, and safe passage to a Muslim country--preferably Iran. If these demands were not met, they promised that the hostages would be killed. The plane was ultimately flown to Don Muang airport, north of Bangkok, Thailand, after a brief stopover in Malaysia, and a stalemate, a Mexican standoff as is known in the vernacular, was underway.

Back in Indonesia, General Yoga Sugamo, the head of Indonesia's civilian intelligence agency, and his deputy, Lieutenant-General Benny Moerdani, began planning a rescue operation--a daring and difficult mission comparable to the Israeli raid on Entebbe and the German mission at Mogadishu. The operation, known as the "Operation Woyla," was staged at 0240 hours on March 31/April 1, 1981; the assault force was commanded by Lieutenant-Colonel Sintong Panjaitan. The task force consisted of fifty Indonesian commandos--all operators from a new unit still to enter the Indonesian military's order of battle--and they flew to Thailand on Indonesian Air Force transports with the support of the Thai authorities. Once in place, the operators approached the aircraft in a slow and deliberate single-file wave; Indonesian personnel, Thai special forces (Royal Thai Air Force commandos) and police units had secured the airfield. Step ladders were used on the wings of the Garuda Indonesian Airlines DC-9 and the doors were forced open. When the front door was opened, a hijacker was shot dead with a point-blank round to the head. A second

During jungle infiltration exercises, operators from Detachment 81 set up their outer-perimeter before a sniper team is infiltrated into position. The operators are armed with SS1-V2 5.56mm assault rifles, copies of the Belgian FN FNC rifle.

Army Special Forces, the new national and overseas Indonesian counter-terrorist unit, stand for inspection at their home base, near Jakarta. Note SS1-V2 5.56mm assault rifles, and marksman carrying Heckler and Koch G3 SG/1 7.62mm sniping rifle.

hijacker, who clumsily stumbled, was apprehended and taken prisoner, and three other hijackers were killed inside. The entire operation lasted three minutes. All fifty-five hostages were rushed down emergency chutes and taken into protective care, but one Indonesian commando, the commander of the mission who was the first through the door in true "Follow Me" fashion, was shot in the groin; Special Forces Lieutenant Achmad Kirang would later die of his wounds. The pilot of the plane, Captain Herman Rante, died two days later, as well, after being hit by a stray shot.

The rescue came hours after the Indonesian government was reported to have bowed to demands, including the release of 80 "political prisoners" in exchange for the hostages. But leaders in Jakarta were adamant in their stance not to succumb to the extortion of terrorists and thugs. The message of "Operation Woyla" was clear: Terrorists would have no future in Indonesia or in attacking Indonesian targets anywhere in the world.

The Indonesian Special Forces, among the most professional and capable in all of Asia, began counter-terrorist training in 1980. At the time of "Operation Woyla," a dedicated counter-terrorist unit had not yet been formed. As a result, the assault force was drawn from the One and Four Groups of the Army Special Forces. In speaking of "Operation Woyla" in an editorial dedicated to the national courage required in fighting and defeating terrorists, the Wall Street Journal noted that the Woyla rescue was on par with the more famous rescues in Uganda and Somalia and that if it weren't for the fact that President Reagan had been shot at the same time and the world's media descending on Washington D.C. at the time, the Indonesian operation would have become world famous. The operation was a brilliant success and not only demonstrated national resolve by the Indonesian Defense Ministry, but professional skill at the hand of the operators. Despite rumors to the contrary, there were no members of the U.S. Delta Force present during the Woyla rescue operation. The assault force was completely comprised of Indonesians.

Shortly after the Woyla operation, the Indonesian Army accelerated the development of a military special forces unit. Known as "Detachment 81" (so named because it was formed in 1981), the unit was officially created under the Headquarters of the Special Forces. The original commander, the legendary Lieutenant-Colonel Prabowo, had just completed courses at Fort Bragg, Fort Benning and in St. Augustin with the GSG-9; he is also reported to have visited Hereford and the 22nd SAS Regiment in the United Kingdom. Detachment 81 was designed and certainly crafted along the lines of the world's other counter-terrorist and hostage rescue forces--a small unit of only 300 men that would be on call twenty-four-hours a day, all year round, to respond to those special missions where only highly specialized training and unique equipment would do the job. In a nation such as Indonesia, a string of 13,000 small and large islands with a population (1993 estimate) of 196,000,000 people,[1] where tribal strife and religious fundamentalism brought about its fair share of terrorist acts, one thing was clear--Detachment 81 would be among the world's busiest units. Most of their operations would remain classified, however, though they are known to have participated in countless operations against rebel targets in East Timor Province and in Aceh Province.

Detachment 81, based in Jakarta, was reported to have been disbanded in the early 1990s, and army counter-terrorist and hostage-rescue absorbed into the main SF groups--the ***Kopassus*** (***Komando Pasukan Khusus,*** or Army Special Forces). In their ten years of existence, they are known to have trained with the U.S. Army's 1st SFOD-D, GSG-9 in Germany, the British and Australian (and New Zealand) SAS, and Malaysian special forces; there has always been rumors to the effect that Detachment 81 has trained with the Israelis, though this has never been confirmed--nor denied--by the Indonesians. They conduct year round training with Indonesian Para-Kommando units throughout the country. Their equipment was always a hodgepodge of gear and weaponry, including Belgian Minimis, American M16s, Israeli Mini-Uzis, and, of course, German MP5s.

For a nation as large as Indonesia, with its ethnic and political difficulties, it would be impossible for one small army unit to assume all counter-terrorist roles and missions and as a result, several units exist.

The Indonesian Navy maintains a maritime counter-terrorist force that is called to intervene in all situations involving the hijacking of vessels or ferries, or when the best means for reaching a ground target (a terrorist safe-house, for example) requires amphibious or underwater skills. This unit, one of the most secretive in the Indonesian order of battle, is called ***"Detachment Jala Mengkara"*** and is a combination of navy frogmen and marine recon operators. They function along similar lines to the British Royal Marines Commachio Group, though they have trained with the U.S. Navy's

SEAL Team SIX, the British Special Boat Service's "M" Squadron, and the Dutch 7 NL SBS. This role is duplicated by one of the army forces combat swimmer units, which was raised in the late 1980s to protect offshore oil rigs from pirates.

The Indonesian Air Force also maintains its own hostage-rescue unit, a small force of anti-hijacking specialists known as "Team Bravo." Trained by Detachment 81, as well as other international units, "Team Bravo" is dedicated solely to the safe and stealthy (if not explosive) entry into a hijacked aircraft and quick termination to any hostage situation on board an aircraft. They are reported to be incredible shots with their 9mm automatics and legend has it that they can empty an automatic's full fifteen-round clip into the very center of a target from thirty feet away.

The military and police have several counter-terrorist/hostage rescue units. From the police, the ***Brimoh*** (Mobile Brigade) is the premier unit. Actually, the unit is much larger than a brigade, with sub-units placed in all the provinces. No doubt some of the members have good training; however, judging from the size of the waistlines one sees on most ***Brimoh*** members in Jakarta, physical fitness is not the

Army Special Forces personnel from the legendary ***Kopassus*** (***Komando Pasukan Khusus,*** Army Special Forces) stand at attention during an award ceremony.

Operators from the ***Komando Pasukan Khusus*** demonstrate their knife-throwing capabilities at a demonstration for visiting Asian counter-terrorist officers.

Army special forces personnel march to inspection after the successful completion of maneuvers in 1992.

Outside a base mess, a ***Kopassus*** officer assembles his men. Photograph shows to advantage ***Kopassus*** insignia, though this officer, as is evident by the "Budweiser" above his right breast pocket, has also passed the U.S. Navy BUD/S training.

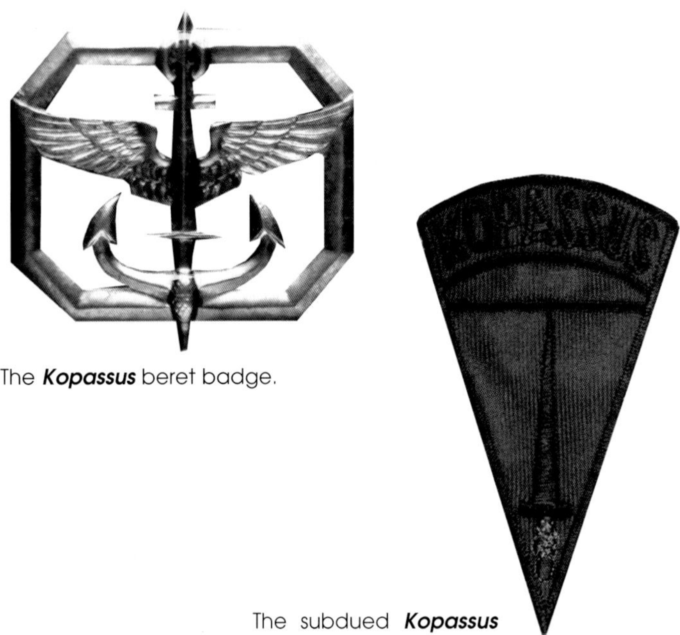

The ***Kopassus*** beret badge.

The subdued ***Kopassus*** patch.

unit's forte. The true police intervention unit is the ***Sat Gegana***, made up of volunteers from the force who are ***all*** Ranger-qualified. Initially, these units were trained by the U.S. Army's 1st Special Forces Group (Airborne) on the island of Okinawa, but have since developed their own unique and highly specialized counter-terrorist and counter-insurgency skills. Although a "police" unit, the ***Sat Gegana*** has seen "combat" in Borneo and in East Timor. They are under the command and control of the National Police HQ in Jakarta, and their training base, a sprawling state-of-the-art facility, is at Kelapa Dua just outside Jakarta.

[1] The Indonesian population is 87% Muslim, 6% Protestant, 3% Roman Catholic, 2% Hindu, 1% Buddhist, and 1% other.

Indonesian Army Master Parachutist Wings.

Navy SCUBA qualification badge--worn by all ***Jala Mengkara*** personnel.

## *Japan*

For nearly twenty years, Japan has faced a unique terrorist phenomenon attacks against the ruling government by both left wing and right wing groups. The Japanese Red Army is by far the most infamous of indigenous Japanese terrorist organizations, though its call to fame has been a series of bloody attacks often carried out in conjunction with, or for, Palestinian terrorist organizations, primarily the Marxist PFLP. Their exploits include the Lod Airport Massacre (June 30, 1972) in which twenty-seven Puerto Rican pilgrims were killed; the July 20, 1973, hijacking of a JAL flight from Paris to Tokyo to Libya; sabotaged Shell oil tanks in Singapore (January 31, 1974); and, occupied the Japanese embassy in Kuwait City on February 6, 1974. From 1977 (following the notorious Dacca incident) to 1986, the Japanese Red Army maintained a low-profile. Since 1986, however, they have once again stepped up their campaign of violence, especially in light of several high profile arrests by police of key organization members. Perhaps most troubling are reports that the Japanese red Army has tightened its alliance with a wide assortment of terrorist groups—including Ahmed Jibril's Popular Front for the Liberation of Palestine General Command (PFLP-GC), the organization responsible for the destruction of Pan Am 103 over Lockerbie, Scotland, on December 21, 1988.

The potential for terrorist chaos is perhaps best illustrated by the fact that there are an estimated 35,000 violent ultra-leftists in Japan today, and nearly 15,000 ultra-right wingers (who, in recent years have shown a growing propensity for violence, including the use of fire-arms and hostage taking. The Internal security mandate in Japan falls under the responsibility of the National Police Agency. The need to maintain order and control in the light of terrorist threats falls under the control of specially trained tactical units within the "Riot Police." In fact, according to Japanese Police publications, the Riot Police play ***the*** central role of counter-terrorism in the security police activities. Each Prefecture Police force has its own riot squad, with a collective force of nearly 15,000 officers. Within each riot squad is a SWAT-type unit, trained in assault skills and proficient in heavy weapons, capable of meeting any serious criminal or terrorist incident, and also trained in hostage-rescue. As Japan is an island, the unit also has some SCUBA skills and maritime abilities should a ferry or passenger liner be taken over by terrorists or guerrillas. It has been published that a

Japanese riot police, respond to a left-wing demonstration where firearms have been spotted. (Courtesy: Japanese Police Attaché, Washington D.C. Embassy)

force specifically trained for hijack rescues on airliners is on permanent on-call status at both Haneda and Narita airports. Virtually no information has been made available on these units, however, and their abilities, equipment and known operations have been kept hidden from public disclosure. Published reports indicate that these Prefecture Police SWAT-squads are quite good, however, and have undergone joint training and instruction with GSG-9 and various state SEKs in Germany, the French GIGN, and the British SAS; joint instruction with the Israeli ***Ya'ma'm*** is also rumored to have transpired, though no firm proof exists.

Clearly, 1995 was the busiest year in Japanese Police history as tactical units throughout the country faced off against the deadly cult of religious-sect leader Shoko Asahara, the Aum Shinrikyo. In March one attack at the Kasamigaseki subway station in central Tokyo, a Sarin (poisonous nerve gas of World War Two origin) attack by the apocalyptic Aum Shinrikyo killed ten civilians and injured an astounding 5,550. It was the most horrific of terrorist attacks to take place on Japanese soil. The Aum Shinrikyo attack galvanized Japanese law enforcement into responsive operations against additional nerve gas attacks (police in NBC gear were seen responding to sightings of potential devices throughout Japanese rail installations) and offensive ones, as well, in the search for the elusive cult leader.

Making the search for Shoko Asahara so difficult and so dangerous was the fact that the cult had reportedly purchased enough chemicals to produce "tons" of Sarin; the cult also had a Russian-made military helicopter in its possession, and many of its followers reportedly received commando training in Russia from former ***Spetsnaz*** instructors. Finally, however, in May 1995 Japanese police units, in full tactical gear and heavy weapons, located Asahara in a cult hide-away. Although ready for a fire-fight, assault rifles at the ready, Japanese police found Asahara laying on his stomach, meditating, smelling as if he hadn't bathed in the fifty-seven days that he was the most wanted man in Japan.

With the cult leader in custody, Japanese police geared for possible terrorist strikes meant to free Asahara by Aum Shinrikyo followers. Such an attack came on June 21, 1995, when an All-Nippon Airways Boeing 747 was hijacked by an ice-pick wielding cult-member; he held 365-passengers and crew hostage. The plane eventually landed at Hakodate, in northern Japan, and a stand-off ensued for the following fifteen hours. Japanese police officials, unaware if the terrorists was armed with a pistol or even plastic explosives (possibly even nerve gas) acted with caution—they commenced negotiations with the hijacker, but prepared a tactical response ready for the green light to move in and take the subject down. When it became clear the hijacker would not surrender, the Riot Police moved in. Borrowing a page from the 1972 Israeli rescue at Lod, approximately twenty heavily-armed police officers, many dressed as All-Nippon Airways mechanics in white coveralls, rushed to the front and sides of the aircraft and, using small collapsible ladders, scrambled into the plane's underbelly.

The hijacker was subdued moments later and taken into custody.

One Japanese National Police Agency ***actively*** involved in preventative counter-terrorism is the NPA's "Escort Service." As the leading nation in Asia, and certainly one of the leading industrial powers in world, Japan is host to thousands of VIPs who attend conferences, meetings and conventions. Seen operating in groups of six (three on each side of a limousine), the Escort Service officers are all volunteers, and all officers who are of sound physical and psychological standing, and who excel in the martial arts and are bulls-eye marksman. Their operational dress is a three-piece business suit, a 9mm automatic, and a bullet-proof attaché case that doubles as a shield. During a report on American television aired prior to an E7 meeting in Tokyo, the force was shown on exercises. A senior police officer, playing the VIP, was flanked by six Escort Service bodyguards walking out of a hotel lobby. A shot was fired and the unit burst into action. The VIP was quickly hurled to the ground where an officer threw himself atop his charge, and the five other squad members drew their holster automatics, knelt to the ground, and opened up their cases turned into ballistic body bunkers.

Japanese riot police race through a daunting wall of fire in response to a Red Army demonstration in Tokyo. (Courtesy: Japanese Police Attaché, Washington D.C. Embassy)

During a hijacking alert, laden-down riot policemen man a vigil at Narita Internatinal Airport. (Courtesy: Japanese Police Attaché, Washington D.C. Embassy)

Japanese police officers train to rappel down a Bell-206 Jet Ranger to perfect their aerial insertion skills. (Courtesy: Japanese Police Attaché, Washington D.C. Embassy)

# Korea

***August 1988. It was a tense time in Korea as the threat of terrorism, or full-scale North Korean attack, was a dire possibility in the days preceding the South's hosting of the 1988 Summer Olympics. Police were everywhere, the South Korean military was on alert, and many feared a North Korean statement of violence to upset the games was more than likely. Journalists, too, wanted to know how South Korea would protect the games of joy and the authorities were eager to show off their best stuff to the international media as well as the leaders in Pyongyang.***

***On one summer's morning, approximately one hundred journalists were told to assemble at a lobby of a five-star Seoul hotel. "Just bring your cameras and recorders," the coordinator told them, "it'll be a great show." As the television reporters and print journalists gathered in the ornate lobby awaiting the anticipated display, a thunderous explosion and a blinding flash of light rocked the building. Nearly fifty men, all wearing black outfits with their faces covered by balaclavas raced through the gathering smoke screeching a war cry that sent chills through most spines. As an officer, also clad in black and concealed by his face mask, spoke through a megaphone in a subdued though understood English, the operators went through the motions of fast-roping down an elevator shaft, engaging in a mock gun battle, and even hurling K-Bar knives at a mannequin simulating a terrorist; Kung-fu style "stars" were also thrown at the mannequin with uncanny accuracy and lethal skill. It was a bit circus-like, a bit bizarre, and reminiscent of a bad martial arts film, but it drove the message home to the journalists racing to file their stories (and clean themselves off). It was also a message to the powers that be in Pyongyang that Seoul was ready for anything and everything that the North was planning to throw its way. Officials had prepared a computerized data-base profiling the 600 top terrorists from over 600 international organizations, police specialists armed with electronic stethoscopes were on alert to seek out the sounds of hidden time bombs, and sixty-four dogs trained to sniff out explosives that machines could not detect patrolled key sites. "Preparing for the Olympics is like preparing for war," claimed Major-General Yook Wan Sik, the man responsible for security during the Seoul games. In light of past terrorist attacks and bombings by the North, including the notorious destruction of a Korean Air Lines jet in 1987, the Republic of Korea had good reason to expect war.***

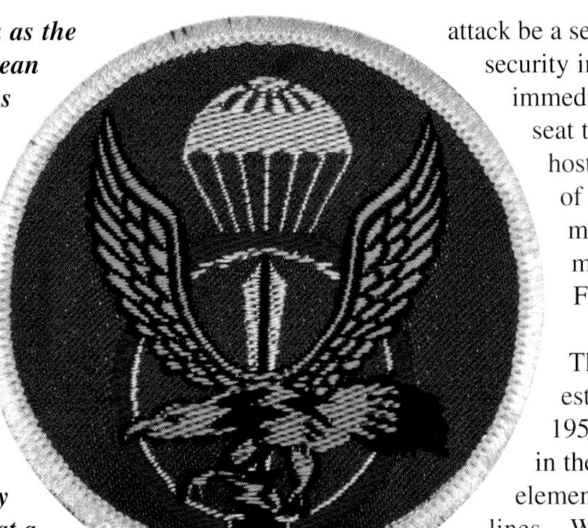
The 707th Special Mission Battalion patch

The unit "forced" into the dog and pony show at the Seoul hotel lobby was a mysterious, though highly capable, force of operators known as Unit 868, a National Police force formed six years earlier tasked with maintaining internal security in the Korean capital in the event of a large-scale terrorist incident. In many ways, Unit 868 was created as a result of Seoul's hosting of the 1988 Summer games, and had been training for nine hours a day, six days a week, for the past six years. Unit 868's primary function was the spearheading of all counter-terrorist operations that might result out of an attack mounted in and around the commencement of the Olympic games. The police operators were highly regarded as world-class caliber, they were expertly trained in the martial arts and in weapons proficiency, and boasted to be the best marksmen in all of Asia. Yet should the terrorist attack be a serious one, it would be a matter of national security importance to neutralize the terrorist threat immediately, then Unit 868 would take a back seat to the ROK's primary counter-terrorist and hostage-rescue force--a unit that the Republic of Korea deploys only in the most sensitive, most dangerous and most important of missions. That unit is the Army Special Forces' 707th Special Mission Battalion.

The Korean Army's special forces were established at battalion strength on April 1, 1958, as a copy of the experiment underway in the United States with a specialized military element functioning in Germany across Soviet lines. Well known in Vietnam for mission achievements, ROK special forces were a highly professional and cohesive combat formation on par with their American counterparts, and certainly with their adversaries in the North. Known, in ROK military slang, as the "Apostles of Justice" and using the phrase "Make the Impossible Possible" as their unit motto, the ROK Special Forces are under the command and control of the SWC--Special Warfare Command, though in wartime it is renamed the Combined Unconventional Warfare Task Force (CUWTF) and is combined with USSOCOM units already stationed in country, and those in the process of deploying. Operators are known as the "black berets" and are modeled along the lines of the U.S. Army's special forces, both in size, mandate and structure; though, it should be noted, ROK special forces possess fourteen-man teams as opposed to the American twelve-man forces, and are not medically trained. ROK Special Forces are divided into brigades; the 1st, 3rd, and 5th are known as the Seoul Brigades as they are all stationed in and around the Korean capital, and the 7th, 9th, 11th and 13th are located throughout the southern portion of the country.

The elite of the elite of the ROK's organized Special Forces is the 707th Special Mission Battalion. Terrorism and proactive sabotage espionage from the North was always a major concern for the South Koreans, and creating a force capable of meeting this threat, one posed by terrorists and saboteurs, frogmen and suicidal bombers, fell on the military. After the Munich Olympic Massacre, when most European and Asian nations were busy filling the gap in their internal defense with the creation of police or Gendarmerie units, the ROK opted on a purely military solution and the 707th Special Missions Battalion was created. Its ranks were to be filled exclusively by known and proven black berets who had exemplary service records and passed exhaustive security checks. The unit would number approximately 300 operators and technicians.

Volunteers in the ROK's special forces endure a six month basic infantry and combat course followed by an additional six months of parachute training and special warfare instruction. The instruction is grueling and almost fanatic by Western standards. Heavy emphasis is placed on physical fitness--especially toughening up the operators to be able to withstand Korea's harsh climactic conditions. Operators are routinely brought out in sub-zero temperatures to perform their calisthenics and physical drills in foot deep snows, and are often ordered to swim naked in frozen lakes and rivers. Great emphasis is also placed in ski and mountain warfare training, and ROK special forces personnel are expert survivalists and ropesmen.

Following the nearly twelve months of instruction, in which the operator has been exposed to the entire gamut of insertion and extraction techniques and tools (from Klepper canoes to UH-60 Blackhawk choppers), has been trained in the rudimentary basics of explosives and charges, and has also been taught to be a cold-killing machine able to use a fist and a rock with the same lethal edge as an automatic rifle. Obviously, through this lengthy training period, the conscript turned operator is transformed into a weapons expert and a lethal shot with his Daewoo K1 and K2 5.56mm assault rifles, M16A2/203 40mm grenade launchers, A4 anti-tank rocket and anti-personnel grenades; ROK black berets are also taught fast driving skills, basic boating skills (especially for Zodiac inflatables) as well as the basic skills required to operate a tank. Prior to the 1988 Olympics, 707th Special Mission Battalion personnel deployed Short Brothers built Javelin man-portable surface-to-air missile to safeguard against low-level terrorist air attack.

Korean Special Forces do not maintain a professional NCO corps, like the U.S. Army's Special Forces Groups (Airborne), and all personnel graduating the special forces training are immediately promoted to the rank of sergeant; in fact, the only way a conscript in the Korean Army can make the rank of staff sergeant is to be a black beret. Having undergone this exhaustive training and having served a minimum of six months in a "regular" black beret brigade, sergeants wishing to volunteer into the 707th SMB must undergo a torturous ten day selection process that usually eliminates nearly ninety-percent of all applicants. As the 707th, like the special forces units, are made up virtually entirely of conscripts doing their mandatory military service, the surviving ten-percent are then asked to sign on for an additional period of service.

The unit's training facility at Maesanri, a few miles southeast of the capital Seoul, is considered the state-of-the-art counter-terrorist training facility in all of Asia. The facility's physical fitness area, obstacle course and firing ranges, both combat drill and static target, are all designed to transform the operator into a dedicated killing machine: terrorists in Korea are not to be negotiated with, promised freedom or allowed to dictate the unraveling of any hostage taking situation. Interestingly enough, the training facility at Maesanri boasts a full-scale mock-up of a Boeing 747 airliner that is situated in a valley. This mock-up allows the unit to train around the clock all year long in the speedy and effective entry into a hijacked aircraft; the mock-up also permits live-fire training inside the confines of a Boeing 747 replica--something that the management of Korean Air and Kimpo International Airport has obvious problems with. If a bus, train, ship or aircraft is hijacked, or if North Korean special forces or saboteurs infiltrate the ROK for the purpose of perpetrating a terrorist act, the 707th Special Mission Battalion is uniquely qualified to "handle" the situation. It should be noted that all 707th SMB personnel are SCUBA-qualified and trained, and have often deployed underwater in training missions and even operationally (though the details of these deployments are classified top-secret by the Korean government).

The 707th Special Mission Battalion's over-aggressiveness in training (as well as, it has been suggested, their never confirmed missions behind enemy lines) has brought them a reputation as a truly special counter-terrorist force. Yet what truly separates them from virtually every other similar unit around the world, even Britain's SAS and Israel's ***Sayeret Mat'kal,*** is the fact that the unit maintains a company of beautiful young ladies, known as the special woman's company, made of forty extremely attractive and extremely lethal female soldiers trained in the art of special warfare and counter-terrorism. Although little is known of this force, outside of training films where they battle their male counterparts in the Tae-kwon-do bouts and when they are shown in tight fitting black Ninja outfits firing suppressed MP5s, it is believed they are used for undercover work and in hostage-rescue scenarios where the terrorists might not suspect that a female would pose any threat--this includes, it is speculated, the hijacking of a Korean Air jet to Seoul's Kimpo International Airport where food or medicine must be brought on board.

Unlike a regular unit in the Korean military, budgetary constraints are few with the 707th, and they are able to purchase the best equipment in the world--either gear produced in the ROK or bought off the shelf in the United States, Europe, or Asia. This include uniforms, protective gear and electronic devices, as well as weaponry. The 707th Special Mission Battalion's principal weapon is the Daewoo K1 and K2 5.56mm assault rifles, modified with forward pistols grips, laser sights and night-vision devices. The unit has recently began experimenting with the Heckler and Koch family of MP5 9mm submachine guns, especially the MP5 SD3 suppressed variant. The primary pistol carried by the 707th SMB is the Colt .45 pistol, though the Daewoo 9mm pistol, considered a fine weapon, has entered service as well. The 707th SMB is not "shotgun crazy," in the words of one U.S. Army 1st Special Force Group (Airborne) operator, but their primary 12-gauge weapons include the Remington Mk. 870 and the Daewoo USAS-12 12 gauge automatic shotgun. 707th Special Mission Battalion snipers, among the most expert in all of Asia, are known to favor both the Heckler and Koch PSG-1 7.62mm weapon, and the American M-24 7.62mm system; unit snipers, it should be noted, also deploy the RAI .50 caliber system.

The 707th Special Mission Battalion's closest foreign ties are obviously with the U.S. Army's 1st SFOD-D, the U.S. Navy's SEAL Team SIX, and the Australian SAS Tactical Assault Group, although ties are known to exist with special force units in Singapore and Indonesia, as well as units and agencies in the Philippines, Thailand, and Hong Kong. It is believed the 707th Special Mission Battalion has forged some sort of ties with the British SAS, Germany's GSG-9 and Israeli special forces, though this is impossible to confirm. Unit 868 and the National Police has forged ties to the FBI's HRT, Germany's BKA and GSG-9, France's GIGN, and Spain's GEO; it is also believed that contacts were established with Israel's ***Ya'ma'm,*** though this, too, has not been confirmed by either side. It is not believed that the unit has established or maintains ties with Japanese units, and this stems from a particular security concern. The Japanese Red Army, supported by Pyongyang, has operated frequently in the ROK on the north's behalf; with as many as 870,000 Koreans residing in Japan, the potential for security being breached by the two nations exchanging tactics and know-how appears to be of considerable concern. Much of these contacts have had to do with actual hostage rescue work. In its VIP security tasks, Unit 868 and the ROK National Police are considered world-wide masters obtaining the respect and admiration from security personnel from South Africa, Israel and the United States.

## Macao

There has always been a Special Duties Unit (SDU) attached to the Police Tactical Unit. It numbered some twenty men until last year when they increased it to approximately seventy men. This was due to the requirement of a cohesive and highly effective counter-terrorist response for the new international airport currently being built, and the rather lively nature of the heavily armed criminals perpetrating armed robberies, kidnappings and organized criminal activities.

The SDU is organized very much along western lines with entry teams, snipers, and communications, EOD and intelligence specialists. Trained ostensibly by the Portuguese GOE to quite a high standard, they are reported to be somewhat "cowboyish" in nature. Although maintaining close-ties to such diverse units as the U.S. Navy SEALs and Hong Kong's SDU, the Macao SDU ***will not*** hold joint training with foreign units, although they do send observers and liaisons to visit other units around the world.

The Macao SDU includes MP5 A3s (Pakistan origin and jams), original Heckler and Koch MP5 SDs, Heckler and Koch PSG-1 7.62mm sniper rifles, and Glock Model 18 9mm automatics (the unit originally used Heckler and Koch P7s--a result of a trip to St. Augustin and the GSG-9 compound).

## New Zealand

***The scene looks so typical in the arena of counter-terrorist training exercises, yet quite peculiar to the non-indigenous eye. On a snow-covered slope reminiscent of a high brow resort atop St. Moritz, a lone cottage sits amid the snow and rock--defended by three men and two women, all carrying AK-47s. Unknown to the gunmen, they are in the sights of three snipers, all gently caressing the trigger housing of their Heckler and Koch PSG-1 7.62mm sniper rifles awaiting the order to fire. As three four-man teams inch their way in the snow, wearing white coveralls over their DPM pattern fatigues, the snipers breathe slowly and in well-rehearsed releases exhale until authorization is received. The teams move closer, still unseen and unheard. FIRE! Three 7.62mm rounds rip across the heads of the two women and the man armed with the Walkie-talkie, and two of the snipers roll around in the snow and quickly engage targets "Four" and "Five." The teams move in at once in a choreographed display of physical prowess and precision. The "A Team" blows the house's front door off its hinges with two dedicated 12-gauge shotgun blasts, while "B Team" provides tactical cover with automatic weapons and "C Team" deploys poised to assist the entry team. Inside the house, a lone hostage is held by two gunmen, all carrying pistols and grenades. The "A Team" operators enter the single-room house and in less than three seconds, pepper the terrorists with barrages of 9mm gunfire from the Heckler and Koch MP5 submachine guns. Mission complete, or is it?***

***The lone hostage in that mountain hideaway was wearing DPM camouflage and the sand-colored beret of "the" squadron. The rank of lieutenant-colonel was worn on his epaulets and in his hands were a clipboard with some notes and a stopwatch. He wasn't happy. The assault took five minutes from the time the operators reached the "point of no return" up the mountain--a hundred meters from the target--and the teams needed to settle themselves into position and be ready to assault in three minutes. The lieutenant-colonel was the commander of the unit, the squadron, and he was determined to make his men intimate players on that peak in southern New Zealand until they got it right.***

New Zealand's 1st Special Air Service Squadron is among the most secretive units in the international community of special operations forces. According to one noted defense writer in the United States, "The New Zealanders make the British SAS look like a public relations office and the Israelis look like an advertising agency." The New Zealand military has released virtually no information on the size and strength of their 1st Special Air Service Squadron, but it is known that they fulfill a duty almost identical to that which their neighbors to the west in Australia fulfill; in fact, the two units, the New Zealand 1st SAS Squadron and the Australian 1st Special Air Service Regiment, often train together. A company of the SAS is on-call twenty-four-hours-a-day in the likelihood of a serious hostage-taking incident in New Zealand or involving New Zealand aircraft or citizens in Asia. They are considered very professional and quite capable--with years of experience in counter-insurgency warfare in Brunei, Borneo, Indonesia, and South Vietnam.

While the New Zealand military has placed incredible information restrictions concerning material released of its armed forces, especially its special operations entities, it is known that the 1st SAS Squadron is based at Papakura Base near Auckland and the unit's primary weapon is the American-produced M16A2 5.56mm assault rifle and the German Heckler and Koch MP5 family of 9mm submachine guns. Their shotgun of choice is the American-made Remington Mk 870 and their principal sniper weapons are the Heckler and Koch PSG-1 7.62mm rifle, and the Remington M24 system.

It is known that the squadron routinely trains with the Australian SAS, as well as Thai and Indonesian special forces, and units from Singapore.

The New Zealand Constabulary also possesses a heavy weapons tactical team of its own to respond to ordinary criminal situations involving hostages or barricaded perpetrators.

## Pakistan

***It is before dawn in the hills outside of Islamabad, and the sounds of gunfire has shattered the eerie silence of the valley's windless hours. Tracer rounds illuminate sources of fire and a fragmentation grenade detonating adjacent to a cave opening turns the dark aqua sky into a multi-colored light show. As the fire directed up toward the peak of the hill intensifies, two Aérospatiale SA 330J Puma choppers race along the summit closely--and dangerously--hugging the mountain's uneven boulders and peaks. As the choppers move in for a landing, a smoke grenade is tossed toward the targeted cave, allowing fifteen operators in each chopper to safely jump off the hovering platform and assault the target with their weapons ablaze. Five minutes later, after nearly five hundred rounds are spent inside the cave, the order to cease-fire is issued in a heavy Baluchi accent. "Not good enough," the CO tells the men as he cleans his pipe against his DPM pattern jacket. "Let's do it again, and this time let's try and not kill the hostages!"***

Counter-terrorism and hostage-rescue operations in Pakistan is the sole domain of the Army's Special Service Group, known more commonly by its acronym title of SSG, and the unit's "Musa Company." The Special Service Group was formed, on an unofficial basis of sorts in 1964, and quickly developed as ***the*** special forces entity of the Pakistani military. The SSG participated in the 1965 Indo-Pakistani war, as well as the 1971 Indo-Pakistan War and the 1973-77 counter-insurgency campaign in western Pakistan against Baluchi insurgents. As terrorist attacks increased in ferocity and frequency following the 1972 Munich Olympic Massacre, the Pakistani Ministry of Defense opted to assign the SSG an additional task--counter-terrorism and hostage-rescue. Initially, "Musa Company" was the ***Army's*** special forces diver unit, but as the SSG expanded and more operators became diver qualified, the company was transformed into the national counter-terrorist force. The unit trained with the 22nd Special Air Service Regiment and the newly created U.S. Army's 1st SFOD-Delta (Airborne), as well as with other Asian special forces units in order to hone it skills, but the Pakistanis proved to be excellent soldiers (the army is a 500,000-man strong professional force) and "Musa Company" quickly gelled into a top-notch rescue force on-call around the clock for the most sensitive missions. As all unit operators were first broken, built and trained by the SSG, Musa Company operators were all airborne qualified, all expert shots with a wide-variety of weaponry, and capable of marching thirty kilometer a night, or crawling an equal range across the most inhospitable terrain in order to reach an objective. All that the newly formed unit needed was a baptism of fire. That opportunity came in late 1981.

On September 30, 1981, Sikh terrorist hijacked an Indian Airlines aircraft to Lahore, and threatened to blow the aircraft up unless concessions were obtained from the government in Delhi. Copying the Israel example from "Operation Isotope 1" in May 1972, the Musa Company operators donned PIA mechanics coveralls and slowly though methodically inched their way toward the hijacked aircraft. Disguised as the cleaning crew, the Musa Company operators removed American-made Colt M1911 .45 caliber pistols from beneath their coveralls and stormed the aircraft. After a brief gun battle, the operators arrested five hijackers and freed the forty-four hostages unharmed. It was a brilliant operation and the true embodiment of the unit's existence.

The second go for the unit would not be as fortunate.

On September 5, 1986, Pan Am Flight 73 from Bombay to New York, a Boeing 747, landed at Karachi International Airport for a routine refueling and passenger stop when four Arabic-speaking men dressed as security guards and brandishing Chinese-produced Model 56 7.62mm assault rifles stormed the aircraft with a burst of gunfire. One passenger, a twenty-nine-year-old naturalized American-citizen was immediately murdered and his body shoved off the plane onto the tarmac below. While the Pan Am crew ***conveniently*** escaped through hatches in the cockpit, over 350 passengers were taken hostage. The terrorists, apparently belonging to the Libyan-backed Arab Liberation Organization, demanded an Arabic-speaking flight crew and that the plane be flown to Cyprus; the terrorists demanded that three terrorists recently arrested in Larnaca, Cyprus, for the brutal 1985 murder of three Israeli nationals, be released.

The stand-off ensued for fifteen grueling hours. Musa Company operators were placed on high-alert the moment news of the hijacking came over the police emergency band from Karachi, and the entire unit was flown to Karachi Airport from the unit headquarters at Cherat, near Islamabad. By the time they arrived, the Pan Am jet was cordoned off and police officers stood behind supply vehicles with their weapons trained on the cockpit. Musa Company operators were positioned in an adjacent hangar where the men practiced storming 747s on a Pakistan International Airlines jet. Police negotiators pleaded with the terrorists to talk and release at least some of the hostages, but the terrorists were adamant--either the demands would be met, or the hostages killed one-by-one. Time was running out, but time--in such situations--usually favored the rescuers as the terrorists tended to lose their resolve, be more open to a peaceful end to the situation, and view a politically reached ending to the ordeal over the bravado and rush of the hostage-taking's first few hours. Sometimes, however, Murphy's Law takes over such scenarios.

The negotiations stretched out for over fourteen hours. The Musa Company commander, Captain B.[1], had by now completed his operational plans, his TAC options and selected his assault team. Inside the hangar, now turned into a mini-command post with computer terminals established and SATCOM phones beaming to Islamabad, the assault units continued to prepare for what they thought was an inevitable assault by executing mock raids on the PIA Boeing 747. Fifteen hours into the foiled hijacking, a generator on board the Pan Am aircraft malfunctioned and the aircraft plunged into darkness. The terrorists panicked, thinking a rescue assault was imminent, and opened fire by spraying the cabin area with automatic weapons fire and tossing grenades toward the rear passenger section. Chaos ensued and the emergency escape chutes were opened and filled with fleeing men, women and children. Musa Company, a good five minute drive away, quickly hopped into their Land Rovers and raced to the smoldering jet. They boarded the aircraft with guns ablaze, further adding to the carnage. In the end, eighteen people were killed in the melee by both terrorist and Musa Company gunfire.

Tragically, as the fire-fight ended and the dead and wounded were laying inside the aircraft and on the tarmac, an advisory team from the U.S. Army's 1st SFOD-Delta (Airborne) arrived from Pope AFB at Karachi International Airport.

Musa Company's most recent--publicized--mission came on February 19, 1994, when a tactical team assaulted the Afghan Embassy in Islamabad after Afghani gunmen entered the building and took five schoolboys and a teacher hostage. The gunmen, armed with a variety of pistols and hand grenades, had been held for three days after their schoolbus had been hijacked; seventy-three children had been released a few days earlier. The kidnappers, whose motives combined political and monetary reasons (they had asked for a US $5,000,000 ransom, along with 2,000 truckloads of food and supplies for the war-ravaged Afghan capital of Kabul), were led to believe that their demands would be met when Musa Company struck--they assaulted the facility and in a flurry of gunfire killed the kidnappers and rescued all the children.

Service in Musa Company, like its parent unit the Special Service Group, is strictly voluntary. Training is divided into two equal phases of twenty-five months in length[2] - the first half is devoted solely to conventional commando instruction and culminates with parachute training at the Peshawar Airborne School. The second-phase of SSG instruction consists of mountain warfare instruction, built-up area skills, intelligence-gathering and reconnaissance work, and sabotage. Once a candidate has passed the grueling training course and is sanctioned to wear the red beret and SSG sword and lightning flash badge of the unit, he must serve in its ranks for at least six months before being permitted to volunteer into Musa Company.

Although the Chinese-produced Model 56 7.62mm assault rifle is among the most popular weapons to be found in the Pakistani military, SSG Musa Company operators are firm believers in the Heckler and Koch family of MP5 9mm submachine guns in all the available variants. The unit's handgun is of choice is the Glock Model 19, though the Colt .45 is widely carried. The unit's primary sniper weapon is the Heckler and Koch PSG-1 7.62mm rifle.

Maritime counter-terrorism, while the domain of Musa Company, is also the responsibility of the Naval Special Service Group (SSGN), based at Karachi, and the Pakistani Navy's special warfare entity. The SSGN has trained together with the U.S. Navy SEALs (including SEAL Team SIX), as well as with the British Special Boat Service.

[1] Identity withheld for security reasons.

[2] Officers training is conducted at the academy at Abbotobab, and lasts twenty-four months in total.

## Singapore

When counter-terrorist instructors teach their classes in tubular assaults, gaining entry into planes, buses and trains, they always stress the point that time is not only of the essence, but the dividing line between life and death. Gaining access to the target is half the battle, racing down the aisle and eliminating any potential terrorist is the other half. It doesn't matter what they are armed with. The entire effort must be handled expeditiously and without hesitation.

On Tuesday March 26, 1991, four Pakistanis hijacked a Singapore Airlines flight after take-off from Kuala Lumpur Airport and eventually ordered it to land at Changi Airport in Singapore. Armed with nothing more than butter knives, the hijackers managed to assume control of the A310 Airbus and demanded that Pakistan release the husband of Benazir Bhutto, Asif Ali Zardari and several of his comrades from the Pakistan People's Party (PPP). The authorities in Singapore would have none of this nonsense. The Airbus was cordoned off to a remote section of Changi Airport, and a group of men wearing black coveralls, balaclavas, and carrying MP5s scurried about behind a supply truck doubling as a CP. The ordeal lasted nine hours. At dawn on March 27, the operators struck. They made forcible entry into the aircraft, and raced through the aisle with MP5s aimed at anything that looked wrong. Their gunsights found the four hijackers, killing the butter-knife wielding terrorists and rescuing all 123 on board.

Counter-terrorist duty in Singapore is the domain of two units. The Police Tactical Team, a unit of 200 operators trained by the SAS, Israel's ***Ya'ma'm***, GSG-9 and the Australian SAS is charged with handling most terrorist incidents. Well-trained, instructed by the world's best, they are considered among the better units in Asia. Their equipment consists of Heckler and Koch MP5s, Glock Model 19 9mm semi-automatics, and Heckler and Koch HK512 12-gauge shotguns, though as a result of the Israeli influence on the unit operators have carried Mini-Uzis and Jerichos into the field.

For the operations outside the boundaries of the city-state, a special troop from the 1st Commando Battalion is tasked with rescuing hostages on board a hijacked Singapore Airlines flight or a Singapore-owned and operated ship. Although not considered to be as capable as the Police Tactical Team, the 1st Commando Battalion is also trained by the British and Australian SAS, as well as Israeli counter-terrorist "advisors" and, it is believed, the U.S. Army's 1st SFOD-Delta.

## Taiwan

Although the island nation of Taiwan has been immune to the scourge of the modern terrorism when compared to the urban terrorist battlefields of the Middle East and Europe, few nations are as prepared to meet a terrorist threat as is the Republic of China (R.O.C.); few nations, in fact, possess the number of elite special forces needed for this special form of warfare as does the R.O.C. Until 1992, the ROC maintained four counter-terrorist units: (1) The First Peace Preservation Police Corps Special Weapons and Tactics Unit; (2) The Military Police Special Service Company (responsible for the north of island including Chiang Kai-Shek International Airport); (3) The Airborne and Special Warfare Command Special Operations Unit (responsible for the center of the country); and, (4) the Chinese Marine Corps Special Operations Unit (responsible for the south of Taiwan). All forces are under the primary administrative and logistic control of the Security Task Force Headquarters (***Wei An***). The Security Task Force reports directly to Prime Minister Mr. Lien Chan. Counter-terrorist duty was once the sole domain of the armed forces but attempts to demilitarize the republic and instill a democratic atmosphere resulted in the National Police SWAT units receiving the responsibility of internal anti-terrorist duties (the above military units remain on alert status as powerful back-up units in case of emergency).

Police SWAT badge

Military Police Special Service Company badge

The Police SWAT Unit was formed in April 1985 and reports directly to the Ministry of The Interior. Under its official mandate, its mission is to "handle" all terrorist and serious criminal operations within the Republic of China, including neutralizing aircraft hijackings and hostage rescue situations; the unit is also tasked with arresting very dangerous criminals. The R.O.C. National Police SWAT unit is based in Shih Lin, in the northern suburbs of Taipei, and consists of ninety men divided into three platoons, each one consisting of 10-12 man teams with additional logistic and training support. Training for this all-volunteer force lasts ten months (with an annual 13-week refresher cycle) with an emphasis placed on weapons proficiency, helicopter insertion, abseiling, hostage-rescue, anti-hijack exercises, and hand-to-hand combat. Special instruction includes sniping, high-speed and evasive driving, EOD and explosive entry. In past years, R.O.C. SWAT unit members have attended Los Angeles Police Department SWAT courses. According to foreign reports, the Taiwanese Police SWAT unit has also trained with Israeli personnel. Weapons deployed by the National Police SWAT unit are: Pistols--Beretta 92F/SC; S&W M10 .30 Spec; S&W 5909, and SIG Sauer; SMGs and Rifles--Mini-Uzi 9mm submachine gun and M16A2 5.56mm assault rifle; and, Sniper Rifle--SIG 2000 7.62mm.

To date there have been nine hijackings of commercial CAAC airliners from the People's Republic of China to Taiwan. Although the Police SWAT units were called to the scene, they were not needed, as the hijackers surrendered immediately to authorities. The unit also participated in the rescue of a kidnapped businessman, the quelling of a prison riot, and in serious narcotic arrests.

Supplementing the capabilities of the national SWAT units, each of the 23 counties in Taiwan maintains a special weapons and tactics unit numbering on between 50-100 men depending on the size of the county. Supporting the national SWAT forces in case of emergency, as mentioned above, are:

(1) Military Police Special Service Company: This force is approximately 90-man strong, organized into three platoons. Formed in 1978 and based at Linkou, mid-way between Taipei and Chiang Kai-Shek International Airport at Taoyuan, this elite force is responsible for:

- Back-up to the Police SWAT unit in aircraft hijackings and hostage-rescue scenarios.
- Providing bodyguards for diplomats, embassies and missions around the world, and are seconded to the National Security Bureau for this duty.
- Escort fissionable material to Taiwan's three nuclear power sites.
- A wartime mission which is classified top-secret and not available for publication.

Training for the Military Police Special Service Company operators lasts nine months, and includes jump training (5 basic static-line), and Ranger training at Ku Kuan in the central mountains.

(2) Army Airborne and Special Warfare Command Special Operations Unit: Formed in 1980s, this is one of Taiwan's true special forces entities, this force of approximately 100 men is situated in Ping Dong, in southern Taiwan, and missions include:

- Insertion into difficult terrain in Taiwan for anti-terrorist operations (such as free-fall parachuting).
- Operations overseas involving threatened Taiwanese citizens
- A classified wartime mission believed, according to foreign reports, to include clandestine operations in Mainland China.

Training for Army Airborne and Special Warfare Command Special Operations unit operators (a volunteer force) is classified, but it is known that some members of the unit attend the U.S. Army Ranger School, as well as the Special Forces 'Q' Course at Fort Bragg, North Carolina.

(3) Chinese Marine Corps Special Operations Unit: This company size entity consisting of approximately 90 men is responsible for all aspects of maritime security including surface swimming, ship-boarding, maritime anti-hijack missions. Many of the volunteers of this force are former frogmen from the marine amphibious reconnaissance battalion and are SCUBA and airborne qualified, although this is not part of the force's training; according to reports, some members of this elite force are attached to the Singapore Navy's diving unit. Their missions include:

- Maritime security, anti-piracy and maritime counter-terrorism.
- A classified wartime mandate believed to include infiltration into Mainland China.

Police Lieutenant-Colonel Liou Shou-Te, commander of the Police SWAT unit, reports to Police General Zhuang, commander of the National Police authority.

The Police SWAT unit strikes a rare pose for the cameras. Note black fatigues, and SWAT unit patches.

Heliborne insertion exercises (courtesy of the Police Air Unit and a Aerospatiale Dauphin) with the SWAT team. The SWAT members are among the nation's best operators in heliborne insertion techniques such as abseiling and fast-roping.

SWAT unit operators test their marksmanship skills with an M16A2 5.56mm assault rifle--the standard--and favorite assault weapon used by Taiwanese special forces.

A SWAT sniper carefully selects his target before squeezing on the trigger of his SIG-2000 7.62mm sniper rifle.

A SWAT operator prepares to fire his Beretta automatic shotgun.

Incredible photograph illustrating the imagination and skill of SWAT operators, as an operator fires his Beretta automatic from the backseat of a motorbike. Interestingly enough, the SWAT team employs "Motorbike shotgun teams."

SWAT team operators train in Tai Kwon Do, Judo, Ch`ina (Chinese Aikido) and Wushu. The SWAT operators are masters with their weapons. They are even deadlier with their hands.

## *Thailand*

Just another morning on the streets of Bangkok in the middle of March, though it would soon turn out to be the type of scenario that every operator, whether he be from a military or police unit, dreads with a full heart. March 11, 1994. On a main thoroughfare in city center, several drivers noticed a truck driven by a Near Eastern individual driving erratically; the vehicle would speed up and slow down at odd intervals. Near a department store in downtown Bangkok, the truck hit several motorbikes parked alongside the curb. When the owners of the motorbikes approached the truck driver demanding insurance forms and compensation, he offered them a wad of foreign currency. The generous offer was refused, and when an argument ensued, he fled on foot blending into the crowded chaos of morning Bangkok traffic. A police tow truck moved the vehicle to an impound station where it sat for a week awaiting its owner to reclaim it. Nobody ever showed up.

Suspicious, police examined the vehicle and were shocked by what they found. Inside the truck's one-ton water tank, police found C-4 plastic explosives and a large amount of ammonium nitrate fertilizer mixed with diesel fuel--almost a carbon-copy of the bomb the blew up the World Trade Center in New York City a year earlier.[1] The tank was loaded into the back of a six-wheeled rental, with the device wired to the truck battery with a detonating switch mounted on the dashboard. Immediately upon discovering the device, bomb-squad officers arrived but security officers feared that the abandoned vehicle was a ruse, a red herring, meant to act as a diversion while perhaps a more sinister attack was underway. SWAT officers from the Bangkok Metropolitan Police, an elite unit known as "Task Force 191," were raced to the embassy while beepers and cellular phones all around, Lopburi, home to the Thai special forces, rang off the wall. To old-timers, the incident sparked flashbacks to December 1972 when Black September terrorists seized the Israeli embassy and held hostages. Thai military units had then surrounded the embassy grounds, but realized that they were ill-equipped to make any tactical moves. A benevolent Egyptian diplomat facilitated negotiations and the hostages release.

Counter-terrorism in Thailand is the responsibility of four separate units tasked with different assignments. For much of its history, the Royal Thai Special Forces (RTSF) participated in counter-insurgency campaigns along the border with Cambodia and Laos through the American involvement in Vietnam and beyond,[2] and they were the military unit originally tasked with counter-terrorist and hostage-rescue operations. Yet the Thai military realized that despatching teams or squadrons of operators to a crisis was a stop-gap--hostage-rescue work was the domain of specialists and a unit tasked solely with hostage-rescue work was created. It was known as "Task Force 90," and was made up of the most physically fit special forces operators, most politically reliable (coups are always a threat in Thailand), and those with the best marksmanship skills. Based at Lopburi, the young unit received a wealth of international instruction and joint-training, including from the U.S. Army's 1st SFOD-Delta, the Australian SAS, the British SAS, the Republic of Korea's 707th Special Mission Battalion, and, it has been reported, Israeli advisors. Little is known of their equipment, other than the fact they use MP5s, CAR-15s, and PSG-1 7.62mm sniper rifles. It is believed their pistol of choice is the Glock Model 19.

In 1989, following an embarrassing performance by the Thai army in a short border conflict with Laos, an airborne Ranger Battalion was raised at the Special Forces Center in Lopburi (with plans to move the battalion to Nakhon Nayon). The unit was slated as a rapid deployment force, with TF 90 placed under its operation control. This battalion had strong backing from then-army commander Chaovalit, who has since become a member of the political opposition.

The Royal Thai Air Force has also gotten into the business of hostage-rescue operations and a unit, a 100-man outfit, within the "201 Squadron/2 Wing" at Lopburi, that is trained specifically for para-rescue and rescuing hostages off of hijacked aircraft. They are known to have trained with the U.S. Army's 1st SFOD-Delta and seven operators from the unit visited Israel where they trained from both army and police units; according to rumor, they have also been trained by British SAS instructors, officers from the Australian SASR, and GSG-9 commanders. They are armed primarily with the Heckler and Koch MP5 SD3 9mm submachine gun, and Browning Hi-Power automatics.

It should also be noted that the Royal Thai Marines Corps' reconnaissance company possess a small anti-terrorist team tasked with shoreline rescue operations, and the Royal Thai Navy SEALs are trained with maritime counter-terrorist and hostage-rescue operations.

Other Thai counter-terrorist units include the Bangkok Metropolitan Police which has a SWAT team known as Task Force 191, and a unit from the extensive paramilitary arm known as the ***Tahan Prahan***, loosely translated as "Rangers." Many foreigners assume that they are an elite unit; in reality, their weapons and training are substandard. There is one exception: a special counter-terrorist unit within the force was raised at Korat and designated for country-wide rural operations, whereas TF 90 was charged with urban operations.

[1] Recently, it was learned that the similarities between the bomb found in Bangkok and the device the blew up underneath the World Trade Center was no coincidence. Authorities now believe that the man behind the Thailand bombing-attempt was none other than World Trade Center bombing master-mind Ramzi Yusef, captured in Pakistan and brought back to New York City on February 8, 1995.

[2] In the mid-1980s, for example, the unit participated in preemptive strikes against Burmese opium warlords and actively trained members of Task Force 838, an elite unit that oversaw the activities along the Cambodian border.